James Payn

Biographia Dramatica

James Payn

Biographia Dramatica

ISBN/EAN: 9783744759953

Printed in Europe, USA, Canada, Australia, Japan

Cover: Foto ©ninafisch / pixelio.de

More available books at **www.hansebooks.com**

BIOGRAPHIA DRAMATICA,

OR,

A COMPANION

TO

THE PLAYHOUSE:

CONTAINING

Historical and Critical Memoirs, and Original Anecdotes, of BRITISH and IRISH DRAMATIC WRITERS, from the Commencement of our Theatrical Exhibitions; amongst whom are some of the most celebrated ACTORS.

ALSO

An Alphabetical Account of their WORKS, the Dates when printed, and occasional Observations on their Merits.

TOGETHER WITH

An INTRODUCTORY VIEW of the RISE and PROGRESS of the BRITISH STAGE.

By DAVID ERSKINE BAKER, Esq.

A NEW EDITION:

Carefully corrected; greatly enlarged; and continued from 1764 to 1782.

THE SECOND VOLUME.

LONDON:

Printed for Mess. RIVINGTONS, St. Paul's Church-Yard; T. PAYNE and SON, Mews-Gate; L. DAVIS, Holborn; T. LONGMAN, and G. ROBINSON, Pater Noster-Row; J. DODSLEY, Pall-Mall; J. NICHOLS, Red-Lion-Passage, Fleet-Street; J. DEBRET, Piccadilly; and T. EVANS, in the Strand.

MDCCLXXXII.

THE COMPANION TO THE PLAY-HOUSE.

1. ABDELAZAR, or, *The Moor's Revenge*. Trag. by Mrs. Aphra, or Afra Behn. Acted at the duke of York's theatre, 4to. 1677. This play is no more than an alteration of Marloe's *Lascivious Queen*, of which see more in its place. From it, however, Dr. Young took the hint of his admirable tragedy of *The Revenge*; the death of a father, and loss of a crown, being the prime motives of resentment equally in *Abdelazar* and *Zanga*. A similar reluctance appears in both at the descending to acts of villainy for the gratification of it, and both alike declare the sum of their crimes at the completion of their revenge. The plot is intricate, much interlarded with trivial circumstances, and the catastrophe on the whole too bloody, yet with a little alteration might be rendered very fit for the present stage.

2. ABDICATED PRINCE, or, *The Adventures of four Years*. Tragi-Com. Anonym. Acted at Alba Regalis, by several persons of great quality, 4to. 1690. This piece is entirely political, and seems not to have been intended for the stage: it contains under feigned names the transactions of the English court and nation during the reign of James II. with the Abdication of that prince, but written with great partiality, the duke of Monmouth being made the hero, and personal abuse proceeding to so extravagant a length in it, as to charge the king with the death of his brother Charles II. This play needs no key, *Alba Regalis* evidently being meant for the English court, and the very names of the personages so closely pointed to real history, as to be obvious to any one ever so slightly acquainted with the public transactions of that period.

3. ABRAHAM'S SACRIFICE. This play, neither Langbaine, Jacob, or Gildon, pretend to have seen, to know the author of, or to assign a date to; but all of them suppose it a translation from Theodore Beza.

Oldys calls it "Abraham his Sacrifice, or, The Tryale of the Hearte, 1560." But Maunsell, in his Catalogue, 1595, p. 55. with more probability speaks of it as as a translation from Beza, by Arthur Golding, under the title of *Abraham's offering his son Isaake*.

4. ABRA-MULE, or, *Love and Empire*. Tr. by Dr. Joseph Trapp. Acted at the new theatre in Lincoln's-Inn-Fields, 4to. 1704. The scene lies in Constantinople, and the plot of it may be more fully seen in a book called *Abra-Mule, or, the true history of the dethronement of Mahomet* IV. by M. Le Noble; translated by S. P. The language of this play is in many places either prosaic or bombast; yet the incidents are in themselves so affecting, and the plot so interesting, that it has generally met with applause in the performance. The two lines which conclude the first act of this tragedy, deserve remembrance, for the sake of a happy parody on them, said to have been produced extempore during the first night of representation:

> My wide dominions o'er the world shall run,
> And my pale *crescent* brighten to a *sun*.
>
> Success and laurels shall attend my sword,
> And turn my *harp* into a *harpsichord*.

5. THE ABSENT MAN. Farce, by Thomas Hull. Acted at Covent-Garden the 28th of April 1764, for the benefit of the author and Miss Miller. N. P.

6. THE ABSENT MAN. Farce, by Isaac Bickerstaffe. Acted at Drury-Lane, 8vo. 1768. The hint of this piece, and that only, the author says, was taken from the character of *Menalcas* in La Bruyere, translated by the *Spectator*. It met with applause.

7. THE ACCOMPLISHED MAID. Com. Op. by Mr. Toms. Acted at Covent-Garden, 8vo. 1766. A translation of *La Buona Figliola*.

8. ACHILLES, or, *Iphigenia in Aulis*. T. by Abel Boyer. Acted at Drury-Lane, 4to. 1700. This is a translation from the *Iphigenia of Racine*. It was acted without any success. On the appearance of the *Victim*, by Charles Johnson, in 1714, Mr. Boyer republished this play, under the title of *The Victim*, or, *Achilles and Iphigenia in Aulis*, 12mo. and in the preface to it says, that it passed the correction and approbation of Mr. Dryden. On the 23d of March 1778, it was revived at Covent-Garden, under the title of *Iphigenia*, for the benefit of Mrs. Barry.

9. ACHILLES. An Opera, by John Gay, 8vo. This piece, which is in the manner of the *Beggar's Opera*, is a ludicrous relation of the discovery of Achilles by Ulysses. The scene lies in the court of Lycomedes. Achilles is in woman's cloaths through the whole play, and it concludes by his marriage with Deidamia. It was acted in 1733, at Covent-Garden.

10. ACHILLES IN PETTICOATS. An Opera, altered from Gay, by George Colman. Acted at Covent-Garden, 8vo. 1774. This alteration met with little success.

11. ACIS AND GALATEA. A Masque, by P. Motteux, from *Ovid's Metam.* Book XIII. set to music by John Eccles, and performed at the theatre royal in Drury Lane by his majesty's servants, 4to. 1701. The scene Sicily. With this Masque are published the rest of the musical entertainments in an Opera, called, *The Mad Lover*.

12. ACIS AND GALATEA. An English Pastoral Opera, in three acts. by John Gay. It is in recitative and air, the story taken from the 13th Book of *Ovid's Metamorphoses*; the music composed by

by Handel, and was performed at the Hay-Market, 1732.

13. ACOLASTUS. This play is no more than a translation, for the use of children, of a Latin play of the same name written by Guil. Fullonius, on the story of the Prodigal Son. It is printed in the old black letter, 4to. and dedicated to the king.

"Joannis Palsgravii Londoniensis, Ecphrasis Anglica in Comediam ACOLASTI.

"The comedye of ACOLASTUS translated into oure englyshe tongue, after such maner as chylderne are taught in the grammar schole, fyrst worde for worde, as the latyne lyeth, and afterwarde accordynge to the sense and meanyng of the Latin sentences: by shewing what they do value and countervayle in our tongue, with admonitions set forth in the margyn, so often as any such phrase, that is to say, kynde of spekyng used of the Latyns, which we use not in our tonge, but by other wordes expresse the said Latyn maners of speakinge, and also adages, metaphores, sentences, or other fygures, poeticall or rhetoricall do require, for the more perfyte instructynge of the lerners, and to leade theym more easilye to see howe the exposytion gothe; and afore the seconde sceane of the fyrst acte, is a brefe introductory to have some general knowledge of the dyvers sortes of meters used of our auctour in this comedy. And afore Acolastus balade is shewed of what kyndes of meters his balade is made of. And afore the syxte sceane of the fourthe acte, is a monition of the rhetorycall composytion used in that sceane, and certayne other after it ensuyinge.

"Interpreted by John Palsgrave, Anno M.D.XL.

"Wylliam Fullonius the maker of this presente comedy, did set it forthe before the bourgeses of Hagen in Holand. Anno M.D.XXIX."

14. ACT AT OXFORD. Com. by Thomas Baker, 4to. 1704. This author, in his Dedication to Lord Dudley and Ward, informs us, it was forbid to be represented, and at the same time disclaims any intention of treating the university of Oxford with rudeness, as it had been reported.

15. ACTÆON AND DIANA. An Interlude, by Mr. Robert Cox, with a pastoral story of the Nymph Oenone, followed by the several conceited humours of Bumpkin the huntsman, Hobinal the shepherd, Singing Simkin, and John Swabber the Seaman, 4to. No date. The story is taken from *Ovid's Metamorphoses.*

16. ADELPHI, or, *The Brothers.* Com. translated from *Terence,* by Richard Bernard, 4to. 1598.

17. ADELPHI. The same play, translated by Laurence Echard, 8vo. 1694.

18. ADELPHI. Com. translated by T. Cook, 12mo. 1734.

19. ADELPHI. Com. translated by S. Patrick, 8vo. 1745.

20. ADELPHI. Com. translated by Gordon, 12mo. 1752.

21. ADELPHI. Com. translated by G. Colman, 4to. 1765.

22. A new translation of the ADELPHI of Terence into blank verse, 8vo. 1774. None of these translations were ever intended for, nor are they by any means adapted to, the English stage.

23. ADRASTA, or, *The Woman's Spleen and Love's Conquest.* Tragi-Com. by John Jones, never acted, but printed in 4to. 1635. Part of it is taken from *Boccace, Day.* 8. *Novel.* 8.

24. THE

24. THE ADVERTISEMENT, or, A Bold Stroke for a Husband. Com. by Mrs. Gardiner. Acted one night, Aug. 9, 1777, at the Hay-Market, for the benefit of the authoress. Not printed.

25. ADVENTURES IN MADRID. C. by Mrs. Pix. Acted at the Queen's Theatre in the Hay-Market; 4to. no date. [1709.]

26. ADVENTURES OF FIVE HOURS. Tragi-Com. by Sir Samuel Tuke, Bart. Acted at Court. Fol. 1663. 4to. 1664. 4to. 1671. D. C. Downes, in his *Roscius Anglicanus*, says, it was written by that gentleman and the earl of Bristol. It is translated from a Spanish play, recommended by king Charles II. was acted with great applause, and has several copies of verses prefixed to it by Mr. Cowley, and other eminent poets of that time.

27. ADVENTURES OF HALF AN HOUR. F. by Christopher Bullock. Acted at Lincoln's-Inn-Fields, 12mo. 1716.

28. THE AFFECTED LADIES. C. by John Ozell. This play is only a literal translation of the *Precieuses Ridicules* of Moliere.

29. AGAINST MOMUS'S AND ZOILUS'S. A dramatic piece, by John Bale, bishop of Ossory, the first English dramatic writer. Of this piece we have no remains but the bare mention of it by himself, in his account of the writers of Britain.

30. AGAINST THOSE WHO ADULTERATE THE WORD OF GOD. A dramatic piece by the last-mentioned author; and of which we have exactly the same kind of knowledge. Neither of them were ever acted or even printed, but in all probability they were written at some time between 1530 and 1540.

31. AGAMEMNON. T. by James Thomson. Acted at Drury-Lane, 8vo. 1738. This tragedy, as Dr. Johnson observes, was much shortened in the representation. It had the fate which most commonly attends mythological stories, and was only endured, but not favoured. It struggled with such difficulties through the first night, that Thomson, coming late to his friends with whom he was to sup, excused his delay by telling them how the sweat of his distress had so disordered his wig, that he could not come till he had been refitted by a barber. He had so interested himself in his own drama, that, it I remember right, as he sat in the upper gallery he accompanied the players by audible recitation, till a friendly hint frighted him to silence. Pope countenanced *Agamemnon* by coming to it the first night.

32. AGAMEMNON. Tr. translated from *Seneca* by John Studly, in queen Elizabeth's reign. He has, however, added a whole scene in the fifth Act.

33. AGAMEMNON. Trag. translated from *Æschylus*, by R. Potter, 4to. 1777.

34. AGIS. T. by John Home, performed at Drury-Lane, 1758, 8vo. This play is founded on a story in the Spartan History; whether the author was only warmed by the spirit of a particular party, or that he chose in this piece to give vent to his resentments against his countrymen for the rigour wherewith they had persecuted him on account of his former tragedy of *Douglas*, it is difficult to determine; but it is at least apparent, that throughout the whole of the piece he has kept up a figurative retrospect of the conduct of the Scots, in regard to king Charles I. and that, in the character of his *Agis*, he has never lost sight of the idea of that unfortunate prince. It was performed

performed with tolerable succeſs, being ſtrongly ſupported, not only by a party zeal in the author's favour, but alſo by the additional advantages of very fine acting, and two pompous and ſolemn muſical proceſſions. Without theſe aſſiſtances, however, it is ſomewhat doubtful whether it might have met with the ſame ſucceſs. On this tragedy, Mr. Gray, in a letter to Dr. Warton, (ſee Maſon's *Memoirs* of the former, 4to. edit. p. 261.) has the following remark: "I cry to think that it ſhould be "by the author of *Douglas*: why, "it is all modern Greek; the "ſtory is an antique ſtatue painted "white and red, frized, and dreſſed "in a negligée made by a York- "ſhire mantua-maker."

35. AGLAURA. Tragi-Com. by Sir John Suckling; acted at the private houſe in Black-Fryars, 8vo. 1646. The author has ſo contrived this play, by means of an alteration in the laſt Act, that it may be acted either as a tragi-comedy, or a perfect tragedy. The ſcene lies in *Perſia*. It was entered by Thomas Walkeley, April 18, 1638, in the books of the Stationers' Company.

36. AGNES DE CASTRO. Tr. by Mrs. Cath. Trotter, afterwards Cockburne, 4to. acted at the Theatre Royal 1696. It is built on a French novel of the ſame name, tranſlated by Mrs. Behn, and deſervedly met with very good ſucceſs.

37. THE AGREEABLE SURPRISE. Com. of one Act, tranſlated from *Marivaux*, 12mo 1766. Performed by the ſcholars of Mr. Ruk's academy at Iſlington. Printed in *Poetical Bloſſoms*, or, *The Sports of Genius*.

38. AGRIPPA KING OF ALBA, or, *The falſe Tiberinus*. Tragi-Com. by John Dancer. This is a tranſlation from M. Quinault; it is in heroic verſe, was performed ſeveral times with great applauſe at the Theatre Royal in Dublin, and was printed at London in 4to. 1675.

39. AGRIPPINA *Empreſs of Rome*, her Tragedy, by Tho. May, Eſq. The ſcene of this play lies in Rome, and the plot is taken from the Roman hiſtorians. It was acted in 1628, and printed in 12mo. 1639 and 1654.

40. AGRIPPINA; by Thomas Gray, 4to. 1775. This piece conſiſts only of two ſcenes of a tragedy, ſo admirably executed as to make one lament that the author did not complete it according to his original deſign. The ſtory was intended to be taken from the 13th and 14th Books of *Tacitus*. The language of this production, though far from wanting ornament, is by no means overloaded with it; and, had our author lived to complete his undertaking, it could not fail to have proved the nobleſt pattern for the ſtyle of imperial Tragedy. Dr. Johnſon however obſerves, "it was no loſs to the Engliſh "ſtage that *Agrippina* was never "finiſhed." The fable indeed could not poſſibly admit of any good character, and therefore only terror could have been excited by it. The loſs of the reader nevertheleſs may have been conſiderable; for, to uſe the critic's own ſentiments concerning our author, "a man like him, of great "learning and great induſtry, "could not but produce ſomewhat "valuable."

41. King AHASUERUS and Queen ESTHER. An Interlude, attributed to Robert Cox, comedian, and is publiſhed in the ſecond part of *Sport upon Sport* 1672.

42. AJAX. Trag. 12mo. 1714. This is only a tranſlation from the Greek

Greek of *Sophocles* by one Mr. Jackson, but revised by Mr. Rowe.

43. AJAX. Trag. translated by George Adams, 8vo. 1729.

44. AJAX. Trag. translated by Thomas Franklin, 4to. 1759.

45. ALAHAM. Trag. by Fulke Greville, lord Brook, Folio, 1633. The scene of this play is laid at the mouth of the Persian Gulph, and the plot taken from some incidents in Herbert's travels. The author has followed the model of the ancients; the Prologue is spoken by a Ghost, who gives an account of every character, and so strictly has he adhered to the rules of the drama, that he has not throughout introduced more than two speakers at a time, excepting in the chorus's between the Acts.

46. ALARBAS. A dram. Opera, written by a gentleman of quality, 4to. 1709. The scene lies in *Arcadia* in Greece. From the Preface it appears not to have been acted.

47. ALARUM FOR LONDON, or, *The Siege of Antwerp: with the ventrous Acts and valorous Deeds of the lame Soldier.* Tragi-Com. Acted by the lord chamberlain's servants, 4to. 1602. This play is not divided into acts, the plot is taken from *The Tragical History of the City of Antwerp.*

48. ALBERTUS WALLENSTEIN, *late Duke of Fridland, and General to the Emperor Ferdinand* II. Trag. by Henry Glapthorne. It was acted at the Globe by the Bank Side, 4to. 1634. The scene lies at *Egers*, and the plot is merely historical, being built on facts not very distant from the time of writing it.

49. ALBINA. Trag. by Mrs. Cowley. Acted at the Hay-Market 1779, 8vo. In a Preface which is suppressed in a second edition of this play, are many complaints against the managers of Drury-Lane and Covent-Garden, and some insinuations of unfair practices towards the author while the play was in their hands. The charges of plagiarism from this piece seem to have no other foundation than in the fancy of the author.

50. ALBION. An Interl. mentioned by Kirkman only, and probably the same as is entered, by Thomas Colwell, in the Stationers' Company's Books of the years 1565 to 1566, under the title of "A Mery Playe, bothe pythy and pleasaunt, of ALBYON Knight."

51. ALBION, or, *The Court of Neptune.* A Masque, by T. Cooke, 8vo. 1724. The scene laid on the British seas.

52. ALBION AND ALBANIUS. An Opera, by J. Dryden. Acted at the Theatre Royal, Fol. 1685. Set to music by Lewis Grabue, Esq. The subject of this piece is wholly allegorical, being intended to expose lord Shaftesbury and his adherents. Downes tells us, that, happening to be first performed at an unlucky time, being the very day on which the duke of Monmouth landed in the West, and the kingdom in a great consternation, it ran but six nights, which not answering half the charge the company had been at in getting it up, involved them very deeply in debt.

53. ALBION QUEENS. See ISLAND QUEENS.

54. ALBION RESTOR'D, or, *Time turn'd Oculist.* A Masque, never acted. 8vo. 1758.

55. ALBION'S TRIUMPH, *personated in a Masque at Court, by the King's Majesty and his Lords* (all whose names are at the end), *the Sunday after Twelfth Night*, 1631, 4to. The scene is Albipolis, the chief city of Albion. Inigo Jones had a share in the invention of this masque.

56. AL-

56. ALBOVINE. *King of the Lombards.* Trag. by Sir W. Davenant, 4to. 1629. The story is found in Bandello, the *Hiſtoires tragiques.* tom. IV. Nov. 19. and ſome of the hiſtorians of the Francs and Lombards. The ſcene lies in Verona.

57. "ALBUMAZAR. Com. preſented before the Kings Majeſtie at Cambridge the 9th of March, 1614. By the gentlemen of Trinitie College, 4to. 1615. 4to. 1634." This play was written by Mr. Tomkis, of Trinity College; and acted before king James on the day above-mentioned. Dryden, in a Prologue compoſed by him for the revival of it, conſiders it as the original of the *Alchymiſt,* and accuſes Ben Jonſon in very poſitive terms with plagiariſm, but without any foundation, as this play was neither acted nor printed until four years after *The Alchymiſt.*

58. ALBUMAZAR. C. by David Garrick. Acted at Drury-Lane, 8vo. 1773. This is an alteration of the above play. Though it had the advantage of the beſt performers, yet neither on this, or a former revival of it in 1748, did it meet with much ſucceſs.

59. ALCAMENES AND MENALIPPA. Trag. Mears, in his Catalogue, aſcribes this play to William Philips. Chetwood, we believe, with his uſual want of fidelity, has given it the date of 1668.

60. ALCHYMIST. C. by Ben. Jonſon. Acted by the king's ſervants, 4to. 1610. This play is too well known and admired to need any comment on, or account of it. Let it ſuffice to ſay, that the deſign of it was to laſh the then prevailing paſſion for Alchymy, and point out how eaſy it is for mankind to be impoſed on where ſome darling folly leads its aid to the impoſture.

61. ALCIBIADES. Trag. by Thomas Otway. Acted at the Theatre Royal, 4to. 1675. 4to. 1687. The ſtory of this play is taken from *Corn. Nepos and Plutarch.* The author has, however, conſiderably departed from the hiſtory, making his hero, Alcibiades, a man of the ſtricteſt honour, who chuſes rather to loſe his life than wrong his defender king Agis, or abuſe his bed; whereas Plutarch gives him a quite different character.

62. ALCIBIADES. Trag. by William Shirley. This play has not yet been printed. It is promiſed, however, in a collection of the author's dramatic works, and appears to have been refuſed by both Mr. Garrick and Mr. Harris.

63. ALEXANDER THE GREAT. by T. Ozell, tranſlated from *Racine,* 12mo. 1714.

64. ALEXANDER THE GREAT. Op. performed at Lincoln's-Ina-Field-, 8vo. 1715.

65. ALEXANDER. Op. by Anthony Henley, Eſq. It does not appear whether the former Opera is the ſame as the preſent, or not. The writer of Mr. Henley's life ſays, he almoſt finiſhed an Opera with this title at the time of his death, and that it was to be ſet by Daniel Purcell.

66. ALEXANDER AND CAMPASPE. A Com. by John Lyly, played before queen Elizabeth, on Twelfth-Night, by the children of Paul's, 4to. 1584. 4to. 1591. 12mo. 1632. Pio: from Pliny's *Nat. Hiſt.* B. 35. Ch. 10.

67. THE ALEXANDRÆAN TRAGEDY; by William Alexander, earl of Stirling, 4to. 1605. The ground-work of this play is laid on the differences which aroſe among Alexander's captains after his deceaſe about the ſucceſſion. Jacob contradicts Langbaine for

ſaying

saying that it is written after the model of the Ancients, yet condemns the play for those very faults which could only arise from the author's having followed that model, and consequently must be mistaken either on one side of the question or the other. The noble author has undoubtedly kept the ancient tragic writers perpetually in his eye, and even borrowed freely from their thoughts, several whole speeches being apparently little more than translations from *Virgil*, *Seneca*, and others. He has kept close to historical fact, even in his episodes, yet has neglected the very essence of the drama, viz. action, the first act being wholly employed by the Ghost of *Alexander* (probably in imitation of Seneca's *Thyestes*); the second having but little to do with the main business of the play, beginning with the council held by Perdiccas, Meleager, and the rest of the commanders; and through the whole remainder of the piece scarce one action is performed in the view of the audience, the whole being little more than a narration, thrown into the mouths of the several characters, of adventures atchieved by themselves and others. The scene lies in Babylon, and the plot is to be found in Quintus Curtius, Justin, and other historians.

68. ALEXIS'S PARADISE. D. Op. 1680.

69. ALEXIS'S PARADISE, or, *A Trip to the Garden of Love at Vauxhall*. Com. by James Newton, L[?]; 8vo. 1722.

70. ALFRED. A Masque; by James Thomson and David Mallet, 8vo. 1740. The scene of this play lies in Britain; and the story from the English history at the time of the Danish Invasion. It was performed the 1st of August, 1740, in the Gardens of Clifden, in commemoration of the accession of George I. and in honour of the birth-day of the prince of Brunswick; the prince and princess of Wales, and all their court, being present. *The Judgment of Paris*, a Masque, and also several scenes out of Rich's pantomines, were performed at the same time.

71. ALFRED. An Opera, as altered from the above play. Acted at Covent-Garden, 8vo. 1745.

72. ALFRED. A Masque, by David Mallet. Acted at Drury-Lane, 8vo. 1751. This is the play of Mr. Thomson and Mallet, entirely new-modelled by the latter, no part of the first being retained, except a few lines. Though excellently performed, it was not very successful. The prologue was written by the earl of Corke.

73. ALFRED. Trag. altered from Mallet, by David Garrick. Acted at Drury-Lane, 8vo. 1773. The alterations in this piece are but trifling, and its success not greater than on its original performance.

74. ALFRED. Trag. by John Home. Acted at Covent-Garden, 8vo. 1778. This play, which is the last production of its author, was so coldly received by the public, that it was performed only three nights.

75. ALFRED THE GREAT; DELIVERER OF HIS COUNTRY. T, 8vo. 1753. This is a despicable performance, written, as the title page declares, by the author of *The Friendly Rivals*.

76. ALL ALIVE AND MERRY. Com. by S. Johnson, the dancing-master. This piece was acted at Lincoln's-Inn-Fields, about the year 1737, without any success, and hath never been printed. For some

some judgment of this gentleman's writings in general, see *Hurlothrumbo*.

77. ALL BEDEVILLED, or, *The House in an Uproar*. A Farce, by Moses Browne, 8vo. 1723. See POLIDUS.

78. ALL FOOLS. C. by George Chapman, 4to. 1605. D. C. The plot is founded on *Terence's Heautontimorumenos*. It was accounted an excellent play in those times, and was acted at the Black-Friars.

79. ALL FOR LOVE, or, *The World well Lost*. Trag. by John Dryden, written in imitation of Shakespeare's style, and acted at the Theatre Royal, 4to. 1678. 4to. 1692. 4to. 1703. This is generally considered by the critics as the most compleat dramatic piece of that justly admired author. There needs, perhaps, no other reason to be assigned for its being so, than that it was the only one (amongst a very large number) which he was permitted to bring to that perfection which leisure and application, added to a most capital degree of genius, might be expected to attain. The plot and general design of it is undoubtedly borrowed from Shakspeare's *Anthony and Cleopatra*; yet justice and candour require this confession at least from us, that as much as he has fallen short of his first model in fire and originality, he has equally surpassed him in point of regularity and poetic harmony; and it may perhaps stand hereafter as a matter of contest, whether this tragedy is, or is not, to be esteemed as an invincible masterpiece of the power of English poetry.

Dryden indeed tells us, that it *is the only play he wrote for himself*; the rest were given to the people. It is by universal consent (as Dr. Johnson observes) accounted the work in which he has admitted the fewest improprieties of style or character; but it has one fault equal to many, though rather moral than critical, that, by admitting the romantic omnipotence of love, he has recommended as laudable and worthy of imitation that conduct which, through all ages, the good have censured as vitious, and the bad despised as foolish.

80. "A moral and pitieful co- " medie, intitled ALL FOR MO- " NEY, plainly representing tne " manners of men and fashion of " the world, now a-dayes." Compiled by Thomas Lupton, 4to. B. L. 1578.

81. ALL FOR THE BETTER, or, *The Infallible Cure*. Com. by F. Manning; acted at the Theatre Royal in Drury-Lane, 1703, 4to. The scene lies in Madrid, and the prologue was written by Farquhar.

82. ALL IN THE RIGHT. F. translated from D*'Allainval*, by Thomas Hull, and acted at Covent-Garden, the 26th of April 1766, for the translator's benefit. Not printed.

83. ALL IN THE RIGHT, or, *The Cuckold in good Earnest*. F. 8vo. 1762. A low, stupid, and indecent piece.

84. ALL MISTAKEN, or, *The Mad Couple*. Com. by the Hon. James Howard, Esq; acted at the Theatre Royal. 4to. 1672. 4to. 1710. The scene lies in Italy.

85. ALL MISTAKEN. Com. by William Shirley. This is an alteration of Shakspeare's *Comedy of Errors*, with great additions. It has not yet been printed or acted.

86. ALL IN THE WRONG. C. by Arthur Murphy, 8vo. 1761. This comedy made its first appearance in the summer season at the Theatre Royal in Drury-Lare, under the conduct of Mr. Foote and

and the author. It met with success, and deservedly. The intention of it is to bring together into one piece, and represent at one view, the various effects of the passion of jealousy in domestic life, acting on different dispositions and different tempers, and under the different circumstances of husband and wife, lover and mistress. The author confesses, in his advertisement prefixed to the piece, that some of his hints have been borrowed from the *Cocu Imaginaire* of Moliere. The plot and conduct in general however must be allowed his own, and to have great merit. The characters are not ill drawn, though perhaps not perfectly finished; the misunderstandings and perplexities produced among them by the wrong-headedness of this absurd passion, are natural and unforced, and the incidents are so happily contrived that, although the audience seem from time to time to have some insight into what should follow, yet something new and unexpected is perpetually starting up to surprize and entertain them. In a word, it is one of the busiest plays I am acquainted with; and, if I may be allowed to hint at a fault in it, it appears to me to be, that in consequence of the variety of incidents and number of characters, the *denouement* seems rather too much hurried on, and to want somewhat of that distinctness which the author with a little more pains might have rendered it capab'e of. On the whole, however, it is a very entertaining comedy, and I cannot help thinking the lady *Restless* in this play more truly a *Jealous Wife*, and, for the importance of the scenes she is introduced into, more highly finished than the Mrs. Oakly of Mr. Colman's comedy; for my sentiments in regard to which

see JEALOUS WIFE. It was afterwards brought again on this same stage by Mr. Garrick for the winter season, and met with the same approbation as in the summer.

87. ALL PLOT, or, *The Disguises*. Com. by Mr. Stroude. Acted at Lincoln's-Inn-Fields, between 1662 and 1671. This play is mentioned by Downes, p. 31. It seems not to have been printed.

88. ALL PUZZLED. Far. Anonym. 1702.

89. ALL'S LOST BY LUST. Tr. by William Rowley. Acted at the Phœnix, 1633, 4to. This play was well esteemed. Its plot is chiefly from Novel 3, of the *Unfortuna'e Lovers*.

90. ALL'S WELL THAT ENDS WELL. Com. by Shakspeare, Fol. 1623. This play, which is supposed to have been sometimes called *Love's Labour Wonne*, was originally taken from Boccace, but came immediately to Shakspeare from Painter's *Gilletta of Narbon*, in the first volume of *The Palace of Pleasure*, 4to. 1566, p. 88. Dr. Johnson says, it " has many de-
" lightful scenes though not suf-
" ficiently probable, and some hap-
" py characters though not new,
" nor produced by any deep know-
" ledge of human nature. Pa-
" rolles is a boaster and a coward,
" such as has always been the
" sport of the stage, but perhaps
" never raised more laughter or
" contempt than in the hands of
" Shakspeare.

" I cannot reconcile my heart
" to Bertram, a man noble with-
" out generosity, and young with-
" out truth; who marries Helen
" as a coward, and leaves her as
" a profligate: when she is dead
" by his unkindness, sneaks home
" to a second marriage, is ac-
" cused by a woman whom he has
" wronged,

A L

" wronged, defends himself by
" falshood, and is dismissed to hap-
" piness."

91. ALL THE WORLD'S A
STAGE. Farce, by —— Jackman.
Acted at Drury-Lane, 8vo. 1777.
This Farce has some humour, and
is still represented.

92. ALL VOWS KEPT. Com.
Acted at Smock-Alley, 12mo.
1733. Printed at Dublin. Scene
Verona.

93. AN ALLEGORICAL MO-
RAL DRAMATIC MUSICAL EN-
TERTAINMENT, by way of Epi-
thalamium, 12mo. 1770. Printed
in a novel, entitled CONSTANTIA,
or, *The Distressed Friend.*

94. ALMANZOR AND ALMA-
HIDE, or, *The Conquest of Granada.*
The second part by John Dryden.
Acted at the Theatre Royal, 4to.
1672. 4to. 1687. See CONQUEST
OF GRANADA.

95. ALMENA. Op. by Richard
Rolt. Acted at Drury-Lane, 8vo.
1764. The musick by Arne jun.
and Battishull. The story taken
from the Persian History.

96. ALMEYDA, or, *The Rival
Kings.* Trag. by Gorges Edmund
Howard, 12mo. 1769. Printed at
Dublin. The story of this play
is taken from *Almoran and Hamet,*
by Dr. Hawkesworth, and it is dedicated to the queen.

97. ALMIDA. Trag. by Mrs.
Celisia. Acted at Drury-Lane,
8vo. 1771. From the excellent
performance of Mrs. Barry (now
Crawford), this play, though a
very poor one, had a considerable
run.

98. ALMYNA, or, *The Arabian
Vow.* Trag. by Mrs. Manley.
Acted at the Theatre Royal in the
Hay-Market, 1707, 4to. The
scene lies in the capital of Arabia,
and the fable is taken from the life
of *Caliph Valid Amanzor,* with some
hints from the *Arabian Nights' En-*

A L

tertainments. The character of *Almyna* is drawn from Dennis's *Essay
on Operas,* wherein is given a view
of what heroic virtue ought to attempt.

99. ALONZO. Trag. by John
Home. Acted at Drury-Lane, 8vo.
1773. By the assistance of excellent acting, this piece obtained a
nine nights' hearing, and then sunk,
as it deserved, into oblivion.

100. ALPHONSO, KING OF NA-
PLES. Trag. by George Powell.
Acted at the Theatre Royal, 1691.
4to. The scene lies in Naples,
and the story is founded on Neapolitan history. This play, however, is taken from the *Young Admiral* of Shirley. Prologue by Joe
Haines ; Epil. Durfey.

101. ALPHONSUS, EMPEROR OF
GERMANY. Tr. by George Chapman, often acted with great applause in Black Fryars, printed in
4to. 1654. This play seems to
have been written in honour of the
English nation, in the person of
Richard, earl of Cornwall, son to
king John, and brother to Henry III.
who was chosen king of the Romans
in 1257, at the same time that Alphonsus, the 10th king of Castile,
was chosen by other electors. In
order to cast an *opprobrium* on this
prince, our author represents him
as a bloody tyrant, and, contrary
to other historians, brings him to an
untimely end ; supposing him to be
killed by his own secretary in resentment for the death of his father,
who had been poisoned by him:
and, to complete his revenge,
he makes him first deny his Sa-
viour in hopes of life, and then
stabs him, glorying that he had at
once destroyed both soul and body.
This passage is indeed related in
Clark's Examples, and some other
authors, but for the true story consult *Mariana de Reb. Hispan.* and
other Spanish historians.

102. AL-

102. ALPHONSUS, KING OF ARRAGON. Hiſtor. Play, by R. G. acted with applauſe, and publiſhed in 4to. 1599.

103. ALTEMIRA. Tr. by Benj. Victor, 8vo. 1776. This play was written fifty years before the publication of it, and had been in rehearſal at Drury-Lane, but was prevented being acted by an accident. The hint of the plot was taken from a volume of Letters, called *Philander and Silvia*, written by Mrs. Manley, on the unhappy fate of lord Grey, who married the eldeſt daughter of earl Berkeley, and afterwards debauched her younger ſiſter; but for the principal ſubject of it, the author was obliged to a ſimilar ſtory in the Hiſtory of Italy, between the ducal houſes of Milan and Bologna.

104. ALTEMIRA. Tr. in rhime, by Roger Boyle, earl of Orrery. Acted in Lincoln's-Inn Fields, 1702. 4to. The ſcene is Sicily. This play being left unfiniſhed by his grandfather Roger, earl of Orrery, the Hon. Charles Boyle, afterwards earl of Orrery, was pleaſed to reviſe it, and to ſeparate from a vaſt variety of wit, and redundance of moral thoughts, which made the whole of an extreme length, the moſt beautiful and inſtructive turns of both, ſo as to reduce the poem within a reaſonable compaſs. The Prologue was written by lord Bolinbroke; the Epilogue by Charles Boyle, Eſq. It was publiſhed by Francis Manning.

105. ALZIRA, or, *The Spaniſh Inſult repented*. Tr. by Aaron Hill. Acted at Lincoln's-Inn-Fields, 8vo. 1736. This play is a tranſlation from Voltaire, and although this's language is very nervous and forcible, yet a ſtrict adherence to the rules of the drama, and that paſſion for long-winded declamation,

ſo prevalent among the French writers, throws a heavineſs into the piece, which, however ſtrongly it may be ſupported, renders it ever tedious and inſipid to the taſte of an Engliſh audience.

106. ALZIRA. A Trag. tranſlated from Voltaire, by William Somerville, Eſq. This was never publiſhed or acted. It is, however, mentioned by lady Luxborough to be in her poſſeſſion in 1750. See her Letters, p. 211.

107. ALZIRA. Trag. tranſlated from Voltaire; printed in Voltaire's works, 12mo. under the name of Dr. Franklin.

108. ALZUMA. Tr. by Arthur Murphy. Acted at Covent-Garden, 8vo. 1778. In this play our author has ſtrove to unite the chief incidents of the *Iphigenia in Tauris*, *Alzira*, and *Semiramis*; but with little ſucceſs. It was deſigned for repreſentation during the laſt Spaniſh war, and from thence would have derived ſome temporary advantages. It is by far inferior to the *Orphan of China*, *Zenobia*, and the *Grecian Daughter* by the ſame hand, and was received with coldneſs throughout its nine nights' exiſtence on the ſtage.

109. ANALASONT, QUEEN OF THE GOTHS. Tr. by John Hughes. This, being a juvenile production of the author, whoſe age when he wrote it was only nineteen, is deemed too imperfect for publication, though ſome of the ſpeeches and ſcenes have evident marks of genius. It was written in 1696, and is now in MS. in the poſſeſſion of the Rev. Mr. Duncombe.

110. AMANA. Dramatic Poem, by Mrs. Elizabeth Griffith, 4to. 1764. The ſtory of this piece is taken from *The Adventurer*, Nº 72 and 73. It was never acted.

111. AMASIS,

111. AMASIS, K. OF EGYPT. Tr. by Charles Marsh. Acted one night at the Little Theatre in the Hay-Market, 8vo. 1738. Scene Memphis.

112. AMAZON QUEEN, or, *The Amours of Thalestris to Alexander the Great.* A Tragi-Com. in heroic verse, by J. Weston, 4to. 1667. The story from Q. Curtius and Strabo. This play was never acted, by reason of the author's hearing of two plays besides on the same subject intended for the stage.

113. THE AMBITIOUS SLAVE, or, *A Generous Revenge.* Trag. by Elkanah Settle. Acted at the Theatre Royal, 4to. 1694. The scene is the frontiers of Persia. This play met with but ill success.

114. THE AMBITIOUS STATESMAN, or, *The Loyal Favourite.* Tr. by J. Crowne. Acted at Theatre Royal, 4to. 1679. This play, though esteemed by the author as one of his best performances, met with very indifferent success. The scene lies in Paris; and for the plot, see *de Serres, Mezeray,* &c.

115. THE AMBITIOUS STEP-MOTHER. Tr. by Nicholas Rowe, 4to. 1700. Acted at Lincoln's-Inn-Fields. The scene lies in Persepolis, and the characters are made Persian, but the design of the play seems to have been taken from the establishing Solomon on the *Throne of David,* by Bathsheba, Zadock the Priest, and Nathan the Prophet. See 1 Kings, ch. i. from ver. 5.

Perhaps none of our author's pieces exhibit so manly a dialogue as that which passes between *Memnon* and *Magas*, at the beginning of the second act. The majestic honesty of the old Persian general by far outweighs the tempestuous ravings of Bajazet, or the philosophic effusions of *Tamerlane* and *Ulysses.*

This play was revived by Mr. Garrick at Drury-Lane in the year 1758; the principal characters being performed by Messieurs Mossop, Fleetwood, Holland, Mrs. Cibber, Mrs. Pritchard, and Miss Macklin.

116. AMBOYNA, or, *The Cruelties of the Dutch to the English Merchants.* Tr. by J. Dryden. Acted at the Theatre Royal, 4to. 1673. 4to. 1691. Scene Amboyna. The plot of this play is chiefly founded on history. See Wanley's *History of Man,* lib. iv. c. 10. *The Rape of Ijabinda,* by Harman, is built on a novel of Giraldi. Decad. 5. Nov. 10. This play, as Dr. Johnson observes, is a tissue of mingled dialogue in verse and prose. It was a temporary performance, written in the time of the Dutch war, to inflame the nation against their enemies; to whom he hopes, as he declares in his epilogue, to make his poetry not less destructive than that by which Tyrtæus of old animated the Spartans. This play was written in the second Dutch war in 1673.

117. AMELIA. Oper. after the Italian manner, by Henry Carey, set to music by J. F. Lampe, and performed at the French Theatre in the Hay-Market, 8vo. 1732.

118. AMELIA. A Musical Entertainment, by Richard Cumberland. Acted at Covent-Garden, 8vo. 1768. This was taken from *The Summer's Tale* of the same author.

119. AMELIA. A Musical Entertainment, by Richard Cumberland. Acted at Drury-Lane, 8vo. 1771. The same piece with some slight alterations.

120. AMELIA, or, *The Duke of Foix.* Translated from Voltaire, in vol. II. of Dr. Franklin's Edition, 12mo. The original play was acted December 1752.

121. AMENDS FOR LADIES; with the merry pranks of *Moll Cutpurse*, or, *The Humours of Roaring.* Com. by Nat. Field, 4to. 1618. 4to.

4to. 1639. Scene London. The plot of Subtle's tempting the wife at the requeſt of the huſband, ſeems founded on the novel of the *Curious Impertinent* in Don Quixote. This play was written by our author, by way of making the ladies amends for a comedy, called *Woman's a Weathercock*, which he had written ſome years before, and whoſe very title ſeemed to be a ſatire on their ſex.

122. AMINTA, the famous. Paſtoral, by Torquato Taſſo, tranſlated by John Dancer, 8vo, 1660.

123. AMINTAS. An Eng. Op. performed at Covent-Garden, 8vo. 1796. An alteration of Roh's *Royal Shepherdeſs*.

124. AMINTA. A Paſtoral, 4to. 1628. tranſlated from the Italian of Taſſo, with Ariadne's complaint, in imitation of *Anguilara*.

125. AMINTAS. Dram. Paſt. tranſlated from Taſſo, by William Ayre, 8vo. [1737.] No date. See AMYNTAS.

126. AMOROUS BIGOT, with the ſecond part of *Teague O'Divelly*. Com. by Thomas Shadwell. Acted by his Majeſty's ſervants.

127. AMOROUS ORONTUS, or, *Love in Faſhion*. Com. in heroic verſe, by J. Bulteel, Gent. 4to. 1665. It is a tranſlation of the *Amour à la Mode* of T. Corneille, the original plot of which is borrowed from a Spaniſh play, called *El amor al uſo*, by Ant. de Solis.

128. AMOROUS MISER, or, *The Younger the Wiſer*. Com. by P. Motteux, 4to. 1705. The ſcene lies in Spain.

129. AMOROUS OLD WOMAN, or, *'Tis well if it take*. Com. attributed by Langbaine to Thomas Duffet. Acted at the Theatre Royal, 4to. 1674. It was afterwards republiſhed with a new title-page, by the name of *The Fond Lady*.

130. AMOROUS FANTASME. Tragi-Com. by Sir William Lower, 12mo. 1660. This play is tranſlated from the *Fantome amoureux* of Quinault, which appeared with great ſucceſs on the French ſtage.

131. AMOROUS PRINCE, or, *The Curious Huſband*. Com. by Mrs. Behn. Acted at the Duke's Theatre, 4to. 1671. The plot of this play is built on the Novel of the *Curious Impertinent*, and on Davenport's *City Night-Cap*. Mrs. Behn has, however, greatly excelled that play, and even improved on the Novel itſelf. Scene the Court of Florence.

132. AMOROUS QUARREL. C. by Ozell, tranſlated from Moliere's *Dépit Amoureux*. From this play Dryden's *Mock Aſtrologer*, and the greateſt part of Ravenſcroft's *Wrangling Lovers*, are apparently borrowed.

133. THE AMOROUS QUARREL. Com. tranſlated from Moliere, and printed in Foote's Comic Theatre, vol. IV.

134. AMOROUS WAR. Tragi-Com. by Jaſper Maine, D. D. 4to. 1648, 8vo. 1659.

135. THE AMOROUS WIDOW, or, *The wanton Wife*, by Betterton, 4to. 1706. This is no more than a tranſlation *ad libitum* of Moliere's George Dandin. Excluſive of ſome little deficiencies in point of delicacy, this may juſtly be eſteemed a very good play, and even now meets with confiderable applauſe whenever it is performed.

136. L'AMOUR A LA MODE, or, *Love a la Mode*. Farce, in three Acts, 8vo. 1760. This is merely a tranſlation from the French, and ſaid to be the work of Hugh Kelly. It is one of thoſe pieces which generally are produced by a ſucceſsful performance. This was publiſhed at the time when Macklin's *Love à la Mode* was acting with great ſucceſs.

137. AMPHITRYON. Tranſlated from Plautus, by Thomas Cooke, 12mo.

12mo. 1746. Dedicated to the earl of Chesterfield. Printed as a specimen of a translation of Plautus, which the author never finished.

The following circumstance was omitted in the account of our author, and is therefore inserted here:

Mr. Cooke is said to have been better versed in the art of collecting money by subscription, than any of his contemporaries. He always procured the earliest intelligence of a young nobleman returned from his travels, an heir lately come of age, or a rich Creole newly landed. On the receipt of such information, he conducted his attack as follows:

He first waited on my Lord, Sir John, or the Esquire, and solicited and received the single subscription of perhaps a guinea. Soon after, he paid a second visit to the same person, pretending to have been but recently informed of his uncommon genius and his zeal to promote the interests of learning, and therefore intreated the honour of dedicating his work to him, which was to be done at the expence of five guineas more. Having obtained this permission, and the cash, his dernier resort was to call on his patron a third time, representing the necessity of prefixing a copper-plate with his arms to the intended dedication. For this piece of service his usual tax was ten additional guineas. By such contrivances he was known to have picked up no inconsiderable sums, especially as he practised the same stratagem on many people, without the least design of inscribing a work to any of them, or even publishing the piece advertised in his proposals.

138. AMPHYTRION, or, *The Two Sosias*. Com. by J. Dryden. Acted at the Theatre Royal, 4to. 1691. This play is founded on the two Amphytrions of Plautus and Moliere. The scene lies in Thebes, and the music of the songs is composed by Purcell.

139. AMPHYTRION. C. translated from Plautus, by L. Echard, 8vo. 1694.

140. AMPHYTRION. C. translated from Moliere, by Ozell.

141. AMPHYTRION, or, *The Two Sosias*. Com. altered from Dryden, with Moliere's Dialogue-Prologue between Mercury and Night, introduced into the first scene, and the addition of some new music; acted at the Theatre Royal in Drury-Lane, 8vo. 1756. This alteration was made by Dr. Hawkesworth at Mr. Garrick's desire.

142. AMPHYTRION. C. translated from Plautus by Bonnel Thornton, 8vo. 1767.

143. AMYNTAS. A translation in Hexameter verse, by Abraham Fraunce, 4to. 1591.

144. AMYNTAS. The very same work, by Oldmixon, 4to. 1698. The before-mentioned translations were not intended for the stage. This, however, was brought on at the Theatre Royal; but, as the Preface informs us, with ill success. Prologue by Dennis.

145. AMYNTAS OF TASSO. Translated from the original Italian, by Percival Stockdale, 8vo. 1770.

146. AMYNTAS, or, *The Impossible Dowry*. Past. by Thomas Randolph. Acted before the king and queen at Whitehall, 4to. 1638.

147. THE ANATOMIST, or, *The Sham Doctor*. Com. by Edward Ravenscroft, 4to. 1697. It was afterwards published in 12mo. 1722: to both editions a musical masque is annexed, or rather inserted in it, called, *The Loves of Mars and Venus*, written by Motteux. Both pieces were

were acted at Lincoln's-Inn-Fields. In its original form, however, it has been long laid afide; but the Doctor being tranflated into a Frenchman, by the name of Monf. le Medecin, and almoft every thing curtailed but the fcenes between him, his maid Beatrice, and Crifpin, it remains in that mangled condition as one of the moft ftandard farces.

148. ANDRIA. Terens in Englyfh, or the tranflacyon out of Latin into Englyfh of the firft comedy of *Tyrens*, callyd ANDRIA, B. L. No date. Suppofed to be printed by Raftell.

149. ANDRIA. C. by Maurice Kyffin, 4to. 1588. I believe this to be the fecond tranflation in our language of any of Terence's works. It is printed in the old black letter, and has the following full title, viz. *Andria, The firft Comædie of Terence, in Englifh. A Furtherance for the Attainment unto the right Knowledge and true Proprietie of the Latin Tong*, &c. It has two Dedications; the firft, I fuppofe, to the eldeft, the fecond to two other fons of lord Buckhurft, to all of whom I imagine Mr. Kyffin had been tutor. In the latter of thefe Dedications he tells us, that feven years before he had tranflated the moft of this comedy into verfe, but that now he had altered his courfe and turned it into profe, as a thing of lefs labour in fhew, and more liberty in fubftance, feeming withal moft accordant to this comical kind of writing. It is recommended by five copies of verfes in Latin, and one in Englifh. Among the former number is one by the famous William Camden.

150. ANDRIA. Com. tranflated from *Terence*, by Richard Bernard, 4to. 1598.

151. ANDRIA. Com. tranflated from *Terence*, by Thomas Newman, 8vo. 1727. This is a tranflation of the fame play, fitted for fcholars' private reprefentation in their fchools.

152. The firft Comedy of *Pub. Terentius*, called ANDRIA, or, *The Woman of Andros*, Englifh and Latin; claufed for fuch as would write or fpeak the pure language of this author after any method whatfoever, but fpecially after the method of Dr. Webb, 4to. 1629.

153. ANDRIA. tranflated by Echard. 8vo.

154. ANDRIA. tranflated by T. Cooke, 12mo. 1734.

155. ANDRIA. tranflated by S. Patrick, 8vo. 1745.

156. ANDRIA. Com. tranflated from Terence, by Mr. Gordon, 12mo. 1752.

157. ANDRIA. tranflated by George Coleman, 4to. 1765.

158. THE ANDRIAN OF TERENCE, Latin and Englifh, 8vo. No date. Printed at Sherborne.

159. ANDROBOROS. A biographical Farce, in three Acts, viz. the Senate, the Confiftory, and the Apotheofis, printed at Monoropolis, fince Auguft, 170 . The Dedication to Don Com. Fiz. Scene, long Gallery in Moorfields. Mr. Coxeter fays that, in a copy of this whimfical piece which he had feen, and which now is in the poffeffion of Thomas Pearfon, Efq; there was a MS. declaring it to be written by Governor Hunter.

160. ANDROMACHE. Trag. by J. Crowne. Acted at the Duke's Theatre, 4to. 1675. This play is only a tranflation of Racine's *Andromaque*, by a young gentleman, chiefly in profe, and publifhed with fome alteration by Crowne. It was brought on the ftage without fuccefs.

16'. ANDROMANA, or, *The Merchant's Wife*. Trag. 4to. 1660. by J. S. (i. e. James Shirley.) The plot is founded on the ftory of

Plangus,

Plangus, in Sir P. Sidney's *Arcadia*. The title in the first page is, *The Tragedy of Andromana; or, The fatal End of Disloyalty and Ambition*.

162. ANDRONICUS COMNENIUS. Trag. by J. Wilson, 4to. 1664. Scene Constantinople. For the story, see Heylin's *Cosmography*, in the description of Greece.

163. ANDRONICUS. Trag. Impietie's long successe, or Heaven's late Revenge, 8vo. 1661. Scene Constantinople. For the plot, see the Life of Andronicus in Fuller's *Holy State*.

164. ANGELICA, or, *Quixote in Petticoats*. C. in two acts. 8vo. 1758.

165. ANNETTE AND LUBIN. Com. Op. of one act, by C. Dibdin. Acted at Covent-Garden, 8vo. 1778. This is taken from a French piece with the same title.

166. THE ANTIGALLICAN. F. by Mr. Mozeen, 8vo. 1762. This piece was performed one night only, for the joint benefit of the author and Mr. Ackman. It has been since published, together with a Collection of Poems, by subscription. It was received with some approbation.

167. ANTIGONE, *The Thebane Princess*. Trag. by Thomas May, 8vo. 1631. Scene in Thebes. The plot from the Antigone of *Sophocles*, Seneca's *Thebais*, &c.

168. ANTIGONE. Trag. translated from Sophocles, by George Adams, 8vo. 1729.

169. ANTIOCHUS. Trag. by M. Motley, 8vo. 1721. Acted at the Theatre Royal in Lincoln's-Inn-Fields. By the dedication to Washington, earl of Ferrers, it appears that the author was nearly related to that nobleman. The plot is built on the well-known story of Seleucus Nicanor giving up his wife Stratonice to his son Antiochus, on being informed by his physician, that his incurable illness was occasioned by his love for her. The scene lies in Antioch.

170. ANTIOCHUS. Tr. on the same story, by Charles Shuckborough, Esq; of Longborough, Gloucestershire: never acted, but printed in 8vo. 1740.

171. ANTIOCHUS THE GREAT, or, *The Fatal Relapse*. Tr. by Mrs. Jane Wiseman. Acted at Lincoln's-Inn-Fields, 4to. 1702.

172. ANTIPODES. Com. by Richard Brome. The scene London. Acted by the Queen's servants at Salisbury-Court, in Fleet-street, 1638. published 4to. 1640.

173. THE ANTIQUARY. Com. by Shakerly Marmion. Acted at the Cock-pit, 4to. 1641. This is a very pleasing play. Aurelio's declaring his marriage to the Duke and Leonardo, from his mistress Lucretia's lodgings, to which he had got admittance through the assistance of her maid, is an incident that has been made use of in several plays, particularly in *Ram-Alley*, *The Parson's Wedding*, and *Woman's a Riddle*. The character of the Antiquary, who cannot endure any thing but what is old, is an admirable hint, original in its execution, and might, under the pen of an able writer, be turned to very great advantage.

174. ANTONY AND CLEOPATRA. Trag. by Shakspeare, Fo. 1623.

Of this play Dr. Johnson says, "it keeps curiosity always busy, "and the passions always inte-"rested. The continual hurry "of the action, the variety of in-"cidents, and the quick succession "of one Personage to another, call "the mind forward without in-"termission from the first act to "the last. But the power of de-"lighting is derived principally "from the frequent changes of the "scene; for, except the feminine "arts,

" arts, some of which are too low, which distinguish Cleopatra, no character is very strongly discriminated. Upton, who did not easily miss what he desired to find, has discovered that the language of Antony is, with great skill and learning, made pompous and superb, according to his real practice. But I think his diction not distinguishable from that of others: the most tumid speech in the play is that which Cæsar makes to Octavia. The events, of which the principal are described according to history, are produced without any art of connexion or care of disposition."

175. ANTONY AND CLEOPATRA. Tr. by Sir Charles Sedley, 4to. 1677. Acted at the Duke's Theatre. As this play is founded on the same story with the last-mentioned one, there can be no room to say any thing farther concerning it, than that, although far from a bad piece, it nevertheless falls greatly short of the merit either of Shakspeare's or Dryden's Tragedy.

176. ANTONY AND CLEOPATRA. An historical Play, fitted for the stage by abridging only. Acted at Drury-Lane, 8vo. 1758. This alteration was made by Mr. Capell, with the assistance of Mr. Garrick. It was acted with considerable applause.

177. ANTONY AND CLEOPATRA. A Trag. by Henry Brooke, Esq; 8vo. 1778. Not acted. Printed in the author's works, 4 vols. 8vo.

178. ANTONIO AND MELLIDA. An historical Play, 4to. 1602.

179. ANTONIO AND VALLIA. Com. by Philip Massinger. This play was entered on the books of the Stationers' Company, and was one of those destroyed by Mr. Warburton's servant.

180. ANTONIO'S REVENGE; or, *The Second Part of Antonio and Mellida.* Tr. These two plays were written by J. Marston. Both were acted by the children of St. Paul's, and both printed in 4to. 1602.

181. THE TRAGEDIE OF ANTONIE. Done into English from the French, by Mary, countess of Pembroke, 12mo. 1595. At the end of the play is this date,—At Ramsbury, 26 of November, 1590.

182. ANY THING FOR A QUIET LIFE. Com. by Thomas Middleton. Acted at Black-Fryars, printed in 4to. 1662.

183. APOCRYPHAL LADIES. Com. by Margaret, duchess of Newcastle. This play is one of those which help to swell the bulk of writing of this voluminous titled Authoress. It is, as many other of her pieces, irregular and unfinished, and is divided into twenty-three scenes, but not reduced to the form of acts.

184. APOLLO AND DAPHNE, or, *The Burgo-Master trick'd,* by Lewis Theobald, 8vo. 1726. This is nothing more than the vocal parts of a Pantomime Entertainment, performed two years before at Lincoln's-Inn-Fields Theatre. It was for many years served up as an after-dish at the Theatre Royal in Covent-Garden.

185. APOLLO AND DAPHNE, or, *Harlequin's Metamorphoses.* A Pantomime, by John Thurmond, 12mo. 1727.

186. APOLLO AND DAPHNE. Op. 4to. 1734.

187. APOLLO AND DAPHNE. A Masque, by J. Hughes, 4to. 1716. The story from which it is taken is too well-known to need any farther notice in this place. The scene lies in the valley of Tempe in Thessaly. It was set to music, and performed at the Theatre Royal in Drury-Lane.

188. APOLLO

188. APOLLO SHROVING. C. 8vo. 1627. The letters E. W. prefixed to it, are initials of the name of a person who, though not the author, occasioned the publication of this piece, which was written by William Hawkins the school-master of Hadleigh in Suffolk, for the use of his scholars, and acted by them on Shrove-Tuesday, Feb. 6, 1626.

189. THE APOTHEOSIS OF PUNCH. A satirical Masque, with a Monody on the Death of the late Master Punch. Acted at the Patagonian Theatre Exeter-Change, 8vo. 1779. This is an attempt to ridicule Mr. Sheridan's Monody on Mr. Garrick's Death.

190. THE APPARITION, or, *The Sham Wedding*. Com. Acted at Drury-Lane, 4to. 1714. written by a gentleman of Christ-Church College, Oxford.

191. THE APPARITION. Com. translated from Plautus, by Richard Warner, 8vo. 1773.

192. APPIUS. Trag. by John Moncrief. Acted at Covent-Garden, 8vo. 1755. with no success.

193. APPIUS AND VIRGINIA. Trag. Com. by R. P. 4to. 1576. in black letter, and not divided into acts, *wherein* (as it is said in the title-page) *is lively expressed a rare example of the vertue of chastity, in wishing rather to be slaine at her owne fa.ber's hands, than to be deflowred of the wicked judge Appius*. This seems to be the same TRAGEDY OF APPIUS AND VIRGINIA as was entered on the books of the Stationers' Company between the years 1577 and 1578, by Kycharde Jonnes.

194. APPIUS AND VIRGINIA. Trag. by J. Webster, 4to. 1654. The scene lies in Rome, and the story is taken from Livy, Florus, &c. This play was afterwards revived and altered by Betterton.

195. APPIUS AND VIRGINIA.

Trag. by J. Dennis. Acted at Drury-Lane, N. D. 4to. (1709.) I cannot on the present occasion well avoid relating a humorous anecdote of this author, whose opinionated and testy disposition is well known, as it is strongly characteristic of that disposition. It is as follows: Mr. Dennis had for the advantage, as he expected, of his play, invented a new kind of thunder, which the actors indeed approved of, and is the very sort made use of to this day in the theatre. Notwithstanding such assistance, however, the tragedy failed; but some nights after, the author being in the pit, at the representation of *Macbeth*, and hearing the thunder made use of, he arose, in a violent passion, and exclaiming with an oath that was his thunder, *See*, said he, *how these rascals use me: they will not let my play run, and yet they steal my thunder*.

196. APPRENTICE. Farce, of two acts, by Arthur Murphy. Acted at Drury Lane, 8vo. 1756. The intention of this farce is entirely to expose the absurd passion so prevalent amongst apprentices and other young people, who, with no talents or education, assemble themselves in bodies composed of noise and nonsense, under the title of *Spouting Clubs*, where, without the gait or accent of Turk, Christian, or man, they unite in committing the most horrible murders on common sense, and the works of poor departed authors, who, could they rise again, would by no means be able to lay claim to the very offspring of their own brains thus defaced as they are by these pitiful retailers of their remnants of remnants; and all this to the loss and destruction of somewhat still more invaluable, their time and reputations. It met with considerable applause, and contributed in some measure, though it could not

not effectually carry the point, to drive this pernicious folly out of doors.

197. THE APPRENTICE'S PRIZE, &c. A Play, by Richard Brome and Thomas Heywood; entered on the books of the Stationers' Company, April 8, 1654; but not printed.

198. APRIL DAY. A Burletta, of three acts, by Mr. Ohara. Acted at the Hay-Market, 8vo. 1777. This was afterwards reduced to two acts, and performed as an after piece.

199. ARCADES. A kind of Masque, by J. Milton. This is only part of an entertainment presented to the countess-dowager of Derby at Harefield, by some noble persons of her family. It is very short and incomplete; yet as it is the work of that first-rate poet, and is published among his poetical pieces, I could not here pass it over unnoticed.

200. ARCADIA. Past. by James Shirley. Acted at the Phœnix in Drury-Lane, 4to. 1640. The plot of this play is founded on Sir Ph. Sidney's *Arcadia*, and is itself the foundation of a modern tragedy, called *Philoclea*.

201. ARCADIA, or, *The Shepherd's Wedding*. A Dramatic Past. 8vo. 1761. This little piece was brought on the stage at Drury-Lane Theatre, and was performed several nights, though with no very extraordinary approbation or success. It is extremely short and simple, being only a compliment to their present majesties on their nuptials. The words are by Mr. Robert Lloyd, and the music composed by Mr. Stanley.

202. ARDEN OF FEVERSHAM. The full title of this play is,

" The lamentable and true tragedie of M Arden of Feversham
" in Kent, who was most wickedlye
" murdered by the means of his
" disloyall and wanton wyfe, who,
" for the love she bare to one
" Mosbie, hyred two desperat ruffins Blackwill and Shagbag to
" kill him." Anon. 4to. 1592. 4to. 1633. and reprinted by Edward Jacob, 8vo. 1770. with a ridiculous preface imputing it to Shakspeare. The plan of this play is formed on a true history, then pretty recent, of one Arden, a gentleman of Feversham, in the reign of Edward VI. who was murthered as he was playing a game at tables with the said Mosebie. The fact is related by Hollingshed, Baker, in Beard's Theatre, and Jacob's History of Feversham.

203. ARDEN OF FEVERSHAM. Trag. by George Lillo. Acted at Drury-Lane, 1759. Printed in 12mo. 1762. This was left imperfect by Mr. Lillo, and finished by Dr. John Hoadly.

204. ARGALUS AND PARTHENIA. Tragi-Com. by H. Glapthorne, Acted at Drury-Lane, 4to. 1639. The plot of this play is also founded on the story of those two lovers in Sir P. Sidney's *Arcadia*, see p. 16, &c.

205. ARIADNE, or, *The Marriage of Bacchus*. Opera, by P. P. 1674. 4to. This piece is a translation from the French, and was presented at the Theatre Royal in Covent-Garden, by the gentlemen of the academy of music.

206. ARIADNE, or, *The Triumphs of Bacchus*. An Opera, by Thomas Durfey. 8vo. 1721. This piece was never performed, but is printed with a Collection of Poems in the year above-mentioned. The scene Naxos, an island in the Archipelago.

207. ARISTIPPUS, or, *The Jovial Philosopher*. By T. Randolph, *demonstrativelie proveing that quartes, pointes, and pottles, are sometimes necessary authors in a scholar's library: presented in a private shew; to which is added*, The Conceited Pedler, *presented*

presented in a strange shew, 4to. 1635.

208. ARISTOMENES, or, *The Royal Shepherd*. Trag. by Anne, countess of Winchelsea. 8vo. 1713. The story of this play is founded on the Lacedæmonian history, and the general scenes are Aristomenes's camp before the walls of Phæræa, sometimes the town of Phæræa, and sometimes the plains among the Shepherds.

209. ARMINIUS. T. by William Paterson, 8vo. 1740. This play was intended for representation at Drury-Lane; but the author, being unluckily acquainted with Mr. Thomson, used to write out fair copies of his friend's pieces for the stage or the press. It happened that the copy of *Edward* and *Eleanora*, which had been refused a licence, was read by the *censor* from one in Mr. Paterson's hand-writing; and this circumstance alone occasioned the present performance sharing the like fate.

210. THE ARRAIGNMENT OF PARIS. A Dram. Pastoral, presented before the Queen's Majesty, by the children of her chapel; and printed in 4to. 1584. Kirkman attributes this piece to Shakspeare, but on no foundation, it being the work of George Peele.

211. ARSASES. Tr. by William Hodson, 8vo. 1775. Not acted.

212. ARSINOE, or, *The Incestuous Marriage*. Tr. by A. Henderson. No date, 8vo. [1752.] This play was never acted, nor indeed ever deserved such an honour. The story is Egyptian; the execution of it truly wretched.

213. ARSINOE QUEEN OF CYPRUS. An Opera, after the Italian manner, by Peter Motteux, performed at the Theatre Royal in Drury-Lane, 1707. 4to. It was published by Thomas Clayton.

214. ART AND NATURE. C. by the Rev. Mr. Miller, 8vo. Acted at Drury-Lane, 1738. The principal scenes in this play are founded on the *Arlequin Sauvage* of M. De l'Isle, and Le Plateur of Rousseau; but it met with no success.

215. ARTAXERXES. Oper. 8vo. 1763. This piece is set to music in the manner of the Italian Operas, and was performed at Covent-Garden Theatre partly by English, and partly by Italian Singers. It met with good success during the run; which, however, was not a very long one, it having been brought on too late in the season. Both the words and music are by that celebrated composer Dr. Thomas Augustine Arne. The former, however, was no more than a most wretched mangled translation of that excellent piece the *Artaserse* of the Abbé Metastasio; in which Dr. Arne has at least shewn, that, however close an alliance poetry and music may have with each other, they are far from being constant companions, since in this performance the former is entirely as contemptible, as the latter is inimitable.

216. ARTAXERXES. Op. translated from *Metastasio*, by John Hoole, 8vo. 1768.

217. THE ARTFUL HUSBAND. Com. by W. Taverner, 4to. N. D. Acted with great applause at the Theatre in Lincoln's-Inn-Fields. Mr. Coxeter mentions his having been informed that this play was chiefly written by Dr. Joseph Browne.

218. THE ARTFUL WIFE. C. also by W. Taverner. Acted in the same place. 8vo. 1718. yet although it is in every respect far superior to the former, it had not the fortune to meet with the same success.

219. ARTHUR'S SHOW. This was probably an interlude, or masque, which actually existed, and was

was very popular in Shakspeare's age; and seems to have been compiled from Mallory's *Morte Arthur*. It is mentioned by *Justice Shallow*, in the Second Part of *King Henry* IV.

220. ARTIFICE. C. by Susanna Centlivre. Acted at the Theatre Royal in Drury-Lane, 1723. 8vo.

221. THE ARTIFICE. A Comic Opera, in two acts, by William Augustus Miles. Acted at Drury-Lane, 8vo. 1780. This piece was acted with little success, yet full as much as it deserved.

222. ART OF MANAGEMENT, or, *Tragedy expelled*, a dramatic piece, by Mrs. Charlotte Charke; performed once at the Concert-room in York Buildings. This piece was intended as a satire on Charles Fleetwood, Esq; then manager of the Theatre Royal in Drury-Lane; but that gentleman and his party found means to put a stop to its further progress on the stage. It was printed in 1735. 8vo. with a humorous dedication to Mr. Fleetwood, who endeavoured to smother it, by purchasing the whole impression. Some few, however, escaped the flames, and have crept into the world.

223. ARVIRAGUS AND PHILICIA. Tragi-Com. in two parts, by Lodovick Carlell, 8vo. 1639. The story of this play is founded on the British History, by Geoffr. of Monmouth and others, concerning Arviragus, who reigned in Britain in the time of Claudius Cæsar. It was since revived, with a new prologue written by Dryden, and spoken by Hart.

224. THE ASSEMBLY. Com. by a Scots gentleman, 12mo, 1722. Scene Edinburgh. This piece is no more than a gross abuse on the Whig party in Scotland, with the most barefaced profession of Jacobitism, and invectives against all who maintained the cause of king William in Scotland. The writer of Dr. Pitcairne's Life, in the *Biographia Britannia*, ascribes it to that gentleman.

225. THE ASSEMBLY. Farce, by James Worsdale. This piece had nothing extraordinary in it, but the excellence of the author in performing the part of an old woman (old Lady *Scandal*) in it.

226. THE ASSIGNATION, or, *Love in a Nunnery*. C. by J. Dryden. Acted at the Theatre Royal, 4to. 1673. 4to. 1692. This play was damned in the representation, and is one of these hasty performances which, at times, threw a cloud over the merit of that prince of poets. The incidents and characters are almost all borrowed, and are very strangely jumbled together. This is the play which the duke of Buckingham has made Mr. Bayes boast of, for introducing a scene of a petticoat and the belly-ach: but when it is considered that this great man was absolutely constrained to write several plays in a year, will it not appear much more amazing that his pieces have any merit at all, than that they have no more?

227. THE ASS-DEALER. Com. translated from Plautus, by Richard Warner, vol. V. 8vo. 1774.

228. ASTREA, or, *True Love's Mirrour*, by Leonard Willan, 8vo. 1651. The plot from a romance of the same name.

229. THE ASTROLOGER. C. As it was *once* acted, says the title-page, at Drury-Lane, 8vo. 1744. This play was taken from *Albumazar*. The author, James Ralph, in his Advertisement, complains that ten years elapsed before it could obtain the favour of a representation; that he was not unknown to the great, nor destitute of private friends; and having devoted the most serious of his studies to the service of the publick, he had some reason to expect the public favour. Yet that the receipts

ceipts of the house upon the First Night were but twenty-one pounds; and when the manager risqued a second to give the author a chance for a benefit, he was obliged to shut up his doors for want of an audience. Prologue spoken by Mr. Garrick; Epilogue written by him, and spoken by Mrs. Woffington.

230. As you find it. Com. by Charles, earl of Orrery. Acted at Lincoln's-Inn-Fields, 4to. 1703. Epilogue by lord Lansdowne.

231. As you like it. Com. by W. Shakspeare, Fol. 1623. The plot of this play is taken from Lodge's *Rosalynd*, or *Euphues' Golden Legacye*, 4to. 1590. and Shakspeare has followed it more exactly than is his general custom when he is indebted to such worthless originals. He has even sketched some of his principal characters, and borrowed a few expressions from it. The characters of *Jaques*, *the Clown*, and *Audrey*, however are entirely of the poet's own formation. Dr. Johnson says, " of " this play the fable is wild and " pleasing. I know not how the " ladies will approve the facility " with which both Rosalind and " Celia give away their hearts. " To Celia much may be forgiven " for the heroism of her friend- " ship. The character of *Jaques* " is natural and well preserved. " The comic dialogue is very " sprightly, with less mixture of " low buffoonery than in some " other plays; and the graver part " is elegant and harmonious. By " hastening to the end of his work, " Shakspeare suppressed the dia- " logue between the usurper and " the hermit, and lost an oppor- " tunity of exhibiting a moral les- " son in which he might have " found matter worthy of his high- " est powers." It may be added, that it is, perhaps, the truest pastoral drama that ever was written; nor is it ever seen without pleasure to all present. In the closet it gives equal delight, from the beauty and simplicity of the poetry. In this play, amongst numberless other beauties, is the celebrated speech on the stages of human life, beginning with, " All " the World's a Stage." The scene lies partly at the court of one of the provincial dukes of France, and partly in the forest of Arden.

232. Athaliah. Trag. by W. Duncombe, 8vo. 1724. 12mo. 1726. This is no more than a translation, with very little liberty, of the *Athaliah* of Racine. The story of it may be seen in 2 Kings, ch. xi. and 2 Chron- xxii. and xxiii. The choruses are elegantly translated; yet as the necessary music must have amounted to a prodigious expence, and as religious subjects do not seem the most peculiarly adapted to dramatic representation, this piece, although capital in merit, was never brought on the stage. The scene lies in the Temple of Jerusalem.

233. The Atheist, or, *The Second Part of the Soldier's Fortune*. C. by Thomas Otway. Acted at the Duke's Theatre, 4to. 1684. This was Otway's last performance, and is very unworthy of the author.

234. The Atheist's Tragedie, or, *The Honest Man's Revenge:* by Cyril Tournuer, 4to. 1612. The plot, of Levidulcia's conveying Sebastian and Tresco out of her chamber, when surprized by the coming of her husband Belleforest, is taken from *Boccace*, Dec. 7. Nov. 6.

235. Athelstan. Trag. by Dr. Browne. Acted at Drury-Lane, 8vo. 1756. This tragedy is founded on the British History, and has great merit, yet seemed not to meet with the success that merit claimed,

claimed, having been scarcely heard or thought of since its first run. The struggles and conflicts of various passion, which Athelstan is made to undergo before his paternal and domestic affections get the better of a resentment which had led him into an act of treason against his prince and country, are finely supported, and perhaps scarcely excelled in any of our modern tragedies.

236. ATHELWOLD. Trag. by Aaron Hill, Esq; Acted at Drury-Lane, 8vo. 1731. This play had made its appearance at the same theatre in 1710, under the title of ELFRID, or, *The Fair Inconstant*, and had met with disapprobation. The author has, however, made great alterations for the better in the present piece. The plot is founded on the well-known story of Athelwold's marrying the fair Elfrida, whom he had been sent, by king Edgar, to see and make his report of, with a view to her becoming his mistress. The poet has greatly heightened the infidelity of Athelwold, by making him, previous to his having seen Elfrida, to have seduced, under the most solemn promises of marriage, a valuable maiden, and her too the object of adoration of his dearest friend Lleolyn; thus making him trebly false to friendship, love, and loyalty. The consciousness of this ill-fated error, blended with the honour, courage and tenderness, which constitute the other parts of Athelwold's character, afford great opportunities to the author of painting the movements of the human heart; nor has he lost those opportunities. The language is poetical and spirited, the characters chaste and genuine, and the descriptions affecting and picturesque. In a word, I cannot help considering this little known tragedy as very far from the least valuable of Mr. Hill's dramatic pieces.

237. THE ATHENIAN COFFEE-HOUSE. Com. This play stands in Mr. Whincop's Catalogue, amongst the anonymous pieces written since the Restoration. In Mr. Coxeter's MS. Notes, it is said to be printed in 4to. and the scene to lie in an upper coffee-room. I suspect it to be the same play with that which in the British Theatre is called the *New Athenian Comedy*, and is said to be a satire on a particular society, i. e. the authors of the *Athenian Oracle*.

238. THE AUCTION. Farce, by Theophilus Cibber. Acted at the Hay-Market, 8vo. 1757. This is no other than a few scenes taken from Fielding's *Historical Register*.

239. AURENGE-ZEBE, or, *The Great Mogul*. Trag. by J. Dryden. Acted at the Theatre Royal, 4to. 1676. 4to. 1692. This play is written in rhyme, yet is far from being the worst of the writings of that great poet. The scene lies at Agra, the capital of the Mogul's territories in India, and the plot may be found in Tavernier's Voyages, vol. I. part. 2. chap. 2. Langbaine accuses the author with having borrowed his characters of *Aurenge-zebe* and *Nourmahal* from the *Hipolytus* and *Phædra* of Seneca, and also with having stolen several hints from Milton's *Sampson Agonistes*. From the first of these charges, however, Jacob takes some pains to vindicate him.

This tragedy, as Dr. Johnson observes, is founded on the actions of a great prince then reigning, but over nations not likely to employ their criticks upon the transactions of the English stage. If he had known and not liked his character, our trade was not in those times secure from his resentment.

His

A U A U

His country is at such a distance, that the manners might be safely falsified, and the accidents feigned; for remoteness of place is remarked, by Racine, to afford the same conveniencies to a poet as length of time.

This play is written in rhyme, and has the appearance of being the most elaborate of all his dramas. The personages are imperial; but the dialogue is often domestic, and therefore susceptible of sentiments accommodated to familiar incideuts. The complaint of life is celebrated, and there are many other passages that may be read with pleasure.

240. AURORA's NUPTIALS. A dramatic performance, occasioned by the nuptials of William prince of Orange, and Anne princess royal of England. Acted at Drury-Lane, 4to. 1734. The musick by John Frederick Lampe.

241. THE AUTHOR. Com. of two acts, 8vo. 1757, by S. Foote, Esq; Acted at Drury-Lane. This piece was written only for the sake of affording to the writer of it an opportunity of exerting his talents of mimickry, at the expence of a gentleman of family and fortune, Mr. Aprice; whose particularities of character, although entirely inoffensive, were made the butt of public ridicu'e in the part of *Cadwallader*. The eager fondness which the world will ever shew to personal slander, added to the inimitable humour of this writer and performer in the representation, for some time, brought crowded houses to it; till at length the resemblance appearing too strong, and the ridicule too pungent not to be seen and felt by the gentleman thus pointed out, occasioned an application for the suppression of the piece, which was therefore

forbidden to be any more performed.

242. THE AUTHORS. Dramatic Satire in two acts, 8vo. 1755.

243. THE AUTHOR AND THE BOOKSELLER. Dramatic piece, by Charlotte M'Carthy, 8vo. N. D. This was merely designed as an introduction to proposals for printing a book, intitled " Justice " and Reason faithful Guides to " Truth. A Treatise under thir- " ty-seven Heads."

244. THE AUTHOR's FARCE. Com. of three acts, by H. Fielding, Esq; 8vo. 1732. This comedy contains a supposed rehearsal of another piece, intituled *The Pleasures of the Town*, designed principally to ridicule the then prevailing fondness for the Italian singers. It was first acted at the little theatre in the Hay-Market with very considerable success, and afterwards revised and altered.

245. THE AUTHOR's TRIUMPH, or, *The Managers managed*. A Farce, which the title-page says should have been acted at Lincoln's-Inn-Fields, April 14, 1737, Anonym. 8vo. This is plainly the work of some disappointed author, whose piece having been refused a reception into a theatre royal, had, however, interest or money enough to procure one night's representation of this little squib of vengeance at one of the smaller theatres. It seems to have met with the contempt its total want of merit rendered it liable to; yet even this was not sufficient to cure the author's vanity; for in a preface to his piece, he attributes its failure entirely to the fault of the actors, and want of judgment in the town. How severe is the fate of a manager, who, whilst he with unwearied diligence, watches over the public sources of entertainment,

A U

ment, carefully keeping away all the rubbish which aims at polluting the stream, finds his own reward, the lying open to every attack on his reputation, his understanding, and even his property, from the unlimited abuse of each petty scribbler, who thinks himself aggrieved, by not being permitted to abuse the judgment of the town, and bring contempt on the very name of dramatic performances!

B.

B A

1. THE BABLER. Com. translated from Voltaire, and printed in Dr. Franklin's Edition, 12mo.

2. THE BANDITTI, or, *A Lady's Distress*. A play, by T. Durfey. Acted at the Theatre Royal 4to. 1686. The scene lies in Madrid, and some part of the plot is taken from Shirley's *Sisters*. This play met with some opposition in the performance, from persons with catcalls; on which account, Durfey has prefixed to it a humorous dedication, in which he seems to aim at some particular character, under the title of Sir Critic Catcall.

3. BAND, RUFF, AND CUFF. See EXCHANGE WARE.

4. BANISH'D DUKE, or, *The Tragedy of Infortunatus*, 4to. Acted at the Theatre Royal, 1690. The scene lies in a village in Belgium, the character of *Infortunatus* is drawn for the duke of Monmouth, and those of *Romanus* and *Papissa*, for king James II. and his queen.

5. THE BANISHMENT OF CICERO. Trag. by Richard Cumberland, Esq; 4to. 1760. This play was never acted, having been refused by Mr. Garrick, to whom it was offered. The plot of it is founded on history, and on the enmity and machinations of Calphurnius Piso, and the family of Clodius against the famous father of his country, Tully. The language of the piece in general is nervous, sentimental, and poetical, and the characters well drawn. Yet I cannot help thinking those of Clodius and his sister too vicious and shocking to come within the decent cloathing of the tragic muse; or if they did, the punishment of their crimes is not sufficiently striking, especially that of Clodius himself, who has not only apparently had an incestuous correspondence with his sister, but is moreover an atheist of that time, a character, which, by the way, I do not remember meeting with in ancient history, but rather seems a refinement in wickedness reserved for the politeness of our more enlightened age. The expectations of the reader, moreover, are raised in one place concerning the consequences of some fact, for which Clodius makes the most horrid preparations before they are informed of what it is, but which, when they come to be acquainted with it, does not appear to have the least connection with the present business

business of the drama, and consequently to be only an act of vice perpetrated for its own sake merely, viz. the debauching of the wife of Pompey even in the very temple of Juno. This is one fault in the conduct of the design, yet I think not the only one; Cicero himself, who ought assuredly to be the hero of the piece, being of much less consequence, and his character more carelessly touched, than those of several others in the play, and the catastrophe itself being too hastily brought on, nor sufficiently prepared for by a train of previous incidents; and, if I mistake not, far from being authorized by the testimony of history. On the whole, however, though the piece might perhaps have given some little scope to the ill-nature of the critics, had it appeared on the stage, yet for the closet it is far from wanting merit.

6. THE BANKRUPT. Com. by Samuel Foote. Acted at the Hay-Market 1773. printed 8vo. 1776. This performance, like the rest by the same author, contains little else than detached scenes without any plot. It exhibits, however, some strong delineations of character, and is far from the worst performance, which Mr. Foote, *catching the manners living as they rose*, gave to the public.

7. OF BAPTISM AND TEMPTATION, two comedies, by bishop Bale. Of these we know no more than the name, as mentioned by himself in the list of his own works.

8. BAPTISTES. A sacred dramatic poem. See *Tyrannical Government*, &c.

9. BARBAROSSA. T. by Dr. Browne. Acted at Drury-Lane, 8vo. 1755. This play is by no means so good a one as the *Athelstan* of the same author above-mentioned. The design seems borrowed from the tragedy of *Merope*. Zaphira's distress and her resolutions, greatly resemble, though they fall far short of *Merope's*. Achmet's declaring himself, and *Eumene's* being suspected, the murderers of their respective selves, are too much alike to allow a claim to much invention in the author of this play; and the character of *Barbarossa* seems to be drawn after *Poliphontes*, with some few strokes of *Bajazet* and the blustering monarch in the *Mourning Bride*. Yet did this tragedy meet with more success than *Athelstan*, from the advantages it appeared under, by the performances of Mr. Garrick and Mr. Mossop, in the parts of *Achmet* and *Barbarossa*; the prologue and epilogue by Mr. Garrick. With the following passage in the latter of these,

" Let the poor devil eat, allow him
" that, &c."

the author was much disgusted, as it represented him in the light of an indigent person. Vanity was undoubtedly one of the most prominent features in Dr. Browne's character.

10. THE BARBER OF SEVILLE. Com. of four acts, 8vo. 1776. This is merely an indifferent translation of Beaumarchais' celebrated piece with the same title, and was not acted.

11. BARTHOLOMEW FAIR. C. by Ben Jonson, 1614. This play has an infinite deal of humour in it, and is, perhaps, the greatest assemblage of characters that ever was brought together within the compass of one single piece. Some of the characters, and indeed the greatest part of the humour in them, may be looked on as extremely low; but the intention of the author,

thor, in rendering them so, was to satirize the taste of the times he lived in (not greatly different from that of our own age), by pointing out, how exalted a degree of applause might be obtained by this light and low manner of writing, at the same time that his *Catiline*, a long-laboured and learned piece, although tolerably received, had not obtained that applause, which he, and every other judicious critic, was and must be convinced its merit had a title to.

12. A BARTHOLOMEW FAIRING, *new, new, new, sent from the raised siege before Dublin, as a preparatory present to the great thanksgiving day. To be communicated only to Independants*. This piece is a mere party affair, and never was performed, but printed in 4to. in five short acts, 1649.

13. THE BASHFUL LOVER. Tragi-Com. by P. Massenger. Acted at the private house in Black Friars, 8vo. 1655.

14. THE BASHFUL LOVERS. Jacob, and after him Whincop, mention a Tragi-Com. with this title, to which are prefixed the letters B. J. whence they seem to infer Ben Jonson to have been the supposed author; but as the other catalogues take no notice of this play, and as the date, size of edition, and place of performance, are all the same as in the last-mentioned piece, I cannot help conjecturing that it may be the same, with only the difference of a spurious title page, to pass it on the world as a work of Ben Jonson's.

15. THE BASSET TABLE. C. by Mrs. Centlivre, 4to. 1706. The scene in Covent-Garden. This play, like most of this lady's writings, contains a great deal of plot and business, without much either of sentiment or delicacy.

16. THE BASTARD. T. 4to. 1652. Some part both of the plot and language is borrowed from the loves of Schiarra in the *English Lovers*, and the incident of Catalina's supplying her mistress Mariana's room on the wedding night, from the story of Roberto and Isidaura, in the *Unfortunate Spaniard*, p. 87. Scene in Seville. Mr. Coxeter attributes this play to Cosmo Manuche.

17. THE BASTARD. Trag. by Robert Lovett, Esq. This play, if it was ever acted, appeared only on the Irish stage. It has not been printed, but is praised in some verses by Mr. Sterling, published in Concanen's poems, 8vo. 1724, p. 261.

18. THE BASTARD CHILD, or, *A Feast for the Church-wardens*. A Dram. Satire of two acts; acted every day within the bills of mortality. By Daniel Downright, 8vo. 1768.

19. THE BATH, or, *The Western Lass*. Com. by T. Durfey. Acted at Drury-Lane, 4to. 1701.

20. THE BATH UNMASK'D. Com. by Mr. Odingsells. Acted at Lincoln's-Inn-Fields, 8vo. 1725.

21. THE BATTLE OF ALCAZAR, with Capt. Stukeley's death. Trag. Anonym. acted by the lord high admiral's servants, 1594, 4to. The story relates to Sebastian, king of Portugal, and Abdelmelech, king of Morocco. The plot taken from Heylin's *Cosmography*, in the History of Spain, &c. Shakspeare has pointed his ridicule at this play, in a parody on the words, *Feed and be fat*, &c. See last edition of Shakspeare's Plays, vol. V. p. 503. It is probable Dryden might take the hint of his *Don Sebastian* from the present tragedy.

22. THE BATTLE OF AUGRIM, or, *The Fall of St. Ruth*. T. by Robert

Robert Ashton. This play is little more than a bombastic narrative of the transactions of the celebrated 11th of July, 1691, when the Irish rebels, under the French general St. Ruth, met with a thorough defeat from the army belonging to king William, under the command of general Gincle, on the plains near Aughrim, in Conaught. The writer has shewn great warmth and zeal to the cause he espouses; but would have done better to have confined himself within the trammels of a prose narrative, than to have attempted the flights of poetry, which appear to be entirely out of his reach. It was published about the year 1727, being dedicated to the then lord lieutenant of Ireland. The scene lies in and before the town of Aughrim.

23. BATTLE OF HASTINGS. Trag. by Richard Cumberland Esq. Acted at Drury-Lane, 8vo. 1778. The coat of Joseph, and the dress of Harlequin, were never composed of patchwork more general than is the style of this performance. An injudicious application of Shakspeare's phraseology throughout all parts of it, continually provokes a comparison unfavourable to our present author. Add to this, that he has grossly violated the truth of history in his representations of *Edgar Atheling*, and *Harold*. Under his hand they may be said to have exchanged characters. He has even neglected to make the name of his play correspond with its subject; for, except from the title-page, we hear nothing of a *battle*. In spite of these defects, however, and many more, his work might have been received without disgust, had not his insatiate vanity prompted him to anticipate its appearance by such a degree of self-commendation as perhaps has never been exceeded. The cool reception afforded to this and three or four later pieces by Mr. Cumberland, has in all probability stopped his dramatic career, which indeed, had he consulted his fame as an author, should have concluded with the *West-Indian*, above which he has never risen. Poets do not seem to be aware that a stock of ideas, like a fund of wealth, by gradual subtraction, may be at length exhausted.

24. BATTLE OF SEDGMOOR. A Farce of one short act, said by Coxeter to have been rehearsed at Whitehall. It was never acted, but injuriously fathered on the duke of Buckingham, and printed among his works, in 2 vols. 8vo. 1707. The scene lies in a drawing room at Whitehall.

25. BATTLE OF THE POETS, or, *The Contention for the Laurel*. Acted at the little theatre in the Hay-Market, 1731, 8vo. It is no more than a few loose scenes to be introduced into the tragedy of *Tom Thumb*, intended to cast an abuse not only on Mr. Cibber, who was made laureat at that time, but also on Aaron Hill, Stephen Duck, and other competitors for the laurel, whom the writer has introduced under the characters of *Sulky, Bathos, Flaile*, &c. as he has done the laureat under that of *Fopling Fribble*. The piece contains much scurrility with very little wit. In a copy which I have seen, the name of Thomas Cooke was put in MS. as the author of it.

26. THE BAWDY HOUSE, or, *The Rake Demolish'd*. Farce, 12mo. 1774. We want words to express our detestation of this infamously obscene production.

27. BAYES's OPERA, by Gab. Odingsells, 8vo. 1730. This is

one

one of the many mufical pieces which the *Beggar's Opera* gave birth to. It was acted at Drury-Lane without fuccefs.

28. THE BEAU DEFEATED, or, *The Lucky younger Brother*. C. Acted at Lincoln's-Inn-Fields, 4to. without a date. The dedication to this play is figned by Mrs. Pix as the author of it. Some of the catalogues afcribe it to a Mr. Barker.

29. THE BEAU MERCHANT. Com. 4to. 1714. Written, according to Coxeter, by one Mr. Blanch, a gentleman near Gloucefter, but was never acted. The fcene lies in a coffee-houfe in Stockjobbing Alley.

30. THE BEAU'S ADVENTURES. Farce, by Phil. Bennet, Efq; 1733, 8vo.

31. THE BEAU'S DUEL, or, *A Soldier for the Ladies*. Com. by Mrs. Centlivre, 4to. 1704. This is one of the moft indifferent amongft that lady's pieces, and is now never acted.

32. THE BEAU'S STRATAGEM. Com. by G. Farquhar. Acted at the Hay-Market, 4to. 1707. This play was begun and ended in fix weeks, the author labouring all the time under a fettled illnefs, which carried him off during the run of his piece. In a fhort advertifement, he acknowledges the friendfhip of Mr. Wilks, to whom he attributes its fuccefs. The frequency of its reprefentation to this day, however, and the pleafure it conftantly affords, are proofs that the piece has an intrinfic merit in itfelf, which cannot need to ftand indebted to the performance of any actor for the applaufe it meets with.

33. BEAUTY IN A TRANCE. A Play, probably a Trag. by John Ford, entered on the books of the Stationers' Company, September 9, 1653, and was among thofe deftroyed by Mr. Warburton's fervant.

34. BEAUTY IN DISTRESS. Trag. by P. Motteux. Acted at Lincoln's-Inn-Fields, 4to. 1698. There are many fine lines in this drama, and a great variety of pleafing incidents. It is not, however, on the lift of acting plays. Prefixed to it is " a Difcourfe of the " lawfulnefs and unlawfulnefs of " plays, lately written in French, " by the learned Father Caffaro, " divinity profeffor at Paris, fent " in a letter to the author by a " divine of the church of England."

35. BEAUTY THE CONQUEROR, or, *The Death of Marc Anthony*. Trag. by Sir Charles Sedley, 1702. This play is written in imitation of the Roman manner, but was never acted.

36. BEAUTY'S TRIUMPH; a Mafque, by Thomas Duffet, prefented by the fcholars of Meff. Hart and Banifter, at their boarding-fchool at Chelfea, and printed 4to. 1676.

37. THE BEGGARS BUSH. T. Com. by Beaumont and Fletcher, F. 1647.

38. BEGGAR'S OPERA, by John Gay. Acted at Lincoln's-Inn-Fields, 4to. 1727. The great fuccefs of this piece, which carried it through a run of fixty-three nights during the firft feafon it was performed, and the frequent repetitions of it fince, have rendered its merits fo well known, that it is unneceffary to fay any thing farther of it in this place. It was written in ridicule of the mufical Italian drama, was firft offered to Cibber and his brethren, and by them rejected.

39. THE BEGGAR'S PANTOMIME, or, *The Contending Columbines*. An Interlude, intermixed with

with ballad songs in the characters of *Polly* and *Lucy*, manager and deputy-manager, with the scenes of *Britannia*, or, *The Royal Lovers*. Acted at Lincoln's-Inn Fields, 12mo. 1736. This is founded on a contention between Mrs. Clive and Mrs. Cibber, for the part of *Polly*.

40. THE BEGGAR'S WEDDING. A Ballad Opera of three acts, by Charles Coffey, 8vo. It was first performed at Dublin with but indifferent success, but being afterwards reduced into one act, and played in London under the title of *Phœbe*, in 1729, it pleased so well as to obtain a run of thirty nights. In the year 1763, it was revived, acted, and printed again in 8vo.

41. BELIEVE AS YOU LIST. Com. by P. Massinger. This play was never in print, but was certainly acted. The licence to it was signed by H. Herbert, and dated the 6th of May, 1631. It was entered at Stationers' Hall, Sept. 9, 1653, and June 29, 1660. This also was one of those sacrificed by Mr. Warburton's servant.

42. BELLAMIRA, or, *The Mistress*, Com. by Sir Charles Sedley. Acted by their majesties' servants, 4to. 1687. The scene of this play lies in London, but the plot is taken from the *Eunuch of Terence*.

43. BELLAMIRA HER DREAM, or, *The Love of Shadows*. Tragi-Com. in two parts, by Thomas Killigrew. These two plays were written during the time that the author was resident in the state of Venice; and were printed with the rest of his works in Fol. 1664.

44. THE BELLE'S STRATAGEM. Com. by Mrs. Cowley. Acted at Covent-Garden 1780. This play has not yet appeared in print, and therefore is scarcely an object of criticism. Its success was very great on the stage during a considerable run. To speak of it as a first-rate performance, would be doing injustice to the piece, as it possesses little originality, either in plot, character, or situation. It however gives pleasure in the exhibition, and affords a hope that the stage may derive considerable support from the future productions of this ingenious writer.

45. BELL IN CAMPO. Trag. in two parts. These two plays are the produce of that indefatigable authoress, Margaret, duchess of Newcastle. They were never acted, but are printed among her works, Fol. 1662.

46. BELISARIUS. Trag. by W. Philips. Acted at Lincoln's-Inn-Fields, 8vo. 1725. Reprinted, 8vo. 1758.

47. BELPHEGOR, or, *The Marriage of the Devil*. Tragi-Com. by John Wilson. Acted at Dorset-Garden, 4to. 1691. The plot of this play is taken from Machiavel. The scene Genoa.

48. BELPHEGOR, or, *The Wishes*. Com. Op. of two acts, by Miles Peter Andrews, performed at Drury-Lane, 1778. The songs only published. The reader will solicit no further acquaintance with so flimsy a performance.

49. BELTESHAZZAR, or, *The Heroic Jew*. A dramatic Poem, by Thomas Harrison. Scene Babylon. Never acted, but printed in 12mo. 1727, and 1729.

50. THE BENEFICE. Com. by Dr. Robert Wild, 4to. 1689. The opinion which the Presbyterians (of whom this author was a very zealous one) entertain of the orthodox clergy, may be collected from this comedy. The design is taken from another play, called *The Return from Parnassus*.

51. THE

51. THE BETRAYER OF HIS COUNTRY. Trag. by Henry Brooke. See THE EARL OF WESTMORLAND.

52. BETTY, or, *The Country Bumpkins*. A Ballad Farce, by H. Carey. This was acted with very little success at Drury-Lane, 1738.

53. BIANCA. Trag. by R. Shepherd. Not acted. Printed at Oxford, 8vo. 1772.

54. BICKERSTAFF'S BURYING, or, *Work for the Upholders*. Farce of three long scenes, by Mrs. Centlivre; acted at the Hay-Market, and dedicated *to the magnificent Company of Upholders*, 4to. no date.

55. BICKERSTAFF'S UNBURIED DEAD. A moral drama. Acted at Lincoln's-Inn Fields, 1743, 8vo.

56. THE BIRD IN A CAGE. Com. by James Shirley. Acted at the Phœnix, Drury-Lane, 4to. 1633. Scene in Mantua. This is an excellent piece, and has prefixed to it an ironical dedication to the famous William Prynne, Esq; who had been a most furious antagonist to plays, but was at that time a state prisoner for high misdemeanors.

57. THE BIRTH-DAY. Entertainment of three acts, by Mrs. Penny. Printed in a quarto volume of poems, 1771.

58. THE BIRTH OF HERCULES. Masque, by William Shirley, set to musick by Dr. Arne, and intended for representation at Covent-Garden, 4to. 1765. This Masque was written in honour of the prince of Wales's birth, and rehearsed in 1763, but afterwards laid aside on account of disturbances in the theatre about admission at half-price.

59. THE BIRTH OF MERLIN, or, *The Child has Lost a Father*. Tragi-Com. by William Rowley. The scene lies in Britain, and the story is taken from Geoffrey of Monmouth. Shakspeare, as the title-page informs us, is said to have assisted in this play, which is not very probable from the poorness of the composition. It was frequently acted with great applause, and was published in 4to. 1662.

60. THE BITER. Com. by Mr. Rowe, 1705, 4to. Acted at Lincoln's-Inn Fields. This was the only attempt of our author in the comic way, and met with no success. Yet it is not without some share of merit, and was meant to expose the *Biters*, a sort of character of that period of time, not much unlike the *Humbuggers* of this age. Dr. Johnson observes, that though this piece was unfavourably treated by the audience, the author himself was delighted with it; for he is said to have sat in the house, laughing with great vehemence, whenever he had in his own opinion produced a jest. But finding that he and the public had no sympathy of mirth, he tried at lighter scenes no more.

61. THE BLACKAMOOR WASH'D WHITE. Com. Op. by Henry Bate. Acted at Drury-Lane, 1776. The songs only printed. This piece met with an ill reception, being acted only about three nights.

62. THE BLACK MAN. An Interlude, attributed to Cox the comedian, and printed in the second part of *Sport upon Sport*, 1659; also in 4to.

63. THE BLACK PRINCE. T. by Roger, earl of Orrery. Acted at the duke of York's theatre, Fol. 1669 and 1672. The story is taken from the English Historians.

64. THE

64. THE BLACK WEDDING. A play with this title was entered on the books of the Stationers' Company, Nov. 29, 1653, but does not appear to have been printed.

65. THE BLAZING COMET. *The Mad Lovers*, or, *The Beauties of the Poets*. A Play, by Samuel Johnson, author of *Hurlothrumbo*. Acted at the Hay-Market, 8vo. 1732. This is, like his other writings, a farrago of madness, absurdity, and bombast, intermingled with some strokes of genius and imagination.

66. THE BLAZING WORLD. Com. by the dutchess of Newcastle. Fol. 1662. There are no more than two acts of this play, the author having never finished it; but it is printed with her other works.

67. THE BLESSINGS OF P*** AND A SCOTCH EXCISE, or, *The Humbug Resignation*. Farce, as it was lately performed (says the title-page at the new theatre in S— A—y street, by his M— company of comedians, 8vo. 1763. Despicable abuse of lord Bute.

68. THE BLIND BEGGAR OF ALEXANDRIA. Com. *Most pleasantly discoursing his various humours in disguised shapes, full of conceit and pleasure*, by George Chapman. It was published in 1598, is the author's first play, and is neither divided into acts or scenes.

69. THE BLIND BEGGAR OF BETHNAL GREEN, *with the merry Humour of Tom Stroud, the Norfolk Yeoman*. Com. by John Day. Acted by the prince's servants, 4to. 1659. For the plot, as far as it concerns history, consult the writers on the reign of Henry VI.

70. THE BLIND BEGGAR OF BETHNAL GREEN. A Ballad Farce, by Robert Dodsley. This is on the same story with the fore-

going. It was acted at Drury-Lane, but without much success, in 1741, and is to be found in a collection of the author's works, published under the modest title of *Trifles*, 8vo. 1748.

71. THE BLIND LADY. Com. by Sir Robert Howard, 8vo. 1661. The scene lies in Poland, and the plot is taken from Heylin's *Cosmography*, lib. 2. This play is printed with divers other poems of the same author.

72. THE BLOODY BANQUET. Trag. printed in 4to. 1620 and 4to. 1639, with the letters T. D. but is, in some of the old Catalogues, ascribed to Tho. Barker.

73. THE BLOODY DUKE, or, *The Adventures for a Crown*. Trag-Com. Acted at the court of Alba Regalis, by several persons of great quality, 4to. 1690. This is a political piece, exposing the Popish plot, &c. and is written by the author of *The Abdicated Prince*, of which see above.

74. THE BLUNDERER. Com. translated from Moliere, printed in Foote's *Comic Theatre*, vol. IV.

75. BLURT, MASTER CONSTABLE, or, *The Spaniard's Night Walk*. Com. by Thomas Middleton, acted by the children of Paul's, 4to. 1602.

76. BOADICEA QUEEN OF BRITAIN. Trag. by Charles Hopkins. Acted at Lincoln's-Inn-Fields, inscribed to Mr. Congreve, 4to. 1697. The story of this queen is to be found in *Tacitus*, and in the English Historians, and is very well conducted in the play before us, more especially the discovery of Camilla's rape in the fourth act. By the dedication to *Friendship Improved*, we find that Boadicea was well received.

77. BOADICEA. T. by Richard Glover. Acted at Drury-Lane, 8vo. 1753. This gentleman's poem

of *Leonidas*, and his known great abilities, occasioned the most sanguine expectations to be formed with respect to this play, which had been many years written before it was brought on the stage. It did not, however, perfectly answer those expectations; there being rather a deficiency both as to incident and characters; yet the language is very poetical, and the descriptions beautiful. In a word, it seems much better adapted to give pleasure in the closet than the theatre. It will so seldom happen, in the course of these volumes, that we shall be able to give the sentiments of a critick in lawn sleeves on any dramatic performance, that we cannot resist the opportunity of exhibiting archbishop Herring's opinion of this play—" to the most material ob- "jections the author would say "(as Shakspeare must in some in- "stances) that he did not make "the story, but told it as he found "it. The first page of the play "shocked me, and the sudden and "heated answer of the queen to "the Roman ambassador's gentle "address, is arrant madness; it is, "indeed, unnatural. It is ano- "ther objection, in my opinion, "that *Boadicea* is really not the "object of crime and punishment, "so much as of pity; and not- "withstanding the strong paintings "of her savageness, I cannot help "wishing she had got the better. "She had been most unjustly and "outrageously injured by those "universal tyrants who ought "never to be mentioned without "horror. However, I admire the "play in many passages, and "think the two last acts admira- "ble. In the fifth, particularly, "I hardly ever found myself so "strongly touched."

78. BOARDING SCHOOL, or, *The Sham Captain*. Opera, by C. Coffey. Acted at Drury-Lane, 8vo. 1733. This is taken from a play of Durfey's, intituled *Love for Money*, which being in itself but a very poor original, it is scarcely to be expected that this cold second-hand service of it should be very palatable, and it consequently met with no success.

79. A BOLD STROKE FOR A WIFE. Com. by Mrs. Centlivre. Acted at Lincoln's-Inn-Fields, 8vo. 1717. In this play she was assisted by Mr. Mottley, who wrote a scene or two entirely. It met with very good success; and indeed, notwithstanding the absurdity and impossibility of the plot, and the poorness of the language, there is so much business and variety in it to keep up the attention of an audience, that it is still generally seen with pleasure.

80. BON TON, or, *High Life above Stairs*. Farce, by David Garrick. Acted at Drury-Lane, 8vo. 1776.

81. THE BONDMAN. An ancient story, by P. Massinger. Acted at the Cock-pit, Drury-Lane, 4to. 1623. 4to. 1638. This is a very excellent tragedy. The scene lies at Syracuse. The plot, of the slaves being seduced to rebellion by *Pisander*, and reduced by *Timoleon*, and their flight at the sight of the whips, is borrowed from the story of the Scythian slaves' rebellion against their masters, in *Justin*, lib. i. cap. 5. It was revived with alterations and additions, and a second title of *Love and Liberty*, and acted at Drury-Lane, 1719, 8vo.

82. THE BOND MAN. Tragi-Com. altered from Massinger, by Richard Cumberland. Acted at Covent-Garden, 1779. Not printed. This alteration was very coldly received, being acted only about six nights.

83. THE

83. THE BOND WOMAN. This play was entered on the books of the Stationers' Company, Sept. 23, 1653, but does not appear to have been printed.

84. BONDUCA. Trag. by Beaumont and Fletcher, Fol. 1647. This play is upon the story of a queen of Britain, who is indifferently styled by the historians Boadicea, and Bonduca. It is esteemed a very good play.

85. BONDUCA, or, *The British Heroine*. Trag. Acted at the Theatre Royal, 4to. 1696. This was published by George Powell, who says it was given him by a friend, and that it was revised and studied in one fortnight.

86. BONDUCA. Trag. altered from Beaumont and Fletcher, by George Colman. Acted at the Hay-Market, 8vo. 1778. A judicious alteration from Beaumont and Fletcher's piece with the same title.—As the style of this play often rises to the most picturesque sublimity, the following lines are added as examples of it.

See Act II. Sc. I.

Go on in full assurance! draw your sword,
As daring and as confident as justice!
The Gods of Rome fight for ye; loud fame calls ye,
Pitch'd on the topless Apennine, where the snow dwells,
And blows to all the under-world, all nations,
The seas and unfrequented deserts; wakens
The ruin'd monuments; and there where nothing
But eternal death and sleep is, informs again
The dead bones with your virtues. Fight and conquer.
Up to your troops, and let your drums beat thunder;
March sudden, like a tempest, &c.

Again:

See that huge battle, moving from the mountains!
Their gilt coats shine like dragons' scales, their march
Like a rough tumbling storm: see they fall, look,
Look where the armed carts stand, a new army!
Look how they hang like falling rocks! as murdering
Death rides in triumph, Curius, fell destruction
Lashes his fiery horse, and round about him
His many thousand ways to let out souls.
Let us to where they charge, and where the mountains
Melt under their hot wheels, and from their ax' trees
Huge claps of thunder plough the ground before 'em!

We must do Mr. Colman the justice to suppose that he would have retained more of his authors, but that he was constrained to cut them down to the ability of his performers.

87. BONOS NOCHIOS. An Interlude. Entered in the books of the Stationers' Company, by Jeffrey Charlton, Jan. 27, 1608, but we believe not printed.

88. The merry conceited humours of BOTTOM THE WEAVER, 4to. N. D. An interlude taken from *The Midsummer's Night Dream*, printed with other pieces ascribed to Robert Cox, comedian.

89. THE BOW-STREET OPERA, in three acts, 8vo. 1773. Abuse of Sir John Fielding.

90. BRAGANZA. T. by Robert Jephson, Esq. Acted at Drury-Lane, 8vo. 1775. A successful tragedy on its original appearance, but one that has fallen into neglect since the first season. The plot of it too nearly resembles some parts of *Venice preserved*.

BR [36] BR

91. THE BRAGGADOCIO, or, *Bawd Turn'd Puritan*. Com. written by a person of quality, 4to. 1691. Scene London.

92. THE BRAGGARD CAPTAIN, Com. translated from Plautus, by Bonnell Thornton, 8vo. 1767.

93. BRAVO TURN'D BULLY, or, *The Depredators*. A Dramatic Entertainment. Founded on some late transactions in America, 8vo. 1740.

94. THE BRAZEN AGE. A History, by Thomas Haywood, in 4to. 1613. The first act contains the death of the centaur Nessus; the second, the tragedy of *Meleager*; the third, the tragedy of *Jason* and *Medea*; the fourth, *Vulcan's Net*; the fifth, the Labours and Death of *Hercules*; being all of them stories taken from Ovid's *Metamorphoses*, lib. iv. vii. viii. and ix.

95. BRENNORALT, or, *The Discontented Colonel*. Trag. by Sir John Suckling. This is printed among his works, in 8vo. 1646.

96. BRIDALS. Com. by the Dutchess of Newcastle, published among her works, Fol.

97. THE BRIDE. Com. by Thomas Nabbes, 4to. 1640. Acted in the year 1638, at Drury-Lane.

98. BRITAIN'S HAPPINESS. A musical Interlude, by P. Motteux, performed at both the Theatres, 4to. 1704. The scene, a prospect of Dover castle and the sea. This interlude had long before been intended only for an introduction to an opera, which, if ever finished, was to have been called *The Loves of Europe*, every act shewing the manner of a different nation in their addresses to the fair sex.

99. BRITANNIA. A Masque, by David Mallet, 8vo. 1755. This piece was set to Music by Dr. Arne, and performed with success at the Theatre Royal in Drury-Lane. Prefixed to it is a prologue, in the character of a drunken sailor reading a play-bill, written in conjunction by Messrs. Mallet and Garrick, and spoken by the latter with universal applause; and which, the subject being extremely popular, as a French war had not been long declared, was called for and insisted on by the audience many nights in the season when the piece itself was not performed.

100. BRITANNIA AND BATAVIA. Masque, by George Lillo, 8vo. 1740, written on the marriage of the prince of Orange and the princess Royal.

101. BRITANNIA. An English Opera, by Mr. Lediard. Acted at the new theatre in the Haymarket, 4to. 1732.

102. BRITANNIA, or, *The Gods in Council*. Dramatic poem, wherein felicity is predicted to Britain, the causes of the present disputes in Europe and America are debated, and their issue prophetically determined, by Robert Avery, 4to. 1756.

103. BRITANNIA REDIVIVA, or, *Courage and Liberty*. An allegorical Masque, performed at the New Wells Clerkenwell, 12mo. 1746. The musick by John Dunn.

104. BRITANNIA TRIUMPHANS. A Masque, by Sir W. Davenant and Inigo Jones. It was presented at Whitehall, by king Charles I. and his lords, on the Sunday after Twelfth-Night, 1637, and was printed in 4to. 1637.

1637, but is not inserted in the folio edition of Sir William's works.

105. BRITANNICUS. Trag. by J. Ozell, 12mo. 1714. This is only a translation of a French play of the same name by M. Racine.

106. THE BRITISH ENCHANTERS, or, *No Magic like Love*; by lord Lansdowne. It was first called a Tragedy, and was acted at the Queen's Theatre in the Hay-Market, 4to. 1706. The author, who took an early dislike to the French and Italian Operas, seems in this attempt to have aimed at reconciling the variety and magnificence essential to operas, to a more rational model, by introducing somewhat more substantial than the mere gratification of eye and ear. Its success was great, but was put a stop to by the division of the theatre and a prohibition of musical pieces.

107. THE BRITISH HEROINE. Trag. by —— Jackson. Acted at Covent-Garden, May 5, 1778, for the benefit of the Author's wife. Not printed.

108. THE BRITON. Trag. by Ambrose Philips. Acted with considerable success at the Theatre Royal in Drury-Lane, 8vo. 1721. Whatever was the reception of this tragedy, says Dr. Johnson, it is now neglected; though one of the scenes, between *Vanoc* the British Prince and *Va'ens* the Roman General, is confessed to be written with great dramatic skill, animated by a spirit truly poetical.

109. BRITONS STRIKE HOME, or, *The Sailors Rehearsal*. A Ballad Farce, by Edward Philips, performed, but without success, at Drury-Lane, 1739. 8vo.

110. THE BROKEN HEART. Tr. by Mr. John Ford. Acted at Black-Friers, 4to. 1633.

111. THE BROKEN STOCKJOBBERS, or, *Work for the Bailiffs*. A Farce, as lately acted in Exchange-Alley, 8vo. 1720.

112. THE BROKER BEWITCH'D. Comic Farce of two acts, 8vo. N. D.

113. THE BROTHERS. Com. by J. Shirley. Acted at Black-Fryars, 1652. 8vo. Scene lies in Madrid.

114. THE BROTHERS. Trag. by Dr. Young. Acted at Drury-Lane, 8vo. 1752. The scene of this play lies in Macedon, and the plot from the History of Macedonia in the reign of the last Philip. The two characters of *Demetrius* and *Perseus* are admirably drawn, and their contest, before their father in the third act, perhaps the finest pieces of oratory in the English language. But there is one particular circumstance relating to this play, which does as much honour to the heart, as the play itself does to the abilities of the author, which is his having not only given up the entire profits of three benefits arising from it, but also even made up the amount of them to the sum of 1000 *l.* and generously bestowed it to the noblest of all purposes, viz. the propagation of the Gospel in foreign parts.

The original compiler of this work might have added, that the speeches of the contending brothers are in great measure translations from *Livy*, and that the play itself was but coldly received, being undramatical in its conduct, and imperfect in its catastrophe. This latter defect indeed is acknowledged in the Doctor's own epilogue, which was never used, the place of it being supplied by a sample of Scottish humour, in which Mr. Mallet expresses himself of our author and his charity in the following

following very delicate terms:

"A scheme forsooth to benefit the
"nation,
"Some queer odd whim of pious pre-
"f gation!
"Lord! talk so, here—the man must
"be a widgeon:
"Drury may propagate—but not reli-
"gion."

This pleasantry might have set the whole clan of the *Mac Gregors* on a roar, but excited contempt only in an English audience, their ears till then having escaped the insult of such vile ribaldry. Dr. Young was much offended by it, nor would suffer it to be printed at the end of his piece. He was scarce less angry with Mr. Garrick, at whose instigation it was written, as well as delivered to Mrs. Clive, who spoke it in her broadest manner.

115. THE BROTHERS. A Com. by Richard Cumberland, Esq. Acted at Covent-Garden, 8vo. 1769. This play (a promising forerunner of the West-Indian) was received with no inconsiderable applause.

116. BRUTUS. Trag. translated from Voltaire; printed in Dr. Franklin's Edition of that author's works, 12mo.

117. BRUTUS OF ALBA, or, *The Enchanted Lovers*. Trag. by Nahum Tate. Acted at the Duke's Theatre, 4to. 1678. The plan of this play is taken from the fourth Book of Virgil's *Æneid*.

118. BRUTUS OF ALBA, or, *Augusta's Triumph*. An Opera. Acted at the Theatre in Dorset-Gardens, 4to. 1697. The scene of this piece lies mostly on the Thames, and the plot is taken entirely from the last-mentioned play, and some of the old dramatic writers. It was published by George Powell and John Verbruggen.

119. BUCKRAM IN ARMOUR. Ballad Opera, 8vo. This piece appears to have been acted, but the title-page was wanting to the only copy we have seen.

120. THE BUGBEARS. Com. by J. Jeffere. This ancient play is in MS. in the library of lord Shelburne, and appears to be a free translation from some Italian drama.

121. THE BURNING OF SODOM. Trag. by Ralph Radcliff. Not printed.

122. THE BURNING OF JOHN HUSS. Trag. by Ralph Radcliff. Not printed.

123. BURY FAIR. Com. by Thomas Shadwell, 4to. 1689. The characters of *Old Wit*, and Sir *Humphry Noddle* in this play, are apparently borrowed from *Justice Spoilwit* and Sir *John Noddy*, in the duke of Newcastle's *Triumphant Widow*, and that of La Roche from the *Precieuses ridicules* of Moliere. In the dedication to the earl of Dorset, the author says that this play
"was written during eight months
"painful sickness, wherein all the
"several days, in which I was able
"to write any part of a scene,
"amounted not to one month,
"except some few which were em-
"ployed in indispensable busi-
"ness."

124. BUSIRIS, *King of Egypt*, Trag. by Dr. Edward Young, 8vo. 1719. It appeared with success on the stage at Drury-Lane, but is written in a glaring ambitious style, like that which we probably should have met with in the dramas of *Statius*, had any of them escaped the wreck of Roman literature. The haughty message sent by *Busiris* to the *Persian Ambassador* is copied from that returned by the *Æthiopian Prince* to *Cambyses* in the third book of *Herodotus*. The plot of this play, we believe, to be of the author's contrivance.

The

The dialogue contains many striking beauties of sentiment and description, but is wanting in that power which not only plays with imagination, but seizes on the heart. Dr. Johnson somewhere observes that of Congreve's three comedies, two are ended by means of a wedding in a mask. With equal justice we may add, that the three tragedies of Dr. Young are concluded by suicides in three pairs, *Memnon* and *Mandane*, *Alonzo* and *Leonora*, *Demetrius* and the *Thracian Princess*. That our poet, who never wanted words, was poor in other dramatic stores, is evident from this closing repetition of the most hackney'd incident that occurs in modern tragedy. "The dagger and the "bowl, says Dryden, are always "at hand to butcher a hero, when "a poet wants the brains to save "him."

125. BUSSY D'AMBOIS. Tr. by G. Chapman, 4to. 1607. 4to. 1608. 4to. 1616. 4to. 1657. This play was often presented at Paul's, in the reign of James I. and after the Restoration was revived with success at the Theatre Royal. The plot of it is taken from the French historians in the reign of Henry III. of France.

126. BUSSY D'AMBOISE, HIS REVENGE. Trag. by the same. Acted at White-Fryers, 4to. 1613 and 1641. This play is neither so good a one, nor so strictly founded on truth, as the foregoing, nor was it received with so much applause upon the stage. By the prologue to the edition of 1641, it appears that Nat. Field had been celebrated in the part of *Bussy d'Amboise*; and, by Durfey's dedication, we find that Hart was equally applauded in it.

127. BUSSY D'AMBOIS, or, *The Husband's Revenge*. Trag. by T. Durfey. Acted at the Theatre Royal, 1691. 4to. This is no more than a revival of Chapman's play, with some improvement on the character of *Tamyra*. For the intrigue of *Bussy* and *Tamyra*, see Rosset's *Histoires Tragiques*, Hist. 17. p. 363. under the feigned names of *Lysis* and *Silvie*. The scene lies at Paris.

128. THE BUSY BODY. Com. by Mrs. Centlivre. Acted at the Theatre Royal in Drury-Lane, 4to. 1709. This play met with so slight a reception from the players, that they even for a time refused to act it, and when prevailed upon so to do, which was not till towards the close of the season, Mr. Wilks shewed so much contempt for the part of Sir *George Airy*, as to throw it down on the stage at rehearsal, with a declaration, that no audience would endure such stuff. The success the piece met with, however, falsified these prognostications; and to do justice to the author it must be confessed, that although the language of it is very indifferent, and the plot mingled with some improbabilities, yet the amusing sprightliness of business, and the natural impertinence in the character of *Marplot*, make considerable amends for the above-mentioned deficiencies, and render it even to this hour an entertaining and standard performance. The dumb scene of Sir *George* with *Miranda*, and the History of the Garden-gate, are both borrowed from Ben Jonson's comedy of the *Devil's an Ass*.

129. BUTHRED. Trag. Acted at Covent-Garden, 8vo. 1778. Buthred (or, as it was called in Scotland, *Burethread*, and in Ireland *Butter-head*) is an anonymous tragedy, acted four nights to very patient audiences. Surely the reception of such pieces is more injurious

jurious to managers, than all the abuse that disappointed authors cou'd throw out against them. It is said, however, to have been the work of Mr. Johnstone, who wrote the *Reverie, Chrysal,* and other pieces of merit. We relate this hear-say circumstance, but do not believe it.

130. BUXOM JOAN. Burletta, by Mr. Willet. Acted at the Hay-Market, 4to. 1778. Taken from the original song sung in *Love for Love.*

C.

1. THE CABAL. As acted in George-street, 8vo. 1763, despicable performance occasioned by the apprehension of Mr. Wilkes.

2. THE CADY OF BAGDAD. Com. Opera, of three acts, by Abraham Portal, performed at Drury-Lane, 1778. The songs only published. This piece had no success.

3. "The Tragedie of CÆSAR AND POMPEY, or, *Cæsar's Revenge.* Acted by the students of Trinity College, in Oxford, 4to. 1607."

4. CÆSAR AND POMPEY. A Roman Tragedy, declaring their wars, out of whose events is evicted this proposition, *only a just man is a free man.* By George Chapman, 4to. 1607. 4to. 1631. Acted at the Black-Friers. The plot of this play is taken from the Roman history. Scene Rome and Pharsalia.

5. CÆSAR BORGIA, *Son to Pope Alexander* VI. Trag. by Nat. Lee. Acted at the Duke's Theatre, 4to. 1680. The scene lies in Rome, and the plot is built on the histories of Guicciardini and Marina, and Ricaut's Lives of the Popes. The play, like many others by this author, has great beauties, mingled with many strokes of rant, bombast, and absurdity, and therefore does not now stand in the list of acting dramas. It met, however, with good success at first.

6. CÆSAR IN EGYPT. Trag. by C. Cibber. Acted at Drury-Lane, 8vo. 1725. Colley Cibber's genius, however pleasing in comedy, is very far from being admired in a tragic cast of writing, nor is this play even considered as his tragic master-piece. The scene of it lies in Alexandria, and the plan is borrowed from the *Pompée* of P. Corneille; but how far it falls short of the merit of that celebrated author, we shall leave to the judgment of those who chuse to be at the pains of comparing the two pieces.

7. *The History and Fall of* CAIUS MARIUS. Trag. by T. Otway. Acted at the Duke's Theatre, 4to. 1680. The scene of this play lies at Rome, and the characters of *Marius,* jun. and *Lavinia,* are taken, and that even in many places verbatim, from those of *Romeo*

Romeo and *Juliet*. The plot into which the story of their love is thus interwoven, may be found in Plutarch's Life of *Caius Marius*, and in Lucan's *Pharsalia*.

8. CALEDON'S TEARS, or, *Wallace*. Trag. by G. Nesbit, 12mo. 1733. This play was printed at Edinburgh, and is said in the title-page to be collected from chronicles and records.

9. CALIGULA, *Emperor of Rome*. Tr. by J. Crowne. Acted at the Theatre Royal, 4to. 1698. The scene lies in the Imperial Palace in Rome, and the plot is taken from Suetonius's Life of that Prince.

10. CALISTA. Op. 8vo. 1731. dedicated to the dutchess of Queensbury. In the title-page it is said to be designed for one of the theatres; but this is hardly probable, as it appears to be built entirely on some scandalous reports of the times.

11. CALISTO, or, *The Chaste Nymph*. A Masque, by J. Crowne, 4to. 1675. It was written by command of king James II's queen, and was oftentimes performed at court by persons of great quality. It has songs between the acts. The scene lies in Arcadia; the duration of it an *artificial day*; and the plot is founded on Ovid's *Metamorphoses*. Lib. ii. Fab. 5, 6. It is dedicated to Lady Mary, afterwards queen to William III. who, together with the princess, afterwards queen Anne, the duke of Monmouth, &c, performed and danced in it.

12. CALYPSO AND TELEMACHUS. Opera, by John Hughes, Esq; 8vo. 1712. performed at the Queen's Theatre in the Hay-Market. The music composed by Mr. Galliard. This opera was an essay for the improvement of theatrical music in the English language, after the model of the Italians. The story on which it is founded, is in Homer, and improved in the adventures of Telemachus by the archbishop of Cambray. Our author has changed some incidents, and added the character of *Proteus*, to give it the greater variety.

13. CALYPSO. Masque, 8vo. 1778. Printed in a volume of Poems, intituled, "Miscellaneous "Poems, consisting of Elegies, "Odes, Pastorals, &c." published by Newberry.

14. CALYPSO. An Opera, by Richard Cumberland. Acted at Covent-Garden, 8vo. 1779. The adventures of Telemachus, in different shapes, have already surfeited the world. Opera, masque, and tragedy, have all maintained this hero in a languishing kind of existence. Mr. Cumberland has been more merciful. He contrived to give him as little pain as possible, by procuring him almost instantaneous damnation.

15. THE CAMP. Dram. Entertainment, by Richard Brinsley Sheridan. Acted at Drury-Lane, 1778. Though the scenery of this after-piece is uncommonly various and characteristic, yet the drama itself must be allowed to possess a still higher degree of merit. All the shifts, impositions, distresses, intrigues, manoeuvres, &c. peculiar to a camp, are described in the dialogue, or exhibited in the dumb show of Mr. Sheridan's performance, which, throughout two seasons, was a considerable favourite with the publick, being well attended, while the plays of Shakspeare were acting to almost empty benches. Such is the success of comic novelty, especially when produced by a hand so masterly as that of our author, assisted by

by the labours of the first scene-painter in Europe, the extent of whose skill was displayed in a most perfect representation of the late encampment at Cox-Heath.

16. CAMBYSES, *King of Persia.* Play in old metre, by Thomas Preston, 4to. without a date. Its running title is, *A Comedie of King Cambises*; and its fuller one as follows: "A lamentable tragedy full "of pleasant mirth, containing the "Life of *Cambises*, King of Persia, "from the beginning of his king- "dome unto his death; his one "good deed of execution, af- "ter the many wicked deeds "and tyranous murders commit- "ted by and through him. And "last of all, his odious death, "by God's judgment appointed, "done in such order as followeth." The story is taken from Herodotus and Justin.

17. CAMBYSES, *King of Persia.* Trag. by Elkanah Settle. Acted at the Duke's Theatre, 4to. 1671. This play is on the same story with the foregoing, and is written in heroic verse. The scene lies in Suza, and Cambyses' camp near the walls of Suza. In a postscript, the author acknowledges that his fellow-student had some hand in the beginning of this tragedy, but dying six months before the finishing of the play, he did not see two acts completed, and that not sixty lines of his remained.

18. CAMILLA. An Opera, by Owen Mac Swiny; first performed at the Theatre Royal in Drury-Lane, and afterwards in the Haymarket, 4to. 1706.

19. THE CAMPAIGNERS, or, *Pleasant Adventures at Brussels.* Com. by T. Durfey, 4to. 1698. Part of the plot is taken from a novel called *Female Falshood*. Scene Brussels. Time thirty-five hours. Prefixed to this play is, "A familiar "Preface upon a late reformer of "the stage [Collier]. Ending with "a satyrical fable of the Dog and "the Otter."

20. CANDLEMAS-DAY, or, *The Killing of the Children of Israel;* by Jhan Parfre, written in 1512. Printed from a copy in the Bodleian library, in Hawkins's *Origin of the Drama*, vol. I. 8vo. 1773. In the preceding year (i. e. 1511, as Mr. Hawkins observes), "we learn "from the prologue to this piece, "the players had represented *The* "*Appearance of the Angels to the* "*Shepherds*, and *The Adoration of* "*the Eastern Sages;* a subject very "susceptible of poetical orna- "ment, and the writer promises "to entertain the publick, in the "next year, with *The Disputation* "*among the Doctors:* but we do not "find that either of these pieces "has been preserved.

"In this rude play, the Hebrew "soldiers swear by *Mahound*, or "*Mahomet*, who was not born till "six hundred years after: Herod's "messenger is named *Watkin*, and "the knights are directed to walk "about the stage, while Mary and "the infant are conveyed into "Egypt. Yet, notwithstanding "these absurdities, there is some "kind of spirit in the character of "*Herod*; and the author (one can "hardly say, the poet) seems to "have distinguished *his* speeches "by a peculiar elevation of lan- "guage."

To these observations of Mr. Hawkins we may add, that in this mystery of the *Massacre of the Holy Innocents*, which is part of the subject of a sacred drama given by the English Fathers at the famous council of Constance, in the year 1417, a low buffoon of Herod's court is introduced, desiring of his lord to be dubbed a knight, that he may be properly

properly qualified to *go on the adventure* of killing the mothers of the children of Bethlehem. This tragical bufinefs is treated with the moft ridiculous levity. The good women of Bethlehem attack our knight-errant with their fpinning-wheels, break his head with their diftaffs, abufe him as a coward and a difgrace to chivalry, and fend him home to Herod with much ignominy. It is certain, that our anceftors intended no fort of impiety by thefe monftrous and unnatural mixtures. Neither the writers nor the fpectators (fays Mr. Warton) faw the impropriety, nor paid a feparate attention to the comic and the ferious part of thefe motley fcenes; at leaft they were perfuaded, that the folemnity of the fubject covered or excufed all incongruities.

21. THE CANTERBURY GUESTS, or, *A Bargain Broken*. Com. by E. Ravenfcroft. Acted at the Theatre Royal, 4to. 1695. This is a very indifferent play, and met with very indifferent fuccefs. Scene Canterbury.

22. THE CAPRICIOUS LOVERS. Com. by Mr. Odingfells. Acted at Lincoln's-Inn-Fields Theatre, 1726. 8vo.

23. THE CAPRICIOUS LOVERS. Com. Op. by Robert Lloyd. Acted at Drury-Lane, 8vo. 1764. The mufic by Mr. Rufh. The ground work of this piece is the *Caprices d'Amour, ou Ninette à la Cour*, by Favart.

24. THE CAPTAIN. Com. by Beaumont and Fletcher, Fol. 1647. This is far from one of the moft capital pieces of thefe united authors, and is now never performed.

25. THE COMEDIE OF CAPTAIN MARIO; by Stephen Goffon. This was never printed.

26. CAPTAIN O'BLUNDER, or, *The brave Irishman*. Farce, by Tho.

Sheridan. Dublin, 12mo. about 1748. This farce has always met with great approbation in Ireland, on account of the favourable light in which the Irifh gentleman, notwithftanding all his abfurdities and frequently forced blunders, ftill appears to ftand. One of the principal, and indeed moft entertaining fcenes in it, is borrowed from the Sieur *Pourceaugnac* of Moliere. It was written by Mr. Sheridan when a mere boy at College: but the original copy being loft, it was fupplied from the memory of the actors, who added and altered in fuch a manner, that hardly any part of the original compofition now remains.

27. THE CAPTIVE. Com. Op. by Ifaac Bickerftaffe. Acted at the Hay-Market, 8vo. 1769. This is taken from the comic fcenes of *Don Sebaftian*. It was fet to mufic by C. Dibden, but was not acted with much applaufe.

28. THE CAPTIVE PRINCESS. Trag. by Dr. Smith. Not acted or printed. See the account of the Author.

29. THE CAPTIVES. Trag. by John Gay. Acted at Drury-Lane, 8vo. 1723. Mr. Victor gives the following anecdote relative to this play: Mr. Gay " had intereft " enough with the late queen " Caroline, then princefs of Wales, " to excite her royal highnefs's " curiofity to hear the author read " his play to her at Leicefter-" Houfe. The day was fixed, and " Mr. Gay was commanded to at-" tend. He waited fome time in " a prefence-chamber with his " play in his hand; but being a " very modeft man, and unequal " to the trial he was going to, " when the door of the drawing-" room, where the princefs fat with " her ladies, was opened for his " entrance, he was fo much con-
" fufed

"fused and concerned about mak-
"ing his proper obeisance, that
"he did not see a low footstool
"that happened to be near him,
"and stumbling over it, he fell
"against a large skreen, which he
"overset, and threw the ladies into
"no small disorder."

30. THE CAPTIVES. Com. translated from Plautus, by Richard Warner, 8vo.

31. THE CAPUCHIN. Com. by Samuel Foote. Acted at the Hay-Market, 8vo. 1778. This was an alteration of *The Trip to Calais*, and was acted in 1776.

32. CARACTACUS. A dramatic Poem, by Mr Mason, 4to. and 8vo. 1759. This piece is written after the manner of the Greek tragedy, with odes and choruses, and was never intended for the English stage. In the closet, however, it must always give ineffable delight to every mind capable of judgment, as it lays the strongest claim to immortality, and is one among a few instances that poetical genius is so far from its decline at this time in these realms, that we have writers now living, some of whose works no British bard whatsoever, Shakspeare, Spencer, and Milton not excepted, would have reason to blush at being reputed the author of.

33. CARACTACUS. Dramatic Poem, by W. Mason. Acted at Covent-Garden, 8vo. 1776. This alteration was made by the author, and was received with applause.

34. THE CARDINAL. Tr. by Ja. Shirley, 8vo. 1652. Acted in Black-Friers. Scene Navarre.

35. THE CARELESS HUSBAND. Com. by C. Cibber. Acted at the Theatre Royal, 4to. 1704. This comedy contains, perhaps, the most elegant dialogue, and the most perfect knowledge of the manners of persons in real high life, extant in any dramatic piece that has yet appeared in any language whatever. Yet such is the natural malevolence of mankind, and such our unwillingness to bestow praise, at least on the living, that Mr. Cibber's contemporaries would not allow him to have been the author of it; some attributing it to the duke of Argyle, to whom it was dedicated, some to Mr. Defoe, some to Mr. Maynwaring, &c. As, however, during a long course of years, in which it has constantly been performed with the greatest success, no claim has been laid to any part of it, we surely may pay the deserved tribute of praise to him who by this prescription stands as the undoubted author of the whole, and to whom the English stage is to this hour greatly obliged for a very considerable share of its comic entertainments during the course of every season. When Mr. Cibber had written two acts of this play, he says, he threw them aside in despair of meeting with a performer capable of doing justice to the character of Lady *Betty Modish*, owing to the ill state of health of Mrs. Verbruggen, and Mrs. Bracegirdle being engaged at another theatre. In this state of suspence, Mrs. Oldfield, whose talents the author had but an indifferent opinion of, exhibited excellences which he had no expectation of seeing, and which encouraged him to complete his work. Near forty years after the representation of this comedy, he says, " Whatever favourable recep-
" tion it met with, it would be un-
" just in me not to place a large
" share of it to the account of Mrs.
" Oldfield; not only from the un-
" common excellence of her ac-
" tion, but even from her per-
" sonal manner of conversing.
" There are many sentiments in
" the

"the character of Lady *Betty Mo-*
"*diſh,* that I may almoſt ſay were
"originally her own, or only
"dreſſed with a little more care
"than when they negligently fell
"from her lively humour: had
"her birth placed her in a higher
"rank of life, ſhe had certainly
"appeared, in reality, what in this
"play ſhe only excellently acted,
"an agreeably gay woman of
"quality, a little too conſcious of
"her natural attractions." (Apol.
p. 249.)

36. THE CARELESS LOVERS. Com. by Edward Ravenſcroft. This play was written after the time that Dryden had attacked our author's *Mamamouchi,* and therefore in the epiſtle and prologue he has endeavoured to revenge his cauſe, by an attack on Dryden's *Almanzor* and his *Love in a Nunnery.* And retorting back on him the charge of plagiariſm, which, notwithſtanding what Mr. Ravenſcroft ſays in his prologue, he is far from being clear of in regard to this very piece, as the ſham ſcene in the fourth act, where Mrs. Breedwell and Clapham bring in their children, and challenge marriage of the lord de Boaltado, is apparently ſtolen from Moliere's M. de *Pourceaugnac,* Act 2. Scene 7. and 8. Whatſoever of that comedy moreover the author had not before made uſe of in his *Mamamouchi,* he has tranſplanted into this piece, which was acted at the duke's Theatre, 4to. 1673. In the epiſtle to the reader, the author ſays " that it was written at
" the deſire of the young men of
" the ſtage, and given them for
" a lenten play; they aſked it not
" above a week before Shrove
" Tueſday. In three days time
" the three firſt acts were made,
" tranſcribed, and delivered to them
" to write out in parts. The two
" laſt acts took me up juſt ſo
" much time: one week compleated it."

37. THE CARELESS SHEPHERD. A Paſtoral. I never ſaw this piece, but it is in all the Catalogues without either author's name or date.

38. THE CARELESS SHEPHERDESS. A Paſtoral Tragi-Com. by Thomas Goffe, 4to. 1656. This play was acted before the king and queen at Saliſbury Court. The ſcene lies in Arcadia. It has however a preludium, whoſe ſcene is placed in Saliſbury Court; and to the play is annexed a catalogue, extremely defective and erroneous however throughout, of all the dramas which had before that time been printed in the Engliſh language.

39. THE CARES OF LOVE, or, *A Night's Adventure.* A Com. by A. Caves. Acted at Lincoln's-Inn-Fields, 4to. 1705. Dedicated to Sir William Read the Oculiſt. The Prologue written and ſpoken by Mr. Booth.

40. THE CARNIVAL. Com. by Thomas Porter. Acted at the Theatre Royal, 4to. 1664. Scene Sevil.

41. THE CARTHAGINIAN. C. tranſlated from Plautus, by Rich. Warner, Eſq; 8vo.

42. CARTOUCHE, or, *The Robbers.* Anonym. 8vo. a comedy. This is a tranſlation from the French, and was acted at the Theatre in Lincoln's-Inn-Fields, 8vo. 1722. The plot is founded on ſome parts of the life of Cartouche, the celebrated French highwayman.

43. THE CASE IS ALTER'D. Com. by Ben Jonſon. Acted by the children of the Black Friers, 4to. 1609. This is not one of the moſt celebrated of this author's works, nor is it at this time ever acted. It is partly borrowed from
Plautus,

Plautus, as will be apparent on a comparison of several scenes in it with the *Aulularia* and *Captivi* of that author.

44. THE CASKET. Com. translated from Plautus, by Richard Warner, Esq; 8vo.

45. CASSANDRA, or, *The Virgin Prophetess*. Opera. Acted at the Theatre Royal, 4to. 1692.

46. CATALINE, HIS CONSPIRACY. Trag. by Ben Jonson, 4to. 1611. This play has great merit, but is too declamatory for the present dramatic taste. Jonson has in this, as in almost all his works, made great use of the Ancients. His *Sylla's* Ghost, at the opening of this play, is an evident copy from that of *Tantalus* at the beginning of Seneca's *Thyestes*, and much is also translated from Sallust through the course of the piece. For the plot, see Sallust, Plutarch's life of Cicero, and L. A. Florus. Scene in Rome.

47. CATALINE, or, *Rome Preserved*. Trag. translated from Voltaire. Printed in Dr. Franklin's translation, 12mo.

48. CATALINE'S CONSPIRACIES. By Stephen Gosson. This piece was never printed.

49. CATHARINE AND PETRUCHIO. Farce, by David Garrick Esq. Acted at Drury-Lane, 8vo. 1756. This is nothing more than an alteration of Shakspeare's *Taming of the Shrew*, by inverting and transposing different parts of it, rejecting the superfluous scenes, and reducing the whole into a regular piece of three acts. But the judgment wherewith this is executed, and the valuable use that the author has made of Shakspeare, whom he has neither deviated from, nor added to, does great honour to his understanding and knowledge of theatrical conduct, and has rendered a comedy, which, from the many absurdities mingled with its numerous beauties, had long been thrown aside, one of the most entertaining of the *petites pieces* on the present acting list.

50. CATO. Trag. by J. Addison. Acted at Drury-Lane, 4to. 1712. This play was performed eighteen times during its first run, is ushered into notice by eight complimentary copies of verses to the author, among which, one by Sir Richard Steele leads up the van, besides a prologue by Mr. Pope, and an epilogue by Dr. Garth, and has ever since been so universally admired, that it appears totally unnecessary to add any thing further in its commendation. As to its faults, if such it has, the contemporary critics have sufficiently endeavoured to point them out. It may not, however, be impertinent to observe in this place, that the beauties of poetry and the spirit of liberty which shine through the whole, scarcely more than compensate for its want of *pathos*, and the deficiency of dramatic business. It cannot, however, surely be thought an ill compliment to the author, to confess, that although as a play it may have many superiors, yet it must ever be allowed to stand foremost in the list of our dramatic poems. The story is founded on history, and the scene lies through the whole piece in the governor's palace at Utica. Of a work so much read, it is difficult (as Dr. Johnson observes) to say any thing new. About things on which the public thinks long, it commonly attains to think right; and of Cato it has not been unjustly determined, that it is rather a poem in dialogue than a drama, rather a succession of just sentiments in elegant language,

than

than a representation of natural affections, or of any state probable or possible in human life. Nothing here excites or assuages emotion; here is no magical power of raising phantastic terror and wild anxiety. The events are expected without solicitude, and are remembered without joy or sorrow. Of the agents we have no care. Cato is a being above our solicitude; a man of whom the gods take care, and whom we leave to their care with heedless confidence. To the rest neither gods nor men can have much attention; for there is not one amongst them that strongly attracts either affection or esteem. But they are made the vehicles of such sentiments and such expression, that there is scarcely a scene in the play which the reader does not wish to impress upon his memory. See also the remarks of Dennis, as quoted by Dr. Johnson in his life of Addison.

51. CATO. Trag. by J. Ozell. Acted at the Theatre in Lincoln's-Inn Fields, 12mo. 1716. This is only a translation from a French play of the same title, by M. Deschamps, to which is added, a parallel between that play and the last mentioned one of Mr. Addison's. Prefixed to it is an address to count de Volkra, the imperial ambassador, representing the author's ill success on his third night, owing to the preparations then making for a masquerade, given by his excellency on the archduke's birth.

52. CATO OF UTICA. Trag. translated from Des Champs, 12mo. 1716. This is different from Ozell's translation, and does not appear to have been acted.

53. THE CAVE OF IDRA. T. by Henry Jones. This was left unfinished by the author. See *The Heroine of the Cave.*

54. *The Tragic Comedye of* CELESTINA, *wherein are discoursed in most pleasant style many philosophicall sentences and advertisements, very necessarye for younge gentlemen, and discoveringe the sleights of treacherous servants, and the subtile cariages of filthye bawdes.* This title is entered on the books of the Stationers' Company, October 5, 1598, by William Aspley, but whether printed or not, I am unable to say.

55. CELESTINA, or, *The Spanish Bawd.* C. 1708. This was written originally in Spanish, by Don Mateo Aleman, one of the most celebrated dramatic authors of that nation, in twenty-one acts, and was translated above an hundred years ago, at the end of Gusman de Alfarache, *The Spanish Rogue.* In the second volume of the new translation, it is reduced to five acts.

56. CENIA, or, *The Suppos'd Daughter.* Trag. 8vo. 1752. This is no more than a literal prose translation of the tragedy of *Cenie,* by Grafigni, from which Dr. Francis borrowed the design of his *Eugenia,* which made its appearance this same year.

57. CEPHALUS AND PROCRIS. Dramatic Masque. With a pantomime Interlude, called *Harlequin Grand Volgi.* Acted at Drury-Lane, 8vo. 1733.

58. CHABOT. ADMIRAL OF FRANCE, by George Chapman and James Shirley. Acted at Drury-Lane, 4to. 1639. The story of it is taken from the French Historians, in their account of the reign of Francis I.

59. A CHALLENGE AT TILT AT A MARRIAGE. A Masque, by Ben Jonson. Fol. 1640.

61. CHAL-

60. CHALLENGE FOR BEAUTY. Tragi-Com. by Thomas Heywood, 4to. 1636. Acted in Black-Friers and the Globe. Scene Portugal.

61. THE CHAMBERMAID. Ballad Opera, of one act, by Edward Philips, performed at the Theatre Royal in Drury-Lane, 1730, 8vo. Taken from the *Village Opera*, by C. Johnson.

62. THE CHANCES. Com. by Beaumont and Fletcher. Fol. 1647. The plot of this play is taken from a Novel of Cervantes, called the Lady *Cornelia*, amongst the collection of Novels in 6 vols. 12mo. which I mentioned before. The scene lies in Bologna.

63. THE CHANCES. Com. by the duke of Buckingham. Acted at the Theatre Royal, 4to. 1682. This is only the preceding play altered and amended. It has been frequently performed with great applause, and indeed the vast variety of business and hurry of intrigue, which is happily produced by the confusion of mistaking two characters so extremely different as those of the *Constantias*, cannot avoid keeping up the attention of an audience, and making the piece appear, if one may so term it, entirely alive. Yet notwithstanding the alterations made in it first by the duke, and since that in the preparing it for some still later representations, there runs a degree of indelicacy through a few scenes, and a libertinism through the whole character of *Don John*, which, to the honour of the present age be it recorded, have for many years past, experienced a very singular disapprobation, whenever they have been attempted to be obtruded on the public.

64. THE CHANCES. C. with alterations, by David Garrick Esq. Acted at Drury-Lane, 8vo. 1773.

65. THE CHANGE OF CROWNES. A play, by Edward Howard, entered on the books of the Stationers' Company, but not printed.

66. CHANGES, or, *Love in a Maze*. Com. by James Shirley. Acted at the private house Salisbury-Court, 4to. 1632. Scene London. This play met with considerable success, not only during the author's life, but for a long time after. A scene in the first act, where *Goldsworth*, on examining his two daughters, finds them both in love with the same person, has been made use of, although indeed considerably improved, by Dryden in his *Maiden Queen*.

67. THE CHANGELING. T. by Thomas Middleton, 4to. 1653, 4to. 1668. Rowley joined with our author in this play, which met with very great success. The scene is Alicant, and the principal foundation of the plot may be found in the story of *Alsemero* and *Beatrice Joanna*, in Reynolds's *God's Revenge against Murder*, book i. ch. viii.

68. THE CHANGLING. Com. by Matthew Heywood. See vol. I. p. 219.

69. THE CHAPLET. A musical Entertainment, by Moses Mendez, 8vo. 1749. Acted at Drury-Lane. This piece had a considerable run, and still stands in a very favourite light among our musical dramatic entertainments. The poetry of it, on the whole, if not great, at least deserves the praise of being very pleasing, and will, perhaps, give pleasure where works of more essential merit may meet with a less kind reception.

70. THE CHAPTER OF ACCIDENTS. Com. by Miss Lee. Acted at the Hay-Market, 8vo. 1780. This play, which is built on *Diderot's Pere de Famille*, without being

ing a servile copy, possesses considerable merit, and was acted with much applause.

71. CHARLES VIII. OF FRANCE, or, *The Invasion of Naples by the French.* An Historical Play, by J. Crowne. Acted at the duke of York's Theatre, 4to. 1672. The plot of this play is taken from *Guicciardini*, and some of the French Historians. Scene Naples. It is written in heroic verse, and is perhaps one of the most striking instances of the insatiable turn of satire which prevailed with the celebrated earl of Rochester, who, notwithstanding the compliment paid him by the writer, in dedicating this play to him, could not avoid ridiculing the piece and its author, in his imitation of the third of Boileau's satires, in which he even mentions Mr. Crowne and his play by name, quotes a peculiar passage from it, and in a remark upon it points it out to that censure which otherwise it might perhaps have escaped.

72. CHARLOTTE, or, *One Thousand Seven Hundred and Seventy-three.* A Play, 8vo. 1775.

73. THE CHARITABLE ASSOCIATION. Com. of two acts, by Henry Brooke, Esq. 8vo. 1778. Not acted. The scene York.

74. A CHASTE MAID IN CHEAPSIDE. Com. by Thomas Middleton. Acted at the Swan on the Bank-side, by the Lady Elizabeth's servants, 4to. 1630.

75. THE CHASTE WOMAN AGAINST HER WILL. Com. This piece was advertised with others at the end of *Wit and Drollery*, 12mo. 1661. as then printing. It seems, however, to have been suppressed.

76 CHAUCER'S MELIBEE. C. by Ralph Radcliff. Not printed.

77. THE CHEAT. Com. translated from Plautus, by Richard Warner, Esq. 8vo.

VOL. II.

78. THE CHEATER CHEATED Interlude, 4to. No date. This piece is printed with some others, attributed to Robert Cox, Comedian.

79. THE CHEATS. Com. by John Wilson, written in the year 1662. 4to. 1663. 4to. 1671. This play met with general approbation; notwithstanding which, the author's modesty induced him to make an apology for its faults, in a preface to the earlier editions. To the fourth edition, which was in 1673, there is the addition of a new song.

80. THE CHEATS OF SCAPIN. A farce, by T. Otway, 4to. 1677. This farce is printed at the end of the tragedy of *Titus* and *Berenice*, which consists only of three acts, and was probably intended to be performed with it in the same manner as we have lately seen some pieces of irregular length destined for a joint performance. It is not much more than a translation of Moliere's *Fourberies de Scapin*; the plot of which, moreover, is borrowed from the *Phormio* of Terence. The scene Dover.

81. THE CHEATS OF SCAPIN. Com. by Ozell. This is only the absolute translation of Moliere's play, was never acted, but is printed among the rest of Ozell's translations from that author.

82. THE CHELSEA PENSIONER. Com. Opera, by C. Dibden. Acted at Covent-Garden, 8vo. 1779. The hint of this piece is taken from the story of Belisarius.

83. THE CHESHIRE COMICS. Com. by S. Johnson, 1730. This piece, written by the author of *Hurlothrumbo*, is, like that, full of madness and absurdity, yet, like that, has in it many strokes of wonderful imagination. I believe it has not been printed.

84. THE

84. THE CHESHIRE HUNTRESS, and *The old Fox caught at last*. Dramatic Tale, 8vo. 1740.

85. CHESTER WHITSUN PLAYS. MS. Harl. 1013. in the British Museum. These mysteries are said (perhaps truly) to have been written and exhibited in 1328, but the Harleian MS. represents t'em as they were played in 1600. There is a better copy of the same collection in the Bodl. Lib. E. N. 115, transcribed by one William Bedford, 1604, but even in that we see (says Mr. Tyrwhitt) but small remains of the original diction and orthography. Among the MSS. Harl. 2124 and 2125 are likewise two other copies. These dramas are taken from both the Old and New Testament, though abundantly disguised by buffoonery. The different trading companies of Chester were employed three days in the representation of them.

The Fall of Lucifer by the Tanners. *The Creation* by the Drapers. *The Deluge* by the Dyers. *Abraham, Melchisedeck,* and *Lot,* by the Barbers. *Moses, Balak,* and *Balaam,* by the Cappers. *The Salutation* and *Nativity* by the Wrightes. *The Shepherds feeding their flocks by night* by the Painters and Glasiers. *The three Kings* by the Vintners. *The Oblation of the three Kings* by the Mercers. *The killing of the Innocents* by the Goldsmiths. *The Purification* by the Blacksmiths. *The Temptation* by the Butchers. *The last Supper* by the Bakers. *The Blind Men and Lazarus* by the Glovers. *Jesus and the Lepers* by the Corvesaryt. *Christ's Passion* by the Bowyers, Fletchers, and Ironmongers. *Descent into Hell* by the Cooks and Innkeepers. *The Resurrection* by the Skinners. *The Ascension* by the Taylors. *The Election of St. Matthias, Sending of the Holy Ghost,* &c. by the Fishmongers. *Antichrist* by the Clothiers. *Day of Judgment* by the Websters. The reader perhaps will smile at some of these COMBINATIONS.

In one of these Adam and Eve are exhibited on the stage naked, and conversing about their nakedness. This very pertinently introduces the next scene, in which they have coverings of fig-leaves. So extraordinary a spectacle was beheld by a numerous assembly of both sexes with great composure: they had the authority of scripture for such a representation, and they gave matters just as they found them in the third chapter of Genesis. It would have been absolute heresy to have departed from the sacred text in personating the primitive appearance of our first parents, whom the spectators so nearly resembled in simplicity: and if this had not been the case, the dramatists were ignorant what to reject and what to retain.

The following is the substance and order of the former part of the play. God enters creating the world: he breathes life into Adam, leads him into Paradise, and opens his side while sleeping. Adam and Eve appear naked and *not ashamed*, and the old serpent enters lamenting his fall. He converses with Eve. She eats of the forbidden fruit, and gives part to Adam. They propose, according to the stage direction, to make themselves *subligacula a foliis quibus tegamus pudenda*. Cover their nakedness with leaves, and converse with God. God's curse. The serpent *exit* hissing. They are driven from Paradise by four Angels, and the cherubim with a flaming sword. Adam appears digging the ground, and Eve spinning. Their children Cain and Abel enter. The former kills his

his brother. Adam's lamentation. Cain is banished, &c.

86. THE CHIMÆRA. Com. by T. Odell. Acted at Lincoln's-Inn Fields, 8vo. 1721. The date and title of this piece are sufficient to point out the design of it, which was to expose the follies and absurdities that mankind were drawn into by the epidemical madness of that extraordinary year.

87. THE CHINESE FESTIVAL. A Ballet or grand Entertainment of Dancing, composed by Mr. Noverre, 1755. This entertainment, being not in itself in any respect dramatic, could not properly claim a place in this work, or indeed be thought deserving of any mention, was it not for its having been the cause of an extraordinary incident in theatrical history, which is one proof among many, how far an unreasonable prejudice, excited by the most trivial apparent cause, may misguide public judgment, and occasion it to crush and overthrow in one point the very fabric which in some other it has been itself attempting to rear. The town had for some seasons been murmuring at the *avaricious* disposition, as it was styled, of the managers, in *presuming* on success with the public, on the *bare merit* of some *trivial* authors, such as Shakspeare, Jonson, Rowe, Otway, &c. and grudging the expence attending on the more necessary decorations of the stage, consisting of *dances*, gay *scenery*, &c. a complaint which from Englishmen could scarce indeed have been expected. Yet the managers, willing to oblige them at any rate, and so fond of the favour and goodwill of their supporters, that, like lord Townly, they were willing " to feed even their very follies to " deserve it," determined to spare no expence in procuring these tinsel trappings to the Muse, this costly garnish to the dish of public taste; and on the recommendation of Mr. Denoyer, senior, engaged Mr. Noverre himself, a Swiss by birth, in their service, and, as they were well convinced of his abilities, gave him a plenipotentiary commission to employ whom he pleased under him. This engagement with Mr. Noverre, however, was entered into long before the declaration of war with France. But the time necessarily employed in procuring a sufficient troop to execute a plan so extensive and magnificent as was proposed, which was to consist of upwards of an hundred persons, and those to be collected from the different parts of the world, some being Italians, some Germans, some Swiss, and some few (but these by much the smallest number) Frenchmen, together with their respective voyages to London, the time taken up in contriving and making up such a numerous variety of suitable habits, and that required for repeated practices of the ballet itself before it could be sufficiently regular to make its appearance, took up a space of about eighteen months, during which time England had come to an open rupture with France, and war had been declared against that nation. Here then arose an opportunity for the private enemies of the manager (and such every manager must necessarily have, among those authors whose vanity has soared to dramatic writing, and yet whose merit, being unequal to the task, has subjected their pieces to a rejection) to exert their spleen, and shew their malevolence. Paragraphs were repeatedly inserted in the public papers; " that the ma- " nagers of Drury Lane were en- " gaging and bringing over a " troop of Frenchmen to the King's " Theatre

"Theatre in London, at the very time that England had just declared war with France." Nay, they did not scruple to add, that the managers had sent over not only for French dancers, but French dresses also, and even that the very carpenters and other manufacturers were to be from that nation. No wonder then if, thus prepossess'd by calumny and falshood, the populace, whose conclusions are generally right, however they may be misguided as to their first motives, became extremely exasperated against the managers for a step, which, had it been really such, would have been so very ill-timed and unpopular. In consequence therefore of this ill-grounded resentment, the piece even on the very first night of its appearance, though honoured with the sanction of his majesty's command and presence, could not escape ill treatment; but on the ensuing one, when it had not that protection to secure it, the tumults were very violent, and the contests between the opponents of the ballet and some young persons of fashion who were desirous of supporting it, rose to so great a height, that even some blows were interchanged. This however lasted only five nights, for on the sixth, being determined absolutely to put a stop to it, the rioters went to such lengths as to do very considerable damage to the theatre; and, not contented with venting their fury on the spot where the supposed offence had been given, they inflamed the mob without doors to join with them in the cause, and proceed to an attack on Mr. Garrick's house in Southampton-street, which, but for the timely interposition of the civil magistrate, it is most probable they would have entirely demolished. The piece however was never afterwards attempted to be performed, and the managers were obliged to sit down contented with the loss of upwards of four thousand pounds, which they had expended on this affair, in gratification, as they intended it, of the public taste. Mr. Foote, in his *Minor*, has with great humour referred to this fact, and ridiculed the folly of this absurd opposition, where he makes *Shift* say, when relating his adventures while a candle-snuffer at the theatres, that " it was in that office he acquired " intrepidity;" " but," adds he, " an unlucky crab-apple applied to " my right eye by a patriot gin- " gerbread-baker in the Borough, " who would not suffer three dan- " cers from Switzerland because " he hated the French, obliged " me to a precipitate retreat."

88. THE CHINESE ORPHAN. Historical Trag. Altered from a specimen of the Chinese tragedy in Duhalde's *History of China*, interspersed with songs after the Chinese manner. By William Hatchet, 8vo. 1741. See farther under ORPHAN OF CHINA.

89. CHIT CHAT. Com. by T. Killigrew, Esq; 8vo. N. D. [1722.] This play is little more than what its title implies, viz. an unconnected piece consisting principally of easy and genteel conversation; yet it met with considerable applause when represented at Drury-Lane Theatre, and so strongly was the interest of the author, who had a place at court, supported by the duke of Argyle and others of his friends, that the profits of this play were said to have amounted to upwards of a thousand pounds.

90. CHLORIDIA, or, *Rites to Chloris and her Nymphs*. Masque, by Ben Jonson, presented at court by

by the queen and her ladies at Shrovetide, 1630, 4to.

91. THE CHOICE. Farce. Acted at Drury-Lane, 1765, for the benefit of Mr. and Mrs. Yates. Not printed.

92. THE CHOICE OF APOLLO. Serenata, by John Potter, performed at the Hay-Market, 4to, 1765. The music by William Yates.

93. THE CHOEPHORAE. Trag. translated from *Æschylus*, by R. Potter, 4to, 1777.

94. THE CHOLERIC MAN. Com. by Richard Cumberland, Esq. Acted at Drury-Lane, 8vo. 1775. This play is taken from *Heautontimorumenos* of Terence. The news-paper criticks of the times charged Mr. Cumberland with having borrowed from Shadwell's *Squire of Alsatia*, a piece of which he declares he had no knowledge. These attacks, which ought to have been treated with silent contempt, drew from Mr. Cumberland a peevish dedication, which seems to prove that he possesses too much sensibility for a happy man.

95. THE CHRISTIAN HERO. Trag. by George Lillo, 8vo. N. D. [1734.] This play is founded on the history of the famous George Castriot, commonly called Scanderbeg, king of Epirus. It was performed at the Theatre in Drury-Lane, and with but very little success. The editor of Whincop's *Scanderbeg* seems, in a preface to that play, to glance a hint of some ungenteel behaviour in Mr. Lillo with regard to it. But as it is well known, that disappointment on one side is sometimes the occasion of injustice towards the other, I cannot think the reality of the accusation in this case seems perfectly authenticated.

96. A CHRISTIAN TURN'D TURK, or *The tragical Lives and Deaths of the two famous Pirates* WARD *and* DANSIKER. Trag. by Robert Daborn, Gent. not divided into acts, 4to. 1612. The story is taken from an account of the overthrow of those two pirates, by Andrew Barker, 4to. 1609.

97. CHRISTMAS, *his Masque*, by Ben Jonson, presented at court, 1616.

98. THE CHRISTMAS ORDINARY. Com. by Trinity-College, Oxford. This piece was entered on the books of the Stationers' Company June 29, 1660, but we believe was not printed.

99. CHRISTMAS ORDINARY. A private Shew, wherein is expressed the jovial freedom of that festival, acted at a gentleman's house among other revels, 4to. 1682. This piece is written by a person who was master of arts, and is signed with the letters W. R.

100. A CHRISTMAS TALE, in five parts, by David Garrick, Esq. Acted at Drury-Lane, 8vo. 1767. A performance yet more contemptible in its composition than *Cymon*, which led the way to this childish and insipid species of entertainment. The success of the *Christmas Tale*, though moderate, was chiefly owing to the assistance of Loutherburgh, who about this period began to exert his talents as a scene-painter, in the service of Drury-Lane theatre. This piece, after being gradually curtailed, and reprobated in the news-papers, was at last hooted and laid aside.

On this occasion we may observe that, when a vicious taste prevails in an audience, a manager should struggle to correct it, instead of seeking to derive advantage

vantage from the reigning fashions or follies of the age.

"The drama's laws the drama's pa-
"trons give,"

says the first of modern criticks; but, as he has elsewhere expressed himself of Dryden, "in a pointed "sentence more regard is com- "monly had to the words than to "the thought, so that it is very "seldom to be rigorously under- "stood." In whatever cause the present times may appear supine and neglectful, the interests of literature have by no means been abandoned. An age that has produced and applauded *Elfrida* and *Caractacus*, cannot justly be suspected of very strong aspirations after such infantine performances as *Cymon* and the *Christmas Tale*. The public taste, in these instances, did not mislead the manager; but the manager availed himself of the ductility of the public, and (artificially enough) created an appetite for such pieces as he himself was capable of producing. The general dissipation of which moralists complain, under proper direction, might in some measure reform itself. Theatrical amusements, of whatever they may consist, are sure to be attended; and where no exhibitions, but such as tend to enlarge the understanding or amend the heart, are offered to an audience, is there need of a Ghost to inform us that no others can be followed? Let us therefore acquit the public taste of depravation, and lay the blame on a quarter where it ought more equitably to fall. The manager, in short, who persists in offering such frivolous entertainments to the public, though placed at the head of a Theatre Royal, is little better in reality than a pandar to dissipation, and deserves not a distinction more honourable than that of master to the first puppet-show in Europe.

101. CHRIST'S PASSION. T. by George Sandys, 8vo. 1640. This play was not intended for the stage, and is only a translation of the *Christus patiens* of Hugo Grotius, with annotations. It was, however, esteemed a very good translation by his contemporaries, and is even strongly commended in a copy of verses prefixed to it by the great lord Falkland.

102. OF CHRIST WHEN HE WAS TWELVE YEARS OLD. Com. This is one of the pieces written by bishop Bale, of which we know nothing more than the name, as handed down to us by himself in a catalogue of his works.

103. CHRONONHOTONTHOLO- GOS. A Mock Trag. by Harry Carey, 8vo. 1734. Acted with success at the Little Theatre in the Hay-Market. This piece, though designed as a ridicule on the extravagance of such tragedies as were in favour about the time it was written, would produce no effect on modern audiences, who have beheld *Zingis*, *Sethona*, and the *Fatal Discovery*, which every way exceed it in tumour, meanness, and improbability.

104. CHUCK, or, *The School Boy's Opera*, 1736. This piece is extremely puerile, yet the author or editor has thought proper to put Mr. Cibber's name to it.

105. THE CHURL. Com. translated from Plautus, by Richard Warner, Esq; 8vo.

106. CICILIA AND CLORINDA, or, *Love in Arms*, Tragi-Com. by Thomas Killegrew. Fol. 1664. This is formed into two plays, the first of which was written at Turin, about 1650, and the second at Florence, in 1651. The scene of both

both pieces lies in Lombardy, and the characters of *Anaxeo, Ducius,* and *Manlius,* seem copies of *Aglatides, Artabes,* and *Megabises,* in the *Grand Cyrus,* Part I Book 3.

107. THE CID. Tragi-Com. by Joseph Rutter. Acted at Court and at the Cockpit-Drury-Lane. This play is also in two parts, both printed in 12mo. the first in 1637, the second in 1640. They are translations at large, and with some alterations, of the celebrated *Cid,* of Corneille, and were undertaken, the first at the request of the earl of Dorset, to whose son the author was tutor, and the second by the command of king Charles I. who was so well satisfied with the first translation, as to order the second part to be put into Mr. Rutter's hands for the same purpose.

108. THE CID, or, *The Heroick Daughter.* Trag. 12mo. 1714. This is a translation from Corneille, by John Ozell.

109. CINNA'S CONSPIRACY. Trag. Anonym. Acted at Drury-Lane, 4to. 1713. The scene Rome. Plot from the Roman History.

110. CIRCE. Dram. Opera, by Dr. Charles D'Avenant. Acted at the duke of York's Theatre, 4to. 1677, 4to. 1685, with considerable applause. Prologue by Dryden, Epilogue by lord Rochester, and the music by Bannister. The scene lies in *Taurica Chersonesus,* and the plot is borrowed from poetical history, viz. Ovid's *Metamorphoses.* Book 14. Boccace, Nat. Comes, &c.

111. THE CITIZEN'S DAUGHTER. Farce. 12mo, No date (about 1775.)

112. THE CITIZEN. Com. of three acts, by Arthur Murphy, 1761. This was one of the new pieces which were brought on the stage in the summer of 1761, at Drury-Lane, under the management of Mr. Foote and its author. It is rather a long Farce than a Comedy, the incidents being all farcical, and the personages *outré.* The character of *Maria,* a girl of wit and sprightliness, who in order to escape a match which she has an aversion to, and at the same time make the refusal come from her intended husband himself, by passing on him for a fool, is evidently borrowed from the character of *Angelique* in the *Fausse Agnes* of *Destouches;* nor has the author been quite clear from plagiarism as to some other of the characters and incidents. It did not meet with so much success as either the *All in the Wrong,* or the *Old Maid* of the same author, which appeared at the same time; and indeed Mr. Murphy has seemed himself to acquiesce in the public judgment, by not having suffered this piece to appear in print as originally acted. It was, however, remarkable for having given an opportunity of shewing the extraordinary talents of a young actress who had never trod the stage before, viz. Miss Elliot, who was extremely pleasing in every various transition of the character of *Maria.*

113. CITIZEN TURNED GENTLEMAN. See MAMAMOUCHE.

114. THE CITY BRIDE, or, *The Merry Cuckold.* Com. by Jos. Harris. Acted at Lincoln's-Inn Fields, 4to. 1696. This play is borrowed almost entirely from Webster's *Cure for a Cuckold,* several whole scenes being the same, but spoiled by the present transposer: so that its success was but very indifferent.

115. THE CITY FARCE, 1737, 8vo. The title page says it was designed for Drury-Lane. Prefixed to it is, An address to the pit.

116. THE

116. THE CITY HEIRESS, or, Sir Timothy Treatall. Com. by Mrs. Behn. Acted at the Duke's Theatre, 4to. 1682. This play was well received, but is in great measure a plagiarism, part of it being borrowed from Middleton's *Mad World my Masters*, and part from Massinger's *Guardian*. From the character of *Sir Timothy Treatall*, and that of Middleton's play from which it was taken, collected together, may be deduced the origin of the *Sir John English*, in C. Johnson's *Country Lasses*. Mrs. Behn has also introduced into this play a great part of the *Inner-Temple Masque*, by Middleton. The Prologue was written by Otway.

117. THE CITY LADY, or, Folly Reclaim'd. Com. by Thomas Dilke. Acted at Little Lincoln's-Inn, 4to. 1697. Scene Covent-Garden. It was acted with success.

118. THE CITY MADAM. C. by Philip Massinger. Acted at Black-Friers, 4to. 1659. This is an excellent comedy, nor can there perhaps be shewn a more perfect knowledge of the disposition of the human mind than is apparent in the behaviour of the city lady and her two daughters to the husband's brother, who is unfortunately fallen into distress, and is become a dependent on the family. The plot, the business, the conduct, and the language of the piece, are all admirable. Mr. Love, in the year 1771, made some alterations in it, with which it was acted at Richmond.

119. THE CITY MATCH. C. by Jasper Maine, D. D. This play was presented before the king and queen at Whitehall in 1639, and there is an edition of it in folio the same year; another in 4to. 1658; and a third in 8vo. 1659. The scene lies in London, and it has been esteemed a very good comedy. See *The Schemers*.

120. THE CITY NIGHT CAP, or, *Crede quod babes et babes*. Com. by Robert Davenport. Acted at the Cock-pit Drury-Lane, 4to. 1661. This play met with very good success. The plot of *Lorenzo*, *Philippo*, and *Abstemia*, is taken from the *Curious Impertinent* in *Don Quixote*; and that of *Ludovico*, *Francisco*, and *Dorothea*, in which the new-married lady is set to do homage to her husband's nightcap, which Mr. Ravenscroft has also introduced into his *London Cuckolds*, is borrowed from Boccace's *Decameron*, Day 7. Nov. 7.

121. CITY POLITIQUES. C. by J. Crown, 4to. 1683. This play was a very severe satire upon the Whig party then prevailing; yet has the author vindicated himself, in his epistle to the reader, from what had been laid to his charge, viz. that he had intended a personal abuse on a certain eminent serjeant at law and his wife, under the characters of *Bartolin* and *Lucinda*, and a doctor under that of *Panchy*.

122. THE CITY RAMBLE, or, *The Playhouse Wedding*. Com. by E. Settle. Acted at the Theatre Royal, 4to. N. D. [17.2.] The two first speeches of this play are taken from Beaumont and Fletcher's *Knight of the Burning Pestle*, and much throughout the whole piece from the *Coxcomb* of the same authors.

123. A CITY RAMBLE, or, *The Humours of the Compter*. Farce, by Charles Knipe. Acted at Lincoln's Inn Fields, 12mo. 1715 and 1736. The name of this Farce is sufficient to point out its subject.

124. THE CITY WIT, or, *The Woman wears the Breeches*. Com. by Richard Brome, 8vo. 1653.

The prologue is a mixture of prose and verse.

125. THE CLANDESTINE MARRIAGE. Com. by George Colman and David Garrick. Acted at Drury-Lane, 8vo. 1766. This is indisputably one of the best comedies produced in the present times. The hint of it came from Hogarth's *Marriage Alamode*, as the prologue confesses. It was received at first with very great applause, and still deservedly continues to be a favourite performance.

126. CLAUDIUS TIBERIUS NERO, *Rome's greatest Tyrant (the Tragedie of) truly represented out of the purest Records of those Times*, 4to. 1607. Dedicated to the right worshipful Sir Arthur Mannering (Sonne and Heyre unto Sir George Mannering, of Eitbfield, in the County of Salop) Carver unto Prince Henry his Grace.

127. CLARICILLA. Tragi-Com. by Thomas Killigrew. Acted at the Phœnix in Drury-Lane, 12mo. 1641. Fol. 1665.

128. CLEMENTINA. Trag. by Hugh Kelly. Acted at Covent-Garden, 8vo. 1771. This play is entitled to some degree of applause, if regarded merely as the work of an unlettered man, but would confer no credit on any author of a higher rank. The language of Clementina, so far from being elevated on tragic stilts, is scarcely raised above the most creeping prose. The performance of Mrs. Yates alone could have counteracted its natural tendency towards damnation.

129. CLEOMENES, or, *The Spartan Hero*. Trag. by John Dryden. Acted at the Theatre Royal, 4to. 1692. This play, notwithstanding the misrepresentation of it by Dryden's enemies at court, was acted with great applause. The plot of it is professedly taken from Plutarch, but improved by the addition of *Cassandra's* love for *Cleomenes*, and the giving him a second wife. The scene lies in Alexandria and the port of that city— and to all the editions is prefixed the life of Cleomenes. Dr. Johnson observes, that this tragedy is remarkable, as it occasioned an incident related in the *Guardian*, and allusively mentioned by Dryden in his preface. As he came out from the representation, he was accosted thus by some airy stripling: *Had I been left alone with a young beauty, I would not have spent my time like your Spartan*. *That, Sir*, said Dryden, *perhaps is true; but give me leave to tell you, that you are no hero*.

130. CLEONE. Trag. by R. Dodsley. Acted at Covent-Garden, 8vo. 1758. An imperfect hint towards the fable of this tragedy was taken from the *Legend of St. Genevieve*, written originally in French, and translated into English in the last century by Sir William Lower. Mr. Pope had attempted in his very early youth a tragedy on the same subject, which he afterwards destroyed. The circumstance of *Siffroy's* giving his friend directions concerning his wife, seems to favour somewhat of *Posthumus's* orders in *Cymbeline*. The last acts, containing *Cleone's* madness over her murdered infant, are wrought to the highest pitch, and received every advantage they could possibly meet with from the inimitable performance of Miss Bellamy, to whose peculiar merit, in this part, it would be doing injustice not to pay that tribute in this place, which the most judicious audience in the world, viz. that of London, afforded her during a long and crowded run of the piece, though

Mr.

Mr. Garrick (who had refused it because it contained no character in which he could have figured himself) did his utmost to overpower it, by appearing in a new part on the very first night of its representation. Annexed to this tragedy is an ode, intituled, *Melpomene*, which does honour to its author.

The Prologue by Mr. Melmoth. The Epilogue by Mr. Shenstone.

131. CLEONICE, *Princess of Bithynia*. Trag. by John Hoole. Acted at Covent-Garden, 8vo. 1775. Mr. Hoole's third production. An ill-fated piece, but not more deserving severity than many others that have escaped it. This author's conduct, after the miscarriage of his play, is worth the imitation of other unsuccessful dramatists. Mr. Hoole returned a part of the money he had received for the copy, observing that he designed it to have been as lucrative to the publisher as to himself, and therefore it was unjust that the chief loss should happen to the former.

132. CLEOPATRA. Trag. by Samuel Daniel, 8vo, 1595. This play is founded on the story of *Cleopatra*, in Plutarch's Lives of Anthony and Pompey, and on a little French book, of which we have a translation by Mr. Otway, intituled, *The History of the Three Triumvirates*. This tragedy was very much esteemed in its time, and there is an edition of it in 1623, in which the author has made various alterations greatly to its advantage. Scene in Alexandria.

133. CLEOPATRA QUEEN OF EGYPT, her Tragedy, by Thomas May, 12mo. 1654. This is upon the same story with the foregoing, and the author, either with an intent of shewing his learning or his candour, has throughout quoted in the margin the historians from whom he took the story, viz. Plutarch, Dion Cassius, Suetonius, Strabo, and Appian. He has, besides, borrowed several other embellishments, particularly Callimachus's Epigram upon Timon, and an annotation on the antient Libyan Psylli, celebrated for curing the venomous wounds given by serpents, by sucking the place. The scene Egypt.

134. CLOACINA. A Comi-Tr. Anonymous. 4to. 1775. This piece (as every reader will suppose from its title) was not intended for exhibition. It contains, however, some pleasant satire on the caprice of managers, and the bad taste displayed by our modern writers of tragedy. The whole is interspersed with strokes of ridicule on particular characters, among which that of an eminent patriotic speaker is delineated in the following couplet:

" The specious B——ke, who talks with-
" out design,
" As Indians paint, because their tints
" are fine."

We do not think our author's censure is absolutely just on the present occasion; but yet, if the orator be such a one as he describes, the comparison in the second line is at once new, happy, and judicious.

135. THE CLOCK-CASE, or, *Female Curiosity*. Interlude; acted May 2, 1777, at Covent-Garden, for Mr. Wilson's benefit.

136. THE CLOUDS. C. translated from Aristophanes, by Thomas Stanley, Esq. Fol. 1656.

137. THE CLOUDS. C. translated from Aristophanes, by James White, 12mo. 1759.

138. THE CLOUDS. Com. by Lewis Theobald, 12mo. 1715. This play was not intended for the stage.

stage, but is only a translation, with notes from Aristophanes.

139. THE COACH-DRIVERS. A Political Comic Opera, adapted to the music of several eminent composers, 8vo. 1766.

140. COALITION. Farce, founded on facts, and lately performed with the approbation, and under the joint inspection, of the managers of the Theatres Royal, 8vo. 1779. Relates to the management of the Theatres.

141. THE COBLER OF PRESTON. Farce of two acts, by Charles Johnson, 8vo. 1716. Acted at Drury-Lane. The plot of this piece is founded on the History of Shakspeare's drunken Tinker, in the *Taming of a Shrew*.

142. THE COBLER OF PRESTON. Farce, by Christopher Bullock. Acted at Lincoln's-Inn Fields, 12mo. 1716. This farce was begun on Friday, finished on Saturday, and acted on the Tuesday following. It was hurried in this manner, to get the start of Mr. Charles Johnson's Farce of the same name.

143. THE COBLER, or, *A Wife of Ten Thousand*. Ballad Opera, by C. Dibdin. Acted at Drury Lane, 8vo. 1774. The hint of this piece was taken from *Blaise la Savetier of Sedan*.

144. THE COBLER OF CASTLEBURY. Music Entertainment, by —— Stewart. Acted at Covent-Garden, 8vo. 1779.

145. THE COBLER'S OPERA. by Lacy Ryan. Acted at Lincoln's-Inn Fields, 8vo. 1729.

146. THE COBLER'S PROPHECY. Com. by Robert Wilson, 4to. 1594.

147. CODRUS. Trag. 8vo. 1774. Not acted.

148. COELIA, or, *The Perjured Lover*. A Play, by Charles Johnson. Acted at Drury-Lane, 8vo. 1733. This play has much pathos in it, and may be considered as very far from a bad piece, yet in the representation it met with no success. Epilogue by Henry Fielding.

149. COELUM BRITANNICUM. A Masque, by Thomas Carew, 4to. 1634. This masque was written at the particular command of the king, and performed by his majesty and the nobles, at the Banquetting House at Whitehall, on Feb. 18, 1633. The decorations were by Inigo Jones, and the music by H. Lawes. This piece was for some time ascribed to Sir William Davenant through mistake, which mistake has been continued so far as to the folio edition of Sir William's works.

150. THE COFFEE-HOUSE. C. by the Rev. James Miller. Acted at Drury-Lane, 8vo. 1737. This piece met with no kind of success, from a supposition, how just I cannot pretend to determine, that Mrs. Yarrow and her daughter, who kept Dick's Coffee-House near Temple-Bar, and were at that time celebrated toasts, together with several persons who frequented that house, were intended to be ridiculed by the author. This he absolutely denied as being his intention; when the piece came out, however, the engraver who had been employed to compose a frontispiece, having inadvertently fixed on that very coffee-house for the scene of his drawing, the Templers, with whom the above-mentioned ladies were great Favourites, became, by this accident, so confirmed in their suspicions, that they united to damn this piece, and even extended their resentments to every thing that was suspected to be this author's for a considerable time after.

151. THE

151. THE COFFEE-HOUSE, or, *The Fair Fugitive*. Com. translated from Voltaire, 8vo. 1760.

152. THE COFFEE-HOUSE. C. translated from Voltaire; printed in Dr. Franklin's Edition.

153. THE COFFEE-HOUSE POLITICIAN, or, *The Justice caught in his own Trap*. Com. by Henry Fielding, 8vo. 1730. This play has no very great share of merit, yet was performed with tolerable success at the Little Theatre in the Hay-Market.

154. COLA'S FURY, or, *Lyrenday's Misery*. Tr. by Henry Burkhead, 4to. 1645. The subject of this play is the Irish rebellion which broke out in the year 1641; and the principal personages who had any concern in the transactions of that time are distinguished under fictitious names, viz. Duke of Ormond, Osiris, Sir John Borlace, Berosus, &c. as may be easily discovered by referring to Temple's, Borlace's, and Clarendon's Histories. This tragedy was never acted, but is commended, in most extravagant terms, in two copies of verses prefixed to it.

155. THE COLLEDGE OF CANONICALL CLERKES. An Interlude; with this title was entered, by John Charlewood, on the books of the Stationers' Company in the years 1566 to 1567; but not printed.

156. THE COLLONELL. A play, by William Davenant, Gent. was entered on the books of the Stationers' Company, by Eph. Dawson, Jan. 1, 1629; but we believe not printed.

157. COLONEL SPLIT-TAIL. Op. Account Versailles, 8vo. 1730. This wretched catchpenny relates to the celebrated Colonel Chartres.

158. THE COMMATE OF CAPPS. A Masque, 1592. This piece is very rare. I have never seen it;

nor did either Langbaine or Jacob, by both of whom it is mentioned without either author's name or date; but the author of the British Theatre, if any reliance can be had on him, appears to have known it better, since in that work alone I find it with the old spelling and date I have here put to it.

159. THE COMBAT OF LOVE AND FRIENDSHIP. C. by Robert Mead, 4to. 1654. This play was presented, during the author's lifetime, by the gentlemen of Christ-Church College, Oxford, but was not published till after his decease.

160. THE COMEDY OF ERRORS, by William Shakespeare, Fol. 1623. This play is founded on the *Menechmi* of Plautus, translated by W. W. 4to. 1595. Mr. Steevens observes that we find in it more intricacy of plot than distinction of character; and our attention is less forcibly engaged, because we can guess in a great measure how the denouement will be brought about. Yet the poet seems unwilling to part with his subject even in the last and unnecessary scene, where the same mistakes are continued till their power of affording entertainment is entirely lost.

161. THE COMEDY OF ERRORS. Altered from Shakspeare, by Thomas Hull. Acted at Covent-Garden, 1779. Not printed.

162. THE COMICAL GALLANT, *with the Amours of Sir John Falstaff*. Com. by J. Dennis. Acted at Drury-Lane, 4to. 1702. The scene of this play lies in Windsor Park, and the town of Windsor; and the piece is no other than a very indifferent alteration of Shakspeare's *Merry Wives of Windsor*; to which is added a large account of the taste in poetry, and the causes of the degeneracy of it.

163. THE

163. THE COMICAL HASH. Com. by the duchess of Newcastle, Fol. 1662.

164. THE COMICAL LOVERS. Com. by C. Cibber, 4to. No date [1707]; acted by subscription at the Queen's Theatre in the Hay-Market. This piece is composed of the comic Episodes of Dryden's *Maiden Queen*, and *Marriage à la Mode* joined together: the alteration cost the author, as he says himself (Preface to *Double Gallant*), six days trouble, and met with a very favourable reception. There are but six characters in it; and these were performed by Mrs. Bracegirdle, Mrs. Oldfield, and Mrs. Porter, Mr. Wilks, Mr. Booth, and Mr. Cibber. A tag to the fourth act seems pointed at the parting of *Moneses* and *Arpasia* in *Tamerlane*, and is a humourous picture of many such parting scenes in some of our lovesick tragedies.

165. THE COMICAL REVENGE; or, *Love in a Tub*. Com. by Sir George Etherege. Acted at the Duke of York's Theatre, 4to.: 669. 4to. 1689. This comedy, though of a mixt nature, some of it being serious and written in heroic verse, and by no means equal to the comic parts of it, yet has generally succeeded very well upon the stage, and met with universal approbation; yet, to the honour of the present taste, this, and several other admirably written pieces, have been for some time past laid aside, on account of the looseness of their characters and expressions; wit seeming in this age not to be considered as a sufficient protection for libertinism, which was too much the case at the period in which this author wrote.

166. THE COMMISSARY. Com. by Samuel Foote. Acted at the Hay-Market, 8vo. 1765. It was performed with success. Besides some persons who are yet living, the celebrated Dr. Arne is introduced and ridiculed in the present comedy.

167. THE COMMITTEE. Com. by Sir Robert Howard, Fol. 1665. This comedy, which has had the second title of *The Faithful Irishman* added to it, was written not long after the Restoration, and was intended to throw an idea of the utmost odium on the Round-head party and their proceedings. The piece has no great merit as to the writing, yet from the drollery of the character of *Teague*, and the strong picture of absurd fanaticism mingled with indecent pride, drawn in those of Mr. Day, Mrs. Day, and Abel, it even now, when every spark of party fire, as to that part of the English history, is absolutely extinct, has established itself as a standard acting comedy, and constantly gives pleasure in the representation.

The character of *Teague* we find was taken from the life. The present duke of Norfolk, in his Anecdotes of the Howard Family, p. 112. says, "When Sir Robert was in Ireland, his son was imprisoned here by the parliament for some offence committed against them. As soon as Sir Robert heard of it, he sent one of his domestics (an Irishman) to England, with dispatches to his friends, in order to procure the enlargement of his son. He waited with great impatience for the return of this messenger; and when he at length appeared with the agreeable news, that his son was at liberty, Sir Robert finding that he had been then several days in Dublin, asked him the reason of his not coming to him before. The honest Hibernian answered, " with

"with great exultation, that he had been all the time spreading the news, and getting drunk for joy among his friends. He, in fact, executed his business with uncommon fidelity and dispatch, but the extraordinary effect, which the happy event of his embassy had on poor Paddy, was too great to suffer him to think with any degree of prudence of any thing else. The excess of his joy was such, that he forgot the impatience and anxiety of a tender parent, and until he gave that sufficient vent among all his intimates, he never thought of imparting the news there where it was most wanted and desired. From this Sir Robert took the first hint of that odd composition of fidelity and blunders which he has so humorously worked up in the character of *Teague*."

168. THE COMMITTEE MAN CURRIED. Com. in two Parts, by S. Sheppard, 4to. 1647. *A Piece discovering the Corruption of Committee Men and Excise Men; the unjust Sufferings of the Royal Party; the devilish Hypocrisy of some Roundheads; the Revolt for Gain of some Ministers. Not without pleasant Mirth and Variety.* These two plays have much more zeal than wit, yet at the same time are most barefaced pieces of plagiarism, there being scarcely any thing of Sir John Suckling's, either in prose or verse, which has escaped the plunder of this dramatic pirate, exclusive of what he has borrowed from the first and third Satires of *Juvenal*, as translated by Sir Robert Stapleton.

169. THE COMMODITY EXCIS'D, or, *The Women in an Uproar*. A new Ballad Opera; as it will be privately acted in the secret apartments of Vintners and Tobacconists. By Timothy Smoke, 8vo. 1733.

The occasion on which this piece was written, is sufficiently evident from its title and date. It is, however, the dullest of dull performances. The matchless obscenity of the last scene may prove agreeable to such readers as delight in *Meretriciads, Courts of Cupid*, &c. but would find no other admirers.

It exhibits a frontispiece representing the Custom-house, Sir Robert Walpole riding on a tun drawn by the English lion and Hanoverian horse, together with other circumstances too gross for description.

170. THE COMMONS' CONDITION. Com. Anonym. 1676. Of this nothing more than the name is mentioned in any of the catalogues.

171. A COMMONWEALTH OF WOMEN. A Play, by Thomas Durfey. Acted at the Theatre Royal, 4to. 1686. This play is borrowed from Fletcher's *Sea Voyage*, and is very indifferently executed. The scene Covent-Garden.

172. THE COMPROMISE, or, *Faults on both Sides*. Com. by Mr. Sturmy, 8vo. 1723. Acted at the Theatre Royal in Lincoln's-Inn Fields.

173. COMUS. A Masque, by Dr. Dalton. Acted at Drury-Lane, 8vo. 1738. This piece is a very judicious alteration of Milton's Masque at Ludlow-Castle, wherein it is rendered much more fit for the stage by the introduction of many additional songs, most of them Milton's own, of part of the *Allegro* of the same author, and other passages from his different works, so that he has rather restored Milton to himself than altered him. It met with great applause on its first appear-

appearance; but it must be confessed, that this was chiefly owing to the lustre of the music. A very good judge observes, that "whilst the musician's skill was applauded to the skies, the poem itself was either not attended to, or only occasioned weariness and satiety. It will be allowed by all, that, had it not been for the ornament of the songs, the dramatic part could not have lived to a second night: and the whole piece, since the music has lost great part of its charms with its novelty, is now scarcely able to hold up its head."

174. COMUS. Masque, altered from Milton, by George Colman. Acted at Covent-Garden, 8vo. 1772.

175. THE CONCEITED LADIES. Com. translated from Moliere. Printed in Foote's Comic Theatre, 12mo. vol. IV.

176. IL CONCLAVE DEL 1774. Drama per Musica. Italian and English, 8vo. 1774.

177. THE CONFEDERACY. C. by Sir John Vanbrugh. Acted at the Hay-Market, 4to. 1705. This is a very pleasing comedy, and full of business; the characters are natural, and although there may seem somewhat improbable in the affair of *Dick* and *Brass*, yet, as many strange things are undoubtedly done in the fortune-hunting scheme, it can scarcely be deemed impossible; the language is pleasing, and the plot of the two wives against their husbands well conceived and admirably executed. It is not, however, to be regarded as the *chef d'Oeuvre* of this witty and ingenious author.

178. THE CONFEDERATES. A Farce, by Joseph Gay, 8vo. 1717. This piece is written in rhyme, and although the name put to it is a fictitious one, contains a considerable share of humour. It is a very severe satire on a farce written in confederacy by the three great geniuses, Pope, Gay, and Arbuthnot, called *Three Hours after Marriage*, which justly met with universal disapprobation. The real author of this farce (which was never acted) was Captain John Durant Breval, whom on this account Mr. Pope has thought proper to lash, as he did every one whom he either disliked or feared, in the *Dunciad*.

179. An exellent new Commedie, intituled THE CONFLICT OF CONSCIENCE. Contayninge a most lamentable example of the dolefull desperation of a miserable worldlinge, termed by the name of *Philologus*, who forsooke the trueth of God's Gospel, for feare of the losse of lyfe, and worldly goods.

Compiled by Nathaniel Woodes, minister in Norwich.

The actors names, devided into six partes, most convenient for such as be disposed, either to shew this Comedie in private houses, or otherwise.

Prologue Mathetes Conscience Pophinitius		Cacon Avarice Suggestion Gilbertus Nuntius	
	for one		for one
Hypocrisie Theologus	for one		
		Philologus	for one
Sathan Tyrranye Spirit Horror Euirbus Cardinal	for one		

At London. Printed by Richarde Bradocke, dwelling in Aldermenburie, a little above the Conduct. Anno 1581. Bl. l.

180. THE CONGRESS OF THE BEASTS. *Under the Mediation of the Goat, for negotiating a Peace between the Fox, the Ass wearing the Lion's*

Lion's skin, the Horse, the Tigress, and other Quadrupedes at war. Farce of two acts, now in rehearsal at a new grand Theatre in Germany, 8vo. 1748. This is entirely political.

181. CONJUGAL FIDELITY. C. translated from Plautus, by Richard Warner, Esq.

182. THE CONJUROR. A Farce, by Miles Peter Andrews, Esq. Acted April 29, 1774, at Drury-Lane, for the benefit of Mr. Brereton. N. P.

The audience acquitted Mr. Andrews of being himself the character from which his performance receives its title.

183. THE CONNAUGHT WIFE. Com. of two acts, performed at Smock-Alley, Dublin, 8vo. 1767.

184. THE CONNOISSEUR, or, *Every Man in his Folly.* A Comedy, by —— Conolly. Acted at Drury-Lane, 8vo. 1736. This play is intended to answer the same kind of purposes of ridicule with Shadwell's *Virtuoso*, and Foote's farce of *Taste*, but is but indifferently executed, and met with very middling success.

185. THE CONQUEST OF CHINA, *by the Tartars.* Trag. by E. Settle. Acted at the Duke's Theatre, 4to. 1676. This play is written in heroic verse, and the plot founded on history, which may be seen by referring to Heylin's *Cosmog.* Palafax's Conquest of *China*, &c. Sir Robert Howard had written a play on the same subject. See Dr. Johnson's *Life of Dryden*.

186. CONQUEST OF GRANADA. Trag. in two Parts, by J. Dryden. Acted at the Theatre Royal, 4to. 1672. 4to. 1681. These two plays met with great success when performed, on which account, as it should seem, Langbaine, who is ever strongly prejudiced against this prince of English poets, has taken amazing pains to point out how much he has borrowed for the forming of these pieces from the celebrated romances of Almahide, Grand Cyrus, Ibrahim, and Guzman. Yet surely this envy was entirely unnecessary, since, as the plot of the piece is built on history, it should rather be esteemed as a merit, than a blemish in the author, that he has, like an industrious bee, collected his honey from all the choicest flowers which adorned the field he was traversing, whether the more cultivated ones of serious, or the wilder of romantic history. They are, however, written in a manner so different from the present taste, that they have been long laid aside.

Dr. Johnson, with his usual energy of style and propriety of criticism, observes that these two plays are written with a seeming determination to glut the public with dramatic wonders; to exhibit in its highest elevation a theatrical meteor of incredible love and impossible valour, and to leave no room for a wilder flight to the extravagance of posterity. All the rays of romantic heat, whether amorous or warlike, glow in Almanzor by a kind of concentration. He is above all law; he is exempt from all restraints; he ranges the world at will, and governs wherever he appears. He fights without enquiring the cause, and loves in spite of the obligations of justice, of rejection by his mistress, and of prohibition from the dead. Yet the scenes are, for the most part, delightful; they exhibit a kind of illustrious depravity, and majestic madness: such as, if it is sometimes despised, is often reverenced, and in which the ridiculous is mingled with the astonishing.

187. THE CONQUEST OF SPAIN. Trag. 4to. 1705. Acted at

at the Queen's Theatre in the Hay-Market. Scene Spain. It was written by Mrs. Pix. See *Downes*. p. 48.

188. THE CONQUEST OF CANADA, or, *The Siege of Quebec.* Historical Tragedy of five acts, by George Cockings, 8vo. 1766.

189. THE CONQUEST OF CHINA. Trag. A play with this title appears to have been written by Sir Robert Howard, and was intended to be revised by Mr. Dryden. It was, however, never either acted or printed, and is now probably lost. See Dr. Johnson's *Life of Dryden*, p. 345.

190. THE CONQUEST OF CORSICA BY THE FRENCH. Trag. by a Lady, 12mo. 1771. Not acted.

191. THE CONSCIOUS LOVERS. Com. by Sir Richard Steele. Acted at Drury-Lane, 8vo. 1721. The general design of this celebrated comedy is taken from the *Andria* of Terence; but the author's principal intention in the writing it was, as he himself informs us, to introduce the very fine scene in the fourth act between young *Bevil* and *Myrtle*, which sets forth, in a strong light, the folly of duelling, and the absurdity of what is falsely called the *Point of Honour*; and in this particular merit the play would probably have ever stood foremost, had not that subject been since more amply and completely treated by the admirable author of Sir *Charles Grandison*, in the affair between that truly accomplished gentleman and Sir *Hargrave Pollexfen*. See Sir *Charles Grandison*, vol. I. and II.

192. THE CONSCIENTIOUS LOVERS. Com. by C. Shadwell. This play is put down in Mears's Catalogue; but we are doubtful whether it was ever printed.

193. THE CONSPIRACY. Tr. by Henry Killigrew, 4to. 1638. This piece was intended for the entertainment of the king and queen at York House, on occasion of the nuptials of lord Charles Herbert with lady Mary Villiers; and was afterwards acted on the Black-Friers stage. It was written at seventeen years of age; and the commendation bestowed on it by Ben Jonson and lord Falkland created the author some envy among his contemporaries. The edition above-mentioned is a surreptitious one, published while Killegrew was abroad, and without his consent or knowledge. He afterwards, however, gave the world a more genuine one, in Fol. 1653; but was so much ashamed of this first edition, that, to prevent its being known to be the same piece, he altered the name of it to *Pallantus* and *Eudora*, which therefore I would recommend to the reader. The scene lies in Crete.

194. THE CONSPIRACY, or, *The Change of Government.* Trag. by Whitaker. Acted at the Duke's Theatre, 4to. 1680. This play is written in rhyme, the epilogue composed by Ravenscroft, and the scene lies in Turkey.

195. CONSPIRACY and *Tragedy of Charles Duke of Byron, Marshal of France.* Two plays, by George Chapman. Acted at Black-Friers, 4to. 1608. 4to. 1625. These pieces are both founded on history, and their plots may be seen in Mezeray, D'Avila, and other historians on the reign of Henry IV. of France.

196. THE CONSPIRATORS. A Tragi-comic Opera, as it was acted in England and Ireland without applause, 8vo. 1749. It was printed at Carrickfergus, as the title declares, and is addressed to the people of Great Britain and Ireland, where the scenes are laid by a much injured person in the drama. It is also

also said to be formed on an event sufficiently notorious.

197. THE CONSTANT COUPLE, or, *A Trip to the Jubilee*. C. by G. Farquhar. Acted at Drury-Lane, 4to. 1700. This is a very genteel, lively, and entertaining piece; it met with great success at its first appearance, and is always well received whenever it is represented. It has been said that the author, in his principal character of *Sir Harry Wildair*, meant to present the public with his own portrait—but as the same has also been surmised with regard to his *Captain Plume*, and his young *Mirabel*, I cannot help making one remark on this opinion, which I think must do honour to the author, viz. that such a general belief could arise from nothing but that resemblance, which must have been apparent to those who knew him, between him and these elegant and pleasing characters. For it is scarcely to be imagined, that a man of the generous, open, familiar, and dissipated cast of character that such a resemblance implies him to have been, could be so much of an egotist as intentionally to make himself the principal in every piece he sent into the world; and yet it is, perhaps, scarce possible for any writer, who is to draw characters in real and familiar life, not to throw into that which he intends to render most amiable and important so much of his own principles, opinions, and rules of action, as to render a resemblance very apparent to those who are familiar with his complexion of mind and general turn of character. Of this we have numerous instances, in writers of other kinds than the dramatic; *Joseph Andrews*, *Tom Jones*, and *Captain Booth*, have been ever acknowledged as the characters of their ingenious author; nor can any one deny a similarity between Sir *Charles Grandison* and his estimable author: and, to conclude the observation, I cannot think it improbable, that, were we closely to examine the comedies of the latter half of the seventeenth century, we might find out in their heroes and heroines the genuine portraits of the Behns, Durfeys, Wycherleys, and Centlivres, of those periods of gallantry and licentiousness. The part we have been speaking of is in itself very elegant, but the peculiar merit of Mr. Wilks, in the performance of it, has certainly been hitherto unequalled; nor can there be a stronger proof of it, than its having been so frequently since performed by women, where a partiality to the sex might be urged to excuse some little deficiency in point of execution.

198. CONSTANTINE. T. by Phil. Francis, 8vo. 1754. Covent-Garden. It met with very bad success, although not by many degrees the worst of the productions of that season.

199. CONSTANTINE THE GREAT, or, *The Tragedy of Love*, by N. Lee. Acted at the Theatre Royal, 4to. 1684. The scene of this play is laid in Rome, and the plot founded on real History, for which see various historians of the life of that emperor, and particularly Ammianus Marcellinus, by whom the story of *Crispus* and *Fausta* is very circumstantially related.

200. THE CONSTANT MAID. Com. by James Shirley. 4to. 1640. The greatest part of this play is borrowed from others, particularly the circumstance of *Hartwell*'s courting the widow *Bellamy* by the advice of his friend *Playfair*;

CO

fair; which, although the basis of all the principal business of the piece, has been made use of in many comedies both ancient and modern.

201. THE CONSTANT NYMPH, or, *The Rambling Shepherd.* A Pastoral. Acted at the Duke's Theatre. Anonym. 4to. 1678. This piece was written by a person of quality, who tells us (as most authors, whose pieces do not succeed, are desirous of finding out any other cause for their failure than want of merit) that it suffered much through the defects of setting it off when it came upon the stage. The scene is Lucia in Arcadia.

202. THE CONTENDING BROTHERS. Com. by Henry Brooke, Esq; 8vo. 1778. Not acted. This play is formed on the plan of Farquhar's *Twin Rivals.*

203. THE CONTENTED CUCKOLD, or, *The Woman's Advocate.* Com. by Reuben Bourne, 4to. 1692. Scene London. This play was never acted.

204. THE CONTENTION BETWEENE LIBERALITIE AND PRODIGALITIE. *A pleasant Comedie play'd before her Majestie,* 4to. 1602. This piece is anonymous, but, notwithstanding the difference of time, I am apt to believe it to be no more than an enlargement and improvement of a much older piece, intituled *Liberalitie and Prodigalitie, a Masque of much Moralitie,* printed so early as 1559. Yet whether this alteration was made by the author of the first, or not, I am entirely unable to determine, although, as upwards of forty years had elapsed, I think it the more rational to surmise in the negative.

205. THE CONTENTION BETWEEN YORK AND LANCASTER, *with the tragical Death of the good*

CO

Duke Humphry, &c. in two parts, 4to. 1600. There is very little difference between this and Shakspeare's second Part of *Henry* VI. as published in 1623 by Hemings and Condell.

206. CONTENTIONS FOR HONOUR AND RICHES. A Masque, by James Shirlev, 4to. 1633. This was originally no more than an Interlude or Entertainment, but was afterwards enlarged by the author to the bulk of a comedy, with the title of *Honoria* and *Mammon.*

207. CONTENTION OF AJAX AND ULYSSES *for the Armour of Achilles.* An Interlude, 8vo. 1659. The plan taken from the 13th book of Ovid's *Metamorphoses.*

208. THE CONTRACT. Com. of two acts, by Dr. Thomas Franklin, performed at the Hay-Market, 8vo. 1776. This is a poor performance founded on D'Estouche's *L'Amour Usé,* and met with no success.

209. THE CONTRACT. See FEMALE CAPTAIN.

210. THE CONTRAST. This play was written by Drs. Benjamin and John Hoadly; and acted at Lincoln's-Inn Fields, 1731. It was performed five times in the month of May, but was never printed. The plan of it was a rehearsal of two modern plays, a tragedy and a comedy, and was intended to ridicule the then living poets, among whom we find, by the Grub-street Journal, Mr. Thomson author of the *Seasons* was to be numbered. At the desire of bishop Hoadly it was suppressed, and every scrap of paper, copy, and parts, recalled by Mr. Rich, and restored to the authors. Mr Fielding availed himself afterwards of the same design in his celebrated and popular performance, called PASQUIN.

F 2
211. THE

CO [68] CO

211. THE CONTRAST. Dram. Past. 8vo. 1752. This was printed in a periodical work, called *The General Review*, N° 5.

212. THE CONTRAST, or, *The Jew and married Courtezan*. Farce, by Mr. Waldron. Acted one night at Drury-Lane, May 12, 1775, for the benefit of himself and Mrs. Greville. Not printed.

213. THE CONTRETEMS, or, *Rival Queens*. A small Farce, as it was lately acted with great applause at H——d——r's private Th——re near the H——y M——s. Anonym. 4to. 1727. This piece was never intended for public representation, but was written only in ridicule of the confusion which at that time reigned in the King's Theatre in the Hay-Market, in consequence of the contests for superiority between the two celebrated Italian singers Signora Faustina and Signora Cuzzoni, the divided opinions of the public with regard to their respective merits, and the insolent airs of importance assumed by them in consequence of the public favour shewn to them. In the Dramatis Personæ, which consists entirely of the persons belonging to that theatre, HEIDEGGER the manager is characterized as high priest of Discord, and that great composer, Mr. Handel, styled Professor of Harmony.

We cannot on this occasion avoid taking notice of the careless manner in which new editions of some authors' works have been executed, from the ignorance of the persons to whose care they are intrusted. In the last republication of Colley Cibber's Plays, this piece is inserted instead of *The Rival Queans*, which see in its place.

214. THE CONTRIVANCES, or, *More Ways than one*. A Farce, by Harry Carey. Acted at Drury-Lane, 12mo. 1715. This is a very entertaining piece, had good success at its first appearance, and sometimes brings crowded houses to this day.

215. THE CONVENT OF PLEASURE. Com. by the Duchess of Newcastle, 1668. This is one among many of the pieces of this voluminous female author, which have never been performed, and perhaps very seldom read.

216. THE COOPER. Musical Entertainment; acted at the Hay-Market, 8vo. 1772. Set to music by Dr. Arne, who was also suspected to be the author of it.

217. THE COQUET, or, *The English Chevalier*. Com. by Charles Molloy, 8vo. 1718. Acted at the Theatre in Lincoln's-Inn Fields with great applause.

218. THE COQUET'S SURRENDER, or, *The Humorous Punster*. Com. Anonym. 1732. This play I have never seen, unless it is the same as was published, in 1733, under the title of *The Court Lady*, or *The Coquet's Surrender*, which is said to have been written by a lady, and, by the Dramatis Personæ, appears to have been acted at the Hay-Market.

219. THE COQUET. Musical Entertainment, by Stephen Storace, sung at Marybone-Gardens, 8vo. 1771. This is a translation from the Italian of Goldoni, and adapted to the original music of Galluppi.

220. THE COQUETTE, or, *The Mistakes of the Heart*. Com. by —— Hitchcock. Acted at York and Hull, 8vo. 1777. Printed at Bath.

221. CORIOLANUS. Trag. by W. Shakespare, Fol. 1623. The plot of this play is taken from history, viz. from Plutarch's Life of *Coriolanus*. The scene lies partly in Rome, and partly in the territories of the Volscians.

Dr.

Dr. Johnson says, it is one of the most amusing of our author's performances: "The old man's merriment in *Menenius*; the lofty lady's dignity in *Volumnia*; the bridal modesty in *Virgilia*; the patrician and military haughtiness in *Coriolanus*; the plebeian malignity and tribunitian insolence in *Brutus* and *Sicinius*; make a very pleasing and interesting variety; and the various revolutions of the hero's fortune fill the mind with anxious curiosity. There is perhaps too much bustle in the first act, and too little in the last."

222. CORIOLANUS. Trag. by James Thomson. Acted at Covent-Garden, 8vo. 1748. Our pleasing poet's principal merit not lying in the dramatic way; and this, though the last, being far from the best of his works, even *in* that way; I cannot pay any very exalted compliments to the piece.

The style of it is, like the rest of the author's writings, ill calculated to excite the passions. Dr. Johnson observes, this tragedy was, by the zeal of Sir George Lyttelton, brought upon the stage for the benefit of Thomson's family, and recommended by a prologue, which Quin, who had long lived with him in fond intimacy, spoke in such a manner as shewed him *to be*, on that occasion, *no actor*. The commencement of this benevolence is very honourable to Quin; who is reported to have delivered Thomson, then known to him only for his genius, from an arrest, by a very considerable present; and its continuance is honourable to both; for friendship is not always the sequel of obligation. By this tragedy a considerable sum was raised, of which part discharged his debts, and the rest was remitted to his sisters, whom, however removed from them by place or condition, he regarded with great tenderness.

* 222. CORIOLANUS, or, *The Roman Matron*. Trag. by Thomas Sheridan. Acted at Covent-Garden, 8vo. 1755. This piece was composed from the two former plays by Shakspeare and Thomson, and, being assisted by a splendid ovation, had some success.

223. CORNISH INTERLUDES. Of these there are three in the Bodleian library, written on parchment. B. 40. Art. In the same place is also another, written on paper in the year 1611. Arch. B. 31. Of the last there is a translation in the British Museum. MSS. Harl. 1867. 2. It is entitled the CREATION OF THE WORLD. It is called a Cornish play or opera, and said to be written by Mr. William Jordan. The translation into English was made by John Keigwin of Mousehole, in Cornwall, at the request of Trelawney, bishop of Exeter. Of this William Jordan I can give no account. Of his translator it may be observed, that among the many valuable MSS. in Lambeth library (806. 16.) there is a very long poem, in stanzas of four lines, intituled, "MOUNT CALVARIE, or "The History of the Passion, Death, "and Resurrection of our Lord "Jesus Christ, written in Cornish "(as it may be conjectured) some "centuries past; interpreted in "the English tongue by John "Keigwin, Gent."

224. THE CORNISH COMEDY. Acted at the Theatre in D.... Gardens, 4to. 1696. Scene Cornwall. This play was published by George Powell, who, in a dedication to Christopher Rich, Esq; says, it was the conception of a few loose hours, and committed by the author to his hands to dispose of in the world.

225. THE

225. THE CORNISH SQUIRE. Com. by Sir John Vanbrugh, Congreve, and Walsh. Acted at the Hay-Market, 1706. This is founded almost entirely on the Sieur Pourceaugnac of Moliere. In the year 1734, this piece was by Mr. Ralph brought on the stage at Drury-Lane, and published in 8vo. In the preface, he says Mr. Congreve and Mr. Walsh were concerned in it.

226. CORONA MINERVÆ, A Masque. "Presented before prince "Charles, his highness the duke "of York his brother, and the "lady Mary his sister, the 27th of "February, at the college of the "Museum Minervæ, 4to. 1635." Chetwood ascribes this piece to Thomas Middleton; but I believe without foundation.

227. THE CORONATION. Tr. Com. by J. Shirley. This play was printed in 4to. 1640. as John Fletcher's; but, as Shirley laid claim to it, I have here restored it to his name. Scene Epirus.

228. THE CORONATION OF QUEEN ELIZABETH, or, *The Restoration of the Protestant Religion, and the Downfal of the Pope*, by W. R. 4to. 1680. This is no more than a droll of three acts, played at Bartholomew and Southwark fairs.

229. THE CORONATION OF DAVID, A Drama, written by Joseph Wise in 1763. Published at Lewes, 8vo. 1766.

230. THE CORPORAL. Play, by Arthur Wilson; entered on the books of the Stationers' Company, Sept. 4, 1646, but we believe not printed.

231. CORRUPTIONS OF THE DIVINE LAWS. A dramatic piece, mentioned by bishop Bale in the catalogue of his own works.

232. THE COSTLY WHORE. A comical History, acted by the company of Revels. Anonym. 4to. 1633. This piece is by Philips attributed to Robert Mead; but Langbaine seems firmly of opinion that it is not his. The scene lies in Saxony.

233. THE COTTAGERS. Opera, by George Savile Carey, 8vo. 1766.

234. THE COTTAGERS. Musical Entertainment; acted at Covent-Garden, 8vo. 1779. This piece, though said to be performed, was never represented under this title. It is the same performance as *William and Nanny*, by Mr. Goodenough: and, having been printed by a bookseller ten or eleven years before it appeared on the stage, was published by the person who had purchased the impression.

235. COVENT-GARDEN. Com. by Thomas Nabbes, 4to. 1638. This piece was first performed in 1632, but was not printed till the time above-mentioned. The title implies where the scene is laid, and it is a representation of the humours of that place at the period when it was written. It is dedicated to Sir John Suckling.

236. COVENT-GARDEN WEEDED, or, *The Middlesex Justice of Peace*. Com. by Richard Brome, 8vo. 1659.

237. THE COVENT-GARDEN TRAGEDY. Farce, by H. Fielding, Acted at Drury-Lane, 8vo. 1733. This is a burlesque, but not equal to some other pieces of the same author; the humours of Covent-Garden, with respect to whores, gamblers, and bullies, being subjects too low for mock tragedy.

238. COVENTRY PLAYS, intituled, *Ludus Coventriæ*, five *Ludus Corporis Christi*. They are now in the British Museum, and may be found by the following distinctions

tions among the Cottonian MSS. Vesp. D. VIII. p. 113. PLUT. IV. A. They are forty in number, and their subjects, like those of similar exhibitions at Chester already described, are chiefly from the Old and New Testament. The language of them, having probably undergone no changes by transcription, is in many places almost as gross as that of some of the Scotch dramatic writers before the year 1600, who employed their talents for the entertainment of our future Solomon. Quotations from such parts of these mysteries as would best support my assertion, might be accompanied by suspicion of profaneness, which of all other charges the editor of the present work would be studious to avoid. A slight extract, however, may serve to shew the indelicacy of the poets, as well as the ancient audiences of Coventry. In the play of the *Woman taken in Adultery*, the appearance of the guilty fair one is preceded by this extraordinary stage-direction and dialogue. Pageant XXI. p. 121.
"—*Hic Juvenis quidam extra currit, caligis non ligatis et* BRACCAS IN MANU TENENS, *et dicat Accusator:*

"*Accusator.*
" Stow that harlot, sum ertheley wyght,
" That ж advowtrye her is sownde."
" *Juvenis.*
" Giff any man flow me yis nyght,
" I shal hym geve a dedly wownde.
" If any man my wey doth stoppe,
" Or we departe, ded shal he be ;
" I shal yis daggar putt in his croppe,
" I shal hem kylle, or he shal me."
" *Pharisæus.*
" Grett goddys curse mut go with the,.
" With such a shrewe wyll I not melle."
" *Juvenis.*
" That same blyssynge I gyff you thre,
" And qwherh you alle to ye devyl of
" helle.
" In feyth I was so for affrayd
" Of yone thre threwys, ye seth to say,

" My breche be nott yett well upteyd,
" I had such hast to renne away.
" Thei shal nevyr catche me in such af-
" fray ;
" I am full glad y' I am gon.
" Adewe adewe a xx devyls way,
" And goddys curse have ye everychon."
" *Scriba.*
" Com forth yᵘ slutte, com forth yᵘ
" scowte,
" Com forth yᵘ bysmar & brothel
" belde,
" Com forth yᵘ hor, & stynkynge bych
" clowte,
" How long hast yᵘ such harlotry
" helde ?
" Com forth yᵘ quene, com forth yᵘ
" icolde
" Com forth yᵘ sloveyn, com forth yᵘ
" slutte ;
" We shal the teche, with carys colde,
" A lytyl bettyr to kepe yⁱ kutte."

These performances began on *Corpus Christi* day, which according to Dugdale was the commencement of the chief fair held in Coventry. They were acted by the Gray Friars, or Franciscans. The theatres were placed on wheels, and drawn to all the eminent parts of the City, for the better advantage of the numerous spectators.

239. OF THE COUNCELLS OF BISHOPS. A Com. by Bishop Bale. See his List in the *British Theatre*, p. 199.

240. THE COUNTERFEIT BRIDEGROOM, or, *The Defeated Widow*. Com. 4to. 1677. This is no other than Middleton's *No Wit like a Woman's*, printed with a new title ; an artifice to give the appearance of novelty, which seems to have been frequently practised in those times, but which would not by any means pass now, when the slightest plagiarism is immediately discovered by the piercing eyes of our stage-hunting critics, by whom resemblances are even formed in their own imaginations only (to the prejudice of real merit), where no more than that general sympathy of conception which all writers,

writers, whose genius enables them to see nature as she is, must have with each other, can give ground for their accusations.

241. THE COUNTERFEIT HEIRESS. Farce, taken from Durfey's *Love for Money*. Acted at Covent-Garden, April 16, 1762, for Mrs. Vincent's benefit. Not printed.

242. THE COUNTERFEITS. C. Acted at the Duke's Theatre, 4to. 1679. J. Leonard has been supposed to be the author of this play, which is very far from being a bad one. The scene lies in Madrid. The plot is taken from a Spanish novel, called *The Trapanner trapanned*; and Mr. Cibber has made great use of it in his comedy of *She wou'd and she wou'd not*.

243. THE COUNTERFEITS. F. taken from Moore's *Gil Blas*. Acted at Drury-Lane, for Mr. Yates's benefit, March 26, 1764. Not printed.

244. THE COUNTESS OF ESCARAGONAS. Com. by J. Ozell. This is only a translation from Mol'ere, and never intended for the stage.

245. THE COUNTESS OF PEMBROKE'S IVY CHURCH, by Abraham Fraunce, 4to. 1591. As this is in some of the old catalogues set down as the name of a play in two parts, I could not omit a mention of it, although it contains nothing dramatic, but one piece in English hexameters, called *Amintas's* Pastoral, which is but a translation of Tasso's *Aminta*.

246. COUNTESS OF SALISBURY. Trag. by Hall Hartson, Esq. 8vo. 1767. This play is taken from Dr. Leland's Romance, called *Longsword Earl of Salisbury*. It was first acted at Dublin, and afterwards at the Hay-Market. We have already hinted, in our brief account of Mr. Hartson, that he was supposed to have received material assistance in this tragedy from the hand of his tutor, Dr. Leland. That the composition was not his own, may also be inferred from a circumstance we shall now relate. An acquaintance complimented our ostensible author on the happy manner in which a speech from Homer is appropriated to the countess of Salisbury. Mr. Hartson disclaimed all knowledge of this circumstance, and denied that the Greek poet had furnished any part of his materials. For the information of our readers, we shall subjoin both these passages.

For ah! no more Andromache shall come,
With joyful tears to welcome Hector home;
No more officious, with endearing charms,
From thy tir'd limbs unbrace Pelides' arms!   Book 27. v. 241, &c.

Never, oh, never more shall Ela run
With throbbing bosom, at the trumpet's sound,
To unlock his helmet conquest-plum'd, to strip
The cuisses from his manly thigh, or snatch
Quick from his breast the plated armour, wont
T' oppose my fond embrace.—Sweet times, farewel,
These tender offices return no more.

The reader will perhaps allow that he who supplied the latter of these speeches, could not be unacquainted with the former.

247. THE COUNTRY CAPTAIN. Com. by the Duke of Newcastle. Acted at Black-Friers, and printed at the Hague, 12mo. 1649.

248. THE COUNTRY GIRL. Com. by Anth. Brewer, 4to. 1649. This play was frequently acted with great applause. The scenes in London and Edmonton.

249. THE COUNTRY GIRL. Com. by David Garrick. Acted at Drury-Lane, 8vo. 1766. This

is an alteration of Wycherly's *Country Wife*, and met with some applause.

250. THE COUNTRY HOUSE. A Farce, by Sir J. Vanbrugh, 12mo. 1715. This is nearly a translation from a French piece.

251. THE COUNTRY COQUET, or, *Miss in her Breeches*. Ballad Opera. As it may be acted at Drury-Lane, 8vo. 1755.

252. THE COUNTRY ELECTION. Farce, in two acts, 8vo. 1768. This is supposed to have been written by Dr. Trusler.

253. THE COUNTRY MADCAP. Farce. Acted at Covent-Garden, 1772. This is only Fielding's *Miss Lucy in Town*, under a different title.

254. THE COUNTRY SQUIRE, or, *A Christmas Gambol*. Com. by Richard Gwinnet, Esq. It was acted by the author, and a number of his neighbours, 8vo. 1732. See *The Glo'stershire Squire*.

255. THE COUNTRY WIFE. A Com. in two acts, as it is performed at the Theatre Royal in Drury-Lane; altered from Wycherly, 8vo. no date. [1765]. This alteration is Mr. Lee's; but since Shakspeare has suffered by the same hand, can Wycherly complain of mutilation?

256. COUNTRY INNOCENCE, or, *The Chambermaid turn'd Quaker*. Com. by John Leanard. Acted at the Theatre Royal, 4to. 1677. This is a most notorious plagiarism, being only Brewer's *Country Girl*, just mentioned, reprinted, with scarcely any difference but that of a new title.

257. THE COUNTRY LASSES, or, *The Custom of the Manor*. Com. by Charles Johnson. Acted at Drury-Lane, 12mo. 1715. This is a very busy and entertaining comedy, and consists of two separate and independent plots, one of which is borrowed from Fletcher's *Custom of the Country*; the other from Mrs. Behn's *City Heiress*, and what she stole is from, viz. Middleton's *Mad World my Masters*. It still stands on the list of acting plays, and is ever sure to give pleasure. The character of Farmer *Freehold* in particular is admirably drawn.

258. THE COUNTRY WAKE. Com. by Thomas Dogget, 4to. 1696. This play was acted with applause at Lincoln's-Inn Fields; and has since been reduced into a ballad-farce, by the name of *Flora*, or *Hob in the Well*, which is one of the best pieces of that kind extant. Scene Gloucester.

259. THE COUNTRY WEDDING AND SKIMMINGTON. A Tragi-comi-pastoral farcical Opera, by Essex Hawker, 8vo. 1729, acted at Drury-Lane. This piece is only one long scene on a bank near the Thames' side at Fulham, with twenty-five airs in it after the manner of *The Beggar's Opera*, and was composed for the young company to act in the summer.

260. THE COUNTRY WIFE. C. by William Wycherley. Acted at the Theatre Royal, 4to. 1675. 4to. 1688. This comedy is, next to the *Plain Dealer*, the best of our author's pieces. It contains great wit, high character, and manly nervous language and sentiment; yet on account of the looseness in the character of *Horner* and other of the personages, it was for some time, and had it not been altered must have been totally, laid aside. The last performer, who excelled in the character of *Pinchwife*, was the late Mr. Quin. Mrs. *Pinchwife* seems in some measure borrowed from Moliere's *Ecole des Femmes*.

261. THE COUNTRY WIT. C. by J. Crowne. Acted at the Duke's Theatre,

Theatre, 4to. 1675. This play contains a quantity of low humour, and was a great favourite with king Charles II. Part both of the plot and language are borrowed from Moliere's *Sicilien, ou l'Amour Peintre.* Scene the Pall-Mall, in the year 1675.

262. THE COURAGIOUS TURK, or *Amurath* I. Trag. by Thomas Goff, 4to. 1632, 8vo. 1656. The plot from the Histories of the Turkish Empire, in the reign of Amurath. It was acted by the students of Christ-Church, Oxford, where the author was a fellow. Compared with the ranting absurdities of this piece, the tragedies of Lee are sober declamations. Our hero, on the appearance of a comet, addresses the following question to the stars:

"Why do you put on perriwigs of fire?"

263. THE COURTEZANS. C. of two acts, founded on truth, and acted every night at Drury-Lane and Covent-Garden, by Charles Townly, Esq. 8vo. 1760. This author's name is a fictitious one.

264. THE COURTEZANS. Com. translated from Plautus by Richard Warner, Esq. 8vo.

265. COURT AND COUNTRY, or, *The Changelings.* Ballad Opera, 8vo. 1743. This piece was never intended for the stage, but is only a satire on the alterations made in the ministry, and the unsteadiness in some of the patriot party, or, as they called themselves, the country interest about that time.

266. THE COURT BEGGAR. C. by Richard Broome. Acted at the Cockpit in 1632, and printed 8vo. 1653.

267. THE COURT LEGACY. Ballad Opera, of three acts, 8vo. 1733. Anonymous, never acted.

268. THE COURT OF ALEXANDER. Opera, by George Alexander Stevens. Acted at Covent-Garden, 8vo. 1770.

269. THE COURT LADY, or, *Coquet's Surrender.* Com. Anonym. 8vo. 1730. This play I find by the dramatis personæ was acted, though I imagine without success. By the dedication, however, which is a satyrical one, *To a great Lady at Court,* it seems to have aimed personal reflection on some particular intrigue at that time pretty well known at court. Be this as it will, the piece in itself has very little merit, either in plot, language, or character. The running title of it is, *The Coquet's Surrender,* or *The Humourous Punster,* which last title is derived from a principal character in the piece, who is perpetually running into the absurdity of puns and quibble, but whom we may safely acquit of the charge either of humour or even common sense.

270. COURT MEDLEY, or, *Marriage by Proxy.* A ballad Op. of three acts, 8vo. 1733.

271. COURTNAY, EARL OF DEVONSHIRE, or, *The Troubles of Queen Elizabeth.* T. 4to. Anonym. No date. This play is dedicated to the duke of Devonshire, but was never acted.

272. THE COURT SECRET. Tragi-Com. by James Shirley, 8vo. 1653. This play was never acted, but was prepared for the stage at Black-Friers, plays being at that time, viz. during the commonwealth, entirely interdicted. The scene lies at Madrid.

273. COURTSHIP A-LA-MODE. Com. by David Craufurd. Acted at Drury-Lane, 4to. 1700. It is dedicated to John Le Neve, Esq; by William Pinkethman the player, to whom the care of the publication had been left. The prologue by Farquhar. In the preface, the play

play is said to have been written in ten mornings.

274. THE COXCOMB. Com. by Beaumont and Fletcher. Fol. 1647. This play has at times been revived and acted with success.

275. THE COZENERS. A Com. in three acts, by Samuel Foote. First acted at the Hay-Market in 1774. Printed in 8vo. 1778.

One character in the piece (that of Mrs. Simony) was designed as a vehicle for satire on the late Dr. Dodd. As some apology for Mr. Foote's stage ridicule, we may observe, that he rarely pointed it at any persons who either met with public respect, or deserved to meet with it.

276. CRAFTIE CROMWELL, or, *Oliver ordering our new State.* Tragi-Com. *Wherein is discovered the traiterous Undertakings and Proceedings of the said* Nol *and his levelling Crew*; written by Mercurius Melancholicus, and printed in 4to. 1648. It consists of five very short acts, and at the end of each act a chorus enters.

277. CRAFTE UPON SUBTILTYES BACKE. An enterlude; entered by Jeffrey Charlton on the books of the Stationers' Company, Jan. 27, 1608; but we believe not printed.

278. THE CRAFT OF RHETORIC. Of this piece, I shall give the full title as follows: *A newe Commodye in English (in Maner of an Enterlude) ryght elygant and full of Craft of Retboryk (wherein is shewed and descrybyd as well the bewte and good properties of Women as their vyces and evyl Condicion) with a moral conclusion and exhortacyon to Vertew.* London, printed by *John Rastell*, 4to. without date. This play is in metre, and in the old black letter; so that it is probable, from every testimonial, to be one of the very earliest of our dramatic pieces.

279. THE CRAFTSMAN, or, *Weekly Journalist.* A Farce, 8vo. 1728. Scene London, in Caleb D'Anvers's chambers in Gray's-Inn. This piece was not intended for the stage, but is a banter on the paper of that title.

280. CREUSA, QUEEN OF ATHENS. Trag. by W. Whitehead. Acted at Drury-Lane, 8vo. 1754. This play is founded on the *Ion* of Euripides; but the plot is extremely heightened, and admirably conducted by our author, nor has there, perhaps, ever been a more genuine and native simplicity introduced into dramatic writing, than that of the youth Ilyssus, bred up in the service of the Gods, and kept unacquainted with the vices of mankind.

281. THE CRISIS, or, *Love and Fear.* Com. Opera, by Thomas Holcraft. Acted at Drury-Lane, May 1, 1778, for the benefit of Miss Hopkins. Not printed.

282. THE CRITICAL MINUTE. Farce, by Dr. Hill. Acted at Drury-Lane, about 1754, one night. Not printed.

283. THE CRITIC, or, *A Tragedy Rehearsed.* Farce, by Richard Brinsley Sheridan, Esq. Acted at Drury-Lane, 1779. Not printed.

The drift of this performance, which abounds with easy wit, unaffected humour, and judicious satire, is perhaps in general misunderstood. It might not have been written with the single view of procuring full houses during its own run, but as a crafty expedient to banish empty ones on future occasions. In short, it is to be regarded in the light of an advertisement published by the manager of Drury-Lane, signifying his wish that no more *modern tragedies* may be offered for representation at his theatre. It has already acted as a caustic on the

the author of *Zoraida*, whose piece immediately followed in the same season. We hear indeed that our Cambridge Quixote imputes all his sufferings to the magic of the fell enchantress *Tilburina*. Let not however this circumstance discourage writers of real genius and judgment. Ludicrous parodies or imitations, do no injury to originals of sterling merit. The most successful ridicule could never drive our Shakspeare's phantom from the stage, though the spectre raised by his would-be rival Voltaire, is known to have faded long ago at the first crowing of the cocks of criticism.

In this after-piece, a well-known author is likewise supposed to be represented under the title of *Sir Fretful Plagiary*. How he happened to deserve such ridicule, in preference to any other playwright of similar pretensions, it is not our present business to enquire. A literary thief, however, is the most tender and irascible of all beings, and, like his brethren who appear every six weeks at the Old Baily, lives in perpetual hostility with those who are qualified to detect his practices, and point out the objects of his plunder. To a dramatist of this description, a general reader, with a retentive memory, is as formidable as an empty house on a third night. The present age exhibits more than one *Sir Fretful*, more than one notorious plagiary.

284. THE CRITIC, or, *Tragedy Rehearsed*. *A literary catchpenny by way of prelude to a dramatic afterpiece, by R. B. Sheridan*, 8vo. 1779.

285. THE CRITIC ANTICIPATED, or *The Humours of the Green Room*. Piece, rehearsed behind the curtain of the Theatre in Drury-Lane, 8vo. 1779. Another despicable catchpenny.

286. THE CRITIC, or, *Tragedy Rehearsed*. A new dramatic piece in three acts, as performed by his majesty's servants, with the greatest applause, 8vo. 1780. This is a third catchpenny produced by the success of Mr. Sheridan's piece. It is of a different kind from the former, being entirely political.

287. CROESUS. T. by W. Alexander, earl of Sterling, 4to. 1604, and Fol. 1639. This is the most affecting of all our author's pieces. The plot is borrowed from Herodotus, Justin, and Plutarch, with an episode in the fifth act from Xenophon's *Cyropaedia*. The scene lies in Sardis.

288. CRONWELL, *Lord Thomas*. Historical Play, 4to. 1613. This drama is in all the Catalogues set down to Shakspeare; but Theobald and other editors of his works have omitted it, together with six pieces more, viz. the *Puritan*, *Pericles*, Prince of *Tyre*, the Tragedy of *Locrine*, the *Yorkshire* Tragedy, Sir *John Oldcastle*, and the *London* Prodigal. All which, though it is probable from some beautiful passages that Shakspeare may have had a hand in them, are on the whole too indifferent to be received as the genuine and entire works of that inimitable genius.

289. CROMWELL'S CONSPIRACY. Tragi-Com. relating to our latter times, beginning at the death of king Charles I. and ending with the happy Restoration of king Charles II. Written by a person of quality, 4to. 1660.

290. CROSS PURPOSES. Farce, by Mr. Obrien. Acted at Covent-Garden, 8vo. 1772. This piece had considerable success.

291. THE CRUEL BROTHER. Trag. by Sir W. Davenant, 4to. 1630. Presented at Black-Friers. The scene Italy.

292. THE

292. THE CRUEL DEBTOR, 4to. 1669. This is only named in Kirkman's and other lists. It is however probably a republication, as I find entered on the books of the Stationers' Company, by Thomas Colwell, in the years 1565 to 1566, "a ballet, intituled, An Interlude, of The Cruell Detter, by Wayer."

293. THE CRUEL GIFT, or, The Royal Resentment. Trag. by Mrs. Centlivre. Acted at Drury-Lane, 12mo. 1717. It was the second attempt made by this lady in the tragedy walk, and is very far from being a bad one. The design is founded on the story of Sigismunda and Guiscardo, which is to be met with in Boccace's Novels, and a poetical version of it very finely done by Dryden, and published among his Fables.

294. THE CRUELTY OF THE SPANIARDS IN PERU. Expressed by instrumental and vocal music, and by art of perspective in scenes, by Sir William Davenant, &c. represented daily at the Cockpit in Drury-Lane, at three in the afternoon punctually, 4to. 1658. The author of the British Theatre mentions a remarkable circumstance in regard to it, which is, that Oliver Cromwell, who had prohibited all theatrical representations, not only allowed this piece to be performed, but even himself actually read and approved of it; the reason assigned for which was its strongly reflecting on the Spaniards, against whom he was supposed to have formed some very considerable designs.

295. THE CRY. Dram. Fable, by Mrs. Sarah Fielding, 3 vols. 12mo. 1754.

296. THE CUCKOLD IN CONCEIT. Com. by Sir John Vanbrugh. This is little more than a translation of Moliere's Cocu Imaginaire. It was acted at the Queen's Theatre in the Hay-Market, 1706, but we believe not printed.

297. CUCKOLD'S HAVEN, or, An Alderman no Conjuror, by N. Tate, Farce. Acted at Dorset-Gardens, 4to. 1685. The plot of this piece is borrowed partly from Eastward Hoe, and partly from the Devil's an Ass, of Ben Jonson.

298. THE CUNNING LOVERS. Com. by Robert Broome, 4to. 1654. This piece was acted at Drury-Lane with considerable applause, and was well esteemed. The scene lies in Verona. For the plot, see The Seven Wise Masters of Rome, and a Novel called The Fortunate deceiv'd, and unfortunate Lovers.

299. THE CUNNING MAN. A Musical Entertainment, by Dr. Burney. Acted at Drury-Lane, 8vo. 1766. This is a translation of Rousseau's Devin du Village. It was produced about the time when the original author came to England, and was adapted to his musick; but notwithstanding these advantages, and the elegance of the translation, it was but coldly received.

300. CUPID AND DEATH. A Masque, by James Shirley, 4to. 1653. This was presented before the Portuguese Ambassador, on the 26th of March, 1653. For the design, see Ogilby's Æsop, vol. 1. fab. 39.

301. CUPID AND HYMEN. A Masque, by John Hughes, 8vo. about 1717.

302. CUPID AND PSYCHE, or, Columbine Courtezan, dramatic pantomime entertainment. Acted at Drury-Lane, 8vo. 1734.

303. CUPID'S REVENGE. T. by Beaumont and Fletcher. Acted by the children of the Revels, 4to. 1615, 4to. 1630, 4to. 1635.

The

The last edition of Beaumont and Fletcher observes that the plot and machinery of this play are equally ridiculous, and that it was a pity so much admirable poetry should be bestowed on so absurd a drama. It was entered on the Stationers' books, April 24, 1615.

304. CUPID'S REVENGE. An Arcadian Pastoral, by Francis Gentleman. Acted at the Hay-Market, 8vo. 1772.

305. CUPID'S WHIRLIGIG. C. by E. S. Acted by the children of the Revels, 4to. 1607, 4to. 1616, 4to. 1630. Coxeter relates that he had been assured by an old bookseller, that this play was entered at Stationers' Hall as Shakspeare's, but at that time thought falsely, in order to make it sell.

306. A CURE FOR A CUCKOLD. Com. by John Webster and W. Rowley, 4to 1661. This play was acted several times with applause.

307. A CURE FOR A SCOLD. Ballad Opera, by James Worsdale. Acted at London and Dublin, 12mo. 1738. This is taken from Shakspeare's *Taming of the Shrew*, but never met with any great success, although some of the songs are far from unentertaining.

308. A CURE FOR JEALOUSY. Com. by John Carey, 4to. 1701. Acted at Lincoln's-Inn Fields. This is not by the same author as the *Generous Enemies*, of which hereafter. The scene lies in Covent-Garden; it met with no success, being performed during the run of Farquhar's *Constant Couple*, which the author in his preface calls a Jubilee Farce, and seems much offended that so great a degree of attention should be paid to it.

309. A CURE FOR DOTAGE. Musical Entertainment, sung at Marybone-Gardens, 8vo. 1771.

310. THE CUSTOM OF THE COUNTRY. Tragi-Com. by Beaumont and Fletcher. Fol. 1647. This was accounted a very good play. The plot is taken from Malespini's Novels, Dec. 6. Nov. 6. and has been made considerable use of by C. Johnson in his *Country Lasses*. The scene lies sometimes at Lisbon, and sometimes in Italy.

Dryden, in the preface to his Tales, says, " There is more bau" dry in one play of Fletcher's, " called *The Custom of the Country*, " than in all ours together. Yet " this has been often acted on the " stage in my remembrance."

311. CUTTER OF COLEMAN-STREET. Com. by Abraham Cowley, 4to. 1663. At the beginning of the civil war (says Dr. Johnson), as the prince passed through Cambridge in his way to York, he was entertained with the representation of the *Guardian*, a comedy, which Cowley says was neither written nor acted, but rough-drawn by him, and repeated by the scholars. That this comedy was printed during his absence from his country, he appears to have considered as injurious to his reputation; though, during the suppression of the theatres, it was sometimes privately acted with sufficient approbation.

When the king was restored, the neglect of the court was not our author's only mortification; having by such alteration as he thought proper fitted his old comedy of the *Guardian* for the stage, he produced it at the duke of York's Theatre, under the title of the *Cutter of Coleman-Street*. It was treated on the stage with severity, and was afterwards censured as a satire on the king's party. Mr. Dryden, who went with Mr. Sprat to the first exhibition, related to Mr. Dennis, " that when
" they

"they told Cowley how little favour had been shewn him, he received the news of his ill success, not with so much firmness as might have been expected from so great a man." What firmness they expected, or what weakness Cowley discovered, cannot be known. It appears, however, from the theatrical register of Downes the prompter, to have been popularly considered (in spite of the author's exculpation of himself) as a satire on the royalists. It has been revived within these thirty years at the theatre in Lincoln's-Inn Fields.

312. CYMBELINE. Trag. by W. Shakspeare. Fol. 1623. The plot of this play is taken from an old story-book, intituled, *Westward for Smelts*. 4to. 1603. Dr. Johnson observes, that it "has many just sentiments, some natural dialogues, and some pleasing scenes, but they are obtained at the expence of much incongruity. To remark the folly of the fiction, the absurdity of the conduct, the confusion of the names, and manners of the different times, and the impossibility of the events in any system of life, were to waste criticism upon unresisting imbecility, upon faults too evident for detection, and too gross for aggravation."

313. CYMBELINE. Trag. altered from Shakspeare, by W. Hawkins. Acted at Covent-Garden, 8vo. 1759. This is what the title implies, it being only fitted to the English stage, by removing some part of the absurdities in point of time and place, which the rigid rules of dramatic law do not now admit with so much impunity as at the time when the original author of *Cymbeline* was living. Thus far our predecessor; but justice obliges us to add, that the play is entirely ruined by Mr. Hawkins's unpoetical additions and injudicious alterations. It had no success when performed for a night or two at Covent-Garden, the hand of the reformer having destroyed all its powers of entertainment, by discarding the part of Jachimo, delaying the appearance of Posthumus till the third act, &c. &c. With a few trivial omissions, the original piece is still a favourite with the public.

314. CYMBELINE. Trag. altered by David Garrick, Esq. Acted at Drury-Lane, 12mo. 1759. This alteration, being less violent, is less defective than many similar attempts on the dramas of Shakspeare. A material fault, however, occurs in it. By omitting the Physician's soliloquy in the first act, we are utterly unprepared for the recovery of Imogen after she had swallowed the potion prepared by her stepmother. To save appearances, this speech was inserted in the printed copy, but was never uttered on the stage. Useless as it might be to those who are intimately acquainted with the piece, it is still necessary toward the information of a common auditor.

315. CYMBELINE, KING OF GREAT BRITAIN. A Tragedy, written by Shakspeare, with some alterations by Charles Marsh, 8vo. 1755. Though Mr. Marsh was not at that time a magistrate, the dullness he displayed in the present undertaking, afforded strong presumptions of his future rise to a seat on the bench at Guildhall, Westminster.

316. CYMBELINE. Trag. by Henry Brooke, Esq. 8vo. 1778. Not acted. This is on the same story as Shakspeare's Play.

317. Cy-

317. CYMON. Dram. Romance, by David Garrick. Acted at Drury-Lane, 8vo. 1767. The hint of this piece was taken from Dryden's Poems. It is, however, a wretched production, equally devoid of wit, humour, and poetry. To the scene-painter and the vocal performers, it was indebted for its success, which (to the shame of taste and common sense) was considerable.

318. CYNTHIA AND ENDYMION, or, *The Loves of the Deities*. A dramat. Op. by T. Durfey, 4to. 1697. This piece was designed to be acted at court before queen Mary II. and after her death was performed at the Theatre Royal, where it met with good success. The story is taken from Ovid's *Metamorphoses*, and *Psyche*, in Apuleius's *Golden Ass*. The scene lies in Ionia and on Mount Latmos. But although there are many lines in the piece greatly superior to the general cast of genius which appears in this author's other works, yet he is inexcuseable in the perversion of the characters from what Ovid has represented them; *Daphne*, the chaste favourite of *Diana*, appearing in this play a whore and a jilt, and the fair *Syrinx* being painted in the ignominious colouring of an envious, mercenary, and infamous woman.

319. CYNTHIA's REVELS, or, *The Fountain of Self-Love*. A comical Satire, by Ben Jonson. This piece was acted, in 1600, by the children of Queen Elizabeth's Chapel.

320. CYNTHIA's REVENGE, or, *Menander's Extasy*, by John Stephens, 4to. 1613. This play runs mostly in verse, and is one of the longest dramatic pieces that ever was written. The plot is from Lucan's *Pharsalia* and Ovid's *Metamorphoses*.

321. CYRUS THE GREAT, or, *The Tragedy of Love*. Trag. by J. Banks. Acted at Lincoln's-Inn Fields, 4to. 1696. This play was at first forbidden to be acted, but afterwards came on, and met with very good success. Downes the prompter says, Mr. Smith having a long part in it, fell ill upon the fourth day, and died. This occasioned it to be laid aside, and it was not acted afterwards. The plot is from Scudery's Romance of the Grand Cyrus. The scene in the camp near Babylon.

322. CYRUS. Trag. by John Hoole. Acted at Covent-Garden, 8vo. 1768. Though our author has founded this tragedy on an opera, his good sense has freed it from the romantic insipidities with which these ridiculous entertainments usually abound. *Cyrus* was performed with great success.

323. CYTHEREA, or, *The Enamoured Girdle*. Com. by J. Smith, 4to. 1677. This play was never acted. Scene the city of York.

324. THE CZAR OF MUSCOVY. Trag. by Mrs. Mary Pix, 4to. 1701. This play was acted in Lincoln's-Inn Fields, and is founded on some of the incidents of the then recent history of the great Czar Peter. The scene Muscovy. It died, however, in obscurity, and has not been heard of since.

D.

D.

1. **DAME DODSON, or, *The Cunning Woman*.** Com. by E. Ravenscroft. Acted at the Duke's Theatre, 4to. 1684. This is translated from a French comedy, called, *La Divineresse ou les faux Enchantemens*; yet although the original met with the highest approbation in France, and was eagerly followed, this copy of it was damned in its representation on the London Theatre.

2. **DAMON AND PHEBE.** Musical Entertainment, by Thomas Horde, jun. Esq; Printed at Oxford, 8vo. 1774.

3. **DAMON AND PHILLIDA.** A Ballad Pastoral, by Colley Cibber, 8vo. 1729. This little Farce is entirely selected out of the *Love in a Riddle* by the same author. Yet notwithstanding that piece fell to the ground on the second night of its appearance, this entertainment was not only then extremely applauded, but has continued so to be ever since; and indeed amongst all our Ballad Farces I scarcely know any thing that can lay a juster claim to applause, the words of all the songs being happily adapted to the music, the music to the words, and the whole mingled with a simplicity of manners and uniformity of conduct that render it most perfectly and truly pastoral. This, however, is an instance among many, how far party prejudice will have an influence on the behaviour of an audience, in over-bearing its cool and candid judgment. The scene Arcadia.

4. **DAMON AND PYTHIAS.** An historical play. Scene Syracuse. Of this neither Langbaine no Jacob give any particular accounts but the piece itself is to be found reprinted in a Collection of old Plays, published by R. Dodsley, in 12 vols. 8vo. to which I refer the reader.

5. **DAMON AND PHILLIDA.** Altered from Cibber into a Comic Opera, by C. Dibdin. Acted at Drury Lane, 12mo 1768.

6. **THE DAMOISELLE, or, *The New Ordinary*.** Com. by Richard Brome, 8vo. 1653. Scene London.

7. **THE DAMOISELLES A-LA-MODE.** Com. by R. Flecknoe, 12mo. 1667. The scene of this play is laid in Paris, and the plot, as the author himself confesses, borrowed from the *Precieuses Ridicules*, the *Ecole des Femmes*, and the *Ecole des Maris* of Moliere.

8. **DAPHNE AND AMINTOR.** Com. Op. by Isaac Bickerstaffe. Acted at Drury-Lane, 8vo. 1765. This, owing to the excellent acting of Miss Wright (afterwards Mrs. Arne), had great success. It is little more than *The Oracle* of Mrs. Cibber, with a few songs interspersed.

9. **DAPHNIS AND AMARYLLIS.** Pastoral, 8vo. 1766. Printed at Exeter. This is Mr. Harris' piece, called *The Spring*, under a new title.

10. **DARAXES.** Pastoral Opera, by Aaron Hill. This little piece, which was to have consisted of two acts only, is to be found in Mr. Hill's posthumous works, published in two vols. 8vo. 1760. One act of it is entirely finished, and a regular plan laid down for the

the conduct of the other; but whether the author wanted time or inclination to execute that plan I know not; the piece however remains incompleat, yet in such a state that some able hand might easily put the concluding stroke to it, so as to render it perfectly what the author himself intended it should be.

11. DARIUS. T. by the earl of Sterling, 4to. Edinburgh, 1603. This was one of his lordship's first performances, and was originally written in a mixture of the Scotch and English dialects; but the author afterwards not only polished the language, but even very considerably altered the play itself. The first London edition of this piece was with his *Crœsus*, under the joint title of *The Monarchick Tragedies*, together with the *Aurora*, containing the first fancies of the author's youth, 4to. 1604. Fol. 1637.

12. DARIUS, KING OF PERSIA. Trag. by J. Crowne. Acted by their majesties servants, 4to. 1688. The scene lies in the plains and town of Arbela in Persia; and the plot of this play, as well as of lord Sterling's, is borrowed from Quintus Curtius, Plutarch, and other historians of the life of *Alexander*.

13. DEAF INDEED! Farce, by —— Topham. Acted at Drury-Lane, 1780. Not printed. Our author has avoided insulting the town, by the publication of this, which is perhaps the most stupid and indecent performance ever permitted to disgrace a Theatre Royal. The good taste of the audience would not suffer so infamous an exhibition to be represented throughout, but very properly condemned it in the middle of the second act.

14. THE DEAF LOVER. Farce, by F. Pilon. Acted at Covent-Garden, 8vo. 1779. This is an alteration of *The Device* after mentioned, and was represented with a moderate share of applause.

15. DEATH OF DIDO. A Masque, by R. C. 1621.

16. THE DEATH OF ADAM. Trag. translated from the German of Mr. Klopstock, by Robert Lloyd, 12mo. 1763. Dr. Kenrick observes, that Mr. Lloyd was not sufficiently acquainted with the original language of this play, to do justice either to it or himself.

17. THE DEATH OF BUCEPHALUS. A Burlesque Tragedy, by Dr. Ralph Schomberg. Acted at Edinburgh, 8vo. 1775. Probably some performer on one of the Northern Theatres came to Bath for the recovery of his health, and was attended there by Dr. Schomberg, who might refuse his fees, provided his patient, at his return, would introduce *Bucephalus* on the stage in Scotland. To some such accident it must have been indebted for representation.

18. THE DEATH OF CÆSAR. Trag. translated from Voltaire, and published in Dr. Franklin's edition, 12mo.

19. THE DEATH OF DIDO. Masque, by Barton Booth. Acted at Drury-Lane, 8vo. 1716. The music by Dr. Pepusch.

20. THE DEATH OF HANNIBAL. Trag. by Lewis Theobald. A play of this title Jacob, in his lives of the dramatic poets, p. 259, informs us the above-mentioned author had prepared for the stage. But it never made its appearance there, nor, I believe, was ever published.

21. THE DEBAUCHEE, or, *The Credulous Cuckold*. Com. Acted at the

the Duke's Theatre, 4to. 1677. Anonym. Though there is no author's name to this comedy, yet whatever difference there is between it and Richard Brome's *Mad Couple well match'd*, of which it is little more than a revival, is the work of Mrs. Behn.

22. THE DEBAUCHEES, or, *The Jesuit Caught*. Com. by H. Fielding. Acted at Drury-Lane, 8vo. 1733. This play is built on the story so recent at that time of Father Girard and Miss Cadiere, and in it the author has by no means spared the characters of the black-hooded gentlemen of that reverend tribe, whose intrigues and machinations seem at length to have rendered them the objects of almost universal disgust and hatred.

23. THE DECEIT. Farce, by Henry Norris, 12mo. 1723. Of this I know no more than the name.

24. THE DECEIT, or, *The Old Fox Outwitted*. Pastoral Farce, of one act, by J. W. As it was designed to have been acted, 8vo. 1743. Printed with a Collection of Poems, called *The Poplar Grove, or, The Amusements of a Rural Life*.

25. THE DECEIVER DECEIVED. Com. by Mrs. M. Pix, 4to. 1698. Acted at the Theatre in Lincoln's-Inn Fields. There are two dialogues in this play, one in the fourth act, by D'Urfey, and the other in the last, by Motteux, both set to music by Eccles. Scene Venice.

26. DECIUS AND PAULINA. A Masque, by L. Theobald, 8vo. 1718. 4to. 1719. To this piece are added musical entertainments as performed at the Theatre in Lincoln's-Inn Fields, in the dramatic opera of *Circe*, set to music by Galliard.

27. THE DECOY. An Opera, by H. Potter. Acted at Goodman's-Fields, 1733. 8vo.

28. THE DELIVERY OF SUSANNAH. Trag. by Ralph Radcliff. Not printed.

29. DEMETRIUS. Opera, translated from *Metastasio*, by John Hoole, 8vo. 1768.

30. DEMOPHOON. Opera, translated from *Metastasio*, by John Hoole, 8vo. 1768.

31. DEORUM DONA. A Masque, by Robert Baron, 8vo. 1648. performed before Flaminius and Clorinda, king and queen of Cyprus, at their regal palace in Nicosia. The scene lies in Nicosia. This piece is part of a romance of this author's, called, *The Cyprian Academy*; but he has been in some measure guilty of piracy, the ditty which is sung by Neptune and his train, being made up from Waller's Poem *to the King on his Navy*, and part of Act 2. Scene 1. nearly transcribed from the same author, on lady Isabella playing on her lute.

32. THE DEPOSING AND DEATH OF QUEEN GIN. An Heroic-Comi-Trag. Farce. Anonymous, 8vo. 1736. This little burlesque piece, which is not devoid of humour, was acted at the New Theatre in the Hay-Market. The design of it is founded on an act of parliament, whereby an additional duty was laid on malt spirits, and the retailing of spirituous liquors of any kinds prohibited to the distillers, by which means the pernicious practice that the commonalty of England, and more especially of this great metropolis, had been for some time infatuated with, of drinking great quantities of the worst and most pernicious kind of spirit distilled from malt, under the name of gin,

was at once greatly checked, and at length, by means of different acts, entirely put an end to. The principal characters in the piece are, *Queen Gin*, the Duke of *Rum*, the Marquis of *Nantz*, and Lord *Sugar-Cane*.

33. THE DESERVING FAVOURITE. Tragi-Com. by Lodowick Carlell. Scene Spain. This piece met with great applause, and was acted several times before the king and queen at Whitehall, and at Black-Friers. It was first printed in 4to. 1629. and afterwards, 8vo. 1659.

34. THE DESERT ISLAND. A dramatic Tale, in three acts, by A. Murphy, 8vo. 1760. This little piece, which is allied to tragedy, although the catastrophe of it is a happy one, was first performed at the Theatre Royal in Drury-Lane on the same night with the *Way to keep him*, a comedy of the same number of acts by the same author. The plan of this piece has its original, according to the author's own confession, in a little drama of a single act, called L'*Isola disabitata*, or *The uninhabited Island*, written by the Abbé Metastasio. Mr. Murphy has greatly extended the original, so that the language, in which there is a considerable share both of poetry and *pathos*, may properly be called his own. But the plan being extremely simple, even for one act, and that stretched into three without the introduction of a single incident or episode, renders it somewhat too heavy and declamatory to give much pleasure in a public representation, though it will bear a close examen and *critique* in the closet. The success of it evinced the truth of this observation, for notwithstanding the great approbation shewn to the other piece brought on at the same time, yet even the sprightliness of that cou'd not secure to this a run of many nights, after which the *Way to keep him* continued an acting piece for the remainder of that season; and, by the addition of two new acts afterwards, still stands on the stock-list of the theatre, while the *Desert Island* became truly deserted, and has never since been represented.

35. THE DESERTER. Musical Drama, by C. Dibden. Acted at Drury-Lane, 8vo. 1773. Taken from a French piece, intituled, *Le Deserteur*; and acted with success.

36. THE DESTRUCTION OF JERUSALEM, by Titus Vespasian. Trag. in two parts, by J. Crowne. Acted at the Theatre Royal, 4to. 1677. They are both written in heroic verse, and were acted with applause; yet the author found it necessary to enter into some kind of vindication of himself, with respect to his character of *Phraartes*. The historical part of these plays is to be met with in Josephus's wars of the Jews, and some other authors.

37. DESTRUCTION OF TROY. Trag. by J. Banks. Acted at the Duke's Theatre, 4to. 1679. This is very far from being a despicable piece, although it met with very indifferent treatment from the critics. It is founded on history, and taken from Homer, Virgil, &c. and Langbaine observes of it, although the language is not equal to that of Shakspeare's *Troilus* and *Cressida*, yet it at least surpasses Heywood's *Iron Age* (which is built on the same plot), and many other tragedies which have met with a more favourable reception.

38. THE DEUCE IS IN HIM. Farce, by George Colman. Acted at Drury-Lane, 8vo. 1763. The first hint of this piece was taken from the *Episode* of *Lindor*, in Marmontel's

Marmontel's *Tales*, and that part of the fable which relates to Madame Florival, from a story originally published in *The British Magazine*. It met with very great and deserved success from the publick. The plan on which this delicate satire on platonic love is founded, has been approved by those who are the strictest advocates for morality in dramatic exhibitions. The piece, though very serious in the main, is extremely laughable in many parts. The disease, as an ingenious critic has observed, is exposed, but not rankled. The author acts like a regular physician, without making a display of his great skill, by wantonly adding corrosives, that he might have the credit of curing the distemper in its last stage; a fault but too common with some of our best English dramatic writers: and the avoiding it gave Moliere the character he so justly bears.

39. THE DEVICE, or, *The Deaf Doctor*. Farce, by F. Pilon. Acted at Covent-Garden, 1779. Not printed. This piece, which was taken from the French, met with no success in its original state. It was afterwards altered, and met with a better fate under the title of *The Deaf Lover*.

40. THE DEVICE, or, *The Marriage Office*. Farce, by —— Richards. Acted at Covent-Garden, May 5, 1777, for the benefit of Mr. Wilson. Not printed.

41. THE DEVIL IS AN ASS. Com. by Ben Jonson. Acted in 1616, and printed Fol. 1641. Jonson is certainly but little chargeable with borrowing any part of his plots, yet *Wittipol's* giving his cloak to *Fitz-dotterel* for leave to court his wife for a quarter of an hour, seems founded on a circumstance of Boccace's *Decameron*, Day 3. Nov. 5. Mrs. *Centlivre* has made her Sir *George Airy* do the same, only converting the cloak into a purse of an hundred guineas.

42. THE DEVIL OF A DUKE, or Trappolin's *Vagaries*. Ballad Farce, by R. Drury, 8vo. 1732. Acted at Drury-Lane. This is only an alteration, with the addition of a few songs, of the comedy of *Duke and no Duke*.

43. THE DEVIL'S CHARTER. Trag. by Barnaby Barnes, 4to. 1607. This tragedy contains the life and death of that most execrable of all human beings, pope Alexander VI. in whose history the author has very closely followed Guicciardini, and seems also to have formed this play, in some measure, after the model of *Pericles Prince of Tyre*; for as the author of that piece raises up Gower, an old English bard, to be his interlocutor, so has Barnes revived Guicciardini for the very same purpose.

44. THE DEVIL'S LAW-CASE, or, *When Women go to Law, the Devil is full of Business*. Tragi-Com. by J. Webster, 4to. 1623. This is a good play, and met with success. The circumstance of Romelio's stabbing Contarino out of malice, and its turning out to his preservation, seems borrowed from the story of Phæreus Jason, related by Valerius Maximus, lib. i. c. 8.

45. THE DEVIL OF A WIFE, or, *A comical Transformation*. Farce, by Thomas Jevon. Acted at the Theatre Dorset-Garden, 4to. 1686. 4to. 1693. 4to. 1695. This little piece Langbaine gives great commendations to, and it met with success in the representation. The plot, however, is a very unnatural one, but is borrowed from the story of Mopsa in Sir Philip Sidney's *Arcadia*. It was imagined that Mr. Jevon had some assistance in it from his brother-in-law, Thomas

Thomas Shadwell. However this be, Coffey has made use of the plan and part of the conduct of it in the *Devil to pay*, or *Wives metamorphos'd*.

46. THE DEVIL TO PAY, or, *The Wives metamorphosed*. Ballad Farce, by C. Coffey, 8vo. 1731. This well-known little piece has itself, perhaps, gone through as many metamorphoses, and had as many hands concerned in the fabrication of it, as ever clubbed together in a business of so little importance. The ground work of it, and indeed the best part, is selected from a farce of three acts, written by Jevon the player before-mentioned. In the year 1730, Coffey and Mottley, each of them undertook the alteration of an act and half, and by adding a number of songs converted it into a ballad opera, still of three acts, under the title of *The Devil to pay*. In this state it was performed in the summer season; but some things in it giving disgust, particularly the part of a nonconforming pastor, made explain to lady Loverule, Theophilus Cibber took it once more in hand, omitted that character, and shortening it throughout, reduced it to one act, adding the second title of *The Wives Metamorphos'd*. In doing this, one song was added by his father C. Cibber, and another introduced written by lord Rochester above fifty years before; so that from the joint labours of six or seven authors, came forth the *petit piece* under consideration; which, however, does no discredit to any of its compilers, constantly giving pleasure whenever it is performed, and stealing on attention from the natural behaviour of the characters, even in spite of the impossibility of the circumstance wherefrom all their actions derive their origin.

One theatrical anecdote, however, must not be omitted in our mention of this piece, which is, that to the part of *Nell*, the great Mrs. Clive owes the rise of her now justly established reputation, that being the first thing she was ever taken any considerable notice of in, which occasioned her salary, then but trifling, to be doubled. Harper, who played *Jobson*, had also his salary raised, from the merit he shewed in the performance.

47. THE DEVIL UPON TWO STICKS, or, *The Country Beau*. Ballad Farce, by Charles Coffey, 1744. This is an alteration, but considerably for the worse, of a very middling comedy, called *The Country Squire*, which see in its place. It was acted one night only, at Shepheard's Wells, May-Fair.

48. THE DEVIL UPON TWO STICKS. Com. by Samuel Foote. Acted at the Hay-Market 1768. Printed in 8vo. 1778. This was one of the most successful of Mr. Foote's performances; but though fraught with wit, humour, and satire of the most pleasant and inoffensive kind, yet seems to have sunk into the grave of its ingenious author.

49. DIDO AND ÆNEAS. An Opera, in three short acts, by N. Tate. This was written for, and performed at Mr. Josiah Priest's Boarding-school at Chelsea, by young gentlemen. The music composed by Henry Purcell.

50. DIDO, QUEEN OF CARTHAGE. Trag. by Christopher Marlow and Thomas Nash. Acted by the children of her majesties' chapel, 4to. 1594. This play is uncommonly scarce.

51. DIDO. Trag. in imitation of Shakspear's style, by Joseph Reed. Acted at Drury-Lane, 1767. Not printed. This tragedy was first performed for the benefit of

of Mr. Holland, and twice afterwards, when it was each time received with applause. It was intended to have been revived in the ensuing season; but the author and manager disagreeing in some particulars, the copy was withdrawn, and it has since lain dormant. It would be a poor compliment to the author to observe, that many pieces of inferior merit have been since successfully represented.

52. DIDO. Com. Opera, by Thomas Bridges. Acted at the Hay-Market, 8vo. 1771. A piece of some humour, but unworthy of the burlesquer of Homer.

53. THE DIFFERENT WIDOWS, or, *Intrigue Alamode*. C. 4to. No date. Anonym. Acted at the New Theatre in Lincoln's-Inn Fields.

54. DIOCLESIAN, or, *The Prophetess*. Dramat. Opera, by Thomas Betterton, 4to. 1690. This is only an alteration, with very little difference, of the *Prophetess* of Beaumont and Fletcher, with an addition of some musical entertainments and interludes to it. It is still sometimes performed, but does not seem much to suit with the present taste. It appeared, for the last time, during the theatrical administration of Mr. Rich, and was then republished in 12mo.

55. DIONE. Past. by John Gay, printed in his Poems, 4to. 1720. This piece, says Dr. Johnson, is a counterpart to *Amynta* and *Pastor Fido*, and other trifles of the same kind, easily imitated, and unworthy of imitation. What the Italians call Comedies, from a happy conclusion, Gay calls a Tragedy, from a mournful event; but the style of the Italians and of Gay is equally tragical. There is something in the poetical *Arcadia* so remote from known reality and speculative possibility, that we can never support its representation through a long work. A pastoral of a hundred lines may be endured; but who will hear of sheep and goats, and myrtle bowers and purling rivulets, through five acts? Such scenes please barbarians in the dawn of literature, and children in the dawn of life; but will be for the most part thrown away, as men grow wise, and nations grow learned.

56. DIPHILO AND GRANIDA. This is one of the six pieces which are published in the second part of *Sport upon Sport*, 1659, and in 4to. and are attributed to Robert Cox the comedian.

57. THE DISAPPOINTED COXCOMB. Com. by Bartholomew Bourgeois, 8vo. 1765.

58. THE DISAPPOINTMENT, or, *The Mother in Fashion*. Com. by Thomas Southerne, Acted at the Theatre Royal, 4to. 1684. The scene lies in Florence, and part of the plot is taken from the *Curious Impertinent* in Don Quixote. Prologue by Dryden.

59. THE DISAPPOINTMENT. Ballad Opera, by John Randal. Acted at the Hay-Market, 8vo. 1732. This is an alteration of Mrs. Centlivre's Farce, called *A Wife well managed*.

60. THE DISCONTENTED COLONEL. By Sir John Suckling, N. D. [1639.] The first sketch of Brennoralt.

61. THE DISCOVERY. A Com. acted at the Theatre Royal in Drury-Lane, 1763. 8vo. This original composition was received with uncommon applause. It is a very moral, sentimental, yet entertaining performance. The characters of Sir *Harry Flutter* and his Lady, are supported with wit and spirit; which, notwithstanding the length and languor of some of the scenes, effectually secured to this

play, the approbation of the gayer part of the audience.

62. THE DISCOVERY. Com. translated from Plautus, by Richard Warner. 8vo 1773.

63. THE DISGUISE. A Dram, Novel, 2 vols. 12mo. 1771.

64. THE DISOBEDIENT CHILD. A pretty and merry Interlude, by Thomas Ingeland, 4to. without date. This author lived in the time of queen Elizabeth; and his piece is written in verse of ten syllables, and printed in the old black letter.

65. THE DISPENSARY. Farce, by Thomas Brown. Printed in that author's works.

66. THE DISSEMBLED WANTON, or, My Son get Money. Com. by Leonard Welsted. Acted at Lincoln's-Inn Fields, 8vo 1726. This is an entertaining comedy, and met with tolerable success; but 'tis probable it might have found a more favourable reception, had it not unfortunately made its appearance just at the time when the town was big with expectation of Smyth's Rival Modes, and therefore paid the less attention to any other new piece.

67. THE DISTRACTED STATE. Trag. by J. Tatham, written in 1641, 4to. This author was a strong party man, and wrote for the distracted times he lived in, to which his present work was extremely suitable. His hatred to the Scots is apparent throughout this play, wherein he introduces a Scotch mountebank undertaking to poison Archias the elected king, at the instigation of Cleander. The scene lies in Cicily. This is the best of our author's pieces, and is introduced by three copies of recommendatory verses.

68. DISTRESSED INNOCENCE, or, *The Princess of Persia*. Trag. by Elk. Settle. Acted at the Theatre Royal, 4to. 1691. This play was received with great applause. The plot is founded on the History of Isdegerdes, king of Persia, and the author declares that whatever fictions he may elsewhere have interwoven, the distresses of his principal characters *Hermidas* and *Cleomira* are true history. He likewise acknowledges great assistance in it from Betterton and Mountford, the latter of whom wrote the last scene and the epilogue.

69. THE DISTRESSES. Tragi-Com. by Sir W. Davenant, Fol. 1673. Scene Cordua.

70. DISTRESS UPON DISTRESS, or, *Tragedy in true Taste* An Heroi-comi-parodi-tragi-farcical Burlesque, in two acts, by George Alexander Stevens, 8vo. 1752. This piece was never performed nor intended for the stage, but is only a banter on the bombast language and inextricable distress aimed at by some of our modern tragedy-writers.

71. THE DISTREST MOTHER. Trag. by Ambrose Philips. Acted at Drury-Lane, and printed in 4to. 1712. This play is little more than a translation from the *Andromaque* of Racine. It is, however, very well translated, the poetry pleasing, and the incidents of the story so affecting, that although it is, like all the French tragedies, rather too heavy and declamatory, yet it never fails bringing tears into the eyes of a sensible audience; and will, perhaps, ever continue to be a stock play on the lists of the theatres. The original author, however, has deviated from history, and Philips likewise followed his example, in making *Hermione* kill herself on the body of *Pyrrhus*, who had been slain by her instigation; whereas on the contrary she not only survived, but became wife to *Orestes*.

How

How far the *Licentia poetica* will authorize such oppositions to well-known facts of history, is, however, a point which I have no time at present to enter into a disquisition in regard to.

Dr. Johnson observes that such a work requires no uncommon powers; but that the friends of Philips exerted every art to promote his interest. Before the appearance of the play a whole *Spectator*, none indeed of the best, was devoted to its praise; while it yet continued to be acted, another *Spectator* was written, to tell what impression it made upon Sir Roger de Coverley; and on the first night a select audience, says Pope, was called together to applaud it.

It was concluded with the most successful epilogue that was ever yet spoken on the English theatre. The three first nights it was recited twice; and not only continued to be demanded through the run, as it is termed, of the play, but whenever it is recalled to the stage, where by peculiar fortune, though a copy from the French, it yet keeps its place, the epilogue is still expected, and is still spoken. It was printed in the name of Budgel, but is known to have been the work of Addison.

72. THE DISTRESSED VIRGIN. Trag. by John Maxwell, a blind person, 8vo. 1761. Printed at York by subscription, for the benefit of the author.

73. THE DISTREST WIFE. C. by J. Gay, 8vo. 1743. This piece was designed by its author for the stage, and entirely finished before his death. It is, however, far from being equal to the generality of his writings.

74. THE DISTREST WIFE. C. altered from Gay. Acted at Covent-Garden, 1772, for the benefit of Mrs. Leffingham.

75. THE DIVERSIONS OF THE MORNING. Farce, by Samuel Foote. Acted at Drury-Lane, 1768. Not printed. This was partly compiled from *Taste* and Mr. Whitehead's *Fatal Constancy*.

76. DIVES AND LAZARUS. C. by Ralph Radcliff. Not printed.

77. DIVES'S DOOM, or, *Man's Misery*. By George L. fly, 8vo. 1664. See Vol. I. p. 281.

78. THE DIVINE COMEDIAN, or, *The Right of Plays*, improved in a sacred Tragi-Com. by Richard Tuke, 4to. 1672. This play is on a religious subject, and I imagine was never acted. It was first printed in the same year, by the title of *The Soul's Warfare*, and is intended to point out the danger the human soul incurs in its probationary state in this world.

79. THE DIVORSE. A Play entered on the books of the Stationers' Company, Nov. 29, 1653, but not printed.

80. THE DIVORCE. Musical Entertainment, by Lady Dorothea Dubois, sung at Marybone Gardens, 4to. 1771.

81. THE DOATING LOVERS, or, *The Libertine tam'd*. Com. by Newburgh Hamilton, 12mo. 1715. Acted at Lincoln's-Inn Fields. Scene London. The prologue by Bullock, jun. This play met with no approbation from the unbiassed part of the audience, but was supported to the third night, when, for the author's benefit, the boxes and pit were laid together at the extraordinary price of six shillings each ticket.

82. DOCTOR FAUSTUS's *Tragical History*, by Christopher Marlow, 4to. 1604. 4to. 1616. 4to. 1624. 4to. 1631. 4to. 1663. Black letter. The last edition of this play, with additions of several new scenes and the actors names, was printed in 4to. 1663. The scene

scene at Rhodes and Wertemberg, and the plot is founded on Camerarius, Wierus, and other writers on magic. It was entered on the books of the Stationers' Company, by Thomas Bushull, Jan. 7, 1607.

83. DOCTOR FAUSTUS, *Life and Death of, with the Humours of Harlequin and Scaramouch*; as they were acted by Mr. Lee and Mr. Jevon. Farce, by W. Mountford; acted at the Queen's Theatre in Dorset Gardens, and revived at the Theatre in Lincoln's-Inn Fields. 4to. 1697.

84. DOCTOR FAUSTUS. See THE NECROMANCER.

85. DOCTOR LAST IN HIS CHARIOT. Com. by Isaac Bickerstaffe. Acted at the Hay-Market, 8vo. 1769. This is a translation of Moliere's *Malade Imaginaire*. The author in a preface acknowledges himself indebted to Mr. Foote for a whole scene in the first act, that of the consultation of physicians. It was performed only six nights.

86. DON CARLOS PRINCE OF SPAIN. Trag. by Thomas Otway. Acted at the Duke's Theatre, 4to. 1676. This play is written in heroic verse, was the second work of the author, and met with very great applause. The plot is taken from a Novel of the same name, by S. Real, and also from the Spanish Chronicles in the Life of Philip II.

In a letter from Mr. Booth to Aaron Hill, he says, "Mr. Betterton observed to me many years ago, that *Don Carlos* succeeded much better than either *Venice Preserved*, or *The Orphan*, and was infinitely more applauded and followed for many years." It is asserted to have been played thirty nights together; but this report, as Dr. Johnson observes, it is reasonable to doubt, as so long a continuance of one play upon the stage is a very wide deviation from the practice of that time; when the ardour for theatrical entertainments was not yet diffused through the whole people, and the audience, consisting of nearly the same persons, could be drawn together only by variety.

87. DON GARCIA OF NAVARRE, or, *The Jealous Prince*. This is only a translation from Moliere by Ozell.

88. THE HISTORY OF DON QUIXOT, or, *The Knight of the ill-favoured Face*. Com. This was never printed, but is advertised as at the press in a list of books at the end of *Wit and Drollery*, 12mo. 1661. Winstanley and Philips ascribe a play with this title to Robert Baron.

89. THE COMICAL HISTORY OF DON QUIXOTE. By Thomas Durfey; acted at Dorset-Gardens, 4to. 1694.

90. THE COMICAL HISTORY OF DON QUIXOTE. By Thomas Durfey; acted at Dorset-Gardens, Part II. 4to. 1694.

91. THE COMICAL HISTORY OF DON QUIXOTE. *The third Part, with the Marriage of Mary the Buxome*. By Thomas Durfey, 4to. 1696. This was not acted with the same success as the two former parts.

92. DON QUIXOTE. Musical Entertainment, performed at Covent-Garden, 8vo. 1776. This was acted only one night for the benefit of Mr. Reinhold.

93. DON QUIXOTE IN ENGLAND. Com. by H. Fielding. 8vo. 1733. Acted at the Little Theatre in the Hay-Market, with success.

94. DON SANCHO, or, *The Student's Whim*. Ballad Opera, of three acts, with MINERVA'S TRIUMPH. A Masque, by Elizabeth Boyd,

Boyd, 8vo. 1739. This piece has only the excuse of its being probably the first and only attempt of a female Muse, to secure it from our severest censure. The whole plot of it is the whim of a student at one of the universities, to have the ghosts of Shakspeare and Ben Jonson raised to their view, but to what purpose it seems impossible to divine. Nor does the author's meaning appear more explicable as to the triumph of *Minerva* in her masque. It does not seem to have been ever acted, but the author, in an advertisement, returns her thanks to Mr. Chetwood, at that time prompter of Drury-Lane Theatre, for having obtained it a reading in the green-room of that play-house.

95. DON SAVERIO. Musical Drama; acted at Drury-Lane, 4to. 1750. The music by Dr. Arne, who also probably wrote the words.

96. DON SEBASTIAN, KING OF PORTUGAL. Trag. by J. Dryden. Acted at the Theatre Royal, 4:o. 1690. 4to. 1692. This is commonly (as Dr. Johnson observes) esteemed either the first or second of Dryden's dramatic performances. It is too long to be all acted, and has many characters and many incidents; and though it is not without sallies of frantic dignity, and more noise than meaning, yet as it makes approaches to the possibilities of real life, and has some sentiments which beam a strong impression, it continued long to attract attention. Amidst the distresses of princes, and the vicissitudes of empire, are inserted several scenes which the writer intended for comic; but which, I suppose, that age did not much commend, and this would not endure. There are, however, passages of excellence universally acknowledged; the dispute and the reconciliation of Dorax and Sebastian has been always admired.

97. DORVAL, or, *The Test of Virtue*. Com. translated from Diderot, 8vo. 1767.

98. THE DOUBLE DEALER. Com. by W. Congreve. Acted at the Theatre Royal, 4to. 1694. This is the second play this author wrote; the characters of it are strongly drawn, the wit genuine and original, the plot finely laid, and the conduct inimitable; yet such is, and ever has been the capricious disposition of audiences, that it met not equal encouragement with his *Old Batchelor* (in some respects a much more exceptionable play), nor had it the same success with his later performances.

99. THE DOUBLE DECEIT, or, *A Cure for Jealousy*. Com. by W. Popple, 8vo. Acted at Covent-Garden, 1736.

100. THE DOUBLE DECEIT, or, *The Happy Pair*. A Comic Farce, printed 8vo. 1745, but never acted.

101. THE DOUBLE DECEPTION. Com. by Miss Richardson. Acted at Drury-Lane, 1779. This play was brought on the stage towards the end of the season, and was performed only four nights. It has not been printed.

102. THE DOUBLE DISAPPOINTMENT. Farce, 1747. Acted at Covent-Garden. This has no great share of merit either as to plot or language, yet it met with considerable success, from the delight which the majority of an audience ever take in the exposing of national character, which is here done in the young lady's two lovers, an Irishman and a Frenchman, both of them fortune-hunters, one of whom proves to have been a rubber in a stable, and the other a valet who has robbed his master.

master. These two parts, during the run of the farce, were very well supported by Messieurs Barrington and Blakes. The author of it was Moses Mendez, Esq. It was not printed until 1760, in 8vo.

103. THE DOUBLE DISTRESS. Trag. by Mrs. Mary Pix, 4to. 1701. Acted at Lincoln's-Inn Fields. Scene Persepolis.

104. THE DOUBLE FALSHOOD, or, *The Distrest Lovers.* Trag. by L, Theobald. Acted at Drury-Lane, 8vo. 1727. This piece Theobald endeavoured to persuade the world was written by Shakspeare. How true his assertion might be, I cannot pretend to determine, but very few I believe gave any credit to it. The play, however, was acted with considerable success, and was the last piece in which Mr Booth appeared. Dr. Farmer is of opinion, that it is a production of Shirley's, or at least not earlier than his time. Mr. Malone inclines to believe it written by Massinger.

105. THE DOUBLE GALLANT, or, *The Sick Lady's Cure.* Com. by C. Cibber. Acted at the Hay-Market, 4to. No date [1707]. Part of this play is borrowed from Mrs. Centlivre's *Love at a Venture,* or a French comedy of *Le Gallant double,* and part from Burnaby's *Visiting Day.*

In a letter from Booth to A. Hill, we learn that this play at its first appearance was, as he expresses it, *bounded* in a most outrageous manner. Two years after, it was revived, met with most extravagant success, and hath continued a stock play ever since.

106. THE DOUBLE MARRIAGE. Trag. by Beaumont and Fletcher, Fol. 1647. Scene Naples. This is not one of their best plays, and on an attempt to revive it about seventy years ago, failed of success.

107. THE DOUBLE MISTAKE. Com. by Mrs. Elizabeth Griffiths. Acted at Covent-Garden, 8vo. 1766.

108. THE DOUBLE TRAITOR ROASTED. A new Scots Opera. Acted by a select company of Comedians, near Westminster-Hall, 8vo. 1748.

109. THE DOUBTFUL HEIR. Trag.-Com. by James Shirley. Acted at the private house in Black-Friers, 8vo. 1652. Part of the story on which this play is built may be found in the *English Adventures,* Part III. Scene lines in Murcia.

110. DOUGLAS. Trag. John Home. Acted at Covent-Garden, 8vo. 1757. This tragedy is founded on the quarrels of the families of Douglas and other of the Scots clans. It has a great deal of pathos in it, some of the narratives are pleasingly affecting, and the descriptions poetically beautiful; yet on the whole it appears rather heavy. The author was a Scotsman, and a clergyman of that church. The piece made its first appearance on the Edinburgh theatre, at that time in no unflourishing condition. This, however, drew the resentment of the elders of the kirk, and many other rigid and zealous members of that sect, not only on the author but the performers, on whom, together with him, they freely denounced their anathemas in pamphlets and public papers. The latter indeed it was out of their power greatly to injure, but their rod was near falling very heavy on the author, &c. whom the assembly repudiated and cut off from his preferments. In England, however, he had the good fortune to meet with friends, and being, through the interest of the earl of Bute and some other persons of distinction, recommended

ed to the notice of his present majesty, then prince of Wales, his royal highness was pleased to bestow a pension on him, and his piece was brought on the stage in London, and met with success.

We may however add, that Mr. Home's Muse cannot be said to have flourished beyond the time when she was rich enough to lend images to Ossian. Her stores of fancy were much exhausted, when afterwards, in the *Fatal Discovery*, she was compelled to supply the want of them by tumid language borrowed from Fingal. Mr. Mason (in a note on one of Mr. Gray's Letters, 4to. edit. p. 281.) has the following observation relative to the originality of a passage in Mr. Home's first and happiest production: "It is remarkable "that the manuscript [of one of "the Erse fragments] in the transl-"lator's own hand, which I have "in my possession, varies considerably from the printed copy. "Some images are omitted, and "others added. I will mention "one which is not in the manu-"script, *The spirit of the mountain shrieks*. In the tragedy of "Douglas, published at least three "years before, I always admired "this fine line, *The angry spirit of* "*the water shriek'd.* Quere, Did "Mr. Home take this sublime "image from Ossian, or has the "translator of Ossian borrowed "it from Mr. Home?"

Mr. Gray, however, had so high an opinion of this first drama of Mr. Home, that in a letter to a friend, dated August 10, 1757, he says, "I am greatly struck with the tragedy of *Douglas*, though it has "infinite faults: the author seems "to me to have retrieved the true "language of the stage, which "had been lost for these hundred "years; and there is one scene "(between *Matilda* and the *Old* "*Peasant*) so masterly, that it "strikes me blind to all the de-"fects in the world." To this opinion every reader of taste will readily subscribe.

Dr. Johnson blames Mr. Gray for concluding his celebrated ode with suicide, a circumstance borrowed perhaps from *Douglas*, in which Lady Randolph, otherwise a blameless character, precipitates herself, like the *Bard*, from a cliff into eternity.

111. THE DOWAGER. By Thomas Chatterton. Some scenes of a play by this extraordinary young man are still in MS.

112. THE DOWNFAL OF THE ASSOCIATION. Comic Trag. in five acts, 8vo. 1771. Printed at Winchester.

113. THE DOWNFAL OF BRIBERY, or, *The honest Man of Taunton*. Ballad Opera, of three acts, by Mark Freeman, of Taunton, in Somersetshire, 8vo. 1733. This was never intended for the stage, nor is the author's name apparently a genuine one. It therefore seems to have been only a party-piece, written on a contested election for Somersetshire in the year 1733, which was the time of a general election for parliament.

114. THE DRAGON OF WANTLEY. A Burlesque Opera, by H. Carey, 8vo. 1738; acted at Covent-Garden. This piece has a great deal of humour in it, and was a very fine burlesque on the Italian operas, at that time so much the passion of the town. The plot, taken from the old ballad of *Moore* of *Moorhall*, is worked up into all the incidents of love, heroism, rivalry, and fury, which most of the Italian operas indiscriminately were stuffed with. To help this forward, the characters were dressed in the utmost extravagance of theatric parade: the machinery truly burlesque,

burlesque, and the songs, though ludicrous to the highest degree, were set perfectly in the Italian taste.

115. A DRAMATIC PIECE. By the Charter-House scholars, in memory of the powder plot, performed at the Charter-House, Nov. 6, 1732, 8vo.

116. THE DRUMMER, or, *The haunted House*. Com. by Addison, 4to. 1715. Nothing perhaps can give a stronger proof of how vague and indecisive as to real merit the judgment of an audience is to be considered, and how frequently that judgment is biassed by names alone, than the success of this comedy, which, coming out at first without any known parent, notwithstanding it had all the advantages of admirable acting, was so universally disliked, that the author chose to keep himself concealed till after his death; when Mr. Tickell having omitted it in his Collection of the Author's works, it was republished by Sir Richard Steele in 4to. 1722; and asserted to be the production of Mr. Addison, or at least written *under his direction*. It is observed, by Sir Richard, that "the *Drummer* made no fi-"gure on the stage, though ex-"quisitely well acted; and when "I observe this, says he, I say a "much harder thing of the stage "than of the comedy." Dr. Warton (Essay on the Genius and Writings of Pope, p. 269.) speaking of this play, calls it "that ex-"cellent and neglected comedy, "that just picture of life and real "manners, where the poet never "speaks in his own person, or to-"tally drops or forgets a character "for the sake of introducing a "brilliant simile or acute remark: "where no train is laid for wit; "no JEREMYS or BENS are suf-"fered to appear." Mr. Theobald (see Notes to Beaumont and Fletcher, vol. 1. p. 317. edit. 1778.) says, he was informed by Mr. Addison, that the character of *Vellum* was sketched out by him from that of Savill in the *Scornful Lady*. Sir Richard Steele dedicated his republication of this play to Mr. Congreve, and is very severe on Mr. Tickell for his omission of it, as well as for other circumstances relative to the publication of Mr. Addison's works.

117. THE DRUIDS. Pantomime Entertainment. Acted at Covent-Garden, 1775.

118. THE DRUNKEN NEWS-WRITER. Comic Interlude. Performed at the Hay-Market, 8vo. 1771.

119. THE DUEL. A Play, by William Obrien. Acted at Drury-Lane, 8vo. 1772. This piece deserved more success than it met with. It was taken from *Le Philosophe sans le sçavoir*; and was acted only one night.

120. THE DUELLIST. Com. by William Kenrick. Acted at Covent-Garden, 8vo. 1773. This was taken from Fielding's *Amelia*. It had no success, and was acted only once. We do not, however, think it had more defects than many other pieces that have enjoyed a nine nights' life on the stage. Yet the ancient custom of immediate damnation is less injurious to managers, than the lingering death by which several modern pieces have been suffered to expire.

121. THE DUENNA. Comic Opera, by Richard Brinsley Sheridan, Esq. Acted at Covent-Garden. 1775. This piece was received with applause by crowded audiences through a run of sixty-five nights during the first season of its appearance. In the following

ing year it was repeated at least thirty times, and still continues a favourite with the publick. It exhibits so happy a mixture of true humour and musical excellence, that it deservedly stands *second* on the list of its kindred performances. The *Beggar's Opera* perhaps will always remain the *first*.

122. THE DUENNA. Comic Opera, in three acts, 8vo. 1776. This is a parody on Mr. Sheridan's celebrated performance, and is entirely political. The supposed author of the present Grub-street piece (which is not the worst of its kind) is Israel Pottinger.

123. DUKE AND NO DUKE. Farce, by N. Tate. Acted by their majesties' servants, 4to. 1685. 4to. 1693. The scene of this piece lies in Florence, and the plot is taken from *Trappolin suppos'd a Prince*. It has several songs in it, but these are now omitted in the performance. *Trappolin's* judicial decisions are taken from the *Contes D'Ouville*; but the whole design is so absurd and impossible, that it appears somewhat wonderful it should be so frequently represented as it is, or meet with so much applause even from the very *Canaille*. Prefixed to it is, "A Preface, con-"cerning Farce. With an ac-"count of the Personæ and Larvæ, "&c. of the ancient theatre."

124. THE DUKE OF GUISE. By Henry Shirley. This play has not been printed, but was entered on the books of the Stationers' Company, Sept. 9, 1653.

125. THE DUKE OF GUISE. Trag. by Dryden and Lee. Acted by their Majesties' servants, 4to. 1683. 4to. 1687. This play, although in many parts it is very fine, met with several enemies at its first appearance upon the stage; the nation being at that time in a ferment about the succession, which occasioned several pamphlets to be written *pro* and *con*. The plot is taken from Davila, Mezeray, and other writers on the reigns of Henry III. and Charles IX. and the story of Malicorn the conjurer, from Rosset's *Histoires Tragiques*. Dryden wrote only the first scene, the whole fourth act, and the first half, or somewhat more, of the fifth. All the rest of the play is Lee's.

126. DUKE HUMPHREY. Tr. This play was among those destroyed by Mr. Warburton's servant. It was entered on the books of the Stationers' Company, June 29, 1660, as the work of William Shakspeare. Could we believe it to have been really written by him, what a subject of regret would its ill fate be to every admirer of our immortal poet!

127. THE DUKE OF MILLAN. Trag. by P. Massinger. Acted at Black-Friers, 4to. 1623. 4to. 1638. The plot partly from Guicciardini, book 8. and partly from Josephus's *History of the Jews*, book 15. ch. 4. where will be found the story of Herod's leaving orders with his uncle Joseph to put his beloved wife Mariamne to death, from which the instructions given by Sforza to his favourite Francisco, for the murther of the duchess Marcelia his wife, seem evidently borrowed.

128. THE DUKE OF MILAN. Tragi-Com. by Richard Cumberland, Esq. Acted at Covent-Garden, 1779. Not printed. This piece consists of Massinger's Play, and Fenton's *Mariamne*, incorporated. The works of these two authors so ill coalesce, that the present performance was coldly received, and acted only three nights.

129. THE DUKE'S MISTRESS. Tragi-Com. by James Shirley. Acted

Acted at the private house, Drury-Lane, 4to. 1638. Scene Parma.

130. THE DUMB BAWD. By Henry Shirley. Not printed; but entered on the books of the Stationer's Company, Sept. 9, 1653.

131. THE DUMB LADY, or, *The Farrier made Physician*. Com. by John Lacy. Acted at the Theatre Royal, 4to. 1672. The plot and much of the language of this play is from Moliere's *Medecin malgre lui*. The scene is laid in London.

132. THE DUMB KNIGHT. An historical Com. by Lewis Machin. Acted by the children of the Revels, 4to. 1608, 4to. 1633. The scene of this play lies in Cyprus, and the most essential incidents of the plot are taken from Bandello's Novels, and are similar to those in a Play, called *The Queen, or, The Excellancy of her Sex*.

133. THE DUPE. Com. by Mrs. Sheridan. Acted at Drury-Lane, 8vo. 1763. Our fair dramatist was less fortunate in the production of this, than in her former comedy. *The Dupe* was damned, on account of a few passages which the audience thought too indelicate. Whether they were not, in this respect, *themselves* rather *too delicate*, is a point which must not be here argued. Certain it is, however, that the rigid sentence passed on this unfortunate play redounds greatly to the honour of our modern audiences, who, whether mistaken or not in their judgments, have herein shewn, that they will tolerate nothing which has but the least appearance of being offensive to the laws of decorum.

134. THE DUTCH ALLIANCE. Farce, 8vo. 1759.

135. THE DUTCH COURTEZAN. Com. by J. Marston. Played Black-Friers, by the children of the Revels, 4to. 1605. The incident of *Cocklede moy's* cheating Mrs. *Mulligrub* the vintner's wife of the goblet and the salmon, is taken from the *Contes du Monde*, or else from the same story related in an English book of Novels, called *The Palace of Pleasure*.

136. THE DUTCHESS OF FERNANDINA. Trag. by Henry Glapthorne. This piece was entered at Stationers's Hall, June 29, 1660, but has not been published.

137. THE DUTCH LOVER. C. by Mrs. Behn. Acted at the Duke's Theatre, 4to. 1673. The scene of this play lies in Madrid, and the plot is founded on the stories of *Eufemie* and *Theodore*, *Don Jaime* and *Frederic*, in a Spanish Novel, called *Don Fenise*. Mrs. Behn, in her address to the reader, prefixed to this play, begins thus: "Good, Sweet, Honey, "Sugar-candied Reader."

138. THE DUTCHESS OF MALFEY. Trag. by John Webster. Acted at Black-Friers and the Globe, 4to. 1623, 4to. 1640. The scene lies in Madrid, and the story of it is well known in history. Lopez de Vega wrote a play on the same subject, called *El Mayordomo de la Duquessa de Amalfi*; and besides the historians of Naples, Goulart has given this tale a place in his *Histoires admirables*, and Bandello has worked it up in one of his Novels.

139. THE DUTCHESS OF MALFEY. Trag. Acted at the Duke's Theatre, 4to. 1678. This is Webster's play adapted to the stage.

140. THE DUCHESS OF SUFFOLK, *her Life*. An historical play, by Thomas Drue, 4to. 1631. The plot is founded on history, and the story may be seen at large in Fox's *Martyrology*, A. D. 1558. and in Clark's *Martyrology*, ch. 11. p. 521. Scene London.

141. THE

141. THE DUTCHMAN. Musical Entertainment, by Thomas Bridges. Acted at the Hay-Market, 8vo. 1775.

142. THE DUTIFUL DECEPTION. Com. of one act. Performed at Covent-Garden, April 22, 1778, for the benefit of Mrs. Bulkeley. Not printed.

143. DYCCON OF BEDLAM. A play of this title was entered on the books of the Stationers' Company, by Thomas Colwell, in the year 1562 to 1563. This play, I believe, was never published. It seems to have been the first sketch of *Gammer Gurton's Needle*, which appeared in 1575, from the same printer, or perhaps is the play itself.

E.

1. THE EARL OF DOUGLAS. A Dramatic Essay, 8vo. 1760.

2. THE EARL OF ESSEX. T. by Henry Jones, 8vo. 1753. Acted at Covent-Garden. This piece the town had been for some years in expectation of, and on its appearance it met with great success, taking a run for twelve nights, and bringing the author some very good benefits since in Dublin. It has been said that he was assisted in the writing it by the earl of Chesterfield, and the late laureat C. Cibber. However that may be, the play can scarcely lay claim to any capital share of merit; for although the language may be an improvement on Banks's tragedy of the same name, yet the conduct of the piece is not so good, nor the incidents so affecting, so that the latter has as much the advantage in *pathos*, as this has in poetry.

3. THE EARL OF ESSEX. T. by Hen. Brooke. Acted at Drury-Lane, 8vo. 1761. As all the pieces of this title are founded on history, on that even of our own country, and of a period the best known to every Englishman, very little liberty can be taken with the story of them. Yet Brooke seems to have varied his conduct, from that of the former plays on the subject, so much as to give it somewhat the air of novelty; and indeed not only from that, but from the spirit and energy of the language, this piece appears to bid the fairest for maintaining its ground, and for a time at least banishing its rivals from the stage.

The representative of the Earl, during the run of the piece, being in conversation with Dr. Johnson, was loud in the praise of Mr. Brooke's sentiments and poetry. The Doctor, who had neither read nor seen the work recommended, desired to be furnished with some specimen of its excellence. On this Mr. Sheridan repeated the tag at the end of the first act, concluding with this line:

"To rule o'er freemen, should themselves be free."

This mode of reasoning, observed the Doctor, is conclusive in such a degree, a degree, that it will lose nothing of its force, even though we should apply it to a more familiar subject, as follows:

"Who drives fat oxen, should himself
"be fat."

So happy a parody ought always to attend the *crambe repetita* of the Earl of Essex. Mr. Brooke indeed, when he republished his play, took care to change the line at which the ridicule had been pointed.

4. THE EARL OF MARR NARR'D, *with the Humours of Jockey the Highlander*. Tragi-comical Farce, by J. Philips, 8vo. 1716. This piece was never acted, being merely political, on the successes of the king's army against the Rebels, headed by the earl of Marr, in the year 1715. See THE PRETENDER'S FLIGHT, &c.

5. THE EARL OF SOMERSET. Trag. by Henry Lucas, 4to. 1780. This is on the same story as Sir Thomas Overbury, and was printed in a volume, entituled "Poems to her Majesty."

6. THE EARL OF WARWICK. Trag. by Dr. Thomas Franklin. Acted at Drury-Lane, 8vo. 1767. This play, which was taken, without any acknowledgment, from another on the same subject, and with the same title, by Monsieur de la Harpe, was acted with applause. The performance of Mrs. Yates was truly excellent.

7. THE EARL OF WARWICK, or, *The King and Subject*. Trag. by Paul Hiffernan, 8vo. 1767. A very indifferent translation of Monsieur de la Harpe's play above-mentioned.

8. THE EARL OF WESTMORLAND. Trag. by Henry Brooke, Esq; 8vo. 1778. This was first acted at Dublin in the year 1741, under the title of *The Betrayer of his Country*, and again 1754, under that of *Injured Honour*. It is founded on the old English history, of the first invasion of the Danes, and was favourably received.

9. EARL OF WESTMORELAND. See BETRAYER OF HIS COUNTRY.

10. EASTWARD HOE. Com. by G. Chapman, Ben Jonson, and John Marston. Acted by the children of her Majesties Revels, in the Black-Friers, 4to. 1605. It is said, that for writing this comedy, wherein the authors were accused of reflecting on the Scots, they were committed to prison, and were in danger of losing their ears and noses. They, however, received pardons, and Jonson, on his releasement from prison, gave an entertainment to his friends, amongst whom were Camden and Selden. In the midst of the entertainment, his mother, more an antique Roman than a Briton, drank to him, and shewed him a paper of poison which she intended to have given him in his liquor, having first taken a portion of it herself, if the sentence for his punishment had passed. This is the story which hath come down to us. The offensive parts are omitted in all but a few copies. From it Hogarth took the plan of his set of prints, called *The industrious and idle Prentices*. And some years ago it was revived, for the entertainment and instruction of the city youth, on lord mayor's night, in the stead of the *London Cuckolds*, which it had for many years been customary to perform on that night, to the insult of the citizens, and the disgrace of morality and good manners. This alteration did not succeed, and lately another has been made

made by Mrs. Lenox. See OLD CITY MANNERS.

An alteration was also made by Tate, under the title of *Cuckold's Haven*, but not so good as the original.

11. EDGAR, or, *The English Monarch*. An heroic Trag. by T. Rymer, 4to. 1678, also in 4to. 1691, under the title of *The English Monarch*. This play is written in heroic verse. The scene is fixed in London; the unity of time is so well preserved, that the whole action lies between 12 at noon and 10 at night; and the plot is taken from W. of Malmesbury, and other old English Historians. Langbaine calls it a much better play than Ravenscroft's *Edgar and Alfreda*; but it falls far short of the merit of Hill's *Athelwold*.

12. KING EDGAR AND ALFREDA. T. C. by E. Ravenscroft. Acted at the Theatre Royal, 4to. 1677. This play is on the same story as the preceding one, but the plot of it seemingly borrowed from a Novel, called *The Annals of Love*. The scene lies in Mercia or Middle-England, and there is prefixed to it a life of Edgar, king of the West Saxons.

13. EDGAR AND EMMELINE. A Fairy Tale, by J. Hawkesworth. Acted at Drury Lane, 8vo. 1761. This little piece met with great success in the representation, and indeed deservedly. The exchange of sex in *Edgar* and *Emmeline*, by the command of the fairies, to enable them to receive the impressions of love unknown to themselves, through the conveyance of friendship, is a new and pretty thought; the conduct of it sensible, rational, and delicate, and the behaviour of those little imaginary beings the fairies, consistent with the ideas we have constantly formed of them. In a word, altogether it is a very pleasing entertainment, and is rendered still more so by the addition of the musical Interludes, whereby the main action is broken in upon and relieved.

14. EDWARD I. An historical play, by Geo. Peele, 4to. 1593. The title at length runs as follows. *The famous Chronicle of King Edward the first, surnamed Longshanks, with his returne from the Holy Land. Also the Life of Llewellen Rebell in Wales. Lastly, the sinking of Queene Elinor, who sunck at Charing Crosse, and rose again at Potter'shith, now named Queenhith.* For the story, see Walsingham, and other English Chronicles.

15. EDWARD II. Trag. by C. Marlow. Acted by the earl of Pembroke's servants, 4to. 1598, 4to. 1612, 4to. 1622. It was entered on the books of the Stationers' Company, July 6, 1593. This play is very far from a bad one, and contains the fall of Mortimer, and the life and death of Piers Gaveston, earl of Cornwall, and chief favourite of that unfortunate prince, together with his own death, and the troublesome events of his reign. The scene lies partly in England, and partly in France, and the story keeps very close to history.

16. EDWARD III. *his Reign*. An History, sundry times played about the City of London. Anon. 4to. 1596, 4to. 1599. This play was reprinted in a Collection of Old Poetry as Shakspeare's, in the year 1760. The plot from our English Chronicles.

17. KING EDWARD III. *with the Fall of Mortimer, Earl of March*. Historical Play, 4to. 1691. Anon. Coxeter, however, attributes it to John Bancroft, who, as he says, made a present of it to Mountfort the actor. The scene lies at Nottingham,

tingham, and the plot is from the English History, and a Novel, called *The Countess of Salisbury*.

18. EDWARD IV. An historical play, in two parts, by Tho. Heywood. B. L. 4to. No date. The fourth edition, 4to. 1626.

19. EDWARD AND ELEONORA. Trag. by James Thomson. As it was to have been acted at Covent-Garden, 8vo. 1739. This play, after the parts of it had been cast, and the whole several times rehearsed, was prohibited to be acted by the Lord Chamberlain. It is suspected from some passages in this play (which are omitted in Murdock's edition) that the author rather wished to have it forbid, than to avoid that sentence against it. By the favour of the Prince of Wales, who at that time was in opposition to the court, it is supposed the poet sustained no loss by this play being refused stage representation. The plot is built on the affecting circumstance of conjugal love in *Eleonora* to *Edward* I. who when her husband, at that time not king, received a wound with a poisoned arrow in the holy wars, cured the wound by sucking out the venom, although to the apparent hazard of her own life.

20. EDWARD AND ELEONORA. Trag. altered from Thomson, by Thomas Hull. Acted at Covent-Garden, 8vo. 1775.

21. EDWARD VI. Play, by Edw. Barnard, 8vo. 1757, printed in a volume, intituled, "Virtue the source of Pleasure."

22. EDWARD THE BLACK PRINCE, or, *The Battle of Poictiers*. Hist. Trag. by W. Shirley, 8vo. 1750. This tragedy was acted at Drury-Lane. It is said to be attempted after the manner of Shakspeare, and is founded on a very glorious circumstance of the English History. It is, however, poorly executed, and consequently, although strongly supported by the performance, met with very indifferent success.

23. EDWARD THE BLACK PRINCE, or, *The Battle of Poictiers*. Trag. by Mrs. Hoper. This piece was performed at the playhouse in Goodman's Fields, about 1748, by a patched-up, wretched set of performers, excepting Miss Budgell, who acted the principal heroine. The author being a woman, and entirely unused to writing, this play proved as bad as the last-mentioned one, and, being ushered into the world under such terrible disadvantages, died in the birth, and was entirely lost in its original obscurity.

24. EDWIN. Trag. by Geo. Jeffreys, 8vo. 1724. Acted in Lincoln's-Inn Fields, with but little success.

25. THE ELDER BROTHER. Com. by John Fletcher. Acted at the Black-Friers, 4to. 1637, 4to. 1651, 4to. 1661. The first and third editions have the name of Fletcher alone. In the second, Beaumont is joined with him.

26. THE ELDERS. Farce, by ——— Cobb. Acted at Covent-Garden, April 21, 1780, for the benefit of Mr. Wilson.

27. THE ELECTION. Com. of three acts, 12mo. 1749.

28. THE ELECTION. A Musical Interlude, by Miles Peter Andrews. Acted at Drury-Lane, 8vo. 1774.

What nauseous potions wi'l not musick wash down the throat of the public!

29. ELECTRA. Trag. by C. W. viz. Charles Wase, 8vo. 1649. This is only a translation from Sophocles.

30. ELECTRA.

30. ELECTRA. T. by Lewis Theobald. Translated from the Greek of *Sophocles*, with notes. 12mo. 1714.

31. ELECTRA. Trag. translated from Sophocles, by George Adams, 8vo. 1729.

32. ELECTRA. Trag. translated from Sophocles, by Dr. Thomas Franklin, 4to. 1759.

33. ELECTRA. Trag. translated from Voltaire by Dr. Thomas Franklin, 12mo. 1761. This piece was acted at Covent-Garden for Mrs. Yates's benefit, 1774, and afterwards at Drury-Lane.

34. ELECTRA. Trag. by W. Shirley, 4to. 1765. This piece is dedicated to the earl of Chesterfield. It is no other than the Electra of Sophocles adapted to the stage, and was written in the year 1745. But though there appears nothing in it liable to a personal application, yet after being rehearsed at Covent-Garden in January 1763, it was denied a licence at the Lord Chamberlain's office.

35. ELFRID, or, *The Fair Inconstant*. Trag. by Aaron Hill. Acted at Drury-Lane, 4to. No date [1710]. The author, dissatisfied with this juvenile production, afterwards entirely new wrote it, and brought it out again at Drury-Lane in 1731, under the title of ATHELWOLD. At the end of the preface he says, he had attempted a translation of Godfrey of Boloyn, and that he intended suddenly to publish a specimen and proposal for printing it by subscription.

36. ELFRIDA. Dram. Poem, by W. Mason, 4to. 1752. This piece was not designed for the stage, but is written after the manner of the Greek Tragedy. To attempt giving any character of a performance so recent and so deservingly celebrated, would be vain and unnecessary. I shall therefore only refer my reader to what I have said of this author's other piece, *Caractacus*, which will equally agree with this. In the drama before us, however, the bard has more strictly adhered to the rules of the ancient tragedy, than in his *Caractacus*, having here admitted no more than three speaking characters, the rest being entirely ode and chorus. He has, moreover, agreed in point of catastrophe with Hill and other dramatic writers on the same story, by making *Elfrida* devote herself to a monastic life, to avoid a marriage with *Edgar*, whom history, on the contrary, assures us she became queen to, and survived, nor founded her monastery till after she had, in order to obtain the succession for her own son, procured the murder of her son-in-law Edward.

37. ELFRIDA. Dram. Poem, by W. Mason. Acted at Covent-Garden, 1772, 8vo. By this alteration of *Elfrida*, in which the lyrick parts are both transposed and curtailed, the author is said to have been much offended, and to have designed an angry address to Mr. Colman (then manager of Covent-Garden Theatre) on the subject. But that gentleman threatening him with the introduction of a chorus of Grecian washerwomen in some future stage entertainment, the bard was silenced, being perhaps of opinion that his classical interlocutors would have suffered by the comparison. *Elfrida* has since been altered by the author, new set by Giardini, and acted at Covent-Garden, 1776.

38. ELFRID. Trag. by Mr. Jackson. Acted at the Hay-Market, 1775. This play was performed only three nights.

39. ELIZA.

39. ELIZA. Mufical Entertainment, by Richard Rolt, 8vo. 1754. Set to mufic by Dr. Arne, and performed at the Hay-Market, where it was prohibited. It was afterwards acted at Drury-Lane with fuccefs.

40. ELLA. A Tragycal Enterlude, or Difcoorfeynge Tragedie. Wroten bie Thomas Rowleie; plaiedd before Mafter Canynge, atte hys howfe nempte the Rodde Lodge (alfo before the duke of Norfolck, Johan Howard) 8vo. 1777. One of thofe pieces printed as performances of the 15th century, but now generally acknowledged to have been the forgeries of Thomas Chatterton.

41. ELMERICK, or, *Juftice Triumphant*. Trag. by George Lillo. Acted at Drury-Lane, 8vo. 1740. Scene the king's palace at Buda. This was a pofthumous work, brought on the ftage after the author's death.

42. THE ELOPEMENT. Farce, by William Havard. Acted at Drury-Lane, 1763, for the benefit of the author. Not printed.

43. THE ELOPEMENT. A Pantomime Entertainment. Acted at Drury-Lane, 1768.

44. ELVIRA, or, *The Worft not always true*. Com. by a perfon of quality (fuppofed to be lord Digby) 4to. 1667. The fcene lies in Valencia. The plot is very intricate and bufy; and from fome part of it Mrs. Centlivre feems to have borrowed the *Wonder*, or *A Woman keeps a Secret*.

45. ELVIRA. A Trag. by D. Mallet. Acted at Drury-Lane, 8vo. 1763. This being looked upon by many as a minifterial play, and the rather as it was brought on at the critical time when our political pack were in full cry, hunting down the Scotch Peace, as they called it, Mr. Mallet's performance was beheld in a very unpopular light. The pacific fentiments, though in themfelves unexceptionable, fuch as the idea of a monarch who places his chief glory, not in that military fpirit which operates to the deftruction of mankind, but in cultivating the arts, which flourifh only in peaceful times; thefe were fufficient, at fuch a juncture, to ftamp the play with the character of a political piece. This, together with the author's being a North Briton by birth, proved very unfavourable circumftances to *Elvira*. It is confeffedly an imitation of Mr. De la Motte's tragedy, founded on the fame melancholy event, viz. a Portuguefe ftory, taken from that excellent poem, *The Lufiad of Camoëns*, which has been fo admirably tranflated by Mr. Mickle. Before this tragedy was rehearfed, Mrs. Pritchard, who was appointed to reprefent the queen, objected againft performing it, and gave the profligacy of the character as the oftenfible reafon of her diflike to it. To this the author with fingular modefty replied—" Why, Madam, you have always played *Lady Macbeth*, juft fuch another part as this I defigned for you, and yet you never complained of the former."

46. EMILIA. Tragi-Com. 8vo. 1672. Dedicated to *the only few*. In this Dedication the anonymous author confeffes that the hint of his plot was taken from the *Coftanza di Rofamondo of Aurelio Aureli*. The fcene lies in Micena, and the unity of place, befides that of time and perfons, is fo exactly obferved, that there is no breaking of the fcene until the end of the act.

47. EMILIA. Trag. by Mark Anthony Meilan, 8vo. No date [1771]. The man who can keep his eyes open over this and the other dramatic pieces by our author, might rival the watchfulness of Argus, and set the strongest dose of opium at defiance. When summing and writing-masters would appear as poets, we may truly observe with Horace—*Optat ephippia bos piger.*—Though turn-spits are occasionally called *Cæsar* and *Pompey*, we cannot help grudging the name of the gallant triumvir to this scribbler of dull plays and teacher of multiplication. The hint of his piece was taken from *The Spectator*, N° 491.

48. THE EMPEROR OF THE EAST. Tragi-Com. by P. Massinger. Acted at Black-Friers and the Globe, 4to. 1632. This is a very good play; the history from the life of the younger Theodosius, and the scene laid in Constantinople. Lee seems in his *Theodosius, or The Force of Love,* to have borrowed some hints from the piece before us; particularly that of *Theodosius's* negligence as to public affairs extending to such a length, as the giving his sister *Pulcheria* an absolute power even over the life of his beloved *Athenais*, by means of a blank signed and delivered to her.

49. THE EMPEROR OF THE MOON. Farce, by Mrs. Behn. Acted at the Queen's Theatre, 4to. 1687. This piece is taken from *Arlequin Empereur dans le Monde de la Lune*, which was originally translated from the Italian. Mrs. Behn, however, has made great alterations, and rendered it extremely full of whimsical and entertaining business. It is indeed, however absurd, many degrees more rational than the dumb shew of pantomimes, without either meaning or possibility, which so repeatedly at this time bring crowded houses, to the utter discouragement of dramatic and theatrical genius.

50. THE EMPEROR OF THE MOON. A Dialogue Pantomime. Written by Mrs. Behn, with alterations. Performed at the Patagonian Theatre, 8vo. 1777.

51. THE EMPRESS OF MOROCCO. Trag. by Elk Settle. Acted at the Duke's Theatre, 4to. 1678. This play is written in heroic verse, and is the first that ever was adorned with cuts. It was in such high esteem, that it was acted at court, and the lords and ladies of the bedchamber performed in it. It however excited the envy of Dryden, Shadwell, and Crown, who all wrote against it; but, Settle's cause being warmly espoused by the duke of Buckingham and lord Rochester, who in their answers handled Dryden very roughly, the play stood its ground, and his opponents appeared to have the worst of the argument.

52. THE EMPRESS OF MOROCCO. Farce. Acted at the Theatre Royal, 4to. 1674, said to be written by Thomas Duffet; the epilogue (spoken by *Hecate* and the three witches) being a new fancy, after the old and most surprizing way of *Macbeth* (which had then lately been revived), performed with new and costly machines, which were invented and managed by the most ingenious operator, Henry Wright, P. G Q.

53. THE ENCHANTED LOVERS. A Pastoral, by Sir Wm. Lower, 12mo. 1658. Scene in the island of Erithrea in Portugal. Printed at the Hague.

54. THE ENCHANTER, or, *Love and Magic*, by David Garrick.

rick. Mufical Entertainment of two acts. Acted at Drury-Lane, 8vo. 1760.

55. ENDYMION. Com. by J. Lilly, 4to. 1592; performed before queen Elizabeth, by the children of the Chapel and of Paul's. The ftory from Lucian's Dialogue between *Venus* and the *Moon*, and other of the Mythologifts.

56. ENDYMION, or, *The Man in the Moon*. A Mafque, 4to. 1698. This is printed at the end of a comedy, called *Impofture Defeated*, which therefore I refer you to.

57. ENGLAND'S GLORY. A Poem, performed in a mufical Entertainment before her majefty (Queen Anne) on her happy birthday. Fol. 1706. Dedicated to the Queen, by James Kremberg, who compofed the mufical parts to this poem, made in the form of an Opera.

58. THE ENGLISH BRITONS. Farce, of one act, infcribed to John Wilkes, Efq; 8vo. 1763. A mere paltry political Squib.

59. THE ENGLISH FRYERS, or, *The Town Sparks*. Com. by J. Crown. Acted by their Majefties' fervants, 4to. 1690. Scene London. That this comedy did not meet with fo much fuccefs as fome other of this author's pieces, may be gathered from the account he himfelf gives of the objections againft it, and his defence in the preface to the play.

60. THE ENGLISH LAWYER. Com. by E. Ravenfcroft. Acted at the Theatre Royal, 4to. 1678. This is only a tranflation, with very little change, of Ruggle's Latin comedy, called *Ignoramus*. The fcene Bourdeaux.

61. THE ENGLISH MERCHANT. Com. by Geo. Colman, Efq. Acted at Drury-Lane, 8vo. 1767. The plot and perfonages of this play are happily adapted from the *Ecoffaife* of Voltaire. Mr. Colman's imitation, though well received, muft have appeared to greater advantage, could an actor like Mr. Quin have been found for the reprefentative of the *Merchant*. There is a fober dignity in this character, that can only be fupported by a performer of weight and confequence. Being allotted, through neceffity, to a comedian not remarkable for his fuccefs in parts that require manlinefs of deportment, gravity, and good-breeding, it loft its chief power on the ftage.

62. THE ENGLISH MONARCH. See EDGAR.

63. THE ENGLISH MONSIEUR. Com. by James Howard, 4to. 1674. This play was acted at the Theatre Royal with good fuccefs; and it is not improbable, from the refemblance of circumftances, that prince *Volfcius's* falling in love with *Parthenope*, at the inftant he is pulling off his boots to go out of town (in *The Rehearfal*), may have been intended to glance at the characters of *Comely* and *Elfbeth* in this comedy. Scene lies in London.

64. THE ENGLISH MOOR, or, *The Mock Marriage*. Com. by Rich. Browne, 8vo, 1659. Scene London.

65. THE ENGLISH PRINCESS, or, *The Death of Richard the Third*. Trag. by J. Caryl, 4to. 1667. Acted at the Duke of York's Theatre. The plot is from Holingfhed, Speed, &c. And the fcenes are laid in the head quarters of king Richard and the earl of Richmond, while they are in the fight of each other. The whole drama is written in rhime.

66. THE ENGLISH ROGUE. C. by Thomas Thomfon, 4to. 1668. Scene Venice.

67. THE

67. THE ENGLISH TRAVELLER. Tragi-Com. by Tho. Heywood. Acted at the Cockpit Drury-Lane, 4to. 1633. The plot and language of young *Lyonel* and *Reginald* are taken from the *Mostellaria* of Plautus; but as to the story of old *Wincote* and his wife *Geraldine* and *Delavil*, the author in his *History of Women*, Lib. 4. p. 269. where he has related it more at large, affirms it to be an absolute fact.

68. THE ENGLISHMAN IN PARIS. Com. of two acts, by Sam. Foote. Acted at Covent-Garden, 8vo. 1753. This little piece met with good success; its first appearance was for Macklin's benefit when that performer acted the part of *Buck*, and Miss Macklin, *Lucinda*, which seemed written entirely to give her an opportunity of displaying her various qualifications of music, singing, and dancing, in all of which she obtained universal applause. The author himself afterwards repeatedly performed the part of *Buck*; yet it is difficult to say, which of the two did the character the greatest justice. The piece seems designed to expose the absurdity of sending our youth abroad to catch the vices and follies of our neighbour nations; yet there is somewhat of an inconsistency in the portrait of the Englishman, that scarcely renders the execution answerable to the intention. This little comedy was imagined to be a burlesque on M. de Boissy's *François à Londres*. On a comparison, however, there does not appear the slightest resemblance.

69. THE ENGLISHMAN RETURN'D FROM PARIS. Com. of two acts, by Sam. Foote. Acted at Covent-Garden, 8vo. 1756. This is a sequel to the foregoing piece, wherein the Englishman, who before was a brute, is now become a coxcomb; from being absurdly averse to every thing foreign, is grown into a detestation of every thing domestic; and rejects the very woman, now possessed of every advantage, whom he before was rushing headlong into marriage with, when destitute of any. This piece is much more dramatic and compleat than the other, and has a greater variety of characters in it, two more especially, *Crab*, and *M'Ruthen*, which are finely drawn; but the circumstance of the catastrophe being brought about by *Lucinda's* pretending to have poisoned Sir *John Buck* in a dish of tea, is stolen from Mrs. Centlivre's *Artifice*.

70. THE ENGLISHMAN FROM PARIS. Farce, by Arthur Murphy. Acted at Drury-Lane, for the benefit of the author, April 3, 1756. Not printed. This piece, which was forestalled by Mr. Foote's *Newly returned Englishman*, was performed only one night. The prologue, spoken by Mr. Murphy, is preserved in *The Literary Magazine*.

71. THE ENGLISHMAN IN BOURDEAUX. Com. translated from Favart, 8vo. 1764. The translator is said to be an English lady, then residing at Paris.

72. ENGLISHMEN FOR MY MONEY, or, *A Woman will have her Will*. Com. 4to. 1616, 4to. 1626, 4to. 1631. Scene Portugal.

73. ENOUGH'S AS GOOD AS A FEAST. Com. This piece is mentioned by Kirkman, but without either date or author's name.

74. ENTERTAINMENT AT K. JAMES THE FIRST'S CORONATION. By Ben Jonson. Fol. 1640. This piece consists only of congratulatory speeches spoken to his majesty at Fenchurch, Temple-Bar, and

in the Strand, in his way to the Coronation, with the author's comments to illustrate them.

75. THE ENTERTAINMENT AT RICHMOND. A Masque; presented by the most illustrious prince Charles to their majesties, 1634.

76. AN ENTERTAINMENT AT RUTLAND HOUSE, by declamation and music, after the manner of the ancients, by Sir W. Davenant, 4to. 1657. The vocal and instrumental music composed by Dr. Charles Coleman, Capt. Henry Cook, Mr. Henry Lawes, and Mr. George Hudson.

77. THE ENTERTAINMENT OF K. CHARLES I. coming into Edinburgh, June 15, 1633, 4to.

78. THE ENTERTAINMENT OF K. JAMES AND Q. ANNE AT THEOBALDS, when the house was delivered up with the possession to the queen by the earl of Salisbury, May 22, 1607, the prince Janville, brother to the duke of Guise, being then present; by Ben Jonson.

79. THE ENTERTAINMENT OF THE KING AND QUEEN, on May-Day in the morning 1604, at Sir William Cornwallis's house at Highgate, by Ben Johson.

80. THE ENTERTAINMENT OF THE QUEEN AND PRINCE at Lord Spencer's at Althorpe, on Saturday, June 25, 1603, as they came first into the kingdom, by Ben Jonson.

81. THE ENTERTAINMENT OF THE TWO KINGS OF GREAT BRITAIN AND DENMARK at Theobalds, July 24, 1606, by Ben Jonson. This entertainment is very short, and consists chiefly of epigrams.

82. AN ENTERTAINMENT ON THE PRINCE'S BIRTH-DAY, by Thomas Nabbes, 4to. 1638.

83. AN ENTERTAINMENT designed for her Majesty's Birth-Day, by Robert Dodsley, 8vo. 1732.

84. AN ENTERTAINMENT designed for the Wedding of Governor Lowther and Miss Pennington, by Robert Dodsley, 8vo. 1732. Both these last are printed in a volume of Poems, called, "A Muse in Livery, or The Footman's Miscellany."

85. THE ENTERTAINMENT given by the Right Hon. the Lord Knowles, at Cawsome-House near Reading, to our most gracious Queen Ann, in her progress toward the Bath, upon the 27th and 28th days of April, 1613. Whereunto is annexed, the Description, Speeches, and Songs of the Lords Maske, presented in the Banquetting-house, on the marriage-night of the High and Mightie Count Palatine and the Royally descended Lady Elizabeth, by Thomas Campion, 4to. 1613.

86. THE EPHESIAN MATRON, Farce of one act, by Charles Johnson, 8vo. 1730.

87. THE EPHESIAN MATRON. Comic Serenata, after the manner of the Italian, by Isaac Bickerstaffe, performed at Ranelagh-House, 8vo. 1762.

88. EPICÆNE, or, *The Silent Woman*. Com. by Ben Jonson. Acted by the King's servants, 4to. 1609. This is accounted one of the best comedies extant, and is always acted with universal applause. The scene lies in London. The long speeches in the first book are translated, verbatim, from *Ovid de Arte Amandi*; and a great deal in other places is borrowed from the 6th satire of *Juvenal* against women.

89. EPICÆNE, or, *The Silent Woman*. Com. written by Ben Jonson. Acted at Drury-Lane, 8vo. 1776. This alteration, which is a very judicious one, was made by Mr. Colman.

90. EPIDICUS. Com. translated from Plautus, by Lawr. Echard, with critical remarks; but never intended

intended for the stage. The scene of this piece lies at Athens. The time about five or six hours.

91. EPPONINA. Dram. Essay, by John Carr, addressed to the ladies, 8vo. 1765. The story of this piece is taken from Dion Cassius and Tacitus.

92. ERMINIA, or, *The Chaste Lady*. Tragi-Com. by Richard Flecknoe, 8vo. 1667. This play was never acted, yet the author has inserted the names of the actors, whom he designed for the performance, opposite to the Dramatis Personæ, in order, as he says, "that the reader might have half "the pleasure of seeing them "acted, by a lively imagination, "which would supply the place "of action." And indeed, as Jacob observes, this was by no means impolitic, since, as he could not get the play acted, it became his next business to endeavour to get it read.

93. EPSOM WELLS. Com. by T. Shadwell. Acted at the Duke's Theatre, 4to. 1676. This piece has so much of the true *Vis comica* about it, that it was greatly admired even by foreigners; the famous St. Evremond, in particular, has made no scruple of ranking it in point of merit with Ben Jonson's *Bartholomew Fair*; yet it could not escape the malevolence and envy of some of the author's contemporaries.

94. Æsop. Com. in two parts, by Sir J. Vanbrugh. Acted at Drury-Lane, 4to. 1697. the second part not added until the third edition, 1702. 4to. This play is taken from a comedy of Bourfaut's, written about six years before it; but the scenes of Sir *Polidorus Hogstye*, the *Players*, the *Senator*, and the *Beaux*, in a word, part of the fourth, and the whole of the fifth act, are entire originals. The play contains a great deal of genuine wit, and useful satire, yet had not the success it deserved to meet with, especially on the two first nights, nor did it run above a week together, notwithstanding that the French, which is not by many degrees so good a piece, held out for upwards of a month at Paris.

95. ÆSOP. Farce; acted at Drury-Lane, 1778. The excellence of Mr. Henderson's manner of reciting poetry occasioned this production which was taken from Sir John Vanbrugh's play above-mentioned, with some slight alterations, as is supposed, by Mr. Sheridan, jun. . But though cleared from much of the grossness and obscenity it formerly abounded with, yet it was not sufficiently refined for the nice ears of the present insipid frequenters of the playhouse. It was acted only one night, and is not printed.

96. ESTHER, or, *Faith Triumphant*. A sacred Tragedy, by Thomas Brereton, 12mo. 1715. This is only a translation at large of the *Esther* of Racine, by whom this play was originally written on the foundation of the nunnery of St. Cyr, and acted by the nuns of that house in the presence of Louis XIV. In the characters of *Ahasuerus* and *Esther*, many very fine compliments are paid to Louis XIV. and Madame de Maintenon, the founders of that convent; and the prologue, in the character of *Piety*, is, perhaps, one of the finest pieces of poetry of its length in the French language.

97. ETHELINDA, or. *Love and Duty*. Trag. by Matthew West, A. B. T. C. D 12mo. 1769. Dublin. In an advertisement prefixed to this tragedy, the author says, that from an aversion to intruding on the public, and diffidence

fidence of the piece's merit (being written merely to amufe a few leifure hours at the age of nineteen), he had declined bringing it on the ftage.

98. AN EVENING ADVENTURE, or, *A Night's Intrigue.* C. from the Spanifh. Anonymous, 1680. This play we have not feen, but imagine it to be *The Evening's Intrigue* after-mentioned.

99. AN EVENING'S INTRIGUE. Com. tranflated from the Spanifh; and the fcene removed into England, by Capt. John Stevens. 8vo. 1709. Printed in a book, called, *The Spanifh Libertines.*

100. AN EVENING'S LOVE, or, *The Mock Aftrologer.* Com. by J. Dryden. Acted at the Theatre Royal, 4to. 1671. 4to. 1691. This play met with good fuccefs, yet it is a mafs of borrowed incidents. The principal plot is built on Corneille's *feint Aftrologue* (borrowed itfelf from Calderon's *El Aftrologo fingido*), and the reft taken from Moliere's *Depit amoureux,* and *Les precieufes ridicules,* and Quinault's *L'Amant indifcret,* together with fome hints from Shakfpeare. The fcene Madrid, and the time the laft evening of the carnival in the year 1665.

101. EVERY MAN IN HIS HUMOUR. Com. by Ben Jonfon. Acted by the Lord Chamberlain's fervants, 1598. Printed in 4to. 1601. This comedy is, perhaps, in point of the redundance of characters and power of language, not inferior to any of our author's works. From the character of *Kitely,* it is pretty evident that Dr. Hoadly took the idea of his *Str Ifland,* in the *Sufpicious Hufband,* in which, however, he has fallen far fhort of the original. This play had lain dormant and unemployed for many years, from its revival after the Reftoration, till Mr. Garrick, in the year 1749, brought it once more on the ftage, with fome few alterations, and an additional fcene of his own; ever fince which time it has continued to be a ftock play, and to be performed very frequently every feafon. Yet I much doubt, if in any future period this piece will ever appear to the advantage it did at that time; fince, exclufive of Mr. Garrick's own abilities in *Kitely,* and thofe of Meffieurs Woodward and Shuter, in the refpective parts of Capt. *Bobadil* and Mafter *Stephen,* there was fcarcely any one character throughout the whole, that could be conceived by an audience in the ftrong light that they were reprefented by each feveral performer: fuch is the prodigious advantage, with refpect to an audience, of the conduct of a theatre being lodged in the hands of a man, who, being himfelf a perfect mafter in the profeffion, is able to diftinguifh the peculiar abilities of each individual under him, and to adapt them to thofe characters in which they are, either by nature or acquirement, the beft qualified to make a figure.

Mr. Whalley obferves, that, in this play as originally written, " the fcenes was at Florence, the " perfons reprefented were Italians, and the manners in great " meafure conformable to the ge" nius of the place; but in this " very play, the humours of the " under characters are local, ex" preffing not the manners of a " Florentine, but the gulls and ' bullies of the times and country " in which the poet lived. And " as it was thus reprefented on the " ftage, it was publifhed in the " fame manner in 4to. in 1601. " When it was printed again in " the collection of his works, " it had a more becoming and " con-

"consistent aspect. The scene was transferred to London; the names of the persons were changed to English ones; and the dialogue, incidents, and manners, were suited to the place of action. And thus we now have it in the folio edition of 1616, and in the several editions that have been printed since."

102. EVERY MAN OUT OF HIS HUMOUR. Com. Satire, by Ben Jonson. Acted 1599. This play is composed of a great variety of characters, interrupted and commented on in the manner of the ancient drama, by a Grex, or company of persons, who being on the stage the whole time, have the appearance of auditors, but are in reality a set of interlocutors, who by their dialogue among themselves explain the author's intention to the real audience. This practice is now almost entirely left off, yet as the characters in this piece are most of them perfect originals, all painted in the strongest colours and apparent likenesses of several well-known existents in real life, I cannot help thinking that, with very little alteration more than an omission of the Grex, this play might be rendered extremely fit for the present stage.

Bishop Hurd, however, says:— "if the reader would see the extravagance of building dramatic manners on abstract ideas in its full light, he needs only turn to Ben Jonson's *Every Man out of his Humour*, which, under the name of a *Play of Character*, is in fact an unnatural, and, as the painters call it *hard*, delineation of a group of *simply existing passions*, wholly chimerical and unlike to any thing we observe in the commerce of real life. Yet this comedy has always had its admirers. And Randolph, in particular, was so taken with the design, that he seems to have formed his *Muses' Looking-Glass* in express imitation of it."

103. EVERY BODY MISTAKEN. Farce, by William Taverner. This is only mentioned in Mears's Catalogue, and was, I believe, never printed.

104. EVERY MAN. b. l. 4to. no date. To this morality is prefixed the following advertisement: *Here begynneth a Treatyse how the hye Father of Heven sendeth dethe to somon every creature to come and gyve a counte of theyr lyves in this worlde, and is in maner of a moralle playe.*

The *Dramatis Personæ* are, Messenger | God | Dethe | Every-man | Felawship | Kyndrede | Good-dedes | Knowlege | Confession | Beaute | Strength | Dyscrefion | Fyve-wyttes | Aungell | Doctour.

The printer's colophon is—*Thus endeth this morall playe of Everyman. Imprynted at London, in Poules chyrche-yard, by me John Skot.*

This morality was published early in the reign of Henry VIII. The design of it was to inculcate great reverence for old mother church and her popish superstitions. It is, as Dr. Percy observes, a grave solemn piece, not without some rude attempts to excite terror and pity, and therefore may not improperly be referred to the class of tragedy. It has been lately reprinted by Mr. Hawkins, in his three volumes of Old Plays, intituled, *The Origin of the English Drama*, 12mo. Oxford, 1773. See vol. I. p. 27. where the curious reader will likewise meet with Dr. Percy's Analysis of this early drama.

105. EVERY WOMAN IN HER HUMOUR. Com. 1609. 4to. Anonymous.

106. EVERY

106. EVERY WOMAN IN HER HUMOUR. Farce of two acts, 1760. This little piece has never yet appeared in print, but was performed at Drury-Lane-House, at the time mentioned above, for Mrs. Clive's benefit, who it is therefore not improbable may be the author of it, as that lady had once before declaredly dipped her fingers in ink. (See *The Rehearsal*, or *Bayes in Petticoats*). There is no extraordinary merit, however, in any part of it, excepting in the character of an old maiden aunt, which Mrs. Clive performed herself.

107. EUGENIA. Tr. by Philip Francis. Acted at Drury-Lane, 8vo. 1752. This play is little more than a free translation of a French comedy, called, *Cenia*, and of which a literal version was published the very same year, under the title of CENIA, or *The Suppos'd Daughter*. Notwithstanding Mr. Garrick played the principal part, and the other characters were well performed, it would not by any means succeed. I believe, however, it ran nine nights. Epilogue, by C. Cibber.

108. EUGENIA. Tr. by Robert Carr and Samuel Hayes, 8vo. 1766.

109. EUNUCHUS. C. A translation of one of Terence's Comedies of this name, by Richard Bernard, 4to. 1598.

110. THE EUNUCH. Trag. by William Hemmings, 4to. 1687. This is only *The Fatal Contract*, by the same author, with a new title.

111. THE EUNUCH, or, *The Darby Captain*. Farce, by Thomas Cooke, 8vo. No date. [1737.] This is taken chiefly from the *Miles gloriosus* of Plautus, and the *Eunuchus* of Terence. It was acted at the Theatre Royal in Drury-Lane.

112. THE EUNUCH. C. translated by Thomas Newman, 8vo. 1727.

113. THE EUNUCH. C. translated by Echard, 8vo.

114. THE EUNUCH. C. translated by T. Cooke, 12mo. 1734.

115. THE EUNUCH. C. translated by S. Patrick, 8vo. 1745.

116. THE EUNUCH. C. translated by George Colman, 4to. 1765.

117. EURIDICE. Tr. by David Mallet. Acted at Drury-Lane, 8vo. 1731. *Euridice* was brought on with alterations at Drury-Lane Theatre in the year 1760, and was republished at the same period. The success of it was never great, though on its revival the principal characters were represented by Mr. Garrick and Mrs. Cibber. The author, however, imputed the cold reception it met with, to the negligence of the actors, who, according to his account, displayed no *pathos* in their performance. This same *pathos* was a thing which Mallet conceived to be so much the characteristic of his own poetry, that he once quarreled with Jones, author of *The Earl of Essex*, for pretending to the least share of it. The dispute ended by his turning the poor Bricklayer out of the room where they were spending the evening together. It is but justice to add, that no man maintained his share in conversation more happily than David Mallet. His wife was either an infidel, or was ashamed to be thought a Christian. One night at Hampton-Court, where both she and David Hume were visiting, she turned towards him, saying — " For you know, Mr. " Hume, we Free-thinkers, &c." Hume turned aside to a friend, and added, " Damn her, if I knew on " what side of any question she
" was,

"was, I would take care never to be on the same."

118. EURIDICE. Farce, by Henry Fielding. As it was d—m'd at the Theatre Royal in Drury-Lane, 8vo. 1735.

119. EURIDICE HISS'D, or, *A Word to the Wise*. Farce, by Henry Fielding, 8vo. 1736. This very little piece is published, and I suppose was acted, at the end of *The Historical Register*. It seems to be intended as a kind of acquiescence with the judgment of the publick, in its condemnation of the last-mentioned Farce, at the same time apologizing for it, as being only a mere *Lusus* of his Muse, and not the employment of any of his more laborious or studious hours.

120. EUROPE'S REVELS *for the Peace, and his Majesty's happy Return*. A Musical Interlude, by P. Motteux, 4to. 1697. This piece was written on occasion of the peace at Ryswick, and was performed at the Theatre in Lincoln's-Inn Fields; annexed to it is a Panegyric Poem which was spoken by way of prologue to it. The music by J. Eccles.

121. THE EXAMPLE. Tragi-Com. by James Shirley. Acted at the private house, Drury-Lane, 4to. 1637.

122. EXCHANGE WARE AT THE SECOND HAND, viz. *Band, Ruffe, and Cuffe lately out, and now newly dearned up, or, A Dialogue*, acted in a shew in the famous Universitie of Cambridge, 2d edit. 4to. 1615.

123. EXCISE. A Tragi-comical Ballad Opera, of three acts, 8vo. 1733. Not intended for the stage.

124. THE EXCOMMUNICATED PRINCE, or, *The False Relick*. Tr. by Capt. William Bedloe, Fol. 1679. To this play the publisher, without the author's concurrence or knowledge, added in the title these words, "*Being the Popish Plot in a Play.*" This induced the public to imagine they should find the design of it to be a narrative of that plot which Capt. Bedloe had so considerable a hand in the discovering. They found themselves, however, disappointed; the plan of this play being built on a story related by Heylin, in his *Cosmography*. The scene lies at Cremen in Georgia, and the play was wholly written in two months time. Some ascribe it, or at least the greatest part of it, to Thomas Walter, an Oxford scholar of Jesus College.

125. THE EXILE. Com. by W. Duke of Newcastle. This play is mentioned in several Catalogues; yet we cannot but doubt the existence of it, as no person pretends ever to have seen it, and it is not to be found in any one of the extensive Collections of Plays now existing.

126. THE EXPERIMENT. Com. of two acts; performed at Covent-Garden, April 16, 1777, for Mrs. Lessingham's benefit. Not printed.

127. THE EXPULSION OF THE DANES FROM BRITAIN. Trag. by Elk. Settle. This was brought to the managers of Drury-Lane about the year 1724; but the death of the author prevented its being acted or printed.

128. THE EXTRAVAGANT JUSTICE. Farce, by James Worsdale. Of this I know nothing but the name.

129. THE EXTRAVAGANT SHEPHERD. A Pastoral Comedy, by T. R. 4to. 1654. This piece is translated from the French of T. Corneille, and is founded on a romance, called, *Lysis,* or *The Extravagant Shepheard*, in Folio.

F.

FA

1. The Factious Citizen, or, *The Melancholy Visioner*, Com. Acted at the Duke's Theatre, 4to. 1685. Scene Moorfields.
2. The Faggot-Binder, or, *The Mock Doctor*. Com. translated from Moliere; printed in Foote's Comic Theatre, vol. 5.
3. The Fair. A Pantomime Entertainment. Acted at Covent-Garden, 1753. In this piece Maddox, the celebrated wire-dancer, was introduced, and, from the novelty of his performance, it met with great success.
4. The Fair Captive. Trag. by Elizabeth Haywood. Acted at Lincoln's-Inn Fields, 8vo. 1721. This tragedy was originally written by Capt. Hurst, who sold it to Mr. Rich. It being thought unfit for representation without being altered, Mrs. Haywood was employed to adapt it to the stage. She, however, so totally new-modelled it, that, except in the parts of *Alphonso* and *Isabella*, there remained not twenty lines of the original play. It was acted without success.
5. Fair Emm, *the Miller's Daughter of Manchester, with the Love of William the Conqueror*. A pleasant Com. Acted by the Lord Strange's servants, 4to. 1631. This piece is not divided into acts.
6. The Fair Example, or, *The Modish Citizens*. Com. by Richard Estcourt, 4to. 1706. Acted at Drury-Lane, with applause. Scene London.
7. The Fair Favorite. Tr. Com. by Sir W. Davenant, Fol. 1673.
8. Fair and Foul Weather. A Play, by John Taylor the Water Poet, 4to. 1615. This piece is mentioned by Dr. Hyde, as being in the Bodleian library, but whether in print or manuscript, does not appear.
9. The Fair Circassian. A dramatic Performance, by Dr. Samuel Croxal, 4to. 1720. This is merely a versification of the *Song of Solomon*.
10. The Fairies. Opera, by David Garrick, 8vo. 1755. The music was composed by Mr. Smith. This little entertainment was acted at Drury-Lane, with great applause, the parts being mostly performed by children. The main design of it, and much of the language, is borrowed from Shakspeare's *Midsummer Night's Dream*, but several songs are introduced into it from many of our most celebrated poetic writers.
11. The Fair Maid of Bristol. As it hath been played at Hampton before the King and Queen. Com. 4to. 1605. In the old black letter.
12. The Fair Maid of the Exchange, *with the merry Humours of the Cripple of Fenchurch*. Com. by Thomas Heywood, 4to. 1625. 4to. 1637.
13. The Fair Maid of the Inn. Tragi-Com. by Beaumont and Fletcher, Fol. 1647. The plot of *Muriana's* disowning *Cæsario* for her son, and the duke's injunction to marry him, is related by *Causin*, in his *Holy Court*. The scene lies in Florence.
14. The Fair Maid of the West, or, *A Girl worth Gold*. Com. in two parts, by Thomas Heywood, 4to. 1631. Both these pieces

pieces met with general approbation, and were favoured with the presence of the king and queen. The scene lies at Plymouth, and the plots are original. Nor can there be a much stronger proof of the estimation they were held in, than John Dancer's having formed from them a novel, called, *The English Lovers*.

15. THE FAIR OF ST. GERMAIN. This is only a translation from Bourfault's *Foire de St. Germains*; and was acted at the Theatre in Little Lincoln's-Inn Fields, by the French company of comedians from Paris, 8vo. 1718.

16. THE FAIR ORPHAN. C. Opera, of three acts, performed at Lynn, 8vo. 1771.

17. THE FAIR PARRICIDE. Trag. Anonymous, 8vo. 1752. This piece was never acted, nor intended for the stage. It is written in prose, and very indifferently executed; but the plan of it is entirely founded on the unfortunate affair of Miss Blandy, who was executed for the murder of her father, instigated thereto, as it appeared on the trial, by her lover captain Cranstoun.

18. THE FAIR PENITENT. Tr. by N. Rowe, 4to. 1703. Acted at Lincoln's-Inn Fields. This, as Dr. Johnson observes, is one of the most pleasing tragedies on the stage, where it still keeps its turns of appearing, and probably will long keep them, for there is scarcely any work of any poet at once so interesting by the fable, and so delightful by the language. The story is domestic, and therefore easily received by the imagination, and assimilated to common life; the diction is exquisitely harmonious, and soft or sprightly as occasion requires.

The character of *Lothario* seems to have been expanded by Richard-
VOL. II.

son into *Lovelace*, but he has excelled his original in the moral effect of the fiction. *Lothario*, with gaiety which cannot be hated, and bravery which cannot be despised, retains too much of the spectator's kindness. It was in the power of Richardson alone to teach us at once esteem and detestation, to make virtuous retentment overpower all the benevolence which wit, and elegance, and courage, naturally excite; and to lose at last the hero in the villain.

The fifth act is not equal to the former; the events of the drama are exhausted, and little remains but to talk of what is past. It has been observed, that the title of the play does not sufficiently correspond with the behaviour of *Calista*, who at last shews no evident signs of repentance, but may be reasonably suspected of feeling pain from detection rather than from guilt, and expresses more shame than sorrow, and more rage than shame. This play is so well known, and is so frequently performed, and always with the greatest applause, that little need be said of it, more than to hint that the groundwork of it is built on the *Fatal Dowry of Massinger*.

19. THE FAIR QUAKER OF DEAL, or, *The Humours of the Navy*. Com. by Charles Shadwell. Acted at Drury-Lane, 4to. 1710. This play has no extraordinary merit in point of language, yet the plot of it is busy and entertaining, and the contrast drawn between the rough brutish tar, and the still more disgustful sea-fop, in the characters of Commodore *Flip* and *Beau Mizen*, is far from being a bad picture of the manners of some of the seafaring gentlemen even of this age, at the same time that their ready reformation, on being convinced of their errors, is
I a just

a juſt compliment to the underſtandings of a ſet of men, who are the greateſt glory of Britain, and the terror of all the reſt of Europe.

20. THE FAIR QUAKER, or, *The Humours of the Navy*. Com. by Capt. Edward Thompſon. Acted at Drury-Lane, 8vo. 1773. The foregoing play very poorly altered. As fore-caſtle jeſts are current only on the ſpot where they are born, or among people to whom coarſeneſs of language is familiar, the repreſentation of this comedy ſhould be confined to Portſmouth or Plymouth, which never fail to produce ſuch audiences as would applaud any performance like this of Captain Thompſon.

21. THE FAIR SPANISH CAPTIVE. Tragi-Com. This play was advertiſed at the end of *Wit and Drollery, Jovial Poems*, 12mo. 1661. as then in the preſs: we believe, however, it never appeared.

22. A FAIRE QUARREL. Com. With new additions of Mr. Changh's and Trimtram's Roaring, and the Baud's Song. Never before printed. Acted before the King by the Prince's ſervants; written by Thomas Middleton and William Rowley, Gent. 4to. 1617. 4to. 1622. Part of the plot of which, viz. the ſtory of *Fitz-Allen, Ruſſel* and *Jane,* may be found in a book, called, *The Complaiſant Companion*; and the incident of the phyſician tempting *Jane,* and afterwards accuſing her, is borrowed from Cynthio's Novels, Dec. 4. Nov. 5. Scene in London.

23. THE FAIRY COURT. Interlude, by Francis Gentleman. Not printed.

24. THE FAIRY FAVOUR. Maſque, 8vo. 1766. This maſque was written by Mr. Thomas Hull, for the entertainment of the prince of Wales. It was acted a few nights at Covent-Garden.

25. THE FAIRY PRINCE. M. by George Colman. Acted at Covent-Garden, 8vo. 1771. The greater part of this maſque was borrowed from Ben Jonſon, with the addition of a few paſſages from Shakſpeare, Dryden, and Gilbert Weſt. It was brought out only to introduce the ceremony of the inſtallation.

26. THE FAIRY QUEEN. Op. Anonym. Acted at the Hay-Market, 4to. 1692. This piece is alſo from Shakſpeare's *Midſummer Night's Dream*. The muſic by Purcell.

27. THE FAITHFUL BRIDE OF GRANADA. A play, by W. Taverner. Acted at Drury-Lane, 4to. 1704. Scene Granada.

28. THE FAITHFUL FRIEND. Com. by Francis Beaumont and John Fletcher. This play was entered on the books of the Stationers' Company, June 29, 1660, but was never printed.

29. THE FAITHFUL GENERAL. Trag. by a young lady, who ſigns herſelf M. N. Acted at the Hay-Market, 4to. 1706. In an advertiſement prefixed to it, the author ſays her firſt intention was only to revive *The Loyal Subject* of Beaumont and Fletcher; but that ſhe afterwards new-formed the epiſodes, altered the main deſign, and put the whole into her own language, ſo that ſcarce any part of Beaumont and Fletcher was retained. Scene the city of Byzantium in Greece.

30. THE FAITHFUL IRISHWOMAN. Farce, by Mrs. Clive. Acted at Drury-Lane, 1765, for her benefit. Not printed.

31. THE FAITHFUL SHEPHERD. A Paſtoral Com. from the Italian, by D. D. Gett. This is taken

taken from the *Pastor Fido* of Guarini. I know not the exact date of it, but find it amongst the productions of the seventeenth century.

32. THE FAITHFUL SHEPHERD. Past. Tragi-Com. 12mo. 1736. Printed in Italian and English. In the preface this translation is said to be chiefly that of Sir Richard Fanshaw, with great improvements, by an ingenious gentleman, who would not permit his name to be mentioned.

33. THE FAITHFUL SHEPHERDESS. A dramatic Pastoral, by J. Fletcher, 4to. [N. D.] 2d edit. 4to. N. D. 3d edit. 4to. 1634. This is the production of Fletcher alone. On its first appearance it met with but an ill reception, but was afterwards represented before the King and Queen on Twelfth night, 1633, and, as the title-page of the third edition says, divers times since with great applause, at the private house in Black-Friers. It was introduced by a dialogue song, written by Sir W. Davenant, between a priest and a nymph, and closed with an Epilogue, which was spoken by the lady Mary Mordaunt.

34. THE FALL OF BOB, or, *The Oracle of Gin*. Trag. by John Kelly, Esq. The former edition of this work says it was acted at the Hay-Market. It was occasioned by the gin-act, and was printed in 12mo. 1736.

35. THE FALL OF CARTHAGE. An historical Trag. by William Shirley. This play was never acted, but is advertised as intended to be printed in the author's dramatick works.

36. THE FALL OF THE EARL OF ESSEX. Trag. by Ja. Ralph, 8vo. 1731. This play is only an alteration from Banks. It was represented at the Theatre in Goodman's Fields, a place too far out of the strong tide of the critical current, to put any piece to that public kind of test whereby merit ought to be determined; yet even there it met with but midling success.

37. THE FALL OF PHAETON. A Pantomime Entertainment. Acted at Drury-Lane; invented by Mr. Pritchard. The music by Arne, and the scenes by Hayman, 8vo. 1736.

38. THE FALL OF PUBLIC SPIRIT. Dramatic Satire in two acts, 8vo. 1757.

39. THE FALL OF MORTIMER. An historical Play. Acted at the Hay-Market, 8vo. 1731. This performance is a completion of Ben Jonson's imperfect play on the same subject.

40. THE FALL OF MORTIMER, *An Historical Play, dedicated to the right honourable the earl of Bute*, 8vo. 1763. This is only a republication of the foregoing by Mr. Wilkes, who was author of the elegant but severe dedication prefixed.

41. THE FALL OF SAGUNTUM. Trag. by Phil. Frowde, 8vo. 1727. Acted at Lincoln's-Inn Fields with but indifferent success, notwithstanding it had very considerable merit, and was highly commended by the critical Journalists of that time.

42. THE FALL OF TARQUIN. Trag. by W. Hunt, 12mo. 1713. The name of this play points out its story, and the scene of it lies at Rome. It is a most wretched performance, and was never acted, or printed any where but at York, where the author was then stationed as collector of the excise.

43. FALSE CONCORD. Farce. Acted at Covent-Garden, March 20, 1764, for the benefit of Mr. Woodward. Not printed.

44. FALSE

44. FALSE DELICACY. Com. by Hugh Kelly. Acted at Drury-Lane, 8vo. 1768. This play, which is supposed to have received some improvements from Mr. Garrick, was acted with considerable success on its original appearance. "The sale of it (says the author "of Mr. Kelly's life) was exceed- "ingly rapid and great; and "it was repeatedly performed "throughout Britain and Ireland "to crowded audiences. Nor "was its reputation confined to "the British Dominions. It was "translated into most of the mo- "dern languages; viz. into Por- "tuguese, by command of the "Marquis de Pombal, and acted "with great applause at the pub- "lic Theatre at Lisbon; into "French by the celebrated Ma- "dame Riccoboni; into the same "language by another hand at the "Hague; into Italian at Paris, "where it was acted at the *Theatre* "*de la Comedie Italienne*; and into "German."

45. THE FALSE COUNT, or, *A New Way to play an old Game*. Com. by Mrs. Behn. Acted at the Duke's Theatre, 4to. 1682. The hint of the haughty *Isabella's* being readily imposed upon by the chimney-sweeper, whom her lover *Carlos* had equipped out as a count, is borrowed from the *Precieuses Ridicules* of Moliere. The humour of this character, however, is somewhat too low and farcical.

46. THE FALSE FAVORITE DISGRAC'D, *and the Reward of Loyalty*. Tragi-Com. by George Gerbier D'Ouvilly, 8vo. 1657. This play was never acted, probably from the deficiency in point of language, which may reasonably be expected in a writer, who was not a native of Britain. Scene Florence.

47. THE FALSE FRIEND, or, *The Fate of Disobedience*. Trag. by Mary Pix. Acted at Little Lincoln's-Inn Fields, 4to. 1699.

48. THE FALSE FRIEND. Com. by Sir J. Vanbrugh, 4to. 1702. Acted at Drury-Lane, with very good success.

49. THE FALSE GUARDIANS OUTWITTED. Ballad Opera, by William Goodal, 8vo. 1740. Printed in a Collection, called, "The true Englishman's Mis- "cellany."

50. THE FALSE ONE. Trag. by Beaumont and Fletcher, Fo, 1647. The story of this play is founded on the adventures of Julius Cæsar while in Egypt, and his amours with Cleopatra, as taken from the historians of those times. Scene, Egypt.

51. FALSTAFF's WEDDING. C. *being a Sequel to the Second Part of the Play of King Henry the Fourth. Written in imitation of Shakspeare*, by Dr. Kenrick, 8vo. 1760.

52. FALSTAFF's WEDDING. C. by Dr. Kenrick. Acted at Drury-Lane, 8vo. 1766. This is an alteration of the former play, and was acted at Mr. Love's benefit in 1766. When Shakspeare's Falstaff is forgotten, Dr. Kenrick's imitation of him may be received on the stage. We should add, however, that the present comedy is no contemptible performance.

53. THE FAMILY OF LOVE. Com. by T. Middleton. Acted by the children of the Revels, 4to. 1608. Scene, London. This play is spoken of by Sir Thomas Barnwell, in Shirley's *Lady of Pleasure*.

54. THE FANCIED QUEEN. An Opera, Anonymous, 8vo. 1733. Acted at Covent-Garden. This was written by Robert Drury.

55. FANCIES CHASTE AND NOBLE, by J. Ford. Acted at Phœnix, Drury-Lane, 4to. 1638.

56. FANCY's

56. FANCY'S FESTIVALS. Masq. in five acts, by Thomas Jordan, 4to. 1657. This piece is said in the title-page to have been privately presented by many civil persons of quality, and at their request printed, with many various and delightful new songs, for the further illustration of every scene.

57. THE FAREWELL AND RETURN, or, *The Fortune of War*. Ballad Farce, Anonymous, 12mo. What the date of this little piece is, when or where, or if even at all presented on the stage, I know not. But from the general tenour of the piece, which is no more than a few songs, put together into the form of a kind of interlude, representing a sailor's farewell to his lass, and return after a successful cruize, the plan seems borrowed from a couple of prints, intituled, *The Sailor's Farewell*, and *The Sailor's Return*, and I should imagine it had been written about the beginning of the last Spanish war, and probably performed by way of an interlude or entertainment between the acts. In the only edition I have seen of it, which appears, however, to be a spurious one, there is printed along with it another little piece of somewhat the same nature, intituled, *The Press-Gang*, which see under its own proper title.

58. THE FARMER'S JOURNEY TO LONDON. Farce, 8vo. 1769.

59. THE FARMER'S RETURN FROM LONDON. Interlude, 4to. 1762. This little piece was written by Mr. Garrick, and is published with a frontispiece designed by Mr. Hogarth. The plan of it is a humorous description in rhyme given by a farmer to his wife and children on his return from London, of what he had seen extraordinary in that great metropolis; in which, with great humour and satire, he touches on the generality of the most temporary and interesting topics of conversation, viz. the illustrious royal pair, the coronation, the entertainments of the theatre, and the noted imposition of the Cock-Lane ghost. It was originally written to do Mrs. Pritchard a piece of service at her benefit, but, meeting with universal applause, was repeated between play and farce many times during the course of the season.

60. FARRE FETCHED AND DEAR BOWGHT YS GOOD FOR LADIES. A Play, entered on the books of the Stationers' Company, by Thomas Hackett, 1566, but I believe never printed.

61. FASHION DISPLAYED. C. by Mrs. Philippina Burton. Acted one night at the Hay-Market, April 27, 1770, for the author's benefit. Not printed.

62. FASHIONABLE FRIENDSHIP. Ballad Opera, by William Shirley, Esq. Not acted. This piece is promised in the author's dramatic works.

63. THE FASHIONABLE LADY, or, *Harlequin's Opera*, by J. Ralph, 8vo. 1730. This piece was performed at Goodman's Fields, and is one of the many motley compositions of speaking and singing, which the great success of the *Beggar's Opera* gave birth to. It met, however, with tolerable success.

64. THE FASHIONABLE LOVER, or, *Wit in Necessity*. Com. Anonymous, 4to. 1706. Scene, London. By the Dramatis Personæ, it appears to have been acted at Drury-Lane.

65. THE FASHIONABLE LOVER. Com. by Richard Cumberland, Esq. Acted at Drury-Lane, 8vo, 1772. This piece followed *The West Indian* too soon for the reputation of its author. It was very coldly received.

66. FAST

66. FAST AND WELCOME. C. by Philip Massinger; entered on the books of the Stationers' Company, June 29, 1660, and was one of those destroyed by Mr. Warburton's servant.

67. THE FATAL BROTHERS. Trag. by Robert Davenport; entered on the books of the Stationers' Company, June 29, 1660, but I believe not printed.

68. FATAL CONSTANCY. Tr. by Hildebrand Jacob. Acted at Drury-Lane, 8vo. 1723. This play was acted, with some applause, at the Theatre in Drury-Lane.

69. FATAL CONSTANCY, or, *Love in Tears*. A sketch of a Tragedy in the heroic taste, by William Whitehead, printed in 12mo. 1754, in a volume of Poems. This performance made part of Mr. Foote's farce of *The Diversions of the Morning*.

70. THE FATAL CONTRACT. A French Tragedy, by William Hemings, 4to. 1653. This play met with great success at its first representations and was revived twice after the Restoration under different titles, viz. first by that of *Love* and *Revenge*, and afterwards, in the year 1687, under that of the *Eunuch*. The scene lies in France; and the plot is taken from the French history, in the reign of Childeric I. and Clotaire II.

71. THE FATAL CURIOSITY. Trag. by George Lillo. Acted at the Hay-Market, 8vo. 1736. This piece consists of but three acts. The story of it, however, is very simple and affecting, and is said to have been founded on a real fact which happened on the western coast of England. The circumstance, of a son long absent from his parents, keeping himself, on his return to visit them, for some time unknown, is natural and unforced, while at the same time their being induced by the depth of their distress and penury to resolve on and perpetrate his murder, for the sake of the treasures he had shewn them he was possessed of, is productive of some very fine scenes of intermingled horror and tenderness, when they come to be informed of the dreadful deed they have committed. In short, the play is in my opinion equal, if not superior, to any of this author's other works, and, when acted where it made its first appearance, met with a very favourable reception.

72. THE FATAL DISCOVERY, or, *Love in Ruins*. Trag. Anonym. Acted at Drury-Lane, 4to. 1698. The scene of this play lies in Venice, but the original design of the plot seems taken from the old story of *Oedipus* and *Jocasta*. The preface contains an answer to a copy of verses written by Dryden, and prefixed to the tragedy of *Heroic Love*.

73. THE FATAL DISCOVERY, A Tragedy, by John Home. Acted at Drury-Lane, 8vo. 1769. This play is a disgrace to the talents that produced the beautiful tragedy of *Douglas*. It is indeed little better than Fingal in verse. The defects of it, however, were not superior to the ridiculous improprieties displayed in its representation. On the stage we saw the youthful Ronan *bounding* with all the vigour and alacrity that age, gout, and rheumatism usually inspire. The heroes of this truly Erse performance,

— who never yet had being,
Or, being, wore no breeches,

were invested in gold and purple, while a Grecian palace was allotted to the monarch of a rock. These circumstances sufficiently prove that a manager ought to be conversant with the customs, habits, arms, and architecture, peculiar to various

various countries, that, when he supplies theatrical decorations, he may avoid anachronisms and abſurdities. *The Fatal Diſcovery* ran its nine nights without reputation, and, as it is ſaid, with very inconſiderable emolument to the author.

This play, however, was patronized by Mr. Garrick, who had refuſed *Douglas* before it was offered to Mr. Rich who received it. Surely a manager ſhould bring with him to his talk a perſpicacity that will enable him to diſtinguiſh real merit, a liberality that will permit him to reward it, and a ſpirit which no faction can over-awe, or betray into partial determinations.

74. THE FATAL DOWRY. Tr. by Ph. Maſſinger and Nathaniel Field. Acted at Black-Friers, 4to. 1632. The pious behaviour of *Charolois* in voluntarily giving up himſelf to impriſonment as a ranſom for the corpſe of his father, in order to obtain for it the rites of interment, is taken from the ſtory of Cimon the Athenian, related by Val. Maxim. lib. v. cap. 4. Mr. Rowe has made uſe of the ſame circumſtance to heighten the amiableneſs of *Altamont* in his *Fair Penitent*; the plot of which, as I have before obſerved, is in great meaſure borrowed from this play. *Nereſtan's* behaviour alſo, in the tragedy of *Zara*, ſeems to owe its origin to this hint, though different in ſome reſpect as to the particular ſituation of the action.

75. THE FATAL ERROR. Tr. by Benjamin Victor, 8vo. 1776. The ſubject of this play is taken from Heywood's *Woman kill'd with Kindneſs*.

76. THE FATAL EXTRAVAGANCE. Trag. by Joſeph Mitchell, 8vo. 1720. This play was originally written in one act, with only four characters, and was performed at the Theatre in Lincoln's-Inn Fields. It was, however, afterwards enlarged into five acts, with two additional characters, and preſented at Drury-Lane with ſucceſs in 1726. The ground-work of it is borrowed from Shakſpeare's *Yorkſhire Tragedy*, but the language is new. It is ſaid that the author had great aſſiſtances in it from Mr. Aaron Hill; nay, Victor, in his Hiſtory of the Stage, vol. II. p. 123. poſitively aſſerts, that the laſt-named gentleman wrote the play, got it acted, and ſupported it on the ſuppoſed author's third night, Mr. Mitchell being at that time in great diſtreſs. It is alſo inſerted in the edition of Mr. Hill's works as one of his productions.

77. FATAL FALSHOOD, or, *Diſtreſſed Innocence*. Trag. in three acts, by J. Hewett. Acted at Drury-Lane, 8vo. no date.

78. FATAL FALSHOOD. Trag. by Miſs Hannah More. Acted at Covent-Garden, 8vo. 1779.

79. THE FATAL FRIENDSHIP. A play, by Mr. Burroughes; entered on the books of the Stationers' Company, Sept. 4, 1646, but never printed.

80. FATAL FRIENDSHIP. Tr. by Cath. Trotter, afterwards Cockburne, 4to. 1698. Acted at Lincoln's Inn Fields, with great applauſe. This play was reprinted in the Collection of Mrs. Cockburne's Works, publiſhed by Dr. Birch, 2 vols. 8vo. 1751. It is the moſt perfect of her dramatic pieces.

81. THE FATAL JEALOUSY. Trag. Acted at the Duke's Theatre, 4to. 1673. Anonymous. It is, however, aſcribed by his contemporaries to Nevil Paine. The ſcene of it is laid in Naples, and the plot borrowed from Beard's Theatre,

Theatre, *The Unfortunate Lovers*, &c. The character of *Jasper* seems to be a bad copy of Iago in *The Moor of Venice*, and the author has rendered this a very bloody tragedy, without paying a due, or indeed any regard to poetic justice. Amongst the Dramatis Personæ, we find Nat. Lee the Poet, who performed the small part of the captain of the guard.

82. THE FATAL INCONSTANCY, or, *The Unhappy Rescue*. Trag. by Mr. R. Phillips, 4to. 1701. This piece and its author I find only mentioned by Coxeter in his MS. notes, who tells us moreover that the scene of it is laid near London, and that the prologue was written by Mr. Johnson.

83. THE FATAL LEGACY. Tr. Anonymous, 1723. Acted at Lincoln's-Inn Fields. This is a translation of Racine's *Thebais*. The author, as appears by the dedication, was a young lady. It was coldly received on the stage. Mears's Catalogue calls her J. Robe.

84. FATAL LOVE, or, *The Forc'd Inconstancy*. Trag. by Elk. Settle. Acted at the Theatre Royal, 4to. 1680. The plot of this play may be traced to its origin by reading the fifth book of Tatius's Romance of *Clitophon* and *Leucippe*.

85. FATAL LOVE, or, *The Degenerate Brother*. Trag. by Osborne Sidney Wandesford, Esq; 8vo. 1730. This play was acted, as the author himself informs us, at the Hay-Market, without success; which failure, however, he in his preface attributes to the performers, by whom it seems to have been curtailed, and negligently acted. Yet perhaps the reader may find a better reason for its want of approbation occur to him on the perusal of it.

86. FATAL LOVE. *A French Tragedy, by George Chapman*. In this manner a play is entered on the books of the Stationers' Company, June 29, 1660, but I believe not printed.

87. THE FATAL MARRIAGE, or, *The Innocent Adultery*. Trag. by Thomas Southerne. Acted at the Theatre Royal, 4to. 1694. This play met with great success at its first coming out, and has been often performed since with as great approbation, the tragical part of it being extremely fine and very affecting. It is, however, like his *Oroonoko*, interwoven with comic scenes, so much inferior in point of merit to the other parts, that it has frequently been laid aside for a considerable time. The scene lies in Brussels; the plot of the tragedy is, by the author's own confession, taken from a novel of Mrs. Behn's, called, *The Nun*, or, *The Fair Vow-breaker*; and the incident of *Fernando's* being persuaded to believe that he had been dead, buried, and in purgatory, seems borrowed from Fletcher's *Night Walker*. Mr. Garrick, however, has since purified this ore from its dross, by clearing the play of all the comic part, excepting so much of the characters of the nurse and porter as are inseparable from the affairs of *Isabella*. That gentleman brought it on at the Theatre Royal in Drury-Lane, in 1758, by the title of *Isabella*, or, *The Fatal Marriage*, and it met with great success.

88. A FATAL MISTAKE, or, *The Plot spoil'd*. Trag. by Joseph Haynes, 4to. 1692. This play in the first edition is said to have been acted.

89. FATAL NECESSITY, or, *Liberty Regain'd*. Trag. *as it was once acted in Rome for the sake of freedom and virtue*. Anonym. 8vo. 1742. This piece was published soon after the general election of repre-

representatives in parliament for the several shires, cities, and boroughs in this kingdom in 1742, and is dedicated by the author, under the character of an *Independent Elector*, to Charles Edwin, Esq; one of the gentlemen chosen representatives for the city of Westminster, after a considerable contest, in which he had been supported by those of the electors who took on themselves that title. The plot is built on the famous and well-known story of *Appius* and *Virginia*; but it is not very apparent what deduction the author aims at in that event, with a reference to the above-mentioned election. It was never represented on the stage.

90. THE FATAL PROPHECY. Dram. Poem, by Dr. John Langhorne, printed in his Poems, 12mo. 1766.

91. THE FATAL RETIREMENT. Trag. by Anth. Brown. Acted one night at Drury Lane, 8vo. 1739. This play would scarcely be worth any farther notice than a mention of its name, were it not for a little theatrical anecdote, which, as it does honour to the proper spirit frequently shewn by a capital veteran of the stage, I shall here relate.

When this play was first offered to the theatre, Mr. Quin refusing to act in it, the author's friends thought proper to attribute its want of success to his not appearing in it, and in consequence of such supposition repeatedly insulted him for several nights afterwards in the pursuance of his profession; till at length coming forwards, and addressing the audience, he with great candour and spirit informed them, " that he had, at the request of " the author, read his piece before " it was acted, and given him his " very sincere opinion of it, that " it was the *very worst* play he had " ever read in his life, and *for that " reason* had refused to act in it." This, however, turned the tide so much in his favour, that his speech was received with a thundering clap, and the insults he had received were put to an entire stop.

92. THE FATAL SECRET. Tr. by Lewis Theobald, 1735. 12mo. Acted at the Theatre Royal in Covent-Garden. This play is made up from Webster's *Duchess of Malfy*. Scene, the duchess's palace in Malfy.

93. THE FATAL VISION, or, *The Fall of Siam*. Trag. by A. Hill, 4to. 1716. Acted at Lincoln's-Inn Fields, with success. The scene is fixed in the city of Sofola in Siam; but the author owns that the fable is fictitious, and the characters imaginary. The moral is to expose the dangerous consequences of the giving way to rage and rashness of determination. It is dedicated to the two critics, Dennis and Gildon.

94. THE FATE OF CAPUA. Tr. by Thomas Southerne. Acted at Lincoln's-Inn Fields, 4to. 1700, Scene, Capua. The prologue by Charles Boyle; the epilogue by Col. Codrington. The domestic scenes of this tragedy have uncommon power over the tender passions. The circumstance on which the distresses of *Virginius*, *Junius*, and *Favonia* depend, is original, neither has it been hackneyed by imitators. The piece, however, on the whole, is oppressed by *a load* which, as Wolsey says, *would sink a navy*, too much patriotism. A *patriot*, to our modern apprehensions, is a dull declamatory being, as much out of nature as *Caliban*, and not quite so entertaining. Many of the long speeches of *Magius*, *Pacuvius*, &c, are copies from Livy. The historian extinguishes the poet.

95. THE

95. THE FATE OF CORSICA, or, *The Female Politician*. Com. written by a Lady of quality, says the title-page, 8vo. 1732. Scene, the Castle of Gallera.

96. THE FATE OF VILLAINY. A Play, by Thomas Walker, 8vo. 1730. This was acted at Goodman's Fields with very indifferent success.

97. THE FATHER. Com. translated from *Diderot*, by the translater of *Dorval*, 4to. 1770. This is a translation of *Le Pere de Famille*.

98. THE FATHERS, or, *The Good-natured Man*. Com. by Henry Fielding, Esq. Acted at Drury-Lane, 8vo. 1778. This comedy had but indifferent success in its representation. It was written many years before the author's death, being mentioned by him in the preface to his Miscellanies published in 1743. The cause of its not appearing sooner arose from its being lent to Sir Charles Hanbury Williams, who mislaid it. It is said to have received some touches from the elegant pen of Mr. Sheridan, jun. but they are not very conspicuous.

99. THE FATHER OF A FAMILY. Com. in three acts, by Carlo Goldoni, 8vo. 1757. This is no more than the translation of a piece, intituled, *Il Padre di Famiglia*, represented for the first time at Venice, during the carnival of 1750. But though it is entitled a Comedy, it has nothing of humour, or even an attempt towards wit, shewn throughout the whole of it, and must have been extremely unentertaining in the representation, being no more than a series of the common occurrences of a large family thrown into dialogue, in order to point out the different requisites for forming the character of an amiable father, and matter of a family, and the errors frequently run into by some of the various relatives in domestic life. This piece is printed in English and Italian, the original page for page opposite to the translation, together with another comedy on the story of *Pamela*, of which farther mention will be made hereafter.

100. THE FAVOURITE. An Historical Tragedy, 8vo. 1770. This is taken from Ben Jonson. It is dedicated to Lord Bute.

101. THE FEIGN'D ASTROLOGER. Com. Anonymous, 4to. 1668. This is translated from Corneille, who borrowed his piece from Calderon's *El Astrologo fingido*. The same plot is made use of by M. Scudery, in his Novel of *The Illustrious Bassa*, where the French marquis takes on himself the fictitious character of an *Astrologer*.

102. THE FEIGN'D COURTEZANS, or, *A Night's Intrigue*. Com. by Mrs. Behn. Acted at the Duke's Theatre, 4to. 1679. This play met with very good success, and was generally esteemed the best she had written. The scene lies in Rome, and the play contains a vast deal of business and intrigue; the contrivance of the two ladies to obtain their differently disposed lovers, both by the same means, viz. by assuming the characters of courtezans, being productive of great variety. It is dedicated to Mrs. Ellen Guin. The following passage is extracted from it as a complete specimen of the meanness and servility of the author: "Your permission, Madam, "has inlightened me, and I with "shame look back on my past "ignorance, which suffered me "not to pay an adoration long "since, where there was so very "much due; yet even now though "secure in my opinion, I make "this sacrifice with infinite fear "and

"and trembling, well knowing that so excellent and perfect a creature as yourself differs only from the divine powers in this; the offerings made to you ought to be worthy of you, whilst they accept the will alone."

103. FEIGN'D FRIENDSHIP, or, *The Mad Reformer*. Com. Anonymous, 4to. without a date. It was, however, about the beginning of this century, acted in Little Lincoln's-Inn Fields. Scene, the Park and houses adjoining.

104. THE FEMALE ACADEMY. Com. by the Duchess of Newcastle, Fol. 1662.

105. THE FEMALE ADVOCATES, or, *The Frantic Stock-jobbers*. Com. by W. Taverner. Acted at Drury-Lane, 4to. 1713. The British Theatre and Whincop's Catalogue have the second title of this play the *Stock-jobbers* only; but, as it is probable they might neither of them have seen the piece itself, I have thus restored it.

106. THE FEMALE CAPTAIN. Farce, by —— Cobb. Acted at the Hay-Market, 1780. This had been once acted at Drury-Lane, April 5, 1779, for Miss Pope's benefit, under the title of *The Contract*.

107. THE FEMALE CHEVALIER. Com. altered from *Taverner*, by George Colman. Acted at the Hay-market, 1778. This is taken from *The Artful Husband*.

108. THE FEMALE FORTUNE-TELLER. Com. by Mr. Johnson, 8vo, 1726. What Mr. Johnson it was by whom this piece was written I cannot come to any certainty about, as no christian name is prefixed to the title-page, but am apt to believe it must have been Mr. Charles Johnson, a tragedy by whom, called *Medea*, has been also omitted by all the writers. This is far from a bad play, and, by the names of particular performers writ-ten opposite to the Dramatis Personæ of the copy I have seen, appears to have been intended for representation at the Theatre Royal in Drury-Lane within these five or six years.

109. THE FEMALE GAMESTER. Tr. by Gorges Edmund Howard, Esq. 12mo. 1778. Printed at Dublin.

110. THE FEMALE OFFICER. Comedy, of two acts, by Henry Brooke, Esq. 8vo. 1778. Not acted. Scene, the British Camp in Portugal. Printed in the author's works, 4 vols. 1778.

111. THE FEMALE PARLIAMENT. *A Seri-Tragi-Comi-Farcical Entertainment. Never acted in Utopia before. Wherein are occasionally exhibited, The Humours of Fanny Bloom and Lady Nice Airs. Together with the Amours of Sir Timothy Fopwell and Justice Vainlove*, 12mo. 1754.

112. THE FEMALE PARSON, or, *The Beau in the Suds*. A Ballad Opera, by C. Coffey, 1730. This piece was brought on at the Little Theatre in the Hay-Market, but was with very good reason damned the first night.

113. THE FEMALE PARRICIDE. Trag. by Edward Crane, of Manchester, 8vo. 1761. This piece is founded on the story of Miss Blandy, and was printed at Manchester.

114. THE FEMALE PRELATE, *being the History of the Life and Death of Pope Joan*. Trag. by Elk. Settle. Acted at the Theatre Royal, 4to. 1680. The plot of this play is taken from Platina's Lives of the Popes; and Cooke's Dialogue, intituled, *Pope Joan*. It is dedicated to the Earl of Shaftsbury.

115. THE FEMALE RAKE, or, *Modern Fine Lady*. A Ballad Comedy. Acted at the Hay-Market, 8vo. 1736,

116. THE

116. THE FEMALE VIRTUOSOES. Com. by Thomas Wright. Acted at the Queen's Theatre, 4to. 1693. This play was performed with great applause, but is no more than an improved translation of the *Femmes Savantes* of Moliere; an author to whom many of our playwriters have been greatly obliged, not only for their plots, but even for the very substance and wit of their pieces.

117. THE FEMALE WITS, or, *The Triumvirate of Poets at Rehearsal*. Com. 4to. 1697. With the letters W. M. in the title. This piece was acted at the Theatre Royal in Drury-Lane for several days successively, and with applause. It consists of three acts, is written in the manner of a rehearsal, and was intended as a banter on Mrs. Manley, Mrs. Pix, and Mrs. Trotter.

118. FERREX AND PORREX. Trag. set forth without addition or alteration, but altogether as the same was shewed on the stage before the Queenes Majestie about nine years past, viz. the 18th day of January, 1561, by the Gentlemen of the Inner Temple, B. L. no date. The first three acts of this play were written by Thomas Norton; the two last by Thomas Sackville, Esq. afterwards Lord Buckhurst. The plot is from the English chronicles.

119. THE FICKLE SHEPHERDESS. A Pastoral, 4to. 1703. This is only an alteration of Randolph's *Amintas*; it was acted at the New Theatre in Lincoln's-Inn Fields, and was played entirely by women. The scene lies in Arcadia.

120. FIDELE AND FORTUNATUS. Whether this piece is tragedy or comedy, what is its date, or whether it was ever acted, are particulars I am at a loss to discover; the old catalogues only naming it, and ascribing it to Thomas Barker. The British theatre, however, fixes its date about 1690. And Coxeter, in opposition to all the other writers, distinguishes this Barker from the author of *The Beau defeated*. It is probably much older than any of the before-mentioned lists suppose. In the books of the Stationers' Company, Nov. 12, 1584, is entered " Fidele and Fortuna-" tus. The Deceipts in Love dif-" coursed in a Comedie of two " Italyn Gentlemen, and translated " into Englishe."

121. FILLI DE SCIRO, or, *Phillis of Scyros*. An excellent Pastorall, written in Italian by C. Giudubaldo de Bonarelli, and translated into English by J. S, Gent. 4to. 1655. By some verses prefixed to this translation, it appears to have been made near twenty years before. A translation was at the same time made of *Pastor Fido*, but both of them were laid aside. Coxeter imagines these translations were produced by Sir Edward Sherborne, who was then only seventeen years old. The initial letters seem to point out James Shirley as the translator.

122. THE FINANCIER. Com. of one act, translated from St. Foix. 8vo. 1771,

123. A FINE COMPANION. C. by Shakerley Marmion, 4to. 1633. Acted before the King and Queen at Whitehall, and at the Theatre in Salisbury-Court. This play was greatly approved of, and it is evident on inspection that Durfey's Capt. *Porpuss*, in his Sir *Barnaby Whig*, is an imitation of Capt. Whibble in this play.

124. THE FINE LADIES AIRS. Com. by Thomas Baker. No date [1709]. It was acted in Drury-Lane with success. The scene lies in London, and the prologue is written by Mr. Motteux.

125. FIRE

125. FIRE AND BRIMSTONE, or, *The Destruction of Sodom.* Drama, by George Lesly, 8vo. 1675.

126. FIRE AND WATER. Ballad Opera, by Miles Peter Andrews. Acted at the Hay-Market, 8vo. 1780. There is more of the insipid than the aspiring element in this production.

127. THE FLEIRE. Com. by Edward Sharpham. Acted at Black-Friers, by the children of the Revels, 4to. 1615. 4to. 1631. The scene of this play lies in London, and the plot seems in a great degree to be borrowed from Marston's *Parasitaster.* It is probably older than the year 1615, as I find it entered by John Trundel, on the books of the Stationers' Company, May 9, 1606.

128. THE FLITCH OF BACON. Ballad Opera, by Henry Bate. Acted at the Hay-Market, 1778. Printed in 8vo. 1779.

129. THE FLOATING ISLAND. Tragi-Com. by William S.rode, 4to. 1655. This play was not published till many years after the author's death, but was performed by the students of Christ-Church on the 29th of August, 1636, before the king, for whose diversion it was purposely written at the request of the dean and chapter. It contained too much morality to suit the taste of the court; yet it pleased the king so well, that he soon after bestowed a canon's dignity on the author.

130. FLORA. Opera. Acted at Lincoln's-Inn Fields, being *The Country Wake,* altered after the manner of *The Beggar's Opera,* 8vo. 1732.

131. FLORA'S VAGARIES. C. by Richard Rhodes. This play was written while the author was a student at Oxford, and after being publicly acted by his fellow-students

in Christ-Church, Jan. 8, 1663, and afterwards at the Theatre Royal, was printed in 4to. 1670. The scene lies in Verona; and part of the plot, viz. the circumstance of *Orante's* making use of the friar in carrying on her intrigues with *Ludovico,* is founded on Boccace's *Dream.* Day 3. Nov. 7.

132. FLORAZENE, or, *The Fatal Conquest.* Trag. by James Goodhall. Not acted, but printed at Stamford, 8vo. 1754.

133. THE FLORENTINE FRIEND. A Play, with this title, was entered on the books of the Stationers' Company, Nov. 29, 1653, but was not printed.

134. FLORIZEL AND PERDITA, or, *The Sheepshearing.* Farce, Anon. 8vo. 1754. This piece is no more than an extract from some scenes of Shakspeare's *Winter's Tale,* so far as relates to the loves of *Florizel* and *Perdita,* formed into two acts, and enlivened with part of the humorous character of *Autolicus.* Who this was executed by I know not, but it was first performed at Covent-Garden Theatre for the benefit of Miss Nossiter, that young lady acting the part of *Perdita,* and Mr. Barry the counterpart of her lover. It has since, however, been frequently represented with success.

135. FLORIZEL AND PERDITA. Dram. Pastoral, in three acts, altered from *The Winter's Tale* of Shakspeare, by David Garrick. Acted at Drury-Lane, 1756; printed in 8vo. 1758.

136. THE FOLLY OF PRIESTCRAFT. Com. Anon. 4to. 1690. Langbaine gives this piece the highest commendations, allotting it, in point of ingenious and judicious satire, the next place in rank to Wycherley's *Plain Dealer;* yet hints that it may give umbrage to the priests and bigots of the Romish religion.

137. THE

137. THE FOND HUSBAND, or, *The Plotting Sisters*. Com. by T. Durfey. Acted at Drury-Lane, 4to. 1676. 4to. 1685. 4to. 1711. This met with very great applause, and is look'd upon as one of Mr. Durfey's best plays.

138. FONDLEWIFE AND LETITIA. Com. of two acts, performed at Crow-ftreet Dublin, 12mo. 1767. Taken from *The Old Batchelor*, and printed at Dublin.

139. A FOOL AND HER MAIDENHEAD SOON PARTED. A play under this title was entered on the books of the Stationers' Company, Nov. 29, 1653; but was not printed.

140. THE FOOL'S OPERA, or, *The Taste of the Age*. Written by Matthew Medley, and performed by his company in Oxford, 8vo. 1731.

141. THE FOOL TRANSFORMED. Com. This play was advertifed as being in the prefs, at the end of *Wit and Drollery, Jovial Poems*, 12mo. 1661, but was not publifhed.

142. A FOOL'S PREFERMENT, or, *The three Dukes of Dunstable*. Com. by T. Durfey. Acted at the Queen's Theatre Dorfet Garden, 4to. 1688. This play is little more than a tranfcript of Fletcher's *Noble Gentleman*, except one fcene relating to Ballet, which is taken from a Novel, called *The Humours of Baffet*.

Sir George Etherege, in a letter to the duke of Buckingham, fays "By my laft packet from England "among a heap of naufeous trafh, "I received the *Three Dukes of* "*Dunftabe*; which is really fo "monftrous and infipid, that I "am forry Lapland or Livonia "had not the honour of producing "it; but if I did penance in read-"ing it, I rejoiced to hear that it "was fo folemnly interred to the "tune of cat-calls."

143. THE FOOLS WITHOUT BOOKE. A play, by William Rowley, entered on the books of the Stationers' Company, Sept. 9, 1653, but not printed.

144. THE FOOL TURN'D CRITICK. Com. by T. Durfey. Acted at the Theatre Royal, 4to. 1678. This, like moft of our author's pieces, is full of plagiarifms. The characters of *Old Wine, Trim*, and *Small Wit*, being taken from *Simo, Ajotus*, and *Balio*, in Randolph's *Jealous Lovers*. Nay, the very prologue is a theft, being the very fame with that to lord Orrery's *Mafter Anthony*.

145. THE FOOL WOULD BE A FAVOURITE, or, *The Difcreet Lover*. Com. by Lodowick Carlell, 8vo. 1657. Acted with great applaufe. The fcene in Milan.

146. THE FOOTMAN. An Opera, 8vo. 1734. Performed at Goodman's-Fields.

147. THE FORC'D MARRIAGE, or, *The Jealous Bridegroom*. Tragi-Com. by Mrs. Behn, 4to. 1671. 4to. 1688. This play was acted at the Queen's Theatre, and is fuppofed by Langbaine to be the firft of this lady's production. Scene in the court of France.

148. THE FORC'D MARRIAGE. Com. by Ozell. This is only a tranflation of the *Marriage Forcé* of Moliere, and was never intended for the ftage.

149. THE FORCED MARRIAGE. Trag. by Dr. John Armftrong, 8vo. 1770. This was written in 1754, and is printed in the fecond volume of the author's Mifcellanies. It is a performance which will not add to the reputation of the elegant author of *The Art of preferving Health*. It had been offered to Mr. Garrick, but was refufed by him.

150. THE

150. THE FORCED MARRIAGE. Com. tranflated from Moliere, printed in Foote's *Comick Theatre*, vol. IV.

151. THE FORC'D PHYSICIAN. Com. by Ozell. This piece is under the fame circumftance with the foregoing, being a tranflation only of Moliere's *Medicin malgre lui.*

152. THE FORCE OF FRIENDSHIP. Trag. by Cha. Johnfon. Acted at the Hay-Market, 4to. 1710. Scene, Verona. At the end of this tragedy is fubjoined a fmall Farce, which was acted with it, called *Love in a Cheft.*

153. THE FORTUNE HUNTERS. Farce. To which is annexed, a humorous new ballad, called *The Female Combatants*, or *Love in a Jail*. As it was acted at Mac L——n's Amphitheatre with great applaufe, 8vo. 1750.

154. THE FORTUNE HUNTERS, or, *The Widow bewitch'd*. Farce, by Charles Macklin. This hath been acted for the author's benefit, but is not printed.

155. THE FORTUNATE ISLES and their union, celebrated in a Mafque defigned for the court on Twelfth Night, 1626, by Ben Jonfon.

156. THE FORTUNATE PEASANT, or, *Nature will Prevail*. Com. by Benjamin Victor, 8vo. 1776. This is taken from the *Payfan Parvenu* of Monfieur de Marivaux. It was never acted.

157. THE FORTUNATE PRINCE, or, *Marriage at Laft*. Ballad Opera in three acts, 8vo. 1734.

158. FORTUNE TO KNOW EACH ONE THE CONDICIONS AND GENTLE MANORS, AS WELL OF WOMEN AS OF MEN, &c. A play entered on the books of the Stationers' Company, 1566; but I believe not printed.

159. FORTUNE'S TRICKS IN FORTY-SIX. An allegorical Satire, 8vo. 1747.

160. FORTUNE BY LAND AND SEA. Tragi-Com. by Thomas Heywood. Acted by the Queen's fervants, 4to. 1655. Our author was affifted by Rowley in the compofition of this play, which met with great applaufe in the performance, but was not printed till after their deceafe. The fcene lies in London.

161. THE FORTUNE-HUNTERS, or, *Two Fools well met*. Com. by Ja. Carlifle. Acted by his Majefties fervants, 4to. 1689. This play met with fuccefs, and Langbaine gives it confiderable commendation; yet at the fame time cites an incident from it which contradicts that good opinion, viz. A perfon's miftaking the hand of another for the handle of a pump, and orange-flower for pump-water. The fcene in Covent-Garden.

162. FORTUNE IN HER WITS. Com. by Charles Johnfon, 4to. 1705. This is but an indifferent tranflation of Cowley's *Naufragium joculare*, and was never prefented on the ftage. The fcene, as it does in the laft-named piece, lies at Dunkirk.

163. THE FOUNDLING. Com. by Edward Moore. Acted at Drury-Lane, 8vo. 1748. This comedy was the firft of Moore's dramatic pieces, but is far fuperior to his fecond comic attempt. It met with tolerable fuccefs during its run, although on the firft night of its appearance, the character of *Faddle* (which it is faid was intended for one Ruffel) gave great difguft, and was therefore confiderably curtailed in all the enfuing reprefentations. It has not, however, fince that time been continued as an acting comedy, being generally

generally considered as bearing too near a resemblance to the *Conscious Lovers*. Yet I cannot help thinking it far preferable to that play, as the intricacy of the plot is much more natural, the characters of a more sprightly turn, and drawn in the general from higher life, unmixed with the pertness of a chambermaid coquet, and kitchen coxcomb; on which, however, the greatest part of the liveliness of Sir Richard Steele's play principally depends.

164. *The Booke of the* FOUR HONOURABLE LOVES. Com. by William Rowley; entered on the books of the Stationers' Company, June 29, 1660, but not printed.

165. THE FOUR PRENTICES OF LONDON, *with the Conquest of Jerusalem*. An Historical Play, by Thomas Heywood. Acted at the Red Bull, 4to. 1615. 4to. 1632. The plot is founded on the exploits of the famous Godfrey of Bulloigne, who released Jerusalem out of the hands of the infidels in 1099. A more ample account of which is to be seen in Tasso's *Goffredo*, and in Fuller's *Holy War*.

156. THE FOUR P's. *A merry Interlude of a* Palmer, *a* Pardoner, *a* Potycary *and a* Pedlar, by John Heywood, 4to. no date, and 4to. 1569. This is one of the first plays that appeared in the English language; it is written in metre, and not divided into acts. The original edition is in the black letter, but it has been republished in Dodsley's Collection of Old Plays.

167. FOUR PLAYS IN ONE, or, *Moral Representations*, by Beaumont and Fletcher. Fol. 1647. These four pieces are entitled as follows, viz. I. *The Triumph of Honour*. This is founded on Boccace, Day. 10. Nov. 5. Scene near Athens, the Roman army lying there. II. *The Triumph of Love*. This is taken from the same author, Day. 5. Nov. 8. and the scene laid in Milan. III. *The Triumph of Death*. This is from Part 3. Nov. 3. of the *Fortunate, Deceiv'd, and Unfortunate Lovers*. The Scene, Anjou. IV. *The Triumph of Time*. The plot of this seems to be entirely the invention of the author. Whether this medley of dramatic pieces was ever performed or not, does not plainly appear. It is composed as if acted at Lisbon, before Manuel, king of Portugal, and his queen Isabella, at the celebration of their nuptials, that court being introduced as spectators, and the king, queen, &c. making remarks upon each representation. The two first may properly be called Tragi-Com. the third a Tragedy, and the last an Opera.

168. THE FOUR SEASONS, or, *Love in every Age*. A Musical Interlude, by P. A. Motteux, 4to. 1699. This little piece was set to music by Mr. Jeremy Clarke, and is printed with the musical entertainments in the opera of *The Island Princess*, or *Generous Portuguese*; but whether or not this did itself belong to that opera, does not at present occur to my remembrance.

169. FREDERIC DUKE OF BRUNSWICK LUNENBURG, Trag. by Elizabeth Haywood, 8vo. 1729. Acted at Lincoln's-Inn Fields, with no success.

170. FREE WILL. Trag. by Henry Cheeke, 4to. Black letter, no date. This is one of the very old moral plays. Its full title runs as follows: *A certayne Tragedie wrytten first in Italian by F. N. B.* (Franciscus Niger Bollentinus) *entituled* FREEWYL; *and translated into English by Henry Cheeke, Esquire;*

in is set foorth in manner of a Tragedie the deuylish Deuise of the Popish Religion, &c.

171. THE FREEMAN'S HONOUR. Play, by William Smith. It is only mentioned in the Epistle Dedicatory of a subsequent one written by the same author, and intituled, *The Hector of Germany*. This play, however, is said to have been " acted by the servants of the King's Majesty, to " dignify the worthy Company of " Merchant-Taylors."

172. THE FRENCH CONJURER. Com. by T. P. Acted at the Duke of York's Theatre, 4to. 1678. The plot of this play is composed from two stories in the Romance of Gusman de Alfarache, *The Spanish Rogue*; the one called *Dorido* and *Cloridia*, the other *The Merchant of Sevil*; and the scene is laid in Sevil.

173. THE FRENCH FLOGGED, or, *The British Sailors in America*. Farce of two acts, performed at Covent-Garden, 8vo. 1767. A piece written for, and acted at Bartholomew Fair. It was also once represented at Covent-Garden. The author is supposed to be Geo. Alex. Stevens.

174. THE FRENCHIFIED LADY NEVER IN PARIS. Com. of two acts, by Henry Dell. Acted at Covent-Garden, 8vo. 1757. Taken from Cibber's *Comical Lovers*.

175. FRENCHMAN IN LONDON. A Comedy. Dedicated to Mr. Foote, 8vo. 1755. This piece was never designed for the English stage, being nothing but a literal translation of the *Francois à Londres* of M. de Boissy, from which it was said Mr. Foote had taken the hint of his *Englishman in Paris*. I can, however, perceive no kind of resemblance between the two pieces, any farther than what arises from a similarity

in their name. In the dedication, the translator says to Mr. Foote, " You remember when walking " once in the Thuilleries, you (by " that art peculiar to your own " genius) represented a French" man to himself; the coxcomb, " far from being struck with the " ridicule, declared you the only " well-bred Englishman he had " seen."

176. THE FRIENDS. Trag. by Mark Anthony Meilan, 8vo. No date [1771]. The story from which this play was taken, is printed in *The Gentleman's Magazine*, January 1766.

177. THE FRIENDLY RIVALS, or, *Love the best Contriver*. Com. 8vo. 1752. This comedy was with great propriety refused by the managers.

178. FRIENDSHIP A LA MODE. Com. of two acts, performed at Smock-Alley Dublin, 8vo. Printed at Dublin, 1766. This is an alteration of Vanbrugh's *False Friend*.

179. FRIENDSHIP IMPROVED, or, *The Female Warrior*. Trag. by Cha. Hopkins. Acted at Lincoln's-Inn Fields, 4to. 1700. To this play is prefixed an humorous prologue, on the subject of the author's commencing merchant, and accumulating wealth, if it may be in the power of a poet so to do.

180. FRIENDSHIP IN FASHION. Com. by Tho. Otway. Acted at the Duke's Theatre, 4to. 1678. Though the original compiler of this work asserts that the piece before us met with great success at first, upon its revival at Drury-Lane in 1749, it was, as Dr. Johnson observes, hissed off the stage for immorality and obscenity.

181. " The Honourable His" torie of FRIER BACON AND " FRIER BONGAY. As it was " plaied

"plaied by her Majeſtie's ſervants, "Made by Robert Greene maiſter "of arts," 1594, 4to. 1630, 4to. 4to. 1655. For the ſtory of this piece, ſee Plot's *Hiſtory of Oxfordſhire*, and Wood's *Antiq. Oxon*.

182. THE FRUITLESS REDRESS. Trag. written in the year 1728. This play is ſtill in manuſcript. See vol. I. p. 370.

183. FUIMUS TROES, ÆNEID 2. THE TRUE TROJANS. *Being a ſtory of the Britaines Valour at the Romanes firſt invaſion: publickely repreſented by the Gentlemen Students of Magdalen-College in Oxford*. 4to. 1633. The author of this performance was Dr. Jaſper Fiſher.

184. FULGIUS AND LUCRELLA. By this name is a piece mentioned by Langbaine, Jacob, Gildon, and Whincop, none of whom pretend to have ſeen it, or to give any account of it. But as the author of the *Britiſh Theatre* is more particular in his deſcription of it, it is reaſonable to imagine he had met with the piece itſelf. It differs from them all in the ſpelling of the ſecond name, calling it FULGIUS and LUCRETTE, a Paſtoral, from the Italian, 1676.

185. FUN. A parodi-tragi-comical Satire, 8vo. 1752. This little piece is entirely burleſque, and was written by Dr. Kenrick. It contains ſome ſevere ſtrokes of ſatire on H. Fielding, Dr. Hill, &c. and was intended to have been performed by a ſet of private perſons at the Caſtle Tavern in Pater-noſter Row. But although it was ſcreened under the idea of a concert of muſic, and a ball, Mr. Fielding, who had received ſome information of it, found means of putting a ſtop to it on the very night of performance, even when the audience were aſſembled. The piece, however, which is entirely inoffenſive, otherwiſe than by ſatyrizing ſome particular works which were then recent, was ſoon after printed, and delivered gratis to ſuch perſons as had taken tickets for the concert.

186. THE FUNERAL, or *Grief a la Mode*. Com. by Sir Richard Steele. Acted at Drury-Lane, 4to. 1702. This is, in my opinion, much the beſt of this author's pieces. The conduct of it is ingenious, the characters pointed, the language ſprightly, and the ſatire ſtrong and genuine. There is indeed ſomewhat improbable in the affair of conveying Lady *Charlotte* away in the coffin; yet the reward which by that means is beſtowed on the pious behaviour of young lord *Hardy*, with reſpect to his father's body, makes ſome amends for it. I know not that the plot of this is borrowed from any other piece; yet the hint of lord *Brumpton*'s feigning himſelf dead to try the diſpoſition of his wife, may perhaps owe its origin to a ſcene in Moliere's *Malade Imaginaire*.

187. THE FURIES. T. Tranſlated from *Æſchylus*, by R. Potter, 4to. 1777.

G.

1. GALATHEA. C. by John Lyly, 4to 1592. Played before Queen Elizabeth at Greenwich on New Year's-Day at night. The characters of Galathea and Phillida are borrowed from Iphis and Ianthe, in the 9th book of Ovid's Metamorphosis.

2. GALLIC GRATITUDE, or, The Frenchman in India. Com. of two acts, by James Solas Dodd, performed at Covent-Garden, 8vo. 1779.

3. GALLIGANTUS. Musical Entertainment, 8vo. 1758. This piece was taken from Mr. Brooke's *Jack the Giant Queller*. It was acted at the Hay-Market, and once at Drury-Lane, for Mrs. Yates's benefit

4. A GAME AT CHESSE. by Tho. Middleton, 4to. This play was sundry times acted at the Globe on the Bank Side, and although it has no date, was published about 1625. It is a sort of religious controversy, the game being played between one of the church of England and another of the church of Rome, wherein the former in the end gets the victory, *Ignatius Loyala* sitting by as a spectator. The scene lies in London.

In a copy of this play, in the possession of Thomas Pearson, Esq; is the following memorandum in an old hand. "After nine
" days, wherein I have heard some
" of the actors say, they took fif-
" teen hundred pounds, the Spa-
" nish faction being prevalent, got
" it suppressed, and the author,
" Mr. Thomas Middleton, com-
" mitted to prison, where he lay
" some time, and at last got out
" upon this petition to King
" James:
" A harmless game coyned only for
 " delight,
" Was play'd betwixt the black house
 " and the white.
" The white house won. Yet still the
 " black doth brag,
" They had the power to put me in the
 " bag.
" Use but your royal hand, 'twill set me
 " free,
" 'Tis but removing of a man, that's me.
 "THOMAS MIDDLETON."

5. THE GAMESTER. Com. by James Shirley. Acted at Drury-Lane, 4to. 1637. This is very far from being a bad play. The plot of it is intricate, yet natural; the characters well drawn, and the catastrophe just and moral. It has been twice altered and brought on the stage under different titles; first by Charles Johnson, who took his play of the *Wife's Relief* almost entirely from it; and afterwards by Mr. Garrick, who brought it on at Drury-Lane by the name of the *Gamesters*. For the plot, see Q. *Margaret's Novels*, Day. 1. Nov. 8. and the *Unlucky Citizen*.

6. THE GAMESTER. Com. by Mrs. Centlivre. Acted at Lincoln's-Inn Fields, 4to. 1705. This is far from being the worst of this lady's pieces, although it is, like most of them, formed on models not her own, the plot of it being almost entirely borrowed from a French comedy, called *Le Dissipateur*. It met with good success, and was, within a few years, revived at Drury-Lane. The prologue was written by Mr. Rowe.

7. THE

7. THE GAMESTER. Trag. by Edward Moore. Acted at Drury-Lane, 8vo. 1753. This tragedy is written in prose, and is the most capital piece Mr. Moore produced. The language is nervous, and yet pathetic; the plot is artful, yet clearly conducted; the characters are highly marked, yet not unnatural; and the catastrophe is truly tragic, yet not unjust. Still with all these merits it met with but middling success, the general cry against it being that the distress was too deep to be borne; yet I am rather apt to imagine its want of perfect approbation arose in one part, and that no inconsiderable one, of the audience from a tenderness of another kind than that of compassion; and that they were less hurt by the distress of *Beverly*, than by finding their darling vice, their favourite folly, thus vehemently attacked by the strong lance of reason and dramatic execution. As the *Gil Blas* of this author had been forced upon the town several nights after the strongest public disapprobation of it had been expressed, it was thought by his friends that any piece acted under his name would be treated with vindictive severity. The Rev. Joseph Spence therefore permitted it, for the first four nights, to be imputed to him, but immediately afterwards threw aside the mask, as he supposed the success of the piece to be no longer doubtful; when, strange to tell! some of the very persons, who had applauded it as his work, were among the foremost to condemn it as the performance of Mr. Moore. Some part of this tragedy was originally composed in blank verse, of which several vestiges remain.

8. THE GAMESTERS. Com. by David Garrick, Esq. Acted at Drury-Lane, 8vo. 1758. This is the piece mentioned above, as an alteration of Shirley's *Gamester*. In this alteration the affair of the duel between the two friends, and the love scenes between them and their mistresses, are very judiciously omitted; yet I cannot help thinking that two very capital scenes, the one between *Volatile* and *Riot*, and the other between *Riot* and *Arabella*, which stand in the last act of the *Wife's Relief*, have too much both of nature and judgment not to injure the piece by the loss of them; and that therefore the alteration of this play would have done more justice to the original author, had they been suffered to remain in the same situation they before possessed.

9. GAMMER GURTON'S NEEDLE. Com. by Mr. S. master of arts, i. e. John Still, afterwards bishop of Bath and Wells, 4to. 1575. It is one of the oldest of our dramatic pieces, and affords an instance of the simplicity which must ever prevail in the early dawnings of genius. The plot of this play, which is written in metre, and spun out into five regular acts, being nothing more than Gammer Gurton's having mislaid the needle with which she was mending her man Hodge's breeches against the ensuing Sunday, and which, by way of catastrophe to the piece, is, after much search, great altercation, and some battles in its cause, at last found sticking in the breeches themselves. The original title of it runs thus: *A Ryght Pythy, Pleasant and merie Comedie: Intytuled Gammer Gurton's Nedle; played on the Stage not longe ago in Christe's Colledge in Cambridge, made by Mr. S. Master of Arts: Imprynted at London in Fleete Streeate beneth the Conduit, at the Signe of St. John Evangelist, by Thomas Colwell*. It is

is printed in the ancient black letter, but is republished in a more legible manner, yet still preserving the ancient way of spelling, in Dodsley's Collection of Old Plays.

It has sometimes happened that those who have been tempted to reprint specimens of the rude poetry of our early writers, have likewise persuaded themselves that these trifles were possessed of a further degree of merit than they may justly challenge as the records of fugitive customs, or the repositories of ancient language. I therefore seize this opportunity to disclaim all pretension to the like partialities in favour of Bishop Still's performance. Could I deceive myself so far in respect to that, or the pieces of Heywood, as to imagine they exhibit any traits of the *beautiful simplicity*, for which many an insipid ballad, like *Chevy Chase*, has been loudly celebrated, my wiser readers would detect my weakness, and punish it with the ridicule it deserved. When *Rowe*, in his Prologue to *Jane Shore*, without exception, declared that

These venerable ancient song-enditers •
Soar'd many a pitch above our modern
writers,

he certainly said what he neither believed himself, nor could wish any part of his audience or his readers to believe. Such literary falshoods deserve to be exposed as often as they are noted. If the reader expresses astonishment that a piece so indelicate as this our first regular Comedy, should have been thrice reprinted within the space of five and thirty years, how much more forcibly must his wonder have been excited, when he discovered it to have been the production of one who was educated for the church, and died in the sacred character of a bishop! The early example, however, of this reverend prelate may be fairly pleaded by all the numerous clergymen who in times more chastised have written for the stage.

10. GARRICK IN THE SHADES, or, *A Peep into Elysium*. Farce. Never offered to the managers of the Theatres Royal, 8vo. 1779. This seems to be the production of some disappointed author, whose resentment extended beyond the grave.

11. GARRICK'S VAGARY, or, *England run mad*; with particulars of the Stratford Jubilee, 8vo. 1769.

12. GASCONADO THE GREAT. A Tragi-comi-political-whimsical Opera, 4to. 1759. This piece was written by James Worsdale the painter, and is a burlesque on the affairs of the French nation during this war, the king of France and Madame de Pompadour being depicted under the characters of *Gasconado* and *Pampelin*. There is some humour in it, more especially in a few of the songs; but it was rejected by the managers of both theatres.

13. THE GENERAL CASHIER'D. A Play, 4to. 1712. This play was never acted, but is printed as designed for the stage, and is dedicated to prince Eugene of Savoy.

14. THE GENERAL LOVER. Com. by Theoph. Moss, 8vo. 1749. This comedy not only was not acted, but is perhaps the worst composition in the dramatic way that was ever attempted even without any view to the stage.

15. THE GENEROUS ARTIFICE, or, *The Reformed Rake*. C. translated from the French; printed in Foote's *Comic Theatre*, vol. III.

16. THE GENEROUS CHOICE. Com. by Francis Manning, 4to. 1703. This piece was acted at Little Lincoln's-Inn Fields. Scene, City of Valencia in Spain.

17. THE

17. THE GENEROUS CONQUEROR, or, *The Timely Discovery*. Trag. by Bevil Higgons. Acted at the Theatre Royal, 4to. 1702. The prologue was written by Lord Lansdown. Scene, Ravenna.

18. THE GENEROUS ENEMIES, or, *The Ridiculous Lovers*. Com. by J. Corye. Acted at the Theatre Royal, 4to. 1672. This play is one entire piece of plagiarism from the beginning to end; the principal design being borrowed from Quinault's *La genereuse Ingratitude*, that of the *Ridiculous Lovers* from Corneille's *Don Bertrans de Ciganal*. Bertram's telly humour to his servants, in the third act, is partly borrowed from Randolph's *Muses Looking-Glass*; and the quarrel between him and Kobatzi, in the fifth, taken wholly and verbatim from the *Love's Pilgrimage* of Beaumont and Fletcher. The scene lies in Seville. Yet, notwithstanding all these thefts, I cannot help thinking this play a good one, and that it might stand a tolerable chance of success, was it to be overlooked by some skilful person, and adapted to the present stage.

19. THE GENEROUS FREE MASON, or, *The Constant Lady*. With the Humours of Squire Noodle and his Man Doodle. A Tragi-comi-farcical Ballad Opera, of three acts, by William Rufus Chetwood, 8vo. 1731. The compiler of Whincop's Catalogue says, it was only performed at Bartholomew Fair.

20. THE GENEROUS HUSBAND, or, *Coffee-House Politician*. Com. by Charles Johnson, 4to. No date [1713]. Scene, London.

21. THE GENEROUS IMPOSTOR. Com. by —— Oburne. Acted at Drury-Lane, 8vo. 1781. This play is borrowed from *Le Dissipateur*; and was performed without the least success.

22. THE GENII. Pantomime Entertainment, by Henry Woodward. Acted at Drury-Lane, 1753.

23. THE GENIUS OF NONSENSE. Pantomime, Hay-Market, 1780. Of this original, whimsical, operatical, pantomimical, farcical, electrical, naval, military, temporary, local Extravaganza (for so it is styled in the bills), we might reverse the title, and call it *The Nonsense of Genius*. It is true, that we have beheld more splendid scenery, more surprizing changes, leaps, flyings, sinkings, &c. but were never so well entertained by any of these, as by the judicious mixture of humorous and grotesque circumstances that engage our attention throughout the present performance. As to the characters of the *Agreeable Companion in a Post-Chaise*, and the *Bottle-Conjuror* of the Adelphi, the one is happily imagined, and the other faithfully delineated. The catch sung by *Dame Turton, Goody Burton*, and *Gammer Gurton*, though not original, is here introduced on the stage, for the first time, with proper concomitants. The words of it indeed may be said to comprize the whole extent of an ancient gossip's conversation, viz. a string of questions, with an insipid remark at the end of them. It were injustice also on this occasion to omit the praise so justly due to Mr. Bannister's mimetic powers, which contributed not a little toward the success of the piece before us. There seems indeed to have been a contest between this young comedian and Mr. Rocker, which should excel in the art of imitation; for we cannot determine whether the *Emperor of the Quacks*, or the *Temple of Health*, more strongly resembles its original. We conceive an acquaintance with the copies, however, to

be

be the fafeft as well as cheapeft entertainment of the two. Mr. Rooker's camp-fcene, which concludes the piece, is perhaps as accurate and mafterly a fpectacle as ever appeared on the more extenfive theatres of Covent-Garden and Drury-Lane. An uncommon humour and fprightlinefs in the dialogues of this whimfical exhibition, induce us to place them among the other dramatic productions of Mr. Colman.

24. THE GENTLEMAN. Com. by Sir Richard Steele. This play was left unfinifhed at the author's death, and may probably be ftill in MS.

25. THE GENTLEMAN CIT. Com. tranflated from the French of Moliere; and printed in Foote's Comic Theatre, vol. V.

26. THE GENTLEMAN CIT. C. by Ozell. This is nothing more than a literal tranflation of Moliere's *Bourgeois Gentilhomme*.

27. THE GENTLEMAN CULLY. Com. Acted at the Theatre Royal, 4to. 1702. In all the catalogues I have feen, there is a play by the name of *The Generous Cully*, anonymous, and without a date, excepting in the *Britifh Theatre*, where it is placed in 1691. Coxeter, however, has erazed that title, placing in its room, as they fhould be, the name and date as above, and pofitively attributes it to Charles Johnfon.

28. THE GENTLEMAN DANCING-MASTER. Com. by W. Wycherley. Acted at the Duke's Theatre, 4to. 1673. This is one of the moft indifferent of all our author's pieces.

29. THE GENTLEMAN GARDINER. A Ballad Opera, by James Wilder. Acted at Smock-Alley, Dublin, 12mo. 1751. This is taken from Dancourt.

30. THE GENTLEMAN OF VE-

NICE. Tragi-Com, by James Shirley. Acted at Salifbury-Court, 4to. 1655. The plot of this play is taken from Gayton's notes on *Don Quixote*, book iv. ch. 6. and the fcene lies in Venice.

31. THE GENTLEMAN USHER. Com. by George Chapman, 4to. 1606. It is doubtful whether this play was ever acted. Langhaine gives it a very indifferent character, yet at the fame time owns that it was not without its partifans and admirers.

32. OF GENTYLNES AND NOBYLITE, *a Dialogue between the Merchaunt, the Knyght, and the Plowman, difputyng who is a verey Gentylman, and who is a Nobleman, and how Men fhould come to Auctoryte, compiled in Manner of an Enterlude, with divers Toys and geftis addyd thereto to make myri paftyme and difport.* This piece is written in metre, and printed in the black letter, by John Raftell, without date. By the fpelling and manner of ftyle, I fhould imagine it to be very ancient indeed.

33. THE GENTLE SHEPHERD. A Paftoral Com. 12mo. 1729. This truly poetical and paftoral piece is written in the Scots dialect, publifhed by the celebrated Allan Ramfay the Scots poet, and introduced to the world as his. There are not, however, wanting perfons who deny him the credit of being its author; but as envy will ever purfue merit, and as in upwards of half a century no other perfon has, and it is now moft probab'e never will lay claim to that honour, reafon I think will lead us to grant it to the only perfon who has been named for it. Be this fact, however, as it will, the excellence of the piece itfelf muft ever be acknowledged, and it may, without exaggeration, be allowed to ftand equal, if

K 4 not

not superior, to either of those two celebrated Pastorals, the *Aminta* of Tasso, and the *Pastor fido* of Guarini. It has been reduced into one act, and the Scotch dialect translated, with the addition of some new songs, by Theophilus Cibber, and was presented at Drury-Lane in 1731. The original Pastoral, as it was written, was also performed a few years ago by a company of Scots people, at the Little Theatre in the Hay-Market.

34. GEORGE A GREENE, THE PINDAR OF WAKEFIELD. Com. Anonym. 4to. 1599. The plot of this play (which is not divided into acts) is founded on history, and the scene lies at Wakefield in Yorkshire. This *George a Greene* was a man of great and ancient renown; there is a peculiar history of his life, written by one N. W. 8vo. 1706, and he is mentioned in *Hudibras*, Part 2. Cant. 2. Line 305. This comedy is to be met with in Dodsley's Collection of Old Plays.

35. GEORGE DANDIN, or, *The Wanton Wife*. Com. by Ozell. A translation from Moliere's *George Dandin*.

36. GEORGE SCANDERBAGE, the true History of, as it was lately played by the Right Hon. the Earle of Oxenforde his servants. This play was entered by Edward Alde on the books of the Stationers' Company, July 3, 1601, but I believe not printed.

37. GERMANICUS. Trag. by a gentleman of the University of Oxford, 8vo. 1775.

38. THE GHOST, or, *The Woman wears the Breeches*. Com. Anon. written in 1640, printed, 4to. 1653. Scene, Paris.

39. THE GHOST OF MOLIERE. This is only the translation of a little piece of 14 scenes, called, *L'Ombre de Moliere*, written by M. Brecourt, a friend of that poet's, after his death, and which is printed in all the editions of Moliere's works. The scene lies in the Elysian Fields.

40. THE GHOST. Com. Acted at Smock-Alley, Dublin, 8vo. 1767. This is taken from Mrs. Centlivre's play of *The Man's bewitched*, or, *The Devil to do about her*. It hath since been acted at Drury-Lane.

41. THE GHOSTS. Com. by Mr. Holden. Acted at the Duke's Theatre between 1662 and 1665. Not printed. See Downes's *Roscius Anglicanus*, p. 26.

42. GIBRALTAR, or, *The Spanish Adventure*. C. by J. Dennis, 4to. 1705. Performed at the Theatre Royal in Drury-Lane, but without success. The first day it being well acted in most of its parts, but not suffered to be heard; the second day for the most part faintly and negligently acted, and consequently not seen. The scene lies at a village in the neighbourhood of Gibraltar.

43. GIL BLAS. C. by Edward Moore. Acted at Drury-Lane, 8vo. 1751. This is by much the least meritorious of the three dramatic pieces of our author, and indeed, notwithstanding its being very strongly supported in the acting, met with the least success. The design is taken from the story of *Aurora*, in the novel of *Gil Blas*, but bears too near a resemblance to the plot of the *Kind Imposter*; and the author has deviated greatly from truth in the manners of his characters, having introduced a Spanish gentleman drunk on the stage, which is so far from being a characteristic of that nation, that it is well known they had formerly a law subsisting among them, though now, perhaps, out of

of force, which decreed that if a gentleman was convicted of even a capital offence, he should be pardoned on pleading his having been intoxicated at the time he committed it, it being supposed that any one who bore the character of gentility would more readily suffer death, than confess himself capable of so beastly a vice as drunkenness.

44. THE GIPSIES. Com. Op. by Charles Dibden. Acted at the Hay-Market, 8vo. 1778. This is a translation of *La Bohemienne*, by Favart.

45. GIRALDO THE CONSTANT LOVER. By Henry Shirley. This play was entered on the books of the Stationers' Company Sept. 9, 1653; but probably was not printed.

46. GIVE A MAN LUCK, AND THROW HIM INTO THE SEA. A Play, with this title was entered on the books of the Stationers' Company, with *The Maid's Metamorphoses*, July 24, 1600. It does not appear to have been printed, but was probably a performance of John Lyly's.

47. THE GLASS OF GOVERNMENT. Tragi-Com. by George Gascoigne, 4to. 1575. This play is thus intituled, because therein are handled as well the rewards for virtues as the punishments for vices. The scene lies at Antwerp.

48. GLORIANA, or, *The Court of Augustus Cæsar*, by N. Lee, Acted at the Theatre Royal, 4to. 1676. This is one of the wildest and most indifferent of all our author's pieces, being made up of little else but bombast and absurdity. The plot is more founded on romance than history, as may be readily discovered by comparing it with the first, fifth, and seventh parts of the celebrated romance of *Cleopatra*, under the characters of *Cæsario*, *Marcellus*, and *Julia*. Scene lies in the palace of Augustus Cæsar at Rome.

49. THE GLOUCESTERSHIRE SQUIRE. This is the same play as *The Country Squire* already mentioned, with only an alteration in the title.

50. THE GOBLINS. Tragi-Com. by Sir John Suckling. Acted at Black-Friers, 8vo. 1646. The scene of this play lies in Francelia, and the author, in the execution of his design, has pretty closely followed the footsteps of Shakspeare, of whom he was a professed admirer, his *Reginella* being an open imitation of *Miranda* in the *Tempest*, and his *Goblins*, though counterfeits, being only thieves in disguise, yet seem to be copied from *Ariel* in the same play.

51. GOD HYS PROMISES. A Tragedie or Interlude, *manyfestynge the chyefe* PROMISES *of God unto Man in all Ages, from the Begynnynge of the Worlde, to the Deathe of* JESUS CHRISTE, *a Mysterie* 1538. The Interlocutors are *Pater cælestis, Justus Noah, Moses sanctus, Esaias propheta, Adam primus Homo, Abraham fidelis, David Rex pius, Joannes Baptista*. This play was written by Bishop Bale, and is one of the first dramatic pieces printed in England. It is reprinted by Dodsley in his Collection.

52. GODFREY OF BULLOIGNE, WITH THE CONQUEST OF JERUSALEM. An Interlude; entered on the books of the Stationers' Company, by John Danter, June 19, 1594; but I believe not printed.

53. GODDWYN. Tr. by Thomas Rowleie, 8vo. 1777. This is one of the pieces supposed to be written by Thomas Chatterton.

54. THE GOLDEN AGE, or, *The Lives of Jupiter and Saturn*. An Historical Play, by Thomas Heywood. Acted at the Red Bull, 4to.

4to. 1611. This piece the author himself calls the Eldest Brother of three ages that had adventured on the stage, in all of which he has introduced Homer as the expositor of each dumb shew, in the same manner as Shakspeare has done by Gower, in his PERICLES *Prince of Tyre*. For the story, we need only consult Galtruchius, and other of the heathen mythologists.

55. THE GOLDEN AGE RE-STOR'D, in a Masque at Court, 1615, by the lords and gentlemen the King's servants, by Ben Jonson. This piece was not printed till 1641. Fol.

56. THE GOLDEN PIPPIN. Burletta, by Kane O'hara. Acted at Covent-Garden, 8vo. 1773. It was first produced in three acts, as *Midas* had been before, but like that performance was not very successful in its original state. It was then reduced to an afterpiece, and was received with universal approbation.

57. THE GOLDEN RUMP. This piece was never acted, never appeared in print, nor was it ever known who was the author of it. Yet I cannot avoid mentioning it here, as it was the real occasion of a very remarkable event in dramatic history, viz. the act whereby all dramatic pieces are obliged to undergo the inspection and censure of the Lord Chamberlain, before they can be admitted to a representation. The fact was as follows: During the administration of a certain *Premier Ministre*, the late Mr. Fielding, whose genuine wit and turn for satire were too considerable to need our expatiating on in this place, had in two or three of his comedies, particularly those of Pasquin and the *Historical Register*, thrown in some strokes which were too poignantly levelled at certain measures then pursuing by those at the head of affairs, not to be severely felt, and their consequences, if not speedily put a check to, greatly dreaded by the minister. Open violence, however, was not the most eligible method to proceed in for this purpose. Not a *Restraint of Liberty* already *made Use of*, but a *Prevention* of *Licentiousness* to *come*, was the proper weapon to employ in such a case. A piece, therefore, *written by somebody or other*, was offered to Mr. Henry Giffard, the manager of Goodman's Fields Theatre, for representation. This piece was entitled the *Golden Rump*. In which, with a most unbounded freedom, abuse was vented not only against the parliament, the council, and ministry, but even against the person of majesty itself. The honest manager, free from design himself, suspected none in others, but imagining that a licence of this kind, it permitted to run to such enormous lengths, must be of the most pernicious consequences, quickly fell into the snare, and carried the piece to the minister, with a view of consulting him as to his manner of proceeding. The latter, commending highly his integrity in this step, requested only the possession of the MS. but, at the same time, that the manager might be no loser by his zeal for the interests of his king and country, ordered a gratuity, equal to what he might reasonably have expected from the profits of its representation, to be paid to him. Being now become master of the piece itself, together with the corroborating circumstance of the necessity of employing the public money to prevent even absolute treason from appearing on the open stage, unless some authority of another kind could be found for

stopping

G O

stopping her mouth, he made such use of it, as immediately occasioned the bringing into, and passing in parliament, the above-mentioned bill.

58. GONDIBERT AND BERTHA. Trag. by W. Thompson, M. A. 8vo. 1758. This piece was never acted, nor I believe intended for the stage, but is published in a volume with some poems of the same author. The subject from Davenant's *Gondibert*.

59. THE GOOD ENGLISHMAN. Ballad Opera, of two acts, by William Shirley. A piece not acted or printed.

60. THE GOODNATURED MAN. Com. by Oliver Goldsmith. Acted at Covent-Garden, 8vo. 1768. Many parts of this play exhibit the strongest indications of our author's comic talents. There is perhaps no character on the stage more happily imagined and more highly finished than *Croaker's*; nor do we recollect so original and succesful an incident as that of the letter which he conceives to be the composition of an incendiary, and feels a thousand ridiculous horrors in consequence of his absurd apprehension. Our audiences, however, having been recently exalted on the sentimental stilts of *False Delicacy*, a comedy by *Kelly*, regarded a few scenes in Dr. *Goldsmith's* piece as too low for their entertainment, and therefore treated them with unjustifiable severity. Nevertheless the *Good-natur'd Man* succeeded, though in a degree inferior to its merit. The prologue to it, which is an excellent one, was written by Dr. *Samuel Johnson*.

61. GORBODUC. Trag. by T. Norton and Thomas Sackville, Lord Buckhurst, B. L. 4to. 1590. Reprinted with a preface by Mr. Spence, 8vo. 1735. These are

[139]

G O

only republications of an imperfect copy of FERREX AND PORREX.

62. THE GORDIAN KNOT UNTY'D. Com. 1691. This is not printed, but appears to have been acted in the before-mentioned year. Motteaux in the *Gentleman's Journal*, January 1691-2, says, "You have often asked me who "was the author of *The Gordian* "*Knot Unty'd*; and wondered with "many more why it was never "printed. I hear that gentleman, "who writ lately a most ingenious "dialogue concerning women, "now translated into French, is "the author of that witty play, "and it is almost a sin in him to "keep it and his name from the "world."

63. THE GOSPEL SHOP. Com. of five acts, with a new Prologue and Epilogue, by R. Hill, Esq; of Cambridge, 8vo. 1778. This is a satire on the Methodists. The author's name probably a fictitious one.

64. GOTHAM ELECTION. F. of one long act, by Mrs. Centlivre, 12mo. 1715. In this piece the fair author has shewn great knowledge of mankind, and of the different occurrences of life. It was never acted, being looked on as a party affair, but was printed, with a dedication to Secretary Craggs, of whom it is recorded, greatly to his honour on this occasion, that being complimented on his liberality by Mrs. Bracegirdle, to whom he gave twenty guineas for the author, and told that his generosity appeared the more extraordinary as the Farce had not been acted, he replied, that he did not so much consider the merit of the piece, as what was becoming a secretary of state to do.

65. THE GOVERNOR. Trag. by Sir Cornelius Formido. This
play

play was among those destroyed by Mr. Warburton's servant. It was entered on the books of the Stationers' Company, Sept. 9. 1653.

66. THE GOVERNOR OF CYPRUS. Trag. by J. Oldmixon, 4to. 1703. Acted at the Theatre in Lincoln's-Inn Fields. Scene, the governor's palace in Cyprus near the sea.

67. GOWRY. Trag. 1604. N. P. The mention of this play I find in the following extract of a letter from Mr. Chamberlaine to Mr. Winwood, dated Dec. 18, 1604. "The tragedy of *Gowry*, "with all action and actors hath "been twice represented by the "King's players, with exceeding "concourse of all sorts of people; "but whether the matter or manner be not well handled, or that "it be thought unfit that princes "should be played on the stage in "their lifetime, I hear that some "great councellors are much displeased with it, and so tis "thought it shall be forbidden."

68. THE GRATEFUL FAIR. Com. by Christopher Smart. Acted at Pembroke-College, Cambridge. Not printed.

69. THE GRATEFUL SERVANT. Com. by James Shirley. Acted at the private house Drury-Lane, 4to. 1630. 4to. 1660. This play met with very great applause when acted, and came forth ushered by eight copies of verses in English, and two in Latin, which the author says were "the free vote of his friends, which he could not in civility refuse," and indeed he must have very little of the poetical warmth about him, if he could be desirous so to do. *Lodowick's* contrivance to have his wife *Artella* tempted by *Piero*, in order that he may procure an opportunity of divorcing her, is the same with *Contarini's* humour and contrivance in *The Humorous Courtier*. Scene, Savoy.

70. THE GREAT DUKE OF FLORENCE. A Comical History, by P. Massinger. Acted at the Phœnix Drury-Lane, 4to. 1636. This play met with very good success, and is recommended, in two copies of verses, by George Donne and John Ford. *Sanasarro's* giving the duke a false account of the beauty of *Lidia*, seems to be a near resemblance to the story of *Edgar* and *Elfrida*.

71. THE GREAT FAVORITE, or, *The Duke of Lerma*. Trag. by Sir Robert Howard. Acted at the Theatre Royal, 4to. 1668. Some scenes of this play are written in blank verse, and some in rhyme; the scene lies at Madrid; and the plot is taken from Mariana, Turquet de Mayern, and other historians of those times.

72. THE GREAT MAN. A play of the last century, among those destroyed by Mr. Warburton's servant.

73. THE GRECIAN DAUGHTER. Trag. by Arthur Murphey, Esq. Acted at Drury-Lane, 8vo. 1772. In a postscript to this play, the author says, "he does not "wish to conceal that the subject "of his tragedy has been touched "in some foreign pieces; but he "thinks it has been only touched. "The *Zelmire* of Monsieur Belloy "begins after the daughter has "delivered her father out of prison. The play, indeed, has "many beauties; and if the sentiments and business of that piece "coincided with the design of "*The Grecian Daughter*, the author would not have blushed to "tread in his steps. But a new "fable was absolutely necessary, "and perhaps, in the present humour of the times, it is not un- "lucky

"lucky that no more than three
"lines could be adopted from
"Monsieur Belloy." It met with
very great success, and was excellently performed in the principal
characters, by Mr. and Mrs. Barry,
now Crawford.

74. THE GRECIAN HEROINE,
or, *The Fate of Tyranny*. A Trag.
by T. Durfey. This piece was
never acted, but was published
with a collection of poems, in
1721. The title-page says it was
written in 1718; but the preface
mentions it as a production of
many years earlier; the characters of *Timoleon* and *Belizaria* being intended for Mr. Betterton
and Mrs. Barry.

75. THE GRENADIER. Interlude. Acted at Sadlers-Wells, 8vo.
1773.

76. GREEN'S TU QUOQUE, or,
The City Gallant. Com. by John
Cooke, 4to. No date, 4to. 1614.
We are told by Heywood, who was
the editor of this play, that it
passed the test of the stage with
general applause. It was at first
performed by the latter title only;
but the inimitable acting of Green,
a celebrated comedian of that time,
in the part of *Bubble* the *City Gallant*, who, in answer to every compliment, comes out with the words
Tu quoque, occasioned the author,
out of regard to him, to add to
it the present first title. Both editions of it had a figure of Green
in the title-page, with a label out
of his mouth, *Tu quoque, to you,
Sir!* The piece itself is republished among Dodsley's Old Plays.

77. GREENWICH PARK. Com.
by W. Mountfort, 4to. 1691.
This is a tolerable comedy, and
met with very good success. It
was acted at Drury-Lane.

78. GRIM THE COLLIER OF
CROYDON, or, *The Devil and his
Dame, with the Devil and St.*

Dunstan. Com. by J. T. 12mo.
1662. The plot of this play is
founded on Machiavel's Novel of
The Marriage of Belphegor. The
scene lies in England.

79. GRIPUS AND HEGIO, or,
The Passionate Lovers. Pastoral,
by Robert Baron, 8vo. 1647. This
play consists of no more than three
acts, and is mostly borrowed from
Waller's Poems, and Webster's
Duchess of Malfy. This, however,
may well be excused, when the
reader is informed that the whole
Romance, in which are this and
the *Deorum Dona*, was composed when the author was no
more than seventeen years of
age.

80. THE GROVE, or, *Love's Paradise*. An Opera, by J. Oldmixon,
4to. 1703, performed at Drury-Lane. The author, in his preface, acquaints the critics that this
play is neither translation nor paraphrase; that the story is entirely
new, and that it was at first intended for a pastoral, though in
the three last acts the dignity of the
characters raised it into the form
of a tragedy. The scene is a province of Italy, near the gulph of
Venice.

81. THE GRUBSTREET OPERA.
by H. Fielding. 1731. 8vo. Acted
at the Little Theatre in the Hay-Market. To this is added, *The
Masquerade*. A Poem. Printed in
1728.

82. THE GRUMBLER. Com. of
three acts, by Sir Charles Sedley.
12mo. 1719.

83. THE GRUMBLER. Farce,
altered from Sedley, by Dr. Goldsmith. Acted at Covent-Garden,
1772; not printed. This alteration was made to serve Mr. Quick
at his benefit, and acted only on
that night.

84. THE GUARDIAN. Comical
History, by P. Massinger, 8vo.
1655.

1655. The incident of Severino's cutting off Calipso's nose in the dark, and taking her for his wife Jolante, is borrowed from Boccace's Novels, Day. 8. Nov. 7. and from a romance, called *The Roman Matron*. Scene lies in Naples.

85. THE GUARDIAN. Com. by A. Cowley. Acted before Prince Charles at Trinity College, Cambridge, the 12th of March, 1641. 1650. 4to. See CUTTER OF COLEMAN STREET.

86. THE GUARDIAN. Com. of two acts, by David Garrick, Esq. Acted at Drury-Lane, 8vo. 1759. This little piece is taken in great measure from the celebrated *Pupille* of M. Fagan. It is a pleasing and elegant performance, the language easy and sentimental, the plot simple and natural, and the characters well supported.

87. THE GUARDIAN OUTWITTED. Comic Opera, by Dr. Thomas Augustine Arne. Acted at Covent-Garden, 8vo. 1764. It was acted only six nights, being a very contemptible performance.

88. GUSTAVUS VASA, or, *The Deliverer of his Country*. Trag. by H. Brooke, 8vo. 1739. This play has great merit, yet was prohibited to be played, even after it had been in rehearsal at Drury-Lane, and the performers were perfect, on account of some strokes of liberty which breathe through several parts of it. The author, however, was not injured by the prohibition, for on publishing the book by subscription, Mr. Victor says he was certain Mr. B. cleared above 1000 *l*. It was, however, acted with some alterations on the Irish stage, by the title of *The Patriot*.

89. GUSTAVUS KING OF SWETHLAND. by Thomas Dekker, Not printed, but entered on the books of the Stationers' Company, June 29, 1660.

90. GUY EARL OF WARWICK. A tragical History, by B. J. 4to. 1661. The plot of this piece is founded on history, and it has been attributed to Ben Jonson; but I am apt to believe it only a conjecture formed from the letters prefixed to it, the execution of the work being greatly inferior to those of that first rate genius.

In the books of the Stationers' Company, I find that John Trundle, on the 15th of January, 1619, entered " A Play, called the Life " and Death of Guy of Warwicke, " written by John Day and Thomas " Dekker." Probably this may be the same piece.

91. GUZMAN. Com. by Roger, Earl of Orrery, Fol. 1693. The scene of this play lies in Spain, and the plot is from a romance of the same name. It was acted at the Duke of York's Theatre many years before the time of its publication.

H.

HA

1. THE HALFPAY OFFICERS. Farce, of three acts, by Charles Molloy. Acted at the Theatre in Lincoln's-Inn Fields, 12mo. 1720. The basis of this play is founded on Sir W. Davenant's

nant's *Love and Honour*, and some other old plays.

2. HAMLET PRINCE OF DENMARK. Trag. by W. Shakspeare, 4to. 1604. 4to. 1605. 4to. 1611. 4to. N. D. 4to. 1637. Dr. Johnson observes, that if "the "dramas of Shakspeare were to "be characterised, each by the "particular excellence which dis- "tinguishes it from the rest, we "must allow to the tragedy of "Hamlet the praise of variety. "The incidents are so numerous, "that the argument of the play "would make a long tale. The "scenes are interchangeably di- "versified with merriment and so- "lemnity; with merriment that "includes judicious and instruc- "tive observations; and solem- "nity, not strained by poetical "violence above the natural sen- "timents of man. New charac- "ters appear from time to time "in continual succession, exhi- "biting various forms of life and "particular modes of conversation. "The pretended madness of Ham- "let causes much mirth; the "mournful distraction of Ophelia "fills the heart with tenderness; "and every personage produces "the effect intended, from the "apparition that in the first act "chills the blood with horror, to "the fop in the last that exposes "affectation to just contempt.

"The conduct is perhaps not "wholly secure against objections. "The action is induced for the "most part in continual progres- "sion; but there are some scenes "which neither forward nor re- "tard it. Of the feigned mad- "ness of Hamlet there appears no "adequate cause, for he does no- "thing which he might not have "done with the reputation of "sanity. He plays the madman "most when he treats Ophelia "with so much rudeness, which "seems to be useless and wanton "cruelty.

"Hamlet is, through the whole "piece, rather an instrument than "an agent. After he has, by the "stratagem of the play, convicted "the king, he makes no attempt "to punish him; and his death is "as last effected by an incident "which Hamlet had no part in "producing.

"The catastrophe is not very "happily produced; the exchange "of weapons is rather an expe- "dient of necessity, than a stroke "of art. A scheme might easily "be formed to kill Hamlet with "the dagger, and Laertes with "the bowl.

"The poet is accused of having "shewn little regard to poetical "justice, and may be charged with "equal neglect of poetical pro- "bability. The apparition left "the regions of the dead to little "purpose; the revenge which he "demands is not obtained but by "the death of him that was re- "quired to take it; and the gra- "tification, which would arise "from the destruction of an usur- "per and a murderer, is abated "by the untimely death of Ophe- "lia, the young, the beauti- "ful, the harmless, the pious." It is recorded of the author, that although his knowledge and observation of nature rendered him the most accurate painter of the sensations of the human mind in his writings, yet so different are the talents requisite for acting from those required for dramatic writing, that the part of the Ghost in this play (no very considerable character) was almost the only one, in which he was able to make any figure as a performer. Scene, Elsinoor.

3. HAMLET, altered by Mr. Garrick.

HA

Garrick. Acted at Drury-Lane, 1771. This alteration is made in the true spirit of *Bottom the Weaver*, who wishes to play not only the part assigned him, but all the rest in the piece. Mr. Garrick, in short, has reduced the consequence of every character but that represented by himself; and thus excluding Ofric, the Grave-diggers, &c. contrived to monopolize the attention of the audience. Our poet had furnished Laertes with a dying address, which afforded him a local advantage over the Prince of Denmark. This circumstance was no sooner observed, than the speech was taken away from the former, and adopted by the latter. Since the death of the player, the public indeed has vindicated the rights of the poet, by starving the theatres into compliance with their wishes to see Hamlet as originally meant for exhibition. Mr. Garrick had once designed to publish the changes he had made in it, and (as was usual with him in the course of similar transactions) had accepted a compliment from the booksellers, consisting of a set of Olivet's edition of Tully; but, on second thoughts, with a laudable regard to his future credit, he returned the acknowledgment, and suppressed the alteration. In short, no bribe but his own inimitable performance, could have prevailed on an English audience to sit patiently, and behold the martyrdom of their favourite author.

4. HAMPSTEAD HEATH. Com. by Thomas Baker. Acted at Drury-Lane, 4to. 1706. This play is little more than an alteration of the *Act at Oxford*, written by the same author. The scene lies at Hampstead.

5. HANGING AND MARRIAGE, or, *The Dead Man's Wedding*. F.

HA

by Henry Carey, 1713. This piece of Mr. Carey's is of a date earlier than any of his other Farces, and therefore probably might be a first and unsuccessful attempt in the dramatic way. I imagine it never was acted.

6. HANNIBAL AND SCIPIO. Historical Trag. by Tho. Nabbes. Acted in 1635, at Drury-Lane, 4to. 1637. This play was acted before women appeared upon the stage. The part of *Sophonisba* being performed by one Ezekiel Fenne. It is addressed, in verses by the author, to the ghosts of *Hannibal* and *Scipio*, with an answer in their names directed to him. The plot is founded on History, and may be traced in Cornelius Nepos and Plutarch; but the unity of place is most excessively broken in upon, the scene of the first act lying in Capua, of the second at the court of Syphax, of the third at Utica, of the fourth at Carthage, and of the fifth in Bythinia.

7. HANS BEER POT, his invisible comedy of *See me, and see me not*, 4to. 1618. This piece is, according to the author's own account of it, neither comedy nor tragedy, as wanting first the just number of speakers, and secondly those parts or acts it should have, which ought to be at the least five, but is a plain conference of so many persons, consisting of three acts and no more. It is said to have been acted by an honest company of health-drinkers. Phillips and Winstanley have attributed the piece to Thomas Nash; but Langbaine, whose judgment all the writers since have followed in this particular, gives it to *Dawbridge-Court Belchier*.

8. THE HAPPY CAPTIVE: An English Opera, by Lewis Theobald, 8vo. 1741. The plot of this piece

piece is taken from a Novel, entitled, *The History of a Slave*, which is to be met with in *Don Quixote*, Part I. Book IV. The author has introduced into it an Interlude in two comic scenes between Sign. Capoccio, a director from the Canary Isles, and Sign. Dorinna, a virtuoso, intended as a ridicule on the Italian Operas.

9. THE HAPPY LOVERS; or, *The Beau Metamorphosed.* An Opera, by Henry Ward. Acted at Lincoln's-Inn Fields, 8vo. 1736. Printed also with other pieces, 8vo. 1746.

10. THE HAPPY MARRIAGE, or, *The Turn of Fortune.* Acted at Lincoln's-Inn Fields. Written by a young gentleman, 12mo. 1727.

11. HARLEQUIN DOCTOR FAUSTUS, with the Masque of the Deities. Composed by John Thurmond, dancing-master, 8vo. 1724. This seems to have been acted at Drury-Lane.

12. HARLEQUIN FREEMASON. A splendid and successful Pantomime. Acted at Covent-Garden, 1781. The contriver of it is said to be Mr. Messink.

13. HARLEQUIN'S FROLICKS. A Pantomime, performed at Covent-Garden, 1776.

14. HARLEQUIN HYDASPES, or, *The Greshamite*. A Mock Opera. Acted at Lincoln's-Inn Fields, 8vo. 1719.

15. HARLEQUIN'S JACKET. A Pantomime, performed at Drury-Lane, 1775.

16. HARLEQUIN INCENDIARY, or *Columbine Cameron*. A Musical Pantomime. Anon. 8vo. 1746. This piece was performed at the Theatre Royal in Drury-Lane, the season after the quelling of the Rebellion in Scotland. The music was composed by Dr. Arne, but it does not appear who was the contriver of the Pantomime,

in which, as usual, *Harlequin* is the favoured lover of *Columbine*, who seems by no means to be distinguished as *Jenny Cameron*, but by some part of the scene being laid in the Highlands of Scotland, and the defeat of the rebel army, which has really no connection with the rest of the piece, though it forms the catastrophe of the whole.

17. HARLEQUIN'S INVASION. A Christmas Gambol, 1759. This Pantomime is still often performed at Drury-Lane. The plan of it is a supposed invasion made by *Harlequin* and his train upon the frontiers and domain of Shakspeare. The characters are made to speak, and the catastrophe is the defeat of *Harlequin*, and the restoration of *King Shakspeare*. Of Harlequin's Invasion, all the dialogue, &c. was furnished by Mr. Garrick, who originally wrote some part of it to serve the interest of a favourite performer at Bartholomew Fair, where it passed under a title rendered designedly long and ostentatious, concluding thus— *The Taylor without a Head,* or *The Battle of the Golden Bridge*.

18. HARLEQUIN'S JUBILEE. A Pantomime, performed at Covent-Garden, 1770. This Pantomime was contrived by Mr. Woodward, and was intended to ridicule *The Jubilee*, acted the preceding season at Drury-Lane. It had, however, little effect.

19. HARLEQUIN MULTIPLIED. A piece of this title I find in Mr. Bathoe's Catalogue, but know not either its date or design, not having been able to come at the sight of it. I imagine it however to have been a Pantomime, and consequently of the produce of these last fifty or sixty years.

20. HARLEQUIN PREMIER. Farce, as it is daily acted, 8vo. 1769

1769. This is a political piece.

21. HARLEQUIN RANGER. Pantomime, by Henry Woodward, performed at Drury-Lane, 1752.

22. HARLEQUIN SHEPPARD. A Night Scene in grotesque characters, by John Thurmond. Acted at Drury-Lane, 8vo. 1724. It is built on the exploits of a notorious house-breaker at that period, who twice made his escape from Newgate. The managers Wilks, Booth, and Cibber, were ridiculed as the contrivers of this piece, by Hogarth in one of his earliest performances. They are represented in the act of forming a Pantomime. One of these personages is employed in drawing up the figure of *Jack Shepherd* out of the aperture in a soricus; and an engraved direction gives us to understand, that when the projected piece was exhibited on the stage, the substance with which this hero was to be covered, would be composed of chewed gingerbread.

23. HARLEQUIN SORCERER, *with the Loves of Pluto and Proserpine.* Pantom. Acted at Lincoln's-Inn Fields, 8vo. 1725. This piece contains a great deal of very fine machinery, and brought crowded houses to the manager of Covent-Garden Theatre for several seasons after its revival in 1753.

24. HARLEQUIN STUDENT, or, *The Fall of Pantomime, with the Restoration of the Drama.* Entertainment. Acted at Goodman's Fields. The music by Mr. Prelleur, 8vo. 1741.

25. HARLEQUIN'S TRIUMPH. A Pantomime, by John Thurmond, 8vo. 1727.

26. THE HARLOT'S PROGRESS, or, *The Ridotto al Fresco.* A Grotesque Pantomime Entertainment, by Theophilus Cibber, performed at Drury-Lane, 4to. 1733.

27. THE HASTY WEDDING, or, *The Intriguing Squire.* Com. by Cha. Shadwell. Scene, Dublin. Time, eight hours, 12mo. 1720.

28. HAVE AT ALL, or, *The Midnight Adventures.* Com. by Joseph Williams. Acted at Drury-Lane in May, 1694. This piece is mentioned in Motteux's *Gentleman's Journal*, but was never printed.

29. HEARTS OF OAK. An Interlude, 1762. This is indeed nothing more than a song and a dance of sailors, the former of which was written by Mr. G. A. Stevens, and, being a mere temporary affair on the declaration of war with Spain, met with good success.

30. HEAUTONTIMORUMENOS. Com. by Terence, translated by Rich. Bernard, 4to. 1598.

31. HEAUTONTIMOROUMENOS. Com. Translated from Terence, by Laurence Echard, 8vo. 1694.

32. HEAUTONTIMOROUMENOS. Com. Translated by T. Cook, 12mo. 1734.

33. HEAUTONTIMOROUMENOS. Com. Translated by S. Patrick, 8vo. 1745.

34. HEAUTONTIMOROUMENOS. Com. Translated by Mr. Gordon, 12mo. 1752.

35. HEAUTONTIMOROUMENOS. Com. Translated by G. Colman, 4to. 1765.

36. HEAUTONTIMOROUMENOS. The Prologue, Interludes, and Epilogue, to this play, as acted at Beverly-school, Christmas, 1756. Fol. 1757. These were written by William Warde the matter.

37. THE HEATHEN MARTYR, or, *The Death of Socrates.* Hist. Trag. In which is shewn that the plague which infested the people of Athens was stayed by the destruction

destruction of the enemies of that divine Philosopher. By George Adams, 4to. 1746.

38. HECATE's PROPHECY. A Drama, printed at the end of "Brief Remarks on the Original and Present State of the Drama, 8vo. 1758." This is a severe satire on Mr. Garrick, and is supposed to be the production of William Shirley.

39. HECTOR. Dramatic Poem, by Richard Shepherd, 4to. 1770.

40. THE HECTORS. Trag. by Edmund Prestwich, 1656. A tragedy of this title is attributed to our author by Phillips and Winstanley; and their authority is followed by Jacob and the author of the *British Theatre*, yet contradicted both by Langbaine and Coxeter, the latter of whom refers the play to the anonymous one, called *The Hectors*, or *The False Challenge*. But as the author of the *British Theatre* has given it the above date (though without any authority), which is five years earlier than the publication of that play, I cannot think myself entitled to omit the mention of it here.

41. THE HECTORS, or, *The False Challenge*. Com. Anonym. 4to. 1656. Langbaine gives this play a very good character. Scene, London.

42. THE HECTOR OF GERMANIE, or, *The Palsgrave prime Elector*. An Honourable History, by Wm. Smith, 4to. 1615. This play is not divided into acts.

43. HECUBA. Trag. by Rich. West, Esq; lord chancellor of Ireland. Acted at Drury-Lane, 4to. 1726. This is a translation from Euripides, and met with no success in the representation. The author in his preface says, "I attempted unsuccessfully, and am not the first martyr to truth.

"I shall offer but one reason more, and I presume it will be allowed a very solid one, why this tragedy did not succeed; and that is, *It was not heard*. A rout of Vandals in the galleries intimidated the young actresses, disturbed the audience, and prevented all attention. And I believe, if the verses had been repeated in the original Greek, they would have been understood and received in the same manner." This play is attributed to the present author, on the authority of *Whincop*.

44. HECUBA. Trag. translated from the Greek of *Euripides*, with annotations chiefly relating to antiquity, by Dr. Thomas Morell, 8vo. 1749.

45. HECUBA. Trag. by Dr. Delap. Acted at Drury-Lane, 8vo. 1762. but met with very indifferent success, its run continuing only long enough to afford the author one single benefit. It is not wholly devoid of merit. The language is poetical and affecting, the characters not drawn greatly amiss, and the distresses of *Hecuba* in some parts properly heightened, and pathetically supported. Yet in abatement of these merits, there is a deficiency of incident, and an indulgence of declamation, which wearies the spirits of an auditor at the same time that his heart remains almost totally uninterested. These faults are besides rendered perhaps still more open to the discernment of the audience, by the author's having divided his play differently from the usual and established method. For though the piece is in reality as long as our modern tragedies at least are accustomed to be, it consists of no more than three acts, which being in consequence so much longer respectively than usual,

sets the tediousness of the declamation and the want of invention in the plot in a more glaring light than they would otherwise perhaps have been viewed in; and therefore, although I am ready to allow the author all the merit he can be imagined to possess, and wish him better success in some future attempt, wherein he may avoid the rocks he struck upon before, yet I cannot blame the public for their judgment, or avoid joining in the opinion, that the piece met with as much approbation as it had any right to claim.

46. HECYRA. Com. This is another of Terence's comedies; for the several translations of which see *Heautontimorumenos*.

47. THE HEIR. C. by Thomas May. Acted by the company of Revels, 1620. second impression, 4to. 1633. The plot, language, and conduct of this play are all admirable; it met with great applause, and is highly commended in a copy of verses by Mr. Carew. It is to be found in Dodsley's Collection. Scene, Syracuse.

48. THE HEIR OF MOROCCO, *with the Death of Gayland*. Trag. by Elk. Settle. Acted at the Theatre Royal, 4to. 1682. Scene, Algiers.

49. THE HEIRESS, or, *The Antigallican*. Farce, by Thomas Mozeen. Acted at Drury-Lane, for the author's benefit, a few years before its appearance in print, which was in " A Collection of " Miscellaneous Essays," 8vo. 1762.

50. HELL'S HIGHER COURT OF JUSTICE, or, *The Tryal of the three Politic Ghosts*, (viz. Oliver Cromwell, the King of Sweden, and Cardinal Mazarine.) 4to. 1661. This play was never acted, it being entirely political.

51. *The Life and Death of* HELIOGABALUS. Interlude; entered by John Danter, June 19, 1594, on the books of the Stationers' Company; but I believe not printed.

52. THE HENPECK'D CAPTAIN, or, *The Humours of the Militia*. Farce, 1749.

53. HENRY AND EMMA, or, *The Nut Brown Maid*. Musical Drama taken from Prior. Acted at Covent-Garden, 1749. The songs of this piece, which were set by Dr. Arne, were printed, 8vo.

54. HENRY AND EMMA. Pastoral Interlude, by Henry Bate, altered from Prior, and acted at Covent-Garden, April 13, 1774, for Mrs. Hartley's benefit.

55. HENRY AND ROSAMOND. Trag. by W. HAWKINS, 8vo. 1749. This play, though never acted, is very far from a bad piece. The plot is taken from the ancient story of Fair Rosamond.

56. HENRY I. AND HENRY II. By William Shakspeare and Robert Davenport. In the books of the Stationers' Company, the 9th of Sept. 1653, an entry is made of the above title; but what species of the drama it was, or whether one or two performances, are facts not ascertained. Whatever it might be, it suffered in the general havock made by Mr. Warburton's servant.

57. HENRY II. or, *The Fall of Rosamond*. Trag. by Thomas Hull. Acted at Covent-Garden, 8vo. 1774. *Quædam mediocria*.

58. HENRY II. KING OF ENGLAND, *with the Death of Rosamond*. Trag. by John Bancroft, 4to. 1693. This piece, which was published by Mountfort the player, is in general tragedy, but with a mixture of comedy; it has not the author's name prefixed to it, yet

it

it met with very good success, and is indeed truly deserving of it. The story of it may be found in the English historians, and represents chiefly that part of this prince's life which relates to Rosamond. The scene lies in Oxford; and the epilogue was written by Dryden.

59. HENRY III. OF FRANCE, *stabbed by a Friar*, with the fall of the Guises. Trag. by Thomas Shipman. Acted at Drury-Lane, 4to. 1678. The story of this play is borrowed from Davila, and the Life of the Duke of Espernon. The scene, Blois, removed in the third act to the camp at St. Cloud before Paris.

60. HENRY IV. An Historical Play, by W. Shakspeare, in two parts. The first containing the Life and Death of *Henry*, sur-named *Hotspur*, 4to. 1598. 4to. 1599. 4to. 1604. 4to. 1608. 4to. 1613. 4to. 1622. 4to. 1632. 4to. 1639; and the second the Death of *Henry* IV. and Coronation of *Henry* V. Acted by the Lord Chamberlain's servants, 4to. 1600. Both these plays are perfect masterpieces in this kind of writing, the tragedy and comedy parts of them being so finely connected with each other, as to render the whole regular and complete, and yet contrasted with such boldness and propriety, as to make the various beauties of each the most perfectly conspicuous. The character of *Falstaff* is one of the greatest originals drawn by the pen of even this inimitable master; and in the character of the Prince of *Wales* the hero and the libertine are so finely blended, that the spectator cannot avoid perceiving, even in the greatest levity of the tavern rake, the most lively traces of the afterwards illustrious character of the conqueror of France.

Dr. Johnson observes, " None " of Shakpeare's plays are more " read than the first and second " parts of Henry the Fourth. Per- " haps no author has ever in two " plays afforded so much delight. " The great events are interest- " ing, for the fate of kingdoms " depends upon them; the slight- " er occurrences are diverting, and, " except one or two, sufficiently " probable; the incidents are mul- " tiplied with wonderful fertility " of invention; and the characters " diversified with the utmost nice- " ty of discernment, and the pro- " foundest skill in the nature of " man."

61. KING HENRY IV. *with the Humours of Sir John Falstaff*. Tr. Com. Acted at Lincoln's-Inn Fields, with alterations by Mr. Betterton, 4to. 1700.

62. HENRY IV. OF FRANCE. Trag. by Charles Beckingham, 8vo. 1719. The plot of this play is taken from the history of that great prince; the piece was written by the author at the age of nineteen, and acted in Lincoln's-Inn Fields with good success.

63. " *The Chronicle History of* " HENRY V. *with the Battel* " *fought at Agincourt, in France,* " *together with Antient Pistoll*. As " it hath bene sundry times played " by the right honourable the Lord " Chamberlaine his servants," 4to. 1600. 4to. 1602. 4to. 1608. This play has also an intermixture of comedy, and is justly esteemed an admirable piece, insomuch that notwithstanding the several alterations that have been attempted to be made in it, the original still stands its ground, and is constantly performed with universal applause. The character of *Fleuellen*, the *Welsh* captain, in particular is admirably drawn. The scene in the beginning lies in England, and afterwards

terwards wholly in France. "This play (says Dr. Johnson) has many scenes of high dignity, and many of easy merriment. The character of the King is well supported, except in his courtship, where he has neither the vivacity of Hal, nor the grandeur of Henry. The humour of Pistol is very happily continued: his character has perhaps been the model of all the bullies that have yet appeared on the English stage.

"The lines given to the chorus have many admirers; but the truth is, that in them a little may be praised, and much must be forgiven; nor can it be easily discovered, why the intelligence given by the chorus is more necessary in this play than in many others where it is omitted. The great defect of this piece is the emptiness and narrowness of the last act, which a very little diligence might have easily avoided."

64. HENRY V. Trag. by the Earl of Orrery, Fo. 1672. This may be traced in the English chronicles of that prince's reign and in the French ones of that of Charles VI. Scene, France. It was acted at the Duke of York's Theatre with great success; the characters being very splendidly dressed, particularly those of King Henry, Owen Tudor, and the Duke of Burgundy, which wore the coronation suits of the Duke of York, King Charles, and Lord Oxford. The actors who performed them were Harris, Betterton, and Smith.

65. *The famous Victories of* HENRY V. containing, *The honourable Battel of Agincourt.* Acted by the King's servants, 4to. no date. This is different from Shakspeare's play before-mentioned of the same name, and is supposed to be one which he availed himself of in the composition of his own performance. It is reprinted in Nichols's *Collection of Six Old Plays*.

66. HENRY V. or, *The Conquest of France by the English.* Trag. by Aaron Hill. Acted at Drury-Lane, 8vo. 1723. This is a very good play. The plot and language are in some places borrowed from Shakspeare, yet on the whole it is greatly altered, and a second plot is introduced by the addition of a new Female character, viz. *Harriet*, a niece to lord *Scroope*, who has been formerly seduced by the king. She appears in men's cloaths throughout, and is made the means of discovering the conspiracy against him.

67. HENRY VI. Historical Play in three parts, by William Shakspeare. Two of these plays were printed in 4to. [N. D.] but the whole were not published together until the folio edition of 1623. These three plays contain the whole life and long unhappy reign of this prince. In consequence of which it is impossible but that all the unities of time, place, and action, must be greatly broken in upon; yet has the author made the most valuable use of the incidents of real history, to which he has very strictly adhered.

"Of these three plays," says Dr. Johnson, "I think the second the best. The truth is, that they have not sufficient variety of action, for the incidents are too often of the same kind; yet many of the characters are well discriminated. King Henry, and his Queen, King Edward, the Duke of Gloucester, and the Earl of Warwick, are very strongly and distinctly painted."

68. HENRY VI. *the First Part, with the Murder of the Duke of Gloucester.*

Gloucester. Tr. by J. Crowne. Acted at the Duke's Theatre, 4to. 1681. This play was at first represented with applause; but at length the Romish faction opposed it, and by their interest at court got it suppressed. Part of it is borrowed from Shakspeare's Plays abovementioned. Scene, the Court at Westminster.

69. HENRY VI. *the Second Part, or, The Miseries of Civil War.* Tr. by J. Crowne. Acted at the Duke's Theatre, 4to. 1680. This play was written before the last-named one, and was first printed by the last title only. This is also in great measure borrowed from Shakspeare.

70. HENRY VI. by Theophilus Cibber, of which the following is the complete title: " *An Historical* " *Tragedy of the Civil Wars in the* " *Reign of* KING HENRY VI. " *Being a Sequel to the Tragedy of* " *Humfrey, Duke of Gloucester, and* " *an Introduction to the Tragical* " *History of King Richard the Third.* " *Altered from Shakspeare in the* " *year* 1720." 8vo. no date. This alteration, I believe, was only acted in the summer.

71. KING HENRY VII. or, *The Popish Impostor.* Trag. by Charles Macklin. Acted at Drury-Lane, 8vo. 1746. This piece is built on the story of Perkin Warbeck, but it met with general disapprobation; and indeed the very impropriety in the title, of mentioning a Popish Impostor in a period of time previous to the introduction of Protestantism in these kingdoms, had an air of absurdity, which seemed even before its appearance to stand as a foretaste of no very elegant or judicious entertainment. When, however, it is considered that it was the six weeks labour only of an actor, who even in that short space was often called from it by his profession, and that the players, for the sake of dispatch, had it to study and act by and, just as it was blotted; and that the only revisals it received from the *brouillon* to the press were at the rehearsals of it, no person will be disappointed in finding so many imperfections contained in it.

72. HENRY VIII. *The famous History of his Life.* Historical Play, by W. Shakspeare, Fo. 1623. This is the closing piece of the whole series of this author's historical dramas; and " is (says Dr. John- " son) one of those which still " keeps possession of the stage by " the splendour of its pageantry. " The coronation about forty " years ago drew the people toge- " ther in multitudes for a great " part of the winter. Yet pomp " is not the only merit of this " play; the meek sorrows and " virtuous distress of Katherine " have furnished some scenes " which may be justly numbered " among the greatest efforts of " tragedy. But the genius of " Shakspeare comes in and goes " with Katherine. Every other " part may be easily conceived " and easily written."

73. HENRY VIII. An Historical Play, by Mr. William Shakspeare, with historical notes by Joseph Grove, 8vo. 1758.

74. HERACLIUS EMPEROR OF THE EAST. Trag. by Lodowick Carlell, 4to. 1604. This is little more than a translation from the *Heraclius* of Corneille. It was intended for the stage, but was never acted, another translation having been preferred before it by the performers, and this piece not returned to the author till the day that the other was acted. The plot of it is from Baronius' Ecclesiastical Annals, but the author has not strictly tied himself down to historical

historical truth. The scene lies in Constantinople. Who was the author of the other translation I cannot learn, nor where it was acted; but, notwithstanding the preference shewn to it, this is very far from being contemptible.

75. HERCULES. An Opera.

76. HERCULES. Musical Drama, by T[...]s Broughton; set to music by Mr. Handel, and performed at the Hay-market, 8vo. 1745.

78. HERCULES FURENS. Tr. by Jasper Heywood, 12mo. 1561. and 4to. 1581. This is only a translation from Seneca.

77. HERCULES OETÆUS. Tr. translated from Seneca by J. Studley, 4to. 1581. This is by some thought to be an imitation of the TRAXINIAI of Sophocles.

79. THE HERMIT CONVERTED, or, *The Maid of Bath married*, 8vo. no date, [1771.] This piece was written by a person who calls himself Adam Moses Emanuel Cook. It is evidently the effect of a distempered imagination.

80. THE HERMIT, or, *Harlequin at Rhodes*. A wretched Pantomime; acted at Drury-Lane, 1766.

81. HERMINIUS AND ESPASIA. Trag. by Mr. Hart, 8vo. 1754. The author of this play was a Scotch gentleman, and it made its first appearance on the Edinburgh stage, but without any great success. It is indeed a very dull and uninteresting performance. In the third line of it, however, we are informed, that † "*friendship* is the *wine* of life." Mr. Dennis long before had assured us that *liberty* was the best *salt* to it, and the author of The Tragedy of Tragedies is of opinion, that *love* is its most poignant *mustard*. Thus by degrees we might discover all the articles necessary to the feast of existence, were not poets too little versed in the doctrine of banquets, and therefore liable to mistakes in their adaptation of sauces.

82. HERMON PRINCE OF CHOREA, or, *The Extravagant Zealot*. Trag. by Dr. Clancy, 8vo. 1746. This tragedy was brought on the stage in Ireland, but the publication of it was reserved for London.

83. HERO AND LEANDER, The Tragedies of, by Sir Robert Stapylton, 4to. 1669. Whether this play was ever acted or not, seems to be a dubious point, although the prologue and epilogue carry an implication of the affirmative. The plot is taken from Ovid's Epistles, and *Musæus's Erotopaignion*. The scene, the towns and towers of Sestos and Abydos, the Hellespont flowing between them.

84. HEROD AND ANTIPATER, *with the Death of Fair Mariam*. Trag. by Gervase Markham and William Sampson. Acted at the Red Bull, 4to. 1622. The plot of this play is taken from Josephus's Antiq. of the Jews, book xiv and xv.

85. HEROD AND MARIAMNE. Trag. by Samuel Pordage, Esq. 4to. 1674. Acted at the Duke's Theatre. This play was given by its author to Mr. Settle, to use and form as he pleased; it was, however, many years before it could be brought upon the stage, but when it did appear it met with very good success. The plot is from Josephus, the story of *Tyridates* in *Cleopatra*, and the *Unfortunate Politic*, or *The Life of Herod*, translated from the French, 8vo. 1639.

86. HEROD THE GREAT. Tr. by the Earl of Orrery. This is on the same story with the two foregoing plays. It was never acted, but was printed in Fo. 1694.

87. HEROD

87. HEROD THE GREAT. Dram. Poem, by Francis Peck, printed with the Life of Milton, 4to. 1740.

88. HEROIC FRIENDSHIP. Tr. 4to. 1719. This is a very paltry and stupid performance, was never acted, nor indeed deserved to be so. It has been pretended by some to have been the work of Mr. Otway, found among his papers after his death; but it was neither in his hand-writing, nor is it by any means of a piece with even the most indifferent of that author's works. Scene lies in Britain.

89. HEROIC LOVE, or, *The Cruel Separation.* Trag. by Lord Lansdowne, 4to. 1698. This play was acted at Lincoln's-Inn Fields with great applause, and is indeed one of the best of the tragedies of that period. The plot is taken from the separation of Achilles and Bryseis, in the first book of Homer; and the scene lies in the Grecian fleet and camp before Troy. The unities are strictly adhered to, and the language sublime, yet easy, the author seeming to have made it his principal aim to avoid all that fustian and bombast wherewith the tragic writers, and more especially those of that time, were but too apt to interlard their works. The conclusion of this play was altered after the first representation, his lordship's reasons for which may be seen in his preface. The prologue by Lord Bolingbroke; epilogue by Bevil Higgons. Mr. Walpole's opinion of Lord Lansdown's poetry is much less favourable than that of many other writers. He says, "It was "fortunate for his lordship, that "in an age when persecution "raged so fiercely against luke- "warm authors, that he had an "intimacy with the inquisitor "general; how else would such "lines as this have escaped the "bathos?

"—— when thy Gods
"Enlighten thee to speak their dark
"decrees."

Dr. Johnson observes, that this tragedy was written, and presented on the stage, before the death of Dryden. It is a mythological tragedy, upon the love of Agamemnon and Chryseis, and therefore easily sunk into neglect, though praised in verse by Dryden, and in prose by Pope. It is thus concluded by the wife Ulysses with this speech:

"Fate holds the strings, and men like
"children move
"But as they're led; success is from
"above."

90. THE HEROIC LOVER, or, *The Infanta of Spain.* Trag. by George Cartwright, 8vo. 1661. This play is not mentioned by Langbaine, and is, in all the later catalogues (which have copied from one another, and consequently perpetuated instead of correcting mistakes) intituled *Heroic Love.* The scene lies in Poland; and the author himself calls it a Poem, consisting more of fatal truth than flying fancy: penned many years ago, but not published till now; and I imagine never acted.

91. THE HEROINE OF THE CAVE. Trag. Acted at Drury-Lane, 8vo. 1775. This play was begun by Henry Jones, under the title of *The Cave of Idra,* from a narrative in the Annual Register. On the death of this unfortunate author, it fell into the hands of Mr. Reddish, for whose benefit it was performed. Not being long enough for an evening entertainment, as originally left by its author, Mr. Reddish put it into the hands of Dr. Hiffernan, who extended

tended the plan, and added some new characters.

92. HE WOU'D IF HE COU'D, or, *An old Fool worse than any*. Burletta, by Isaac Bickerstaffe. Acted at Drury-Lane, 8vo. 1771.

93. HEWSON REDUC'D, or, *The Shoemaker return'd to his Trade*. "Being a shew, wherein is repre-"sented the honesty, inoffensive-"ness, and ingenuity of that pro-"fession, when 'tis kept within its "own bounds, and goes not be-"yond the Last." 4to. 1661.

94. HEY FOR HONESTY, DOWN WITH KNAVERY. Com. by Tho. Randolph, 4to. 1651. This is little more than a translation from the Plutus of Aristophanes. It was augmented and published by F. J. The scene lies in London; and it is introduced by a dialogue between Aristophanes, the translator, and Cleon's ghost.

95. HIBERNIA FREE'D. Trag. by Capt. W. Phillips, 8vo. 1722. Acted at the Theatre in Lincoln's-Inn Fields.

96. HIC ET UBIQUE, or, *The Humours of Dublin*. Com. by Rich. Head, 4to. 1663. This play is said to have been acted privately with general applause. Scene, Dublin.

97. THE HIGHLAND FAIR, or, *The Union of the Clans*. An Opera, by Joseph Mitchell, 8vo. 1731. The plot of this piece is built on the fatal and bloody consequences which but too frequently used to happen at some of the highland fairs, from the quarrels which were apt to arise on the meeting of persons of the several clans, whose strong family connections and party-attachments rendered each clan in some degree a separate nation either in alliance, or in a state of warfare with every other neighbouring one. This the author, being himself a Scotchman, was well acquainted with; but the subject being too local for the English stage, when brought on at the Theatre Royal in Drury-Lane, it met with little or no success.

98. HIGH LIFE BELOW STAIRS. Farce. Acted at Drury-Lane, 8vo. 1759. This little piece seems to aim at two points for the reformation of morals. The first to represent as in a mirrour to persons in high life some of their own follies and fopperies, by cloathing their very servants in them, and shewing them to be contemptible and ridiculous even in them. The second and more principal aim is to open the eyes of the great, and convince persons of fortune what impositions, even to the ravage and ruin of their estates, they are liable to, from the wastefulness and infidelity of their servants, for want of a proper inspection into their domestic affairs. It possesses a considerable share of merit, and met with most amazing success in London. In Edinburgh, however, it found prodigious opposition from the gentlemen of the party-coloured regiment, who raised repeated riots in the play-house whenever it was acted, and even went so far as to threaten the lives of some of the performers. This insolence, however, in some degree brought about the very reformation it meant to oppose, and in part the intention of the farce, being the occasion of an association immediately entered into by almost all the nobility and gentry of SCOTLAND, and publicly subscribed to in the periodical papers, whereby they bound themselves mutually to each other to put a stop to the absurd and scandalous custom of giving vails, prevalent no where but in these kingdoms. This piece has been often ascribed to Mr. Townley, master of Merchants-Taylors'

Taylors' school; but we are assured he only allowed his name to be used as the reputed parent of it, the real author being Mr. Garrick.

99. HIPPOLITUS. Trag. by E. Prettwich, 8vo. 1651. This is a translation from Seneca, is made entirely in rhyme, with comments on every scene, and six copies of recommendatory verses by Shirley, Cotton, &c.

100. HIPSIPILE. Opera, translated from Metastasio by John Hoole, 8vo. 1768.

101. HIREN, or, *The Fair Greek*. Trag. by W. Barkited, 8vo. 1611. Though this is noticed as a dramatic piece, I have some doubt of its being such. It appears, however, from Dr. Hyde's Catalogue, to be in the Bodleian library.

102. THE HISTORICAL REGISTER, for the year 1736. Com. by Henry Fielding. Acted at the Hay-Market, 8vo. 1737. To some reflexions on the ministry thrown out in this piece, and in the *Pasquin* of the same author, was owing an act of parliament for laying a restraint on the stage, by limiting the number of theatres, and submitting every new dramatic piece to the inspection of the lord chamberlain, previous to its appearance on the stage.

103. THE HISTORY OF CARDENIO. A Play, by Mr. Fletcher and Shakspeare; entered on the books of the Stationers' Company Sept. 9, 1653; but I believe never printed. It has been suggested, that this play may possibly be the same as *The Double Falshood*; afterwards brought to light by Mr. Theobald.

104. HISTRIOMASTIX, or, *The Player whipp'd*. Com. Anonymous, 4to. 1610.

105. HOB, or, *The Country Wake*. A Farce, by Mr. Cibber. Acted at Drury-Lane, 12mo. 1720. This is only Dogget's *Country Wake*, reduced to the size of a farce. It has since had the addition of some songs, and was performed under the title of *Flora*, or *Hob in the Well*.

106. HOB'S WEDDING. Farce, by John Leigh, 8vo. 1721. This is partly taken from, and partly a continuation of, the same play with that from which the last-named piece is borrowed.

107. THE HOBBY HORSE. Farce, by Capt. Edward Thompson. Acted once at Drury-Lane, April 16, 1766, for the benefit of Mr. Bensley. We hope it proved beneficial to the actor. It would do no credit to any author that ever existed. It was, however, preceded by a very good prologue, written by Mr Colman, and printed in *The Muses Mirrour*.

108. *The Tragedy of* HOFFMAN, or, *A Revenge for a Father*. Acted at the Phœnix, Drury-Lane. Dedicated, by the publisher Hugh Perry, to Master Richard Kilvert, 4to. 1631. It was entered in the books of the Stationers' Company, by John Grove, Feb. 26, 1629.

109. THE HOGGE HATH LOST HIS PEARLE. Com. *divers Times publickly acted by certain London Prentices*, 4to. 1614. The part of the plot, from which the piece derives its name, is the elopement of the daughter of one Hogge an usurer, who is one of the principal characters in the play. The scene lies in London.

110. THE HOLLANDER. Com. by Henry Glapthorne, written and acted 1635, at the Cockpit, Drury-Lane, and at Court, and printed in 4to. 1640. Scene, London.

111. HOLLAND'S LEAGUER. Com. by Shakerley Marmyon. Acted at Salisbury-Court, 4to.

1632. This piece met with great applause. The story was printed the same year in 4to. but there is no incident in this play taken from it, except a detection of the sin of pandarism. The author has, however, borrowed several circumstances from Petronius Arbiter, Juvenal, and other of the classic writers. Scene, in London.

112. THE HONEST CRIMINAL, or, *Filial Piety*. Drama, 8vo. 1778. This is a translation from the French.

113. THE HONEST ELECTORS, or, *The Courtiers sent back with their Bribes*. Ballad Opera, of three acts, 8vo. No date [1733.]

114. THE HONEST LAWYER. Com. by S. S. Acted by the Queens Majesties servants, 4to. 1616.

115. AN HONEST MAN'S FORTUNE. Tragi-Com. by Beaumont and Fletcher, Fol. 1647. The incident of *Lamira's* preferring *Montaigne* to be her husband in the time of his greatest adversity, and when he had the least reason to expect it, seems borrowed from Heywood's *History of Women*, book ix. Scene, in Paris.

116. THE HONEST WHORE. Com. by Thomas Dekker, 4to. 1604. 4to. 1615. 4to. 1616. 4to. 1635. The first part contains *The Humours of the Patient Man and the Longing Wife*, and was acted with applause. The second part contains the humours of *The Patient Man and the Impatient Wife*, the *Honest Whore* persuaded by strong arguments to turn *Courtezan* again; her bravely refuting these arguments; and, lastly, the comical passage of an *Italian Bridewell*, where the scene ends. Neither part is divided into acts, and I believe the latter was never acted. The incident of the Patient Man and his impatient Wife going to fight for the breeches, may be found in Sir John Harrington's Epigrams published at the end of his translation of *The Orlando Furioso*, Book I. Epigr. 16.

117. THE HONEST YORKSHIREMAN. See THE WONDER.

118. HONESTY IN DISTRESS, BUT RELIEV'D BY NO PARTY. T. *as it is basely acted by her Majesty's subjects upon God's Stage the World*, 8vo. 1705. This piece consists of three short acts. The scene laid in London, and was written by Edward Ward, the author of *The London Spy*, but was never intended for the stage.

119. HONORIA AND MAMMON. Com. 8vo. 1659. The Scene of this piece lies at Metropolis, or New Troy. See farther under CONTENTION FOR HONOUR AND RICHES.

120. HONOUR IN THE END. Com. This piece is advertised at the end of *Wit and Drollery*, 12mo. 1661, as in the press. It, however, never appeared.

121. HONOUR REWARDED, or, *The Generous Fortune-Hunter*. Farce, of three acts, by John Dalton, of Clifton, 8vo. 1775. Printed at York.

122. HOOPS INTO SPINNINGWHEELS. Tragi-Com. by J. Planch, 4to. 1725. Printed at Gloucester. It is impossible to conceive any thing more stupid and ridiculous than this performance, which nothing but the dotage of its author could have suffered to be printed.

123. HORACE. Trag. by Charles Cotton, 4to. 1671. This is only a translation of the *Horace* of P. Corneille. The plot of the original piece is taken from the several Roman historians of the story of the *Horatii* and *Curiatii*. It is a very good translation.

124. Ho-

124. HORACE. Trag. by Mrs. Cath. Phillips, Fol. 1678. This is a translation of the same piece as the foregoing, and was very justly celebrated. The fifth act was added by Sir John Denham, and it was presented at court by persons of quality, the prologue being spoken by the Duke of Monmouth.

125. HORATIUS. Roman Trag. by Sir William Lower, 4to. 1656. This is also a translation from Corneille, but is not equal to either of the preceding two. The scene is in Rome in a hall of Horatius's house.

126. AN HOSPITAL FOR FOOLS. A Dram. Fable. Acted at Drury-Lane, 1739. 8vo. The songs set by Arne. This piece, being known to be Miller's, was damned, the disturbance being so great, that not one word of it was heard the whole night. The reason of this partial prejudice against it may be traced under the account already given of *The Coffee-House.*

127. THE HOTEL, or, *The Double Valet.* Farce, by Thomas Vaughan, Esq. Acted at Drury-Lane, 8vo. 1776. By the assistance of excellent acting, this trifling piece was performed with more success than it deserved.

128. AN HOUR BEFORE MARRIAGE. Farce, of two acts. As it was attempted to be acted at Covent-Garden, 8vo. 1772. This piece was not suffered to be heard throughout. What gave so much offence cannot be discovered in the perusal of it, and indeed it seems to have deserved a better fate.

129. *A Pleasant conceited Comedie, Wherein is shewed,* HOW A MAN NAY CHUSE A GOOD WIFE FROM A BAD. Com. Anonymous, 4to. 1602. 4to. 1605. 4to. 1621. 4to. 1630. 4to. 1634. Acted by the Earl of Worcester's servants. The foundation of this play is taken from Cynthio's Novels, Dec. 3. Nov. 5. but the incident of Anselme's saving young Arthur's wife out of the grave, and carrying her to his mother's house, is related in a Novel, called *Love in the Grave,* in *The Pleasant Companion,* and is the subject of several plays. The scene is in London. In Mr. Garrick's Collection, this piece is ascribed in manuscript to Joshua Cooke, probably the author of *Green's Tu quoque.*

130. HUDIBRASSO. Burlesque Opera, of two acts, performed at the Theatre Royal at Voluptuaria, 8vo. 1741. Printed in an indecent pamphlet, intituled, " A " Voyage to Lethe, by Captain " Samuel Cock, some time com- " mander of the good ship the " Charming Sally."

131. THE HUMOROUS COURTIER. Com. by James Shirley. Acted at the private house, Drury-Lane, 4to. 1640. This play was acted with very good success. Scene, Mantua.

132. HUMOROUS DAY'S MIRTH. by George Chapman, 4to. 1599.

133. THE HUMOROUS LIEUTENANT. Tragi-Com. by Beaumont and Fletcher, Fol. 1647. This is an exceeding good play. It was the first that was acted, and that for twelve nights successively, at the opening of the Theatre in Drury-Lane, April 8, 1663. The plot in general is taken from Plutarch's Life of Demetrius, and other writers of the Lives of Antigonus and Demetrius; and the incident of *The Humorous Lieutenant* refusing to fight after he has been cured of his wounds, seems borrowed from the story of Lucullus's soldier

soldier related by Horace in the second book of his Epistles, Ep. 2. Scene, Greece.

134. THE HUMOROUS LOVERS. Com. by the Duke of Newcastle. Acted at the Duke's Theatre, 4to. 1677. This comedy is said by Langbaine to be a very good one. The scene lies in Covent-Garden.

135. THE HUMOURIST. Com. by Thomas Shadwell. Acted at Drury-Lane, 4to. 1671. The scene of this piece is laid in London in the year 1670, and the intention of it was to ridicule some of the vices and follies of the age. Yet this very design, laudable as it was, raised the author many enemies who were determined to damn it, right or wrong, and compelled him to mutilate his play, and expunge his main design, to avoid giving offence. The duration of the scene is twenty-four hours.

136. HUMOUR OUT OF BREATH. Com. by John Daye, 4to. 1607.

137. THE HUMOURS OF A COFFEE-HOUSE. Com. as it is daily acted at most of the Coffee-houses in London, by Edward Ward.

138. THE HUMOURS OF COURT, or, *Modern Gallantry*. Ballad Opera, 8vo. 1732.

139. THE HUMOURS OF AN ELECTION. Farce, by F. Pilon. Acted at Covent-Garden, 8vo. 1780.

140. THE HUMOURS OF EXCHANGE-ALLEY. Farce, by W. R. Chetwood, 1720.

141. THE HUMOURS OF AN IRISH COURT OF JUSTICE. Dram. Satire, 8vo. The Dedication is signed a Freeman Barber, and dated London, Dec. 12, 1750. It was never acted.

142. THE HUMOURS OF OXFORD. C. by James Miller. Acted at Drury-Lane, 8vo. 1729. This was the first and the most original of all our author's dramatic pieces. It met with middling success on the Theatre, but drew on Mr. Miller the resentment of some of the heads of the colleges in Oxford, who looked on themselves as satirized in it. Scene lies in Oxford.

143. THE HUMOURS OF PORTSMOUTH, or, *All is Well that ends Well*. Farce, of three acts, 8vo. No date, about 1760.

144. THE HUMOURS OF PURGATORY. Farce, by Benj. Griffin. Acted at Lincoln's-Inn Fields, 12mo. 1716. The plot of this play seems borrowed from the comic part of Southerne's *Fatal Marriage*.

145. THE HUMOURS OF WAPPING. Farce, 12mo. 1703. This piece I never saw.

146. THE HUMOURS OF WHIST. Dramatic Satire, *as it is acted every day at White's and other Coffee-houses and Assemblies*, 8vo. 1743. Anonym. This piece was never intended for the stage, but only designed as a representation of the various characters which present themselves to observation among the frequenters of the gaming tables in the highest scenes of life. It is, however, very far from being well executed. It was republished in 1753, with the additional title of *The Polite Gamester*.

147. THE HUMOURS OF THE AGE. Com. by Thomas Baker. Acted at Drury-Lane, 4to. 1701. This play was written in two months, and that when the author was but barely of age. The grand scene is in a boarding-house, and the time 12 hours, beginning at ten in the morning.

148. THE HUMOURS OF THE ARMY. Com. by Cha. Shadwell. Acted at Drury-Lane, 4to. 1713. This play met with very good success.

cess. The scene lies in the camp, near Elvas. The time six hours.

149. THE HUMOURS OF THE ROAD, or, *A Ramble to Oxford*. Com. Anonym. 8vo. 1738.

150. THE HUMOROUS QUARREL, or, *The Battle of the Greybeards*. Farce. Acted at Southwark Fair, 8vo. No date [1761].

151. HUMPHRY DUKE OF GLOUCESTER. T. by Ambrose Philips. Acted at Drury-Lane, 8vo. 1722. The plot of this play is founded on history; and the piece itself met with great applause, but at present, as Dr. Johnson observes, it is only remembered by its title.

152. THE HUNTINGTON DIVERTISEMENT, or, *An Enterlude for the general Entertainment at the County Feast, held at Merchant Taylor's Hall*, June 20, 1678, 4to. This piece has the letters W. M. and is dedicated to the nobility and gentry of the county. The scene lies in Hinchinbroke Grove, Fields, and Meadows.

153. HURLOTHRUMBO. Com. by Sam. Johnson, 8vo. 1729. This piece was performed at the Little Theatre in the Hay-Market, and had a run of above thirty nights. The oddity, whimsicalness, and originality of it was what occasioned this amazing success, the play itself being one of the most absurd compages of wild extravagant incidents, incoherent sentiments, and unconnected dialogues. The author himself performed the principal part, viz. that of Lord *Flame*, sometimes in one key, sometimes in another; sometimes fidling, sometimes dancing, and sometimes walking in very high stilts. The celebrated Dr. Byrom, the inventor of a peculiar kind of short-hand, wrote a prologue to it, in which his intention was to point out, by a friendly hint to the author, the absurdity of his play. Mr. Johnson however, so far from perceiving the ridicule, looked on it as a compliment, and had it both spoken and printed to the piece. Yet, notwithstanding all that has here been said, it contains in some places certain strokes both of sentiment and imagination that would do honour even to the most capital genius, and which speak the author, if a madman, at least a madman with more than ordinary abilities.

154. THE HUSBAND HIS OWN CUCKOLD. Com. by John Dryden, jun. Acted at Lincoln's-Inn Fields, 4to. 1696. The story on which this play is founded was an accident which happened at Rome. The author, however, has transferred the scene to England. The prologue is written by Congreve, and the preface and epilogue by Mr. Dryden, sen.

155. HYCKE-SCORNER, 4to. b. l. no date. *Emprynted by me Wynkyn de Worde*. This piece, as Dr. Percy observes, bears no distant resemblance to comedy. Its chief aim is to exhibit characters and manners. Bating a few moral and religious reflections, it is of a comic cast, and contains a humorous display of some of the vices of the age. Indeed the author has generally been so little attentive to allegory, that we need only substitute other names to his personage, and we have real characters and living manners. This play has been reprinted by Hawkins in his three volumes of Old Plays, intituled *The Origin of the English Drama*, 12mo. Oxford, 1773. See vol. I. p. 69. where the reader will likewise meet with Dr. Percy's curious analysis of so extraordinary a performance.

156. HYDE-PARK. Com. by James

H Y

James Shirley. Acted at the private houſe Drury-Lane, 4to. 1637.

157. HYMENÆI, or, *The Solemnities of a Maſque and Barriers at a Marriage*, by Ben Jonſon, 4to. 1606. To this piece the author has annexed many very curious and learned marginal notes for the illuſtration of the ancient Greek and Roman cuſtoms.

158. HYMEN'S TRIUMPH. Paſtoral Tragi-Com. by Sam. Daniel, 4to. 1623. This piece was preſented at an entertainment given to King James I. by his queen at her court in the Strand, on the nuptials of lord Roxborough, and is dedicated to the ſaid queen. It is introduced by a very pretty prologue, in which *Hymen* is oppoſed by *Avarice, Envy*, and *Jealouſy*, the three greateſt diſturbers of matrimonial happineſs. It is entered in the Stationers' books, Jan. 13. 1614.

159. HYPERMNESTRA, or, *Love in Tears*. Trag. by Rob. Owen, 4to. 1703. 12mo. 1722. The ſcene lies in Argos. The ſtory is built on Hiſtory, and the time the ſame as that of the repreſentation. The play, however, was never acted.

160. THE HYPOCHONDRIACK. Com. by Mr. Ozell. This is only a tranſlation of Moliere's *Malade imaginaire*.

162. THE HYPOCHONDRIAC, Farce, Anonym. borrowed from the foregoing; but never acted.

161. THE HYPOCRITE. Com. by Iſaac Bickerſtaffe. Acted at Drury-Lane, 8vo, 1769. This is an alteration of Cibber's *Nonjuror*. Scarce any thing more than the character of *Mawworm* was written by the preſent author. Few plays have had the advantage of better acting, and in conſequence, few have had a greater ſhare of ſucceſs.

163. HYPPOLITUS. Trag. Tranſlated from Seneca, by J. Studley, 4to. 1581.

J.

J A

1. JACK DRUM'S ENTERTAINMENT, or, *The Pleaſant Comedy of Paſquil and Katharine*. Anon. 4to. 1601. 4to. 1616. 4to. 1618. acted by the children of Paul's. The incident of *Mammon's* poiſoning *Katharine's* face, ſeems borrowed from *Demagoras's* treatment of *Parthenia* in *Argalus* and *Parthenia*.

2. JACK JUGGLER. This is called a comedy in Jacob, Langbaine, and all the old Catalogues, whoſe authors do not pretend to have ſeen it, or to aſſign any date to it; but in the *Britiſh Theatre* it ſtands with the appearance of authority as follows, viz. *A merrie Interlude of Jack Juggler*, 1587; but the authority of Cheſwood is too ſlender to rely upon, and if this play was printed at all, I imagine it muſt have been earlier, as I find an Interlude, intituled, "Jack Juggeler and Mrs. Boundgrace," entered by William Copland in the Stationers' books, from the year 1562 to 1563.

3. JACK STRAW'S LIFE AND DEATH, *a notable Rebel in England*,

who was killed in Smith-Field, by the Lord Mayor of London, 4to. 1594. This play is divided very oddly, consisting of no more than four acts. The plot is taken from the English chronicles in their relation of this remarkable event in the reign of Richard II. It is entered on the books of the Stationers' Company, by John Danter, Oct. 23, 1593.

4. JACK THE GIANT-KILLER. Comi-Tragical Farce, 8vo. 1730.

5. JACK THE GIANT QUELLER. An Operatical Play, by Hen. Brooke. This satirical and ingenious piece was performed at the theatre in Dublin in 1748, but there being in it two or three satirical songs against bad Governors, Lord Mayors, and Aldermen, it was prohibited after the first night's representation. The songs however, in the words of which the greatest part of its satyr is contained, were published by themselves in an 8vo. Pamphlet, 1749. In the year 1754 it was altered by the author, and brought again on the stage at Dublin, when it met with no success; it being performed the second night to half a house, and the third for the author's benefit to one not above three parts full. It was not published compleat, untill 1778, when it appeared in the author's works.

6. JACOB AND ESAU. An Interlude, 4to. 1568. This is a very early piece. It is written in metre, and printed in the old Black Letter. Its full title runs as follows: *A new, merry and wittie Comedie or Enterlude, newlie imprinted, treating upon the Historie of* JACOB AND ESAU, *taken out of the 27th chapter of the first Book of Moses, entituled Genesis.* In the title-page are *The Partes and Names of the Players, who are to be* considered to be Hebrews, and so should be apparailed with Attire. "*Ragau* the servant. *Esau* a young man, his maister. *Ragau* entreth with his horn at his back, and his huntyng staffe in hys hande, and leadeth iij greyhounds, or one, as may be gotten.—Here he counterfaiteth how his maister calleth hym up in the mornings, and of his answeres."

7. JAMES IV. KING OF SCOTLAND, by Robert Green, 4to. 1599. The design of this piece is taken from the History of that brave, but cruel king, who lost his life in a battle with the English at Flodden Hill in the beginning of the sixteenth century; for farther particulars of which, see Buchanan and other Scots Historians. There is, probably, an earlier edition of this play, as I find it entered on the books of the Stationers' Company, by Thomas Creede, May 13, 1594.

8. JANE SHORE. Trag. by N. Rowe. Acted at Drury-Lane, 4to. 1713. This is a very excellent Tragedy, and is continually acted with great success. The scene lies in London, and the author in the plot of it has in great measure followed the History of this unhappy fair one, as related in a collection of Novels in 6 vols. 12mo. which I have elsewhere also quoted. It is said to be written in imitation of Shakspeare's *style*. In what he thought himself an imitator of Shakspeare, it is not (as Dr. Johnson observes) easy to conceive. The numbers, the diction, the sentiments, and the conduct, every thing in which imitation can consist, are remote in the utmost degree from the manner of Shakspeare, whose dramas it resembles only as it is an English story, and as some of the persons have their names in history.

history. This play, consisting chiefly of domestick scenes and private distress, lays hold upon the heart. The wife is forgiven because she repents; and the husband is honoured, because he forgives. This therefore is one of those pieces which we still welcome on the stage.

Pope, in his *Art of Sinking in Poetry*, which was published after the death of Rowe, has the following observation. "I have seen "a play professedly writ in the "style of Shakspeare, wherein the "resemblance lay in one single "line,

"And so good morrow t'ye, good master lieutenant."

The satirist, however, was mistaken. The line is not in *Jane Shore*, but in *Jane Gray*, which professes no imitation of Shakspeare; nor is the quotation a fair one, being interpolated to render it ridiculous.

"And so good morning, good master "lieutenant,"

is the verse as printed by Rowe. Dr. Warton says, "*Jane Shore* is "I think the most interesting and "affecting of any he (Rowe) has "given us: but probability is "sadly violated in it by the neg-"lect of the unity of time. For "a person to be supposed to be "starved, during the represent-"ation of five acts, is a striking "instance of the absurdity of this "violation. In this piece, as in "all of Rowe, are many florid "speeches utterly inconsistent with "the state and situation of the "distressful personages who speak "them." Of this charge the same writer produces several instances, and concludes by observing, that "the interview betwixt *Jane* "*Shore* and *Alicia*, in the middle "of the fifth act, is very affecting;

"where the madness of *Alicia* is "well painted." Essay on the Genius and Writings of Pope, p. 271.

9. IBRAHIM, *the illustrious Bassa*. Trag. In heroic verse, by Elk. Settle. Acted at the Duke's Theatre, 4to. 1677. 4to. 1694. This play is written in heroic verse, the plot taken from Scudery's Romance of the same name, and the scene laid in Solyman's Seraglio.

10. IBRAHIM XII. *Emperor of the Turks.* Trag. by Mary Pix, 4to. 1696. In the title-page, he is, by some mistake, called, *Ibrahim XIII*. This play is not replete with much sublimity of expression, nor advantaged by a harmony of numbers, yet the distress of *Morena* is truly affecting, and the conduct far from contemptible. The plot is to be found in Sir Paul Ricaut's continuation of the Turkish History.

11. THE JEALOUS FARMER OUTWITTED, or, *Harlequin Statue*. Pantomime. Acted at Covent-Garden. This formerly used to be acted on the benefit night of Mr. Lalauze, the celebrated Pierot.

12. JEALOUS HUSBAND. See RAMBLING JUSTICE.

13. THE JEALOUS LOVERS. Com. by Tho. Randolph, 4to. 1632. 4to. 1634, presented by the students of Trinity-College, Cambridge. This play, which is esteemed the best of our author's works, is commended by no less than four copies of English, and six of Latin verses, from the most eminent wits of both universities; and was revived with very great success in 1682. Scene, in Thebes.

14. JEALOUS WIFE. Com. by Geo. Colman, 8vo. 1761. This piece made its appearance at Drury-Lane Theatre with prodigious

gious success. The ground work of it is taken from Fielding's History of *Tom Jones*, at the period of Sophia's taking refuge at Lady Bellaston's house. The characters borrowed from that work, however, only serve as a kind of under plot to introduce Mr. and Mrs. Oakley, viz. the *Jealous Wife* and her husband. It must be confessed that the passions of the lady are here worked up to a very great height, and Mr. Oakley's vexation and domestic misery, in consequence of her behaviour, very strongly supported. Yet, perhaps, the author would have better answered his purpose with respect to the passion he intended to expose the absurdity of, had he made her appear somewhat less of the virago, and Mr. Oakley not so much of the henpecked husband; since she now appears rather a lady, who, from a consciousness of her own power, is desirous of supporting the appearance of jealousy, to procure her an undue influence over her husband and family, than one, who, feeling the reality of that turbulent yet fluctuating passion, becomes equally absurd in the suddenness of forming unjust suspicions, and in that hastiness of being satisfied, which love, the only true basis of jealousy, will constantly occasion.

15. JEAN HENNUYER, BISHOP OF LIZIEUX, or, *The Massacre of St. Bartholomew*. Dramatic Entertainment, in three acts, translated from the French, 8vo. 1773.

16. JEHU. Farce. Acted at Drury-Lane 1779. Not printed. This piece was not suffered to be represented throughout. It is said, however, by some who were present, to have merited less severity than it met with. The author hath kept himself concealed.

17. JERONYMO, or, *The Spanish Tragedy, with the Wars of Portugal*. Anonymous, 4to. 1605. This play contains the life and death of Don Andrea.

18. THE JERUSALEM INFIRMARY, or, *A Journey to the Valley of Jehosaphat*. Farce, as it will be acted next Southwark Fair. Anonymous. *Venice*, 8vo. 1749. This piece never was, nor ever is intended to be acted. It is a piece of the most unintelligible, and at the same time abusive, jargon I ever saw, and is written with a view to expose and calumniate a number of private personal characters among the Jews, and some design, as it should seem, at that time on foot, by some of that sort of people, towards the establishment of an infirmary, which place is made the scene of action, and the president (who is a *monkey*) the principal person in the drama. It refers to some public print at that time also put forth with the like design; but as I do not immediately call to mind the particular event on which it turns, I shall conclude with only observing, that it is so execrably bad, as neither to be worthy of a moment's loss of time spent in the perusal of it, or the waste of any farther notice of it in this place.

19. THE JEW DECOY'D, or, *The Progress of an Harlot*. A Ballad Opera, 8vo. 1733. This piece was never performed, but is founded on the plan of Hogarth's celebrated prints of the *Harlot's Progress*.

20. THE JEW OF MALTA. Tr. by Christ. Marlowe, 4to. 1633. This play was not published till many years after the author's death, when Heywood ushered it into the Court, and presented it at the Cockpit, with the prologue and epilogue annexed to this edition of it, at which time it met with very great and deserved applause. Scene, Malta. It was entered on the books

M 2

books of the Stationers' Company the 17th of May, 1594, by Nicholas Ling and Thomas Millington.

21. THE JEW OF VENICE. C. by lord Lansdowne. Acted at Lincoln's-Inn Fields, 4to. 1701. This play is altered from Shakspeare's *Merchant of Venice*, and in some respects with judgment. The introducing the feast, more particularly where the *Jew* is placed at a separate table, and drinks to his money as his only mistress, is a happy thought; yet, on the whole, his lordship has greatly lessened both the beauty and effect of the original, which, notwithstanding this modernized piece, aided by magnificence and music, still stands its ground, and will ever continue one of the darling representations of the theatre. The Prologue was written by Bevil Higgons, in which the ghosts of Shakspeare and Dryden are made to rise crowned with laurel; and in the second act is introduced a musical Masque written by his lordship, called, *Peleus* and *Thetis*. In this play, as Rowe remarks, the character of *Shylock* is made comic, and we are prompted to laughter instead of detestation.

22. THE JEW OF VENICE, by Thomas Dekker. This play was entered on the books of the Stationers' Company, Sept. 9, 1653, but has not been printed.

23. THE JEW'S TRAGEDY, or, *Their fatal and final Overthrow*, by Vespasian and Titus his son. By William Hemings, 4to. 1662. This play was not printed till some years after the author's death. The plot is founded on the siege and destruction of Jerusalem, as related by Josephus in the 6th and 7th Books of his Wars of the Jews.

24. THE JEWELLER OF AMSTERDAM, or, *The Hague*. A Play, by John Fletcher, Nathaniel Field, and Philip Massinger, entered on the books of the Stationers' Company, April 8, 1654, but not printed.

25. THE JEWISH GENTLEMAN. A Play, by Richard Brome, entered on the books of the Stationers' Company, with others, Aug. 4, 1640, but not printed.

"26. IF IT BE NOT GOOD THE "DIVEL IS IN IT. A new Play, "as it hath bin lately acted with "great applause by the Queenes "Majesties servants, at the Red "Bull; written by Thomas Dek- "ker, 4to. 1612." The principal plot of this piece is built on Machiavel's *Marriage of Belphegor*, which is to be found in the select collection of Novels I have before mentioned. The name is founded on a quibble, the *Devil* being a principal character in the play. Scene, Naples.

27. IF YOU KNOW NOT ME, YOU KNOW NOBODY, or, *The Troubles of Queen Elizabeth*, in two parts, by Thomas Heywood, part 1st, 4to. 1606. 4to. 1608. 4to. 1613. 4to. 1632. part 2d, 4to. 1605. 4to. 1623. 4to. 1633. The second part contains the building of the Royal Exchange, and the famous victory of queen Elizabeth in the year 1588. These plays were printed without the author's consent or knowledge, and that so corruptly as not even to be divided into acts; on which, at the revival of it at the Cockpit, one and twenty years after its first representation, he thought it necessary to write a Prologue to it, in which he particularly inveighs against, and disclaims the imperfect copy.

28. IGNORAMUS. Com. by R. C. 4to. 1662. This is a translation of the Latin play of the same name. The two annexed letters are

are explained by Coxeter to stand for Rob. Codrington.

29. IGNORAMUS, or, *The English Lawyer*. C. Acted at Drury-Lane, 12mo. 1736.

30. AN ILL BEGINNING HAS A GOOD END, AND A BAD BEGINNING MAY HAVE A GOOD END. Com. by John Forde, entered on the books of the Stationers' Company, June 29, 1660, and was among those destroyed by Mr. Warburton's servant.

31. THE ILL-NATUR'D MAN. Com. Acted every day in this Metropolis, 8vo. 1773.

32. THE ILLUMINATION, or, *The Glazier's Conspiracy*. A Prelude, by F. Pilon. Acted at Covent-Garden, 8vo. 1779. This trifle was produced by the rejoicings on the acquittal of Admiral Keppel. The writer of it has a very happy talent at catching temporary subjects for the exercise of his dramatic powers.

33. THE IMAGE OF LOVE. This is one of Bishop Bale's dramatic pieces, mentioned by himself in his Catalogue.

34. THE IMAGINARY CUCKOLD. Com. by Ozell. This is only a translation of Moliere's *Cocu imaginaire*. From this piece hints have been taken for the plots of several English comedies, as I shall point out wherever they occur to my knowledge.

35. THE IMAGINARY OBSTACLE. Com. Translated from the French, and printed in Foote's *Comic Theatre*, vol. II.

36. THE IMPERIAL CAPTIVES. Trag. by John Mottley, 8vo. 1720. This piece has merit, and was acted with some success in Lincoln's-Inn Fields. Scene, Carthage.

37. IMPERIALE. Trag. by Sir Ralph Freeman, 4to. 1655. Langbaine gives this play a most excellent character, placing it on an equal rank with most of the tragedies of that period, and speaks of the catastrophe as being extremely affecting. The plot is taken from Beard's *Theatre*, Goulart's *Hist. Admirab.* &c, and the Scene laid in Genoa. The author has prefixed some testimonies from Aristotle, &c. to manifest the value which the writers of antiquity had for tragedy.

38. THE IMPERIAL. Trag. Anon. Fol. 1669. The greatest part of this play is taken from a Latin one. The plot is built on the History of *Zeno*, the twelfth Emperor from Constantine, and the scene lies in Constantinople. Both Langbaine and Jacob have ascribed this play to Sir William Killigrew. But in the former edition of this work, the editor expresses his doubts of its being assigned to him with truth; the principal of his reasons being grounded on the supposed death of Sir William Killigrew in 1665, who lived until the year 1693. I shall therefore leave him in possession of all the credit arising from this tragedy, which cannot boast of much excellence.

39. THE IMPERIAL LOVERS, or, *The Coquet at her Wit's End*. Com. 8vo. Anonym. 1723.

40. THE IMPERTINENT LOVERS. Com. by Francis Hawling. This is mentioned in Mears's Catalogue, but was, I believe, not printed.

41. THE IMPERTINENTS. C. by Ozell. Translation from the *Facheux of Moliere*.

42. THE IMPOSTOR. Trag. by Henry Brooke, Esq; 8vo. 1771. This tragedy is on the same subject as Miller's *Mahomet*. It was not acted.

43. THE IMPOSTOR DETECTED, or, *The Vintner's Triumph over Brooke*

B[rook]e *and* H[ellie]r. A Farce, *occasioned by a Case lately off——d to the* H——e *of* C———ns, *by the said* B———ke *and* H———r, 4to. 1712. The scene, London and Westminster. This piece was evidently never intended for the stage, but was only a political and party affair, which may be known by looking into the proceedings of parliament of that year.

44. The Imposture. Tragi-Com. by James Shirley. Acted at the private house, Black-Friers, 8vo. 1652. Scene, Mantua.

45. Imposture Defeated, or, *A Trick to cheat the Devil.* Com. by George Powell, 4to. 1698. The author himself says, that this trifle of a comedy was only a slight piece of scribble for the introduction of a little music, being no more than a short week's work, to serve the wants of a thin playhouse and long vacation. Scene, Venice. At the end is a Masque, called, Endymion, *the Man in the Moon.* They were performed at the Theatre in Drury-Lane.

46. Of the Impostures of Thomas Becket. This is another piece on Bishop Bale's list.

47. The Impromptu of Versailles, by Ozell, translated from Moliere's Comedy of the same name.

48. The Inchanted Lovers. A Dramatic Pastoral, by Sir William Lower, 12mo. 1658. Scene, the Island of Erithrea in Portugal.

49. Incle and Yarico. Trag. of three acts, by the Author of *The City Farce,* 8vo. 1742. Not acted; but it is said to have been intended to be performed at Covent-Garden. The story from *The Spectator,* vol. I. No 11.

50. The Inconsolables, or, *The Contented Cuckold.* Dramatic Farce, Anonymous, 8vo. 1738. This piece was never acted, and is indeed by no means deserving of a representation. I imagine it to have a reference to, and to have been intended as an exposure of, some particular event in private life, which might have for some time supplied the favourite kind of scandal to the card and tea-tables of this metropolis at that period.

51. The Inconstant, or, *The Way to win Him.* Com. by George Farquhar. Acted at Drury-Lane, 4to. 1702. This is a very lively and entertaining comedy, although there are some incidents in it which scarcely come within the limits of probability. The author in his Preface, and Rowe in the Epilogue, say the hint of the play only was taken from Beaumont and Fletcher's *Wild Goose Chace,* though, in fact, the main plot and whole scenes were borrowed from thence; but the catastrophe of the last act, where young Mirabel is in danger of his life at a courtezan's house, and is delivered by the carefulness of his mistress Oriana disguised as his page, owes its origin, it is said, to an affair of the like nature, which the author had himself some concern in, when on military duty abroad. The scene lies in Paris.

52. The Inconstant Lady. Com. by Arthur Wilson; entered on the books of the Stationers' Company, Sept. 9, 1653, but not printed. It was among those destroyed by Mr. Warburton's servant.

53. The Independent Patriot, or, *Musical Folly.* Com. by Fran. Lynch. Acted at Lincoln's-Inn Fields, 8vo. 1737.

54. Indian Emperor, or, *The Conquest of Mexico by the Spaniards.* Tragi-Com. by J. Dryden, 4to. 1667. 4to. 1668. 4to. 1692. This play is a sequel to the *Indian Queen.* Of this connection notice was given

ven to the audience by printed bills, diſtributed at the door; an expedient ſuppoſed to be ridiculed in the *Rehearſal*, when *Bayes* tells how many papers he has printed to inſtill into the audience ſome conception of his plot. It is written in heroic verſe, the plot is taken from the ſeveral hiſtorians who have written on this affair, and met with great ſucceſs in the repreſentation. The ſcene lies in Mexico, and two leagues about it.

55. THE INDIAN EMPEROR, or, *The Conqueſt of Peru by the Spaniards*. Trag. by Francis Hawling. This was acted in the year 1728, and was promiſed in a ſecond collection of this author's Poems, which never appeared.

56. INDIAN QUEEN. Trag. by Sir Robert Howard and Mr. Dryden, Fo. 1665. This is likewiſe in heroic verſe, and met with great applauſe. Scene, near Mexico.

57. THE INDISCREET LOVER. Com. by Abraham Portal. Acted at the King's Theatre in the Hay-Market, for the benefit of the Britiſh Lying-Inn Hoſpital, in Brownlow-ſtreet, 8vo. 1768.

58. THE INFLEXIBLE CAPTIVE. Trag. by Miſs Hannah More, 8vo. 1774. This is on the ſtory of *Regulus*, and was acted one night at Bath.

59. THE INFORMERS OUTWITTED. A Tragi-comical Farce, Anonymous. This piece was never acted, but was printed in 1738. 8vo.

60. INGRATITUDE OF a COMMONWEALTH, or, *The Fall of Caius Martius Coriolanus*. Trag. by N. Tate. Acted at the Theatre Royal, 4to. 1682. This play is founded on Shakſpeare's *Coriolanus*, and was choſen by the author, as he acknowledges, on account of the reſemblance between the buſy faction of his own time and that of Coriolanus. Scene, the cities of Rome and Corioli.

61. INJUR'D INNOCENCE. Tr. by Fettiplace Bellers, 8vo. 1732. Acted at the Theatre Royal in Drury-Lane, with ſome ſucceſs.

62. INJUR'D LOVE, or, *The Cruel Huſband*. Trag. by N. Tate, 4to. 1707. This tragedy was prepared for the ſtage, and deſigned to have been acted at the Theatre Royal; but by ſome means or other, it was never performed.

63. INJUR'D LOVER, or, *The Lady's Satisfaction*. Com. Acted at Drury-Lane, 4to. N. D.

64. THE INJUR'D LOVERS, or, *The Ambitious Father*. Trag. by W. Mountfort. Acted at Drury-Lane, 4to. 1688. This play met with but indifferent ſucceſs, and indeed ſeems not to have merited better. Langbaine charges the author with having, like Sir *Courtly Nice*, written for his diverſion, but without regarding wit.

65. THE INJUR'D PRINCESS, or, *The Fatal Wager*. Tragi-Com. by T. Durfey. Acted at the Theatre Royal, 4to. 1682. The foundation and ſome part of the language of this play is taken from Shakſpeare's *Cymbeline*, and the ſcene lies at Luds Town, alias London. The author has alſo made uſe of the epilogue to the *Fool turn'd Critick* (a play of his own) by way of prologue to this piece. Its running title is, *The Unequal Match, or The Fatal Wager*.

66. INJUR'D VIRTUE, or, *The Virgin Martyr*. Trag. by Benj. Griffin, 12mo. 1715. Acted at Richmond by the D. of Southampton and Cleveland's ſervants. The ſcene, Cæſarea. This piece is nothing more than an alteration of an old play with the latter title, written by Maſſinger and Decker.

67. THE INNER TEMPLE MASQUE, or, *Maſque of Heroes*.

by Thomas Middleton, 4to. 1619. 4to. 1640. This was presented as an entertainment for many worthy ladies, by the gentlemen of that ancient house. Mrs. Behn has borrowed very confiderably from it in her *City Heirefs.*

68. THE INNER TEMPLE MASQUE. by William Browne, performed about the year 1620; printed from a manufcript in Emanuel college library 1772, in Davies'sedition of this author's works. Mr. Warton fuppofes this mafque to have fuggefted the hint to Milton of his *Mafque of Comus.* See Hiftory of Poetry, vol. II. 403.

69. INNOCENCE BETRAY'D, or, *The Royal Impoftor*, by Meffieurs Daniel Bellamy, fen. and jun. 8vo. 1746. This piece was never acted, but is one of fix dramatic pieces written in concert by thefe two gentlemen, father and fon, and publifhed by them in a volume, together with fome mifcellanies in profe and verfe.

70. INNOCENCE DISTRESS'D, or, *The Royal Penitents.* Trag. by Mr. Gould, 8vo. 1737. This play was never acted. It was publifhed by fubfcription for the benefit of the author's daughter, who dedicates it to the duchefs of Beaufort. The fcene is in the Great Duke's Palace in Mofco.

71. THE INNOCENT MISTRESS. Com. by Mrs. M. Pix, 4to. 1697. This play was acted at the Theatre in Little Lincoln's-Inn Fields, and in the fummer feafon, yet met with very good fuccefs. It is not however original, feveral incidents in it being borrowed from other plays; particularly from Sir George Etherege's *Man of Mode.* Scene, London. Prologue and epilogue by Mr. Motteux.

72. THE INNOCENT USURPER, or, *The Death of the Lady* JANE GRAY. Trag. by J. Banks, 4to. 1694. This play was prohibited the ftage on account of fome miftaken cenfures and groundlefs infinuations that it reflected on the government. The author in his dedication, however, has vindicated himfelf from that charge, by fetting forth that it was written ten years before, fo that it could not poffibly have been meant to caft a reflection on the prefent government. It is far from being the worft of his dramatic writings; and although, in point of language and beauty of poetry, it falls fhort of Mr. Rowe's Tragedy on the fame ftory, yet it excels it with refpect to the *fatbos*, and a ftrict adherence to hiftorical fact. The plot is built on the fufferings of that fair unfortunate victim to the ambition of her relations; and the fcene lies in the Tower.

73. THE INOCULATOR. Com. by GeorgeSaville Carey, 8vo. 1766.

74. THE INQUISITION. Farce, by J. Philips, 8vo. 1717. This piece was never performed, but is fuppofed to be acted at Child's Coffee-houfe, and the King's-Arms Tavern in St. Paul's Church-yard. The fubject of it is the controverfy between the Bp. of Bangor and Dr. Snape, which controverfy is here faid to be fairly ftated and fet in a true light. As other pieces publifhed about this time, with the fame name, are afcribed to Dr. Sewel, I imagine this alfo to be by the fame hand. See PRETENDER'S FLIGHT.

75. THE INSATIATE COUNTESS. Trag. by J. Marfton, 4to. 1603. 4to. 1613. 4to. 1631. As it was a common cuftom with this author to difguife his ftory, and perfonate real perfonages under feigned characters, Langbaine conjectures that by *Ifabella*, the infatiable countefs of *Suevia*, is meant *Joan*
the

the first queen of Jerusalem, Naples, and Sicily. Nor is this writer the only one who has made use of her story under a false title, her tale being related in Bandello's Novels, and by *Belleforest*, tom. II. Nov. 20. under the character of the Countess of *Celant*, as also in *God's Revenge against Adultery*, Ep. 5. by the title of *Anne Duchess of Ulme*.

76. THE INSIGNIFICANTS. C. of five acts, by Dr. Bacon, 8vo. 1757. In the argument the author says, "In this piece all the triflers, "upon whom the wholsome pre- "scriptions given in the preced- "ing satires have not had their "wished-for effect, are considered "as dead persons, and proper "care is taken to provide for their "funerals." See *The Tatlers*.

77. THE INSOLVENT, or, *Filial Piety*. Trag. by Aaron Hill. Acted at the Hay-market, 8vo. 1758. This play was acted when that theatre was under the direction of Theo. Cibber. It was altered by Mr. Hill from an old manuscript play, called, *The Guiltless Adultress, or, Judge in his own Cause*, which had long been in the hands of the managers of Drury-Lane, and was supposed to have been written by Sir William Davenant. The opening of the piece was palpably founded on Massinger's *Fatal Dowry*.

78. THE INSTITUTION OF THE ORDER OF THE GARTER. Dramatic Poem, by Gilb. West, 4to. 1742. This piece was never intended for the stage, yet is truly dramatic, and has many very fine things in it. It is republished in Dodsley's Collection of Poems in six volumes, 12mo. Dr. Johnson observes, that this piece is written with sufficient knowledge of the manners that prevailed in the age to which it is referred, and with great elegance of diction; but, for want of a process of events, neither knowledge nor elegance preserve the reader from weariness.

79. THE INSTITUTION OF THE GARTER, or, *Arthur's Round Table restored*, Masque. Acted at Drury-Lane 1771. This is partly an alteration by Mr. Garrick of the preceding, and was intended to introduce a procession at the installation of Knights of the Garter.

80. AN INTERLUDE BETWEEN JUPITER, JUNO, AND MERCURY, by Henry Fielding, 1743. This piece was never performed, nor indeed intended to be so by itself, it being only a beginning or introduction to a projected comedy, intituled, *Jupiter upon Earth*.

81. A NEWE INTERLUDE OF IMPACYENTE POVERTE, *newlye Imprinted*. M. V. L. X. (I suppose 1560.) 4to. This piece is in metre, and in the old black letter; and the title-page says, " Four *Men may well and easelye playe this Interlude*."

82. AN INTERLUDE OF WELTH END HELTH, *full of Sport and mery Pastyme*. Printed 8vo. in the old black letter, without date. The persons of the play are in the title-page, viz. *Welth, Helth, Liberty, Illwyll, Shrewdwit, Hance, Remedy*. In which also we are told that Four may easily perform this play. This I have entirely from Coxeter's notes.

83. THE INTERLUDE OF YOUTH. 4to. [N. D.] This is an old, serious, moral, and instructive piece, written in verse, and printed in the black letter, by John Waley. Ames, on what authority does not appear, puts the date of 1557 to it.

84. THE INTRIGUES AT VERSAILLES, or, *A Jilt in all Humours*. Com. by T. Durfey. Acted at Lincoln's-Inn Fields, 4to. 1697.

This play did not meet with so much success as the author expected from it, and in his dedication he condemns the taste of the town for preferring others of his plays before it. It is, however, like most of his pieces, a complication of plagiarisms. *Ternezre's* disguising himself in women's cloaths, and his mistress's husband (Count *Brisac*) falling in love with him in that habit, is borrowed from a Novel, called *The Double Cuckold*; and the character of *Vandosin* appears to be a mixture of Wycherley's *Olivia* in *The Plain Dealer*, and Mrs. Behn's *Myrtilla* in *The Amorous Jilt*. The scene, Versailles.

85. THE INTRIGUING CHAMBERMAID. A Ballad Farce, by H. Fielding, 8vo. 1733. This piece is borrowed almost entirely from the *Dissipateur*. It was performed at Drury-Lane with good success, and still continues on the list of acting farces.

86. THE INTRIGUING COURTIERS, or, *The Modish Gallants*. Com. Anonymous, 8vo. 1732, wherein, says the title-page, the secret histories of several persons are faithfully represented. In which is introduced an interlude (after the manner of a rehearsal), called the MARRIAGE PROMISE, or, *The Disappointed Virgin*; consisting of variety of new songs, set to several English, Irish, and Scotch ballad tunes, and country dances. It was never performed any where; but seems to have been occasioned by some pieces of gallantry in the amorous history of the English court at that time.

87. THE INTRIGUING MILLINERS, or, *Attorney's Clerks*. Farce, 1738. This is merely a burlesque; and although anonymous, was written by Mr. Robinson, of Kendal.

88. THE INTRIGUING WIDOW, or, *Honest Wife*. Com. printed in 4to. and dedicated to Lady Rivers, by J. B. The title-page was wanting in the only copy of this play I ever saw.

89. THE INVADER OF HIS COUNTRY, or, *The Fatal Resentment*. Trag. by John Dennis. Acted Drury-Lane, 8vo. 1720. This is an alteration of Shakspeare's *Coriolanus*, and was unsuccessful in its representation. The author, in a dedication to the Duke of Newcastle, makes a formal complaint against the players for not doing him justice. First, in producing his play on a Wednesday, which occasioned his benefit to fall upon a Friday. "Now, says he, my "Lord, Friday is not only the very "worst day of the week for an "audience; but this was that particular Friday when a hundred "persons, who designed to be "there, were either gone to meet "the king, or preparing here in "town to do that duty which was "expected from them at his arrival." The epilogue was writen by Mr. Cibber, who is very heartily abused for it by Mr. Dennis in an advertisement.

90. THE INVASION. Farce, 8vo. 1759. This piece was never acted, nor intended for the stage, but is only a ridicule on the unnecessary apprehensions some persons entertained on account of the threatened invasion of the flat-bottomed boats from France on the coast of England in that year.

91. THE INVASION, or, *A Trip to Brighthelmstone*. Farce, by F. Pilon. Acted at Covent-Garden, 8vo. 1778. This was performed with considerable success.

92. THE HISTORY OF JOBE, by Robert Green. This piece was among those destroyed by Mr. Warburton's servant.

93. Jos's

93. JOB'S AFFLICTIONS. Tr. by Ralph Radcliff. Not printed.

94. JOCASTA. Tr. 4to. 1566! This is a translation from *Euripides*, by George Gascoigne and Francis Kinwellmarshe. The scene lies at Thebes.

95. THE TALE OF JOCONDO AND ASTOLFO. Com. by Thomas Dekker. Entered on the books of the Stationers' Company the 29th of June, 1660; but not printed. This was one of those destroyed by Mr. Warburton's servant.

96. OF JOHN KING OF ENGLAND. A dramatic Piece, by Bishop Bale. This is one among the numerous pieces of this prelate's works, which he has given us a list of in his account of the writers of Britain.

97. *The Troublesome Raigne of* JOHN KING OF ENGLAND, *with the Discoverie of King Richard Cordelion's base Son, vulgarly named the Bastard Fawconbridge: also the Death of King John at Swinstead Abbey.* As it was (sundry times) publikely acted by the Queene's Majesties players in the honourable Citie of London, &c. 1591. b. letter.

From a circumstance in the prologue to this play, it should seem to have been the production of Marlowe. It was republished in 1611 and 1622, with the letters W. Sh. prefixed to it, that it might be mistaken for the work of Shakspeare. See Mr. Malone's Supplement to the edition of Shakspeare's Plays published in 1778, vol. I. p. 163.

This spurious drama has been thrice republished. By the Editor of *Miscellaneous Pieces of ancient English Poesie*, 12mo. 1764; by Mr. Steevens as one of *Twenty of the Plays of Shakspeare*, 8vo. 1766; and by Mr. Nichols in *Six Old Plays on which Shakspeare founded*, &c. printed for S. Leacroft, crown 8vo. 1778.

98. KING JOHN. Trag. by William Shakspeare, Fo. 1623. This is the genuine work of our matchless bard. The plot is from the English historians; and the scene lies sometimes in England, and sometimes in France. Dr. Johnson observes, that though it is not written with the utmost power of Shakspeare, it is varied with a very pleasing interchange of incidents and characters. The Lady's grief is very affecting; and the character of the bastard contains that mixture of greatness and levity which our author delighted to exhibit.

99. KING JOHN AND MATILDA. Trag. by Robert Davenport. Acted at the Cockpit, Drury-Lane, 4to. 1655. This play was acted with great applause, and was published by one Andrew Pennycuicke, who himself acted the part of *Matilda*, no women having at that time ever appeared on the stage. The plot is taken from some circumstances in the same reign with the foregoing play, and the scene laid in England.

100. JOHN THE BAPTIST. An Interlude, by Bishop Bale, 4to. 1538. This was the second dramatic piece printed in England; it is in metre, and in the old black letter, and the full title is as follows: *A brefe Comedie or Interlude of Johan Baptystes preachynge in the Wyldernesse, openynge the craftye Assaultes of the Hypocrytes, wyth the gloryouse Baptysme of the Lord Jesus Chryste.*

101. JOHNNE THE EVANGELISTE. An Interlude, 4to. 1566. Anonymous.

102. JONAS. Trag. by Ralph Radcliff. Not printed.

103. JOSEPH ANDREWS. Farce, by Robert Pratt. Acted at Drury-Lane, for Mr. Bensley's benefit, April 20, 1778. Not printed.

104. JOSEPH's

104. JOSEPH'S AFFLICTIONS. By this title is an Interlude mentioned by Langbaine, who confesses, however, he never saw it, and therefore pretends not to give any date to it. Jacob, Gildon, Whincop, and other catalogues, have followed his example, and taken the name for granted; but the *British Theatre* has it as follows, viz. *Joseph bys Afflictiones*, 1567.

105. JOVIAL CREW, or, *The Devil turn'd Ranter*. An Interlude full of pleasante myrth. Anonymous, 4to. 1598. This is a character of the Roaring Ranters of those times represented in a comedy.

106. THE JOVIAL CREW, or, *The Merry Beggars*. Com. by Rich. Brome. Acted at the Cockpit, Drury-Lane, in the year 1641, 4to. 1652. Dedicated to Thomas Stanley, Esq. This play met with great success at its first appearance, and was frequently revived and performed with the same applause; it was afterwards altered into a Ballad Opera, by the addition of several songs by Mr. Roome and Sir William Young, and brought on the stage with its former title at Drury-Lane Theatre in the year 1732, in which form it was since revived at Covent-Garden, where it took a very successful run for several nights together, and afterwards brought many crowded houses as well then as in succeeding seasons. It is certain that it is far from an unentertaining piece, especially to those who are fond of the musical drama; yet it is mingled with so many absurdities and indelicacies, that I cannot help looking on the great approbation it met with, as a kind of reflection on the public taste.

107. A JOURNEY TO BRISTOL, or, *The Honest Welshman*. Farce, by John Hippisley, [1729.] No date. This is but an indifferent piece, and seems more calculated for the latitude of Bristol, to which place the author used annually to go at the head of a company of comedians, that to that of London. It was performed at Lincoln's-Inn Fields Theatre, but with very little success.

108. IPHIGENIA. Trag. by J. Dennis, 4to. 1700. This was brought on at Lincoln's-Inn Fields, but was damned. The scene is a wild country on the top of a mountain before the Temple of Diana Taurica. The Epilogue by Col. Codrington.

109. IPHIGENIA IN AULIS. Trag. translated from *Euripides*, printed in 8vo. 1780. with three other pieces from the same author.

109 *. IPHIGENIA IN AULIS. Opera, translated from *Algarotti*, 12mo. 1767. Printed in " An " Essay on the Opera.

110. IPHIGENIA IN TAURIS. Trag. translated from *Euripides*, by Gilb. West, Esq; 4to. 1749. Printed with his translation of Pindar.

111. IPHIS AND IANTHE, or, *A Marriage without a Man*. Com. This piece was entered on the books of the Stationers' Company, June 29, 1660, in the name of William Shakspeare. It was never printed. I take this opportunity of observing, that the several plays mentioned in the present work, from the records of Stationers' Hall, are set down with the hope that some of them may be yet existing. As it is known that many ancient manuscript plays are in being, the possessors of them would render an acceptable service to the publick, if they caused a few copies of each to be printed for the perusal of such as are curious in dramatic history.

112. IRENE,

112. IRENE, or, *The Fair Greek*. Trag. by Cha. Goring. Acted at Drury-Lane, 4to. 1708. This play is founded on the celebrated story of the Sultan Mahomet, who being reproved by his grandees for giving too indulgent a loose to his passion for a beautiful Greek named *Irene*, who was his favourite mistress, to the neglect of his state affairs and the prejudice of his empire, took off her head with his own hand in their presence, as an atonement for his fault. The author declares it to be only the product of a few leisure hours during his residence at the university. The scene lies in the Seraglio at Constantinople, about three years after the conquest of that city.

113. IRENE. Trag. by Samuel Johnson. Acted at Drury-Lane, 8vo. 1749. This is the only dramatic piece among all the writings of this celebrated author. It is founded on the same story with the foregoing; the author, however, has taken some trifling liberties with the history, *Irene* being here made to be strangled by order of the emperor, instead of dying by his own hand. The unities of time, place, and action are most rigidly kept up, the whole coming within the time of performance, and the scene, which is a garden of the Seraglio, remaining unmoved through the whole play. The language of it is, like all the rest of Dr. Johnson's writings, nervous, sentimental, and poetical. Yet, notwithstanding these perfections, assisted by the united powers of Mr. Garrick, Mr. Barry, Mrs. Pritchard, and Mrs. Cibber, all together in one play, it did not meet with the success it merited, and might therefore justly have expected.

114. IRELAND PRESERV'D, or, *The Siege of Londonderry*. Tragi-Com. Written by a gentleman, who was in the town during the whole siege. Printed at Dublin, 8vo. 1738-9. This play was written by John Michelborne, one of the governors of Londonderry, during the siege of it. There was an earlier edition in 1707. See vol. I. p. 313.

115. IRISH HOSPITALITY, or, *Virtue rewarded*. Com. by Cha. Shadwell, 12mo. 1720. This is one of five plays by this author, which were written for the latitude of our sister island, and were all performed in Dublin with great applause. The scene of this lies at Mount Worthy in Fingall, and I should apprehend conveys a secret compliment to some person of distinction in that part of Ireland. The time eight hours.

116. THE IRISH FINE LADY. Farce, by Charles Macklin. Acted at Covent-Garden one night only, November 28, 1767. Not printed. It had appeared in Ireland with considerable applause.

117. THE IRISH MASQUE AT COURT. by Ben. Jonson, Fol. 1640. This piece is said to have been presented by gentlemen, the King's servants. At what time, however, I cannot pretend to say, but it is printed among his other works.

118. THE IRISH WIDOW. C. of two acts, by David Garrick, Esq. Acted at Drury-Lane, 8vo. 1772. The intention of this piece seems to have been merely to introduce Mrs. Barry, now Crawford, to the public in a new light, and was very successfully executed. The several performers did great justice to their respective characters.

119. THE IRON AGE. An History, in two parts, by Tho. Heywood, 4to. 1632. The first part contains the rape of *Helen*, the siege

siege of *Troy*, the combat between *Hector* and *Ajax*; the deaths of *Troilus* and *Hector*, the death of *Achilles*; the contention of *Ajax* and *Ulysses*, the death of *Ajax*, &c. The second includes the deaths of *Penthesilea, Paris, Priam*, and *Hecuba*, the burning of *Troy*, and the deaths of *Agamemnon, Menelaus, Clytemnestra, Helen, Orestes, Egisthus, Pylades, King Diomed, Pyrrhus, Cethus, Symon*, and *Therfites*. The plots and much of the language of both these plays are borrowed from the classical writers, and the whole is a compage of incidents and narratives thrown together without the least regard to any dramatic rules. Yet they met with very great success, having been, as the author himself tells us, often publickly acted by two companies upon one stage at once, and at sundry times thronged three several theatres with numerous and mighty auditories.

120. ISABELLA, or, *The Fatal Marriage*. Play, altered from Southerne, by David Garrick, Esq; 8vo. 1758. A judicious alteration of *The Fatal Marriage*, leaving out the comic part.

121. THE ISLAND OF SLAVES. Com. of two acts, 1761. This is little more than a literal translation of the *Isle des Esclaves* of M. Marivaux. It has not made its appearance in print, yet I think has at least as much merit as many of the *Petites Pieces* which we see frequently performed on the stage. It was acted one night only for the benefit of Mrs. Clive, and was the occasion of an epistolary dispute in print between her and Mr. Shuter, whose benefit happened to fall on the same night.

122. THE ISLAND PRINCESS. Tragi-Com. by Beaumount and Fletcher, Fol. 1647.

123. THE ISLAND PRINCESS. Tragi-Com. by Nahum Tate, altered from Beaumont and Fletcher, and acted at the Theatre Royal; 4to. 1687.

124. THE ISLAND PRINCESS, or, *The Generous Portuguese*. Opera, by P. A. Motteux, 4to. 1699. This is only the principal parts of Fletcher's *Island Princess* formed into an Opera, and performed at the Theatre Royal. The scene lies in the Spice Islands; and the music was composed by Mr. Daniel Purcell, Mr. Clarke, and Mr. Leveridge.

125. THE ISLAND QUEENS, or, *The Death of Mary Queen of Scotland*. Trag. by J. Banks, 4to. 1684. This piece was prohibited the stage, for which reason the author thought proper to publish it, in defence of himself and his tragedy. The story is founded on the Scotch and English histories, to which the author has closely and impartially adhered, and well preserved that power of affecting the passions which appears through all his works, and sometimes makes ample amends for want of poetry and language. It was reprinted in 1704, with the title of the ALBION QUEENS, or, *The Death*, &c. To this edition are the names added of Wilks, Booth, Oldfield, Porter, &c. in the Dramatis Personæ. From which it seems that it was afterwards allowed the liberty of being performed.

126. THE ISLANDERS. Comic Opera, by Charles Dibden. Acted at Covent-Garden, 8vo. 1780.

127. THE ISLE OF DOGS. By Thomas Nash. This comedy was never published. In a pamphlet, called, *Lenten Stuff*, 1599, the author says, that having begun the induction and first act of it, the other four acts, without his consent, or the least guess at his drift or scope, were supplied by the players.

What

What the nature of this piece was, I cannot learn; but the consequence of it was very serious to poor Nash, who was, as he says, sequestered from the wonted means of his maintenance, and obliged to conceal himself for near two years, part of which time he resided at Yarmouth, and there wrote the pamphlet above-mentioned.

128. THE ISLE OF GULLS. Com. by J. Daye. Acted at Black-Friers, by the children of the Revels, 4to. 1606. 4to. 1633. This is a very good play, and met with great success. The plot is taken from Sir Ph. Sidney's *Arcadia*.

129. THE ITALIAN HUSBAND. Trag. by Edward Ravenscroft, 4to. 1698. Acted at Lincoln's-Inn Fields. The story of this play is barbarous and bloody, and the villainy carried on it to bring about the catastrophe, deep and horrid; but the piece itself has but little merit more than that of exciting the passions of horror and terror. The scene lies at Radiano in Italy. Besides the Prologue, there is prefixed to this play what the author calls a Prelude, being a dialogue between the Poet, a Critic, and a Friend of the Poet's. The Epilogue written by Jo. Haines.

130. THE ITALIAN HUSBAND, or, *The violated Bed avenged.* A moral drama. By Edward Lewis, M. A. 8vo. 1754. It will be unnecessary to inform those who have read this unaccountable performance, that it was never acted; for no theatre past or present would have received it, neither can we persuade ourselves that any future manager would suffer a line of it to be rehearsed within his walls. We subjoin the following speech to justify our opinion of its defects:

" *Fortis.* You know his lordship's
" bailiff Giovanni
" Lives in a farm near to his castle
" gate.
" Whilst he at dinner sat, a favourite
" hen
" Came cackling, and at's feet lay'd
" a live chick,
" Perfect with wings and claws, with
" eyes and voice,
" Which ran without delay after its
" mother.
" But lo! a greater wonder justly fills
" All hearts with horror and amazement dire:
" Just underneath the table th' earth
" gap'd wide
" And did disclose a bubbling spring
" of blood,
" Whence drops resulting sprinkled
" all the board.
" Fix'd in suspense at this, one, from
" the cellar,
" Ran and declar'd the wine was in a
" ferment,
" Tho un'd before, and boil'd in every
" vessel,
" As if set o'er a fire intense and large.
" Mean while a serpent's carcase they
" beheld
" Dragg'd out of doors, with eager
" haste, by weasels;
" A shepherd's bitch came gaping,
" from whose jaws
" Leap'd forth a lively, large, tun-
" belly'd toad:
" A ram ran full against a dog spontaneous,
" And at one fatal stroke brake the
" dog's neck."

So much for the solemnity of our author's prodigies. At the conclusion of his piece, however, not content, like *Tancred*, to present the lover's heart in a vase to his mistress, or, like *Albovine*, to convert his scull into a drinking cup for her use, he has made an " electuary" of his hero's vitals, and compelled his heroine to swallow it. Some hypocondriac may thank us for having recommended this tragedy to his perusal. Whether it be the production of incurable insanity, or absurdity in the extreme, let more sagacious criticks determine.

131. THE

131. THE ITALIAN NIGHT PIECE, or, *The Unfortunate Piety.* By Philip Massinger. Entered on the books of the Stationers' Company Sept. 9, 1653; and was among those destroyed by Mr. Warburton's servant.

132. THE ITALIAN PATRIOT, or, *The Florentine Conspiracy.* Trag. by Charles Gildon. Acted at Drury-Lane, 4to. 1703. This is the same play as THE PATRIOT, and published by a different bookseller, who says, in the preface, that he was excluded from his share in the other publication, although he had paid part of the copy-money for it; he also asserts, that there is one third more in this copy, which he styles the true original, than in the other.

133. ITE IN VINEAM. Com. by John Bourchier, Lord Berners. Acted, as Wood says, at Calais after vespers. It has not been printed.

134. IT SHOULD HAVE COME SOONER. Farce, by Francis Hawling. This is only mentioned in Mears's Catalogue, and was probably never printed.

135. THE JUBILEE. Dram. Entertainment, by David Garrick, Esq. Acted at Drury-Lane, 1769. Not printed. A spectacle rendered interesting by mute representations of a principal scene in each of the plays of Shakspeare. These groups were originally designed to form a part of the real Jubilee at Stratford. That attempt, however, having failed ridiculously, leaving Mr. Garrick, the steward and inventor of it, several hundred pounds out of pocket, by means of the present exhibition (which was Mr. Wilson the portrait-painter's contrivance) he at once reimbursed himself, and more successfully entertained the public for upwards of ninety evenings in the first season of the piece.

136. THE JUDGE, or, *Believe as you List.* By Philip Massinger. See BELIEVE AS YOU LIST.

137. THE JUDGMENT OF MIDAS. Masque, by Christopher Smart, printed in his " Poems on " Several Occasions." 4to. 1752.

138. THE JUDGMENT OF PARIS, A Masque. by W. Congreve, 4to. 1701. This is a very pretty piece of poetry, and is now frequently performed to music, by way of an *Oratorio*. It was originally composed by John Eccles, Mr. Singer, Mr. Purcell, and Mr. Weldon.

139. THE JUDGMENT OF PARIS. An Entertainment of five Interludes, by Abraham Langford, 8vo. 1730. Printed at the end of " Bellaria, or, The Fair Unfor-" tunate." A Romance.

140. THE JUDGMENT OF PARIS, or, *The Triumph of Beauty.* Pastoral Ballad Opera of one act, performed at Lincoln's-Inn Fields, 8vo. 1731.

141. THE JUDGMENT OF PARIS. A dramatic Pantomime, by John Weaver, 1732.

142. THE JUDGMENT OF PARIS. An English Burletta in two acts, by Dr. Ralph Schomberg. Performed at the Hay-Market with that degree of success that commonly attends our author's literary undertakings, 8vo. 1768.

143. JUGURTHA. A Tragedy, by Dr. Ridley. This performance is still in manuscript.

144. JULIANA, *Princess of Poland.* Tragi-Com. by John Crown, 4to. 1671. Acted at the Duke of York's Theatre. This is the first and indeed the most indifferent of all Mr. Crown's pieces. The story is founded on history, and the scene laid at Warsaw in Poland,

Poland, at the meeting of the *Ban* and *Arcer Ban*, armed in the field, for the election of a king.

145. JULIUS CÆSAR. Trag. by Alex. earl of Sterling, 4to. 1604. Fol. 1637. This is much the most regular dramatic piece of this noble author, at least in respect to the unity of action; yet he has run into the very same fault which Shakspeare had done before him, viz. the not closing the piece with the most natural and affecting catastrophe, viz. the death of Cæsar. Shakspeare, however, has made a noble use of his conspirators, and has drawn the characters of *Antony*, *Brutus*, and *Cassius*, in a manner that gives delight even in despight of the non-necessity of continuing the story. But this author has rendered them so cold and languid, that the reader is apt to wish he had sacrificed them all at once to the manes of the murdered emperor. His style is sententious, yet neither pure nor correct, for which however his lordship pleads his country. Scene, Rome.

146. JULIUS CÆSAR. Trag. by W. Shakspeare, Fol. 1623. The story of this tragedy is from History. What may be considered as faulty in it I have hinted at in my mention of the last-named play, but the beauties of it are innumerable and inimitable. The speeches of *Brutus* and *Antony* over *Cæsar's* body, are perhaps the finest pieces of oratory in the English language, the first appearing unanswerable till the second comes to overthrow its effect; nor can there be a finer scene of resentment and reconciliation between two friends, than that of *Brutus* and *Cassius* in the 4th act. The duke of Buckingham, however, aware of the faults I took notice of in regard to the catastrophe,

has divided the two revolutions in this piece, and formed out of them two plays; the one called JULIUS CÆSAR, the other MARCUS BRUTUS. Under the account of the latter, the reader will find the reason why neither of them came on the stage.

147. JULIUS CÆSAR. Trag. by J. Sheffield, duke of Buckingham, with a prologue and chorus, 4to. 1722.

148. THE TRAGEDY OF JULIUS CÆSAR, *with the Deaths of Brutus and Cassius, written originally by Shakspeare; altered by Sir William Davenant and John Dryden*. Acted at Drury-Lane, 12mo. 1719. This seems to be a publication of the playhouse-copy, with alterations for the stage, which perhaps were traditionally ascribed to Davenant and Dryden; how truly, let any person determine, after reading the following ridiculous rant which is added at the close of the fourth act, and was spoken by Mr. Walker when he performed the character of *Brutus* at Covent-Garden Theatre:

Sure they have rais'd some devil to their aid,
And think to frighten Brutus with a shade:
But ere the night closes this fatal day,
I'll send more ghosts this visit to repay.

149. JULIUS CÆSAR. Trag. Translated from Voltaire, and printed in Dr. Franklin's edition of that author's works.

150. JUNIUS BRUTUS. See LUCIUS JUNIUS BRUTUS.

151. THE JUNTO, or, *The interior Cabinet laid open*. A state Farce, 8vo. 1770. A despicable political catchpenny.

152. THE JUROR. Farce, by W. B. formerly of St. John's-College Cambridge, 8vo. 1718. Never acted.

153. THE JUST GENERAL. T. C. by Cosmo Manuche, 4to. 1652. This piece was intended for the stage, but never acted. Yet, although it was a first attempt of the author's, it is very far from contemptible.

154. THE JUST ITALIAN. T. Com. by Sir W. Davenant. Acted at Black-Friers, 4to. 1630. Scene, Florence.

155. JUSTICE BUSY. A Com. by John Crown. Acted at Lincoln's-Inn Fields about 1699. Not printed. Downes the prompter, who alone mentions it, says it was "well acted, yet proved not a living play: however, Mrs. Bracegirdle, by a potent and magnetic charm in performing a song in it, caused *the stones* of the streets to fly in the men's faces."

156. JUSTICE TRIUMPHANT, or, *The Organ in the Suds*. Farce of three acts, 8vo. 1747. This piece relates to some proceedings then lately transacted in a village near London.

157. IXION. Masque, by W. Taverner. This is only mentioned in Mears's Catalogue, and was, I believe, never printed.

K.

1. THE KEEPERS DISTRACTED. Farce. This is only mentioned in Mears's Catalogue, and was probably never printed.

2. KENSINGTON GARDENS, or, *The Pretenders*. Com. by John Leigh, 8vo. 1720. This was acted at Lincoln's-Inn Fields playhouse, with some success.

3. THE KENTISH ELECTION. Com. by L. N. 8vo. 1735.

4. THE KIND KEEPER, or, *Mr. Limberham*. A Com. by J. Dryden. Acted at the Duke's Theatre, 4to. 1680. This play was intended as an honest satire against the crying sin of keeping; but in short it exposed the keeping part of the town in so just a manner, and set them in so ridiculous a light, that unable to stand the lash of the poet's pen, aided by the force of comic representation, they found means to stop the play after a run of only three nights. There are, however, several parts of it by much too loose for modest ears, or for a moral and well-regulated stage. The author has borrowed some of his incidents from French and Italian Novels; for instance, Mrs. Saintly's discovering *Goodall* in the chest, taken from Cynthio's Novels, part 1. Dec. 3. Nov. 3. and Mrs. Brainsick's pinching and pricking him, from M. de St. Bremond's *Triumph of Love over Fortune*. The scene lies at a boarding house in London.

5. KING AND NO KING. Tr. Com. by Beaumont and Fletcher, 4to. 1619. This play was very roughly handled by Rymer; but, as he dealt no less severely with the works of the immortal Shakspeare, his censures ought to have but little influence over our opinions; and

and this piece amongst others stands up in evidence against his judgment, it having always met with success whenever acted or revived. For a farther account of it, see a criticism on it by Dryden, in the preface to his *Troilus* and *Cressida*. Scene, for the most part of the play, in Iberia. The first edition says it was acted at the Globe, the others at Black Friers.

6. THE KING AND THE MILLER OF MANSFIELD. Farce, by R. Dodsley. Acted at Drury-Lane, 8vo. 1737. The plot of this little piece is built on a traditional story in the reign of our King Henry II. The author, however, has made a very pleasing use of it, and wrought it out into a truly dramatic conclusion. The dialogue is natural, yet elegant; the satire poignant, yet genteel; the sentimental parts such as do honour both to the head and heart of its author, and the catastrophe though simple, yet affecting, and perfectly just. The scene lies in and near the Miller's house in Sherwood Forest, near Nottingham.

7. KING ARTHUR, or, *The British Worthy*. A dramatic Opera, by John Dryden. Acted at the Queen's Theatre, 4to. 1691. This play is a kind of sequel to the *Albion* and *Albanius* of the same author, and seems to have been written rather for the sake of the singing and machinery, than with any view to the more intrinsic beauties of the drama, the incidents being all extravagant, and many of them very puerile. The whole affair of the *Enchanted Wood*, and the other wonders of *Osmond's* art, are borrowed from Tasso, who has made his *Rinaldo* perform every thing that *Arthur* does in this play. The fabulous History of this prince is to be met with in *Geoffrey* of *Monmouth*, as also in the first volume of Tyrrel's *History of England*. The scene lies in Kent. The genius of Dryden, however, struggles through the puerilities with which the story of our legendary prince is encumbered. The contrast of character between *Philadel*, a gentle aerial spirit, friendly to the christians, and *Grimbald*, a fierce earthy goblin, engaged on the adverse party, is not only well designed, but executed with the hand of a master.

8. KING ARTHUR, or, *The British Worthy*. Dramatic Opera, altered by David Garrick. Acted at Drury-Lane, 8vo. 1770. By the assistance of splendid scenery, this alteration was very successful.

9. THE KING CANNOT ERR, &c. Com. 12mo. The title-page of this strange incoherent performance is too long to be here inserted. The author of it, who was evidently disordered in his senses, dedicates *to his Infant Royal Highness the Prince of Wales, on the eighth day of his birth, by way of desert to his Christening, who was born on the twelfth day of the eighth month, in the twelfth year of the last two hundred and fifty years, which make the twenty-fourth part of six thousand years*. He signs his name Ame Cooke.

10. KING CHARLES I. Trag. by W. Havard, 8vo. 1737. This piece was performed at the Theatre in Lincoln's-Inn Fields with very good success; and indeed there are some parts of it which seem to approach as near to the style of Shakspeare, as any of the attempts that have been made to imitate him. Some of the characters are well drawn, and the catastrophe pathetic and affecting. Lord Chesterfield, in his speech, on the Licensing Act, mentioning

this play, says, "the catastrophe was too recent, too melancholy, and of too solemn a nature to be heard of any where but in a pulpit."

11. THE KING AND QUEEN'S ENTERTAINMENT AT RICHMOND, *after their Departure from Oxford; in a Masque presented by the most illustrious Prince, Prince Charles (afterwards King Charles* II.) Sept. 12th, 1634. 4to. The occasion of this masque was the Queen's desire of seeing the prince dance, who was then not much above six years old. The dances were composed by Simon, and the music by Charles Hopper; and the parts of the *Captain* and *Druid* were performed to the greatest degree of excellency by the then lord Buckhurst, and Mr. Edward Sackville.

12. THE FAMOUS TRAGEDY OF KING CHARLES I. *Basely butchered by those who are*

*Omne nefas proni patrare, pudoris inanes,
Crudeles, vi lasti, importunique tyranni,
Ad nuces, faedi, perverh, perfidi se,
Fad si a, is, faeit verbis infanda loquentes.*

4to. 1649. 8vo. 1709. This play seems to have been written by some very strong party man, who thought at so critical a juncture the declaration of his name would have been attended with hazard, perhaps even of life; yet was hardy enough to declare his principles under the protection and secrecy of the press, at a time, and in a manner, wherein he must, if known, have rendered himself liable to the most rigid ministerial resentment. Nor is this, perhaps, the only instance which might urge us to wish that warm integrity and fertile genius were ever constant companions.

13. THE KING'S ENTERTAINMENT AT WELBECK in Nottinghamshire, a seat of the earl of Newcastle, at his going to Scotland in 1633, by Ben Jonson, Fol. 1640.

14. *A Pretie new Enterlude, both pithie and pleasaunt, of the story of* KYNG DARYUS. *Being taken out of the third and fourth Chapter of the thyrd Booke of Esdras.*

The names of the Players.
The Prolocutor.

Iniquitie.	Charytie.
Importunitye.	Parcyalytie.
Equytie.	Daryus Kinge.
Agreable.	Perplexitie.
Ireparatus.	Curyosytie.
Juda.	Persya.
Medey.	Aethyopia.
Constancie.	Optymates.
Anagnostes.	Stipator primus.
Stipator secundus.	Zorobabell.

Sixe persons may easely play it.
Imprynted at London, in Fleetstreet, beneath the Conduite, at the sygne of St. John Evangelyst, by Thomas Colwell. Anno Domini MDLXV. in October.

15. THE KING'S MISTRESS. This play was entered on the books of the Stationers' Company, Sept. 9, 1653; but seems not to have been printed.

16. A KNACKE HOW TO KNOWE A KNAVE. Com. Anonym. 4to. 1594. This piece seems to have been like some of the drolls or medleys performed at our fairs. It is said to have been sundry times played by Edward Allen, with Kemp's applauded merriments of the men of Goteham, in receiving the king into Goteham. The serious part of this play is the story of *Edgar*, *Atterwold*, and *Elfreda*. It is printed in the old black letter, and exposes the vices of the age as detected by honesty.

17. A KNACK HOW TO KNOWE AN HONEST MAN. *A pleasant conceited Comedie*, several times acted. Anonym. 4to. 1596. The scene

scene lies in Venice, and the piece is not divided into acts. It was entered on the books of the Stationers' Company, Nov. 26, 1596, by Cuthbert Burbye.

18. THE KNAVE IN GRAINE, or, *Jack Cottington*. A Play, entered on the books of the Stationers' Company, June 18, 1639, but probably not printed.

19. THE KNAVE IN GRAIN NEW VAMPT. Com. Acted at the Fortune, 4to. 1640, by J. D. The incident of *Julio's* cheating his drunken guests, is repeated by Kirkman in his *English Rogue*, part 3. ch. 13. as is also that of his cheating the countryman of the piece of gold, in the account of the hard frost of 1684. in 8vo. p. 41. But, contrary to the usual custom, these writers have stolen these incidents from the play, instead of the play being founded on their writings. Scene, Venice.

20. A KNAVE IN PRINT, or, *One for another*. Com. by William Rowley, entered on the books of Stationers' Company, Sept. 9, 1653, but not printed.

21. THE KNAVES. A Play, acted in the year 1613. Not printed. See Mr. Malone's Attempt to ascertain the order of Shakspeare's Plays, p. 331.

22. KNAVERY IN ALL TRADES, or, *The Coffee-house*. Com. Anon. 4to. 1664. This play was acted by a company of London Apprentices in the Christmas holidays, and, as it is said in the title-page, with great applause. This applause, however, was probably no more than their own self-approbation, it being a very indifferent performance, and not entitled to success in any one of the regular theatres.

23. THE KNIGHT OF MALTA. Tragi-Com. by Beaumont and Fletcher, Fol. 1647. Scene, Malta.

24. THE KNIGHT OF THE BURNING PESTLE. Com. by Beaumont and Fletcher, 4to. 1613. 4to. 1635. From the dedication of the first edition of this play, it appears to have been written in 1611, and not well received, when acted on the stage. The names of Beaumont and Fletcher are not on the title-page of the first publication of it. See Supplement to Shakspeare, vol. I. p. 194. After the Restoration it was revived with a new prologue, spoken by Mrs. Ellen Guyn, instead of the old one in prose, which was taken verbatim from that before Lylly's *Sapho* and *Phao*. The citizen and his wife introduced on the stage in this play, are probably in imitation of the four gossips, lady-like attired, in Ben Jonson's *Staple of News*, who remain on the stage during the whole action, and criticise upon each scene.

25. THE KNIGHTS. Com. of two acts, by Samuel Foote, 8vo. 1754. This piece made its first appearance at the Little Theatre in the Hay-Market, about the year 1747; and at that time terminated with a droll concert of vocal music between two cats, in burlesque of the Italian comic Operas. As this, however, was only temporary, the author, to adapt it more properly to true dramatic taste, and render it a more perfect Farce, has wound up a conclusion for it, which however, even as it now stands, is scarcely so conclusive or so natural as it could be wished. This fault, however, is amply made amends for by its possessing in the highest degree a much more essential excellence of comedy, viz. great strength of character, and the most accurate and lively colouring of nature. His two knights, Sir *Penurious Trifle* and Sir *Gregory Gazette*,

K N

Gazette, the first of which has the strongest passion for perpetually entertaining his friends with a parcel of stale trite insignificant stories, and the latter, who is possessed with a most insatiable thirst for news, without even capacity sufficient to comprehend the full meaning of the most familiar paragraph in a public Journal, are very strongly painted. The first of them received additional life from the admirable execution of the author in his representation of the character, in which indeed it has been reported, that he mimicked the manner of a certain gentleman in the West of England; and the other seems to have afforded a hint to a writer since, viz. Mr. Murphy, in his *Upholsterer*, to expatiate still more

K N

largely on this extravagant and absurd kind of folly. His other characters of *Tim* and Miss *Suck*, with the scene of courtship introduced between them, though not absolutely new in the first conception, yet are managed after a new manner, and always give great entertainment in the representation. It was acted at Drury-Lane.

26. A new scene for the Comedy, called, THE KNIGHTS, or, *Fresh Tea for Mr. Foote*, 8vo. 1758.

27. THE KNOT OF FOOLS. Play, acted in the year 1613. (See Mr. Malone's Attempt, p. 331.)

28. KNOW YOUR OWN MIND. Com. by Arthur Murphy, Esq. Acted at Covent-Garden, 1777, with considerable success. Printed, 8vo. 1778.

L.

L A

1. THE LADIES CHOICE. Petite Piece, of two acts, by Paul Hiffernan, performed at Covent-Garden, 8vo. no date [1759.] It was acted a few nights, but with no success.

2. THE LADIES FROLICK. Opera, altered from *The Jovial Crew*, by James Love. Acted at Drury-Lane 1770. Not printed.

3. THE LADIES OF THE PALACE, or, *The New Court Legacy*, Ballad Opera, of three acts, 8vo. 1735. Court Scandal.

4. THE LADIES SUBSCRIPTION. Dram. Performance, designed for an introduction to a dance, by John Cleland, 8vo. 1760. Printed at the end of *Titus Vespasian*.

L A

5. THE LADLE. Entertainment of Music, altered from Prior, 8vo. 1773. One of the interludes performed at Sadlers Wells.

6. LADY ALIMONY, or, *The Alimony Lady*. Com. Anonymous, 4to. 1669. Said in the title-page to be duly authorized, daily acted, and frequently followed.

*7. THE LADY CONTEMPLATION. Com. in two parts, by the Duchess of Newcastle, Fol. 1662. Three scenes in the first, and two in the second part, were written by the Duke.

8. THE LADY ERRANT. Tragi-Com. by W. Cartwright, 8vo. 1651. This was by some esteemed an excellent comedy. The scene lies in Cyprus.

9. LADY

9. LADY JANE GREY. Trag. by N. Rowe. Acted at Drury-Lane, 4to. 1715. This is an admirable play, and is frequently performed with success to this day, though not absolutely on the acting list of plays. Mr. Edmund Smith had an intention of writing a tragedy on the subject of Lady *Jane Grey*, according to the history which Mr. Banks followed; and at his death left some loose hints of sentiments, and short sketches of scenes. From the last of these Mr. Rowe acknowledges he borrowed part of one which he has inserted in this play, viz. that between Lord *Guilford* and Lady *Jane Grey* in the third act. The quarrel and reconciliation between Lord *Guilford* and Lord *Pembroke* are very fine; and the scene of Lady *Jane*, previous to her mounting the scaffold, has abundance of the *pathos* in it. On the whole, I think I may venture to pronounce it equal to any, and superior to most, of the dramatic pieces of this admirable author. The scene lies in London.

10. THE LADY OF MAY. A Masque, by Sir Philip Sidney. This piece was presented to Q. Elizabeth in the gardens at Wanstead in Essex, and is printed together with some Poems at the end of the *Arcadia*.

11. THE LADY OF THE MANOR. Com. Op. by Dr. Kenrick. Acted at Covent-Garden, 8vo. 1778. This is taken from Charles Johnson's *Country Lasses*, or *The Custom of the Manor*.

12. THE LADY OF PLEASURE. Com. by Ja. Shirley. Acted at the private house, Drury-Lane, 4to. 1637. The incident of *Kickshaw's* enjoying *Aretina*, and thinking her the devil, is a circumstance that this author has also introduced into his *Grateful Servant*, and Mrs. Behn has copied it in her *Lucky Chance*. Scene, the Strand.

13. THE LADY'S LAST STAKE, or, *The Wife's Resentment*. Com. by C. Cibber. Acted at the Hay-Market, 4to. no date, [1707.] This is very far from a bad comedy. The plot of it is in some measure borrowed from Burnaby's *Reformed Wife*, but the manners, the style, and many of the incidents, are original, and do honour to their author.

14. THE LADY'S PRIVILEDGE. Com. by Hen. Glapthorne. Acted at Drury-Lane, and twice at Whitehall before their Majesties, 4to. 1640. Scene, Genoa.

15. THE LADY'S REVENGE, or, *The Rover reclaim'd*. Com. by William Popple, Esq. Acted at Covent-Garden, 8vo. 1734.

16. THE LADY'S TRYAL. Tragi-Com. by John Ford. Acted at Drury Lane, 4to. 1639. The scene lies in Genoa, and the Prologue is subscribed by Mr. Bird; but whether it was written, or only spoken by him, is not absolutely apparent.

17. THE LADY'S TRIUMPH. Comic Opera, by Elk. Settle, 12mo. 1718. This piece was performed by subscription at the Theatre in Lincoln's-Inn Fields. The entertainments set to music, amongst which was *Decius and Paulina*, were written by Mr. Lewis Theobald.

18. THE LADY'S VISITING DAY. Com. by Charles Burnaby, 4to. 1701. Acted at Lincoln's-Inn Fields. Scene, London.

19. THE LAME LOVER. Com. by Samuel Foote. Acted at the Hay-Market, 8vo. 1770. This piece, though little inferior to any performance of the same writer, did not meet with equal success. Sir *Luke Limp*, the Serjeant, and his son, are admirable portraits.

20. THE LANCASHIRE WITCH-ES. Com. by Thomas Heywood. Acted at the Globe, 4to. 1634. The author was assisted by Mr. Brome in the composition of this play. The foundation of it in general is an old English novel; but that part of it in which *Whetstone*, through the means of his aunt, revenges himself on *Arthur*, *Shakstone*, and *Bantam*, for their having called him *Bastard*, is borrowed from the History of John Teutonicus, a German, who was a known bastard and a noted magician, and whose story is related at large by the author in his *Hierarchy of Angels*.

21. THE LANCASHIRE WITCH-ES, *and Teague O'Dively the Irish Priest*. Com. by Thomas Shadwell. Acted at the Duke's Theatre, 4to. 1682. This play is in some measure on the same foundation with the foregoing one. It was, however, written in the time of high contests between the *Whig* and *Tory* parties, and therefore met with strong opposition from the Papists, on account of the character of *Teague O'Dively*. Its own merit, however, and a very strong party which was raised to support it, enabled the piece to stand its ground in spite of all enmity and ill-nature.

22. LANDGARTHA. Tragi-Com. by Henry Burnell, 4to. 1641. Acted at Dublin with great applause. The author having failed in a former dramatic attempt, insures the success of this by introducing it to the world with a prologue spoken by an Amazon with a battle-ax in her hand, in imitation of Ben Jonson's Prologue to the *Poetaster*. The plot of the play is founded on the Swedish history, being the conquest of Fro (or Frollo) king of Sweden, by Regner (or Reyner) king of Denmark, with the repudiation of Regner's Queen Langartha. The dedication has also somewhat very whimsical in it, being, *To all Fair, indifferent Fair, Virtuous that are not Fair, and magnanimous Ladies*. Scene, Suevia, or Suethland.

23. THE LANGUISHING LOVER, or, *An Invocation to Sleep*. A Musical Interlude, by D. Bellany, 12mo. 1746.

24. THE LATE REVOLUTION, or, *The Happy Change*. Tragi-Com. Acted throughout the English Dominions, in the year 1688, 4to. 1690. It is said in the title-page to be written by a person of quality. From the time in which this piece was produced, it will readily be concluded to be, as it really is, intirely political.

25. THE LAW AGAINST LOVERS. Tragi-Com. by Sir W. Davenant, Fo. 1673. This play is a mixture of the two plots of Shakspeare's *Measure for Measure*, and *Much ado about Nothing*. The characters, and almost the whole language of the piece are borrowed from that divine author, all that Sir *William* has done being to blend the circumstances of both plays together, so as to form some connexion between the plots, and to soften and modernize those passages of the language which appeared rough or obsolete. The scene, Turin.

26. THE LAWS OF CANDY. Tragi-Com. by Beaumont and Fletcher, Fol. 1647. This is one of the most indifferent of these authors plays, and has not been acted for many years. The scene in Candia.

27. THE LAW CASE. A Play. Entered on the books of the Stationers' Company Nov. 29, 1653, but not printed.

28. THE LAW OF LOMBARDY. Trag. by Robert Jephson. Acted

at Drury-Lane, 8vo. 1779. This play, which in its plot resembles *Much ado about Nothing*, was not so successful as the former production of the same author. It was acted nine nights, and then laid aside.

29. LAW TRICKS, or, *Who would have thought it?* Com. by John Day. Acted by the children of the Revels, 4to. 1608. This is an admirable play.

30. THE LAWYERS FEAST. Farce, by Ja. Ralph, 8vo. 1744. This little piece was performed at the Theatre Royal in Drury-Lane, with some success.

31. THE LAWYERS FORTUNE, or, *Love in a hollow Tree*. Com. by William, lord Visc. Grimstone, 4to. 1705. This piece was never acted but by a strolling company of comedians at Windsor, and is certainly full of absurdities; but some indulgence ought surely to be allowed it, when it shall be known that the author was only a schoolboy, and but thirteen years of age at the time he wrote it; and so conscious did his modesty and good sense afterwards render him of its numerous deficiencies, that as far as was in his power he attempted to buy in the impression. In consequence of an election, however, at St. Albans, where his lordship stood for candidate, the old duchess of Marlborough, who was a strong opponent to his interest, caused a new edition of it to be printed at her own expence, and dispersed among the electors, with a frontispiece, in which his lordship was treated with the utmost indecency and ill manners, being represented as an elephant dancing on a rope. This edition also he bought up as nearly as he was able, but could not succeed so far as to prevent some of the copies from getting into the world. The scene lies in a country town.

32. OF LAZARUS RAIS'D FROM THE DEAD. A Comedy, by Bishop Bale. This is one of those pieces mentioned in his own list of his writings.

33. LEANDER AND HERO. Tr. 8vo. 1769. This tragedy is anonymous, and seems to have been printed merely to gratify the vanity of its author, as it never was publicly sold. It is written in prose.

34. KING LEAR. The full title of this play, in the original edition, stands thus: "M. William Shakspeare his true Chronicle History of the Life and Death of King LEAR and his three Daughters; with the unfortunate Life of Edgar, Sonne and Heire to the Earle of Gloucester, and his sullen and assumed humour of *Tom of Bedlam*. As it was plaid before the King's Majesty at Whitehall uppon S. Stephen's night in Christmas hollidaies. By his Majesties servants, playing usually at the Globe on the Banck-side." 4to. 1608. 4to. 1655. This play is founded on the English history, and is one of the Chef d'Oeuvres of this capital master. The distinction drawn between the real madness of the king, and the feigned frenzy of Edgar, is such, as no pen but his own was capable of. The quick, hasty, choleric disposition of *Lear*, supported in the midst of tenderness, distress, and even lunacy, and the general tenor of his whole conversation, which even in all the wild extravagant ramblings of that lunacy still tend as towards a centre to the first great cause of it, the cruelty of his daughters, is painting only to be reached by Shakspeare's happy pencil.

pencil. In a word, to attempt to enumerate all its beauties, would take a larger portion of our work, than the destined limits of it would permit me to bestow on any single piece. The play, however, as it is now acted, is only an alteration of the original piece, made by N. Tate.

Dr. Johnson says, "this play is deservedly celebrated among the dramas of Shakspeare. There is perhaps no play which keeps the attention so strongly fixed; which so much agitates our passions, and interests our curiosity. The artful involutions of distinct interests, the striking opposition of contrary characters, the sudden changes of fortune, and the quick succession of events, fill the mind with a perpetual tumult of indignation, pity, and hope. There is no scene which does not contribute to the aggravation of the distress or conduct of the action, and scarce a line which does not conduce to the progress of the scene. So powerful is the current of the poet's imagination, that the mind, which once ventures within it, is hurried irresistibly along.

"On the seeming improbability of Lear's conduct, it may be observed, that he is represented according to histories at that time vulgarly received as true. And, perhaps, if we turn our thoughts upon the barbarity and ignorance of the age to which this story is referred, it will appear not so unlikely as while we estimate Lear's manners by our own. Such preference of one daughter to another, or resignation of dominion on such conditions, would be yet credible, if told of a petty prince of Guinea or Madagascar. Shakspeare, indeed, by the mention of his earls and dukes, has given us the idea of times more civilized, and of life regulated by softer manners; and the truth is, that though he so nicely discriminates, and so minutely describes the characters of men, he commonly neglects and confounds the characters of ages, by mingling customs ancient and modern, English and foreign."

35. KING LEAR. Trag. by N. Tate. Acted at the Duke's Theatre, 4to, 1681. This is only an alteration of Shakspeare's Lear. "I found (says Mr. Tate in his dedication to Thomas Boteler, Esq;) that the new-modelling of this story would force me sometimes on the difficult task of making the chiefest persons speak something like their character, on matter whereof I had no ground in my author.——I found the whole to answer your account of it, a heap of jewels unstrung and unpolished, yet so dazzling in their disorder, that I soon perceived I had seized a treasure. 'Twas my good fortune to light on one expedient to rectify what was wanting in the regularity and probability of the tale, &c." Mr. Tate has therefore omitted entirely the character of the fool, but has interwoven with the main business of the play an under-plot of the loves of Edgar and Cordelia. He has also altered the catastrophe of the play by making Lear and Cordelia survive with a fair prospect of becoming very happy. Yet, whatever by this means he may gain with respect to poetical justice, he certainly loses as to pathos; nor can I think this piece, as it is now altered, is on the whole equal to what it was in the original form; yet, as it is in some measure rendered more suitable to the present theatrical taste, by this alteration,

it now ſtands forwards, and is conſtantly acted inſtead of the original.

36. THE HISTORY OF KING LEAR, by George Colman. Acted at Covent-Garden, 8vo. 1768. A judicious alteration of the two foregoing pieces.

37. "The true Chronicle Hiſtory "of KING LEIR, and his three "Daughters, Gonorill, Ragan, "and Cordella. As it hath bene "divers and ſundry times lately "acted." 4to. 1605. This play is on the ſame ſtory as Shakſpeare's celebrated Tragedy, and is ſuppoſed to be the ſource from whence he drew his materrials. It is a very contemptible performance, but has been lately twice reprinted. See Steevens's Twenty Plays of Shakſpeare, and Nichols's Six Old Plays.

38. THE LEARNED LADIES. Com. by Ozell. A tranſlation only of the *Femmes ſçavantes* of Moliere.

39. THE LEGACY, or, *The Fortune Hunter*. Com. tranſlated from the French, and printed in Foote's *Comic Theatre*.

40. LETHE. Dramatic Satire, by David Garrick. Acted at Drury-Lane, 8vo. 1748. This piece conſiſts only of a number of ſeparate characters, who, coming by Pluto's permiſſion to drink of the waters of forgetfulneſs, relate to Æſop, who is appointed the diſtributor of theſe waters, the ſeveral particulars which conſtitute the diſtinguiſhing parts of their ſeveral diſpoſitions. In the execution of this deſign, there is ſcope given for very keen and poignant ſatire on the reigning follies of the age. Yet ſo true is it, that the ſtricken deer will ever weep, and the galled jade wince, that notwithſtanding the wit and ſenſible manner in which this ſatire is conveyed, notwithſtanding beſides the admirable performance of the piece, in which the author himſelf during its firſt run acted no leſs than three of the characters, it met with conſiderable oppoſition ; nor was it till ſome time after that it made its ſtand firmly, and became, as it now is, one of the conſtant and regular petite pieces of the Engliſh ſtage. It made its appearance ſome years before at the Theatre in Goodman's Fields, and was printed in 1745, 12mo. under the title of LETHE, or *Æſop in the Shades*. It is, however, conſiderably altered by the dreſs it now appears in, and in the latter editions Mr. Garrick has added a new character called Lord Chalkſtone.

41. LETHE REHEARSED. Dramatic Performance, 8vo. about the year 1749.

42. THE LETTER WRITERS, or, *A new Way to keep a Wife at home*. Com. by Henry Fielding. 8vo. 1732. This play was acted at the Little Theatre in the Hay-Market with ſome ſucceſs ; but, like the reſt of that author's larger dramatic pieces, has never been revived ſince its firſt run. In ſhort, Fielding's happy turn of humour, more eſpecially for ſcenes in lower life, rendered almoſt all his farces ſucceſsful, but was not ſo well adapted to the more elegant parts of genteel and regular comedy.

43. THE LEVEE. Farce, by John Kelley, Eſq; 8vo. 1741. This piece was never acted ; it was indeed offered to, and accepted for repreſentation, by Fleetwood the manager of Drury-Lane Theatre, but was denied a licence by the inſpector of farces.

44. THE LEVELLERS LEVELL'D, or, *The Independents' Conſpiracy to rout Monarchy*. An Interlude, written by Mercurius Pragmaticus,

maticus, 4to, 1647. The author of this piece is unknown; but the very title of it implies him to have been a warm royalist, as does also his dedication, which is to King Charles II. He also appears a stroug enemy to Lilly the Almanack-maker, whom he lashes severely under the name of Orlotto.

45. LEUCOTHÖE. Dram. Poem, by Isaac Bickerstaffe, 8vo. 1756. This little piece, which was never acted, nor seems intended by the author for reprefentation, is a kind of tragic opera, founded on the story of Apollo's love for Leucothöe, the daughter of Orchamus, king of Perfia, and her transformation into a tree of *frankincense*, in confequence of the difcovery made to her father of their amour by Clytie, a former mistress of Phoebus. The story is related in Ovid's *Metamorphoses*; but the author of this piece has deviated from the Latin poet in one particular, viz. that, instead of transforming the jealous Clytie into a sun-flower, which always keeps its face towards the sun, the former object of her passion, he has only made her by the power of Phoebus, and at her own request, be converted into a statue.

The poetry of this little piece is pleafing, and the conduct of it ingenious.

46. THE HISTORY OF LEWIS XI. KING OF FRANCE. Tragi-Com. advertifed at the end of *Wit and Drollery*, 12mo. 1661. as then printing, but which never appeared.

47. THE LIBERTINE. Trag. by Thomas Shadwell. Acted by their Majesties Servants, 4to. 1676. 4to. 1692. This play met with great succefs, and is by some esteemed one of the best of this author's writings. It is on a subject which has employed the pens of the first-rate writers in different languages, there being besides this, two French plays on the story (one by Corneille, the other by Moliere), one Italian, and one Spanish one. Yet I cannot help hinting as my own particular judgment in regard to it, that the incidents are so crammed together in it, without any confideration of time or place as to make it highly unnatural, that the villainy of Don John's character is worked up to such an height, as to exceed even the limits of poffibility, and that the cataftrophe is fo very horrid, as to render it little lefs than impiety to reprefent it on the stage. And, indeed, it is now many years fince it has been permitted to make its appearance there.

48. THE LIBERTINE. Trag. by Ozell. This is only a tranflation of Moliere's play on the fame fubject.

49. THE LIBERTINE, or, *Hidden Treafure*. Com. tranflated from the French, and printed in Foote's *Comic Theatre*.

50. LIBERTY ASSERTED. Tr. by J. Dennis, 4to. 1704. This play was acted with great succefs at the Theatre in Lincoln's-Inn Fields, and is dedicated to Anthony Henley, Efq; to whom the author owns himfelf indebted for *the happy hint upon which it was formed*. The scene is laid at Agnie (which name, he fays, for the fake of a better sound, he has altered to Angie) in Canada; and the plot an imagined one, from the wars carried on among the Indian nations. The extravagant and enthusiastic opinion Dennis himfelf had of the merit and importance of this piece, cannot be more properly evinced than by the following anecdotes, which are related of him with regard to it.

He imagined there were some
Strokes

Strokes in it so severe upon the French nation, that they could never be forgiven, and consequently that Louis XIV. would not consent to a peace with England, unless he was delivered up a sacrifice to national resentment. Nay, so far did he carry this apprehension, that when the congress for the peace of Utrecht was in agitation, he waited on the duke of Marlborough, who had formerly been his patron, to intreat his interest with the plenipotentiaries that they should not acquiesce to his being given up. The duke told him with great gravity, that he was sorry it was out of his power to serve him, as he really had no interest with any of the ministers at that time, but added, that he fancied his case not to be quite so desperate as he seemed to imagine, for that indeed he had taken no care to get *himself* excepted in the articles of peace, and yet he could not help thinking that he had done the French *almost* as much damage as Mr. Dennis himself.

Another effect of this apprehension prevailing with him is told as follows; that being invited down to a gentleman's house on the coast of Sussex, where he had been very kindly entertained for some time, as he was one day walking near the beach, he saw a ship sailing, as he imagined, towards him. On which, taking it into his head that he was betrayed, he immediately made the best of his way to London, without even taking leave of his host who had been so civil to him, but on the contrary proclaiming him to every body as a traitor who had decoyed him down to his house only in order to give notice to the French, who had fitted out a vessel on purpose to carry him off, if he had not luckily discovered their design. So strange is the mixture of vanity and suspicion which is sometimes to be met with in men of understanding and genius!

51. LIBERTY CHASTISED, or, *Patriotism in Chains*. Tragi-comi-political Farce. As it was performed by M———s S———ts in the year 1268. Modernised by Paul Tell-Truth, Esq; 8vo. 1768. This, I believe, is a production of George Saville Carey.

52. THE LIFE AND DEATH OF CAPTAINE THOMAS STUKELEY, *with his Marriage to Alderman Curteis Daughter, and valiant ending of his Life at the Battaile of Alcazar*. As it hath been acted. Printed for Thomas Pavyer, and are to be sold at his shop at the entrance into the Exchange, 1605. 4to. b. l.

53. LIKE MASTER LIKE MAN. Com. of two acts, performed at Smock-Alley, 12mo. 1770. Taken from Vanbrugh's *Mistake*, and printed at Dublin.

54. LIKE WILL TO LIKE, QUOTH THE DEVIL TO THE COLLIER. An Interlude, by Ulpian Fulwell, 4to. 1587. This is entirely a moral piece, intended to point out the benefits that attend on a virtuous, and the punishments that await on a licentious life. It is printed in the old black letter, the prologue written in alternate verse, and the whole piece in rhime; and is contrived so as to be easily performed by five persons. A play with the same title is entered on the books of the Stationers' Company, by John Alde, 1567 to 1568.

55. LILLIPUT. A dramatic Entertainment, by David Garrick, Esq. Acted at Drury-Lane, 8vo. 1757. This piece was acted by children. In the year 1777, it was

was revived at the Hay-Market, when an additional scene was introduced into it.

56. LINGUA, or, *The Combat of the Tongue and the five Senses for Superiority*. A pleasant comedy. Anon. 4to. 1607. 4to. N. D. 4to. 1617. 4to. 1622. 4to. 1632. 8vo. 1657. Winstanley has attributed it to Anth. Brewer, and tells us moreover, that at the first performance of it at Trinity-College in Cambridge, Oliver Cromwell acted the part of *Tactus* in it, from which he first imbibed his sentiments of ambition. The scene is *Microcosmus*, in a grove. The time from morning till night.

57. LIONEL AND CLARISSA. Com. Op. by Isaac Bickerstaffe. Acted at Covent-Garden, 8vo. 1768. In this Opera, which was acted with much approbation, the author boasts that he had borrowed nothing. It was afterwards altered, and acted at Drury-Lane with the new title of *The School for Fathers*.

58. THE LITIGANTS. Com. by Mr. Ozell, 12mo. 1715. This is no more than a translation from the *Plaideurs* of Racine, which is itself borrowed from the *Wasps* of Aristophanes, and is an admirable satire on those persons who engage in, and pursue long and expensive law-suits merely for the sake of litigation. The scene lies in a city of Lower Normandy.

59. THE LITTLE FRENCH LAWYER. Com. by Beaumont and Fletcher, Fol. 1647. The plot of this play is taken from *Gusman de Alfarache*, or the *Spanish Rogue*, Part 2. Ch. 4. the story of Dinant, Clerimont, and Lamira, being borrowed from that of Don Lewis de Castro, and Don Roderigo de Montalva. The scene lies in France.

60. THE LITTLE FRENCH LAWYER. Com. of two acts, from Beaumont and Fletcher. Acted at Covent-Garden, April 27, 1778, at Mr. Quick's benefit. This alteration is said to have been made by Mrs. Booth of Covent-Garden Theatre.

61. THE LITTLE ORPHAN OF THE HOUSE OF CHAO. A Chinese Trag. Translated from the French version of P. Du Halde's *Description de l'Empire de la Chine*, by Dr. Percy. Printed in "Miscellaneous Pieces relating to the "Chinese," vol. I. 12mo. 1762.

62. THE LIVERPOOL PRIZE. Farce, by F. Pilon. Acted at Covent-Garden, 8vo. 1779. with success.

63. THE LIVERY RAKE AND COUNTRY LASS. A Ballad Opera, by Edward Philips, 8vo. 1733. This was performed at the Haymarket with some success.

64. " The lamentable Tragedie
" of LOCRINE, the eldest Sonne
" of King Brutus, discoursing the
" warres of the Britaines and
" Hunnes, with their discomfi-
" ture; the Britaines victory, with
" their accidents; and the death
" of Albanact. No lesse pleasant
" then profitable. Newly set foorth
" overseene, and corrected by
" W. S." 4to. 1595. This play is one of those which have by some been considered as the production of Shakspeare, but more generally rejected. It is certain that, if any judgment can be formed from the style and manner, it is not to be ascribed to our great bard, and is indeed very unworthy of him. The plot is founded on history, and includes a space of twenty years. For farther particulars consult Milton's *History of England*, Book I. p. 14.

65. LODOWICK SFORZA, DUKE OF MILAIN. Trag. by Robert Gomersal,

Gomersal, 12mo. 1633. The story of this play is to be found in Guicciardini, Philip de Comines, and Mezeray, in the reign of Charles VIII. of France. The scene, Milain.

66. LONDON CHANTICLEERS. Com. Anonymous, 4to. 1659. This piece is rather an interlude than a play, not even being divided into acts. It is entirely of the *Basse Comedie* of the French, the scene lying wholly amongst persons of the lowest rank. Yet it has a good deal of humour in it, answers the title, which calls it *A witty Comedy, full of various and delightful Mirth*, and was often acted with great applause.

67. THE LONDON CUCKOLDS. Com. by Edward Ravenscroft. Acted at the Duke's Theatre, 4to. 1682. This play met with very great success, and has, till within a very few years past, been frequently presented on our stages; particularly on *Lord Mayor's* day, in contempt and to the disgrace of the city. Yet its sole ability of pleasing seems to consist in the great bustle of business and variety of incidents which are thrown into it; it being not only a very immoral, but a very ill-written piece. In short, it is little more than a collection of incidents taken from different novels, and jumbled together at bold hazard, forming a connection with each other as they may. The characters of *Wiseacre* and *Peggy*, and the scene of *Peggy's* watching her husband's nightcap in armour during his absence, are from Scarron's *Fruitless Precaution*. *Loveday's* discovering *Eugenia's* intrigue, and screening it by pretending to conjure for a supper, from the *Contes D'Ouville*, Part II. p. 235. *Eugenia's* contrivance to have *Jane* lie in her place by her husband while she goes to *Ramble*, from the *Mescanza dolce*, at the end of Torriano's Grammar, ch. 16. her scheme for the bringing off *Ramble* and *Love-Day*, by obliging the former to draw his sword and counterfeit a passion, from Boccace, Dec. 7. Nov. 6. *Doodle's* obliging his wife *Arabella* to answer nothing but *No* to all questions during his absence, and the consequence of that intrigue with *Townly*, from the *Contes D'Ouville*, Part II. p. 121. and *Eugenia's* making a false confidence to her husband *Dashwell*, and sending him into the Garden in her cloaths, to be beaten by *Love-Day*, from the *Contes de Fontaine*: in a word, it is no more than a long chain of thefts from beginning to end. Yet, furnished as it is by the amassing of all this plunder, it seems calculated only to please the upper galleries, being of a kind of humour too low for any thing above the rank of a chambermaid or footboy to laugh at, and intermingled with a series of intrigue, libertinism, and lasciviousness, that nothing more virtuous than a common prostitute could sit to see without a blush. It is, however, at length totally banished from the stage.

68. THE LONDON GENTLEMAN. Com. by Edward Howard. Entered on the books of the Stationers' Company Aug. 7, 1667, but not printed.

69. THE LONDON MERCHANT. Play, by John Ford. Entered on the books of the Stationers' Company June 29, 1660, and was amongst those destroyed by Mr. Warburton's servant.

70. THE LONDON MERCHANT, or, *The History of George Barnwell*. Trag. by George Lillo, 8vo. 1730. This play was acted at the Theatre Royal in Drury-Lane with great success. It is written in prose, and

and although the language is consequently not so dignified as that of the buskin is usually expected to be, yet it is well adapted to the subject it is written on, and exalted enough to express the sentiments of the characters, which are all thrown into domestic life. The plot is ingenious, the catastrophe just, and the conduct of it affecting. And no lesson surely can be more proper or indeed more necessary to inculcate among that valuable body of youths, who are trained up to the branches of mercantile business, so eminently estimable in a land of commerce such as England, and who must necessarily have large trusts confided to their care, and consequently large temptations thrown in the way of their integrity, than the warning them how much greater strength will be added to these temptations, how almost impossible it will be, for them to avoid the snares of ruin, if they suffer themselves but once to be drawn aside into the paths of the harlot, or permit their eyes once to glance on the allurements of the wanton, where they will be sure to meet with the most insatiable avarice to cope with on one hand, and an unguarded sensibility proceeding at first from the goodness of their own hearts, on the other, which will excite the practice of the most abandoned artifices in the first, and render the last most liable to be imposed on by them, and plunge headlong into vice, infamy, and ruin. This warning is strongly, loudly given in this play; and indeed I cannot help wishing that the performance of it was more frequent, or at least that the managers would make it a rule constantly to have it acted once at least in each house during the course of every period of those holidays in which the very youth to whom this instruction is addressed almost always form a considerable part of the audience. It has often been disputed whether plays, in which the plots are taken from domestic life, should be written in prose or metre, and the success of the present performance, and Mr. Moore's *Gamester*, must incline one very strongly in favour of the former. A great author, however, appears to be of a different opinion. Mr. Gorges Edmund Howard says, that having communicated his play of *The Female Gamester* to Dr. Samuel Johnson, that gentleman observed, " that he could hardly consider a " prose tragedy as dramatic; that " it was difficult for the performers " to speak it; that, let it be either " in the middling or in low life, " it may, though in metre and " spirited, be properly familiar " and colloquial; that many in " the middling rank are not without " erudition; that they have " the feelings and sensations of " nature, and every emotion in " consequence thereof, as well as " the great; that even the lowest " when impassioned raise their " language; and that the writing " of prose is generally the plea " and excuse of poverty of genius."

71. THE LONDON PRODIGAL. Com. by W. Shakspeare, played by the King's Majesties servants, 4to. 1605. Upon this play Mr. Malone observes, that one knows not which most to admire, the impudence of the printer in affixing our great poet's name to a comedy publicly acted at his own theatre, of which it is very improbable that he should have written a single line, or Shakspeare's negligence of fame in suffering such a piece to be imputed to him without taking the least notice of it.

72. " A

72. "A very mery and pythie Commedie, called, THE LONGER THOU LIVEST, THE MORE FOOLE THOU ART. A myrrour very necessarie for Youth, and specially for such as are like to come to dignitie and promotion: as it maye well appeare in the matter folowynge. Newly compiled by W. Wager. bl. l. no date. Imprinted at London, by Wyllyam How for Richarde Johnes, and are to be folde at his shop under the Lotterie-house." B. L. No date.

The Players names.

Prologue.   Fortune.
Moros.   Ignorance.
Discipline.   Crueltie.
Exercitation.   People.
Idlenesse.   Gods Judgment.
Incontinency.   Confusion.

Foure may playe it easely.

The Prologue. Exercitation. }
Wrath. Crueltie.   } for one.
Goddes Judgment.   }

Moros.   } for another.
Fortune.   }

Discipline. Incontinence. }
Impietie.   Confusion.   } for another.

Pietie.   Idlenes. } for another.
Ignorance.   People.   }

73. LOOK ABOUT YOU. Com. Anonymous. Acted by the Lord high Admiral's servants, 4to. 1600. This is a very diverting play, and the plot of it is founded on the English historians of the reign of Henry II.

74. LOOKE TO THE LADIE. Com. by James Shirley. Entered on the books of the Stationers' Company March 10, 1639; but not printed.

75. A LOOKING-GLASS FOR LONDON AND ENGLAND. Tragi-Com. by Thomas Lodge and Robert Green, 4to. 1598. 4to. 1617. The plot is founded on the story of Jonas and the Ninevites in sacred history.

76. LORD BLUNDER'S CONVOL. II.

FESSION, or, *Guilt makes a Coward*. A Ballad Opera, Anonymous, 8vo 1733. This piece was never acted. It was written by the author of *Vanella*, and apparently alludes to some recent transaction.

77. THE LORD OF THE MANOR. Comic Opera. Acted at Drury-Lane, 8vo. 1781. The author of this flimzy piece has kept himself concealed. It was, however, well set to music by Mr. Jackson, and met with some success.

78. OF THE LORD'S SUPPER AND WASHING THE FEET. A Comedy. This is one of the many religious dramas mentioned by Bishop Bale as his own.

79. THE LOST LADY. Tragi-Com. by Sir William Barclay, Fol. 1639.

80. THE LOST LOVER, or, *The Jealous Husband*. Com. by Mrs. De la Riviere Manley. Acted at the Theatre Royal, 4to. 1696. Though this piece did not succeed on the stage, yet the dialogue of it is very genteel, and the incidents not uninteresting; and, indeed, if we make proper allowances for the sex of its author, the time it was wrote in, and its being a first essay in that arduous way of writing, it may very justly be confessed, that it deserved a much better fate than it met with.

81. THE LOST PRINCESS. Tr. by Murrough Boyle, Lord Visc. Dessington, 8vo. without date, but belongs to the writings of the present century.

82. THE POTS. Com. translated from Plautus, by Richard Warner, vol. V. 8vo. 1774.

83. THE LOTTERY. Com. 8vo. 1728. This play was acted at the New Theatre in the Hay-Market. The scene, London.

84. THE LOTTERY. A Ballad Farce, by Henry Fielding, 8vo. 1731. This is a lively and entertaining

taining piece, was acted at Drury-Lane with confiderable fuccefs, and ftill remains on the lift of acting farces, efpecially near the time of drawing the ftate lotteries, when the fcene of the wheels, &c. in Guild-hall gives great pleafure to the nightly refidents of the upper regions of the theatre.

85. LOVE-A-LA-MODE. Com. Anonymous, 4to. 1663. This play, which was acted at Middlefex-houfe with great applaufe, is faid in the title-page to have been written by a perfon of honour, and (according to his preface which is figned T. S.) in the firft year of the Reftoration. Who this perfon of honour was, I have not been able to guefs; but it might poffibly be known by tracing back the alliances of the Colbrand family, as the firft of three recommendatory copies of verfes prefixed to this play is fubfcribed R. Colbrand, Baronet, and directed to his honoured brother the author, who by the letters figned to the preface appears to have been his brother-in-law, or half-brother.

86. LOVE-A-LA-MODE. Farce, by Charles Macklin, 1760. This farce has never been wholly printed, but was brought on at the Theatre Royal in Drury-Lane, where after fome ftruggles between two parties, the one prejudiced for, the other againft its author, it at length made its footing good, and had a very great run, to the confiderable emolument of the writer, who, not being paid as an actor, referved to himfelf a portion in the profits of every night it was acted. The piece does not want merit with refpect to character and fatire, yet has the writer's national partiality carried him into fo devious a path from the manners of the drama, as among four lovers who are addreffing a young lady of very great fortune, viz. an Irifh officer, a Scots baronet, a Jew broker, and an Englifh country fquire, to have made the firft of them the only one who is totally difinterefted with refpect to the pecuniary advantages apparent from the match. A character fo different from what experience has in general fixed on the gentlemen of that kingdom, who make their addreffes to our Englifh ladies of fortune, that although there are undoubtedly many among the Irifh gentlemen, poffeffed of minds capable of great honour and generofity, yet this exclufive compliment to them, in oppofition to received opinion, feems to convey a degree of partiality, which every dramatic writer at leaft fhould be ftudioufly careful to avoid. The Scotchman, and the Englifh gentleman jockey are, however, admirably drawn; but the thought of the cataftrophe is borrowed from Theophilus Cibber's comedy of *The Lover*; and the character of the *Irifhman* bears too much refemblance to Sheridan's *Capt. O'Blunder*, to entitle its being looked on as an entire original. One act of it was printed in the Court Mifcellany, April 1766. The great fuccefs of this piece has given rife to a retort, that it was not really written by Mr. Macklin; and one gentleman I have heard has even whifpered among his friends, that he was in fact the author of it. The meannefs and difingenuity of fuch a proceeding are too obvious to need being enlarged upon. If the perfon to whom I allude has any pretenfions to claim the credit of this performance, it would furely be more honourable to make them in a manner lefs clandeftine, in order that the offenfible and, I believe, real author might affert his right in the face of the public.

In

In the mean time the publick will pay no regard to such unsupported insinuations; and Mr. Macklin may console himself, that some of the best writers in the English language have suffered in the same manner. Mr. Pope observes, that it was said Garth did not write his own *D.spensary*; Denham likewise was charged with purchasing *Cooper's Hill*; Cibber was frequently upbraided as incapable of producing such a piece as *The Careless Husband*; and even Mr. Pope himself was suspected of not being the author of *The Essay on Criticism*. In such company Mr. Macklin need not repine at his own fate.

87. LOVE AND AMBITION. Trag. by Ja. Darcy, 8vo. 1732. This play was brought on the stage in Dublin, and met with some success.

88. LOVE AND A BOTTLE. C. by Geo. Farquhar. Acted at Drury-Lane, 4to. 1699. This is a very sprightly and entertaining play; yet on account of the looseness of the character of *Roebuck* (which, however, is perhaps the best drawn rake we have ever had on the stage), and some other strokes of licentiousness that run through the piece, it has not been acted for many years past. The part of *Mockmode* seems to be borrowed from the *Bourgeois Gentilhomme* of Moliere.

89. LOVE AND DUTY, or, *The Distress'd Bride*. Trag. by John Sturmy, 8vo. 1722. Performed at the Theatre Royal in Lincoln's-Inn Fields.

90. LOVE AND DUTY. Trag. by John Slade, 8vo. 1756. It was acted one night at the Hay-Market by the author and his friends.

91. LOVE AND FOLLY. Serenata in three interludes, set to music by Mr. Galliard. Acted at the King's Theatre in the Hay-Market, 4to. 1739. Between these interludes were performed the choruses to the Duke of Buckingham's Tragedy of *Julius Cæsar*.

92. LOVE AND FRIENDSHIP, or, *The Rival Passions*. As it was acted before the three mock kings Phyz, Trunk, and Ush, 8vo. 1723. Printed at the end of a pamphlet, intituled, "To Diaboloumenon, or The Proceedings at the Theatre Royal in Drury-Lane."

93. LOVE AND FRIENDSHIP. Serenata, set to music by Mr. W. Defesch, 4to. 1734.

94. LOVE AND FRIENDSHIP, or, *The Lucky Recovery*. Com. 8vo. 1754. Never acted.

95. LOVE AND GLORY. A Masque, by T. Philips, Gent. set to music by T. Arne, and acted at Drury-Lane, 8vo. 1734.

96. LOVE AND HONOUR. Tragi-Com. by Sir W. Davenant. Acted at the Black-Friers, 4to. 1649. This play met with very good success. The scene lies in Savoy.

97. LOVE AND HONOUR. Dramatic Poem, by Theo. de la Mayne, 12mo. 1742. Though this piece was not intended for public representation, nor is even rendered in many particulars conformable to the rules of the theatre, yet, as in other respects it is truly dramatic, I cannot deny it a place in this collection. The design of the author is to reduce all the circumstances of the Æneid, which have a reference to the loves of Dido and Æneas, into the limits of a drama somewhat more extensive than a common tragedy. To this end he has made it to consist of seven Cantos, or more properly acts, in which he has introduced the principal personages of the Æneid as interlocutors, and although he has added some characters, and omitted others, enlarged upon certain passages, bor-

rowed

rowed hints from some, and entirely suppressed others, yet he has no where deviated from the general tenor of the poem. His piece opens with the landing of Æneas, and the catastrophe closes with his departure and the death of Dido. In a word, he has formed it into a tragedy, though somewhat irregular, under the modest title of a dramatic Poem only. He has, throughout the whole, quoted the passages made use of from the original, with great candour, and although his versification may not have all that nervous power and dignity which shines through the works of some of our writers, yet it is far from contemptible, or the piece itself from being undeserving of notice and approbation.

98. LOVE AND INNOCENCE. Pastoral Serenata, performed at Marybone, 8vo. 1769.

99. LOVE AND LIBERTY. Tr. by Charles Johnson, 4to. 1709. This play was intended for the Theatre Royal in Drury-Lane, but was not acted. It is dedicated to the judicious critics throughout the town. The scene lies in Naples.

100. LOVE AND REVENGE. Trag. by Elk. Settle. Acted at the Duke's Theatre, 4to. 1675. This play is in great measure borrowed from Hemming's *Fatal Contract*; the plot of which, as well as of this piece, is founded on the French chronicles of Mezeray, De Serres, &c. Settle, in his Postscript to this piece, very harshly attacks Shadwell, who has answered him as severely in his Preface to the *Libertine*.

101. LOVE AND REVENGE, or, *The Vintner outwitted*. Ballad Op. Anonymous, 1729. This is little more than the *Match in Newgate* converted into an opera, by the addition of some songs. It was acted with success at the Little Theatre in the Hay-Market.

102. LOVE AND WAR. Trag. by Thomas Meriton. This is a very middling piece, and was never acted, but printed in 4to. 1658.

103. LOVE AND WINE, being a sequel to Love and Friendship, a Comedy, 8vo. 1754. By the author of *The Friendly Rivals*.

104. LOVE AT A LOSS, or, *Most Votes carry it*. Com. by Mrs. Cath. Trotter, afterwards Cockburne. Acted at Drury-Lane, 4to. 1701. This play was printed in so very incorrect and mutilated a manner, that the author wished to call in and suppress the edition. Many years after she reviewed this performance, and made great alterations in it, intending to bring it again on the stage under the title of *The Honourable Deceivers*, or *All Right at the Last*.

105. LOVE AT A VENTURE. Com. by Mrs. Centlivre, 4to. 1706. This play was acted by the Duke of Grafton's servants, at the New Theatre at Bath.

106. LOVE AT FIRST SIGHT. Com. by David Craufurd, 4to. no date [1704] This play was acted at the Theatre in Little Lincoln's-Inn Fields, but was not published till the above year, though written four years before.

107. LOVE AT FIRST SIGHT, or, *The Wit of a Woman*. Ballad Opera, of two acts, by Joseph Yarrow, 8vo. 1742. This little piece was never acted any where but in the York company of comedians, in which the author was a performer at the time of its publication. The hint on which the whole plot of the piece turns, of the young lady's discovering her inclination to her lover, and making an assignation with him for her elopement, under the pretence of acquainting her father that he had

formed

formed such a design, is apparently borrowed from *Miranda's* appointment with Sir *George Airy* for the garden-gate at the hour of eight in Mrs. Centlivre's *Busy Body*.

108. LOVE AT FIRST SIGHT. Ballad Farce, by Thomas King. Acted at Drury-Lane, 8vo. 1765.

109. LOVE BETRAY'D, or, *The Agreeable Disappointment*. Com. by Mr. Burnaby, 4to. 1703. Acted at Lincoln's-Inn Fields. The author confesses that he borrowed part of his plot, and about fifty lines of this comedy, from Shakspeare, whose play of *Twelfth Night* was that which Mr. Burnaby availed himself of.

110. LOVE CROWNS THE END. A Pastoral, by John Tatham, 12mo. 1640. This was acted by, and, I suppose, written for the scholars of Bingham in Nottinghamshire, in the year 1632. It was printed at the end of a volume, called, "Fancies Theatre," is very short, and not divided into acts. Prefixed to the volume are no less than thirteen copies of verses by Brome, Nabbes, &c. Scene, a Grove, wherein is Lover's Valley.

111. LOVE DRAGOON'D. Farce, by Mr. Motteux. But when or where acted, or of what date the publication, I know not, but imagine it to have been about 1700.

112. LOVE FOR LOVE. Com. by W. Congreve, 4to. 1695. This play is so extremely well known, and so frequently acted with the approbation it justly merits, that it would be unnecessary to say much of it. I shall therefore only just mention that with this piece the new theatre and company opened at Lincoln's-Inn Fields, at which time it met with so much success, that Betterton and the other managers of that house made the author an offer, which he accepted, of a whole share with them in their profits, on condition of his furnishing them with a new play every year. This comedy (as Dr. Johnson observes) is of nearer alliance to life, and exhibits more real manners, then either the *Old Batchelor* or the *Double Dealer*. The character of *Foresight* was then common. Dryden calculated nativities; both Cromwell and King William had their lucky days; and Shaftsbury himself, though he had no religion, was said to regard predictions. The *Sailor* is not accounted very natural, but he is very pleasant.

113. LOVE FOR MONEY, or, *The Boarding-School*. Com. by Tho. Durfey. Acted at the Theatre Royal, 4to. 1691. 4to. 1696. This play met with some opposition in the first day's representation, but, getting the better of that, stood its ground, and had tolerable success. The plot in general is original, yet the piece on the whole is very far from a good one. The scene lies at Chelsea, by the river's side. The time thirty-six hours. Coffey stole from this his farce called *The Boarding-School Romps*.

114. LOVE HATH FOUND OUT HIS EYES. A Play, by Thomas Jourdan. Entered on the books of the Stationers' Company June 29, 1660; and was amongst those destroyed by Mr. Warburton's servant.

115. LOVE FREED FROM IGNORANCE AND FOLLY. A Masque of her Majesties, by Ben Jonson. I know not on what occasion this piece was written, or at what time performed or first published. It is, however, to be found among his works.

116. LOVE IN A CHEST. See FORCE OF FRIENDSHIP.

117. LOVE IN A FOREST. C. by Cha. Johnson, 8vo. 1732. Acted

ed at Drury-Lane Theatre. The plot and part of the language of this play is from Shakſpeare's *As You like it*. Yet, as it has generally happened in every attempt at an amendment of that great author's works, it is ſo much injured by the alteration, that were he at preſent in exiſtence, he might with great juſtice enter an indictment on the maiming act, againſt theſe his pretended reformers.

118. LOVE IN A HURRY. C. by Anth. Aſton. Acted at Smock-Alley, Dublin. Chetwood ſays it was acted with no ſucceſs, and dates it in 1709. I imagine it was printed Ireland.

119. LOVE IN A MAZE. Com. Acted at the King's Theatre about 1672. Not printed, but mentioned by Downes, p. 25.

120. LOVE IN A MIST. A Farce, by John Cunningham. Acted at Dublin, 12mo. 1747.

121. LOVE IN A PUDDLE. C. Anonymous, and without date, but ſince 1700.

122. LOVE IN A RIDDLE. A Paſtoral, by C. Cibber. Acted at Drury-Lane, 8vo. 1729. This was the firſt piece written in imitation of *The Beggar's Opera*, and came out in the ſucceeding year. It met, however, with a moſt ſevere and undeſerved reception, there being a general diſturbance throughout the whole firſt repreſentation, excepting while Miſs Raftor (the preſent Mrs. Clive) was ſinging; and on the ſecond night the riot was ſtill greater, notwithſtanding the late Frederic Prince of Wales was preſent, and that for the firſt time after his arrival in theſe kingdoms, nor would it have been appeaſed, had not Mr. Cibber himſelf come forward, and aſſured the audience that if they would ſuffer the performance to go on quietly for that night, out of reſpect to the royal preſence, he would not inſiſt on the piece being acted any more, although the enſuing night ſhould in right have been his benefit. Which promiſe he faithfully kept. Yet, as a proof that it was party prejudice againſt the author, and not want of merit in the piece itſelf that was the occaſion of all this violent oppoſition, when ſome time afterwards the farce of *Damon* and *Philida*, taken entirely from this play, was brought on the ſtage as a novelty, and not known to be Cibber's, it was very favourably received, and has ever ſince continued to be acted, and conſtantly with great applauſe.

123. LOVE IN A SACK. Farce, by Benjamin Griffin, 12mo. 1715. Acted at Lincoln's-Inn Fields. Scene, Covent-Garden.

124. LOVE IN A VEIL. Com. by Richard Savage. Acted at Drury-Lane, 8vo. 1719. It met with no ſucceſs.

125. LOVE IN A VILLAGE. Com. Opera, by Iſaac Bickerſtaffe. Acted at Covent-Garden, 8vo. 1763. This performance, though compiled from Charles Johnſon's *Village Opera*, and other muſical pieces, yet met with ſo much favour from the town, that it was acted the firſt ſeaſon almoſt as many times as the *Beggar's Opera* had formerly been, and nearly with as much ſucceſs.

126. LOVE IN A WOOD, or, *St. James's Park*. Com. by W. Wycherley. Acted at the Theatre Royal, 4to. 1672. 4to. 1694. This play has been but ſeldom acted ſince its firſt run, and indeed, although there are fine things in it, it is not equal to the author of the *Country Wife* and *Plain Dealer*. Dedicated to the dutcheſs of Cleveland.

127. LOVE IN A WOOD, or, *The*

The Country Squire. Farce, by G. J. (Giles Jacob) 12mo. 1734. This piece was never acted, and was composed by the author in three or four days, and at a time when he was wholly unacquainted with the stage or dramatic writings.

128. LOVE IN ITS EXTASY, or, *The Large Prerogative.* Dramatic Pastoral, by Peaps, 4to. 1649. This piece was composed by the author when a student at Eton, being then only seventeen years of age, but was never acted, and not printed till many years after. Scene, Lilybæus.

129. LOVE IN SEVERAL MASQUES. Com. by H. Fielding, 8vo. 1727. Acted at the Theatre Royal, in Drury-Lane. This play immediately succeeded *The Provoked Husband,* which continued to be acted twenty-eight nights with great and just applause. Considering this as a first attempt, it must be allowed to possess considerable merit.

130. LOVE IN THE CITY. Comic Opera, by Isaac Bickerstaffe. Acted at Covent-Garden, 8vo. 1767. Whether this opera was disliked on account of its supposed insufficiency in dramatic and musical merit, or whether it was condemned by a party of Cheapside wits, who thought themselves reflected on by its title, &c. we are unable to determine, nor is the matter of much importance. An annual representation of the *London Cuckolds,* formerly kept Messieurs *Tape, Drugget,* and *Dripping,* in a proper degree of awe, nor did they dare to offer themselves as judges of theatrical performances. But, since the piece already mentioned has ceased to appear, no critics are more clamorous on some occasions than our Aldermen and Common Council.

Love in the City, however, in spite of its faults, was too good for their entertainment, and contains one character that recommends itself by unusual warmth of colouring, we mean *Miss Priscilla Tomboy,* an unmanageable Creole wench, brought to London, and placed in a Grocer's family, for education.

131.-LOVE IN THE DARK, or, *The Man of Business.* Com. by Sir Fra. Fane. Acted at the Theatre Royal, 4to. 1675. This is a busy and entertaining comedy, yet is the plot borrowed from various novels. The affair of Count *Sforza* and *Parthella* being from Scarron's *Invisible Mistress.* The affair of *Bellinganna, Cornanto's* wife, sending *Scrutinio* to *Trivultio* to check him for making love to her, from Boccace, Day. 3. Nov. 3. which has also been made use of by Ben Jonson, in his *Devil's an Ass,* and by Mrs. Centlivre, in her *Busy Body.* *Hircania's* wife catching him with *Ballinganna,* is built on the story of Socrates and his wife Mirto, in *The Loves of great Men.* p. 59. and *Trivultio's* seeming to beat *Bellinganna,* is grounded on Boccace, Day. 7. Nov. 7. The scene lies in Venice. From the character of *Scrutinio,* Mrs. Centlivre seems to have borrowed the hint of her *Marplot,* which, however, she has greatly improved and heightened.

132. LOVE WITH HONOUR, or, *The Privateer.* Farce, Anonymous. Never acted. Printed at Ipswich, 8vo. 1753.

133. "THE LOVE OF KING "DAVID AND FAIR BETHSABE. "*With the Tragedie of Absalon.* "As it hath been divers times "plaied on the stage." Written by George Peele, 4to. 1599. Mr. Hawkins, who republished this play in his *Origin of the Drama,* observes, that it abounds in luxuriant descriptions and fine imagery, and that

that the author's genius seems to have been kindled by reading the Prophets and the Song of Solomon.

134. LOVE THE LEVELLER, or, *The Pretty Purchase*, by G. B. Gent. 4to. 1704. It appears by the Epilogue, or at least seems implied in opposition to the author's assertion in the epistle to the reader, that it met with but indifferent success. And indeed it seems astonishing, that it should ever have been performed at all, that the managers should receive, the actors study, or the audience permit a thorough hearing to so execrable a piece. It is neither tragedy nor comedy; the plot, if it deserves that title, is full of the most unnatural incidents, the characters the most unmeaning, and the language the most trifling, bald, and insipid, that I almost ever met with. And its being at all endured might probably have been owing to what the author grievously complains of in his Epistle, viz. some correcting friends having with an unsparing hand lopped away, as he calls it, whole limbs, and mangled it into a barbarous deformity, that is to say, I imagine, curtailed so much of it, as to leave scarcely any thing for the public severity to exercise itself upon. The scene lies in Crete, and it is said in the title-page to have been acted at the New Theatre in Bridge's-Street, Covent-Garden, viz. the Theatre Royal in Drury-Lane.

135. LOVE MAKES A MAN, or, *The Fop's Fortune*. Com. by C. Cibber, 4to. to date, [1700.] Acted at Drury-Lane with great success, and continues still to give equal pleasure whenever it makes its appearance. The plot of it is taken partly from Beaumont and Fletcher's *Custom of the Country*, and partly from the *Elder Brother*

of the same authors. There are numberless absurdities and even impossibilities in the conduct of the piece, yet the sprightliness in the character of *Clodio*, the manly tenderness and openness of *Carlos*, and the entertaining testiness of Don *Choleric*, form so pleasing a mixture of comic humour as would atone for even greater faults than are to be found in this drama.

136. THE LOVE MATCH. Farce, Anonym. 1762. This little piece made its appearance at Covent Garden Theatre, but without success. It was indeed greatly deficient in some of the dramatic requisites, the plot being rather a compage of unconnected episodes, and some of the incidents rather forced and unnatural. Yet the language was far from being bad, and there were some of the characters not ill drawn, more particularly that of lady *Bellair*, which in all probability might of itself have protected the piece, and even procured it a run, had it not unluckily made its appearance immediately after that of a much more finished character of the same kind, viz. that of *Sophia*, in the *Musical Lady*. The *Love Match* therefore expired after the second night; nor has the author, who is entirely unknown, as yet thought proper to let it appear in print.

137. LOVE RESTOR'D, in a Masque at Court, acted by gentlemen the King's servants; by Ben Jonson, Fol. 1640.

138. THE LOVER. Com. by Theo. Cibber, 8vo. 1730. Acted at the Theatre in Drury-Lane with no great success, yet is far from being a bad play. It is dedicated to his first wife Mrs. Cibber, to whose performance in it he modestly attributes what approbation it did meet with.

139. THE

139. THE LOVER HIS OWN RIVAL. Ballad Opera, by Abraham Langford. Acted at Goodman's Fields, 8vo. 1736.

140. THE LOVERS OF LOODGATE. A Play, among those destroyed by Mr. Warburton's servant.

141. LOVERS LUCK. Com. by Thomas Dilke, 4to. 1696. This was acted at Little Lincoln's-Inn Fields with general applause, although most of the characters are but copies; particularly Sir Nicholas Purflew, from the *Antiquary of Marmion*; and *Goosandelo*, from Crown's *Sir Courtly*; and Sir *George Etheredge's* Sir *Fopling Flutter*. The scene lies in London.

142. THE LOVER'S MELANCHOLY. Tragi-Com. by John Ford. Acted at Black-Friers and the Globe, 4to. 1629. This play is highly commended in four copies of verses by friends of the author; and he has himself greatly embellished it by an apt introduction of several fancies from other writers, particularly the story of the contention between the musician and the nightingale, from Strada's Prolusions, and the description and definition of melancholy, from Burton's *Anatomy of Melancholy*. This play was acted in the same week, and by the same company, which performed Ben Jonson's comedy of *The New Inn*. The success of them was totally opposite to each other: Ford's play was received with great applause, while Ben's met with general disapprobation. Whoever will recollect the spleen which the latter is acknowledged to have possessed, will not be surprized to find that he resented the fate of his performance in very warm terms; and, to be revenged on Ford, who headed the supporters of Shakspeare's fame, against Jonson's invectives, he charged him with having stolen *The Lovers Melancholy* from Shakspeare's papers, with the connivance of Hemings and Condel, who, with Ford, had the revisal of them. In this dispute the poets of the times took part with either party, as passion or interest directed them; and, among other pieces, which the contest produced, was a pamphlet, intitled, "Old Ben's Light Heart made heavy, by young John's Melancholy Lover;" a performance once in the possession of Mr. Macklin the player, but now lost. An account of it, as well as the other circumstances attending this dispute, as far as they can at present be recovered, are printed in the last edition of Shakspeare, vol. I. p. 219.

143. THE LOVER'S OPERA. Farce, by W. R. Chetwood, 8vo. 1730. The piece was performed at the Theatre in Drury-Lane, and met with some success.

144. THE LOVER'S PROGRESS. Tragi-Com. by Beaumont and Fletcher, Fol. 1647. The plot of this play is founded on a French romance, called *Lisander and Calista*, written by M. Daudiguier; and the scene is laid in France.

145. LOVE'S ADVENTURES. Com. in two parts, by the Duchess of Newcastle, Fol. 1662.

146. LOVE'S ARTIFICE, or, *The Perplex'd Squire*. Farce, of two acts, by John Wignell, 8vo. 1762. This was intended for the compiler's benefit at York, but never performed.

147. LOVE'S A JEST. Com. by P. Motteux, 4to. 1696. This piece was acted with success at the Theatre in Little Lincoln's-Inn Fields. In the two scenes in which love is made a jest, the author has introduced many passages from the Italian

Italian writers. The scene is laid in Hertfordshire. The time of action from noon to night.

148. LOVE'S A LOTTERY, AND A WOMAN THE PRIZE. Com. by Jof. Harris. Acted at Lincoln's-Inn Fields, 4to. 1699. The scene, London. To this piece is annexed a masque, intituled, *Love and Riches reconciled*, which was performed with it at the same theatre.

149. LOVE'S CONTRIVANCE, or, *Le Medecin malgre lui*. Com. by Mrs. Centlivre. Acted at Drury-Lane, 4to. 1703. This is almost a translation of Moliere's comedy of the last of these two titles, with only an enlargement of the plot and characters. The scene, London.

150. LOVE'S CRUELTY. Trag. by James Shirley. Acted at the private house, Drury-Lane, 4to. 1640. The concealment of Hippolito and Chariana's adultery from her servant, through the contrivance of her husband Bellamonte, is taken from Q. Margaret's Novels, Day 4. Nov. 6. and Cynthio's *Hecatomithi*, Dec. 3. Nov. 6.

151. LOVE'S CURE, or, *The Martial Maid*. Com. by Beaumont and Fletcher, Fol. 1647. The scene, Seville.

152. LOVE'S DOMINION. A dramatic Piece, by Richard Flecknoe, 8vo. 1654. It is said in the title-page to have been written as a pattern for the *Reformed Stage*, and to be full of excellent morality. The scene lies at Amathante in Cyprus. The time only from morning till night.

153. THE LOVE-SICK COURT, or, *The Ambitious Politic*. Com. by Richard Brome, 8vo. 1658. Of this play a distich in the title shews us, that the author himself had a very modest and humble opinion. The scene lies in Thessaly.

154. THE LOVE-SICK KING. An English Tragical History, *with the Life and Death of Cartesmunda, the fair Nun of Winchester*, by Anth. Brewer, 4to. 1655. The historical part of the plot is founded on the invasion of the Danes in the reigns of King Ethelred and Alfred, and which may be seen in the writers on the English affairs of that time. The scene lies in England. This play was revived at the King's Theatre, and printed again in 1680, under the new title of *The Perjur'd Nun*.

155. THE LOVE-SICK MAID, or, *The Honour of Young Ladies*. Com. by Richard Brome. Entered on the books of the Stationers' Company Sept. 9, 1633; but, I believe, not printed.

156. LOVE'S KINGDOM. A Pastoral Tragi-Com. by Richard Flecknoe, 12mo. 1664. Not as it was acted at the Theatre near Lincoln's-Inn Fields, but as it was written and since corrected; with a short treatise on the English Stage, &c. This is little more than *Love's Dominion*, altered by its author, with the addition of a new title. It was brought on the stage, but had the misfortune to miscarry in the representation; yet it is so very regular, that the author boasts of *All the Rules of Time and Place* being so exactly observed, that whilst for time 'tis comprized in as few hours as there are acts, for place it never goes out of the view or prospect of *Love's Temple*. The scene is laid in Cyprus.

157. LOVE'S LABOUR'S LOST. Com. by W. Shakspeare. Acted at the Black-Friers and the Globe, 4to. 1598. 4to. 1631. This is one of those pieces which consist of such a mixture of irregularities and beauties, such a chequerwork of faults and perfections, as have occasioned some to suspect it not to be

be the work of this author; yet, as all the editors through whose hands his works have passed, have thought proper to let it keep its place among them, I have on that authority fixed his name to it in this catalogue. It is written for the most part in rhime, which, together with the turn for quibble, that was so much the fashion of the time, that Shakspeare has himself hinted at it in one of his best plays, where he makes his *Hamlet* say, "*We must speak by the Card, or Equivocation will undo us*," are its principal faults; yet through these the real spirit of dramatic genius seems to shine, the sprightliness of *Biron's* character being inimitably supported, and the conduct of his two friends and their *Inamoratas* finely conducted for bringing on the principal design, and working up the plot to its height. The scene lies in the king of Navarre's palace, and the country round it. Dr. Johnson says, that "in this "play, which all the editors have "concurred to censure, and some "have rejected as unworthy of our "poet, it must be confessed that "there are many passages mean, "childish, and vulgar; and some "which ought not to have been "exhibited, as we are told they "were, to a maiden queen. But "there are scattered through the "whole many sparks of genius; "nor is there any play that has "more evident marks of the hand "of Shakspeare."

158. LOVE's LABOUR WON. Com. Meres mentions a play under this title as written by Shakspeare. It is, however, supposed to be no other than *All's well that ends well*.

159. LOVE's LABYRINTH, or, *The Royal Shepherdess*. Tragi Com. by Thomas Forde, 8vo. 1660.

It is uncertain whether this play was ever acted or not. Part of it, however, is borrowed from Gomersal's Tragedy of *Sforza Duke of Milan*. Scene in Arcadia.

160. LOVE's LAST SHIFT, or, *The Fool in Fashion*. Com. by C. Cibber. Acted at the Theatre Royal, 4to. 1696. As it was the first attempt this gentleman made as an author, so was the performance of the part of Sir *Novelty Fashion* in it the means of establishing his reputation as an actor, in both which lights he for many years afterwards continued a glittering ornament to the English stage. The plot of it is original; yet is there some degree of improbability in *Loveless's* not knowing his own wife after a very few years absence from her; however, this little fault is made ample amends for by the beauty of the incident, and the admirable moral deduced from it. The author, in his Apology for his Life, p. 173, has given a very entertaining account of the difficulties and discouragements he met with in getting his piece acted, the prejudices he had to overcome, and the success it met with, which last fully answered his expectations.

161. LOVE's MARTYR, or, *Wit above Crowns*. Play, by Mrs. Anne Wharton. Entered on the books of the Stationers' Company Feb. 3, 1685; but, I believe, not printed.

162. LOVE's MASTERPIECE. Comedy, by Mr. Heywood. Entered on the books of the Stationers' Company May 22, 1640; but, perhaps, never printed.

163. LOVE's METAMORPHOSES. by John Lyly, 4to. 1601. First played by the children of Paul's, and now by the children of the chapel. Entered on the books of the Stationers' Company Nov. 25, 1600.

164. LOVE's

164. LOVE's METAMORPHOSES. Farce, by Thomas Vaughan, Esq. Acted at Drury-Lane, April 15, 1776, for Mrs. Wrighten's benefit. Not printed.

165. LOVE's MISTRESS, or, *The Queen's Masque.* by T. Heywood, 4to. 1636. This Play was three times presented before both their Majesties, within the space of eight days, in the presence of sundry foreign ambassadors, besides being publicly acted at the Phœnix in Drury-Lane. "When this play came "the second time to the royal "view (the author tells us), her "gracious majesty then entertain-"ing his highness at Denmark 'house upon his birth-day, Mr. "Inigo Jones gave an extraordi-"nary lustre to every act, nay al-"most to every scene, by his ex-"cellent inventions; upon every "occasion changing the stage to "the admiration of all the specta-"tors." The design of the plot is borrowed from Apuleius's *Golden Ass*; Apuleius and Mydas beginning the play, and closing every act by way of a chorus.

166. THE LOVES OF EMILIUS AND LOUISA. Trag. by John Maxwell being blind, 8vo. 1755. Printed by subscription at York for the benefit of the author.

167. LOVES OF ERGASTO. A Pastoral, represented at the opening of the Queen's Theatre in the Hay-Market. Composed by Signior Giacomo Greber, 4to. 1705. The scene, Arcadia.

168. THE LOVES OF MARS AND VENUS. A Play set to Music, by P. Motteux. Acted at Little Lincoln's-Inn Fields, in three acts, 4to. 1697. The author in his preface owns the story to be from Ovid, and that he has introduced a dance of Cyclops which bears a resemblance to, yet is very different from Mr. Shadwell's *Psyche*, which

he says is borrowed almost *verbatim* from Moliere, who in his turn took his from an old Italian opera, called *Le Nozze de gli Dei*. The Prologue, or introduction, and the first act, are set to music by Mr. Finger, and the second and third acts by Mr. J. Eccles. It was written to be inserted in Ravenscroft's *Anatomist*. See ANATOMIST.

169. THE LOVES OF MARS AND VENUS. Dramatic Entertainment of Dancing, attempted in imitation of the Pantomimes of the ancient Greeks and Romans, by John Weaver. Acted at Drury-Lane, 8vo. 1717.

170. LOVE's PILGRIMAGE. C. by Beaumont and Fletcher, Fol. 1647. The foundation of this play is built on a novel of Cervantes, called *The Two Damsels*. The scene in the first act between *Diego* the host of *Ossuna*, and *Lazaro* his ostler, is stolen, or rather borrowed from Ben Jonson's *New Inn*, since it is not improbable, as that play miscarried in the action, that Jonson might give them his consent to make use of it.

171. LOVE's REVENGE. Dramatic Pastoral. By Dr. John Hoadley, 8vo. 1745. This piece was set to music by Dr. Green. The scene lies in Arcadia, and it is divided into two interludes or acts. The subject is a revenge vowed by *Cupid* for some slight received from *Psyche*, which he puts in execution by exciting a fit of jealousy between two lovers, whom he afterwards, however, on a return of *Psyche's* kindness, reconciles to each other.

172. LOVE's RIDDLE. A Pastoral Comedy, by Abraham Cowley, 12mo. 1638. The plot of this play, as well as of all our author's dramatic pieces, is entirely original and unborrowed; and although
perhaps

perhaps it is not to be looked on as a first rate performance, yet, when it is considered that it was written while the author was a king's scholar at Westminster school, candour may be allowed not only to let it pass uncensured, but even to be low some share of commendation on it, especially as the author himself in his dedication apologizes for it as a puerile piece of work. This comedy (as Dr. Johnson observes) is of the pastoral kind, which requires no acquaintance with the living world, and therefore being composed while the author was yet at school, it adds little to the wonders of his minority. It was not published till he had been some years at Cambridge.

173. LOVE's SACRIFICE. T. by John Ford. Acted at the Phœnix, Drury-Lane, 4to. 1633. This play was generally well received, and has a complimentary copy of verses prefixed to it by Mr. James Shirley. The scene lies in Pavia.

174. LOVE's TRIUMPH, or, *The Royal Union.* Trag. by Edw. Cooke, 4to. 1678. This play is written in heroic verse. The plot is from the celebrated Romance of *Cassandra*, Part 5. Book 4. and the scene placed in the Palace of Roxana at Babylon. It never, however, appeared on the stage.

175. LOVE's TRIUMPH. Opera, by P. Motteux. Acted at the Hay-Market, 4to. 1708.

176. LOVE's TRIUMPH THROUGH CALLIPOLIS. Performed in a Masque at Court, 1630. by his Majesty King Charles I. with the lords and gentlemen assisting. The words of this piece were by Ben Jonson, the decorations of the scene by Inigo Jones. It was printed in Fol. 1641.

177. LOVE's VICTIM, or, *The Queen of Wales.* Trag. by Cha. Gildon, 4to. 1701. Acted at the Theatre in Lincoln's-Inn Fields, but without success.

178. LOVE's VICTORY. Tragi-Com. by William Chamberlaine, 4to. 1658. This play was written during the troubles of the civil wars, and intended by the author to have been acted, had not the powers then in being suppressed the stage, on which account he was obliged to content himself with only printing it. See *Wits led by the Nose*, or *A Poet's Revenge*. Scene, Sicilia.

179. LOVE's WELCOME, by Ben Jonson, Fol. 1641. This is farther intituled, The King and Queen's Entertainment at Bolsover, at the earl of Newcastle's, the 30th of July, 1634.

180. LOVE THE BEST PHYSICIAN. Com. by Ozell. The literal translation of Moliere's *L'Amour Medecin*, not intended for the stage.

181. LOVE THE CAUSE AND CURE OF GRIEF. A Tragedy, of three acts, by Thomas Cooke, 8vo. 1744. Acted at Drury-Lane Theatre, but justly damned. The fable taken from an old legal story in one of our books of reports. Scene in the county of Kent.

182. LOVE TRIUMPHANT, or, *Nature will prevail.* Tragi-Com. by J. Dryden. Acted at the Theatre Royal, 4to. 1694. This piece is the last Dryden wrote for the stage; and although it did not meet with the success that most of his plays had been indulged with, yet it must be acknowledged that in several parts of it the genius of that great man breaks forth, especially in the discovery of *Alphonso's* victorious love, and in the very last scene, the catastrophe of which is extremely affecting, notwithstanding that it is brought about contrary to the rules

rules of Aristotle, by a change of will in *Veramond*. The plot of it appears to be founded on the story of Fletcher's *King and no King*; at least on the corrections of the fable of that play, made by Rymer in his reflections on the tragedies of the last age. Thus, as Dr. Johnson observes, Dryden began and ended his dramatic labours with ill success.

183. LOVE TRIUMPHANT, or, *The Rival Goddesses*. A Pastoral Opera, by D. Bellamy, sen. Acted by the young ladies of Mrs. Bellamy's Boarding-School, second edition, 12mo. 1722. The plot of it is founded on the judgment of Paris.

184. LOVE WILL FIND OUT THE WAY. Com. By T. B. 4to. 1661. This is Shirley's *Constant Maid*, with a new title.

185. LOVE WITHOUT INTEREST, or, *The Man too hard for the Master*. Com. 4to. 1699. Who was the author of this piece I know not, but the dedication is subscribed by Penkethman, and is directed to six Lords, six Knights, and twenty-four Esquires; yet, notwithstanding this splendid patronage, it met with very little success on its appearance at the Theatre Royal.

186. THE LOVING ENEMIES. Com. by L. Maidwell. Acted at the Duke of York's Theatre, 4to. 1680. The epilogue of this play was written by Shadwell, from whose *Virtuoso* the original hint of this comedy seems to have been derived; the part of *Circumstantio* bearing a great resemblance to the humour of Sir *Formal Trifle*, as may be seen by comparing the description of the *Magpie's* sucking a *Hen's* egg, in the fourth act of this play, with that of the *Mouse* taken in a trap towards the end of the third act of the *Virtuoso*. The scene is laid in Florence.

187. LOW LIFE ABOVE STAIRS, Farce, Anonymous, 8vo. 1759. This was never acted, nor intended for the stage, but only a wretched catch-penny for the selling a pennyworth of blotted paper for a shilling, encouraged by the great success of *High Life below Stairs*, which see in its place.

188. THE LOYAL BROTHER, or, *The Persian Prince*. Trag. by Thomas Southern, 4to. 1682. This was our author's first play. The plot of it is taken from a novel, called *Tachmas Prince of Persia*. The prologue and epilogue are written by Dryden. The scene lies at Ispahan in Persia.

189. THE LOYAL GENERAL. Trag. by N. Tate, 4to. 1680. Acted at the Duke's Theatre.

190. THE LOYAL LOVERS. Tragi-Com. by Cosmo Manuche, 4to. 1652. The author in this play has severely lashed the old committee-men and their informers in the persons of *Gripeman* and *Sodom*. And Langbaine ventures a surmise that under the characters of *Phanaticus* and *Flyblow* he has meant to expose an adventure of the famous Hugh Peters, with a butcher's wife of St. Sepulchre's, with his revenge thereon; observing at the same time that if his conjecture is right, it is but a piece of justice that Peters should find himself personated on the stage, who had so frequently ridiculed others when he acted the clown's part in Shakspeare's company of comedians.

191. THE LOYAL SHEPHERDS, or, *The Rustic Heroine*. Dramatic Pastoral, by T. Goodwin, 8vo. 1779.

192. THE LOYAL SUBJECT. Tragi-Com. by Beaumont and Fletcher,

Fletcher, Fol. 1679. The scene lies at Mosco; and some parts of the plot and characters are ingenious and well supported, yet on the whole I cannot esteem it as one of the best pieces of these authors. Mrs Sheridan, however, thought it worth while to revive it on his Theatre at Dublin some years ago, and reprint it with a few alterations of his own.

193. LUCINDA. Dramatic Entertainment of three acts, by Charles Jenner. Printed at the end of Letters from *Lotharia* to *Penelope*, two volumes, 12mo. 176.

194. LUCIUS, *the first Christian King of Britain*. Trag. by Mrs. Manley. Acted at Drury-Lane, 4to. 1717. This play is founded on the legendary accounts of this monarch, given by the Monkish writers, improved with a considerable share of agreeable fiction of her own. It met with good success, and is dedicated to Sir Richard Steele, who, although she had formerly abused him in the *Atalantis*, was now so well reconciled to her, that he wrote the Prologue to this piece, as Mr. Prior did the Epilogue. The scene lies in the Capital of Aquitaine.

195. LUCIUS JUNIUS BRUTUS, Father of his Country. Trag. by Nathaniel Lee. Acted at the Duke's Theatre, 4to. 1681. This is a very fine play, being full of great manly spirit, force, and vigour, with less of the bombast than frequently runs through this author's works. The plot of it is partly from the real Histories of *Florus, Livy, Dionys. Halic.* &c. and partly from the fictions in the Romance of *Clelia*. The scene between *Vindicius* and the elder *Brutus* seems to bear a great resemblance to that between *Hamlet* and *Polonius*. The scene lies in Rome. Gildon, in his Preface to *The Patriot*, says, this play was forbid, after the third day's acting, by Lord Chamberlain Arlington, as an antimonarchial play.

196. LUCIUS JUNIUS BRUTUS. Trag. by Mr. Duncombe. Acted at Drury-Lane, 8vo. 1735. 12mo. 1747. This play is built upon Voltaire's *Tragedy of Brutus*. For a history of its progress to the stage, see Duncombe's Letters, vol. III. p. 144. It was acted six nights.

197. LUCIUS JUNIUS BRUTUS, or, *The Expulsion of the Tarquins*. Historical Play, by Hugh Downham, M. D. 8vo. 1779. An attempt to restore the familiar blank verse which was used in the last century. This play was never acted, but possesses great merit.

198. THE LUCKY CHANCE, or, *An Alderman's Bargain*, by Mrs. Behn. Acted by their Majesties servants, 4to. 1687. This play was greatly exclaimed against by the critics of that time, whose objections the author has endeavoured to obviate in her preface. The crime laid to her charge was indecency and an intrigue bordering both in action and language on obscenity. From this she has vindicated herself, if retorting the accusation on others, and proving herself only guilty in a lesser degree than others had been before her, may be esteemed a vindication. But, in short, the best excuse that can be made for her, is the fashionable licentiousness of the time she wrote in, when the bare-faced intrigue of a court and nation of gallantry, rendered those things apparently chaste and decent, which would at this time be hissed off the stage as obscene and immoral. As to the plot, it is for the most part original, excepting only the incident

cident of *Gayman's* enjoying Lady *Fullbank*, and taking her for the devil, which is copied from *Kickshaw* and *Aretina* in the *Lady of Pleasure*, by Shirley. The scene, London.

199. THE LUCKY DISCOVERY, or, *The Tanner of York*. A Ballad Opera, Anonymous. Acted at Covent-Garden, 8vo. N. D. [1738.] It was also performed at the same theatre about the year 1754, for the benefit of Mr. Arthur, who then claimed it as written by himself.

200. THE LUCKY ESCAPE. Musical Farce, by Mrs. Robinson. Acted at Drury-Lane, April 30, 1778, for the benefit of the authoress.

201. LUDUS FILIORUM ISRAELIS. Represented by the Guild of Corpus Christi, at Cambridge, on that festival, in the year 1355. See Masters's Hist. C. C. C. C. p. 5. vol. I.

202. LUMINALIA, or, *The Festival of Light*, 4to 1627. Presented in a masque at Court, by the Queen's Majesty and her ladies, on Shrove-Tuesday night, 4to. 1637. At her Majesty's command the celebrated Inigo Jones, who was at that time surveyor of the board of works, took on himself the contrivance of machinery for this masque, the invention of which consisted principally in the presenting *Light* and *Darkness*; *Night* representing the anti-masque or introduction, and the subject of the main-masque being *Light*.

203. THE LUNATICK. Com. Dedicated to the Three Ruling B————s, at the new house in Lincoln's-Inn Fields, 4to. 1705.

204. LUPONE, or, *The Inquisitor*, by Alexander Gordon, 8vo. 1731.

205. LUST'S DOMINION, or, *The Lascivious Queen*. Trag. by Christopher Marloe, 12mo. 1657.

12mo. 1661. This is very far from being a bad play in itself; but was afterwards altered by Mrs. Behn, and acted under the title of *Abdelazar*, or *The Moor's Revenge*, which see in its proper place.

206. An *Enterlude called* LUSTY JUVENTUS, *hyerly describing the Frailtie of Youth: of Nature prone to Vyce: by Grace and good Councell traynable to Vertue*. 4to. b. l. 1561.

The *Dramatis Personæ* are:
Messenger | Lusty Juventus | Good Counsaill | Knowledge. Sathan the devyll | Hypocrisie | Felowshyp | Abhominable-lyving | an Harlot | God's-mercifull-promises. |

The following is the Printer's colophon:

Finis, quod R. Wever. Imprinted at London in Paule's churche-yeard, by Abraham Dele at the signe of the Lambe.

As in the ancient interlude of EVERY MAN occasion is taken to inculcate great reverence for old mother church, so (as Dr. Percy observes) our poet, Master R. Wever, with equal success, attacks both. In *Lusty Juventus*, chapter and verse are every where quoted as formally as in a sermon. From this play we learn that most of the young people were *New Gospellers*, or friends to the Reformation, and that the old were tenacious of the doctrines imbibed in their youth. Hence the Devil is introduced lamenting the downfal of superstition; and in another place Hypocrisy complains that the younger part of the world is growing too wise for his interests.

207. THE LYAR. Com. of three acts, by Samuel Foote, 1762. Printed 8vo. 1764. This piece was originally intended to have been represented during the summer partnership between Mr. Murphy and the author,

thor, but the run of those pieces they had before brought on, and the unexpected necessity of their performing the *Wishes*, having exhausted the time limited for their representation, this was obliged to be deferred till the ensuing winter, when it was represented for the first time at the Theatre in Covent-Garden. Its success was but very indifferent; and indeed it must be confessed that it was in itself far from equal to the generality of this gentleman's works. As to the plot, it is almost entirely borrowed from Sir Richard Steele's *Lying Lover*; which was itself founded on the *Menteur* of Corneille, which was moreover little more than a translation from a dramatic piece written by Lopez de Vega. It is not much to be wondered, therefore, if the dish, thus served up at a fourth hand, did not retain the whole of its original relish. And though there were here and there some strokes of humour which were not unworthy of their author, and some few touches of temporary satire, yet the character of the *Lyar* had certainly neither native originality enough in it to please as a novelty, nor additional beauties enough either in his dress or demeanour to excite a fresh attention to him as a new acquaintance. And what seemed still more extraordinary, the author, who himself performed the part, and therefore one would imagine might have had an eye to his own peculiar excellencies in the writing it, had not even aimed, as he has most usually done, at affording himself any opportunity in it for exerting those amazing talents of mimickry which he has ever been so remarkable for, and so inimitable in. In short, on the whole, it was rather tedious and unentertaining, having neither enough of the *Vis comica* to keep up the attention of an audience through so many acts as a farce, nor a sufficiency of incident and sentiment to engage their hearts, if considered under the denomination of a comedy. It has since been often acted as a Farce.

208. THE LYAR. Com. in three acts, 8vo. 1763. A catchpenny intended to be imposed on the public for Mr. Foote's play of the same name.

209. LYCIDAS. Masque. Not acted, 4to. 1762. Printed with some poems.

210. LYCIDAS. Musical Entertainment, performed at Covent-Garden, 8vo. 1767. The words altered from Milton, and intended as a Dirge on the duke of York's death. It was acted only one night.

211. THE LYING LOVERS, or, *The Ladies' Friendship*. Com. by Sir Richard Steele. Acted at Drury-Lane, 4to. 1704. As this author borrowed part of all his plots from other authors, it is not at all to be wondered at if we find that to be the case with this piece among the rest, the main groundwork of the design being taken from the *Menteur* of P. Corneille, the characters of *Old* and *Young Bookwit* from the *Geronte* and *Dorante* of that piece, and many of the incidents very closely copied. How far Sir Richard has fallen short of, or improved on, his original, is a point that I shall not take on me in this place to determine, but shall only observe that I do not think it by any means equal to any one of his other plays.

212. THE LYING VALET. C. in two acts, by David Garrick, 8vo. 1740. This little piece made its first appearance at the Theatre

in Goodman's Fields; but the author, soon quitting that place for the Theatre Royal in Drury-Lane, brought his Farce with him, which was there acted with great and deserved applause. Some of the nibblers in criticism have charged this piece as being borrowed from some French comedy; but as I have never yet heard the title of the supposed original mentioned, I cannot avoid, as far as to the extent of my own knowledge, acquitting the author from this accusation. A charge, however, which, wherever laid, I am ever apt to suspect as rather the effect of envy, than of a love of justice or the public, as it has ever been the practice of the very best writers in all ages and nations to make use of valuable hints in the works of their neighbours, for the use and advantage of those of their countrymen, to whom those works may not be so familiar as to themselves. No man in his senses would, I think, quarrel with a fine nosegay, because some of the most beautiful flowers in it happened to have been gathered in a neighbouring country; nor is the world much less obliged to the person who favours it with a good translation of a good author, than to that author himself, or one of equal excellence at home. Intreating pardon, however, for this small digression, I shall now proceed to the little dramatic work under consideration, which, whether original, translation, or copy, has undoubtedly great merit, if character, plot, incident, and a rank of diction well adapted to those characters, can give it a just title to the praise I have bestowed on it. Nor can there be stronger evidence borne to its deserts, than that approbation which constantly attended on it through the numerous repetitions of it at both our Theatres.

M.

1. THE MACARONI. Com. by —— Hitchcock, performed at York, 8vo. 1773. It was once acted at the Hay-Market.

2. MACBETH. Trag. by W. Shakspeare, Fol. 1623. This play is extremely irregular, every one of the rules of the *Drama* being entirely and repeatedly broken in upon. Yet, notwithstanding, it contains an infinity of beauties, both with respect to language, character, passion, and incident. The incantations of the witches are equal, if not superior, to the *Canidia* of Horace. The use this author has made of *Banquo's* ghost towards the heightening the already heated imagination of *Macbeth*, is inimitably fine. Lady *Macbeth*, discovering her own crimes in her sleep, is perfectly original and admirably conducted. *Macbeth's* soliloquies, both before and after the murder, are master-pieces of unmatchable writing; while his readiness of being deluded at first by the witches, and his desperation

tion on the discovery of the fatal ambiguity and loss of all hope from supernatural predictions, produce a catastrophe truly just, and formed with the utmost judgment. In a word, notwithstanding all its irregularities, it is certainly one of the best pieces of the very best master in this kind of writing that the world ever produced. The plot is founded on the Scottish History, and may be traced in the writings of Hector Boethius, Buchanan, Holingshed, &c. in Heywood's *Hierarchy of Angels*, and in the first book of Heylin's *Cosmography*. The entire story at large, however, collected from them all, is to be seen in a work in three volumes, 12mo. intituled *Shakspeare illustrated*, vol. I. The scene in the end of the fourth act lies in England. Through all the rest of the play it is in Scotland, and chiefly at *Macbeth's* Castle at Inverness.

"This play, says Dr. Johnson, "is deservedly celebrated for the "propriety of its fictions, and "solemnity, grandeur, and va- "riety of its action, but it has no "nice discriminations of cha- "racter; the events are too great "to admit the influence of par- "ticular dispositions, and the "course of the action necessarily "determines the conduct of the "agents.

"The danger of ambition is "well described; and I know not "whether it may not be said, in "defence of some parts which now "seem improbable, that in Shak- "speare's time it was necessary to "warn credulity against vain and "illusive predictions.

"The passions are directed to "their true end. Lady *Macbeth* "is merely detested; and though "the courage of *Macbeth* pre- "serves some esteem, yet every "reader rejoices at his fall."

3. MACBETH. Trag. with all the alterations, amendments, additions, and new songs. Acted at the Duke's Theatre, 4to. 1674. This alteration was made by Sir William Davenant.

Downes the prompter says, that Nat Lee the Poet having an inclination to turn actor, had the part of *Duncan* assigned to him on this revival, but did not succeed in it. His name, however, stands against the character in the printed copy. It was performed with great splendor. The music by Mr. Lock.

4. MACBETH, the Historical Tragedy of, (written originally by Shakspeare). Newly adapted to the stage with alterations, by J. Lee, as performed at the Theatre in Edinburgh, 8vo. 1753. Language is not strong enough to express our contempt of Mr. Lee's performance. If sense, spirit, and versification, were ever discoverable in Shakspeare's play, so sure has our reformer laid them all in ruins. Criticism disdains to point out each particular mischief of this monkey hand; but yet, gentle reader, accept the following specimen of its attempt to improve the well-known incantation with which the fourth act begins:

1. *Witch.*
No milk-maid yet hath been bedew'd.
2. *Witch.*
But thrice the brinded cat hath mew'd.
3. *Witch.*
Twice and once the hedge-pig whin'd,
Shutting his eyes against the wind.
1. *Witch.*
Up hollow oaks now emmets climb.
2. *Witch.*
And Hecate cries, 'tis time, 'tis time.
3. *Witch.*
Then round about the cauldron go,
And poison'd entrails in it throw.
1. *Witch.*
Toad (that under mossy stone,
Nights and days has thirty one,
Swelter'd venom sleeping got)
Boil first in the inchanted pot, &c. &c.

5. MA-

5. MADAM FICKLE, or, *The Witty False One*. Com. by Thomas Durfey. Acted at the Duke's Theatre, 4to. 1677. This author, who, in regard both of plot and character, was certainly one of the greatest plagiaries that ever existed, has prefixed to this play a motto from Horace, viz. *Non cuivis Homini contingit adire Corinthum*, which Langbaine has humourously enough explained to imply, "That he could not write a play without stealing." At least, however, he has given no proof to the contrary of such explanation in the piece before us, which is wholly made up from other comedies. For instance, the character of Sir *Arthur Old-Love* is a plain copy of Veterano, in the *Antiquary*; as is also the incident of *Zeebiel's* creeping into the Tavern Bush, and *Tilburn's* being drunk under it, &c. of the scene of Sir *Reverence Lamard* and *Pimpwell*, in the *Walks of Islington and Hogsdon*. There are also several hints in it borrowed from Marston's *Fawn*. The scene is laid in Covent-Garden.

6. THE MAD CAPTAIN. Opera, by Robert Drury. Acted at Goodman's Fields, 8vo. 1733. Prologue spoken by the author.

7. THE MAD COUPLE WELL MATCH'D. Comedy, by Richard Brome, 8vo. 1653. This play met with good success, and was revived with some very trivial alterations by Mrs. Behn, under the title of *The Debauchee, or The Credulous Cuckold*, and reprinted in 4to. 1677.

8. THE MAD-HOUSE. A Rehearsal of a new Ballad Opera, burlesqued, called THE MADHOUSE, after the manner of *Pasquin*, by R. Baker. Acted at Lincoln's-Inn Fields, 8vo. 1737.

9. THE MAD LOVER. Tragi-Com. by Beaumont and Fletcher, Fol. 1647. This play is particularly commended by Sir Aston Cockain, in his copy of verses on Fletcher's Plays. The scene lies at Paphos. The plot of *Cleanthe's* suborning the priest to give a false oracle in favour of her brother Syphax is borrowed from the story of *Mundus* and *Paulina*, in Josephus, Book 18. Ch. 4.

10. THE HISTORY OF MADOR KING OF BRITAIN. By Francis Beaumont. Entered on the books of the Stationers' Company June 29, 1660; but not printed.

11. MADRIGAL AND TRULLETTA. A Mock Tragedy, 8vo. 1758. This piece was written by Mr. Reed. It was performed at the Theatre Royal in Covent-Garden one night only, under the direction of Theoph. Cibber. It is intended as a ridicule upon some of the later performances of the buskin, and is executed with much humour.

12. A MAD WORLD MY MASTERS. Com. by Thomas Middleton. Acted by the children of Paul's, 4to. 1608. 4to. 1640. This is a very good play, and has been since borrowed from by many writers; particularly by Mrs Behn, in her *City Heiress*; and by C. Johnson, in his *Country Lasses*.

13. THE MAGIC GIRDLE. Burletta, by George Saville Carey. Acted at Marybone-Gardens, 4to. 1770.

14. THE MAGICIAN OF THE MOUNTAIN. Pantomime. Acted at Drury-Lane, 1763. The good sense of the audience condemned this piece to oblivion after, I think, two representations.

15. THE MAGNET. Musical Entertainment, performed at Marybone-Gardens, 4to. 1771.

16. THE MAGNETIC LADY, or, *Humours reconcil'd*. Com. by Ben Jonson, Fol. 1640. This play is in general esteemed a very good one,

one, yet did not escape the censure of some critics of that time; particularly Mr. Gill master of Paul's school, or his son, wrote a satire against it, which Ben Jonson wrote a reply to, with equal, if not greater severity. Those who are curious to see both will find them in Langbaine, 8vo. 1691, p. 292.

17. MAGNIFICENCE.] A goodly Interlude and a me|ry deuyſed and made by|mayſter Skelton poet| laureate late de|ceaſyd.∴ See University Library, Cambridge, D. 4. 8. It contains 60 folio pages in the black letter, muſt have taken up a conſiderable time in the repreſentation, and was printed by Raſtell in about 1533. It begins with a dialogue between *Felicite* and *Lyberte:*

    Fylycite.
Al thyngys contryvyd by mannys reaſon,
The world envyrenyd of hygh and low eſtate,
Be it erly or late welth hath a ſeaſon;
Welth is of wyſdome the very trewe probate.

The ſubſtance of the Allegory, ſays Mr. Warton, (who had never ſeen any other copy than Mr. Garrick's, of which the firſt leaf and title are wanting) is briefly this, *Magnificence*, becomes a dupe to two ſervants and favourites, *Fanſy*, *Counterfet Countenance*, *Crafty Convoyance*, *Clockyd Colufion*, *Courtly Abuſion*, and *Foly*. At length he is ſeized and robbed by *Adverſyte*, by whom he is given up as a priſoner to *Poverte*. He is next delivered to *Deſpare* and *Miſchefe*, who offer him a knife and a halter. He ſnatches the knife, to end his miſeries by ſtabbing himſelf; when *Good Hope* and *Redreſſe* appear, and perſuade him to take the *rubarbe of repentance* with ſome *goſtly gummes*, and a few *drammes of devotyon*. He becomes acquainted with *Circumſpecyon* and *Perſeverance*, follows their directions, and ſeeks for happineſs in a ſtate of penitence and contrition. There is ſome humour here and there in the dialogue, but the alluſions are commonly low. Although many *Moralities* were written about this period, *Magnificence* and the *Nigramanſir*, by Skelton, are the firſt that bear the name of their author.

18. THE MAGNIFICENT LOVERS. Com. by Ozell. This is only a tranſlation, intended for the cloſet alone, of *Les Amans Magnifiques* of Moliere.

19. MAHOMET, *the Impoſtor*. Tr. by J. Miller. Acted at Drury-Lane, 8vo. 1744. This is little more than a good tranſlation of *The Mahomet* of Voltaire, whoſe writings indeed breathe ſuch a ſpirit of liberty, and have contracted ſuch a reſemblance to the manners of the Engliſh authors, that they ſeem better adapted to ſucceed on the Engliſh ſtage without much alteration, than thoſe of any other foreign writer. This play met with tolerable ſucceſs, its merits having fair play from the ignorance of the prejudiced part of the audience with regard to its author, who unfortunately did not ſurvive to reap any advantage from it, for being unable to put the finiſhing hand to it, he received ſome aſſiſtance in the completing of it from Dr. John Hoadly. The author died during its run; and not long after his death, Fleetwood, then manager of Drury-Lane Theatre, permitted the widow to attempt the performing of it at that houſe for her benefit; when notwithſtanding the diſpute which had been for a long time ſubſiſting between that manager and the town, with regard to the abating the advanced prices on entertainments (and which, as his patent was

was very near expired, he was by no means anxious to reconcile) had arisen to such an height, as to occasion nightly riots at the house, and a determination on the side of the audience to permit no representation till their proposed reformation was complied with, yet so favourable was the town on this occasion, that the play not only went off without the least interruption, but the house was so full, as to enable the widow to clear upwards of an hundred pounds by the profits of it.

This was also the play which, in the year 1753, was the innocent cause of a considerable revolution in the dramatic world, in another kingdom, viz. that of Ireland, and which finally terminated in the entire abdication of a theatrical monarch, although he had with great labour and affiduity brought his domain into a more flourishing state than any of his predecessors had done: for through the too great warmth of party-zeal in a considerable part of the audience, which infilled on a repetition of certain passages in this play, which appeared to them applicable to some persons then in power, and perhaps a too peremptory manner of opposing that zeal on the side of Mr. Sheridan, then manager of the Theatre Royal in Smock-Alley, Dublin, a disturbance ensued, in consequence of which, Sheridan was obliged to quit first the house for the security of his person, and afterwards the kingdom for the support of his fortune. The theatre was shut up for the remainder of that season; and the management of it, after divers ineffectual struggles made by Sheridan for some time, partly by deputation, and partly in person, to reinstate himself in the quiet possession of it, has at length devolved totally into other hands.

This play was revived at Drury-Lane in the year 1765, and has since been frequently acted with applause.

20. THE MAIDEN'S HOLY-DAY. Com. by Christopher Marlow and John Day. Entered on the books of the Stationers' Company April 8, 1654; and was amongst those destroyed by Mr. Warburton's servant.

21. A MAIDENHEAD WELL LOST. Com. by Thomas Heywood, 4to. 1634.

22. THE MAID OF BATH. Com. by Samuel Foote, Esq. Acted at the Hay-Market in 1771. Printed in 8vo. 1778. A transaction which happened at Bath, in which a person of fortune was said to have treated a young lady celebrated for her musical talents in a very censurable manner, afforded the ground-work of this extremely entertaining performance. The delinquent is here held up to ridicule under the name of Flint, and it will be difficult to point out a character drawn with more truth and accuracy than the present, especially in the second act. The parts of Lady *Catherine Coldstream*, Sir *Christopher Cripple*, and *Billy Button*, are also all highly finished, and render the piece one of the most pleasing of this writer.

23. THE MAID OF HONOUR. Tragi-Com. by Phil. Massinger. Acted at the Phœnix, Drury-Lane, 4to. 1632. 4to. 1638. This play met with great applause, and has a copy of verses prefixed by Sir Aston Cockain.

24. THE MAID OF KENT. Com. by —— Waldron, 8vo. 1778. This was originally acted at Drury-Lane 1773, for the author's benefit.

25. THE MAID IN THE MILL. Com. by Beaumont and Fletcher, Fol. 1647. This is a very excellent

lent play, and was one of those which after the Restoration were revived at the Duke of York's Theatre. The serious part of the plot, viz. that which relates to *Antonio*, *Ismenia*, and *Aminta*, is borrowed from a Spanish romance, called, *Gerardo*; and the comic part, with the affair of *Orante's* seizing *Florimel*, the Miller's supposed daughter, and attempting her chastity, from Belleforest's *Histoires Tragiques*, Tom. 1. Hist. 12. The scene lies in Spain.

26. THE MAID OF THE MILL. Com. Opera, by Isaac Bickerstaffe. Acted at Covent-Garden, 8vo. 1765. This is taken from Richardson's Novel of *Pamela*, and was performed with great success.

27. THE MAID OF THE OAKS. Dramatic Entertainment, by John Burgoyne, Esq. Acted at Drury-Lane, 8vo. 1774. The style of this performance is less offensively affected than that of certain proclamations, which induced the Americans to style our author *the Chrononhotonthologos of War*. The *Maid of the Oaks*, in short, is a piece that confers no honour, and brings no disgrace on its parent. A few bold touches from Mr. Garrick's pen are supposed to have sent it with additional force on the stage. As the work of a patriot, a patriot manager may revive it; but perhaps few audiences will thank him for his zeal, or (to use Burgoynian phrase) applaud his *scale of talent* in the direction of a theatre, and declare that he consults the public inclination *to a charm*.

This piece was occasioned by the *Fête Champetre* given at the *Oaks* in Kent, on the marriage of the Earl of Derby and Lady Betty Hamilton, June 9, 1774.

28. THE MAID'S LAST PRAYER, or, *Any rather than fail*. Com. by Thomas Southerne. Acted at the Theatre Royal, 4to. 1693. Scene, London. There is a song in this play by Congreve.

29. THE MAID'S METAMORPHOSES. Com. by John Lyly, 4to. 1600. This play was frequently acted by the children of Paul's, and is one of those pieces in which the author has attempted to refine the English language. The greatest part of the play, and particularly the whole first act, is written in verse.

30. THE MAID'S REVENGE. T. by Ja. Shirley. Acted at the private house, Drury-Lane, 4to. 1630. The plot is taken from Reynolds's *God's Revenge against Murder*, Book 2. Hist. 7. and the scene lies at Lisbon. This is said to be the second play Shirley wrote.

31. THE MAID'S TRAGEDY, by Beaumont and Fletcher. Acted at the Black-Friers, 4to. 1622. 4to. 1630. 4to. 1638. 4to. 1641. 4to. 1650. 4to. 1661. This play is an exceeding good one, and ever met with universal approbation. It has not, however, been introduced to any of our audiences for some years past. Scene, Rhodes.

32. THE MAID'S TRAGEDY, by Edm. Waller. See the preceding article. In this play the catastrophe is rendered fortunate. Mr. Fenton observes, that Langbaine mistook in affirming that King Charles the Second would not suffer the play to appear on the stage, being assured by Mr. Southerne, that in the latter end of that reign he had seen it acted at the Theatre Royal as originally written, but never with Waller's alterations.

33. MAJESTY MISLED, or, *The Overthrow of Evil Ministers*. Tr. 8vo. 1734. The title-page says it was intended to be acted at one of the theatres, but was refused for certain reasons.

34. MAJESTY MISLED. Trag. 8vo. 1770.

35. MAKE A NOISE TOM. Farce, occasioned by the lighting of a loyal bonfire, with that brush of iniquity Mr. B——y, who was burnt in effigy at the town of Wakefield in Yorkshire, 8vo. 1718. This piece seems to be both local and temporary. Scene, Wakefield.

36. THE MAL-CONTENT. T. Com. by John Marston. Acted by the King's servants, 4to. 1604. Of this play there are two editions in the same year. To one of the copies are added an Induction, a new character, and other particulars, by John Webster. It is dedicated in the warmest and most complimentary manner possible to Ben Jonson; yet so fickle and uncertain a thing is friendship, especially among poets whose interests both in fame and fortune are frequently apt to clash with each other, that we find this very author, two years afterwards, in the epistle prefixed to his *Sophonisba*, casting very harsh and severe, though oblique reflections, on the *Sejanus* and *Catiline* of the writer whom he at this time addressed as the most exalted genius of the age he lived in. Some of Marston's enemies represented this play as designed to strike at particular characters; but Langbaine endeavours to vindicate the author from that charge, calling it an honest general satire.

37. THE MALE COQUETTE, or, *Seventeen Hundred Fifty-Seven*. Farce, by David Garrick, Esq. Acted at Drury-Lane. 8vo. 1758. This little piece was planned, written, and acted, in less than a month. It first appeared at Mr. Woodward's benefit, and is intended to expose a kind of character no less frequent about this town than either the *Flashes* or *Fribbles*, but much more pernicious than both, and which the author has distinguished by the title of *Daffodils*; a species of men who, without hearts capable of sensibility, or even manhood enough to relish, or wish for enjoyment with the sex, yet, from a desire of being considered as gallants, make court to every woman indiscriminately; whose reputation is certain to be ruined from the instant these insects have been observed to settle near her, their sole aim being to obtain the credit of an amour, without ever once reflecting on the fatal consequences that may attend thereon in the destruction of private peace and domestic happiness. This character, although a very common one, seems to be new to the stage, and is, in the importance to the world of rendering it detestable to society, undoubtedly worthy of an able pen. The author of this farce has taken as broad steps towards this point as the extent of so small a work would give scope for, yet his catastrophe is somewhat unnatural, and his hero's disgrace not rendered public enough to answer the end entirely. As to the second title of it, there seems no apparent reason for the annexing it, unless it is to afford occasion for a humorous prologue written and spoken by Mr. Garrick, the author of the piece.

38. THE MALL, or, *The Modish Lovers*. Com. by J. D. Acted at the Theatre Royal, 4to. 1674. This play has been ascribed to Dryden, yet its style and manner bear but little resemblance to those of that author, and therefore it is more reasonable to imagine it the work of some obscurer writer.

* 39. MALCOLM. Trag. by Miss Roberts, 8vo. 1779. This tragedy was never acted. The time of the action

action is, when Edgar Atheling fled into Scotland from William the Conqueror.

40. MAMAMOUCHI, or, *The Citizen turn'd Gentleman*, by Edward Ravenscroft, 4to. 1675. This play is wholly borrowed, and that even without the least acknowledgment of the theft, from the *M. of. Pourceaugnac* and the *Bourgeois Gentilhomme* of Moliere. It was printed under the latter title only, 4to. 1672, and was acted at the Duke's Theatre. At the end is an epilogue, spoken at the Middle Temple, by which it appears that the author was a student there.

41. MANGORA, KING OF THE TIMBUSIANS. Tr. by Sir Thomas Moore, 4to. 1718. This play was brought on the stage at the Theatre in Lincoln's-Inn Fields, but was very deservedly damned; it being both with respect to plot, language, and every other essential of dramatic writing, a most contemptible piece.

42. THE MAN HATER. Com. by Ozell. This is only a translation from the *Misantbrope* of Moliere.

43. THE MAN HATER. Com. translated from the French, and printed in Foote's *Comic Theatre*, vol. V.

44. THE MANAGERS. Com. 4to. 1768. Relates to the differences then subsisting amongst the proprietors of Covent-Garden Theatre.

45. THE MANAGER IN DISTRESS. Prelude, by George Colman. Acted at the Hay-Market, 8vo. 1780.

46. MANHOOD AND WISDOME, *A Masque of muche Instructioune*. Anonymous, 4to. 1563.

47. MANLIUS CAPITOLINUS. Trag. by Ozell, 12mo 1715. This is a translation in blank verse from the French of Monsf. de la Fosse. I believe it was never intended for the English stage, but was acted at Paris for threescore nights running, at the time that the earl of Portland was ambassador at the French court. The subject of it is from history, and is to be found in the 6th book of Livy's 1st *Decade*. The translator observes, that La Fosse studied some time at the University of Oxford.

48. MAN AND WIFE, or, *The Shakspeare Jubilee*. Com. by Geo. Colman. Acted at Covent-Garden, 8vo. 1770. This short piece was composed for the purpose of introducing a procession of Shakspeare's characters, before Mr. Garrick's *Jubilee* could be prepared for representation at Drury-Lane.

49. THE MAN OF BUSINESS. Com. by George Colman. Acted at Covent-Garden, 8vo. 1774. This performance was acted with moderate success.

50. THE MAN OF FAMILY. A Sentimental Com. by Charles Jenner, 8vo. 1771. Dedicated to Mr. Garrick, and taken from Diderot's *Pere de Famille*.

51. THE MAN OF HONOUR. Com. by Francis Lynch. At what time this play was written or published I cannot exactly know, but imagine it must have been about 1730, or between that time and 1740, as *The Independent Patriot*, by the same author, came out in 1737.

52. THE MAN OF THE MILL. Burlesque Tragic Opera. The music compiled and the words written by Seignor Squallini, 8vo. 1765. A parody on *The Maid of the Mill*.

53. THE MAN OF MODE, or, *Sir Fopling Flutter*. Com. by Sir George Etheredge. Acted at the Duke's Theatre, 4to. 1676. 4to. 1684. This is an admirable play; the

the characters in it are strongly marked, the plot agreeably conducted, and the dialogue truly polite and elegant. The character of *Dorimant* is perhaps the only completely fine gentleman that has ever yet been brought on the English stage, at the same time that in that of Sir *Fopling* may be traced the ground-work of almost all the *Foppingtons* and *Petit Maitres* which appeared in the succeeding comedies of that period. It is said that Sir *George* intended the part of *Dorimant* as a compliment to the famous earl of Rochester, designing in that character to form a portrait of his lordship, in which all the good qualities he possessed (which were not a few) were set forth in the most conspicuous light, and a veil thrown over his foibles, or at least such a gloss laid on them as to make them almost appear so many perfections.

54. THE MAN OF NEW-MARKET. Com. by Edward Howard. Acted at the Theatre Royal, 4to. 1678. Scene, London.

55. THE MAN OF QUALITY. Farce, by Mr. Lee. Acted at Drury-Lane, 8vo. 1776 A poor alteration of Vanbrugh's *Relapse*.

56. THE MAN OF REASON. Com. by Hugh Kelly. Performed at Covent-Garden, 1776. This was acted only one night, and is not printed. The author of Mr. Kelly's Life says, "it must be "acknowledged that it was in- "ferior to his other works, and "was supposed to have suffered "greatly by the misconception of "the actor (Mr. Woodward), who "performed the principal cha- "racter in it."

57. THE MAN OF TASTE. Com. by J. Miller, 8vo. 1731. This play was acted at Drury-Lane with considerable success.

The plot of it is borrowed partly from the *Ecole des Maris*, and partly from the *Precieuses Ridicules* of Moliere.

58. THE MAN OF TASTE. Farce, Anonymous, 1752. This piece was performed at Drury-Lane, but is nothing more than the foregoing piece cut into a farce by throwing out that part of the plot which is taken from the *Ecole des Maris*, and retaining only that which is borrowed from the *Precieuses Ridicules*.

59. THE MAN'S BEWITCHED, or, *The Devil to do about Her*. Com. by Mrs. Centlivre. Acted at the Hay-Market, 4to. no date. [1710.] This is by no means one of the best, nor is it the worst, of this lady's dramatic pieces. The language is extremely indifferent, and has a very great deficiency both of wit and sentiment; but the plot is agreeably intricate and busy, and the thought of *Faithful's* releasing his Mistress *Laura* from her old guardian Sir *David Watchum*, by pretending to be bewitched, as well as the incident of the imagined ghost in the last act, although they are somewhat too farcical and out of probability, yet are, as far as I know to the contrary, original, and have no disagreeable effect to those who go to a comedy principally with a view of being made to laugh, without entering into too rigid a scrutiny of the adherence to dramatic rules.

60. THE MAN'S THE MASTER. Com. by Sir W. Davenant, 4to. 1669. This is the last play this author wrote, being finished not long before his death, which happened in 1668. The plot of it is borrowed from two plays of M. Scarron, viz. *Jodelet*, or *Le Maitre Valet*, and the *Heritier Ridicule*. The scene is laid in Madrid, and

throughout

throughout the whole in one houfe. It is efteemed a good comedy, and was often acted with approbation. It was alfo revived in 1776, at Covent-Garden, by Mr. Woodward, who acted *Jodelet*, and printed in 8vo.

61. THE MAN TOO HARD FOR THE MASTER. Com. Anonymous. Of this play I know not the author's name, nor any thing more than that it was publifhed fince the Reftoration; nor do I find it mentioned any where but in the appendix to the *Britifh Theatre*.

62. MARCELLIA, or, *The Treacherous Friend* Tragi-Com. by Mrs. Frances Boothby. Acted at the Theatre Royal, 4to. 1670. The fcene lies in France, the plot an invention.

63. THE MARCHES DAY. Dram. Entertainment, of three acts, 8vo. 1771. Printed at Edinburgh.

64. MARCIANO, or, *The Difcovery*. Edinburgh, 4to. 1663. This piece, it is faid in the title-page, was acted with great applaufe before his majefty's high commiffioner and others of the nobility, at the abbey of Holyrud-houfe (at Edinburgh) on St. John's night, by a company of gentlemen. The fcene of this play is laid in Florence.

65. MARCUS BRUTUS. Trag. by John Sheffield, Duke of Buckingham, 4to. 1722. To enrich this very poor play, two of the choruffes were furnifhed by Mr. Pope; but they had (fays the editor of his works) the ufual effects of ill-adjufted ornaments, only to make the meannefs of the fubject the more confpicuous.

66. MARCUS TULLIUS CICERO, *that famous Roman Orator, his Tragedy*, 4to. 1651. It is uncertain whether this play was ever acted or not, but it is written in imitation of Ben Jonfon's *Cataline*. The fcene lies at Rome; and for the ftory, it may be found in Plutarch's Life of Cicero, &c.

67. MARGARET OF ANJOU. Hiftorical Interlude, by Edward Jerningham, Efq. Acted at Drury-Lane, March 11, 1777, for Mifs Younge's benefit. From the acknowledged poetical merit of the author, the public were led to expect a more excellent performance than this was found to be on its reprefentation. The plan of it is French, and will add but little to the fame of its author, who has not thought proper to fubject it to criticifm by allowing it to be printed.

68. MARGERY, or, *A worfe Plague than the Dragon*. Burlefque Opera, by H. Carey, 8vo. 1739. This piece is a fequel or second part of *The Dragon of Wantley* (which fee in its place), and was acted with great applaufe at Covent-Garden Theatre; yet, though it has fome merit, it is far from being equal to the firft part.

69. MARIAM, *the fair Queen of Jewry*. Trag. by Lady Elizabeth Carew, 4to. 1613. This piece it is probable was never acted, yet, confidering thofe times and the lady's fex, it may be allowed to be well penned. It is written in alternate verfe, and with a chorus, which chorus is compofed of *Settines*, or ftanzas of fix lines, the four firft of which are interwoven, or rhyme alternately, the two laft rhyming to each other, and forming a couplet in bafe.

70. MARIAMNE. Trag. by Elijah Fenton. Acted at Lincoln's-Inn Fields, 8vo. 1723. This play is built on the fame ftory with the laft-mentioned one, for which fee *Jofephus*, Book 14 and 15. It was acted with great fuccefs, and was indeed the means of fupporting and

and reconciling the town to a theatre, which for some time before had been almost totally neglected, in favour of Drury-Lane house. Dr. Johnson observes, that to this tragedy Southerne, at whose house it was written, is said to have contributed such hints as his theatrical experience supplied. When it was shewn to Cibber, it was rejected by him, with the additional insolence of advising Fenton to engage himself in some employment of honest labour, by which he might obtain that support which he could never hope for from his poetry. The play was acted at the other theatre, and the brutal petulance of Cibber was confuted, though perhaps not shamed, by general applause. Fenton's profits are said to have amounted to near a thousand pounds.

71. MARIAMNE. Trag. translated from Voltaire, and printed in Dr. Franklin's edition of that author.

72. MARINA. A Play of three acts, by Mr. Lillo. Acted at Covent-Garden, 8vo. 1738. Taken from Pericles, Prince of Tyre.

73. MARPLOT, or, *The Second Part of the Busy Body*. Com. by Mrs. Centlivre. Acted at Drury-Lane, 4to. 1711. This play, like most second parts, falls greatly short of the merit of the first. At its original appearance, however, it met with considerable approbation, and the duke of Portland, to whom it was dedicated, complimented the authoress with a present of forty guineas. The scene lies on the Terriera de Passa in Lisbon.

74. MARPLOT IN LISBON. Com. 12mo. 1760. This is nothing more than Mrs. Centlivre's comedy of *Marplot*, or the second part of *The Busy Body*, which, with this title, and some few alterations in the body of the piece by Mr. Henry Woodward, joint manager with Mr. Barry of the Theatre Royal in Crow-street, Dublin, was represented at that theatre. It has been also still farther pruned, and being reduced into three acts performed two or three nights last season by way of a farce at the Theatre Royal in Covent-Garden.

75. MARRIAGE A LA MODE. Com. by J. Dryden. Acted at the Theatre Royal, 4to. 1673. 4to. 1691. 4to. 1698. Though this piece is called a Comedy in the title-page, yet it might, without any great impropriety, be considered as a Tragi-Comedy, as it consists of two different actions, the one serious and the other comic. The designs of both, however, appear to be borrowed. For example, the serious part is apparently founded on the story of *Sesostris* and *Timareta* in the *Grand Cyrus*, Part 9. Book 3. the characters of *Palamede* and *Rhodophil*, from the history of *Timantes* and *Parthenia*, in the same romance, Part 6. Book 1. the character of *Doralice*, from *Nogaret* in the *Annals of Love*; and the hint of *Melantha*'s making love to herself in *Rhodophil*'s name, from Les Contes D'Ouville, Part 1. p. 3.

76. MARRIAGE A LA MODE. Farce, 1760. This piece was never printed, but was acted in the winter of the above-mentioned year for Mr. Yates's benefit at Drury-Lane. It is, however, nothing more than Capt. Boden's *Modish Couple* cut down into a farce.

77. THE MARRIAGE BROKER, or, *The Pander*. Com. by M. W. 12mo. 1662. The plot of this play is taken from the English chronicles in the reign of Sebert, king of the West-Saxons. The scene lies in London.

78. THE

78. THE MARRIAGE CONTRACT. Com. of two acts, by Henry Brooke, Esq; 8vo. 1778. Not acted. Printed in the author's works, 4 vols. 8vo.

79. THE MARRIAGE HATER MATCH'D. Com. by T. Durfey. Acted at the Theatre Royal, 4to. 1692. The high opinion the author himself had of this piece may be gathered from an epistle to him, prefixed to it by Mr. Charles Gildon, in which the author, through that gentleman, informs the public that this is the best of all his comedies; yet I cannot very readily subscribe to that opinion. The admirable performance of a part in this play, however, was what first occasioned the afterwards celebrated Mr. Dogget to be taken notice of as an actor of merit. It appears to have been acted six nights successively. See Motteux's *Gentleman's Journal*, Feb. 1691-2. The scene in the Park near Kensington. The time thirty hours.

80. THE MARRIAGE NIGHT. Trag. by H. Lord Visc. Falkland, 4to. 1664. This play contains a great share of wit and satire, yet it is uncertain whether it was ever acted or not.

81. THE MARRIAGE PROMISE. See THE INTRIGUING COURTIERS.

82. THE MARRIAGE OF OCEANUS AND BRITANNIA. An Allegorical Fiction, really declaring England's riches, glory, and puissance by sea. To be represented in music, dances, and proper scenes. Invented, written, and composed by Richard Flecknoe, 12mo. 1659.

83. THE MARRIAGE OF WITTE AND SCIENCES. An Interlude. Anonymous, 1606. This piece I have not seen, but suspect it to be older; as I find a play with the same title was entered, by Thomas Marshe, on the books of the Stationers' Company 1569 to 1570.

84. THE MARRIED BEAU, or, *The Curious Impertinent*. Com. by J. Crowne. Acted at the Theatre Royal, 4to. 1694. This play was esteemed a good one, and was frequently acted with general approbation. It has, however, been long laid aside. The story of it is taken from Don Quixote, and the scene lies in Covent-Garden. In the preface to this piece the author has attempted a vindication of himself from the charges brought against his morals, and the looseness of his writings, by some of his contemporaries.

85. THE MARRIED COQUET. Com. by J. Baillie, 8vo. 1746. This play was never acted, nor even printed till after the author's death. It is no very contemptible piece, nor has it any extraordinary merit, yet to the modesty and amiable diffidence of its author, perhaps, was owing its not being published in his life-time. Was every writer possessed of these good qualities, the town would not be so frequently pestered with the complaints of disappointed play-wrights, nor would so many poor performances force their way into the world from beneath the press, which had judiciously been denied access to the theatres.

86. THE MARRIED LIBERTINE. Com. by Charles Macklin, 1761. This play was brought on the stage at Covent-Garden Theatre, yet, after its first run, was no more performed, nor has yet appeared in print. A very strong opposition was made to it during every night of its run, which were no more than the nine necessary to entitle the author to his three benefits. Prejudice against the author seemed, however, to have been in great measure the basis of
this

this oppofition, which, although in fome meafure overborne by a ftrong party of his countrymen, who were determined to fupport the play through its deftined period, yet fhewed itfelf very forcibly even to the laft. I cannot, however, help thinking its fate fomewhat hard; for although it muft be confeffed that there were many faults in the piece, yet it muft alfo be acknowledged that there were feveral beauties; and I own myfelf apt to believe, that, had the play made its firft appearance on Drury-Lane ftage, with the advantages it might there have received from the acting, and had the author remained concealed till its fate had been determined, it might have met with as favourable a reception as fome pieces which have paft on the public uncenfured. What perhaps might alfo add to the prejudice againft it, was a conjecture that was fpread about the town, that Mr. Macklin, in his character of Lord *Belville*, had a view towards that of a man of quality then living and extremely well known; but this I imagine muft have been *merely* conjecture.

87. MARIE MAGDALENE. A Myftery, written in 1512. In this piece a Heathen is introduced celebrating the fervice of *Mahound*, who is called *Saracenorum fortiffimus*; in the midft of which, he reads a leffon from the Alcoran, confifting of gibberifh, much in the metre and manner of Skelton. In the fame performance, one of the ftage-directions is, " Here " enters the prynfe of the devylls " in a ftage, with hell onderneth " the ftage." MS. Digb. 133. in the Bodleian Library.

88. THE MARRIED PHILOSOPHER. Com. by John Kelly. Acted at Lincoln's-Inn Fields, 8vo. 1732.

89. MARRY OR DO WORSE. Com. by W. Walker, 4to. 1704. This piece was acted at Lincoln's-Inn Fields. Scene, in London.

90. THE MARSHAL OF LUXEMBOURG, UPON HIS DEATH-BED. Tragi-Com. Done out of French, 12mo. Said in the title-page to be printed at Collen 1635, and reprinted in 1710.

91. THE MARTYR'D SOLDIER. Trag. by Henry Shirley. Acted at Drury-Lane, 4to. 1638. This play met with great applaufe, but was not publifhed till after the author's death. The plot is taken from hiftory, during the time of the eighth perfecution, for which fee *Baronius*, &c.

92. MARY MAGDALEN, HER LIFE AND REPENTANCE. An Interlude, by Lewis Wager, 4to. 1567. The plot is taken, as it is faid in the prologue, from the feventh chapter of St. Luke. The piece is printed in the old black letter, and contrived fo as to be eafily performed by four perfons; which, from this and the title-pages of other interludes which mention the fame particular, I am apt to imagine was the ftated number for a fet of performers for thefe kind of pieces. Entered on the books of the Stationers' Company, 1566 to 1567.

93. THE MARTYRDOM OF IGNATIUS. Trag. by John Gambold, 8vo. 1773. This tragedy was written in the year 1740, more than thirty years before it was publifhed.

94. A MASQUE prefented at Bretbie in Derbyfhire, on Twelfth-Nighth, 1639, by Sir Afton Cockain, 12mo. 1659. This piece is printed in the body of this author's poems. It was prefented before Philip, the firft earl of Chefterfield, and his countefs; two of their fons acting in it.

95. A MASQUE,

95. A Masque, a Description of, with the nuptial songs at, the Lord Visc. Haddington's marriage at Court, on Shrove-Tuesday at night, 1608. by Ben Jonson, Fol. 1640.

96. A Masque presented at the House of Lord Haye, for the Entertainment of Le Baron de Tour, the French ambassador, on Saturday, Feb. 22, 1617, by Ben Jonson, Fol. 1617.

97. "The Description of a "Masque presented before the "Kinge's Majestie, on Twelfth- "Night, in honour of Lord Haye's, "and his bride-daughter and heir "to the honourable the Lord "Dennye, their marriage having "been the same day at Court so- "lemnized; by Thomas Cam- "pion, Doctor of Physic, 4to. "1607."

98. A Masque presented at Ludlow-Castle, 1634, on Michael-masse-Night, before the right honourable John, Earl of Bridgewater, Viscount Brackly, Lord President of Wales, and one of his Majestie's most honourable privie counsel, by John Milton, 4to. 1637. The greatest of Milton's juvenile performances (says Dr. Johnson) is *The Masque of Comus*, nor does it afford only a specimen of his language; it exhibits likewise his power of description, and his vigour of sentiment, employed in the praise and defence of virtue. A work more truly poetical is rarely found; allusions, images, and descriptive epithets, embellish almost every period with lavish decoration. As a series of lines therefore, it may be considered as worthy of all the admiration with which the votaries have received it.

As a drama it is deficient. The action is not probable. A Masque, in those parts where supernatural intervention is admitted, must indeed be given up to all the freaks of imagination; but, so far as the action is merely human, it ought to be reasonable, which can hardly be said of the conduct of the two brothers; who, when their sister sinks with fatigue in a pathless wilderness, wander both away together in search of berries too far to find their way back, and leave a helpless lady to all the sadness and danger of solitude. This, however, is a defect over-balanced by its convenience. What deserves more reprehension is, that the prologue spoken in the wild wood by the attendant Spirit is addressed to the audience; a mode of communication so contrary to the nature of dramatic representation, that no precedents can support it.

The discourse of the Spirit is too long; an objection that may be made to almost all the following speeches: they have not the spriteliness of a dialogue animated by reciprocal contention, but seem rather declamations deliberately composed, and formally repeated, on a moral question. The auditor therefore listens as to a lecture, without passion, without anxiety.

The song of *Comus* has airiness and jollity; but, what may recommend Milton's morals as well as his poetry, the invitations to pleasure are so general, that they excite no distinct images of corrupt enjoyment, and take no dangerous hold on the fancy.

The following soliloquies of *Comus* and the *Lady* are elegant, but tedious. The song must owe much to the voice, if it ever can delight. At last the brothers enter, with too much tranquillity; and when they have feared lest their sister should be in danger, and hoped that she is not in danger, the Elder makes a speech in praise of chastity, and
the

the Younger finds how fine it is to be a philosopher.

Then descends the Spirit in form of a shepherd; and the brother, instead of being in haste to ask his help, praises his singing, and enquires his business in that place. It is remarkable, that at this interview the brother is taken with a short fit of rhyming. The Spirit relates that the Lady is in the power of *Comus*; the brother moralises again; and the Spirit makes a long narration, of no use because it is false, and therefore unsuitable to a good Being.

In all these parts the language is poetical, and the sentiments are generous; but there is something wanting to allure attention.

The dispute between the *Lady* and *Comus* is the most animated and affecting scene of drama, and wants nothing but a brisker reciprocation of objections and replies to invite attention and detain it.

The songs are vigorous, and full of imagery; but they are harsh in their diction, and not very musical in their numbers.

Throughout the whole, the figures are too bold, and the language too luxuriant for dialogue. It is a drama in the epic style, inelegantly splendid, and tediously instructive.

99. A MASQUE written at Lord Rochester's request for his Tragedy of *Valentinian*, by N. Tate. This is printed in Mr. Tate's Miscellanies, 8vo. 1685, p. 17. The scene is a Grove and Forest.

100. THE MASQUE OF AUGURES, with the several Antimasques, presented on Twelfth-Night, 1621, by Ben Jonson, 4to. 1621. Fol. 1640.

101. THE MASQUE OF FLOWERS. Anonym. 4to. 1614. This masque was presented by the gentlemen of Gray's-Inn, at the Court

at Whitehall in the Banquetting House upon Twelfth-Night, 16:3, and was the last of the solemnities and magnificencies which were performed at the marriage of the Earl of Somerset with the Lady Frances, daughter to the Earl of Suffolk.

102. A MASQUE OF OWLS AT KENILWORTH, presented by the ghost of Captain Cox mounted on his hobby-horse, 1626, by Ben Jonson, Fol. 1640.

103. A MASQUE in the Opera of the *Prophetess*, by Thomas Betterton, printed with that piece.

104. A MASQUE OF THE TWO HONOURABLE HOUSES, OR INNS OF COURT, THE MIDDLE TEMPLE, AND LINCOLN'S-INN, presented before the King at Whitehall on Shrove-Monday at night, Feb. 15, 1613, by Geo. Chapman, 4to. no date. This masque was written and contrived for the celebration of the nuptials of the Count Palatine of the Rhine with the Princess Elizabeth. The machinery and decorations were by Inigo Jones. From Dugdale's *Origines Juridiciales*, p. 346. we find that this masque cost the Society of Lincoln's-Inn no less than 2400 *l*.

105. A Royal MASQUE of the four Inns of Court, performed about *Allhollandtide*, 1633. Anonymous. Of this masque a very full account is given in Whitlock's Memorials of English Affairs, p.18. But whether this piece itself was ever printed, I know not.

106. " THE MASQUE OF THE
" INNER TEMPLE AND GRAYE'S-
" INN, GRAYE'S-INNE AND THE
" INNER TEMPLE, presented be-
" fore his Majestie, the Queene's
" Majestie, the Prince Count Pa-
" latine and the Lady Elizabeth
" their Highnesses, in the Banquet-
" ting House at Whitehall on Sa-
" turday the twentieth day of Fe-
" bruarie,

"bruarie, 1613." By Francis Beaumont. 4to. no date. This masque was represented with the utmost splendor and magnificence, and at a great expence to both the societies. By Dugdale's *Origines* we learn, that at Gray's-Inn the readers on this occasion were assessed at 4 *l.* each; the ancients, or such as were of that standing, at 2 *l.* 10 *s.* each; the barristers 2 *l.* apiece, and the students 20 *s.* each, out of which so much was to be taken as the Inner Temple did then allow.

107. THE MASQUERADE. C. by Charles Johnson, 8vo. N. D. [1719.] Acted at the Theatre Royal in Drury-Lane. This comedy was represented at the same time that Sewel's *Sir Walter Raleigh* was performing at Lincoln's-Inn Fields. At the conclusion of the Epilogue to the latter, are these lines:

" Wit cannot fall so fast, as Folly rises;
" Witness the Masquerade—at double
" prices.
" Yet if you are not pleas'd with what
" We've plaid,
" Go see old Shirley drest in Masque-
" rade."

108. THE MASQUERADE, or, *An Evening's Intrigue.* A Farce, of two acts, by Benj. Griffin, 12mo. 1717. This was performed at Lincoln's-Inn Fields, with some success.

109. MASQUERADE DU CIEL. A Masque, presented to the great Queen of the Little World. A celestial map, representing the true site and motions of the Heavenly Bodies, through the years 1639, 1640, &c. by J. S. 4to. 1640.

110. THE MASSACRE AT PARIS. Trag. by Nat. LEE. Acted at the Theatre Royal, 4to. 1690. The plot of this play is founded on the bloody massacre of the Protestants, which was perpetrated at Paris on St. Bartholomew's day. 1572, in the reign of Charles IX.

VOL. II.

for the particulars of which see *De Serres, Mezeray,* &c. The scene, Paris.

111. THE MASSACRE AT PARIS, *with the Death of the Duke of Guise.* Trag. by Christopher Marlow, 8vo. without date. This play is upon the same story with the last-mentioned one, but takes in a larger scope with respect to time, beginning with the unfortunate marriage between the king of Navarre and Marguerite de Valois, sister to Charles IX. which was the primary occasion of the massacre, and ending with the death of Henry III. of France. This play is not divided into acts, yet it is far from a bad one, and might probably furnish the hint to Mr. Lee.

112. THE FAMOUS HISTORY OF THE RISE AND FALL OF MASSIANELLO, in two parts, by Thomas Durfey, 4to. 1700. second part, 1699. This is on the same story as *The Rebellion of Naples*, and partly borrowed from it.

113. MR. TASTE THE POETICAL FOP, or, *The Modes of the Court.* Com. by the Author of *Vanella*, 8vo. 1734.

114. MASTER ANTHONY. C. by the Earl of Orrery, 4to. 1690. Though this piece bears the above date, yet it appears to have been acted many years before, at the Duke's Theatre in Lincoln's-Inn Fields, by having the names of Mr. Angel and Mrs. Long in the drama, who had at that time been dead some years. See Downes 28.

115. MASTER TURBULENT, or, *The Melancholics.* Com. Anonymous, 4to. 1682. The scene of this play is laid in Moorfields.

116. A MATCH AT MIDNIGHT. Com. by William Rowley. Acted by the children of the Revels, 4to. 1633. Part of the plot of this comedy,

Q

comedy, viz. the defign of *Jarvii's* hiding *Bloodhound* under the widow's bed, is the fame as an old ſtory in the *Engliſh Rogue*, Part 4. Chap. 19.

117. THE MATCH-MAKER FITTED, or, *The Fortune-Hunters rightly ſerved.* Com. 12mo. 1718. This play was intended for the ſtage, but not accepted by the performers. Nor, if it had, could it have ſtood a chance of favour with the public. The language, though far from being low or devoid of underſtanding, yet is heavy, declamatory, and unadapted to comedy; and the characters ſhew the author to have made no very ſtrict obſervations on thoſe diſtinguiſhing features of the mind which mark out the varieties of nature's oddities. Yet there is ſomewhat in the plot which is original, and capable of being extended on to advantage, viz. the circumſtance of the deſigning guardian of a woman of no fortune, who, having by the aſſiſtance of her own artifices, and the ſpreading a belief of her being poſſeſſed of a large eſtate, procured conſiderable ſums by ſelling his conſent by turns to ſeveral different fortune-hunters, and tricked them all into the juſt puniſhment of ridiculous and improper matches, is himſelf at laſt enwrapped into marriage with the girl herſelf. Such a deſign, executed by an able hand, enlivened with juſtly drawn characters, and adorned with pleaſing and dramatic dialogues, might produce a piece not undeſerving the approbation of the public. It is dedicated to Mother Wilſon, of Wildſtreet, Counteſs of Drury, under the character of *Surly* her chaplain. This Mother Wilſon appears to have been a bawd of repute at that time, and probably might have miſuſed the author. Yet there ſeems to be but very little connection between thoſe private occurrences, and the general deſign of the piece.

118. MATCH ME IN LONDON. Tragi-Com. by Thomas Dekker. Preſented firſt at the Bull, in St. John's Street, and afterwards at the private houſe, in Drury-Lane, called the Phœnix. 4to. 1631. Scene, Spain. This is eſteemed a good play.

119. MATILDA. Trag. Of this I know no more than the name, and that it was written in the reign of Henry VII. both which I gather from the Index to Jacob's *Poetical Regiſter*, where alone I find it mentioned, but without any reference to the body of the book, or any farther particulars relating to it. If, however, the laſt circumſtance be true, it will render it the very earlieſt dramatic piece we know any thing of in theſe kingdoms, as that monarch *died* in 1509.

120. MATILDA. Trag. by Dr. Thomas Franklin. Acted at Drury-Lane, 8vo. 1775. This is almoſt a tranſlation from Voltaire's *Duc de Foix*.

121. MATRIMONIAL TROUBLE, in two parts, by the Ducheſs of Newcaſtle, Fol. 1662. The firſt of theſe is a Comedy, the ſecond a Comi-Tragedy.

122. MAY-DAY. Com. by George Chapman. Acted at Black-Friers, 4to. 1611.

123. MAY-DAY. Ballad Opera, by David Garrick. Acted at Drury-Lane, 8vo. 1775.

124. THE MAYOR OF GARRAT. A Comedy, of two acts, by Samuel Foote. Performed at the Theatre in the Hay-Market, 1763. Printed in 8vo. 1769.

In this very humorous and entertaining piece, the character of Major *Sturgeon*, a city-militia officer, is entirely new, highly wrought up, up, and was most inimitably performed by Mr. Foote, with prodigious applause.

125. THE MAYOR OF QUINBOROUGH. Com. by Thomas Middleton. Acted at Black-Friers, 4to. 1661. This play was often performed with great applause. The plot is taken from Stow, Speed, &c. in the reign of Vortiger; and the author has introduced into the piece several dumb shews, the explanation of which he puts into the mouth of Rainulph, monk of Chester, whose *Polychronicon* he has pretty closely followed.

126. MEASURE FOR MEASURE. A Play, by William Shakspeare. Fol. 1623. This is a most admirable play, as well with respect to character and conduct, as to the language and sentiment, which are equal to any of this inimitable author's pieces. The duke's soliloquy on life, and the pleadings of *Isabella* for her brother's pardon with *Angelo*, as well as *Claudio's* own arguments with his sister to yield herself up for his preservation, and her reply to them, are masterpieces of eloquence and power of language. The play is still frequently performed, and always with assured approbation. The plot is built on a novel of *Cinthio Giraldi*, Dec. 8. Nov. 5. The scene lies at Vienna.

Dr. Johnson says, " Of this
" play the light or comic part is
" very natural and pleasing, but
" the grave scenes, if a few passages be excepted, have more labour than elegance. The plot
" is rather intricate than artful.
" The time of the action is indefinite; some time, we know not
" how much, must have elapsed
" between the recess of the Duke
" and the imprisonment of Claudio; for he must have learned
" the story of Mariana in his disguise, or he delegated his power
" to a man already known to be
" corrupted. The unities of action and place are sufficiently
" preserved."

127. MEASURE FOR MEASURE, or, *Beauty the best Advocate*. Com. by Charles Gildon. Acted at Lincoln's-Inn Fields, 4to. 1700. An alteration of Shakspeare's *Measure for Measure*.

128. MEDEA. Trag. by Sir Edward Sherburne, 8vo. 1648. 8vo. 1701. This is only a translation from Seneca, with annotations; but never intended for the stage. To it is annexed a translation of Seneca's answer to Lucilius's query, Why good men suffer misfortunes?

129. MEDEA. Trag. by J. Studley, 8vo. 1563. This is the same play as the foregoing, only translated by a different hand, and with an alteration of the chorus to the first act.

130. MEDEA. Trag. by Charles Johnson. Acted at Drury-Lane, 8vo. 1731. The preface consists almost entirely of complaints of the ill treatment this play met with from a set of gentlemen belonging to the Inns of Court, who came determined to condemn it unheard. There are also a few strokes at Mr. Pope, who, in the *Dunciad*, had, it is said without provocation, introduced the author into that satire. (See, however, *The Suitors*.) The part of *Medea* was performed by Mrs. Porter; *Jason*, by Mr. Wilks.

131. MEDEA. Trag. by Richard Glover, 4to. 1761. This play was not written with a design for stage-representation, being professedly formed after the model of the ancients, each act terminating with a chorus. The author has indeed shewn a good deal of erudition and a perfect acquaintance with

with the ancient classics. Some parts of his language are poetical, the sentimental passages forcible, and the *Ordo Verborum*, though somewhat stiff, yet not pedantic or turgid. Nevertheless, there is a languid coldness that runs through the piece, and robs it of the great essence of tragedy, pathetic power. The whole is declamatory, and the author seems to have kept the *Medea* of Seneca very constantly before his eyes; and it must be apparent to every one of but ordinary judgment, that long declamations, pompous invocations of ghosts, and powers of witchcraft, and choruses composed in the uncouth measure of iambic, dithyrambic, &c. are by no means adapted to the fashion of the English stage. If it should be urged, that these kind of pieces are not written for the theatre, but for the closet, I cannot think even that excuse obviates the objection, or clears an author who writes in this manner from the charge of affectation or singularity, any more than it would avail a man who should dress himself in the short cloke, trunk-hose, &c. of king James the First's times, and though he paid and received visits in this habit, should plead by way of apology that he did not chuse to dance in it at an assembly, or go to court on a birth-day. And, indeed, I can perceive no juster reason for our cloathing our language, than for the decorating our persons after the fashions made use of two thousand years ago. Taste is periodical and changeable, and though it may not always be absolutely right, it is very seldom totally wrong; and consequently a compliance with it, in a moderate degree, will ever be less blameable than an opposition to it, which has not some very peculiar advantages of convenience or pleasure to urge in its excuse. It has been often performed at Drury-Lane and Covent-Garden for Mrs. Yates's benefit.

132. THE MEETING OF THE COMPANY, or, *Bayes's Art of Acting*. Prelude, by David Garrick, Esq. Acted at Drury-Lane at the opening of the Theatre in 1774. Not printed.

133. MELICERTA. An heroic Pastoral, by Ozell. This is only a translation from a piece of the same name by Moliere, who wrote the original at the command of the French king, whose impatience would not wait for the finishing it, so that it was acted in an imperfect state at Versailles, in which condition it remained ever after; the author, I suppose, not thinking it worth while to compleat it.

134. MELITE. Com. Translated from Corneille, 12mo. 1776.

135. MENÆCHMI. Com. by W. W. 4to. 1595. This is only a loose translation from Plautus. From this play the plot of the *Comedy of Errors* is borrowed. It is reprinted in Six Old Plays published by J. Nichols, 8vo. 1779, vol. I.

136. THE MERCANTILE LOVERS. Dramatic Satire, by Geo. Wallis. Acted at York, 8vo. 1775.

137. THE MERCHANT OF VENICE. Tragi-Com. by William Shakspeare, 4to. 1600. 4to. 1637. 4to. 1652. This is an admirable piece, and still continues on the list of acting plays. The story is built on a real fact which happened in some part of Italy, with this difference indeed, that the intended cruelty was really on the side of the Christian, the Jew being the unhappy delinquent who fell beneath his rigid and barbarous resentment. Popular prejudice however vindicates our author in the alteration

alteration he has made; and the delightful manner in which he has availed himself of the general character of the Jews, the very quintessence of which he has enriched his *Shylock* with, makes more than amends for his deviating from a matter of fact which he was by no means obliged to adhere to. The decision of *Portia's* fate by the choice of the caskets affords a pleasing suspense, and gives opportunity for a great many inimitable reflections. The trial scene in the fourth act is amazingly conducted; the anxiety both of the characters themselves, and of the audience, being kept up to the very last moment; nor can I close my mention of that scene without taking notice of the speech put into *Portia's* mouth in praise of mercy, which is perhaps the finest piece of oratory on the subject, (though very fully treated on by many other writers) that has ever appeared in our or any other language. The scene lies partly at Venice, partly at Belmont, the seat of *Portia* on the Continent. For the alterations which lord Lansdowne has made in this play, see JEW OF VENICE.

"Of *The Merchant of Venice*," says Dr. Johnson, " the style is " even and easy; with few pecu-
" liarities of diction, or anomalies
" of construction. The comic part
" raises laughter, and the serious
" fixes expectation. The proba-
" bility of either the one or the
" other story, cannot be maintain-
" ed. The union of two actions
" in one event, is in this drama
" eminently happy. Dryden was
" much pleased with his own ad-
" dress in connecting the two
" plots of his *Spanish Fryer*, which
" yet I believe the critic will find
" excelled by this play."

138. THE MERCHANT. Com. Translated from Plautus, by G. Colman; printed in Thornton's translation of that author.

139. MERCURIUS BRITANNICUS, or, *The English Intelligencer.* Tragi-Com. Acted at Paris with great applause, 4to. 1641. This piece is wholly political, the subject of it being entirely on the ship-money, which was one of the great points that occasioned the troubles of King Charles I. Several of the judges are attacked in it under feigned names, particularly Justice Hutton and Justice Croke, under the names of Hortensius and Corvus Acilius; as is also *Prynn*, who is introduced under the character of *Prinner*. It consists of only four short acts, and of the fifth is laid in the *Epilogue* as follows: " *It is determined by the Ædils, the Masters of publicke Plays, that the next Day (by Jove's Permission) the fifth Act shall be acted upon Tyber, I should say Tyburne, by a new Society of Axalamites. Vive le Roy.*" Before the first act is prefixed this other title, viz. *The Censure of the Judges,* or *The Court Cure.* From Wood's *Athenæ Oxonienses*, vol. II. p. 517. we find it to be the production of Richard Braithwaite.

140. MERCURY HARLEQUIN. Pantomime, by Henry Woodward. Acted at Drury-Lane, 1756.

141. MERCURY VINDICATED *from Alchymists at Court,* by gentlemen the King's servants, by Ben Jonson. Fol. 1640.

142. MERLIN, or, *The British Inchanter, and King Arthur the British Worthy.* Dramatic Opera. Acted at Goodman's Fields, 8vo. 1736. An alteration of Dryden's *King Arthur.*

143. MERLIN, or, *The Devil of Stonehenge,* by Lewis Theobald. Acted

Acted at Drury-Lane, 8vo. 1731. This is the musical part of a Pantomime.

144. MEROPE. Trag. by G. Jefferys. Acted at Lincoln's-Inn Fields, 8vo. 1731. This is taken from the Italian play. The scene, Messene. Prologue, by Aaron Hill.

145. MEROPE. T. by Aaron Hill. Acted at Drury-Lane, 8vo. 1749. This play was, and still continues to be, acted with great applause. It is chiefly borrowed from the *Merope* of Voltaire, yet has Mr. Hill, whose manner and style are very peculiar and original, made it entirely his own by his manner of translating it. Some critics there are indeed who have found fault with this gentleman as a turgid and bombast writer; to their opinions, however, I cannot subscribe, for although it may be allowed that a peculiar *Ordo Verborum*, and a frequent use of compound epithets, which seem to be the true characteristics of Mr. Hill's writings, may give an apparent stiffness and obscurity to a work, yet when once perfectly digested and properly delivered from the lips of oratory, they certainly add great force and weight to the sentiment,—nor can it surely be considered as paying this author any very exalted compliment to rank the Tragedy of *Merope* as superior to any one which has hitherto appeared since; nor can there, perhaps, be a stronger evidence in its favour, than the use which some of the later tragic writers have made of the design of this play, having more or less adopted the plot as the groundwork of their own pieces, as witness the Tragedies of *Barbarossa*, *Creusa*, *Douglas*, &c. The story of *Merope* is well known in history; and the scene lies at Mycene. Soon after the run of this piece the author died.

146. MEROPE. Trag. Translated from Voltaire, printed in Dr. Franklin's edition of that author.

147. MEROPE. Trag. by M. de Voltaire, translated by Dr. John Theobald, 8vo. 1744. This is a mere translation, and was never brought on the stage.

148. MEROPE. Trag. by Mr. Ayre. Italian and English, 8vo. 1740. This is only the literal translation of an Italian Tragedy on the same subject of the foregoing pieces, having the original printed with it page by page, for the use and instruction of persons inclined to become masters of the Italian language.

149. THE MERRY COBLER, A farcical Opera of one act, by Charles Coffey, 1735. This is a second part of the *Devil to pay*, or *The Wives Metamorphosed*; but being in no degree equal to the first, it was deservedly damned the first night at the Theatre Royal in Drury-Lane.

150. THE MERRY COUNTERFEIT, or, *The Viscount Alamode*. Farce, taken from Mrs. Behn. Acted at Covent-Garden, 1762, for the benefit of Mr. Shuter. Not printed.

151. THE MERRY DEVIL OF EDMONTON. Com. Acted at the Globe. Anon. 4to. 1608. 4to. 1617. 4to. 1626. 4to. 1631. 4to. 1655. This comedy is attributed by Kirkman to Shakspeare, but on what foundation I know not, as there do not appear in the piece itself any marks that tend to the confirmation of such a suggestion. Coxeter takes notice of an old MS. of this play that he has seen, which speaks it to have been written by Michael Drayton. The plot is founded on the History of
one

one Peter Fabal, of whom more particular mention is made in Fuller's *Church History*, and in the Chronicles of Henry VI's reign. Scene, Edmonton.

152. THE MERRY MASQUE-RADERS, or, *The Humorous Cuckold*. Com. Anonymous, 8vo. 1732. Not acted.

153. THE MERRY MIDNIGHT MISTAKE, or, *Comfortable Conclusion*. Com. by David Ogborne, 8vo. 1765. The *Merry Midnight Mistake* we apprehend to have been a real incident. Mr. Ogborne dreamed that he was intended for a comic writer; and to shew how little such nocturnal visions are to be trusted, on his awaking sat down and composed this dramatic performance.

154. THE MERRY MILKMAID OF ISLINGTON. See MUSE AT NEWMARKET.

155. THE MERRY MILLER, or, *The Countryman's Ramble to London*. Farce, by Thomas Sadler, 8vo. 1766. Printed at Salop, with Poems by the same author.

156. THE MERRY PRANKS, or, *Windmill Hill*. Farce, Anonymous, 1704. This I never saw.

157. THE MERRY SAILORS, or, *Landlord bit*. A Farce, 1707. This piece is mentioned no where but in the *British Theatre*, and by the title I should rather conceive it to have been a droll acted at some of the fairs, than a regular farce for a theatre.

158. THE MERRY WIVES OF WINDSOR. Com. by W. Shakspeare. Acted by the Lord Chamberlain's servants, 4to. 1602. 4to. 1619. 4to. 1630. This piece is allowed by the critics to be the master piece of our author's writings in the comic way. There is perhaps no comedy in our own or any other language, in which so extensive a groupe of perfect and highly finished characters are set forth in one view. In the delineation of Justice *Shallow* he has gratified a very innocent revenge on a certain magistrate, who, in his adolescent years, had been unreasonably harsh upon him; yet he has done it with so inoffensive a playfulness as bears strong testimony to his own good-nature, having only rendered him laughable without pointing at him any of the arrows of malevolent or poignant satire. Dryden allows this play to be exactly formed; and as it was written before the time that Ben Jonson had introduced the taste for a cold elaborate regularity, it plainly proves that our immortal bard was by no means incapable of polishing and regulating his plots to an equal degree of exactness, had not his choice of historical plans very frequently compelled him, and the unbridled strength of his imagination as often induced him, to o'erleap the bounds of those dramatic rules which were first established by writers who knew not what it was to write, to act, and to think, above all rule.

The editions of 1602 and 1619 are of the first flight sketch, which the author afterwards altered, enlarg'd, and improved. Dr. Johnson says, "Of this play there is "a tradition preserved by Mr. "Rowe, that it was written at the "command of queen Elizabeth, "who was so delighted with the "character of Falstaff, that she "wished it to be diffused through "more plays; but suspecting that "it might pall by continued uniformity, directed the poet to "diversify his manner, by shewing him in love. No task is "harder than that of writing to "the ideas of another. Shak- "speare knew what the queen, if
"the

"the story be true, seems not to have known, that by any real passion of tenderness, the selfish craft, the careless jollity, and the lazy luxury of Falstaff must have suffered so much abatement, that little of his former cast would have remained. Falstaff could not love, but by ceasing to be Falstaff. He could only counterfeit love; and his professions could be prompted, not by the hope of pleasure, but of money. Thus the poet approached as near as he could to the work enjoined him; yet, having perhaps in the former plays compleated his own idea, seems not to have been able to give Falstaff all his former power of entertainment.

"This comedy is remarkable for the variety and number of the personages, who exhibit more characters appropriated and discriminated than perhaps can be found in any other play.

"Whether Shakspeare was the first that produced upon the English stage the effect of language distorted and depraved by provincial or foreign pronunciation, I cannot certainly decide. This mode of forming ridiculous characters can confer praise only on him, who originally discovered it, for it requires not much of either wit or judgment: its success must be derived almost wholly from the player, but its power in a skilful mouth, even he that despises it, is unable to resist.

"The conduct of this drama is deficient; the action begins and ends often before the conclusion, and the different parts might change places without inconvenience; but its general power, that power by which all works of genius shall finally be tried, is such, that perhaps it never yet had reader or spectator, who did not think it too soon at an end."

The adventures of Falstaff in this play seem to have been taken from the story of the *Lovers of Pisa*, in an old piece, called "*Tarlton's Newes out of Purgatorie.*"

159. MESSALINA, *The Roman Empress*, her Tragedy. by Nath, Richards, 12mo. 1640. The plot of this play is from Suetonius, Pliny, Juvenal, and other authors who have written on the vicious character of that insatiate woman. It is ushered in by six copies of verses. Scene, Rome.

160. THE METAMORPHOSES, or, *The Old Lover outwitted*. Farce, by John Corey, 4to. 1704. It was acted at the Theatre in Lincoln's-Inn Fields. Jacob has made a confusion in regard to this farce, giving it in two different places to authors of the same name, and calling it in one place a translation from Moliere, and in the other an alteration of Albumazar. The latter, however, is the right, it consisting only of that part of the plot of the said comedy, which relates to the over-reaching of *Pandolpho* by means of the pretended transformation of *Trincalo*. This mistake, however, has arisen from confounding Mr. Corey, the author of *The Generous Enemies*, with Mr. Corey the comedian, who was the compiler of this piece.

161. THE METAMORPHOSES. Com. Op. by Charles Dibdin. Acted at the Hay-Market, 8vo. 1776. This is taken from Moliere's *Sicilien*, and George Dandin.

162. THE METAMORPHOS'D GYPSIES. A Masque, by Ben Jonson, Fol. 1641. This piece was thrice presented before King James I. First at Burleigh on the Hill,

Hill, next at Belvoir Castle, and lastly at Windsor in Aug. 1621.

163. THE METHODIST. Com. Being a continuation and completion of the plan of the *Minor*, written by Mr. Foote, 8vo. no date. [1761.] This piece was never acted, nor intended so to be, and is no more than a most impudent catch-penny job of Israel Pottinger, whom the great success of Mr. Foote's *Minor* had induced to write this sequel to it, which is contrived in such a manner from the arrangement of the title-page, as to appear to the unwary purchaser the product of the same author. But there is somewhat worse in this piece than even the imposition on the public, which is the gross reflection thrown on the private character of the chief of the Methodists, contrary to the intention of the author of the *Minor*. For although that gentleman has made a very just and ingenious attack on enthusiasm itself, and exposed the sanction which the promoters of vice and venders of lewdness lay claim to under the mask of religion, and the protection of some mistaken and pernicious tenets, yet he has not endeavoured to cast so severe a censure on men of any holy profession, however misled by blind zeal or enthusiastic madness to inculcate and propagate those tenets, as to hint at their being themselves either the abettors or encouragers of those pests of society, who screen themselves under their doctrine, or may pretend to enlist themselves under their banners. This the present writer has done, who, by a continuation of the characters and plot of the *Minor*, has made Dr. Squintum and Mrs. Cole, that is to say, an old bawd and a methodist preacher, coadjutors and joint instruments in carrying on the purposes of debauchery, and bringing to perfection all the infamous transactions of a common brothel: a charge, which if, just, would not only cast an *opprobrium* on a whole sect of teachers, which it is to be hoped not one among them could possibly deserve, but also be a severe reflection on the legislature itself, for not having entered into a stricter inquisition on a nest of vipers, which, lying closely concealed under the shadow of religion, are empoisoning and destroying the very fountain of piety and virtue.

164. MICHAELMAS TERME. Com. by Thomas Middleton, 4to. 1607. 4to. 1630. This play was sundry times acted by the children of Paul's. It is of a moderate length, but is not divided into acts.

165. MICROCOSMUS. A moral Masque, by Thomas Nabbes. Acted at Salisbury Court, 4to. 1637. This has two copies of verses prefixed, one of them by Richard Brome.

166. MIDAS; an English Burletta. Acted at Covent-Garden, 8vo. 1764. The burlesque in this humorous performance turning chiefly on heathen deities, ridiculous enough in themselves, and too absurd for burlesque, the aim of which is to turn *great* things to *farce*, the present mock-opera was not altogether so successful at first, as in many respects it deserved to be.

167. MIDSUMMER NIGHT'S DREAM. Com. by W. Shakspeare. Acted by the Lord Chamberlain's servants, 4to. 1600. Two copies in the same year. This play is one of the wild and irregular overflowings of this great author's creative imagination. It is now never acted under its original form, yet it contains an infinite number

number of beauties, and different portions of it have been made use of separately in the formation of more pieces than one. The parts of *Oberon* and *Titania*, for example, are the ground-work of *The Fairies*; the story of *Pyramus* and *Thisbe* has been also performed singly under the form of an opera; and the still more comic scenes of it have been printed by themselves in quarto under the title of *Bottom the Weaver*, and used frequently to be acted at Bartholomew Fair, and other fairs in the country, by the strolling companies. The scene is in Athens, and a wood not far from it.

"Wild and fantastical as this play is (says Dr. Johnson), all the parts in their various modes are well written, and give the kind of pleasure which the author designed. Fairies in his time were much in fashion; common tradition had made them familiar, and Spenser's Poem had made them great."

168. A MIDSUMMER NIGHT'S DREAM, written by Shakspeare, with alterations and additions, and several new songs. As it is performed at the Theatre Royal in Drury-Lane. By Mr. Colman, 8vo. 1763. This piece was acted only once, when the spectators were uncommonly few, and therefore not in the best humour. Respect for Shakspeare, however, kept them silent; but that silence likewise induced them to sympathize with Lysander and Helena, Demetrius and Hermia, who in one scene are all lying fast asleep on the stage. After the representation was over, Mr. Colman, who did not escape the narcotic qualities of the dose he had administered, took away a third part of its ingredients, and prevailed on his patients to try the effects of it a second time. But in this contracted form it succeeded less, inspiring drowsiness without the benefit of repose. We have reason to think, however, that our theatrical physician had still further hopes of gaining somewhat by his prescription, having, if we are not deceived, compelled those under his regimen at the Hay-Market to swallow it once more, though he could never contrive to make it a popular medicine.

169. THE MILESIAN. Com. Opera, by Mr. Jackman. Acted at Drury-Lane, 8vo. 1776.

170. MINERVA'S SACRIFICE. A Play, by Philip Massinger. Entered on the books of the Stationers' Company Sept. 9, 1653, and was amongst those destroyed by Mr. Warburton's servant.

171. THE MINIATURE PICTURE. Com. by Lady Craven. Acted at Drury-Lane, 1781. Not printed. This piece was first performed in a private Theatre at Newberry. It was produced very late in the season at Drury-Lane, and acted only three or four nights.

172. THE MINOR. Com. of three acts, by Samuel Foote, 8vo. 1760. This piece was first presented in the summer season at the Little Theatre in the Hay-Market, and though it was performed by an entirely young and unpractised company, it brought full houses for thirty-eight nights in that time of the year, and continues still one of the stock pieces for the winter also. As the principal merit of all this gentleman's writings consists in the drawing peculiar characters well known in real life, which he heightened by his own manner of personating the originals on the stage, it will be necessary to inform posterity that in the characters of Mrs. Cole and Mr. Smirk, the

the author represented those of the celebrated Mother Douglas, and Mr. Langford the auctioneer; and that in the conclusion, or rather epilogue to the piece spoken by Shift (which the author performed, together with the other two characters), he took off to a great degree of exactness the manner and even person of that most noted enthusiastic preacher, and chief of the methodists, Mr. George Whitfield. And indeed, so happy was the success of this piece in one respect, that it seemed more effectually to open our eyes (those of the populace especially) in regard to the absurdities of that pernicious set of politic enthusiasts, than all the more serious writings that had ever been published against them. Mr. Foote has been accused of borrowing not only the hint, but even the whole of the character of Mrs. Cole, from another piece which was at that time only in *Embrio*. What justice there is in this charge, however, we may perhaps canvass further in another part of this work, when we come to make mention of that piece.

173. An Additional Scene to the Comedy of THE MINOR, 8vo, 1761. In this Mr. Foote is pretty smartly animadverted upon for making it his practice to expose the harmless peculiarities of private persons upon the public stage.

174. MINORCA. Trag. by Henry Dell, 8vo. 1756. This piece was printed just when the place from which it is named was taken. Nothing can be more contemptible than it is in every point of view. For a specimen, the following lines are selected:

" You call me superstitious, and for
" why?
" Because I believe in dreams, and be-
" lieve I will,—

" —— France do your worst,
" I fear you not, and though by force
" compell'd,
" Will never yield."

175. MIRACLE PLAY OF ST. KATHARINE. By Geoffery, afterwards Abbot of St. Alban's, a Norman, who had been sent over by Abbot Richard to take upon him the direction of the school of that monastery; but, coming too late, went to Dunstable, and taught in the abbey there, where he caused this dramatic piece to be acted (perhaps by his scholars). This was long before year 1110; and probably within the eleventh century. The above play was, for aught that appears to the contrary, the first spectacle of this sort exhibited in these kingdoms; and, as M. L'Extant observes, might have been the first attempt towards the revival of dramatic entertainments in all Europe, being long before the representations of *Mysteries* in France; for these did not begin till 1398. Matthew Paris, who first records this anecdote of the play of. *St. Katharine*, says, that Geoffery borrowed copes from the sacrist of the neighbouring abbey of St. Alban'., to dress his characters.

176. THE MIRACULOUS CUPE, or, *The Citizen outwitted*. Farce, compiled by Brownlow Forde, 12mo. 1771. Taken from Cibber's *Double Gallant*, and printed at Newry.

177. THE MIRROR, or, *Harlequin every where*. Pantomimical Burletta, by Charles Dibdin. Acted at Covent-Garden, 8vo. 1780.

178. THE MIRROUR. A Com. in three acts, by Henry Dell, 8vo. 1757. Never acted. This is merely an alteration of Randolph's *Muses Looking-Glass*.

179. MIRZA. Trag. by Robert Baron, 8vo. 1647. This tragedy

is founded on real facts which happened not long before, and is illustrated with historical annotations. The story of it is the same as that which Denham made the ground-work of his *Sophy*, and which may be found in Sir Thomas Herbert's Travels; yet has Mr. Baron handled it in a very different manner from that author, having finished three complete acts of this before he saw that tragedy; nor found himself then discouraged from proceeding, on a consideration of the great difference in their respective pursuits of the same plan. Baron has made Jonson's *Cataline* in great measure his model, having not only followed the method of his scenes, but even imitated his language; and any one may perceive that his ghost of *Emirhamze Mirza* is an evident copy of that of *Sylla* in *Cataline*. It is, however, a good play, and is commended by five copies of verses by his Cambridge friends, but whether ever acted I know not.

180. THE MISANTHROPE. C. This is a translation from Voltaire.

181. THE MISER. Com. by Thomas Shadwell, 4to. 1672. This play by the author's own confession is founded on the *Avare* of Moliere, which is itself also built on the *Aulularia* of Plautus. Shadwell, however, has by no means been a mere translator, but has added considerably to his original.

182. THE MISER. Com. by Henry Fielding, 8vo. 1732. This play was acted with great applause at the Theatre Royal in Drury-Lane, and is the piece which now continues to be performed annually. It has, as Mr. Murphy observes, the value of a copy from a great painter by an eminent hand.

183. THE MISER. Com. by J. Hughes. This is only a first act of a translation from Moliere, which the author either did not think worth while preserving, or else was prevented by the stroke of death from finishing. It is, however, published with his other dramatic and poetical works.

184. THE MISER. Com. by J. Ozell, 12mo. 1732. This is nothing more than a literal translation of the celebrated French play of Moliere, from which all the above-mentioned pieces have been borrowed. Prefixed to it are some strictures on a new translation of Moliere just then published.

185. THE MISER of Moliere, translated by Michael de Boissy, 12mo. 1752.

186. THE MISER. Com. translated from Plautus, by Bonnel Thornton, 8vo. 1767.

187. THE MISFORTUNES OF ARTHUR (*Uther Pendragon's sonne*) *reduced into tragicall notes by Thomas Hughes, one of the Societie of Grayes-Inne. And here set downe as it past from under his hands, and as it was presented, excepting certain wordes and lines, where some of the actors either helped their memories by brief omission, or fitted their acting by alteration. With a note at the ende of such speeches as were penned by others in lue of some of these hereafter following.*

This dramatic piece has the following general title:

Certaine Devises and Shewes presented her Majestie by the Gentlemen of Grayes-Inne at her Highnesse Court in Greenwich, the twenty-eighth day of Februarie, in the thirtieth yeare of her Majestie's most happy raigne. At London. Printed by Robert Robinson, 1587.

The play is preceded by a prologue, to which this extraordinary stage-direction is annexed.

An Introduction penned by Nicholas Trotte

Trotte Gentleman, *one of the Society of Grayë's-Inne ; which was pronounced in manner following, viz. Three Muses came upon the stage apparelled accordingly, bringing five Gentlemen Students with them astyred in their usuall garments, whom one of the Muses presented to her Majestie as Captives ; the cause whereof she delivered by speech as followeth.*

To every act of this performance there is an argument, a dumb show, and a chorus. At the conclusion of it, is a note specifying, that the Dumb Shews and additional speeches were partly devised by William Fulbeck, Frauncis Flower, Christopher Yelverton, Frauncis Bacon, John Lancaster, and others, who with Maister Penroodocke and Lancaster directed these proceedings at Courte.

The piece is beautifully printed in the black letter, and has many cancels consisting of single words, half lines, and entire speeches. These were reprinted and pasted over the cancelled passages; a practice, I believe, very rarely seen.

The names of the Speakers.
Gorlois, Duke of Cornwall's ghost.
Gueneuora, the Queene.
Fronia, a Lady of her trayne.
Angharad, sister to the Queene.
Mordred, the Usurper.
Conan, a faithfull Counseller.
Nuntius of Arthur's landing.
The Herald from Arthur.
Gawin, King of Albanie.
Gilla, a Brittshe Earle.
Gillamor, King of Ireland.
Cheldrick, Duke of Saxonie.
The Lord of the Pictes.
Arthur, King of Great Brytain.
Cador, Duke of Cornwall.
Hoel, King of Little Brittaine.
The Herald from Mordred.
Aschillus, King of Denmarke.
The King of Norwaye.
A number of Souldiers.
Nuntius of the last battell.
Gildas, a noble man of Brytain.

Of so great a curiosity we should gladly give a more ample account, were we not circumscribed by the limits of our work. The author of this piece, however, was well read in *Virgil, Lucan, Seneca,* &c.

188. THE MISERIES OF INFORCED MARRIAGE, by George Wilkins, 4to. 1607. 4to. 1629. 4to. 1637. To this comedy Mrs. Behn is indebted for great part of the plot of her TOWN FOP, or Sir *Timothy Tawdry*. She has, however, considerably improved on this play, which is not divided into acts.

189. MISS IN HER TEENS, or, *The Medley of Lovers.* Farce, by David Garrick. Acted at Covent-Garden, 8vo. 1747. This farce met with great success, and indeed deservedly so, it being a laughable and diverting piece. The characters of *Flash* and *Fribble* may perhaps be considered as somewhat *outré*, and too much on the *Caricature*, but that has ever been allowed in farce, or what the French call the *Basse Comedie*, where probability is frequently sacrificed to invention, and a strict adherence to nature, or humour, and ridicule. And, moreover, the inimitable performances of the author and Mr. Woodward in these characters seemed to overbear even the slightest reflection of this kind that might arise, since even in the representation of what might itself exceed the bounds of nature, the enchanted audience could scarcely perceive that they were not walking in her very straitest and most limited paths.

190. MISS LUCY IN TOWN. Farce, by Henry Fielding. Acted at Drury-Lane, 8vo. 1742. This piece, which is a sequel or second part of *The Virgin unmasked,* was presented for some nights, and met with applause. But it being hinted that a particular man of quality was pointed at in one of the characters,

ters, an application was made to the lord chamberlain, who sent an order to forbid it being performed any more.

191. THE MISSION FROM ROME INTO GREAT BRITAIN IN THE CAUSE OF POPERY AND THE PRETENDER. Scenically represented, 4to. No date, about 1746.

192. THE MISTAKE. Com. by Sir John Vanburgh. Acted at the Hay-Market, 4to. 1706. This is an admirable play, and always meets with applause. The quarrelling scene between *Carlos* and *Leonora* is perhaps as highly touched as any we have in the whole list of English comedies. Prologue by Steele; Epilogue by Motteux.

193. THE MISTAKES, or, *The Happy Resentment*. Com. by the late Lord Cornbury, 8vo. 1758. The author of this piece was the learned, ingenious, and witty Lord Cornbury. It was, however, never acted, being a very juvenile performance, and unequal to the very deserved reputation his lordship's abilities afterwards acquired. He made a present of it to that great actress Mrs. Porter, to make what emolument she could by it; and that lady, after his death, published it by subscription, at five shillings each book, on which occasion the remembrance of Mrs. Porter's former merits with the public in her profession, and the respect due to the worth of the author, induced the nobility to exert themselves so largely, some subscribing for twenty, others for forty, and some even fourscore or an hundred books, that the whole number of copies disposed of amounted to three thousand. The general tenor of the piece is to form a kind of vindication of the fair sex, by drawing, in his Lord and Lady *Thoughtless*, a contrast and counterpart to the character of Cibber's Lady *Townly*, in the comedy of *The Provoked Husband*. I cannot pay any great compliment to his lordship's genius from the execution of this design, yet there breathe through the whole such sentiments of honour and virtue, as reflect the brightest lustre on a much more valuable quality, viz. his intrinsic goodness of heart. Prefixed to it, is a Preface by Mr. Horace Walpole, at whose press at Strawberry-Hill it was printed.

194. MISTAKEN BEAUTY, or, *The Lyar*. Com. Acted at the Theatre Royal, 4to 1685. Anonymous. This is little more than a translation of the *Menteur* of Corneille. Mr. Hart was much admired for acting the part of *Dorant* in this play, yet it met with no great success. There is an earlier edition of it, under the latter title only, in 1661.

195. THE MISTAKEN HUSBAND. Com. by Dryden. Acted at the Theatre Royal, 4to. 1675. This play is on the model of Plautus's *Menechmi*, and is extremely farcical. It is not, however, Mr. Dryden's, being only adopted by him and enriched with one good scene from his hand. The real author is, I believe, unknown.

196. THE MISTAKES, or, *The False Report*. Com. by Joseph Harris, 4to. 1690. This play was written by another person, but falling into this gentleman's hands, he made many alterations in it considerably for the worse. Yet Dryden bestowed a prologue on it, Tate an epilogue, and Mountfort a whole scene in the last act, and many other corrections. Notwithstanding which, it remains a tedious disagreeable piece, and many of the scenes which are printed in this edition of it, were

obliged

obliged to be omitted in the representation. It is dedicated to Godfrey Kneller, Esq.

197. MITHRIDATES, KING OF PONTUS. Trag. by Nath. Lee. Acted at the Theatre Royal, 4to. 1678. This play is founded on history, for which see *Appian*, *Florus*, and *Plutarch*. The scene lies in Sinope. The epilogue written by Mr. Dryden.

198. THE MOCK DOCTOR, or, *The Dumb Lady cured*. A Ballad Farce, by Henry Fielding. Acted at Drury-Lane, 8vo. 1733. This *Petite Piece* is taken wholly from the *Medecin malgré lui* of Moliere, excepting the songs, which are not very numerous. Some other writers have made use of that comedy as the ground-work of their pieces, but by attempting to enlarge on and improve it have absolutely spoiled it. This author, however, whose natural bent of genius had the same kind of turn with that of Moliere himself, has been contented with only giving a sprightly and happy translation of him, varying no more from his original with respect to plot, incident, or conduct, than the different taste of the two nations rendered absolutely necessary; by which means he has introduced the foreigner amongst us possessed of all his natural vivacity and humour, and with no other alteration than that which his own *Politesse* would necessarily occasion, viz. the being dressed in the full mode of the country he is visiting. How far the author was right in the adoption of this method, the success of the piece sufficiently evinces; it having been received with universal approbation at its first appearance, and continuing to this day one of the constant standing deserts to our dramatic collations, notwithstanding the infinity of *Petites Pieces* that have appeared since.

199. THE MOCK DUELLIST, or, *The French Valet*. Com. by P. B. 4to. 1675. This play was acted at the Theatre Royal with some success, and is, in consequence of the letters affixed to it, attributed by Langbaine and Jacob to one Mr. Peter Belon. Scene, Covent-Garden.

200. THE MOCK LAWYER, Ballad Opera, by Edw. Phillips, 8vo. 1733. This was acted at Covent-Garden with some success.

201. THE MOCK MARRIAGE. Com. by Thomas Scot. Acted at Dorset-Gardens, 4to. 1696. This play was the first attempt of a young author in the dramatic way, and was performed in an indifferent part of the season; yet it met with considerable approbation. The scene is laid in London, the plot I believe original.

202. THE MOCK PREACHER. A satyric comical allegorical Farce. Acted to a crowded audience at Kennington-Common, and many other Theatres, with the humours of the mob, 8vo. 1739.

203. THE MOCK PHILOSOPHER. A new, pleasant and diverting Comedy, representing the humours of the age, by Samuel Harper, 12mo. 1737.

204. THE MOCK TEMPEST, or, *The Enchanted Castle*, by Tho. Duffet, 4to. 1676. This piece was acted at the Theatre Royal, and written purposely in a burlesque style. The design of it was to draw away the audience from the other theatre, to which at that time there was a very great resort, drawn thither in consequence of the applause given to Dryden's alteration of the *Tempest*, which was then in its full run: but it was intermixed with so much scurrility and ribaldry, that although

it met with some little success at first, it presently fell to the ground; and when it came to be presented in Dublin, several ladies and persons of the best quality testified their dislike of such low and indecent stuff, by quitting the house before the performance was half over.

205. MOCK THYESTES. Farce, by James Wright, 12mo. 1674. This piece is written in burlesque verse, and is one proof among many that burlesques are not always intended (as they are most generally mistaken to be) as a ridicule on those authors who are either parodized or travestied in them, but only as the *Jeu d'Esprit* of a lively and ingenious imagination; since the very piece of Seneca on which Mr. Wright has built the plan of his Mock-Tragedy, the very same gentleman has taken the greatest pains in a serious translation of, which he executed with great accuracy and elegance, and which was printed and published together with this burlesque.

206. A MODERN CHARACTER. Introduced into Æsop as acted at the Hay-Market, 8vo. 1751.

207. MODERN COURTSHIP. Com. in two acts, 8vo. 1768.

208. THE MODERN GALLANTS. Com. 8vo. 1733. This is *The Intriguing Courtiers*, with only a new title page.

209. THE MODERN HUSBAND. Com. by Henry Fielding, 8vo. 1734. This play was acted at the Theatre Royal in Drury-Lane with some success, but never revived since.

210. MODERN POETASTERS, or, *Directors no Conjurors*. A Farce, Anonymous, 1725, *on the famous Ode Writers, Satyrists, Panegyrists, &c. of the present Times, and their Patrons, &c.* This piece I have never seen, nor find any account of but in Coxeter's MS. where it is mentioned by the above title. It was never acted, and seems by its denomination to be only a piece of personal satire and partial abuse, neither intended nor fit for the stage.

211. THE MODERN PROPHETS, or, *New Wit for an Husband*. Com. by Thomas Durfey. Acted at Drury-Lane, 4to. no date [1707.] This piece is an excessive bad one, having no kind of merit but the exposing, with some little humour, a set of absurd enthusiasts who made their appearance at that time under the title of *The French Prophets*.

212. THE MODERN RECEIPT, or, *A Cure for Love*. Com. altered from Shakspeare, 12mo. 1739. This is an alteration of *As you like it*.

213. THE MODERN WIFE, or, *The Virgin her own Rival*. Com. by J. Stevens, 8vo. 1744. This piece was, as the title-page informs us, acted gratis at the Theatre in the Hay-Market, by a company of gentlemen for their diversion. The name affixed to it is that of a bookseller, who was remarkable for clandestinely obtaining copies of any little poetical or other performances that he could lay hands on, and publishing them not only without, but even against the consent of their authors; and therefore, as his own abilities appeared scarce equal to the production of a dramatic piece, of even so indifferent a degree of merit as this, which by the way, he published by subscription for his own emolument, it will not appear, perhaps, too uncharitable to suspect that it was not his own, but only procured, like his other publications, by stealth.

214. THE MODISH COUPLE. Com. by Capt. Bodens, 8vo. 1732. This play was acted at Drury-Lane without any great success. Yet I think it seems entitled to

an equal share with most of the comedies of about that period. There is no great intricacy in the plot, nor striking novelty in the characters; yet the dialogue is easy and unforced, and there is nothing either in the conduct or sentiment that disgusts, which is perhaps as much as can be said of most of our modern comedies. From it has since been taken a farce, called *Marriage-à-la-Mode*, performed at Mr. Yates's benefit in the year 1760. Which see in its proper place.

215. THE MODERN HUSBAND. Com. by Charles Burnaby, 4to. 1702. This play was performed at Drury-Lane, and was damned. Yet some excuse is to be made for it, as it appears by the preface to have been written in a month's time, that is to say, if *any* excuse *ought* to be made for the affront thrown on the public by authors, in protruding on them their hasty unfinished performances.

216. THE MODISH WIFE. C. by Francis Gentleman. Acted at the Hay-Market, 8vo. 1774. Prefixed to it is an account of the author.

217. THE MOHOCKS. A Tragicomical Farce, *as it is acted* (says the title-page) *near the Watch-house in* Covent-Garden, 8vo. 1712. This piece was never acted, but is printed with a dedication to Mr. D*** (Dennis), and has been attributed in general to Mr. Gay, but how truly I cannot pretend to affirm. The subject of it is an exposition of the behaviour of a set of mischievous young men who were distinguished by the title of *Mohocks* (as those of the present time are by that of *Bucks* and *Bloods*), and who used, on the presumption of their being protected by rank or fortune from punishment for their errors, to mistreat

every inoffensive person whom they met abroad, under the idea of frolicks. These pernicious beings have almost always subsisted under one title or other, and it seems remarkable that they have ever distinguished themselves by such as in some degree point them out to be the *Feræ Naturæ*: the modern race, however, seeming to have rather more of the monkey than the bear in them, confine themselves to less savage kinds of mischief than those hinted at here, who used to stop at no barbarity, cutting and maiming innocent persons with their swords, &c. and indeed imitating the unpolished nation whose name they assumed.

218. MOMUS TURN'D FABULIST, or, *Vulcan's Wedding*. Opera, Anonym. 8vo. 1729. This piece has a considerable share of merit, the character of Momus being well supported, and almost every song contrived to be a fable prettily told, and conveying a pleasing satirical moral. It was acted at Lincoln's-Inn Fields with success.

219. MONARCHICAL IMAGE, or, *Nebuchadnezzar's Dream*. Dramatical Poem, by Robert Fleming, 8vo. 1691. Printed with other pieces in a volume, intituled, " The Mirror of Divine Love un- " veiled, in a Poetical Paraphrase " of the high and mysterious Song " of Solomon."

220. MONEY IS AN ASS. Com. by Thomas Jordan, 4to. 1668. This play was acted with applause; the part of Capt. Penniless, the principal character in it, having been performed by the author. It is one of the pieces published by Kirkman; and Langbaine surmises from the style, that it is older than the date of its publication.

221. Mo-

221. MONEY'S THE MISTRESS. Com. by Thomas Southerne, 8vo. 1725. This author's comedies are by no means equal to his tragedies, nor is this even the best of the former. It met with no approbation on its appearance at Lincoln's-Inn Fields. The author was sixty-five years of age when it was performed; it may therefore be considered as the very last dying embers of his poetical fire.

222. MONSIEUR DE POURCEAUGNAC, or, *Squire Trelooby*. Anonym. 4to. 1704. This piece was acted at the subscription music at the Theatre Royal in Lincoln's-Inn Fields, March 20, 1704, by a select company from both houses. It is done into English from Moliere's comedy of the same name, which was made and performed for the diversion of the French king. The scene of this lies in London, and it has a prologue by Dr. Garth, whom Coxeter's MS. hints to have been the translator of the whole.

223. MONSIEUR DE POURCEAUGNAC, or, *Squire Trelooby*, by Ozell. A mere translation of Moliere's play, never intended for the stage.

224. MONSIEUR D'OLIVE. C. by George Chapman, 4to. 1606. This play was was esteemed a good one, and met with success. It was acted by her Majestie's children at Black-Friers.

225. MONSIEUR THOMAS. C. by John Fletcher. Acted at Black-Friers, 4to. 1639. In this comedy the author was unassisted by his friend Beaumont (who probably was dead before the writing of it) or any other person; but it was not published till after his death by Richard Brome, who dedicated it to Charles Cotton, as a great admirer of the dead author's works and memory. It was afterwards revived on the stage by Thomas Durfey, under the title of *Trick for Trick*. The scene, London.

226. MONTEZUMA. Trag. by Henry Brooke, Esq. 8vo. 1778. Not acted. Printed in the author's works, in four volumes, 8vo.

227. THE MONUMENT IN ARCADIA. A dramatic Poem, in two acts, 4to. 1773, by George Keate, Esq. As no writer can be much injured by comparison with himself, we shall not hesitate to affirm that the pastoral drama before us is by far the least valuable of Mr. *Keate's* productions; and perhaps the wreath of bays which he so well deserves to wear on other occasions, would appear more green in the eyes of futurity, were this discoloured leaf permitted silently to drop out of it. If we are not misinformed, our author communicated the present work to his friend Mr. Garrick, who pronounced it to be of too grave a cast for representation. Mr. *Keate* is likewise said to have altered the *Semiramis* of *Voltaire*; but its appearance on the stage, unluckily for the public, was anticipated by a similar attempt of one *Captain Ayscough*, whose production would have disgraced a barn in Wales, and yet was suffered to impoverish the managers of a theatre royal in London, throughout a run of more than nine nights.

228. MORE DISSEMBLERS BESIDES WOMEN. Com. by Thomas Middleton, 8vo. 1657. Scene, Milan.

229. THE MORAL QUACK. Dramatic Satire, by Dr. Bacon, 8vo. 1757.

230. THE MORNING RAMBLE, or, *The Town Humours*. Com. Anonymous, 4to. 1673. The scene in London. This is a good play, and by Downes ascribed to Nevil Paine.

231. MOR-

231. MORTIMER'S FALL. Tr. by Ben Jonson. This piece is to be found amongst Jonson's works, but is no more than a fragment, just begun, and left imperfect by means of the author's death. What it would have been, however, may in some measure be gathered from the arguments of each several act, which are published to it for the reader's satisfaction. The loss of it is the more to be regretted, as it is the only plan this author had proceeded on for a dramatic piece, on any story taken from the history of our own domestic affairs.

232. MOTHER BOMBIE. Com. by John Lilly, M. A. 4to. 1594. Acted by the children of Paul's.

233. THE MOTHER-IN-LAW, or, *The Doctor the Disease*. Com. by James Miller, 8vo. 1734. This comedy was acted with very great success at the Theatre in Drury-Lane. The scene of it is laid in London, and the plot is compounded of those of two comedies of Moliere, viz. the *Monsieur Pourceaugnac*, and the *Malade imaginaire*. The author received some helps in the composition from Mr. Henry Baker; and being at that time in orders, and somewhat apprehensive of the effects that a known application to theatrical writing might have on his promotion in the church, he prevailed on that gentleman to pass as the sole author of the piece, which was dedicated to the countess of Hertford. In consequence of the success it met with, however, he afterwards, on a publication of his works all together, resumed his claim to this piece, among the rest, and, if I mistake not, without so much as acknowledging the assistances he had had from his friend.

234. MOTHER SHIPTON, *her Life*. Com. by Thomas Thomson, 4to. N. D. This play, it is said, was acted nineteen days successively with great applause, yet what merit it has can by no means be called its own, all the characters, excepting those which relate to Mother *Shipton*, being stolen from Massinger's *City Madam*, and Middleton's *Chaste Maid in Cheapside*. It has not the author's name at length, but only the initials; which appears as if he was ashamed of his plagiarism.

235. MOTHER SHIPTON. Pantomime. Acted at Covent-Garden, 4to. 1770.

236. THE MOURNFUL NUPTIALS, or, *Love the Cure of all Woes*. Trag. by Thomas Cooke, 8vo. 1739. This was afterwards altered, and brought out at Drury-Lane in 1744, under the title of *Love the Cause and Cure of Grief*, or, *The Innocent Murderer*.

237. THE MOURNING BRIDE. Trag. by W. Congreve. Acted at Lincoln's-Inn Fields, 4to. 1697. This is the only tragedy our author ever wrote, and met with more success than any of his other pieces, yet it is certainly greatly inferior to the very worst of them; for although the story is a pleasing and affecting one, and well told, yet the language has so much of the bombast, and so little of real nature in it, that it is scarcely credible it could be the work of an author so remarkable for the contrary, in the easy flowing wit of his comedies. Dr. Johnson however observes, " that, if he were to select from the whole mass of English poetry the most poetical paragraph, he knows not what he could prefer to an exclamation in this tragedy:

Almeria.
It was a fancy'd noise, for all is hush'd.
Leonora.
It bore the accent of a human voice.
Almeria.

Almeria.

It was thy fear, or else some transient wind
Whistling through hollows of this vaulted isle:
We'll listen ——

Leonora.

Hark!

Almeria.

No, all is hush'd, and still as death.—'Tis dreadful!
How reverend is the face of this tall pile;
Whose ancient pillars rear their marble heads,
To bear aloft its arch'd and ponderous roof,
By its own weight made stedfast and immoveable,
Looking tranquillity! It strikes an awe
And terror on my aching sight; the tombs
And monumental caves of death look cold,
And shoot a chilness to my trembling heart.
Give me thy hand, and let me hear thy voice;
Nay, quickly speak to me, and let me hear
Thy voice—my own affrights me with its echoes."

He who reads these lines enjoys for a moment the powers of a poet; he feels what he remembers to have felt before, but he feels it with great increase of sensibility; he recognizes a familiar image, but meets it again amplified and expanded, embellished with beauty, and enlarged with majesty." The scene is laid in the Court of the King of Valentia.

238. A most pleasant Comedy of MUCEDORUS, the King's Sonne of Valentia, and Amadine, the King's Daughter of Arragon. With the merry Conceits of the Mouse. Amplified with new additions, as it was acted before the King's Majesty at Whitehall on Shrove-Sunday Night. By his Highnesse servants, usually playing at the Globe, 4to. 1615. 4to. 1629. 4to. 1668. This piece is in some of the old catalogues said to be Shakspeare's. It is rather a kind of droll or farce than a regular comedy, and used frequently to be performed for the diversion of country people at Christmas time. It was first printed 1598. 4to.

239. MUCH ADO ABOUT NOTHING. Com. by W. Shakspeare. Acted by the Lord Chamberlain's servants, 4to. 1600. This comedy, though not free from faults, has nevertheless numberless beauties in it, nor is there perhaps in any play so pleasing a match of wit and lively repartee as is supported between Benedict and Beatrice in this; and the contrivance of making them fall in love with one another, who had both equally forsworn that passion, is very pleasingly conducted. The scene lies in Messina, and that part of the plot which relates to Claudio and Hero, with the Bastard's scheme of rendering the former jealous by the assistance of Margaret the waiting-maid, and Borachio, is borrowed from the fifth book of Ariosto's *Orlando furioso*, in the story of *Ariodant* and *Geneura*. The like story is also related in Spenser's *Fairy Queen*, Book 2. Canto 4. Mr. Steevens observes, that " this play
" may be justly said to contain two
" of the most sprightly characters
" that Shakspeare ever drew. The
" wit, the humourist, the gentle-
" man, and the soldier, are com-
" bined in Benedict. It is to be
" lamented, indeed, that the first
" and most splendid of these dis-
" tinctions, is disgraced by unne-
" cessary profaneness; for the
" goodness of his heart is hardly
" sufficient to atone for the licence
" of his tongue. The too sarcastic
" levity, which flashes out in the
" conversation of Beatrice, may
" be excused on account of the
" steadiness of friendship so ap-
" parent in her behaviour, when
" she urges her lover to risque his
" life by a challenge to Claudio.
" In the conduct of the fable, how-
" ever,

"ever, there is an imperfection similar to that which Dr. Johnson has pointed out in the *Merry Wives of Windsor:*—the second contrivance is less ingenious than the first:—or, to speak more plainly, the same incident is become stale by repetition. I wish some other method had been found to entrap Beatrice, than that very one which before had been successfully practised on Benedict."

240. THE MULBERRY GARDEN. Com. by Sir Charles Sedley. Acted at Drury-Lane, 4to. 1668. 4to. 1675. This was esteemed a very good comedy. There appears, however, an evident similarity of Sir John Everyoung and Sir Samuel Forecast to the Sganerelle and Arifte of Moliere's *Ecole des Maris.* Scene, the Mulberry-Garden near Saint James's.

241. MULEASSES THE TURK. Trag. by John Mason, 4to. 1610. Whatever merit this play might really possess, the author himself had a most exalted opinion of it, as is apparent from its title-page, in which he not only styles it a worthy tragedy, but quotes the following line from Horace for its motto, viz. *Sume superbiam quæsitam meritis;* and in another edition of it in 4to. 1632, it is called, *An excellent Tragedy of* MULEASSES *the Turk,* and BORGIAS *Governor of Florence.* Full of interchangeable variety, beyond expectation. Divers times acted (with general applause) by the children of his Majesty's Revels. Scene, Florence. It was entered on the books of the Stationers' Company March 10, 1608. This tragedy has some beautiful lines and speeches, which, however, are disgraced by intrusions of the lowest and most obscene comedy that has hitherto appeared on the stage.

242. THE MUSE OF NEWMARKET, 4to. 1681. This is only an assemblage of three drolls acted at Newmarket, all stolen from other plays. The names of them are as follows: I. THE MERRY MILKMAIDS OF ISLINGTON, or, *The Rambling Gallants defeated.* II. LOVE LOST IN THE DARK, or, *The Drunken Couple.* III. THE POLITICK WHORE, or, *The Conceited Cuckold.* What plays they are taken from, has not yet come to my knowledge.

243. THE MUSES LOOKING-GLASS. Com. by Thomas Randolph, 4to. 1638. This is, perhaps, one of the most estimable and meritorious of all the old pieces extant. It contains an assemblage of characters whose height of painting would do honour to the pen of Shakspeare or Jonson: the language is at the same time natural and poetical, the sentiments strong, the satire poignant, and the moral both absolutely chaste and clearly conspicuous. In a word, there is nothing but the difference of the manners, and the want of intricacy in the plot, which could prevent its becoming one of the favourites of the present stage. The author first gave it the title of *The Entertainment;* and to the last edition, which is in 8vo. 1706, it has the second title of *The Stage reviv'd.* The scene lies in London, near Black-Friers.

244. THE MUSE OF OSSIAN. Dram. Poem, of three acts. Extracted from the several poems of Ossian, the son of Fingal, by David Erskine Baker. Performed at Edinburgh, 12mo. 1763. Printed at Edinburgh.

245. THE MUSES IN MOURNING. Opera, by A. Hill, 8vo. 1760. This little piece was never acted, but is printed in Mr. Hill's

posthumous works. It is like the *Snake in the Grass* of the same author, a burlesque on the prevailing taste for Operas and Pantomimes, under the idea of a lamentation made by the Tragic and Comic Muse, for the apparent neglect shewn to them by the public.

246. MUSICK, or, *A Parley of Instruments*, 4to. 1676. This little piece is no more than the composition of some master of music, for his scholars at a ball.

247. THE MUSICAL LADY. Farce, by George Colman. Acted at Drury-Lane, 8vo. 1762. In the piece before us, Mr. Colman has attacked the ladies on the affectation of a passion for musick, and a taste in composition, without either feeling the one or possessing the other, and there by becoming dupes to fashionable absurdity, and an easy prey to the interested views of a set of foreign fidlers and Italian impostors, to the neglect of real and superior merit, because British, or at the best imagining those qualifications the only title to encouragement, which never thrive perfectly but in a land of luxury and effeminacy, and ought by no means to be set in composition with those manly virtues and generous qualities, which are the distinguishing characteristics of our more hardy countrymen. In this attempt the author has succeeded better than in his former; his *Sophia* is a more finished character than his *Polly Honeycomb*, and the use made of her darling folly by Mr. *Mask*, much more judicious and conducive to her reformation, than the well-laid design of Mr. *Scribble*. The characters are all finely drawn; nor are those of Old *Mask* and even the *Launderess* less delicately finished, than the more important ones of Young *Mask* and *Sophy*. The language is lively and sensible, and the plot, though simple, sufficiently dramatic. In a word, I cannot avoid giving it as my opinion that, notwithstanding the success of the *Jealous Wife*, the *Musical Lady* still stands foremost in point of merit among all Mr. Colman's writings. Yet, though that merit might fully entitle it to the approbation it met with, it would scarcely be just to omit taking notice, that its success was greatly contributed to by the admirable performance of perhaps the most promising young actress that has appeared on this stage for many years past, viz. Miss Pope, who supported the character of *Sophia*, with a sprightliness tempered with judgment, and an elegance heightened by ease, that might have done honour to a performer of three times the experience in life that her years then afforded her an opportunity of acquiring. The prologue was written by Mr. Garrick, and spoken by Mr. King; and the scene lies partly at *Mask's* chamber in the Temple, and afterwards at *Sophia's* house.

248. MUSTAPHA *the Son of* SOLYMAN *the Magnificent*. Trag. by Roger, earl of Orrery, Fol. 1672 and 1690. The scene of this play is laid in Hungary, and the foundation of the story is on historical facts, for which see *Thuanus*, Lib. 12. Knolles's *Turkish History*, &c. It is esteemed a good play, and was acted at the Duke of York's Theatre.

249. MUSTAPHA. Trag. by Fulk Greville, Lord Brooke, Fol. 1613. As this play is built on the same foundation with the preceding one, it will be needless to refer to any other authorities than those abovementioned. There is

an earlier edition of it in 4to. 1606, but it may rather be called a fragment than a play, being not only incorrect, but extremely imperfect, and probably came out without his lordship's knowledge. The folio edition, however, is perfectly corrected.

250. MUSTAPHA. Trag. by David Mallet. Acted at Drury-Lane, 8vo. 1739. This play is also upon the same general plan as the foregoing ones, but the language being more modern and poetical, and the conduct of the plot more adapted to the present taste, it may justly be called the author's own; it was played with success.

251. MYDAS. Com. by John Lyly, 4to. 1592. The story of this play is related at large by Apuleius in his *Golden Ass*. See also Ovid's *Metamorphoses*, Book II. Galtruchius, &c.

252. MYRTILLO. A Pastoral Interlude, by Colley Cibber, 8vo. 1716. Performed at Drury-Lane with no very great success. It is set to Music by Dr. Pepusch.

253. THE MYSTERIOUS MOTHER. Trag. by Horace Walpole, 8vo. 1768. This dramatic piece was printed by our author at Strawberry-hill, and distributed among his particular friends, but with such strict injunctions of secrecy, that, knowing its merit, we cannot but express our surprize that its author should with to withhold it from the public. Mr. Walpole has given the story of it in the following words: " I had
" heard when very young, that a
" gentlewoman, under uncommon
" agonies of mind, had waited on
" Archbishop Tillotson, and be-
" sought his counsel. A damsel
" that served her had, many years
" before, acquainted her that she
" was importuned by the gentle-
" woman's son to grant him a pri-
" vate meeting. The mother or-
" dered the maiden to make the
" assignation, when she said she
" would discover herself, and re-
" primand him for his criminal
" passion; but, being hurried away
" by a much more criminal pas-
" sion herself, she kept the assig-
" nation without discovering her-
" self. The fruit of this horrid
" artifice was a daughter, whom
" the gentlewoman caused to be
" educated very privately in the
" country; but proving very love-
" ly, and being accidentally met
" by her father-brother, who
" never had the slightest suspicion
" of the truth, he had fallen in
" love with, and actually married
" her. The wretched guilty mother
" learning what had happened,
" and distracted with the conse-
" quence of her crime, had now
" resorted to the Archbishop to
" know in what manner she should
" act. The prelate charged her
" never to let her son and daugh-
" ter know what had passed, as
" they were innocent of any cri-
" minal intention. For herself,
" he bad her almost despair."

On this ground-work Mr. Walpole built the admirable play now under consideration, which after he had finished, he discovered to have an earlier origin than he had before known; being to be found in the Novels of *The Queen of Navarre*, vol. I. Nov. 30; and with a strange concurrence of circumstances between the story as there related, and as he had adapted it in the present performance. The tradition, however, was by no means an uncommon one. It had been published at least four times before in the English language, and twice in a dramatic form. The reader may find it related in the Works of Mr. Perkins, a puritan divine of the last century, and from thence extracted in the ninth volume of *The Spectator*, p. 274.

Mr. Walpole has candidly acknowledged, that the subject of this performance rendered it totally unfit for the stage. "The subject, "says he, is so horrid, that I "thought it would shock rather "than give satisfaction to an au- "dience. Still I found it so truly "tragic in the two essential springs "of terror and pity, that I could "not resist the impulse of adapt- "ing it to the scene, though it "should never be practicable to "produce it there. I saw too "that it would admit of great situ- "ations of lofty characters, and "of those sudden and unforeseen "strokes which have singular effect "in operating a revolution in the "passions, and in interesting the "spectator. It was capable of "furnishing not only a contrast of "characters, but a contrast of vice "and virtue in the same charac- "ter: and by laying the scene in "what age and country I pleased, "pictures of ancient manners "might be drawn, and many al- "lusions to historic events intro- "duced to bring the action nearer "to the imagination of the spec- "tator. The moral resulting from "the calamities attendant on un- "bounded passion, even to the "destruction of the criminal per- "son's race, was obviously suited "to the purpose and object of "tragedy."

That the production of such a tragedy as the present, on the modern stage, would be extremely hazardous, we are ready to admit; but we cannot but observe at the same time, that the delicacy of the present times is frequently carried to a ridiculous degree of affectation. Vices of greater magnitude are daily represented, and without exciting the smallest disgust in the spectator. We are by no means convinced that any consequences, unfavourable to the interests of society, could arise from the representation of the result of crimes even so shocking as those which are the basis of the present play, especially when they are painted in such colours as those in which Mr. Walpole's canvas exhibits them. It is certain, that writers of the last century would not have avoided the story for any of the reasons for which the present author has condemned his piece to oblivion; nor do we apprehend that a play, written with the pathos and energy of the present, would have then been refused by managers, or neglected by the town. That former authors, patentees, and audiences, were less scrupulous, may be inferred from this circumstance, that a contemptible performance, intituled, *The Fatal Discovery, or Love in Ruines*, was actually brought before the publick at Drury Lane in 1698. This tragedy is founded on the same circumstances which are the principal objects of the present. The heroine is guilty of incest in the same manner; has a daughter who is brought up unconscious of her real parents, banishes her son, who returns just at the opening of the play; he falls in love with his

his sister-daughter, and marries her. The discovery is made, the lady goes mad, and in her frenzy kills her daughter, and afterwards herself. In the old play the incestuous commerce between the son and mother is softened, by making the latter ignorant of the person with whom she had been guilty, until after the horrid event. The same circumstance has been again introduced by Mr. Gould, in another worthless piece, called *Innocence distressed, or the Royal Penitents*. 8vo. 1737.

Of the present tragedy we may boldly pronounce, that for nervous, simple, and pathetick language, each appropriated to the several persons of the drama; for striking incidents; for address in conducting the plot; and for consistency of character uniformly preserved through the whole piece; it is equal, if not superior, to any play of the present century. We intended to have given the reader a specimen of it; but having learnt that the sensibility of the author (to whom every respect is due) would be wounded by such an exhibition, we deem ourselves bound to suppress it, however reluctantly.

N.

1. THE NABOB. Com. by Samuel Foote. Acted at the Hay-Market, 1772. Printed in 8vo. 1778. A severe, but, I believe, ill-founded satire on the greater part of those gentlemen who have acquired wealth in the East-Indies. At the time this play was produced, a general odium had been excited against the members of the East-India Company, which was kept alive by every art which virulence and party could suggest. Mr. Foote, ever attentive to avail himself of popular subjects, seized the present occasion to entertain the town at the expence of some individuals. The character of Sir Matthew Mite was intended for a gentleman who had risen from the low situation of a cheesemonger. How far it resembles the original must be left to the determination of those who have an opportunity of making the comparison.

2. NANCY, or, *The Parting Lovers*. A Musical Interlude, by H. Carey, 8vo. 1739. This piece was acted with success at the Theatre Royal in Drury-Lane.

3. NANINE. Com. translated from Voltaire, and printed in Dr. Francklin's edition of that author.

4. NAR-

4. NARCISSUS, or, *The Self Admirer.* Com. translated from J. J. Rousseau, 12mo. 1767. This was first acted at Paris, Dec. 18, 1752. It is printed in the translation of this Author's Miscellaneous Works, vol. II.

5. NATIONAL PREJUDICE. Com. of two acts, performed at Drury-Lane, April 6, 1768, for Mrs. Abington's benefit. Not printed.

6. *A new interlude and a mery, of the* NATURE OF THE iiij ELEMENTS, *declarynge many proper poyntys of phylysophy naturall, and of dyvers straunge landys, and of dyvers straunge effects and causis; whiche interlude yf the hole matter be playd wyl conteyue the space of an hour and a halfe; but yf ye lyst ye may leve out muche of the sad mater, as the messengers pte, and some of naturys pte, and some of experyens pte, and yet the matter wyl depende conveyently, and than it wyl not be paste thre quarters of an hour of length.*
Here folow the namys of the pleyers.
The messengere | nature naturate | humanyte | studious defire | senfuall appetyte | the taverner | experyence | Also yf ye lyst, ye may brynge in a dysgysinge.

This piece was published by the learned typographer Rastall, brother-in-law to Sir Thomas More. It might have been the composition of either the one or the other; at least they are not disgraced by the supposition. This sort of spectacle had hitherto been confined to moral allegory, or religion blended with buffoonery; but the present performance is rendered the vehicle of science and philosophy.

7. NATURE WILL PREVAIL. A Dramatic Proverb. Acted at the Hay-Market, 1778. Not printed.

8. NATURE'S THREE DAUGHTERS, BEAUTY, LOVE AND WIT. Com. in two parts, by the Duchess of Newcastle, Fol. 1662.

9. NECK OR NOTHING. Farce, by David Garrick, Esq. Acted at Drury-Lane, 8vo. 1766. This piece is an imitation of the *Crispin Rival de son Maitre* of Le Sage.

10. THE NECROMANCER, or, *Harlequin Dr. Faustus.* Pantomime. Acted at Lincoln's-Inn Fields, 8vo. 1731.

11. NECROMANTIA. A dialoge of the Poete Lucyen between Menippus and Philonides, for his Fantelye faynyd for a mery pastyme, &c. *Rastall me fieri fecit.* As the author, whoever he was, has reduced this dialogue into English verse after the manner of an *interlude*, we have not hesitated to class it among dramatic performances. If Rastall was only the printer of it, which may be doubted, we might fairly enough ascribe it to the festive genius of his brother-in-law, Sir Tho. More.

12. NEGLECTED VIRTUE, or, *The Unhappy Conqueror.* A Play, acted at the Theatre Royal, 4to. 1696. This play was published by Mr. Horden the player, into whose hands it was put, and who wrote the prologue to it, as did Mr. Motteux the epilogue; yet it had very little success. Scene, the Capital City of Parthia.

13. NEPTUNE'S TRIUMPH FOR THE RETURN OF ALBION. A Masque, by Ben Jonson, performed at Court on Twelfth Night, 1624.

14. NERO EMPEROR OF ROME, his Trag. by Nath. Lee. Acted at the Theatre Royal, 4to. 1675. This tragedy is written in a mixed style, part being in prose, part in rhyme, and part in blank verse. The plot may be traced in the historical writings of Suetonius, Tacitus, Aurelius Victor, &c. The scene, Rome.

15. NERO, *the Tragedy of*. Anonymous, 4to. 1624. 4to. 1633. This play is in the title-page, called *Nero newly written*, becauſe it was written after that of *Claudius Tiberius Nero*, which Kirkman has by miſtake called Nero's Life and Death. See *Claudius Tiberius Nero*. It is on the ſame foundation with Lee's play, and the ſcene laid in the ſame place.

16. THE NEST OF PLAYS, by Hildebrand Jacob. Acted at Covent-Garden, 8vo. 1738. This was the firſt dramatic entertainment licenced by the Lord Chamberlain, after the paſſing of the act for reſtraining the liberty of the ſtage; which was of itſelf aſſigned as a reaſon for its want of ſucceſs. Be that as it will, the work was damned the firſt night. It conſiſts of three ſhort diſtinct comedies, whoſe names are as follows, viz. I. THE PRODIGAL REFORMED. II. THE HAPPY CONSTANCY. III. THE TRIAL OF CONJUGAL LOVE. All intended together to form the amuſement of one evening.

17. THE NEW ACADEMY, or, *The New Exchange*. Com. by Rich. Brome, 8vo. 1658.

18. THE NEW ATHENIAN COMEDY, by J. S. 4to. 1693, *containing the Politics, Oeconomics, Tactics, Cryptics, Apocalyptics, Styptics, Sceptics, Pneumatics, Theologics, Poetics, Mathemetics, Sophiſtics, Pragmatics, Dogmatics*, &c. *of that moſt learned Society*. This piece was not intended for the ſtage; it conſiſts only of three acts, and is a low piece of banter on the Athenian ſociety. Scene, S[mith's] Coffeehouſe, Stocks-Market.

19. NEW BROOMS! An occaſional Prelude, by George Colman. Performed at Drury-Lane, at the opening of the theatre, Sept. 21, 1776. 8vo.

20. A NEW BULL-BAYTING, or, *A Match play'd at the Town Bull of Ely*, 4to. 1659. This is rather a dialogue than a play.

21. A NEW COMEDY. Acted by the French King and his Privy Council, tranſlated out of French, 4to. 1704.

22. NEWE CUSTOM. An Interlude, Anonymous, 4to. 1573. The whole title of it is as follows: "*A new Enterlude, no leſs wittie than pleaſant, intitled*, New Cuſtome; *deviſed of late, and for diverſe Cauſes now ſet forth, never before this Tyme imprinted*. The Dramatis Perſonæ, which are eleven in number, are in the title-page, and ſo diſpoſed therein, as to evince the poſſibility of what is ſaid, viz. *that Fowre may play this Enterlude*, or, in the preſent theatric phraſe, to point out all the doubles that may be made uſe of in the caſting of it. It is printed in the black letter, and is written in Engliſh hexameter rhymes. I cannot, however, avoid making one remark in this place, which has frequently occurred to me on the ſight and peruſal of ſome of theſe earlieſt of our dramatic pieces, viz. that from the ſpelling and general turn of the phraſeology and verſification, they muſt have been much longer written than appears from the date of their publication, or elſe that the works of Shakſpeare, Spenſer, Sidney, and others of thoſe brilliant ſtars which adorned the Britiſh hemiſphere at a certain period, muſt have made a moſt amazingly ſudden reformation and improvement in the Engliſh language, both with reſpect to poetry and proſe, neither of which are now, after near two centuries being elapſed, ſo much altered from their manner of writing, as that manner is from the ſtyle and complexion of ſome even of their contemporaries.

23.

22. NEW HIPPOCRATES. Farce, 1761. This piece made its appearance for two several benefits on Drury-Lane stage, and is said to have been written by Dr. Hiffernan. The intent of it is to expose the folly of persons of fortune confiding the conduct of their health and constitutions to foreign empiricks, to the prejudice of deserving regular-bred gentlemen of the faculty, who, possessed of great learning, skill, and judgment, are nevertheless often neglected and denied that encouragement, which is at the same time unreasonably lavished on these pernicious beings; to whom, from their absolute deficiency of every one of those qualities, it would be madness to entrust the management of even the most trivial concerns in life, exclusive of life itself. The design so far may be good, but the execution of it is puerile, and defective in almost every essential to the drama; character, incident, and probability, being all alike wanting in it; the foreign quack being made an absolute Englishman, and the only attempt at real character which is that of Miss Griseldine Waponrake, a Yorkshire, galloping, foxhunting, female rustic, dragged in by head and shoulders without any previous expectation, or subsequent consequence, or, in a word, without any farther connexion to this piece, than it might be made to have equally well to any other. The success it met with, which was a kind of cold contemptuous disregard, was surely as much as its merit could demand, and indeed the author seems to have shewn a consciousness of the same judgment, by not publishing the piece.

24. THE NEW INN, or, *The Light Heart*. Com. by Ben Jonson, 8vo 1631. Nothing, perhaps, can give a stronger idea of the self-opinion, haughtiness, and insolence of this writer, whose merit, great as it was, must be greatly eclipsed by those ill qualities, than his behaviour with regard to this play, which not succeeding according to the exalted idea he had himself formed of its worth, he published it with the following title-page, which I shall here transcribe at large: *The New Inn; or, The Light Heart. A Comedy, never acted, but most negligently played by some of the King's Servants, and more squeamishly beheld and censured by others the King's Subjects*, 1629. *Now at last set at Liberty to the Readers, his Majesty's Servants and Subjects, to be judged*. Nay, not satisfied with this general glance at their judgements in the title, he has annexed to the play an ode, in which he openly and insolently arraigns the public for want of taste, and threatens to quit the stage. Such was the resentment shewn by this opinionated genius on one single slight shewn to him by an audience from whom he had before received repeated favours. This ode, however, drew upon him an answer from Mr. Feltham, which could not fail of severely wounding a mind so susceptible of feeling, and so avaricious of praise, as Jonson's. Nor do I hint this by way of casting any reflection on the memory of this truly great genius, whose merits in some respects are, and ever will remain, unequalled; but only as a hint, how greatly even the the most exalted merit may degrade itself by too apparent a self-consciousness, and how vastly more amiable must have been the private characters of the modest Shakspeare and humble Spenser, who constantly mention themselves with the utmost humility, and others with the highest respect, than that of the overbearing Jonson;

son; who, tender as he thus was as to any attacks made on himself, was nevertheless perpetually carping and cavilling at the works of others, the due commendations given to which his envious disposition would not permit him to bear with patience, nor acquiesce to with unreserve or candour. But such is the frailty of human nature, and such the errors which persons of great abilities are perhaps more epidemically liable to than others whose consciousness of defect abates and antidotes the pride of nature.

25. NEW MARKET, or, *The Humours of the Turf*. Com. of two acts, by George Downing, 12mo. 1763. Printed at Halifax. This piece has been since acted at Drury-Lane.

26. NEW MARKET FAYRE, or, *A Parliamentary Outcry of State Commodities set to sale*. Tragi-Com. Part I. Printed at *You may go look*, 4to. 1649. Scene, Westminster.

27. NEW MARKET FAYRE, or, *Mrs. Parliament's new Figaries*. Tragi-Com. Part II. Written (as the title says) by *The Man in the Moon*, and printed at *You may go look*. These two satirical plays, each of which consists of little more than one scene, were written by some loyalist, to satirize and expose the proceedings of the rebels, whose power was at that time arisen to its greatest height; but whether published before or after the martyrdom, I know not.

28. A NEW REHEARSAL, or, *Bays the Younger*. Anon. 8vo. 1714. Containing an examen of *The Ambitious Step-mother*, *Tamerlane*, *The Biter*, *Fair Penitent*, *Royal Convert*, *Ulysses*, and *Jane Shore*; all written by N. Rowe, Esq; also a word or two upon Mr. Pope's *Rape of the Lock*. This piece is written in imitation of the Duke of Buckingham's *Rehearsal*, Mr. Rowe's plays, however, being rendered in it the sole subject of examination and criticism. It is in three acts, and the scene laid at the Rose Tavern, Covent-Garden. Prefixed to it is a preface in Vindication of Criticism in general, collected from the works of the Earl of Shaftesbury. This piece, although anonymous, was written by Cha. Gildon.

29. NEWS FROM PARNASSUS. Prelude, by Arthur Murphy. Acted at Covent-Garden, 1776. Not printed.

30. NEWS FROM PLYMOUTH. Com. by Sir W. Davenant, Fol. 1673. Scene, Plymouth.

31. NEWS FROM THE NEW WORLD DISCOVER'D IN THE MOON. A Masque, by Ben Jonson, Fol. 1641. Presented at Court before King James I. 1620.

32. A NEW TRICK TO CHEAT THE DEVIL. Com. by R. Davenport, Gent. 4to. 1639. This play met with good success. The scene lies in London. Slightall's Instructions to the Gentlemen (Act 1. Scene 2.) are borrowed from *Ovid de Arte Amandi*, lib. II. and the plot of Fryar John's discovering the intrigue between the constable and the woman, and pretending to conjure for victuals at the husband's return (Act 3. Scene 1.) has not only been copied by M. D'Ouville, in his Tales, but has also been since made use of by Ravenscroft, in his *London Cuckolds*.

33. A NEW WAY TO PAY OLD DEBTS. Com. by P. Massinger. Acted at the Phoenix, Drury-Lane, 4to. 1633. This play is very deservedly commended in two copies of verses by Sir Henry Moody and Sir Thomas Jay. It is one of the best of the old comedies, and I think the very best of this author's writing. The plot is good and well

well conducted, the language dramatic and nervous, and the characters, particularly that of Sir Giles Over-reach, highly and judiciously drawn. It was revived at Drury-Lane Theatre some few years ago; but whether from any fault in the performance, or want of taste in the audience, I know not, but it did not meet with that success which might have been expected from its merit, and which some of its contemporaries, not possessed of more, have since received on a revival.

34. A NEW WONDER, A WOMAN NEVER VEXT. Com. by W. Rowley, 4to. 1632. This is a diverting play, and met with success. The circumstance of the widow's finding in the belly of a fish the ring which she had dropped in crossing the Thames, seems borrowed from Herodotus' story of *Polycrates*, in his *Thalia*.

35. THE NICE LADY. Com. by George Smith Green, 8vo. 1762. Not acted. In the preface to this play our author says, that being informed Mr. Garrick had declared he would give a thousand guineas for a good comedy, he was excited to be a candidate for the prize, and accordingly completed his performance (of which half the first act had been written ten years before) in six weeks time. Thus finished, it was transmitted to Mr. Garrick for his *liking*; but that gentleman, being supposed equally able to judge of the value of money as of plays, happened to have a greater affection for his thousand guineas than for the present work, and therefore returned it to the author, who expresses much resentment against him for his refusal. Whoever will take the trouble of reading Mr. Green's performance, will not censure the manager for his conduct on this occasion.

36. NICE VALOUR, or, *The Passionate Madman.* Com. by Beaumont and Fletcher, Fol. 1647. Scene, Genoa.

37. THE NICE WANTON. A pleasaunt Comedie, Anonymous, 1634.

38. NICOMEDE. Tragi-Com. by John Dancer. Acted at the Theatre Royal in Dublin, 4to. 1671. This is a translation from the French of Corneille, and is one of the pieces which that author valued himself the most upon, and whose several beauties he has enumerated in an *Examen.* The story is from *Justin*, Book 34. Chapter the last; and the scene is laid at Nicomedia.

39. A NIGHT's INTRIGUE. Farce, Anonymous, 8vo. without date, but written since 1700. This is probably *The Evening's Intrigue*, by Capt. Stevens.

40. THE NIGHT WALKER, or, *The Little Thief.* Com. by John Fletcher. Acted at Drury-Lane, 4to. 1640. 4to. 1661. Scene, London. This was Fletcher's only, unassisted by his colleague Beaumont.

41. *The* NIGRAMANSIR, *a morall Enterlude and a pithie, written by Maister Skelton laureate, and plaid before the king and other estatys, at Woodstoke, on Palme Sunday.* It was printed by Wynkin de Worde in a thin quarto, in the year 1504. It must have been presented before King Henry VII. at the royal manor or palace, at Woodstock in Oxfordshire, now destroyed. The characters are a Necromancer, the devil, a notary publick, simonie, and Philargyria or avarice. It is partly a satire on some abuses in the church; yet not without a due regard to decency, and an apparent respect for the dignity of the audience. The story, or plot, is the trial of *Simony* and *Avarice*:

the

the devil is the judge, and the notary publick acts as an assessor or scribe. The prisoners, as we may suppose, are found guilty, and ordered into hell immediately.

There is no sort of propriety in calling this play the *Necromancer*; for the only business and use of his character, is to open the subject in a long prologue, to evoke the devil, and summon the court. The devil kicks the necromancer, for waking him so soon in the morning; a proof, that this drama was performed in a morning, perhaps in the chapel of the palace. A variety of measure, with shreds of Latin and French, is used; but the devil speaks in the octave stanza. One of the stage-directions is *Enter Balsebub with a Berde*. To make him both frightful and ridiculous, the devil was commonly introduced on the stage, wearing a visard with an immense beard. Philargyria quotes Seneca and St. Austin, and Simony offers a bribe. The devil rejects her offer with much indignation, and swears by the *foule Eumenides*, and the hoary beard of Charon, that she shall be well fried and roasted in the unfathomable sulphur of Cocytus, together with Mahomet, Pontius Pilate, the traitor Judas, and King Herod. The last scene is closed with a view of hell, and a dance between the devil and the necromancer. The dance ended, the devil trips up the necromancer's heels, and disappears in fire and smoke. Great must have been the edification and entertainment which King Henry VII. and his court derived from so elegant and rational a drama!

42. *The Tragedie of* NINUS AND SEMIRAMIS, the first monarche of the World. This play was entered on the books of the Stationers's Company May 10, 1595, by John Hardye; but, I believe, not printed.

43. NOAH'S FLOOD, or, *The Destruction of the World*. An Opera, by Edward Ecclestone, 4to. 1679. This piece is of the same nature with Dryden's *State of Innocence*, but falls infinitely short of the merit of that poem. The first edition of it not selling off according to the expectations of the bookseller, they put to it at different times two new title-pages, viz. *The Cataclism*, or, *General Deluge of the World*, 1684. and 2dly, *The Deluge*, or, *The Destruction of the World*, 1691. with the addition of several ornamental sculptures. Besides this, another edition of it came out in 12mo. 1714. with the title of *Noah's Flood*, or, *The History of the general Deluge*; and the names of several eminent booksellers, who joined in an imposition upon the world of this piece as a new one, and the parent unknown, as may be seen in the preface.

44. THE NOBLE CHOICE, or, *The Orator*. A Play, by Philip Massinger. Entered on the books of the Stationers' Company Sept. 9, 1653; but, I believe, not printed.

45. THE NOBLE FORESTERS, or, *Human Life reflected*. Interlude, taken from *As you Like it*, and printed in the *Theatrical Museum*, 8vo. 1776.

46. THE NOBLE GENTLEMAN. Com. by Beaumont and Fletcher, Fol. 1647. Scene, France. This play was revived with very little alteration by Mr. Durfey, under the title of *The Fool's Preferment*, or, *The three Dukes of Dunstable*, of which see mention made in its proper place.

47. THE NOBLE INGRATITUDE. A Pastoral Tragi-Com. by Sir William Lower, 12mo. 1659. This is a translation from the French of M. Quinault. Scene, in the

Forest

Forest of Argier. Printed at the Hague.

48. THE NOBLE PEDLAR. Burletta, performed at Marybone, 4to. 1770.

49. THE NOBLE RAVISHERS, a Play, was entered on the books of the Stationers' Company Nov. 29, 1653; but, I believe, not printed.

50. THE NOBLE SOLDIERS, or, *A Contract broken justly revenged*. Trag. by Samuel Rowley, 4to. 1634. This piece was not published till after the author's decease, though according to the editor's preface it had met with success in the representation; but where it was acted it is not easy to trace, any more than the foundation of the story, the former not being mentioned at all, nor any mention made as to the other, or what king of Spain it was who was guilty of the act of perjury with Onælia, on which the plot of this piece turns. The running title of this play is, *The Noble Spanish Soldier*; and Nicholas Vavasour the publisher, on the 9th of December, 1633, entered it under that title as written by Thomas Decker. See also *The Spanish Soldier*.

51. THE NOBLE STRANGER. Com. by Lewis Sharpe. Acted at the private house in Salisbury Court, 4to. 1640. Langbaine gives this play a good character, particularly recommending the parts of Pupillus and Mercutio, and the description given of several poets, amongst whom is Ben Jonson, in the fourth act.

52. THE NOBLE TRYAL. Tragi-Com. by Henry Glapthorne. Entered on the books of the Stationers' Company June 29, 1660, but not printed.

53. THE NOBLEMAN. Tragi-Com. by Cyril Tourneur. This play was entered on the books of the Stationers' Company Feb. 15, 1611. It was never printed, but was destroyed by Mr. Warburton's servant.

54. THE NOBLEMAN. Com. by Mrs. Cooper. Acted at the Hay-Market, about May 1736. Not printed. See Davies's Life of Garrick, vol. I. p. 225.

55. NOBODY AND SOMEBODY, with the true Chronical Historie of ELYIDURE, who was fortunately three times crowned Kinge of England. Acted by the Queen's servants, 4to. no date. This play is not divided into acts. The story is taken from our English chronicles.

56. NO FOOLS LIKE WITS, or, *The Female Vertuosoes*. Com. Acted at Lincoln's-Inn Fields, 8vo. 1721. This is only a republication of Wright's *Female Virtuosoes*, by Mr. Gay, and was set up and acted in opposition to Mr. Cibber's *Refusal*, which was partly borrowed from the same play, or at least from the same original, viz. the *Femmes sçavantes* of Moliere. I cannot, however, think this comedy equal in merit to the *Refusal*.

57. NO ONE'S ENEMY BUT HIS OWN. Com. by Mr. Murphy. Acted at Covent-Garden, 8vo. 1764. Although this play contains a great deal of spirited dialogue, properly characterised, and well supported; yet the character of Careless, whom the author intends for the person who is *No One's Enemy but his own*, being that of a worthless wretch, without honour or probity, the piece was totally disliked by the public.

58. NO WIT LIKE A WOMAN'S. Farce. Acted at Drury-Lane, 1769. This was acted at some of the benefits. It was taken from *George Dandin* of Moliere, and has not been printed.

59. NO WIT, NO HELP LIKE A WOMAN'S. Com. by Thomas Middleton,

Middleton, 8vo. 1657. The scene in London.

60. THE NONESUCH. Com. by William Rowley. Entered on the books of the Stationers' Company, June 29, 1660; and was among those destroyed by Mr. Warburton's servant.

61. THE NONJUROR. Com. by Colley Cibber. Acted at Drury-Lane, 8vo. 1717. The general plot of this comedy is borrowed from the *Tartuffe* of Moliere; and the principal character in it, viz. that of Doctor Wolfe, is a close copy from that great original. The conduct of the piece, however, is so greatly altered as to render it perfectly English, and the Coquet *Maria* is truly original and most elegantly spirited. The principal intention, however, of the author, who was a man warmly attached to the illustrious family then not long established on the British throne, and which had been very lately disturbed in the possession of it by a most unprovoked rebellion; his intention I say was, by clothing Moliere's *Tartuffe* in a habit very little different from his own, viz. " that " of an English popish priest, lurk-" ing under the doctrine of our " own church, to raise his fortune " upon the ruin of a worthy gen-" tleman, whom his dissembled " sanctity had seduced into the " treasonable cause of a Roman " Catholic outlaw," (see Cibber's Apology) to point out the mischiefs and ruin which were frequently brought into the most noble and valuable families by the self-interested machinations of those skulking and pernicious vipers, those wolves in sheep's cloathing, who at that troublesome and unsettled period, covering their private views beneath the mark of public zeal and sanctity, acted the part of the great serpent of old, first tempting to sin, and then betraying to punishment. The play met with great success in the representation, taking a run of eighteen nights; the subject itself being its protection, and its enemies not daring to shew any more at that time than a few smiles of silent contempt. The consequence however was what the author foresaw; that is to say, the stirring up a party against him, who would scarcely suffer any thing he wrote afterwards to meet with fair play, and making him the constant butt of Mist's *Journal*, and all the *Jacobite* faction. Nor do I think it by any means an improbable surmise, that the enmity and inveteracy of his antagonist Mr. Pope, and the set of wits who were connected with him, might have their original foundation traced from the appearance of this play. Scene, London. Prologue by Mr. Rowe.

62. THE NORTHERN HEIRESS, or, *The Humours of York*. Com. by Mrs. Mary Davis. Acted at Lincoln's-Inn Fields; 12mo. 1716 and 8vo 1725. Scene in York.

63. THE NORTHERN HEROES, or, *The Bloody Conquest, between Charles the Twelfth, King of Sweden, and Peter the Great, Czar of Muscovy*. With the Loves of Count Gillensternia and the Princess Elimira. With a comic Interlude, called *The Volunteers*, or, *The Adventures of Roderick Random, and his Friend Strap*, &c. Acted at Bartholomew Fair, 8vo. 1748.

64. THE NORTHERN LASS, or, *A Nest of Fools*. Com. by Richard Brome. Acted at the Globe and Black-Friers, 4to. 1632. This is one of the best of this author's pieces; it met with good applause in the representation,

and is commended by his contemporary Ben Jonson. It was revived and reprinted in 4to. 1684. with a new Prologue by Jo. Haynes, and an Epilogue. And, new songs being added to it, the music of which was composed by Dan. Purcell, it was again reprinted in 4to. 1706. It has no less than six copies of complimentary verses prefixed to it.

65. NORTHWARD HOE. Sundry times acted by the children of Paul's, by Thomas Decker and John Webster, 4to. 1607. A part of the plot, viz. that of Greenshield and Featherstone's pretending to Mayberry that they have both lain with his wife, and of their coming to a knowledge of each other by means of her ring, is borrowed from Malespini's Novels, Part 1. Nov. 2.

66. NORTHUMBERLAND. T. by Mark Anthony Meilan, 8vo. No date. This is on the same story as Rowe's Lady Jane Gray, and was never acted.

67. THE NORWICH MERCHANT, or, *The Happy Reconciliation*. Farce, 12mo. no date. Printed at Norwich.

68. THE NOTE OF HAND, or, *Trip to Newmarket*. Farce, by Richard Cumberland, Esq. Acted at Drury-Lane, 8vo. 1772. This is a good Farce, and met with success.

69. NOVELLA. Com. by Rich. Brome. Acted in 1632, but not printed till 1653, in 8vo. Langbaine gives this play a very good character. Scene in Venice.

70. THE NOVELTY, or, *Every Act a Play*, by P. Motteux. Acted at Lincoln's-Inn Fields, 4to. 1697. The model of this compound of pieces seems to be taken from the hint of Sir William Davenant's *Playhouse to be let*. It consists, as the title implies, of five distinct short dramatic pieces, all of them of different kinds, as follows: viz. I. A *Pastoral*, called THYRSIS. It was written by Mr. Oldmixon, and the scene of it lies on a green before a wood. II. A *Comedy*, called ALL WITHOUT MONEY. Scene, The Pallmall. III. A *Masque*, entitled HERCULES, the scene of which lies in the Lydian Court. Both these are original, and written by Mr. Motteux himself. IV. A *Tragedy*, called THE UNFORTUNATE COUPLE, which is only the latter part of Dr. Filmer's *Unnatural Brother*. Scene, Lyons. V. This last is called NATURAL MAGIC, and is a Farce written in imitation of part of a French Comedy of one act, after the Italian manner. The scene laid in a country house.

71. THE NUPTIALS. Masque, on the marriage of his Grace James, Duke of Hamilton and Lady Anne Cochran, 8vo. 1723. Prefixed to this performance, which was written by Allan Ramsay, and performed Feb. 11, 1723, is an Introduction concerning Masques.

72. THE NUPTIALS OF PELEUS AND THETIS, by James Howel, 4to. 1654. This piece consists of a Masque, and a Comedy from whence the Masque is taken, and was acted at Paris six times by the King in person, the Dukes of Anjou and York, the Princess Royal, the Princess of Conti, and several other illustrious personages. The Masque is borrowed from an Italian Comedy. The scene lies in Thessaly; and the story is to be found in Ovid's *Metamorphoses*, Book 11.

73. THE NUTBROWN MAID. Comic Opera, by George Savile Carey, 12mo. 1770.

O.

[259]

O.

O C

1. **THE OAKS**, or, *The Beauties of Canterbury.* Com. by Mrs. Burgefs. Acted at the Theatre in Canterbury, 8vo. 1780. This play takes its name from a place near the cathedral of the city, where it was acted and printed. The author of it is a pastry-cook, a mantua-maker, and wife of a parish-clerk.

2. **OBERON THE FAIRY PRINCE.** A Masque of Prince Henry's, by Ben Jonson. Fol. 1640. The author has himself written annotations on this play.

3. **THE OBSTINATE LADY.** Com. by Sir Aston Cockain, 4to. 1657. This play is written in imitation of Massinger's *Very Woman*, as may be easily perceived on a comparison between the characters of Don John, Antonio, and Almira, in that comedy, and those of Carionil and Lucora in this. Scene, London.

4. **AN OCCASIONAL PRELUDE.** Performed at the opening of Covent-Garden Theatre, Sept. 21, 1772, by George Colman, 8vo. 1776.

5. **OCTAVIA.** Trag. by Tho. Nuce, 4to. 1581. This is only a translation of the *Octavia* of Seneca. Scene, Rome. For the History, fee Suetonius's Life of Cicero, Tacitus, &c.

6. **THE OCULIST.** Farce. Anon. 8vo. 1747. I have never seen this piece; it was never acted, nor do I find it mentioned any where but in the *British Theatre*. I am apt to imagine it was only written as an abuse or banter on Dr. Taylor the oculist, who,

O D

about that time was much talked of.

7. **THE OCULIST.** Dramatical Entertainment of two acts, by Dr. Bacon, 8vo. 1757.

8. **ODE,** upon dedicating a building and erecting a statue to Shakspeare, at Stratford upon Avon, 4to. 1769. A performance entitled to our notice here, because for a few evenings it was recited at Drury-Lane Theatre, in lieu of a dramatic after-piece. Minute criticism would be misemployed on a work to which no man will afford a second reading. We shall therefore content ourselves to observe, that, however this ode might be applauded by a handful of company assembled to see the puppet-show at Stratford, it met with colder treatment from the judicious audiences of London. To these, the art of the speaker, matchless as it was, appeared but a weak substitute for poetic spirit and imagination. The success of Mr. *Garrick's* attempts as a comic writer, we have often acknowledged; but in his present effort, after climbing up with considerable labour into the Pindaric saddle, he serves only to remind us of poor *Tom Thumb*, when he rode the great horse for the entertainment of King *Arthur's* court. Let other unqualified ode-adventurers take warning, and forbear to imitate a bard by whose fire they are untouched, and with whose manner and language they have no acquaintance. This piece was reprinted with a whimsical parody on it, intituled, " The

S 2 " Ode

"Ode on dedicating a building and erecting a statue to Le Stue, cook to the Duke of Newcastle at Clermont," in a collection of fugitive pieces, published by Dilly, called THE REPOSITORY.

9. OEDIPUS. Trag. by Alex. Neville, 4to. 1581. This is a translation from Seneca, who himself borrowed part of it from Sophocles.

10. OEDIPUS COLONEUS. T. by George Adams, 8vo. 1729. This is only a very flat translation from Sophocles, with notes, but not intended for the stage.

11. OEDIPUS COLONEUS. T. by Thomas Franklin 4to. 1759. Printed in Dr. Franklin's edition of Sophocles.

12. OEDIPUS TYRANNUS. T. by George Adams, 8vo. 1729. This is another of the translations from Sophocles.

13. OEDIPUS TYRANNUS. T. by Thomas Franklin, 4to. 1759. Printed in Dr. Franklin's edition of Sophocles.

14. OEDIPUS TYRANNUS, by Thomas Maurice, 4to. 1779. This is a free translation of the same play, and was printed in a volume of the author's works, 4to.

15. OEDIPUS. Trag. translated from Voltaire, and printed in Dr. Franklin's edition of that author.

16. OEDIPUS KING OF THEBES. Trag. by J. Dryden and N. Lee. Acted at the Duke's Theatre, 4to. 1679. 4to. 1687. 4to. 1692. 4to. 1701. This is a very excellent Tragedy, being one of the best executed pieces that either of those two celebrated authors were concerned in; yet the critics have justly found fault with the impropriety of Oedipus's relishing an embrace from Jocasta after he had quitted his crown, and was gone to such extremity of distraction, as to have pulled out his own eyes. The plot is from H story; and the authors have happily availed themselves of several beauties both in Sophocles and Seneca. The scene lies at Thebes. This Tragedy was performed about twenty-five years since, and never failed to affect the audience very strongly. Nor can I in this place avoid relating an anecdote in regard to the power it has shewn of this kind, which is, that some years ago at a representation of it in Dublin, where Elrington acted the part of Oedipus, one of the instrumental performers, who was sitting in the Orchestra to see the piece, was affected in so violent a manner with the feigned distraction of that monarch, that he was immediately seized with a real madness, which, if I am not mistaken, never left him but with life. The first and third acts were written by Dryden, who drew the machinery of the whole; the remainder by Lee.

17. OEDIPUS KING OF THEBES. Trag. by Lewis Theobald, 12mo. 1715. This is only a translation from Sophocles, with critical notes by the translator.

18. OENONE. Pastoral, 4to. No date. Printed with other pieces, attributed to Robert Cox, comedian.

19. OITHONA. Dram. Poem, taken from Ossian; set to music by Mr. Barthelemon: performed once at the Hay-Market, 8vo. 1768.

20. THE OLD BATCHELOR. Com. by W. Congreve. Acted at the Theatre Royal, 4to. 1693. This was the first piece of this justly admired author's writings, being brought on the stage when he was only twenty-one years old. Such a comedy, written at such an age (as Dr. Johnson observes) requires some consideration. As the

the lighter species of dramatic poetry professes the imitation of common life, of real manners, and daily incidents, it apparently presupposes a familiar knowledge of many characters, and exact observation of the passing world; the difficulty therefore is to conceive how this knowledge can be obtained by a boy.

But if the *Old Batchelor* be more nearly examined, it will be found to be one of those comedies which may be made by a mind vigorous and acute, and furnished with comic characters by the perusal of other poets, without much actual commerce with mankind. The dialogue is one constant reciprocation of conceits, or clash of wit, in which nothing flows necessarily from the occasion, or is dictated by nature. The characters both of men and women are either fictitious and artificial, as those of *Hartwell* and the Ladies; or easy and common, as *Wittol* a tame ideot, *Bluff* a swaggering coward, and *Fondlewife* a jealous puritan; and the catastrophe arises from a mistake not very probably produced, by marrying a woman in a mask.

Yet this gay comedy, when all these deductions are made, will still remain the work of a very powerful and fertile mind: the dialogue is quick and sparkling, the incidents such as seize the attention, and the wit so exuberant that it *o'er-informs its tenement.*

21. OLD CITY MANNERS. C. by Charlotte Lennox. Acted at Drury-Lane, 8vo. 1773. This is an alteration of *Eastward Hoe.*

22. THE OLD COUPLE. Com. by Thomas May, 4to. 1658. This is a very good play, and the principal design is to point out the folly, absurdity, and detestableness of avarice.

23. OLD FORTUNATUS. Com. by Thomas Decker. Acted before the Queen at Christmas by the earl of Nottingham's servants, 4to. 1600. This play is printed in the black letter. The plan of it is founded on the ancient story of *Fortunatus*, and his inexhaustible purse and wishing hat. But the author has made such admirable use of the various circumstances of the tale, and taken the advantage of throwing in such sentiments and strokes of morality, that, notwithstanding the wildness and improbability of every part of the plot, I know not on the whole among the plays of that time many that have a juster claim to approbation than this piece. The scene lies partly at Fama Gosta, in the Island of Cyprus, and partly in the Court of England, during the reign of Athelstan.

24. OLD INTEREST. A Farce, of forty-three acts, 8vo. 1754. A mere election squib.

25. THE OLD LAW, or, *A New Way to please ye.* Com. by P. Massinger, Thomas Middleton, and William Rowley. Acted at Salisbury House, 4to. 1656. At the end of the edition here mentioned, is printed a catalogue, but a very imperfect one, of the dramatic pieces extant before that time, and which, besides abundance of typographical mistakes, has many other gross errors in it, several pieces being inserted as plays, which are entirely of another species of writing. The scene is in Epire.

26. THE OLD MAID. A Comedy of two acts, by A. Murphy, 1761. This *Petite Piece* was performed several times with great approbation at the Theatre Royal in Drury-Lane, during the summer theatrical partnership of the author and Mr. Foote. It has certainly great merit. The subject

ject of it, and part of the fable, were taken from *L'Etourderie* of Monsieur Fagan. The ambiguity and perplexity produced by Clermont's first mistake of the wife for the maiden, is natural and well supported, and the conduct and behaviour of that gentleman and the other characters in consequence of this circumstance, which, though kept unknown to them till the absolute period of the *Denouement*, is sufficiently discovered to the audience to give them the full enjoyment of their mutual energy, does honour to the skill and judgment of the author. The *Old Maid's* character is admirably kept up, and indeed, to speak of it on the whole, I know not any farce at present extant, which seems to lay a juster claim to a continuance of that public favour which was at first paid it, and which seemed to grow upon the audience in every subsequent representation, than the piece before us.

27. AN OLD MAN'S LESSON AND A YOUNG MAN'S LOVE. 4to. 1605. Though so early a piece, Langbaine has taken no notice at all of it or its author; but Jacob and Gildon have both attributed it to one Nicholas Breton. In this particular, however, they are both mistaken, having named the editor for the author, that gentleman in his preface declaring himself ignorant whom it was written by. It appears moreover to be much older than the time of its publication, being only an interlude, or indeed, to speak more properly, a bare dialogue between a father and son, the former of whom is a widower, and the latter a traveller, who, after a long absence, is returned to his father's house.

28. THE OLD MAN TAUGHT WISDOM, or, *The Virgin unmask'd*. A Farce, by Henry Fielding, 8vo. 1734. This farce was acted with good success at Drury-Lane Theatre, and continues on the acting list to this day. The characters are all outré to the greatest degree, and the piece is entirely devoid of even the shadow of a plot, yet there is somewhat laughable in it on the whole; and therefore as it pleases the Canaille, it is in general more frequently performed, than many farces of an infinitely greater share of merit.

29. THE OLD MODE AND THE NEW, or, *Country Miss with her Furbelow*. Com. by Thomas Durfey. Acted at the Theatre Royal, 4to. no date [1709.] Scene, Coventry. This is a very indifferent play.

30. THE OLD TROOP, or, *Monsieur Raggout*. Com. by John Lacy. Acted at the Theatre Royal, 4to. 1672. Scene, in London. Langbaine imagines this play, by the style, to be founded on some French original, yet candidly acknowledges this supposition to be nothing more than bare conjecture.

31. AN OLD WIFE'S TALE. C, Anonymous. Neither Langbaine, Jacob, or Gildon, pretend to have seen this play, or to know either its author or date; but the compiler of the *British Theatre* seems to be better acquainted with it, having boldly named and dated it, viz. *An Olde Wyfe her Tale*, 1598. In the books of the Stationers' Company, " A booke or interlude, " intituled a pleasant conceipte " called THE OWLDE WIFE's " TALE," is entered by Raphe Hancock, April 16, 1595. I am informed, it is in the collection of a gentleman now residing in London, but it has not fallen in my way to see it.

32. OLINDO AND SOPHRONIA. Trag. by Abraham Portal, 8vo. 1758. This play is a very indifferent

ferent one, and was never brought on the ſtage. The ſtory of it is taken from Taſſo's *Gieruſalemme liberata*.

33. OLIVER CROMWELL. An Hiſtorical Play, by George Smith Green, 8vo. 1752. Never acted, though probably intended for the ſtage by its author, and refuſed by the managers for reaſons not unobvious.

34. OLYMPIA. Trag. tranſlated from Voltaire, and printed in Dr. Franklin's edition of that author, 12mo.

35. THE OLYMPIAD. Opera, tranſlated from Metaſtaſio, by John Hoole, 8vo. 1768.

36. ONCE A LOVER AND ALWAYS A LOVER. Com. by Lord Lanſdowne. This is no more than an alteration of *The She Gallants*, which had been written when his lordſhip was very young, but which at a maturer time of life he reviſed, and improved by the addition and amendment of ſeveral ſcenes, which he particularly ſpecifies in an advertiſement prefixed to it. It is to be found in the third volume of an edition of his Lordſhip's works, in 12mo. 1736. But what is ſomewhat extraordinary, none of the writers take any notice of it under this title; nor does it appear, although *The She Gallants*, with all its imperfections on its head, was acted with great approbation, that this improved comedy was ever brought on the ſtage; nay, it is reaſonable to conjecture the contrary, as there are no performers' names annexed to the Dramatis Perſonæ.

37. AN OPERA, alluding to the Peace, by Mr. Grimes, and performed by his ſcholars at Cordwainers-Hall, 8vo. 1712.

38. THE OPERA OF OPERAS, or, *Tom Thumb the Great*, by Mr. Hacket and Mrs. Heywood. Acted at the Hay-Market, 8vo. 1733. This is no more than Fielding's *Tragedy of Tragedies* (which ſee in its place), transformed into an opera, by converting ſome paſſages of it into ſongs, and ſetting the whole to muſic.

39. THE OPERATOR. Ballad Opera, 4to. 1740.

40. THE OPPORTUNITIE. C. by Ja. Shirley. Acted at the private houſe in Drury-Lane, 4to. 1640. The hint of part of this play is borrowed from Shakſpeare's *Meaſure for Meaſure*.

41. THE ORACLE. Com. Anonymous, 8vo. 1741. This piece is taken no kind of notice of either in the *British Theatre*, or by Whincop, which are the only catalogues publiſhed ſince the date of it, nor have I myſelf ever ſeen it; but as I find its name in the monthly liſts of the publications of that year, I can by no means refuſe it a place here. That it was never preſented on any ſtage, is a point, however, which will not admit a diſpute.

42. THE ORACLE. Com. of one act, by Mrs. Cibber. Acted at Covent-Garden, 8vo. 1752. This little piece is a tranſlation from the French, and was, I believe, only intended as a means of aſſiſting the authoreſs in a benefit. It is, however, very prettily executed, and not only gave great pleaſure at the firſt repreſentation, but even continued, for a conſiderable time afterwards, a ſtanding theatrical collation. The character of Cynthia is ſimple and pleaſing, and although all thoſe kind of characters apparently owe their origin to Shakſpeare's *Miranda*, yet a very little variation in point of circumſtance or behaviour, will ever beſtow on them a novelty, which, added to the

delight we conſtantly take in impotence, cannot fail of giving pleaſure.

43. THE ORATORS. Com. of three acts, by Samuel Foote, 8vo. 1762. This piece met with very good ſucceſs. It was performed at the Little Theatre in the Hay-Market in the middle of the day, during ſome part of the ſummer of 1762. The bills publiſhed for it were under the idea of *Lectures* on *Engliſh Oratory*, and indeed part of the firſt act is taken up in an ironical kind of lecture on that ſubject. The two laſt, however, are an illuſtration of ſome of the principles laid down in the ſaid lecture, by examples with regard to the ſeveral methods of arguing and declaiming, peculiar to the oratory of the bar, and that of *ſome public aſſemblies*. The former is an imaginary trial of that ideal being, the *Ghoſt* of Cock-Lane, and the other is a ſuppoſed meeting of mechanics and labouring men at the noted *Robinhood Society*. In the purſuance of this plan, in order to point out the abſurdities which are frequently run into both in the matter and manner of argumentation, Mr. Foote has thrown into his deſign a great variety of characters, ſome of which have been ſuppoſed to be drawn from real life, particularly one of an eminent printer of a neighbouring kingdom, who, with all the diſadvantages of age, perſon, and addreſs, and even the deficiency of a leg, is perpetually giving himſelf the airs of the greateſt importance, continually repeating ſtories of his wit, and, not contented with being a moſt tireſome egotiſt in other reſpects, is even continually talking of his amours, and boaſting of being a favourite with the fair ſex. Such a character is ſurely a genuine object of ridicule; the ſtage ſeems to demand it as a ſacrifice at the ſhrine of *Common Senſe*; nor can I think the dramatic writer juſtly chargeable with perſonality, who, ſeeing ſo extraordinary a flower growing in nature's garden, does not exclude it from the noſegay he is gathering, becauſe it grew in a particular ſpot, and that its glaring colours had happened to have been obſerved by hundreds beſides himſelf.

44. THE ORDINARY. Com. by William Cartwright, 8vo. 1651. Scene, London. That this play was eſteemed a good one, may be inferred from the compoſer of a book called *Love Dialogues* having tranſcribed part of the firſt act, viz. the ſcene between the widow Potluck, Slicer, and Hearſay, and republiſhed it in his works, p. 81. under the name of the *Old Widow*.

45. ORESTES. Trag. by Tho. Goffe, 4to. 1633. 8vo. 1656. This play was acted by the ſtudents of Chriſt-Church, Oxford; the prologue being ſpoken by the author. The plot is borrowed from the *Oreſtes* of Euripides, and the *Electra* of Sophocles.

46. ORESTES. Trag. by John Hughes, 8vo. 1717. This is alſo from Euripides, but was never acted, the author dying before he had rendered it complete.

47. ORESTES. Dram. Opera, by Lewis Theobald. Acted at Lincoln's-Inn Fields, 8vo. 1731. This piece, though in the title ſtyled an Opera, is in reality a regular tragedy of five acts, with nothing to give it a right to the former title but ſome few pieces of muſic introduced in various parts of it. The ſcene lies in Scythia Taurica, and the ſtory of the plot is that of the expedition of Oreſtes and Pylades to that country, in order to bear away the ſtatue of Diana,

Diana, which had been sent down thither from heaven; an exploit they at length atchieved by the assistance of Iphigenia, the sister of Orestes, at that time, though unknown to them, a priestess of that goddess in her temple at Tauris, where the sought-for statue was deposited.

48. ORESTES. Trag. translated from Voltaire, by Dr. Franklin. Acted at Covent-Garden, March 13, 1769, for Mrs. Yates's benefit, and since at Drury-Lane. Printed in the translation of Voltaire's works.

49. ORESTES. Trag. translated from Euripides; printed with three other plays in a volume, intituled, "Select Tragedies of Euripides," 8vo. 1780.

50. ORGULA, or, *The Fatal Error*. Trag. by L. W. 4to. 1658. To this play is annexed a preface discovering the true nature of *Porse*, with the proper use and intention of such public divertisements. The scene is laid in Segusia, the antique name of a city and province in the East-Gaul, or France.

51. "The Historie of ORLANDO "FURIOSO, one of the twelve "Pieres of France. As it was plaid "before the Queen's Majestie," 4to. 1594. This play was written by Robert Green. It is a very irregular one, being not divided into acts, and most of it taken with very little difference, but that of national language, from the *Orlando Furioso* of the celebrated Italian poet Ariosto.

52. ORNASDES, or, *Love and Friendship*. Tragi-Com. by Sir William Killigrew, 8vo. 1664. Fol. 1666. The scene, in the Island of Citherea.

53. OROONOKO. Trag. by Tho. Southerne. Acted at the Theatre Royal, 4to. 1696. 4to. 1699. This play met with very great success when it first appeared, and has ever since continued to give pleasure in the tragic parts of it to every sensible and feeling auditor, the love of Oroonoko to Imoinda being, perhaps, the tenderest, and at the same time the most manly, noble, and unpolluted, that we find in any of our dramatic pieces; his firmness and resolution, alike perfect in action and in suffering, are truly heroic, and I think unequalled. But the intermixture of the low, trivial, and loose comedy of the widow Lackit and her son Daniel, with the addresses of Charlotte Weldon in breeches to the former, are so greatly below, and indeed so much empoison, the merit of the other parts, that nothing but the corrupt taste of the period in which the author first imbibed his ideas of dramatic writing, can stand in any degree of excuse for his having thus enwrapped a mass of sterling ore in rags and filthiness. The scene is laid in some of the English colonies in America, and the plot professedly borrowed from Mrs. Behn's novel of the same name. The epilogue by Congreve.

54. OROONOKO. Trag. by J. Hawkesworth, 8vo. 1759. This piece was acted at Drury-Lane Theatre, and is only an alteration of the foregoing play, in which the Augæan stable is indeed cleansed, the comic parts being very properly quite omitted. Yet still there seems somewhat more wanting than such a mutilation, to render this play what one would wish it to be; for as the comedy took up so considerable a share in the length of a drama of no immoderate extent, the story of the tragedy was apparently not sufficiently full of business to make out the catastrophe of an entire piece, without the addition of more incidents.

And

And though Dr. Hawkſworth in his alteration has greatly amended this play in point of omiſſion, yet the little further extent that he has given to the characters of Aboan and Hotman ſeems not ſufficient to fill up the hiatus which thoſe omiſſions have occaſioned, and I cannot help thinking therefore, it is ſtill to be wiſhed that ſome other writer of ability would conſider it as worth his while once more to reviſe this admirable groundwork of a tragedy, and by interweaving with its preſent texture ſuch additional incidents as Mrs. Behn's extenſive novel might very amply furniſh, by which means the whole might be rendered equally intereſting, and the piece become entitled to that immortality its merit is entitled to, pay a pleaſing and grateful tribute to the memory of an author, whoſe value ſeems likely to ſink almoſt into oblivion, for want of ſome ſuch care.

55. OROONOKO. Trag. altered from Southerne, 8vo. 1760. To this piece the editor added near 600 lines in place of the comic ſcenes, and two new characters.

56. OROONOKO, or, *The Royal Slave*. Tr. altered from Southerne, by Francis Gentleman. Acted at Edinburgh, 12mo. 1760 Printed at Glaſgow. In an advertiſement prefixed to this alteration, Mr. Gentleman ſays, that the deſign of it was firſt hinted to him by a noble perſonage, who had diſtinguiſhed himſelf in the literary world, and who recollected to have heard Mr. Southerne declare in his latter days, that he moſt heartily regretted his complying with licentious taſte by writing any thing ſo offenſive to modeſty, as the comic part of his works; eſpecially that which was ſo unnaturally joined to the tragedy of this play. This alteration appears to have been well received at Edinburgh.

57. THE ORPHAN, or, *The Unhappy Marriage*. Trag. by Thomas Otway. Acted at the Duke's Theatre, 4to. 1680. This play, from its frequent repetitions on the theatre, is too well known to need our ſaying much in regard to it. The plot is founded on the Hiſtory of Brandon, in a novel called *Engliſh Adventures*. The language is truly poetical, tender, and ſentimental, the circumſtances affecting, and the cataſtrophe diſtreſsful. Yet there is ſomewhat improbable and bungling in the particular on which all the diſtreſſes are founded; and I muſt own myſelf ſomewhat of the opinion of that perſon, who on the firſt ſeeing it, exclaimed, "O! *What an infinite deal of Miſchief would a farthing ruſh-light have prevented!*" Nor can I avoid remarking, that the compaſſion of the audience has commonly appeared to me miſplaced, it lighting in general on the whining, irreſolute Caſtalio, inſtead of falling where it ought to do, on the more ſpirited and open hearted Polydore, who, in conſequence of concealments on the ſide of his brother, which he could not have any reaſon to expect, and by which he is really injured, is tempted in his love and reſentment to an act which involves him in greater horror and diſtreſs than any of the other characters can undergo, from the more bloody effects it produces. This partiality has, however, always appeared to me to ariſe from ſome ſtrokes of libertiniſm thrown into the early parts of Polydore's character, which give an air of looſeneſs to it, and prejudice the audience againſt him through the whole play. As Dr. Johnſon obſerves,

ferves, it is one of the few pieces that keep poffeffion of the ſtage, and has pleaſed for almoſt a century, through all the viciſſitudes of dramatic faſhion. Of this play nothing new can eaſily be ſaid. It is a domeſtic tragedy drawn from middle life. Its whole power is upon the affections; for it is not written with much comprehenſion of thought, or elegance of expreſſion. But if the heart is intereſted, many other beauties may be wanting, ye: not be miſſed.

58. THE ORPHAN OF CHINA. Trag. tranſlated from Voltaire, 8vo. 1755. This was the firſt tranſlation of Voltaire's play.

59. THE ORPHAN OF CHINA. Trag. tranſlated from Voltaire; printed in Dr. Franklin's edition of that author's works. This play was originally acted at Paris the 20th of Auguſt, 1755.

60. THE ORPHAN OF CHINA. Trag. by A. Murphy. Acted at Drury-Lane, 8vo. 1759. The foundation of this play is to be ſeen in a dramatic piece tranſlated from the Chineſe language, in Du Halde's Hiſtory of China. The ſubject had before been handled by M. de Voltaire, in his *Orphelin de la Chine*. Mr. Murphy has, however, greatly varied from the French poet in the conduct of his plot, by very properly introducing the orphan, who in that play is an infant, and only ſpoken of, as a youth advanced in life, and one of the capital characters in the piece. On a cloſe examination, perhaps, he may be found to have made ſome uſe of the *Heraclius* of Corneille; but whatever aſſiſtances he may have had recourſe to for the laying his foundation, the ſuperſtructure muſt be allowed his own; and though this gentleman's genius ſeems to be more naturally devoted to the comic than the tragic Muſe, it would be injuſtice to him, not to confeſs that this is far from ſtanding the laſt on the liſt of our modern tragedies; nor would it be perhaps ſaying too much, to obſerve, that, was the whole play, or indeed even the laſt act of it, equal to the merit of the fourth, it would ſtand a very fair chance of being eſteemed the very foremoſt on that liſt. But it ſeems to be the conſtitutional error of our preſent tragic writers, to value themſelves more on a pompous, poetical, and correct ſtyle, than on a novelty of plot, on pathos, or natural cataſtrophe; in conſequence of which, a degree of ſameneſs ſeems to run through them all. The repreſentation of this play gave Mrs Yates the firſt opportunity of diſplaying her theatrical powers, and confirmed her reputation as one of the moſt excellent tragic actreſſes who have trod the Engliſh ſtage. In the year 1777, Mr. Murphy made ſome alterations in this drama, when it was revived at Covent-Garden, but with ſucceſs very inferior to its original appearance.

61. THE ORPHAN OF VENICE. Trag. by Ja. Darcy, 1749. This play I have never ſeen, nor know whether it ever was in print. It was acted at the Theatre Royal in Dublin.

62. ORPHEUS. An Engliſh Opera, by J. Hill, Fo. 1740. This little piece was, I believe, the firſt attempt in writing of an author who has ſince been more voluminous, than generally read. For this alone it is remarkable, and for having been the occaſion of giving the firſt vent to that ſpirit of vindictiveneſs and abuſe, which has ſince flowed in ſuch abundant torrents from the pen of its author. This piece had, I believe, been the work of a few lei-

sure juvenile hours. The natural self-love and ambition of a young author induced him to carry it to Mr. Rich the manager of Covent-Garden Theatre, by whom, after it had been for some short time in his hands, it was returned with the usual reply, that it would not do. In the season following, however, Mr. Rich brought on the stage his celebrated Pantomime Entertainment of *Orpheus* and *Euridice*, on which Mr. Hill immediately in a most gross and abusive letter to Mr. Rich in print, publickly accused that gentleman with having infamously stolen from this piece while in his hands, the greatest part, if not the whole, of that Pantomime. This charge, however, Mr. Rich fully cleared himself from, by publishing an answer to the said letter, in which he not only proved that there was no resemblance between his piece and Mr. Hill's, but also produced affidavits of several persons who had been employed by him in preparations for his Pantomime above twelve years before.

63. ORPHEUS. An ancient play under this title was amongst those destroyed by Mr. Warburton's servant. On the same subject, there is a fragment of a drama perhaps far more ancient, in The British Museum.

64. ORPHEUS AND EURIDICE. An Opera set to music, by J. F. Lampe, 8vo. 1740. It is the speaking parts and music of the above-mentioned Pantomime. The author Lewis Theobald.

65. ORPHEUS AND EURIDICE, with the Pantomime Entertainment. As acted at Lincoln's-Inn Fields, 4to. 1740. By Mr. Henry Somner.

66. ORPHEUS AND EURIDICE. A Masque, by Martin Bladen, 4to. 1704. This Masque is published at the end of a Tragi-Comedy, called *Solon*.

67. ORPHEUS AND EURIDICE. A Masque, by J. Dennis. This piece is printed in the *Muses Mercury*, for Feb. 1707.

68. ORPHEUS AND EURIDICE. A Dramatic Entertainment of Dancing, attempted in imitation of the ancient Greeks and Romans, by John Weaver. Acted at Drury-Lane, 8vo. 1718. The story on which all these several pieces are founded, may be seen in Ovid's *Metamorphoses*, Books X. and XI. The scene, partly in Thrace, and partly in the Infernal Regions.

69. OSMAN. Trag. by Francis Gentleman. This piece has never yet appeared in print, although about the year 1751 proposals were published both for the printing and acting it by subscription, each subscriber for a ticket at the performance of it at the little theatre in the Hay-Market being, by the proposal, entitled to a copy of the play in large or small paper, according to the part of the house for which he chose to take the ticket. This design, however, was laid aside, most probably for want of sufficient encouragement to the subscription. Yet the play did not want merit, and being afterwards brought on the stage at Bath, met with approbation. See THE SULTAN.

70. OSMAN. Trag. by Christ. Arnold, 4to. 1757. This play was not acted. It is founded on a catastrophe, which happened at Constantinople in the year 1624.

71. OSMOND THE GREAT TURK, otherwise called, *The Noble Servant*. Trag. by Lodowick Carlell, 8vo. 1657. The main action of this play is, in reality, the taking of Constantinople by Mahomet

Mahomet II. in the year 1453, a particular account of which may be seen in Knolles's *Turkish History*, and all the writers on the life of that monarch, as also in *A true Relation of the Murther of Osman the great Turk, and five of his principal Bashaws*, &c. printed in 4to. 1622. Yet the author has transferred his scene from Greece to Barbary, and altered the names of Mahomet and Irene, into those of Melchofus and Despina; probably in imitation of Beaumont and Fletcher's *Bloody Brother*, in which those authors have degraded Antoninus and Geta, from Emperors of Rome to Dukes of Normandy, giving them the names of Rollo and Otto. The underplot of Orcanes, Calibus, and Ozaca, is founded on the story of Mustapha, son of Mahomet the Second, Achmet Bassa, and his wife. The scene in Constantinople.

72. OTHELLO, *The Moor of Venice*. Trag. by W. Shakspeare. Acted at the Globe and Black-Friers, 4to. N. D. 4to. 1622. 4to. 1630. 4to. 1655. This is generally allowed to be one of the *Chef-d'Oeuvres* of this admirable author, notwithstanding all the several cavils and censures thrown on it by Rymer. Dr. Johnson says, "The "beauties of this play impress "themselves so strongly upon the "attention of the reader, that "they can draw no aid from cri"tical illustration. The fiery "openness of Othello, magnani"mous, artless, and credulous, "boundless in his confidence, ar"dent in his affection, inflexible "in his resolution, and obdurate "in his revenge; the cool ma"lignity of Iago, silent in his re"sentment, subtle in his designs, "and studious at once of his in"terest and his vengeance; the "soft simplicity of Desdemona, "confident of merit, and con"scious of innocence, her artless "perseverance in her suit, and her "slowness to suspect that she can "be suspected; are such proofs of "Shakspeare's skill in human na"ture, as, I suppose, it is vain to "seek in any modern writer. The "gradual progress which Iago "makes in the Moor's conviction, "and the circumstances which he "employs to inflame him, are so "artfully natural, that, though it "will perhaps not be said of him "as he says of himself, that he is "*a man not easily jealous*, yet we "cannot but pity him, when at "last we find him *perplexed in the* "*extreme*.

"There is always danger, lest "wickedness, conjoined with abi"lities, should steal upon esteem, "though it misses of approba"tion; but the character of Iago "is so conducted, that he is from "the first scene to the last hated "and despised.

"Even the inferior characters "of this play would be very con"spicuous in any other piece, not "only for their justness, but their "strength. Cassio is brave, be"nevolent, and honest, ruined "only by his want of stubborn"ness to resist an insidious invi"tation. Roderigo's suspicious "credulity, and impatient sub"mission to the cheats which he "sees practised upon him, and "which by persuasion he suffers "to be repeated, exhibit a strong "picture of a weak mind betrayed "by unlawful desires to a false "friend; and the virtue of Æmilia "is such as we often find worn "loosely, but not cast off, easy "to commit small crimes, but "quickened and alarmed at atro"cious villainies.

"The scenes from the begin"ning to the end are busy, varied "by happy interchanges, and re"gularly

"gularly promoting the progression of the story; and the narrative in the end, though it tells but what is known already, yet is necessary to produce the death of Othello.

"Had the scene opened in Cyprus, and the preceding incidents been occasionally related, there had been little wanting to a drama of the most exact and scrupulous regularity."

The story is borrowed from Cinthio's Novels. Dec. 3. Nov. 7.

73. OVID's TRAGEDY, by Sir Aston Cockain, 8vo. 1669. Langbaine observes the title of this play to be a misnomer, Ovid having scarcely any thing to do with the main plot of the piece, which is the jealousy of Bassane, and the murther of his bride Clorina and his friend Pyrontus in consequence of it, not very much unlike that of Alonzo, Carlos, and Leonora, in the *Revenge*. The incident of Captain Hannibal's inviting the dead carcass of Helvidius to supper with him, is the same with the catastrophe of Don John in the *Libertine*, and was probably borrowed from the same original, viz. An Italian play, called *Il Atheisto fulminato*. Some part also of the plot and language derive their source from Ovid's Elegies.

74. THE OXFORD ACT. Ballad Opera, 8vo. 1733. This was occasioned by the act then held at Oxford.

75. THE OXONIAN IN TOWN. Com. by George Colman. Acted at Covent-Garden, 8vo. 1770. The representation of this piece, after a few nights, was in danger of being interrupted by means of a set of Irish sharpers and gamblers, who applied some passages in the performance personally to themselves. The good sense of the majority, however, interfered, and frustrated the designs of a set of beings who are a disgrace to society.

P.

P A

1. THE PADLOCK. Com. Opera, by Isaac Bickerstaff. Acted at Drury-Lane, 8vo. 1768. This very pleasing entertainment was set to music by Mr. Dibden, who performed the part of Mungo in it. Few pieces have been more applauded than this was during the first season of its representation.

2. PAGEANTS, *performed at the Inauguration of the Lord Mayors of the City of London*. Of these performances, which are generally of a dramatic cast, the compilers of our theatrical catalogues have inserted only a few out of the great number which have appeared in print. The reader, who may have the curiosity to search after, and the perseverance to peruse these obsolete specimens of city manners, will not entertain the highest opinion of the taste, though he cannot but be struck with the magnificence with which these annual spectacles of Prætorian exaltation were exhibited. They generally consist of personifications of industry, commerce, the city of London,

London, the Thames, and beings of the like kind, intermixed with heathen gods and goddesses, and seem to have afforded great delight to the rude and uncultivated understandings of those for whose entertainment they were intended. The last pageant exhibited was in the year 1707; that designed for the 29th of October, 1708, being suppressed on account of the death of George, Prince of Denmark, which happened on the preceding day. From that period pageants were discontinued, and, on the death of Elkanah Settle, the office of city poet was likewise laid aside. The following list is more perfect than any which hath yet been published, though I am not without apprehension that some pieces may have escaped my search.

1585 By George Peele, 4to.
1605 By Anth. Munday, 4to.
1611 By the same, 4to.
1612 By Thomas Dekker, 4to.
1613 By Thomas Middleton, 4to.
1614 By Ant. Munday, 4to.
1615 By the same, 4to.
1616 By the same, 4to.
1619 By Thomas Middleton, 4to.
1620 By John Squire, 4to.
1621 By Thomas Middleton, 4to.
1624 By John Webster, 4to.
1626 By Thomas Middleton, 4to.
1631 By Thomas Heywood, 4to.
1632 By the same, 4to.
1633 By the same, 4to.
1634 By John Taylor, 4to.
1637 By Thomas Heywood, 4to.
1638 By the same, 4to.
1639 By the same, 4to.
1656 By J. B.
1657 By John Tatham, 4to.
1658 By the same, 4to.
1659 By the same, 4to.
1660 By the same, 4to.
1661 By the same, 4to.
1662 By the same, 4to.
1663 By the same, 4to.
1671 By Thomas Jordan, 4to.
1672 By the same, 4to.
1673 By the same, 4to.
1674 By the same, 4to.
1675 By the same, 4to.
1676 By the same, 4to.
1677 By the same, 4to.
1678 By the same, 4to.
1679 By the same, 4to.
1680 By the same, 4to.
1681 By the same, 4to.
1682 By the same, 4to.
1683 By the same, 4to.
1684 By the same, 4to.
1685 By Matt. Taubman, 4to.
1686 By the same, 4to.
1687 By the same, 4to.
1689 By the same
1691 By Elkanah Settle, 4to.
1692 By the same, 4to.
1693 By the same, 4to.
1694 By the same.
1695 By the same.
1698 By the same, Fo.
1699 By the same, Fo.
1700 By the same, Fo.
1701 By the same, Fo.
1708 By the same, Fo.

3. THE PAINTER'S BREAKFAST. Dram. Satyr, by Mr. Brenan, 12mo. 1756. This piece was printed at Dublin, but it does not appear to have been acted.

4. PALLADIUS AND IRENE. Drama in three acts, 8vo. 1773.

5. PALAMON AND ARCYTE. Com. in two parts, by Richard Edwards. These are very old pieces, being published together with the author's songs, &c. in 1585. The story of them is professedly taken from Chaucer's celebrated poem of *The Knight's Tale*. Queen Elizabeth's observations on the persons of the last-mentioned piece, deserve notice; as they are at once a curious picture of the romantic pedantry of the times, and of the characteristical turn and predominant propensities of her majesty's mind. When the play was over, she summoned the poet

into

Into her presence, whom she loaded with thanks and compliments: and at the same time turning to her levee remarked, that Palamon was so justly drawn as a lover, that he certainly must have been in love indeed: that Arcite was *a right martial knight, having a swart and manly countenance*, yet with the aspect of a Venus clad in armour: that the lovely Emilia was a virgin of uncorrupted purity and unblemished simplicity; and that although she sung so sweetly, and gathered flowers alone in the garden, she preserved her chastity undeflowered. The part of Emilia, the only female part in the play, was acted by a boy of fourteen years of age, a son of the Dean of Christ-Church, habited like a young princess; whose performance so captivated her majesty, that she gave him a present of eight guineas.

6. PAMELA. A Comedy. As it is performed gratis at the late Theatre in Goodman's Fields, 8vo. 1742. The late Mr. Love of Drury-Lane Theatre was author of this play, but it does little credit to his memory. It may be observed, however, that *Jack Smatter*, a foppish character in it, was performed by —— *a gentleman*. That gentleman was Mr. Garrick, who, during the infancy of his genius and his art, is said to have written the character he represented.

7. PAMELA, or, *Virtue rewarded*. Com. Anonymous, 1742. This play is on the same plan with the foregoing one, but much worse executed, and was never acted at all.

8. PAMELA. Com. by Carlo Goldoni, 8vo. 1757. This piece is founded entirely on the celebrated novel of that title, written by Mr. S. Richardson. The original is in Italian, and a translation in English is printed with it page for page. The language of the former, however, is mere dialogue, entirely undramatical, and little more than a recapitulation of scenes infinitely better related in the novel itself; and as for the translation, it is still more flat and insipid than the original. They are printed with the *Father of a Family* above-mentioned.

9. PAN AND SYRINX. Opera, of one act, by Lewis Theobald, 8vo. 1717. Set to music by Mr. Galliard, and performed in Lincoln's-Inn Fields. For the story consult Ovid's *Metamorphoses*, Book 1. Fab. 12.

10. PAN's ANNIVERSARIE, or, *The Shepherd's Holiday*. A Masque, by Ben Jonson, Fol. 1640. presented at Court before King James, 1625. The author was assisted in the decorations of this, as well as of some other of his masques, by that ingenious and celebrated architect Inigo Jones.

11. PANDORA, or, *The Conquests*. Tragi-Com. by Sir William Killigrew, 8vo. 1664. Fo. 1666. Scene, in Syracuse.

12. PANDORA. Com. translated from Voltaire, and printed in Dr. Franklin's edition of that author.

13. THE PANTHEONITES. Dramatical Entertainment, by Francis Gentleman. Acted at the Haymarket, 8vo. 1773.

14. PAPAL TYRANNY IN THE REIGN OF KING JOHN. Trag. by C. Cibber. Acted at Covent-Garden, 8vo. 1744. This play is not an alteration from Shakspeare, though founded on the same portion of the English history as his King John; nor is it by any means so good a play as his; although, had that author never had existence, this might very well have passed as a good one among the

course of modern tragedies. The author, after having for several years quitted the stage, once more launched forth into public character in the part of Pandulph the Pope's nuncio in this piece, which he had probably written with a view to his own manner of acting; and notwithstanding his great age, being then about seventy-three, and the loss of several of his teeth, whereby his articulation must necessarily have been greatly injured, yet a grace and dignity appeared in his attitudes, action, and general deportment, which could not fail inspiring a reverential awe for this valuable and valued veteran of the stage, who, worn out in the service of the public, seemed on this occasion to endeavour at convincing the town how warmly, to the very last moment of life, his zeal excited him to contribute as much as his exhausted powers would permit, towards their entertainment, both in the light of a writer and a performer. And, indeed, an equal inclination seemed apparent in the audience to reward this zeal by the highest encouragement both to the author and his piece.

15. THE PARASIDE, or, *Revenge for Honour*. By Henry Glapthorne. A play with this title was entered on the books of the Stationers' Company Nov. 29, 1653; but, I believe, not printed.

16. THE PARASITE. Com. translated from Plautus by Richard Warner, and printed in his edition of that author, 8vo. 1773.

17. PARASITASTER, or, *The Fawn*. Com. by John Marston. Acted at Black-Friers by the children of the Revels, 4to. 1606. The scene of this play is laid in Urbino, and part of the plot, viz. that of Dulcimel's imposing on the duke by a pretended d scovery of Tiberio's love to her, is borrowed from the story told by Philomena in Boccace's *Decameron*, Dec. 3. Nov. 3. as also the disposition of Nymphadoro of a general love for the whole fair sex from Ovid. *Amor.* Lib. 2. Eleg. 4.

18. THE PARLIAMENT OF BEES, with their proper characters, or a beehive furnished with twelve honey-combs, as pleasant as profitable, being an allegorical description of the actions of good and bad men in these our daies. A Masque, by John Daye, 4to. 1640. This piece is interred in all the old Catalogues as a species of play, but is indeed nothing more than a conversation between twelve characters, or colloquists, in rhyme.

19. THE PARLIAMENT OF LOVE. Com. by William Rowley. Entered on the books of the Stationers' Company, June 29, 1660, and was among those destroyed by Mr. Warburton's servant.

20. THE PARRICIDE. Trag. by J. Sterling. Acted at Goodman's Fields, 8vo. 1736.

21. THE PARRICIDE, or, *Innocence in Distress*. Trag. by William Shirley, 8vo. 1739. This play was acted at Covent-Garden Theatre; and from the dedication to John Rich, Esq; appears to have met with a very unjustifiable opposition the single time it was performed. Scene, a Village in Kent.

22. THE PARSON'S WEDDING. Com. by Thomas Killigrew, Fol. 1664. This play was revived with considerable success at the Theatre in Lincoln's-Inn Fields, and acted entirely by women. The scene lies in London; and the plot, made use of by Careless and Wild to circumvent Lady Wild and Mrs. Pleasance into marriage, seems borrowed from like circumstances

in the Antiquary and Ram-Alley. The author has, however, made good use of his theft, having conducted his Denouement in a more pleasing manner than in either of the other two plays.

23. PARTHENIA, or, *The Lost Shepherdess.* An Arcadian Drama, 8vo. 1764.

24. THE PARTHIAN EXILE. Trag. by George Downing. Acted at Coventry and Worcester, 8vo. 1774.

25. THE PARTHIAN HERO. Trag. by Matthew Gardiner, 8vo. 1741. Of this I know nothing more than the mention of it in the *British Theatre.* It was never acted in London; but it is not improbable that it might be both represented and published in Dublin.

26. PASQUIN. A Dramatic Satire on the Times, by Henry Fielding. Acted at the Hay-Market, 8vo. 1736. This piece contained several very severe satirical reflections on the ministry, which being taken notice of, as well as some others, in a succeeding play of the same author, and performed at the same house, were the occasion of a bill being brought into the house of commons for limiting the number of playhouses, and restraining the liberty of the stage.

27. OF THE PASSION OF CHRYST. Two Comedies. These two pieces are by Bishop Bale, and only mentioned in his own list of his works.

28. THE PASSIONATE LOVERS. Tragi-Com. by Lodowick Carlell, in two parts. Twice acted before the King and Queen at Somerset-House, and afterwards at Black-Friers, 4to. 1655. 8vo. 1655. Scene, Burgony and Neuftrea.

29. IL PASTOR FIDO. or, *The Faithful Shepherd,* translated out of Italian into English. 4to. 1602. 12mo. 1633. By Mr. Dymock. Prefixed to the 4to. edition are verses by Samuel Daniel to Sir Edward Dymock, who is called Kinsman of the Translator; and a Dedication to the same gentleman by the publisher Simon Waterson, in which Mr. Dymock is spoken of as then dead. The 12mo. edition is dedicated by John Waterson to Charles Dymock, Esq; son of the gentleman who translated the piece.

30. IL PASTOR FIDO, or, *The Faithful Shepherd.* A Pastoral, by Sir R. Fanshaw, 4to. 1647. This is only a translation of Guarini's celebrated pastoral of that name, written originally on occasion of the young duke of Savoy, Charles Emanuel's marriage with the infanta of Spain. The scene lies in Arcadia. Prefixed to it are verses by Sir John Denham.

31. PASTOR FIDO, or, *The Faithful Shepherd,* Pastoral, by Elk. Settle, 4to. 1677. 4to. 1694. This is nothing more than the foregoing translation somewhat altered and improved, and adapted to the stage. It was performed at the Duke of York's Theatre.

32. PATHOMACHIA, or, *The Battle of Affections, shadowed by a feigned Siege of the Citie of Pathopolis.* Com. Anonymous, 4to. 1630. The running title of this piece is *Love's Loadstone.* Who the author of it was I know not, but it was not published till some time after his death, by Fr. Constable, the bookseller.

33. PATIE AND PEGGY, or, *The Fair Foundling.* A Scotch Ballad Opera, by Theophilus Cibber. Acted at Drury-Lane, 8vo. 1730. This is Ramsay's *Gentle Shepherd,* reduced into one act; and *The Scotch Dialect* translated, with the addition of new songs. The author says it was planned and finished in one day.

34. PA-

34. PATIENT GRISELE. Com. by Ralph Radcliff. Not printed.

35. PATIENTE GRIZZELE. C. Anonymous, 1603. The plot of this piece is founded on Boccace's Novels, Dec. 10. Nov. 10. The story is also to be found very finely told in a poem, called *Gualtherus and Grisalda*, which is a translation or modernized versification of one of Chaucer's *Canterbury Tales*. This piece was entered, by Cuthbert Burby, on the books of the Stationers' Company March 28, 1600.

36. THE PATRIOT, or, *The Italian Conspiracy*. Trag. by C. Gildon. Acted at Drury-Lane, 4to. 1703. This play is taken from Lee's *Lucius Junius Brutus*. Prologue by Dennis; epilogue by Farquhar. Scene, Florence.

37. THE PATRIOT, being a dramatic History of the Life and Death of William the first Prince of Orange, founder of the Republick of Holland, 4to. 1740.

38. THE PATRIOT. Trag. by W. Harrod, 8vo. 1769.

39. THE PATRIOT KING, or, *The Irish Chief*. Trag. by Francis Dobbs. Acted at Smock-Alley, Dublin, 8vo. 1774. This play had been rejected both at Drury-Lane and Covent-Garden.

40. PATRIOTISM. Farce. Acted by his Majesty's servants, 8vo. 1763. Despicable political nonsense.

41. THE PATRON, or, *The Statesman's Opera*, of two acts, by Thomas Odell, 8vo. [1729.] Acted at the Little Theatre in the Hay-Market. N. D.

42. THE PATRON. A Comedy of three acts, performed at the Hay-Market, 8vo. 1764. The hint borrowed from one of Marmontel's Tales. The character of the patron, said to be Lord Melcombe, is that of a superficial pretender to wit and learning, who, being a man of fashion and fortune, affords his countenance and protection to a set of contemptible witlings, for the sake of the incense offered by them to his vanity. The character of a mere antiquarian, a favourite object of ridicule with Mr. Foote, is here introduced with great pleasantry, Mr. Rust having fallen in love with a fine young lady, because he thought the tip of her ear resembled that of the princess Poppæa. Sir Peter Pepperpot, a rich West-India merchant, comes in likewise, with his account of barbecues and turtle-feasts; and a miserable poet, with a low Moorfields bookseller, serve to complete the entertainment. Mr. Foote, in a dedication to Lord Gower, speaks of this piece as the best in his own estimation that he had then written.

43. PAUL THE SPANISH SHARPER. Farce, of two acts, by James Wetherbey, 8vo. 1730. Never acted.

44. PAUSANIAS, THE BETRAYER OF HIS COUNTRY. Trag. 4to. 1696. This play was brought on the stage by Mr. Southern, who in the dedication informs his patron that it was put into his hands by a person of quality. We find, by Dr. Garth's *Dispensary*, that Mr. Norton was the author of it. The story of it may be found in Plutarch. The scene is laid in Lacedæmon, and the piece built on the model of the antients, and written according to the reformation of the French stage.

45. THE PEDLER. Com. by Robert Davenport. It was entered on the books of the Stationers' Company, by Mr. Allott, April 8, 1630; but, I believe, not printed.

46. THE

46. THE PEDLER'S PROPHECIE. Com. Anonymous, 4to. 1595. This is rather an interlude than a regular play. It is very old, and undivided into acts.

47. A PEEP BEHIND THE CURTAIN, or, *The New Rehearsal*. Farce, by David Garrick, Esq. Acted at Drury-Lane, 8vo. 1767. This is a very pleasing entertainment, and received every advantage which it could derive from excellent acting. It contains several temporary allusions to the then state of the theatres, which met with approbation from the public.

48. PELEUS AND THETIS. A Masque, by Lord LANSDOWNE. See JEW OF VENICE.

49. PENELOPE. A Farce, by Thomas Cocke and John Mottley, 8vo. 1728. Almost the whole first act of this piece was written by the last-named author some years before the other gentleman had any hand in it, or had ever seen it. It is a mock-tragedy, and was probably intended as no more than a burlesque drama without any particular aim. But as it was brought on the stage soon after the publication of Mr. Pope's translation of the *Odyssey* of Homer, that gentleman considered it as a ridicule on his work, and has in consequence of that supposition treated Mr. Cooke somewhat severely as the author of it in his notes to the *Dunciad*. The piece, as a burlesque, is not without merit, but met with no success in the representation, from making its first appearance at the little French Theatre in the Hay-Market, and being performed by a most contemptible set of actors; by which means, exclusive of the enmity its subject drew on it, had by no means fair play with the public.

50. KING PEPIN'S CAMPAIGN. Burlesque Opera, by William Shirley. Acted at Drury-Lane 1745. Printed, 8vo. 1755.

51. PERCY. Trag. by Miss Hannah More. Acted at Covent-Garden, 8vo. 1778. This was a successful piece. The author, in an advertisement, says, that the French Drama founded on the story of Raoul de Coucy, suggested some circumstances in the former part of this tragedy.

52. THE PERFIDIOUS BROTHER. Trag. by Lewis Theobald. Acted at Lincoln's-Inn Fields, 4to. 1715. The model of this play is somewhat like that of the *Orphan*, the whole scene of it being laid in a private family at Bruffels. It appears to have been acted without success; and in the Preface the author attempts to vindicate himself from the charge of having borrowed it from Mr. Meflayer.

53. THE PERFIDIOUS BROTHER. Trag. by Henry Meftayer, 12mo. 1716. The author of this play, who was a watch-maker, complains, in a Dedication to Mr. Theobald, of that gentleman's purloining his piece from him, and getting it represented as his own.

54. PERIANDER KING OF CORINTH. Trag. by John Tracy, 8vo. 1731. This tragedy, though very far from a contemptible one, met with but middling success when performed at the Theatre in Lincoln's-Inn Fields. The plot is taken from well-known History. The late Dr. Ridley was present when this Tragedy was read at a tavern, where the author gave a magnificent supper on the occasion. The Doctor being asked how he and his brother critics liked the piece, he replied, that they were unanimous in praise of——the supper.

55. PE-

55. PERICLES PRINCE OF TYRE. Trag. by William Shakſpeare. Acted at the Globe, 4to. 1609. 4to. 1619. 4to. 1630. 4to. 1635. This is one of thoſe pieces which the editors of Shakſpeare's works have generally agreed to reject. The laſt publiſher, however, of this play, Mr. Malone, entertains a more favourable opinion of it, and declares himſelf thoroughly convinced, that if not the whole, at leaſt the greater part, of the Drama was written by Shakſpeare, into whoſe works he hopes to ſee it admitted in ſome future publication of them, inſtead of *Titus Andronicus*. The ſtory on which it is formed is of great antiquity. It is found in a book once very popular, intituled, *Geſta Romanorum*, which is ſuppoſed by the learned editor of *The Canterbury Tales of Chaucer*, 1775, to have been written five hundred years ago. One of the earlieſt editions of that work was printed in 1488, and therein the Hiſtory of *Appollonius, King of Tyre*, makes the 153d chapter. It is likewiſe related by Gower, in his *Confeſſio Amantis*, Lib. viii. p. 157—185. edit. 1554. There is alſo an ancient Romance on this ſubject, called *King Appolyn of Thyre*, tranſlated from the French by Robert Copland, and printed by Wynkin de Worde in 1510. As the author has introduced Gower in this piece, it is reaſonable to ſuppoſe that he chiefly followed the work of that poet.

56. THE PERJUR'D DEVOTEE, or, *Force of Love*. This is one of the pieces publiſhed under the title of a volume of Miſcellanies in 8vo. 1716, by Meſſrs. Daniel Bellamy, ſen. and jun. of which, however, none were brought on the ſtage.

57. THE PERJUR'D HUSBAND, or, *The Adventures of Venice*. Trag. by Mrs. Centlivre. Acted at Drury-Lane, 4to. 1700. This is the firſt of this lady's attempts for the Drama; and although her writings afterwards took the comic turn for the moſt part, yet both this piece and the *Cruel Gift* ſhew her very capable of making a figure in the ſervice of the Tragic Muſe. The ſcene lies at Venice in Carnival Time.

58. THE PERJUROR. Farce, of one act, by Chriſtopher Bullock, 8vo. 1717. Acted at Lincoln's-Inn Fields. The ſcene of this little piece lies in a Country Market-Town, and the deſign, if it has any, ſeems to be to point out the colluſions and combinations that are or may be carried on between ill-deſigning juſtices of the peace, and the conſtables and other officers whom they employ under them, to the great injury of the rights of the ſubject and of public juſtice in general. It is, however, a very poor performance.

59. PERKIN WARBECK, the chronicle Hiſtory of. A Strange Truth, by John Ford. Acted at the Phœnix, Drury-Lane, 4to. 1634. 12mo. 1714. This is not a bad play. It is founded on the Hiſtory of that ſtrange Pretender to the crown, who ſet himſelf up, and cauſed himſelf to be proclaimed king of England, declaring himſelf to be Richard duke of York, brother to Edward V. who loſt his life in the Tower, as may be ſeen in the Engliſh Hiſtorians of the reign of Henry VII. Scene, England.

60. PERULLA AND IZADORA. Trag. by C. Cibber. Acted at the Theatre Royal, 4to. No date, [1706]. As this author's *Taſte* was very far from lying in the tragic ſtrain of writing, it is not to be wondered at that this play, together

together with some others of his tragedies, have been entirely set aside from the theatre, and even forgot in the closet, since the period of their first appearance. In the Dedication to Charles, earl of Orrery, the author makes his acknowledgments for the assistance he received from that nobleman; by means of which, he says, the play reached the sixth day.

61. THE PERPLEX'D COUPLE, or, *Mistake upon Mistake*. Com. by Charles Molloy. Acted at Lincoln's-Inn Fields, 12mo. 1715. This play is for the most part borrowed from Moliere's *Cocu Imaginaire*; which indeed has been the foundation of several other English dramatic pieces.

62. THE PERPLEX'D LOVERS. Com. by Mrs. Centlivre. Acted at Drury-Lane, 4to. 1712. The greatest part of the plot of this play is, by the author's own confession, borrowed from a Spanish play, the name of which however she has not informed us of. The scene lies in London; the time from five in the evening to eight in the morning.

63. THE PERPLEXITIES. Com. by Thomas Hull. Acted at Covent-Garden, 8vo. 1767. This is only an alteration from Sir Samuel Tuke's *Adventures of Five Hours*; and, like most other comedies of Spanish origin, is a chaos of balconies, cloaks, rapiers, and dark lanthorns. Mr. Beard both spoke and sung in the prologue to it, a circumstance as worthy of record as the piece itself.

64. THE PERSIAN PRINCESS, or, *The Royal Villain*. Trag. by Lewis Theobald. Acted at Drury-Lane, 12mo. 1715. 4to. 1717. The author, in his preface to this play, asserts it to have been written and acted before he was full nineteen years of age. The plot of it, notwithstanding the title, seems to be entirely invention, there being no incident in the Persian History from which the story appears in the least to be borrowed.

65. THE PERSIAN. Com. translated from Plautus by Richard Warner, and printed in the fifth volume of that gentleman's edition, 8vo. 1774.

66. THE PERSIANS. Trag. translated from Æschylus by R. Potter, 4to. 1777.

67. PERSEUS AND ANDROMEDA, *with the Rape of Columbine*, or, *The Flying Lovers*, in five Interludes; three serious, and two comic. The serious composed by Monsieur Roger, and the comic by John Weaver, dancing-masters. Acted at Drury-Lane, 8vo. 1728.

68. PERSEUS AND ANDROMEDA. Pantomime. Acted at Lincoln's-Inn Fields, 4to. 1730. This is the same performance as hath frequently been represented at Covent-Garden, and was probably the production of Lewis Theobald.

69. THE PETTICOAT PLOTTER. Farce, of two acts, by Newburgh Hamilton, 12mo. 1720, performed at the Theatre Royal in Drury-Lane and Lincoln's-Inn Fields.

70. THE PETTICOAT PLOTTER, or, *More Ways than one for a Wife*. A Farce, of two acts, by Henry Ward, performed at York, 8vo. 1746.

71. PHÆBE. Pastoral Opera, by Dr. John Hoadly, set to music by Dr. Greene, 8vo. 1748.

72. PHÆDRA. Trag. translated from Corneille, 8vo. 1776.

73. PHÆDRA AND HIPPOLITUS. Trag. translated from Seneca, by Sir Edward Sherburne, 8vo. 1701.

74. PHÆDRA AND HIPPOLITUS,

TUS. Trag. by Edmund Smith. Acted at the Hay-Market, 4to. no date. [1707.] This play, as Dr. Johnson observes, pleased the critics, and the critics only. It was hardly heard the third night. Addison, in *The Spectator*, mentions this neglect of it as disgraceful to the nation, and imputes it to the fondness for operas then prevailing. The authority of Addison is great; yet the voice of the people, when to please the people is the purpose, deserves regard. In this question, I cannot but think the people right. The fable is mythological, a story which we are accustomed to reject as false, and the manners are so distant from our own, that we know them not by sympathy but by study: the ignorant do not understand the action, the learned reject it as a school-boy's tale; *incredulus odi*. What I cannot for a moment believe, I cannot for a moment behold with interest or anxiety. The sentiments, thus remote from life, are removed yet further by the diction, which is too luxuriant and splendid for dialogue, and envelopes the thoughts rather than displays them. It is a scholar's play, such as may please the reader rather than the spectator; the work of a vigorous and elegant mind, accustomed to please itself with its own conceptions, but of little acquaintance with the course of life.

75. PHÆDRA AND HIPPOLITUS. Opera, composed by Mr. Thomas Roseingrave, 8vo. 1753. Printed at Dublin. This piece (strange as it may seem) is no other than the foregoing tragedy by Mr. Smith, turned into an opera by abbreviation, and the addition of songs. It does not appear to have been acted.

76. PHÆNISSÆ. Trag. transl-

lated from Euripides; printed with three other pieces of the same author, 8vo. 1780.

77. PHAETON, or, *The Fatal Divorce*. Trag. by Charles Gildon, 4to. 1698. This play is written in imitation of the ancients, was acted at the Theatre Royal, and met with good success. The plot, and a great many of the beauties of it, the author himself owns to have been taken from the *Medea* of Euripides, and he has evidently made use of many hints from the French play of *Phaeton*. The scene is in a Grove and adjoining temple in the Land of Egypt. To it is annexed some reflections on Collier's Short View of the Immorality and Prophaneness of the Stage.

78. A PHANATIC PLAY. First Part, presented before and by the Lord Fleetwood, Sir Arthur Haslerig, Sir Henry Fane, Lord Lambert, and others, with Master Jester and Master Pudding, 4to. 1660. It consists but of one scene. This, by its title, I should imagine to be a party play, probably intended just at the period of the Restoration to ridicule and expose the Roundheads. I have never seen it, nor do I find it mentioned by any of the writers but Jacob; from whom, and Coxeter's MS. note on him, I have selected the full title I have here inserted.

79. PHARNACES. Opera, altered from the Italian, by Thomas Hull. Acted at Drury-Lane, 8vo. 1765.

80. THE PHOENIX. Tragi-Com. by Thomas Middleton. Acted by the children of Paul's, 4to. 1607. 4to. 1630. This is a good play. The plot of it is taken from a Spanish novel, called *The Force of Love*; and the scene is laid in Ferrara.

81. PHOENIX IN HER FLAMES. Trag. by Sir W. Lower, 4to. 1639. Scene, Arabia. Langbaine supposes this to have been the author's first attempt, it having been written before he was knighted.

82. PHILANDER. A Dramatic Pastoral, by Mrs. Lennox, 8vo. 1758. A piece not intended, nor indeed of merit sufficient, for the stage.

83. PHILASTER, or, *Love lies a Bleeding*. Tragi-Com. by Beaumont and Fletcher, 4to. 1622. This was the first piece that brought these afterwards most justly celebrated authors into any considerable estimation, and is even now considered as one of the most capital of their plays. It was presented at the Old Theatre in Lincoln's-Inn Fields, when the women acted by themselves; a circumstance recorded by Mr. Dryden, who wrote a prologue for them, which may be found among his *Miscellany Poems*. The scene lies in Cilicia.

84. PHILASTER, or, *Love lies a Bleeding*. Tragi-Com. Acted at the Theatre Royal; revised, and the two last acts new-written, by Elkanah Settle, 4to. 1695.

85. PHILASTER. A Trag. by Beaumont and Fletcher. Acted at Drury-Lane, 8vo. 1763. The revival of this piece was greatly approved by the public; as Mr. Colman's alterations were extremely judicious. This play has been generally considered as one of the best produced by the twin-writers above-named; but, on account of the indecencies in some parts of it, hath been deemed unfit to appear before a modern audience. These blemishes and other improprieties being removed, the tragedy thus new-modelled was brought on, with this additional advantage, that Mr. Powell first appeared on the stage, in the representation thereof, in the character of Philaster. Mrs. Yates also displayed new graces on this occasion, and the editor's prologue has been both greatly admired and criticised. Of the former revivals of this play, we have already given an account.

86. PHILENZO AND HIPPOLITA. Tragi-Com. by Philip Massinger. Entered on the books of the Stationers' Company Sept. 9, 1653; and was among the number destroyed by Mr. Warburton's servant.

87. PHILETUS AND CONSTANTIA. This is one of six pieces supposed to be written by Robert Cox comedian, which are printed in the second part of *Sport upon Sport*, 1699. and in 4to. N. D.

88. PHILIP OF MACEDON. A Tragedy, by David Lewis. Acted at Lincoln's-Inn Fields, 8vo. 1727. That Mr. Pope, to whom this tragedy is dedicated, should have perused it throughout, may excite some astonishment in a reader who imposes the same task on himself. But what will he say, when he is told by the dedicator that the dedicatee did not only peruse but commend it? Certes, he will imagine that some partial kindness for the said David must at once have strengthened the patience and influenced the decision of the said Alexander. We know not otherwise (to borrow the words of the dedication) how "a per-
"formance like this could be ap-
"proved in all its parts by
'his discerning and consummate
"judgment." May we not, however, suppose that the smooth, insinuating oil of flattery will occasionally supple the toughest of the critic tribe?

89. PHILLIS AT COURT. Comic Opera, of three acts, performed at Crow-

Crow-street, Dublin, 8vo. 1767. This is an alteration of Lloyd's *Capricious Lovers*, new set to music by Giardini.

90. PHILOCLEA. Trag. by M'Namara Morgan. Acted at Covent-Garden, 8vo. 1754. This play is founded on part of Sir Philip Sidney's celebrated romance of the *Arcadia*, the same story which had been long before reduced into a tragedy by James Shirley. The piece before us is crowded with an immense number of absurdities both in language and plot, the first being alternately bombast and puerile, and the other incorrect, imperfect, and contradictory. Yet did this tragedy meet with better success than plays of much greater merit that appeared in that and some of the ensuing seasons. This success, however, may be in great measure attributed to the manner in which the more tender and sensible parts of the audience could not fail being affected by the passionate scenes of love in it, which gave so fine an opportunity for a display and exertion of fine figure, and tenderness of expression, in Mr. Barry and Miss Nossiter.

91. PHILOCTETES. Trag. translated from Sophocles, by Dr. Thomas Sheridan, 8vo. 1725. Printed at Dublin.

92. PHILOCTETES. Trag. translated from Sophocles, by George Adams, 8vo. 1729.

93. PHILOCTETES. Trag. translated from Sophocles, by Dr. Thomas Franklin, 4to. 1759.

94. PHILODAMUS. Trag. by Thomas Bentley, Esq. 4to. 1767. It is said, in The Biographia Brittannica, vol. II. p. 247. that this piece was esteemed, by the late Mr. Gray, as one of the most capital poems in the English language. Accordingly, say the same author, he wrote a laboured and elegant commentary upon it, which abounds with wit, and is one of his best productions. It is to be lamented that this work is withheld from the public. The extraordinary merit ascribed to Mr. Bentley's piece is not very conspicuous in the perusal of it.

95. THE PHILOSOPHIC WHIM, or, *Astronomy*. Farce, by Dr. Hiffernan, 4to. 1774.

96. PHILOTAS. Trag. by Sam. Daniel, 4to. 1605. 4to. 1623. This play is esteemed a good one, but met with some opposition, not on account of any deficiency in the poetry or in the conduct of the design, but from a suspicion propagated by some of the author's enemies, that he meant to personalize, in the character of Philotas, that unfortunate favourite of queen Elizabeth's, the earl of Essex; which obliged him to enter on his vindication from that charge in an apology printed at the end of it. In this play, as well as in his tragedy of *Cleopatra*, he has shewn great judgment by treading in the steps of the ancients in the modelizing his fable and the working of his morals; the two principal, but frequently disregarded branches of tragedy. According to their manner also, he has introduced choruses between the acts.

97. PHILOTAS. Trag. by Philip Frowde, 8vo. 1731. This tragedy was acted at Lincoln's-Inn Fields Theatre, with very little success; yet I cannot help looking on it as a very admirable play. The characters of Clytus, Alexander, and Philotas, are very finely supported; those of Antigona and Cleora beautifully contrasted; the language bold and spirited, yet poetical and correct; the plot ingenious, and the catastrophe interesting.

ing. The design of this, as well as the foregoing play, is taken from Quintus Curtius and Justin, and the scenes of both are laid in Persia.

98. PHILOTUS. *Ane verie excellent and delectabill Treatise intitulit* Philotus. *Quhairin we may persave the greit inconveniences that falles out in the mariage betwene age and zouth. Imprinted at Edingburgh be Robert Charteris. Cum privilegio regali.* 4to. 1603. 4to. 1612.

The names of the Interloquitors.
Philotus, the auld man.
The Plesant.
Emilie, the Madyn.
The Macrell.
Alberto, the Madynis father.
Flavius, ane zoung man.
Stephano, Albertois servant.
Philerno, Albertois sone.
Brisilla, Philotus his Dochter.
The Minister.
The Huir.
The Messinger.

The piece concludes thus:

"Lest, Sirs, now let us pray with ane accord,
"For to preserve the persoun of our King,
"Accounting ay this gift as of the Lord,
"Ane prudent prince above us for to ring.
"Thanglair to God, and graithis let us sing,
"The Father, Sone, and Halie Gayst our
"gyde,
"Of his mercies us to conduct and bring
"To Hevin for ay, in pleisoures to abyde."

Here follows an advertisement of which the last line is cut off.

"The printer of this present Treatise hes (according to the Kings Majesties licence grantit to him) printit sindrie uther delectabill discourses undernamit, sic as are, Sir David Lyndesayis play, The Preistis of Pebles, with merie tailes ——"

This *delectabill treatise* is by far the most offensive drama ever produced, nor does it leave us room to suppose its author was at all superior in point of delicacy or decency to a Hottentot. The words so frequently scribbled in chalk on pales and shutters are here printed at full length; a sufficient proof of the barbarous state in which Scotland remained till civilized by its intercourse with England. As an additional support to our remark, we may add, that in one of the Scotch libraries there is a MS. comedy by Sir David Lindsay. In the course of this performance, a husband being resolved to ensure the fidelity of his wife, applies a padlock to her on the stage. The same couple complete the ceremony of their final separation, by kissing each other's posteriors.

To the play of *Philotus* the figures of *Justice* and *Religion*, with sacred mottoes, are prefixed, as if the author, or editor, was determined to match his obscenity with an equal degree of profaneness.

99. PHORMIO. Com. by Rich. Bernard, 4to. 1598. This is only a translation from Terence, with some critical and useful notes, and additions for the use of learners. This play has been also translated by Hoole, Patrick, Echard, Cooke, Gordon, and Colman, but never brought on the stage in its own form, although two very celebrated poets, viz. Moliere among the French, and Otway among the English writers, have made great use of the plot in their respective comedies of the tricks of Scapin.

100. PHYSICK LIES A BLEEDING, or, *The Apothecary turned Doctor*, Com. Acted every day in most apothecaries shops in London, by Thomas Brown, 4to. 1698.

101. THE PICTURE. Tragi-Com. by Ph. Massinger. Acted at the Globe and Black-Friers, 4to. 1630. This play met with good success, and indeed very deservedly, it having great merit. The entire

tire plot, incidents, &c. are taken from the 28th Novel of the second volume of *Painter's Palace of Pleasure*, intituled, *A Lady of Boeme*, p. 292. edit. 1567. It was performed by Lowin, Taylor, Benfield, and all the most capital performers of that age, whose names are opposite their respective parts.

102. THE PICTURE, or, *The Cuckold in Conceit*. A Ballad Opera, 8vo. 1745. This piece was written by James Miller, and was acted at Drury-Lane, after the death of the author. It is taken from the *Cocu Imaginaire* of Moliere.

103. PIETY AND VALOUR, or, *Derry defended*. Tragi-Com. Anonymous, 1692. This play I find no where mentioned but in *The British Theatre*, and as it is of the same date with a tragi-comedy, called, *The Siege of Derry*, and that is not very frequent to see two plays on the same subject (though this, indeed, was at that time a very popular one), I think it not improbable that these might be only two editions of the same piece, or perhaps (which has not been an uncommon practice) the same edition vamped up with a new title-page, in hopes to quicken the heavy and slow sale of a very indifferent performance, which lay on the bookseller's hands.

104. PIETY IN PATTINS. Farce, by Samuel Foote, Esq. Acted at the Hay-market, 1773. This piece was first introduced to the stage in an entertainment, called, *The Primitive Puppet-Shew*.

105. PIGMY REVELS. Pantomime. Acted at Drury-Lane, 1773.

106. THE PILGRIM. Com. by Beaumont and Fletcher, Fol. 1647. This is a very good play, and met with approbation on its first appearance; besides which, it was in the year 1700, altered and revived by Sir John Vanbrugh at the Theatre Royal in Drury-Lane, with a new prologue and epilogue, and a secular masque, by Mr. Dryden, being the last of that great poet's works, and written a very little before his death. Yet do they stand as a proof, with how strong a brilliancy his poetic fires glowed even to the last. The prologue is pointed with great severity against Sir Richard Blackmore, who, though by no means a first-rate poet, yet I cannot help thinking deserving of more immortality, than either the envy or ill-nature of his brother wits have, by their ridicule on his works, permitted the prejudices of mankind, ever easily led aside by what they imagine a superior judgment, to grant him. This comedy, however, when revived about thirty years ago, together with the secular masque, by the managers of Drury-Lane Theatre, though very well, nay, in some of the characters, very greatly performed, did not meet with the applause it might reasonably have expected. Such is the difference of taste at different periods.

107. THE PILGRIM. Trag. by Thomas Killigrew, Fol. 1664. This play was written at Paris 1651, while the author was on his travels. The scene, Millain.

108. THE PILGRIMS, or, *The Happy Converts*. A dramatic entertainment, by W. Harrison, 4to. 1701. This was never acted, yet is very far from being totally devoid of merit. The scene is laid in London.

109. THE PILGRIMAGE TO PARNASSUS. Com. by the author of *The Return to Parnassus*. This play was never printed, but is mentioned by Mr. Malone as having once existed.

110. THE PIRATE. A play by Robert

Robert Davenport. Not printed. See Mr. Malone's Attempt to ascertain the dates of Shakspeare's Plays, p. 331.

111. PISO'S CONSPIRACY. Trag. Anonym. 4to. 1676. Acted at the Duke's Theatre. This is no more than the *Tragedy of* NERO, printed with a new title.

112. PITTY THE MAID. Play, entered on the books of the Stationers' Company, Nov. 29, 1653, but not printed.

113. THE PLAGUE OF RICHES, or, *L'Embarras des Richesses*. Com. French and English, 8vo. 1735. This is only a translation by Ozell of a French comedy, but never intended for the stage.

114. THE PLAIN DEALER. Com. by W. Wycherley. Acted at the Theatre Royal, 4to. 1676. 4to. 1677. 4to. 1678. 4to. 1681. 4to. 1691. 4to. 1702. This play is looked upon as the most capital of our author's pieces, and indeed Dryden has given it the character of being the boldest, most general, and most useful satire, that was ever presented on the English stage. The plot, however, and particularly the two most principal characters in it, viz. Manly and Olivia, seem in some measure borrowed from the *Misantrope* of Moliere, as does also that of Major Oldfox from Scarron's *City Romance*. Yet, notwithstanding, he is scarcely to be condemned for these little thefts, since he has applied them to so noble an use, and so greatly improved on his originals. The character of Lord Plausible is said to have been intended for George Lord Berkeley, who was created Earl of Berkeley by King Charles II. a nobleman of strict virtue and piety, and of the most undistinguished affability to men of all ranks and parties. Scene, London.

115. THE PLAIN DEALER. Com. by Isaac Bickerstaffe. Acted at Drury-Lane, 8vo. 1766. In this alteration from Wycherley's comedy with the same title, the principal character is wretchedly mutilated. Much of his manly satire is omitted, while all his misanthropy is preserved.

116. THE PLATONICK LADY. Com. by Mrs. Centlivre. Acted at the Hay-Market, 4to. 1707. This is not one of her best plays, and is now never acted. The Prologue was written by Captain George Farquhar. The scene, London.

117. THE PLATONIC LOVERS. A Tragi-Com. by Sir W. Davenant. Acted at Black-Friers, 4to. 1636. Scene, Sicilia.

118. THE PLATONIC WIFE. Com. by Mrs. Griffiths. Acted at Drury-Lane, 8vo. 1765. The hint of this drama was taken from one of the *Contes Moraux* of Marmontel, styled *L'Heureux Divorce*. It met with little success, being acted only six nights.

119. THE PLAY OF CARDS. This play was never printed. It is, however, mentioned by Mr. Malone, in his Attempt, &c. p. 331.

120. A PLAY *betwene* JOHAN *the Husband*, TYB *the Wife*, and *Sir* JOHAN *the Priest*, by John Heywood, 4to. *Imprynted at London by William Rastall, the* XII *Day of February*, 1533. This piece, and some others of this author's, which we shall presently have occasion to speak of, are mentioned in *The Museum Ashmoleanum*. They are printed in the old black letter, written in metre, and not divided into acts, and are, I believe, some of the earliest, if not the very earliest, dramatic pieces printed in London.

121. A PLAY *betwene the* Pardoner

doner *and the* Fiere, *the* Curate, *and Neybour* Pratte. An Interlude, by John Heywood. *Imprynted by Wyllyam Rastall*, 5th of April, 1533. Black letter, 4to. See Ames, 182.

122. A PLAYHOUSE TO BE LET. A Com. by Sir W. Davenant, Fol. 1673. This piece is only an assemblage of several little detached pieces in the dramatic way, written in the time of Oliver Cromwell, and during the prohibition of theatrical representations. These are connected with one another by the addition of a first act by way of introduction, each act afterwards being a separate piece, viz. the second is a translation of Moliere's *Cocu Imaginaire*, purposely thrown into a kind of jargon or broken English, like that spoken by Frenchmen who have not been long in England. The third and fourth acts are tragical, or rather a species of Opera, representing, by vocal and instrumental music, and by the art of perspective in scenes, the History of Sir Francis Drake, &c. and the cruelty of the Spaniards in Peru: and the fifth a tragedie travestie, or farce in burlesque verse, on the actions of Cæsar, Antony, and Cleopatra. The last of these pieces was also performed separately at the Theatre in Dorset Gardens, by way of Farce, after the Tragedy of *Pompey*, written by Mrs. Katherine Philips.

123. PLYMOUTH IN AN UPROAR. Com. Op. by Mr. Neville. Acted at Covent-Garden, 8vo. 1779. A temporary trifling performance, occasioned by the alarm excited at Plymouth, on the appearance of the French Fleet before that place in the summer of 1779.

124. THE PLAY IS THE PLOT. Com. by John Durant Breval. Acted at Drury-Lane, 4to. 1718. This play the author himself confesses to be meer farce, and it consequently met with but indifferent success. Part of it seems to be translated from some of the French Interludes in the *Theatre Italien*. The scene lies at a village in Bedfordshire.

125. A PLAY *of* Gentilness *and* Nobilitie. An Interlude, in two parts, by John Heywood, 4to. This has no date, but is, I suppose, about 1535.

126. A PLAY OF LOVE. An Interlude, by John Heywood, 4to. 1533.

127. A PLAY *of the Weather*, called, *A new and very merry Interlude of all Manner of Weathers*, by John Heywood, Fol. 1533. These three last pieces, with the two mentioned above, and the four P's, make up the whole of the dramatic works of this author, who was the second writer whose dramatic works were printed. An edition of this play was printed by Robert Wyer, in 12mo. See Ames, 157.

128. THE PRINCELY PLEASURES AT KENNELWORTH CASTLE. A Masque, in prose and rhime, by George Gascoigne, 4to. 1575. This is a relation of the entertainment given to Queen Elizabeth at Kenelworth, by Robert Dudley, Earl of Leicester, on the 9th, 10th, and 11th of July, 1575.

129. PLEASURE RECONCIL'D TO VIRTUE. A Masque, by Ben Jonson, presented at Court before King James I. 1619; with an additional masque *for the Honour of Wales*, in which the scene is changed from the Mountain Atlas as before to Craig-Eriri. This latter part is mentioned in some of the catalogues, but erroneously, as a distinct piece of itself.

130. THE PLOT. A Pantomimical

mical Entertainment, 8vo. 1735. This piece was acted at Drury-Lane.

131. A PLOT AND NO PLOT. Com. by J. Dennis. Acted at Drury-Lane, 4to. No date [1697]. This play was intended by its author as a satire upon the credulity of the *Jacobite* party of those days. It is extremely regular, and bears testimony in favour of the writer, not only as a man of wit, but as a perfect master of the arts of the stage, and of the strict rules of the drama.

132. THE PLOTTING LOVERS, or, *The Dismal Squire*. Farce, by Charles Shadwell, 12mo. 1720. This piece was acted in Dublin. It is a translation, with liberty, of Moliere's *Monf. de Pourceaugnac*, that is to say, that whole play of three acts is reduced into one, every incident and humourous passage of any consequence, however, being preserved in it. The scene, Dublin, the time one hour.

133. PLUTO FURENS ET VINCTUS, or, *The Raging Devil bound*. A Modern Farce, 4to. 1669. Dedicated to Sir John James, Sir William Greene, Sir Samuel Starlyn, Sir John Forth, sheriff of London, John Breden, John Bucknall, aldermen, Emery Hill, Esq; with the rest of the worshipful Corporation of Brewers. The title says it was printed at Amsterdam.

134. PLUTUS, or, *The World's Idol*. by Lewis Theobald, 12mo. 1715. This is only a translation from the Greek of Aristophanes, with notes, and a discourse prefixed containing some account of Aristophanes, and his two comedies of *Plutus* and the *Clouds*. It was not intended for the stage.

135. PLUTUS THE GOD OF RICHES. 8vo. 1742. This is another translation of the same piece, executed jointly by Mr. Henry Fielding and the Reverend Mr. Young, being designed as a specimen of a proposed complete translation of all the comedies of Aristophanes by those two ingenious gentlemen, for which they delivered proposals, but which were never carried into execution.

136. POETASTER, or, *The Arraignment*. Comical Satyr, by Ben Jonson. Acted by the children of the Queen's Chapel, in 1601. 4to. 1602. This piece is a satire on the poets of that age, more particularly Decker, who is severely lashed under the title of *Crispinus*, yet has very spiritedly returned it in his *Satyromastix*. It is adorned with many translations from Horace, Virgil, Ovid, and others of the antient poets, whom Ben Jonson was on every occasion fond of shewing to the world his intimate acquaintance with.

137. ΠΟΙΚΙΛΟΦΡΟΝΗΣΙΣ, or, *The Different Humours of Men*, represented in an Interlude *at a Country School*, Dec. 15, 1691, by Samuel Shaw, 8vo. 1692.

138. THE POLITE GAMESTER, or, *The Humours of Whist*. Dram. Satire, 8vo. 1753. This is a republication of *The Humours of Whist*.

139. THE POLITIC BANKRUPT, or, *Which is the best Girl*. Comedy. Entered on the books of the Stationers' Company Sept. 9, 1653; but, I believe, not printed.

140. THE POLITIC QUEEN, or, *Murther will out*. By Robert Davenport. This play was entered on the books of the Stationers' Company June 29, 1660; but, I believe, not printed.

141. THE POLITICAL REHEARSAL. HARLEQUIN LE GRAND, or, *The Tricks of Pierrot le Premier*, &c. Tragi, comic, pantomimical Performance, of two acts, 12mo. 1742.

142. THE

142. THE POLITIC WHORE, or, *The Conceited Cuckold.* Acted at New-Market, 4to. 1680. See *The Muse at New-Market.*

143. THE POLITICIAN. Trag. by James Shirley. Acted at the private house, Salisbury-Court, 4to. 1655. The scene of this play lies in Norway, and the plot seems borrowed from the story of the King of Romania, the Prince Antissus and his Mother-in-law, in the Countess of Montgomery's Urania.

144. THE POLITICIAN CHEATED. Com. by Alexander Greene, 4to. 1663. This play was printed at the time above-mentioned, but never made its appearance on the stage. The scene, in Spain.

145. THE POLITICIAN REFORMED. Drama, in one act, 8vo. 1774. This was published in "An appeal to the Public from "the Judgment of a certain Ma- "nager (Mr. Garrick), with ori- "ginal Letters."

146. POLIDUS, or, *Distress'd Love.* Trag. by Moses Browne, 8vo. 1723. The author of this play seems to have been a very young gentleman, and indeed some such excuse is necessary to atone for its deficiencies. It was never acted at any of the regular theatres, but was performed by young gentlemen, for their diversion, at the private theatre in St. Alban's-street. Annexed to it, is a Farce, called, ALL BEDEVILLED, or, *The House in a Hurry,* by the same author, possessed of the same share of merit, and performed at the same time and place.

147. POLITICKS IN MINIATURE, or, *The Humours of Punch's Resignation.* Tragi, comic, farcical, operatical Puppet-Shew, 12mo. 1742. This piece, and *The Political Rehearsal,* were printed together. They are entirely political and temporary, and originally appeared in *The Westminster Journal.*

148. POLLY. An Opera, by John Gay, 4to. 1729. This is a second part of *The Beggar's Opera,* in which, according to a hint given in the last scene of the first part, Polly, Macheath, and some other of the characters, are transported to America. When every thing was ready, however, for a rehearsal of it at the Theatre Royal in Covent-Garden, a message was sent from the Lord Chamberlain, that *it was not allowed to be acted, but commanded to be suppressed.* What could be the reason of such a prohibition, it is not very easy to discover, unless we imagine it to have been by way of revenge for the numerous strokes of satire on the court, &c. which shone forth in the first part, or some private pique to the author himself; for the opera before us is so totally innocent of either satire, wit, plot, or execution, that, had not Mr. Gay declaredly published it as his, it would, I think, have been difficult to have persuaded the world that their favourite Polly could ever have so greatly degenerated from those charms which first brought them into love with her, or that the author of *The Beggar's Opera* was capable of so poor a performance as the piece before us. But this is frequently the case with second parts, undertaken by their authors in consequence of some extraordinary success of the first, wherein the writer, having before exhausted the whole of his intended plan, hazards, and often loses in a second attempt, for the sake of profit, all the reputation he had justly acquired by the first.

Yet notwithstanding this prohibition, the piece turned out very advantageous to Mr. Gay, for being
per-

persuaded to print it for his own emolument, the subscriptions and presents he met with on that occasion, from persons of quality and others, were so numerous and liberal, that he was imagined to make four times as much by it as he could have expected to have cleared by a very tolerable run of it on the stage.

149. POLLY HONEYCOMBE. A dramatic Novel, by George Colman, 8vo. 1760. This little piece was brought on the stage at Drury-lane house, and met with most amazing success. Its design is to expose the mischiefs which may arise to young girls from the fashionable taste of novel reading; but this is far from being rendered clear in the *Denouement*. Its greatest merit appears to be in the portrait of a ridiculous couple, who in the decline of life, and after having been for many years united, not only affect to keep up the fondness of a honeymoon, but are even perpetually shewing before company such a degree of fulsome tenderness to each other as not only renders them ridiculous in themselves, but disgusting and troublesome to all their friends and acquaintance.

150. POLLY. Opera, a'tered from Gay, by George Colman. Acted at the Hay-Market, 8vo. 1777. At the distance of near fifty years from its original publication, Mr. Colman ventured to produce this piece before the public, when it completely justified all the censures which had been passed upon it, being as insipid and uninteresting a performance as ever appeared on the English stage. After a few nights representation it sunk into its former obscurity, and will hardly be revived again. One circumstance deserves notice. The duchess of Queensberry, the patroness of the author and the piece, was still living, and, though extremely old, attended the performance several times before her death, which happened a few weeks afterwards.

151. POLYEUCTES, or, *The Martyr*. Trag. by Sir William Lower, 4to. 1655. The foundation which the story has in truth may be traced in Coeffeteau's *Hist. Rom.* in *Surius de Vitis Sanctorum*, &c. But the several incidents of Paulina's dream, the love of Severus, the baptism of Polyeuctes, the sacrifice for the Emperor's victory, the dignity of Felix, the death of Nearchus, and the conversion of Felix and Paulina, these, I say, are all the invention, and do honour to the abilities of the author. The scene lies in Felix's palace at Militene, the capital city of Armenia.

152. POMPEY. Trag. by Mrs. Katherine Philips, 4to. 1663. This play is a translation from the *Pompée* of Corneille, undertaken at the request of the earl of Orrery, and published in obedience to the commands of the countess of Corke, to whom, in consequence, it was dedicated by its fair and ingenious author. It was frequently presented with great applause, and at the end of it most commonly was acted the *Travestie*, or Mock Tragedy, which forms the fifth act of Sir W. Davenant's PLAY-HOUSE TO BE LET. Which see above.

153. POMPEY THE GREAT. Trag. by Edm. Waller, 4to. 1664. This is a translation of the same play as the foregoing, and was acted by the Duke of York's servants. Mr. Waller, who translated only one act, was assisted in it by the Earl of Dorset and Middlesex.

154. POM-

154. POMPEY THE GREAT HIS FAIR CORNELIA'S TRAGEDY, *effected by her Father and Husband's Downcast, Death, and Fortune*, by Thomas Kyd, 4to. 1595. This is only a translation from an old French author, one Robert Garnier. The translation is in blank verse, with only now and then a couplet, by the way of closing a paragragh or long sentence, and choruses which are written in various measures of verse, and are very long and sententious. It was first published under the title of *Cornelia*, 4to. 1594.

155. PONTEACH, or, *The Savages of America*. Trag. by Major Richard Rogers, 8vo. 1766.

156. THE POOR MAN's COMFORT. Tragi-Com. by Robert Daborne. Acted at the Cockpit, Drury-Lane, 4to. 1655.

157. THE POOR SCHOLAR. Com. by Robert Neville, 4to. 1662. This play was never acted, but is commended in three copies of verses.

158. POOR VULCAN! Burletta, by Charles Dibdin. Acted at Covent-Garden, 8vo. 1778.

159. PORSENNA's INVASION, or, *Rome preserved*. Trag. 8vo. 1748. Printed for the author, but never acted.

160. THE PORTRAIT. Burletta, by George Colman, Esq. Acted at Covent-Garden, 8vo. 1770. This piece is founded on a French drama, performed at the Italian comedy at Paris, intituled, *Le Tableau Parlant*.

161. THE PORTSMOUTH HEIRESS, or, *The Generous Refusal*. Com. Anonymous, 4to. 1704. This play was never acted. The plot of it is probably founded on some real and well-known fact, and the time of it is made to be during the king of Spain's residence at that place.

162. PRAISE AT PARTING. Interlude, by Stephen Gosson. Not printed.

163. THE PRAGMATICAL JESUIT NEW LEAVEN'D. A Comedy, by Richard Carpenter, 4to. no date. The author of this piece was a very religious man, and has endeavoured throughout the whole to promote, as much as possible, the cause of morality and virtue, and point out the difference between hypocrisy and true religion. He has also made it his business to expose all the numerous subtilties and artful inventions made use of by the Romish clergy, for the gaining over of proselytes, and promoting their own religion.

164. THE PRECEPTOR, or, *The Loves of Abelard and Heloise*. A Ballad Opera, of one act, by W. Hammond, 8vo. 1740. The very title of this piece informs us of its subject, which seems in its own nature to be more adapted for the ground-work of a tragedy, than a ballad opera. I imagine, therefore, it might be a mere *Jeu d'Esprit*, and that as it never was, so also it might probably never be intended to be brought on the stage.

165. THE PRECEPTOR. Com. in two acts, by Thomas Warboys, 8vo. 1777. Not acted.

166. THE PREJUDICE OF FASHION. Farce, acted at the Hay-Market, Feb. 22, 1779. Not printed.

167. THE PRESBYTERIAN LASH, or, NOCTROFFE's *Maid Whipp'd*. A Tragi-Comedy, *acted in the great Room at the Pye Tavern at Aldgate, by Noctroffe the Priest, and several of his Parishioners, at the cutting of a Chine of Beef*. Anonymous, 4to. 1661. This piece was

was written just after the Restoration, at which time the Puritan and Presbyterian party were so obnoxious to the government and to the loyalists, that every kind of satire, scandal, or abuse, was permitted to have its full vent, and to take an entire and unlimited scope against them. That it was sometimes unjust, I make no doubt; and so probably might the piece before us be, which is entirely a personal satire on Zachary Crofton, a violent Presbyterian teacher then living. It is dedicated to master Zach. Ncstroffe, by K. F. and consists only of thirteen scenes, not divided into acts.

168. THE PRESENCE. Com. by the Duchess of Newcastle, Fol. 1662. This very voluminous writer had composed twenty-nine additional scenes to this piece, which she intended to have interwoven with the general texture of the comedy, but finding they would render it too long for a single drama, she omitted them; but has printed them separately, and published them with the play.

169. THE PRESS-GANG, or, *Love in Low Life*. Ballad Farce, by Henry Carey, 8vo. 1755. This piece was performed at Covent-Garden on the prospect of the last war. It was, however, originally written about 1739, and is now frequently performed as an interlude under the title of *True Blue*.

170. PRESUMPTUOUS LOVE. A Dramatic Masque. Anonymous, 4to. 1716. This masque was performed at the Theatre in Lincoln's-Inn-Fields, in a comedy, called, *Every Body mistaken*, which was never printed, and was only an alteration of Shakspeare's *Comedy of Errors*. The story of the masque is taken from the Heathen Mythology, and the scene laid in the Plains of Thessaly. The music,

after the Italian taste, was composed by Mr. W. Turner, who, says the author, has a happy genius in naturalizing Italian music into a true English manner, without losing the force of the original in the imitation, or the masterly touches of the art in the composition. As Mears ascribes a piece, called, *Every Body mistaken*, to William Taverner, it will be no improbable conjecture, that this piece may be by the same author.

171. THE PRETENDERS, or, *The Town unmask'd*. Com. by Tho. Dilkes. 4to. 1608. Scene, Covent-Garden. This piece was acted, but without success, at the Theatre in Lincoln's-Inn Fields.

772. THE PRETENDER'S FLIGHT, or, *A Mock Coronation, with the Humours of the facetious Harry St. John*. Farce, by John Phillips, 8vo. 1716. Of this piece very little seems needful to be said, since its date points it out to have been written at the close of the rebellion in 1715, when the Chevalier quitted Scotland in the most abrupt and dastardly manner. The under-plot is intended as a ridicule on the famous Lord Bolingbroke, whose adherence to that mistaken party drove him for several years into exile. The name of the author seems to be a fictitious one, as the piece is ascribed to Dr. Sewell, in an advertisement prefixed to *The Maid's the Mistress*, 12mo. 1732.

173. THE PRINCE OF AGRA. Trag. by Hugh Kelly. Acted at Covent-Garden one night, April 7, 1774, for Mrs. Leffingham's benefit. It is an alteration of Dryden's *Aurenzebe*. At this period Mr. Kelly, being apprehensive of an opposition to any piece which he should bring on the stage, prevailed on Mr. Addington to allow his name to be used as the author of

of *The School for Wives*, which was produced at Drury-Lane the same feafon as this appeared at Covent-Garden, and with the like deception. Not printed.

174. THE PRINCE OF PRIGG'S REVELS, or, *The Practices of that grand Thief Captain James Hind*. Relating divers of his pranks and exploits never heretofore publifhed by any. Repleat with various conceits and Tarltonian mirth fuitable to the fubject. Written by J. S. 4to. 1658.

175. THE PRINCE OF TUNIS. Trag. by Henry Mackenfie. Acted at Edinburgh, 8vo. 1773.

176. THE PRINCESS, or, *Love at firft Sight*. Tragi-Com. by Thomas Killegrew, Fol. 1663. This play was written while the author was at Naples. The fcene is laid in Sicily and Naples, and the plot probably from fome traditional ftory in the Neapolitan hiftory.

177. THE PRINCESS OF CLEVE. Tragi-Com. by Nat. Lee. Acted at Dorfet-Gardens, 4to. 1689. This play is founded on a French romance of the fame title; and the famous invective againft women, which is fpoken by Poltrot in the fifth act, is borrowed from a romance, called *The French Rogue*. The fcene is laid in Paris.

178. THE PRINCESS OF ELIS, or, *The Pleafures of the Enchanted Ifland*. A Dramatic Piece, in three parts, by Mr. Ozell. This is only a tranflation from Moliere. The original was written to add a fpirit to the gallant and magnificent entertainments given by Lewis XIV. at Verfailles on the 7th of May, 1664, and was performed by his majefty, the princes of the blood, and the other nobility of that then glorious and illuftrious court.

179. THE PRINCESS OF PARMA. Trag. by H. Smith, 4to.

1699. This play was acted at the Theatre in Lincoln's-Inn Fields. The fcene is laid in Genoa; and the epilogue was written by Mr. Motteux.

180. THE PRINCESS OF PARMA. Trag. by Richard Cumberland, Efq. This play has not yet appeared in print. It was acted on the 20th and 21ft of October, 1778, at the private Theatre of Mr. Hanbury at Kelmarfh, in Northamptonfhire. The performers were the author, Mr. Cradock, and fome friends. A farce, called *The Election*, was exhibited at the fame time, but whether written by the fame auth— is not certain. The prologue and epilogue were printed in the newspapers foon after the reprefentation.

181. THE PRISON BREAKER, or, *The Adventures of John Shepherd*. A Farce. Anonymous, 8vo. 1725. Intended (by its author, I fuppofe) to be acted at Lincoln's-Inn Fields.

182. THE PRISONER, or, *The Fair Ancloress*. Tragi-Com. by Philip Maffinger. This play was entered on the books of the Stationers' Company (Sept. 9, 1653); but was never printed.

183. THE PRISONERS. Tragi-Com. by Thomas Killigrew. Acted at the Phœnix, Drury-Lane. 12mo. 1640. The fcene, Sardinia.

184. THE PRODIGAL. Com. tranflated from Voltaire, and printed in Dr. Franklin's edition of that author.

185. THE PRODIGAL, or, *Recruits for the Queen of Hungary*. Com. by Thomas Odell, 8vo. 1744. This is little more than an alteration of Shadwell's *Woman Captain*. It was acted with fome fuccefs at the Little Theatre in the Hay-Market, it being at a period when the Emprefs Queen was as

great a favourite with the English people, as the heroic Prussian monarch has since been.

186. THE PRODIGAL SCHOLAR. Com. by Thomas Randall. It was entered on the books of the Stationers' Company June 29, 1660; but not printed.

187. A PROJECTOR LATELY DEAD. Com. not printed. This play is mentioned in a pamphlet, called, A Collection of Judgments upon Sabbath-breakers, 1636. p. 45. "His (Attorney-General
"Noy's) clients the players, for
"whom he had done knight's
"service, to requite his kindness
"the next terme following, made
"him the subject of a merry co-
"medy, styled, *A Projector lately
"dead*, wherein they bring him
"in his lawyer's robes upon the
"stage, and openly dissecting him,
"find 100 proclamations in his
"head, a bundle of moth-eaten
"records in his maw, &c."

188. THE PROJECTORS. Com. by J. Wilson, 4to. 1665. This play met good success on the stage. Scene, London.

189. THE PROJECTORS. Com. Anonymous, 8vo. 1737. This is a very middling piece, and was never acted. Its design is to ridicule that class of people who are ready to encourage any proposed scheme, however romantic and absurd, which offers the most distant and airy prospect of gain to themselves, and who consequently, by grasping at a shadow, do for the most part lose the substance which they already possess.

190. PROMOS AND CASSANDRA. Com. in two parts, by George Whetstone, 4to. 1578. black letter. The full title is as follows: "*The right excellent and famous Historye of Promos and Cassandra; divided into two comical Discourses. In the first Parte is shewne* the unsufferable Abuse of a lewde Magistrate; the virtuous Behaviours of a chaste Ladye; the uncontrowled Lewdeness of a favoured Courtisan; and the undeserved Estimation of a pernicious Parasyte. *In the second Parte is discoursed* the perfect Magnanimitye of a noble Kinge, in checking Vice and favouring Vertue. *Wherein is shewne*, the Reigne and Overthrow of dishonest Practices, *with the* Advauncement of Upright Dealing." Both these plays are written in verse, for the most part alternate. The scene lies at Julio in Hungary, and Shakspeare made some use of them in his *Measure for Measure*. Reprinted in *The Six Old Plays*, 8vo. 1779. Vol. I.

191. PROMETHEUS. Pantomimime. Acted at Covent-Garden, 1776.

192. PROMETHEUS CHAINED. Trag. translated from Æschylus, by R. Potter, 4to. 1777.

193. PROMETHEUS IN CHAINS. translated from the Greek of Æschylus, by Thomas Morell, 8vo. 1773.

194. THE PROPHETESS. A Tragical History, by Beaumont and Fletcher, Fol. 1647. This play is founded on the History of the Emperor Dioclesian, to whom, when in a very low station in life, it was foretold by a *Prophetess* that he should become emperor of Rome, when he should have killed a mighty *Boar (quando* Aprum *interfecerit)*; in consequence of which prediction, he applied himself more particularly to the hunting of those animals, but in vain. The prophecy, however, was at last fulfilled by his putting to death Aper, the father-in-law of the Emperor Numerianus, whose many tyrannies and acts of cruelty, and particularly the murder of his son-in-law,

in-law, had occasioned a mutiny among the people, which Dioclefian heading, immediately mounted the throne he had so long been waiting for. The story is to be found at large in Nicephorus, Eusebius, Baronius, &c.

195. THE PROPHETESS, or, *The History of Dioclesian*, with alterations and additions, after the manner of an opera, by T. Betterton. Acted at the Queen's Theatre, 4to. 1690. This is the above play, altered into the form of an opera by the addition of several musical entertainments, composed by Mr. Henry Purcell. It has been also brought on the stage again several times, and particularly during the theatrical administration of the late Mr. Rich; but is very far from being a pleasing play.

196. PROTEUS, or, *Harlequin in China*. Pantomime, by Mr. Woodward, 1755. This piece was performed at the Theatre Royal in Drury-Lane, with great success; for the author of it, although no writer, had an admirable aptness at the invention of this kind of entertainments, so as to render them pleasing and shewy, without such an extreme of expence as these affairs have been frequently suffered to extend to.

197. THE PROVOK'D HUSBAND, or, *A Journey to London*. Com. by C. Cibber. Acted at Drury-Lane, 8vo. 1727. This comedy was begun by Sir John Vanbrugh, but left by him imperfect at his death, when Mr. Cibber took it in hand, and finished it. It met with very great success; yet such is the power of prejudice and personal pique in biassing the judgment, that Mr. Cibber's enemies, ignorant of what share he had in the writing of the piece, bestowed the highest applause on the part which related to Lord Townly's provocations from his wife, which was mostly Cibber's, at the same time that they condemned and opposed the *Journey to London* part, which was almost entirely Vanbrugh's, for no other apparent reason but because they imagined it to be Mr. Cibber's. He soon, however, convinced them of their mistake, by publishing all the scenes which Sir John had left behind him, exactly from his own MS. under the single title of THE JOURNEY TO LONDON.

198. PROVOK'D WIFE. Com. by Sir John Vanbrugh. Acted at Lincoln's-Inn Fields, 4to. 1697, and 4to. 1699. This Comedy has a great many very fine scenes in it, and the character of Sir John Brute is very highly and naturally drawn. Yet it has in the language, as well as conduct of it, too much loose wit and libertinism of sentiment to become the theatres of a moral and virtuous nation; since no behaviour of a husband, however brutal, can vindicate a wife in revenging her cause upon herself, by throwing away the most valuable jewel she possesses, her innocence and peace of mind. Lady Brute's conduct, moreover, seems rather to proceed from the warmth of her own inclinations, than a spirit of resentment against her husband; nay, she seems so far to have lost even the very sense of honour, that a little matter appears capable of inducing her to turn pander to her niece Belinda. Had Lady Brute, indeed, appeared to the audience strictly virtuous through the whole transaction, yet had carried on such a deception to her husband, as to have alarmed all those suspicions which a consciousness of his own behaviour towards her would authorize him in entertaining the belief of, and then

then reformed him by a perfect clearing up of those suspicions, and, by shewing him how near he might have been to the brink of a precipice, taught him to avoid for the future the path that was leading him towards it, the moral would have been compleat; whereas, as it now stands, all that can be deduced from it is, that a brutish husband deserves to be made a cuckold, and that there can be no breach of virtue in giving him that desert, provided he can afterwards, either by the persuasions of his wife, or the bluster of her gallant, be soothed or frightened out of an intention of resenting it on her, a maxim of the most happy tendency to persons inclinable to gallantry and intrigue; since the same practices may equally answer against the good and indulgent, as against the surly and brutal husband. This play was one of those which were severely censured by Mr. Collier, on account of its immorality. When it was revived in 1725, the author thought proper to substitute a new scene, in the fourth act, in place of one in which in the wantonness of his wit he had made a rake talk like a rake in the habit of a clergyman; to avoid which offence, he put the same debauchee into the undress of a woman of quality; and with this alteration it has ever since been performed.

199. THE PROSE. or, *Love's Aftergame*. Com. Entered on the books of the Stationers' Company Nov. 29, 1673, but not printed.

200. THE PRUDE. Com. translated from Voltaire, and printed in Dr. Franklin's edition of that author.

201. THE PRUDE. Com. Opera, by Elizabeth Ryves, 8vo. 1777. Not acted. Printed in a Collection of her Poems.

202. PRUNELLA. An Interlude, by Richard Estcourt, 4to. without date. This piece was performed for Mr. Estcourt's benefit, between the acts of the *Rehearsal*, and must have been before the year 1713. It was intended as a burlesque on the Italian operas in general, and particularly on those of *Arsinoe, Camilla,* and *Thomyris*, at that time greatly in vogue. The sense and music, says the title-page, collected from the most famous masters. He lays his scene in Covent-Garden, which, in imitation of the pompous manner of the Italian scenery, he humourously describes as follows: "*Scene*, a flat piece of ground without hedge or stile, the prospect of a church in view, and *Tom's Coffee-house* at a distance." Some of the songs in the above-mentioned operas are parodized in it.

203. PSYCHE. A Trag. by Thomas Shadwell. Acted at the Duke's Theatre, 4to. 1675. This is the first piece this author wrote in rhyme, for which some of his contemporary critics were very severe upon him. His intention in his work was not to produce a perfect regular dramatic piece, but only to entertain the town with a variety of music, dancing, scenery, and machinery, rather than with fine writing or exactness of poetry. The plot of it is partly founded on Apuleius's *Golden Ass*, and partly on the French *Psyche*, which he very candidly acknowledges the use he has made of in his preface. It met with great success, and indeed deservedly, since all the first-rate masters in music, dancing, and painting of that time, were employed about it.

204. PSYCHE. An Opera, by Mr. Ozell. This is a literal translation of *The Psyche* of Molière, from which, as I have said before,

the last-mentioned piece is partly borrowed.

205. PSYCHE DEBAUCH'D. C. by Thomas Duffet. Acted at the Theatre Royal, and printed in 4to. 1678. This piece is a mock opera. It was intended to ridicule Shadwell's *Psyche*, and written purposely to injure the *Duke's* house, which at that time was more frequented than the *King's*. It is, however, nothing but a mass of low scurrility and abuse, without either wit or humour; and met with the contempt it merited.

206. PUBLIC WOOING. Com. by the Duchess of Newcastle, Fol. 1662. Several of the suitors speeches, particularly those of the soldier, the countryman, and the spokesman for the bashful suitor, were written by the duke; as were also two other scenes, and the two songs at the end of the play.

207. THE PURITAN, or, *The Widow of Watling-Street*. Com. by W. Shakspeare. Acted by the children of Paul's, 4to. 1607. This play is not unentertaining, yet it is one of the seven which have been rejected by the editors of Shakspeare's works. Scene, London. It is reprinted in the Supplement to the edition of Shakspeare 1778.

208. THE PURITAN MAID, MODEST WIFE, AND WANTON WIDOW. Com. by Thomas Middleton. This was entered on the books of the Stationers' Company Sept. 9, 1653; and was among those destroyed by Mr. Warburton's servant.

209. PYRRHUS AND DEMETRIUS. Oper. by Owen M'Swiny, 4to. 1709. This is a translation from the Italian of Scarlatti, and was performed at the Queen's Theatre in the Hay-Market. Scene, in Epirus.

210. PYRRHUS KING OF EPIRUS. Trag. by Charles Hopkins. Acted at Lincoln's-Inn Fields, 4to. 1695. This is the least meritorious and least successful of this author's performances, but has his great youth at the time he wrote it to plead in its defence. It has, however, many strokes in it which an older writer need by no means have been ashamed of. The story of it may be found in Livy, in Plutarch's Life of *Pyrrhus*, &c. The scene is the City of Argos, besieged by Pyrrhus, with the camp of the Epirotes on the one side, and that of the Macedonians, who came to its relief, on the other. Prologue by Mr. Congreve.

211. PYRAMUS AND THISBE. A Comic Masque, 12mo. 1716. This piece was performed at Lincoln's-Inn Fields Theatre. Mr. Richard Leveridge dressed it out in recitatives and airs after the present Italian manner, from the interlude in Shakspeare's *Midsummer Night's Dream*.

212. PYRAMUS AND THISBE. Mock Opera, set to music by Mr. Lampe. Acted at Covent-Garden, 8vo. 1745. Taken from Shakspeare's *Midsummer Night's Dream*.

Q.

QU

1. THE QUACKS, or, *Love's the Physician*. Com. by Owen M'Swiny, 4to. 1705. This piece consists only of three acts, and is a translation from the *L'Amour Medecin* of Moliere. Scene, London. It was twice rejected or forbidden at the Theatre Royal in Drury-Lane; but was at last introduced to the public at that theatre, of which, I believe, Mr. M'Swiny was then in part, if not sole manager. It met, however, with little success.

2. THE QUACKS, or, *Love's the Physician*. Farce, by Owen M'Swiny. Acted at Drury-Lane, 8vo. 1745. This is the before-mentioned piece reduced to one act.

3. THE QUAKER. Comic Opera, by Charles Dibdin. Acted at Drury-Lane, 8vo. 1777.

4. THE QUAKER'S OPERA, by Thomas Walker. Acted at Lee and Harper's Booth in Bartholomew Fair, 8vo. 1728. This is one of many very indifferent pieces which the world since of applause no *Beggar's Opera* had met with, hatched into life. Mr. Walker, mo..., might have another motive... make him hope success in a ballad opera, from the great approbation he had been favoured with in the part of Capt. Macheath.

5. THE QUAKER'S WEDDING. Com. by Richard Wilkinson, Gent. printed in 1.mo. 1728. It was acted at Drury-Lane 1703, and is only V. B RECLAIM'D, &c. with a new title.

6. THE QUEEN, or, *The Excellency of her Sex*. Tragi-Com.

Anonymous, 4to. 1653. This excellent old play is said to have been found out by a person of honour, and given to the editor Alexander Goughe, to whom three copies of verses are addressed on the publication of it. Part of the plot, viz, the affair of Solafsa's swearing Velasco not to fight, is taken from Belleforest's *Histoires tragiques*, Novel 13. Scene lies at Arragon.

7. THE QUEEN AND CONCUBINE. Com. by Richard Brome, 8vo. 1659. Scene, Sicily.

8. QUEEN CATHERINE, or, *The Ruins of Love*. Trag. by Mary Pix. Acted at Lincoln's-Inn Fields, 4to. 1698. The scene lies in England, and the plot from the English history in the reigns of Edward IV. and Henry VI. The epilogue was written by her contemporary Mrs. Trotter.

9. QUEEN HESTER. A Play; entered on the books of the Stationers' Company in the year 1560 to 1561, but not printed.

10. QUEEN MAB. Pantomime, by Henry Woodward, performed at Drury-Lane 1752.

11. THE QUEEN OF ARRAGON, Tragi-Com. by William Habington, Fol. 1640.

12. THE QUEEN OF CORINTH. Tragi-Com. by Beaumont and Fletcher, Fol. 1647.

13. THE QUEEN OF CORSICA, Trag. written by Francis Jaques, anno Domini 1642. This play is yet in manuscript in the library of the earl of Shelburne.

14. THE QUEEN OF SPAIN; by James Worsdale. This piece I never saw, but find it mentioned

in

in *The British Theatre*, yet without date, or any notice whether it is Tragedy or Comedy. By the title one would be apt to imagine it the former; yet, as Mr. Worfdale's genius has always appeared to take a comic turn, I should rather conclude it to be the latter.

15. THE QUEEN'S ARCADIA. A Pastoral Tragi-Com. by Samuel Daniel, 4to. 1606. 4to. 1623. This piece was presented to Queen Anne, wife of James I. and her ladies, by the university of Oxford, in Christ-Church in August, 1605, and is dedicated in verse to her majesty. The scene lies in Arcadia. The characters of Corinus and Amintas in one of their scenes resemble those of Filme and Daphnis in M. Quinault's *Comedie sans Comedie*: as do two other scenes between them and their mistress Clomire, bear a likeness to that between the swains Damon and Alexis, and the inconstant nymph Laurinda in Randolph's *Amyntas*.

16. THE QUEEN'S EXCHANGE. Com. by Richard Brome, 4to. 1657. This play was acted at Black-Friers with great applause. Scene lies in England. It was afterwards printed with a new title, and called " The Royal Ex- " change," 4to. 1661.

17. THE QUEEN'S MASQUE OF BEAUTY. by Ben Jonson, Fol. 1640. This piece was personated at court by Anne, queen to king James I. and her ladies, on Twelfth Night, 1605.

18. THE QUEEN'S MASQUE OF BLACKNESS. by Ben Jonson, Fol. 1640. This piece, as well as the foregoing, was presented at court by the queen and her ladies, only this was performed on the Sunday night after Twelfth Night, 1608. It was at the palace of Whitehall that both these dramas made their appearance, the celebrated architect Inigo Jones assisting in the machinery and decorations.

19. QUEEN TRAGEDY RE- STOR'D. A Dramatic Entertain- ment, by Mrs. Hooper, 8vo. 1749. This piece, which is a strange in- coherent jumble of repeated absur- dities, though intended by its au- thor as a burlesque on the modern writers, and a means of restoring tragedy to her ancient dignity, was performed one night only at the Little Theatre in the Hay- Market, by a set of performers of equal merit with the piece; the author herself, who had never trod a stage before, appearing in the part of *Queen Tragedy*. As the house was almost entirely filled with her own friends, a silent dis- gust and ennui was all the re- ception it met with; but on at- tempting to bring it on a second night, the fame it had acquired was apparent, from there not being an audience sufficient even to pay the expences of music and candles.

20. QUERER PER SOLO QUER- ER. *To love only for Love's Sake.* Dramatic Romance, by Sir Richard Fanshaw, 4to. 1671. This is only a translation, or rather paraphrase from the Spanish of Antonio de Mendoza, made by Sir Richard during his confinement at Tank- ersly Castle in 1654, when he was taken prisoner by Oliver at the battle of Worcester. The original was written in 1623, in celebra- tion of the birth-day of Philip IV. of Spain, and is dedicated to Eliza- beth his queen. It was repre- sented at court at Aranjuez, be- fore those sovereigns, by the Me- ninas, who are a set of ladies, the daughters or heiresses of the grandees of Spain, who attend on the queen, but who, though only children in years, stand higher in rank than her majesty's ladies of honour.

honour. The piece consists but of three acts or *Jornados*, according to the Spanish custom. Annexed to it is the *Fiestas de Aranjuez, Festivals at Aranjuez*, translated from the same author.

21. THE QUIDNUNCS. Moral Interlude, 4to. 1779. The title-page adds, intended to have been represented at one of the theatres, but for particular reasons suppressed. The whole of it is reprinted in *The London Review*, January, 1779.

R.

R A

1. THE RAGGED UPROAR, or, *The Oxford Roratory*. Dramatic Satire, in many scenes, and in one very long act, in which is introduced the Alamode System of Fortune-telling. Originally planned by Joan Plotwell, and continued by several truly eminent hands well versed in the art of designing; the whole concluding with an important scene of witches, gypsies, and fortune-tellers; a long jumbling dance of politicians; and an epilogue spoken by Mary Squires, &c. flying on broomsticks, 4to. no date. [1754.]

2. THE RAGING TURK, or, BAJAZET II. Trag. by Thomas Goffe, 4to. 1631. 8vo. 1656. The plot of this play may be found by consulting Knolles Turkish History, Calchocondylas, and other writers on that reign. It was acted by the students of Christ-Church, Oxford, to which society the author belonged, but was not published till after his death.

3. RAM-ALLEY, or, *Merry Tricks*. Com. by Lodowick Barrey. Acted by the children of the Revels, 4to. 1611. 4to. 1636. The incident of William Smallshank's decoying the widow Taffeta, is also a circumstance in Killegrew's *Par-son's Wedding*, as likewise in *The English Rogue*, Part IV. Chap. 19. Scene, in London.

4. THE RAMBLING JUSTICE, or, *The Jealous Husbands, with the Humours of John Twyford*. Com. by John Leonard. Acted at Drury-Lane, 4to. 1678. Great part of this play is borrowed from Middleton's *More Dissemblers besides Women*, particularly the scene between Sir General Amourous and Bramble in the second act; Petulant Easy's being disguised like a Gipsy in the same act, and the scene between Bramble and the Gipsies in the third. The scene is laid in London, and the time twenty-four hours. In the year 1680, it was republished with a new title in 4to. and called, "THE JEALOUS HUSBANDS, *with the Humours of Sir John Twyford and the Rambling Justice*."

5. THE RAMPANT ALDERMAN, or, *News from the Exchange*. Farce, Anonymous, 4to. 1685. This farce is one entire piece of plagiarism, being stolen from Marmien's *Fine Companion*, and several other plays.

6. THE RAPE, or, *The Innocent Impostors*. Trag. by Dr. Brady. Acted at Drury-Lane, 4to. 1692. This

This piece was introduced on the stage by Mr. Shadwell, who wrote an epilogue to it.

7. THE RAPE. Trag. Acted at Lincoln's-Inn Fields, 8vo. 1730.

8. THE RAPE OF EUROPA BY JUPITER. A Masque. Anonymous. 4to. 1694. Sung at the Queen's Theatre in Dorset-Gardens by their Majesty's servants.

9. THE RAPE OF HELEN. A Mock Opera, by John Breval, Esq. Acted at Covent-Garden, 8vo. 1737. Scene, Mycenæ, capital of Argos.

10. THE RAPE OF LUCRECE. A true Roman Tragedy, by Thomas Heywood, 4to. 1638. The plot is selected from Livy, Florus, Valerius Maximus, and other Roman historians. In it are introduced several songs sung by Valerius the merry Lord among the Roman Peers.

11. THE RAPE OF PROSERPINE, by Lewis Theobald, 4to. 1727. Acted at the Theatre Royal in Lincoln's-Inn Fields. The music to this piece was composed by Mr. Galliard, and the scene lies in Sicily. This is part of a pantomime which frequently to this day makes its appearance in Covent-Garden Theatre, and, to the great reproach of public taste, has repeatedly drawn crowded audiences to the most trivial and insignificant pieces of the drama, and those even very indifferently performed, at times when the almost supernatural works of Shakspeare, Jonson, &c. supported by every thing that human exertion and abilities could add to them in the acting, have made their appearance to almost empty benches.

12. RAPE UPON RAPE, or, *The Justice caught in his own Trap*. By this title, Fielding's *Coffee-House Politician* was first printed.

13. THE RAREE SHOW, or, *The Fox trap't*. Opera, by Joseph Peterson, comedian, 8vo. 1739. This was printed at York, where it was performed.

14. RAUF RUSTER DUSTER. A Play, with this title, is entered on the books of the Stationers' Company in 1566; but, I believe, never printed.

15. RAYMOND DUKE OF LYONS. This play was acted in the year 1613; but supposed to be never printed. See Mr. Malone's Attempt, &c. Shakspeare, edit. 1778. p. 331.

16. THE REAPERS, or, *The Englishman out of Paris*. Opera, 8vo. 1770. A translation of *Les Moissonneurs*.

17. THE REBELLION. Trag. by Thomas Rawlins. Acted by the company of Revels, 4to. 1640. Scene, Sevil. This play was acted with great applause, and seems to have been held in high estimation, there being no less than eleven copies of commendatory verses prefixed to this first edition of it.

18. REBELLION DEFEATED, or, *The Fall of Desmond*. Trag. by John Cutts, 4to. 1745. This tragedy was never acted, yet is not absolutely devoid of merit. The scene of it lies in Ireland, and the plan is founded on the Irish rebellion in 1582, headed by Gyrald Fitz Gyrald, earl of Desmond.

19. THE REBELLION OF NAPLES, or, *The Tragedy of Massinello* (but rightly Tomaso Annello di Malfa, general of the Neapolitans), 8vo. 1651. This play is said to have been written by a gentleman who was himself an eyewitness to the whole of that wonderful transaction, which happened at Naples in 1647. The scene lies at Naples, and the story may be seen more at large in Giraffi's History of Naples.

20. RE-

20. RECRUITING OFFICER. C. by George Farquhar. Acted at Drury-Lane, 4to. 1707. This most entertaining and lively comedy, which is at this time, and probably will ever continue to be, one of the most standard and established amusements of the British stage, was written on the very spot where the author has fixed his scene of action, viz. at Shrewsbury, and at a time when he was himself a recruiting officer in that town, and, by all accounts of him, the very character he has drawn in that of Captain Plume. His Justice Ballance was designed, as he tells you himself, as a compliment to a very worthy country gentleman in that neighbourhood. He has dedicated the play in a familiar and at the same time grateful manner, to all friends round the Wrekin; and his epilogue is a sprightly and martial one, adapted to the successes of the British arms at that glorious period, being introduced by the beat of drum with the Grenadier-march. The characters are natural, the dialogue genteel, and the wit entirely spirited and genuine. In short, to say the least we can in its praise, we can scarcely keep within the limits assigned us; and, were we to say the most, we could scarcely do justice to its merit.

21. THE RECRUITING SERJEANT. Musical Entertainment, by Isaac Bickerstaffe. Acted at Drury-Lane, 8vo. 1770.

22. REDOWALD. Masque, by Joseph Hazard, 12mo. 1767. Printed at Chelmsford. This piece was written when the author was only sixteen years old; and, making allowance for so early an age, will reflect no discredit on him.

23. THE REFORMATION. C. 4to. 1673. Acted at the Duke's Theatre. Scene, Venice. This piece is ascribed to one Mr. Arrowsmith, M. A. of Cambridge.

24. THE REFORM'D WIFE. C. by Mr. Burnaby. Acted at Drury-Lane, 4to. 1700. From this play, which was unsuccessful, Mr. Cibber has borrowed great part of his *Double Gallant*.

25. THE REFUSAL, or, *The Ladies Philosophy*. Com. by C. Cibber. Acted at Drury-Lane, 8vo. 1720. The ground-work of that part of this play which relates to the second title, is built on the *Femmes Sçavantes* of Moliere, which Wright's *Female Virtuosoes* is also borrowed from. But Mr. Cibber, who always greatly improved those hints which he took from others, has introduced a second plot into it, by making the circumstances of his catastrophe depend on the absurdities of that year of folly and infatuation in which this play made its appearance, when the bubbles of the South-Sea scheme rendered even men of understanding *Fools*, and then subjected them to the designing views of knaves. His Sir Gilbert Wrangle, whom he has made a South-Sea director, is an admirably drawn, an exceeding natural, and yet I think an original character; and although the prejudice which the author had raised against himself on another occasion (see *Nonjuror*) permitted this piece to run for no more than six nights, and that with repeated disturbances at every one of them, yet I cannot help looking on it as one of the most finished of our author's comedies. With the revival of this play, if I do not mistake, Mr. Garrick opened the Theatre Royal at Drury-Lane in the year 1747, being the first of his management; nor can I in justice omit taking notice of the great merit shewn

shewn by Mr. Macklin in the performance of the part of Sir Gilbert.

26. THE REGICIDE, or, *James the First of Scotland.* Trag. by Dr. Smollet, 8vo. 1749. The plot of this piece is founded on the Scottish history of the reign of that monarch, who was basely and barbarously murdered by his uncle Walter Stuart, earl of Athol, in the year 1437. This play was offered to the managers of the theatres, but rejected, a particular account of which the author has given, under feigned characters, in his adventures of *Roderic Random*, in which he has displayed a great deal of wit and humour, but with how much justice I cannot pretend to determine. It was published afterwards by subscription, very much, I believe, to its author's emolument. As therefore it stands in print, and open to every one's examination, I shall by no means here enter into any particular investigation of its merits, but leave it entirely to the decision of the public how far the author and managers were or were not in the right in their respective parts of the contest.

27. THE REGISTER OFFICE. Farce, of two acts, by Joseph Reed, 8vo. 1761. This little piece, which was performed at the Theatre Royal in Drury-Lane with great applause, is intended to expose the pernicious consequences that may, and probably do, frequently arise from Offices of Intelligence, or, as they are called, Register Offices, where the management of them happens to be lodged in the hands of wicked and designing men. This design is surely a laudable one, as the stage ought certainly to be made a vehicle to convey to the public ear and eye, not only the representation of general vice and folly, but also the knowledge of any particular evil or abuse, which may occur to a few persons indeed, but those perhaps either too unconsequential or too indolent to attempt a redress of it, and which cannot therefore by any means so readily as by this be brought forth to open daylight, and in consequence to public redress. In the execution of this, the plan of which is rendered as simple as possible, several characters are introduced; the generality of which are well drawn, particularly the provincial ones of an Irish spalpeen, a Scotch pedlar, and a Yorkshire servant-maid, as also that of a military male *Slip-slop*, whose ignorance leads him into the perpetual use of hard words whose meaning he does not understand, and consequently mispronounces, and whose impudence secures him from a blush on the detection of his absurdity. There is also another character in it, which was omitted in the representation, viz. that of Mrs. Snare, an old puritanical bawd, which treads so close on the heels of the celebrated Mrs. Cole in Mr. Foote's *Minor*, not only in the general portrait, but in the particular features of sentiment and diction, that we should certainly be ready to fly out in exclamation against the author as the most barefaced and undaunted plagiary, had he not, in an advertisement annexed to the piece, assured us that the said character was written previous to the appearance of *The Minor*, and even that the MS. had been lodged in Mr. Foote's own hands, under an expectation of that gentleman's bringing it on the stage in the year 1758, two years before he brought out his own piece of *The Minor*. A few years after it first appeared, it was revived; and

a new

a new character, Mrs. Doggrel, a female author, excellently performed by Mrs. Pope, was introduced in it.

28. THE REGISTER OFFICE. An Entertainment, in two acts, by E. Morton, 12mo. 1758. Printed at Salop.

29. THE REGULATORS. Com. by George Lillo. This piece was advertised to be printed, among the other works of this author, in certain proposals which were circulated for some time. But the intended edition not meeting with encouragement, the play has never appeared, and is now probably lost.

30. REGULUS. Trag. by John Crown. Acted by their Majesties servants, 4to. 1694. The title of this play declares what the subject of its plot must be, the story of *Regulus* being perfectly well known as one of the noblest examples of honour and constancy to be met with throughout the whole Roman history. It is to be found in Livy, Florus, &c.

31. REGULUS. Trag. by W. Havard, 8vo. 1744. This play is on the same subject with the beforementioned one, and was presented at the Theatre Royal in Drury-Lane, with some success.

32. THE REHEARSAL. Com. by the Duke of Buckingham. Acted at the Theatre Royal, 4to. 1672. This play was acted with universal applause, and is indeed the truest and most judicious piece of satire that ever yet appeared. Its intention was to ridicule and expose the then reigning taste for plays in heroic rhime, as also that fondness for bombast and fustian in the language, and clutter, noise, bustle, and shew in the conduct of dramatic pieces, which then so strongly prevailed, and which the writers of that time found too

greatly their advantage in not to encourage by their practice, to the exclusion of nature and true poetry from the stage. This play was written, and had been several times rehearsed before the plague in 1665, but was put a stop to by that dreadful public calamity. It then, however, wore a very different appearance from what it does at present, the poet having been called Bilboa, and was intended for Sir Robert Howard; afterwards, however, when Mr. Dryden, on the death of Sir W. Davenant, became laureat, and that the evil greatly increased by his example, the duke thought proper to make him the hero of his piece, changing the name of Bilboa into Bayes; yet still, although Mr. Dryden's plays became now the more particular mark for his satire, those of Sir Robert Howard and Sir W. Davenant by no means escaped the severity of its lash. This play is still repeatedly performed, constantly giving delight to the judicious and critical parts of an audience. Mr. Garrick, however, introduced another degree of merit into the part of Bayes, having rendered it by his inimitable powers of mimickry not only the scourge of poets but of players also, taking off, in the course of his instructions to the performers, the particular manner and style of acting of almost every living performer of any note. And although that gentleman for some years past laid aside this practice, perhaps esteeming mimickry below the province of a performer of capital merit, yet his example has been followed by several actors who have played the part, and will perhaps continue to be so by every one whose powers of execution are equal to the undertaking, one performer

former at prefent of Covent-Garden excepted, whofe humanity forbids him to exert this dangerous talent, which he is known to poffefs in the extreme of perfection.

33. THE REHEARSAL. A Farce, or, *A second Part of Mrs. Confufion's Trevail and hard Labour she endured in the Birth of her first Monstrous Offspring, the Child of Deformity, the hopeful Fruit of seven Years Teeming, and a precious Babe of Grace, delivered in the Year* 1648, by *Mercurius Brittannicus, printed in the Year* 1718. 4to. The dedication to Monf. Pillioniere. This is one of the pieces produced in the Bangorian controverfy, occafioned by Bifhop Hoadly's famous Sermon before the King. The scene, Gray's-Inn.

34. THE REHEARSAL, or, *Bays in Petticoats*, by Mrs. Clive. Com. in two acts, performed at Drury-Lane, 8vo. 1753. This piece was originally written three years before, and acted for the author's benefit.

35. THE REHEARSAL OF KINGS. Farce, 1692. Anonymous. What kind of piece this is, I know not, only finding a bare mention made of it in Whincop and the *British Theatre.*

36. A RELATION of the late Royal Entertainment given by the right honourable the Lord Knowles at Cawfome-Houfe, neere Redding, to our moft gracious Queene Anne, in her progreffe toward the Bathe, upon the seven and twentieth daye of April, 1613. Whereunto is annexed, the defcription, fpeeches, and fongs of the Lords Mafke, prefented in the banquetting-houfe on the marriage night of the high and mightie Count Palatine, and the royally defcended the Ladie Elizabeth. Written by Thomas Campion, 4to. 1613.

37. THE RELAPSE, or, *Virtue in Danger*. Being the fequel of *The Fool in Fashion*. Com. by Sir John Vanbrugh. Acted at Drury-Lane, 1697. 4to. 1708. 4to. In this continuation of Cibber's *Love's last Shift*, all the principal characters are retained, and finely supported to the complexion they bore in the firft part. It was, however, an hafty performance, being written in fix weeks time, and fome broken fcenes that there are in it may be deemed an irregularity. There are, indeed, much wit, great nature, and abundance of fpirit, which run through the whole of it, yet it muft be acknowledged there is a redundancy of licentioufnefs and libertinifm mingled with them, and that two or three of the fcenes, particularly thofe between Berinthia and Lovelefs, and that (which is indeed now omitted in the reprefentation) between Coupler and Young Fafhion, convey ideas of fo much warmth and indecency as muft caft a very fevere reflection on fuch audiences as could fit to fee them without being ftruck with difguft and horror. The tafte, however, of the age Sir John Vanbrugh lived in, alone could juftify his committing fuch violence on the chaftity of the Comic Mufe; and whoever will perufe Cibber's prologue to the *Provok'd Hufband*, will be fatisfied from the teftimony of one who certainly was well acquainted with this gentleman's fentiments, that he was, before his death, not only convinced of, but determined to reform this error of tafte. See *A Trip to Scarborough.*

38. RELIGIOUS. A Tragi-Com. by the Duchefs of Newcaftle, Fol. 1662.

39. THE RELIGIOUS REBEL, or, *The Pilgrim Prince*. Trag. Anonymous, 4to. 1671. Scene, in Germany.

40. THE

40. THE RENEGADO. Tragi-Com. by Phil. Massinger. Acted at Drury-Lane, 4to. 1630. This was esteemed a good play, and is recommended by two copies of verses by Shirley and Daniel Larkyn. The scene, Tunis.

41. THE REPRISAL, or, *The Tars of Old England.* Com. of two acts, by Dr. Smollet. Acted at Drury-Lane, 8vo. 1757. However indifferent this author's success might be in tragedy, yet his comic genius has shewn itself very conspicuously in this little piece, in which there are four characters, viz. a French, Scotch, and Irish man, and an English sailor, as highly drawn and as rationally distinguished as in any dramatic piece I know in the English language. It met with good success in the representation; yet, to speak my real and unbiassed opinion, not equal to what its merit might have justly claimed.

42. THE RESTORATION, or, *Right will take Place.* Tragi-Com. without date. This play was never acted; it is a very paltry performance, yet has been attributed, but injuriously, to the duke of Buckingham.

43. THE RESTORATION OF KING CHARLES II. or, *The Life and Death of Oliver Cromwell.* An Histori-Tragi-Comi-Ballad Opera, by Walter Aston, 8vo. 1733. To this piece, which was forbid to be performed, is annexed a preface in vindication of the author from certain aspersions which had been thrown on him with regard to it.

44. THE RETURN FROM PARNASSUS, or, *A Scourge for Simony.* Com. Anonymous. 4to. 1606. This piece was publicly acted in St. John's College, Cambridge, by the students. The poets of that time are treated with much severity in it, and from the hints thrown out in it against the clergy, Doctor Wild laid the foundation of his play called *The Benefice.*

45. THE REVENGE. Trag. by E. Young. Acted at Drury-Lane, 8vo. 1721. This play met, and justly, with very great success, as it is undoubtedly the master-piece in the dramatic way of that great and valuable author. The design of it seems to have been borrowed partly from Shakspeare's *Othello,* and partly from Mrs. Behn's *Abdelazar;* the plot favouring greatly of the former, and the principal character, viz. Zanga, bearing a considerable resemblance to the latter. Yet it will not surely be saying too much, to observe that Dr. Young has in some respects greatly improved on both. If we compare the Iago in one with the Zanga in the other tragedy, we shall find the motives of resentment greatly different, and those in the latter more justly as well as more nobly founded than in the former. Iago's cause of revenge against Othello is only his having let a younger officer over his head on a particular and single vacancy, notwithstanding he himself still stands most high in his esteem and confidence, and consequently in the fairest light, for being immediately preferred by him to a post of equal if not greater advantage. To this, indeed, is added a slight suspicion, which he himself declares to be but bare surmise, of the general's having been too great with his wife, a particular which Othello's character and cast of behaviour seems to give no authority to; and on these slight motives he involves, in the ruin he intends for the Moor, three innocent persons besides, viz. Cassio, Desdemona, and Roderigo. Far different is Zanga's cause of rage, and differently

ferently pursued. A father's assured death, slain by Alonzo, the loss of a kingdom, in consequence of his success, and the indignity of a blow bestowed upon himself from the same hand; all these accumulated injuries, added to the impossibility of finding a nobler means of revenge, urge him against his will to the subtilties and underhand methods he employs. Othello's jealousy is raised by trifles, the loss of a poor handkerchief which Desdemona knew not was of value, and only pleading for a man's forgiveness who had been cashiered on a most trivial fault, are all the circumstances he has to corroborate the vile insinuations of Iago. He therefore must appear too credulous, and forfeits by such conduct some of our pity. Alonzo, on the contrary, long struggles against conviction of this kind, nor will proceed to extremities, till, as he says himself, " *Proofs rise on proofs, and still the last the strongest!*" The man his jealousy stands fixed on, is one who had for three years been not only his wife's lover but her destined husband. He finds a letter (forged indeed, but so as to deceive him) from Carlos to his wife in rapturous terms, returning thanks for joys long since bestowed on him; he finds his picture hid in a private place in his wife's chamber, is told a positive and circumstantial story by one whose perfect truth he had long confided in; and lastly is confirmed in all his apprehensions by that unwillingness to sooth them which Leonora's conscious innocence urges her pride to assume. Such are the advantages the piece before us has with respect to plot over Othello. And notwithstanding that Abdelazar has been rendered by Mrs. Behn a very spirited character, yet any one on inspection will easily perceive how much more highly coloured Zanga is, and what advantages, even in the subtilty and probability of success in his machinations, the one has above the other. In a word, we may, I think, with great justice, assign to this piece a place in the very first rank of our dramatic writings.

46. THE REVENGE, or, *A Match in Newgate*. Com. Acted at the Duke's Theatre, 4to. 1680. This play was attributed to Mr. Betterton, but is in reality no more than Marston's *Dutch Courtezan*, revived with some very trifling alterations.

47. REVENGE FOR HONOUR. Trag. by George Chapman, 4to. 1659. The plot of this play is Eastern, and the scene laid in Arabia.

48. THE REVENGE OF ATHRIDATES. English Opera. Acted at Smock-Alley, Dublin, 8vo. 1765. Anonymous. The music selected by Tenducci. This is an alteration of *Pharnaces*.

49. THE REVENGER'S TRAGEDY, by Cyril Tourneur. Acted by the King's servants, 4to. 1607. 4to. 1608. Scene, Italy.

50. THE REVENGEFUL QUEEN. Trag. by William Phillips. Acted at Drury-Lane, 4to. 1698. The plot of this play is taken from Machiavel's *Florentine History*, and the scene laid in Verona. Sir William Davenant had many years before written a tragedy on the same story, viz. ALBOVINE KING OF THE LOMBARDS. That, however, the author declares he knew nothing of, till after the writing and publication of this piece.

51. THE REVOLTER. Tragi-Com. Anonymous. Acted between the Hind and Panther and Religio Laici, &c. 4to. 1687. This cannot

not be called a dramatic piece. It is a satire on Mr. Dryden.

52. THE REVOLUTION OF SWEDEN. Trag. by Catharine Trotter, afterwards Cockburne. Acted at the Hay-Market, 4to. 1706. The scene, Stockholm, and the Camp near it.

53. THE REWARDS OF VIRTUE. Com. by John Fountain, 4to. 1661. This play was not intended for the stage by its author; but after his death, Mr. Shadwell, who perceived it to have merit, made some few alterations in it, and revived it under the title of *The Royal Shepherdess*, in the year 1669.

54. REX ET PONTIFEX, being an attempt to introduce upon the stage a new species of Pantomime. Robert Dodsley, 8vo. 1745. Printed in a volume of his works, called *Trifles*.

55. RHODON AND IRIS. A Pastoral, by Ralph Knevet, 4to. 1631. This piece is recommended by four copies of verses; it was presented at the Florists feast at Norwich, May 3, 1631. The scene, Thessaly.

56. KING RICHARD THE FIRST. By Dr. George Sewell, 8vo. 1728. This consists only of a few imperfect scenes left unfinished by the author, and published after his death.

57. KING RICHARD THE SECOND. Trag. By. W. Shakspeare. Acted at the Globe, 4to. 1597. 4to. 1598. 4to. 1608. 4to. 1615. 4to. 1634. This play has not been acted for many years. Dr. Johnson observes, that it is extracted from Holinshed, in which many passages may be found which Shakspeare has with very little alteration transplanted into his scenes; particularly a speech of the Bishop of Carlisle, in defence of King Richard's unalienable right and immunity from human jurisdiction.

This play is one of those which Shakspeare has apparently revised; but as success in works of invention is not always proportionate to labour, it is not finished at last with the happy force of some other of his tragedies, nor can be said much to affect the passions or enlarge the understanding.

58. THE HISTORY OF KING RICHARD THE SECOND. By Nahum Tate. Acted at Drury-Lane, under the name of *The Sicilian Usurper*, 4to. 1681.

59. KING RICHARD THE SECOND. Trag. by L. Theobald, 8vo. 1720. This is only an alteration from Shakspeare, in which, however, the writer has taken some considerable liberties as well with the facts of history as with his original author. Scene, the Tower. It was acted at the Theatre in Lincoln's-Inn Fields with success; and is dedicated to the Earl of Orrery, who, on that occasion, made Mr. Theobald a present of a bank note of an hundred pounds, inclosed in an Egyptian pebble snuff-box of about twenty pounds value.

60. KING RICHARD THE SECOND. Trag. altered from Shakspeare, and the style imitated by James Goodhall, 8vo. 1772. Printed at Manchester. This piece was offered to Mr. Garrick for representation, but refused by him.

61. KING RICHARD THE THIRD. Trag. by W. Shakspeare. Acted by the King's servants, 4to. 1597. 4to. 1598. 4to. 1602. 4to. 1612. 4to. 1624. 4to. 1629. 4to. 1634. Dr. Johnson says, " This is
" one of the most celebrated of our
" author's performances; yet I
" know not whether it has not
" happened to him as to others, to
" be praised most when praise is
" not most deserved. That this
" play has scenes noble in them-
" selves,

"selves, and very well contrived to strike in the exhibition, cannot be denied. But some parts are trifling, others shocking, and some improbable."

This play originally took in a long series of events belonging to the reign of Richard the Third, but was very different from the form in which it now makes its appearance on the stage.

62. KING RICHARD THE THIRD. Trag. altered from Shakspeare, by Colley Cibber. Acted at Drury-Lane, 4to. 1700. The original compiler of our work has been very lavish of his praise of this alteration; but as his encomiums do not appear to be well founded, we think it unnecessary to insert them. The flowery descriptive lines, appropriated to a chorus in *King Henry the Fifth*, are very absurdly put into the mouth of the anxious Richard, whose crown and life depended on the battle for which he was then preparing. When this piece was first introduced to the stage, the licencer expunged the whole first act, assigning as his reason for it, that the distresses of King Henry the Sixth, who is killed by Richard in that part of the play, would put weak people too much in mind of King James, then living in France. In this mutilated state it was acted several years before the proscribed part was admitted. It has, however, always been a very popular and successful performance.

63. RICHARD IN CYPRUS. Tr. by T. Teres. 8vo. no date. [1769.]

64. THE RICHMOND HEIRESS, or, *A Woman once in the Right*. C. by Thomas Durfey. Acted at the Theatre Royal, 4to. 1693. This play did not meet at first with all the success the author expected from it, but being revived afterwards, with alterations, was very favourably received.

65. THE RICHMOND HEIRESS. Com. altered from Tom Durfey, by —— Waldron, and acted at Richmond 1777. Not printed.

66. RICHMOND WELLS, or, *Good Luck at last*. A Comedy, by John Williams. Acted at Mr. Pinkethman's Theatre in Richmond, 12mo. 1723. Scene, Richmond, and the Wells. The author, in his preface, complains of the negligence of the actors in the performance of his piece, and from the motto he appears to have been very young when he produced it.

67. THE RIDER, or, *The Humours of an Inn*. Farce, of two acts, 8vo. 1768. It is said to have been acted with general approbation, and intended for the theatres in London. The last of these assertions may perhaps be true; the former is totally incredible.

68. THE RIGHTS OF HECATE. Pantomime Entertainment. Acted at Drury-Lane 1764.

69. A RIGHT WOMAN, Com. by Francis Beaumont and John Fletcher. Entered on the books of the Stationers' Company June 29, 1660; but, I believe, not printed.

70. RINALDO. Opera, 8vo. 1711. Performed at the Queen's Theatre in the Hay-Market. The plan of this piece was laid by Aaron Hill; but that gentleman's design was filled up with Italian words by Sig. Giacomo Rossi, and the music composed by Handel. The hint of the story is taken from Tasso, and the scene in and near Jerusalem.

71. RINALDO AND ARMIDA. Trag. by J. Dennis. Acted at Lincoln's-Inn Fields, 4to. 1699. The hint of the chief characters in this, as well as the last-mentioned piece, is from Tasso's *Gierusalemme*, but the manners of them being

ly our author thought unequal to that great Italian, he has taken the liberty to change them, and form his characters more agreeable to the subject. His reasons for so doing he has given, not only in his preface to the play, but also in the *Prologue*, which he confesses to be a sort of preface to it. How far he has succeeded in his design, must, however, be left to the judgment of every reader. The scene lies on the top of a mountain in the Canaries. The musical entertainments in it were composed by Mr. John Eccles, excepting a chorus in the fourth act, which is borrowed from Mr. H. Purcell's Frost Scene.

72. THE RIVAL BROTHERS. Tr. Anonym. Acted at Lincoln's-Inn Fields, 4to. 1704. The running title of this play is, *A Fatal Secret*, or, *The Rival Brothers*. Scene, England.

73. THE RIVAL CANDIDATES. Com. Opera, by Henry Bate. Acted at Drury-Lane, 8vo. 1775. This was acted with great applause, and still continues to be favourably received.

74. THE RIVAL FATHER, or, *The Death of Achilles*. Trag. by William Hatchett, 8vo. 1730. This play was acted at the New Theatre in the Hay-Market. It is founded on the well-known story in the Greek annals of the death of that great hero, by a wound in the heel (the only part in which he was vulnerable) by an arrow shot from the bow of Paris, as he was kneeling at the altar, to dedicate his vows to Polyxena, the daughter of Priam (who is here, however, made to be in love with, and ardently beloved by, his son Pyrrhus), as the guarantee of a peace between the Greeks and Trojans. The conduct of the piece in general is borrowed from the *Mort D'Achille* of Corneille, and the author confesses his having taken some hints from the *Audromache* of Racine, and endeavoured to imitate the simplicity of style which Phillips has preserved in his *Distress'd Mother*. He has, however, fallen greatly short of all his originals, and rendered his piece too heavy and declamatory from a want of incident, and a super-abundance of long uninterrupted speeches, which must ever tire an audience, and abate that power which affecting circumstances would otherwise have over their minds. Yet, on the whole, there is some merit in it; and it will not be saying too much to confess, that there have been many pieces since its appearance, which have not been so deserving of approbation, that have met with good success. The scene lies in the Grecian camp before Troy.

75. THE RIVAL FATHER. Farce, 8vo. 1754. This piece was never acted, nor deserved to be so; it was, however, printed in Dublin, and, though published anonymous, has been acknowledged by one Mr. Preston, an itinerant actor, as his offspring.

76. THE RIVAL FOOLS. Com. by C. Cibber. Acted at Drury-Lane, 4to. no date. [1709.] This play is partly borrowed from Fletcher's *Wit at several Weapons*. It met, however, with very bad success. There happened to be a circumstance in it, which, being in itself somewhat ridiculous, gave a part of the audience a favourable opportunity of venting their spleen on the author; viz. a man in one of the earlier scenes on the stage, with a long angling rod in his hand, going to fish for Miller's Thumbs: on which account, some of the spectators took

occasion

occasion whenever Mr. Cibber appeared, who himself played the character, to cry out continually Miller's Thumb.

77. THE RIVAL FRIENDS. C. by Peter Hausted, 4to. 1632. The title of this play has somewhat whimsical in it, and bears testimony to the author's uneasiness under censure. He tells you in it, that it was acted before the King and Queen's Majesties, when, out of their princely favour, they were pleased to visit the university of Cambridge, on the 19th day of March, 1631. *Cry'd down by Boys, Faction, Envy, and confident Ignorance, approved by the judicious, and exposed to the public Censure by the Author.* His dedication is in the same style, being a copy of verses, inscribed *to the Right Honourable, Right Reverend, Right Worshipful, or whatsoever he be, shall be, or whom he hereafter shall call Patron.* From hence it appears that it had met with some criticisms, which he knew not how to bear. Yet it is commended by a copy of Latin verses, and two in English. It has an introduction, by way of dialogue, between Venus, Phœbus, and Thetis, sung by two trebles and a bass, in which Venus (being Phosphorus, as well as Vesper) appears at a window above, as risen, calling to Phœbus (or Sol) who lies in Thetis' lap, at the east side of the stage, canopied by an azure curtain. The scene between Loveall, Mungrell, and Hammershin, in the third act, is copied from that between Truewit, Daw, and La Foole, in the fourth act of Ben Jonson's *Silent Woman.*

78. THE RIVAL GENERALS. Trag. by J. Sterling. Acted at Dublin, 8vo. 1722.

79. THE RIVAL KINGS, or, *The Loves of Oroondates and Statira.* Trag. by John Banks. Acted

at the Theatre Royal, 4to. 1677. This is one of the least known of this author's pieces, and bears the strong characteristic of all his writings, viz. the being affecting in its conduct, without having one good line in its composition. It is written in rhyme, and the plot taken almost entirely from the romance of Cassandra, excepting what relates to Alexander, the foundation of which may be traced in Quintus Curtius and Justin. The scene, Babylon.

80. THE RIVAL LADIES. Tragi-Com. by J. Dryden. Acted at the Theatre Royal, 4to. 1664. 4to. 1669. 4to. 1675. The dedication to this play is a kind of preface in defence of black verse. The scene lies in Alicant; the dispute betwixt Amideo and Hypolito, and Gonsalvo's fighting with the pirates, is borrowed from Encolpius, Giton, Eumolphus, and Tryphena's boarding the vessel of Lycas, in Petronius Arbiter; and the catastrophe has a near resemblance to that of Scarron's *Rival Brothers.*

81. THE RIVAL LOVERS. C. in two acts, by Thomas Warboys, 8vo. 1777. Not acted.

82. THE RIVAL MILLINERS, or, *The Humours of Covent-Garden.* A tragi, comic, farcical, operatical, fantastical Farce, by Robert Drury, 8vo. 1735. This is a burlesque or mock tragedy, and was performed at the Little Theatre in the Hay-Market, with some applause.

83. THE RIVAL MODES. Com. by Ja. Moore Smyth. Acted at Drury-Lane, 8vo. 1727. The reputed genius of this gentleman gave the highest expectations of this piece for a long time before its appearance, which, however, it was very far from answering, and consequently very soon dropt into oblivion.

X 3 84. THE

84. THE RIVAL MOTHER. C. Anonymous. 8vo. 1678.

85. THE RIVAL NYMPHS, or, *The Merry Swain*, by Meff. Daniel Bellamy, fen. and jun. 1746. This is one of the dramatic pieces publifhed by thefe gentlemen in conjunction. I imagine it to be a comedy.

86. THE RIVAL QUEENS, or, *The Death of Alexander the Great*. Trag. by Nath. Lee. Acted at the Theatre Royal, 4to. 1677. This is looked on as one of the beft of this author's pieces, and is to this day frequently reprefented on the ftage; yet with confiderable alterations from what Mr. Lee left it. It muft be confeffed, that there is much bombaft and extravagance in fome parts of it; yet in others there is fo much real dignity, and fuch beautiful flights of imagination and fancy, as render even the madnefs of the true genius more enchanting than even the more regular and finifhed works of the cold laborious playwright of fome periods fince his time. The fcene is in Babylon, and the ftory may be found in the hiftorians of that hero's life.

87. THE RIVAL QUEANS, *with the Humours of Alexander the Great*. A comical Tragedy, by C. Cibber. Acted at Drury-Lane, 8vo. 1729. This piece is a burlefque on the laft-mentioned play, almoft every fcene being parodized with a good deal of humour. This piece was not printed till the time of the above date, and then only in Dublin. Yet it had appeared at Drury-Lane early in the prefent century.

88. THE RIVAL PRIESTS, or, *The Female Politician*. Com. by Meff. Bellamy, 1746. None of the writings of thefe gentlemen were ever acted at the public theatres.

89. THE RIVAL THEATRES, or, *A Play-houfe to be Let*. Farce, To which is added, *The Chocolate Makers, or Mimickry expofed*. An Interlude, by George Stayley, comedian. Acted at Dublin, 12mo. 1759.

90. THE RIVALS. Tragi-Com. 4to. 1668. This play is printed without any author's name; but Langbaine, on the authority, as he fays, of the publifher, afcribes it to Sir W. Davenant. The fcene lies in Arcadia. It was acted at the Duke of York's Theatre, and is only an alteration of *The Noble Kinfmen*, by Fletcher and Shakfpeare.

91. THE RIVALS. Com. by Richard Brinfley Sheridan, Efq. Acted at Covent-Garden, 8vo. 1775. This was the firft dramatic piece of an author, who has fince reached the higheft point of excellence in the leaft eafy and moft hazardous fpecies of writing. The prefent play is formed on a plot unborrowed from any former drama, and contains wit, humour, character, incident, and the principal requifites to conftitute a perfect comedy. It notwithftanding met with very harfh treatment the firft night, and was with difficulty allowed a fecond reprefentation.

92. THE RIVAL SISTERS, or, *The Violence of Love*. Trag. by Robert Gould. Acted at Drury-Lane, 4to. 1696. The reprefentation of this play appears, by the author's complaint in his Epiftle, to have been for fome time delayed after his firft offer of it to the ftage; but, when it was acted, met with a favourable reception. The plot is in great meafure borrowed from Shirley's *Maid's Revenge*, but the original ftory is to be found in *God's Revenge againft Murder*. The fcene

scene lies at Avon, a village in Portugal. The prologue and epilogue written by D'Urfey.

93. THE RIVAL WIDOWS, or, *The Fair Libertine*. Com. by Mrs. E. Cooper, 8vo. 1735. This Piece was acted at the Theatre Royal in Covent-Garden, with some success; the principal character being performed by the authoress on her own benefit, and on the other nights by Mrs. Horton.

94. THE ROARING GIRL, or, *Moll Cutpurse*. Com. by Thomas Middleton and Thomas Dekkar. Acted at the Fortune Stage by the Prince's players, 4to. 1611.

95. ROBERT CYCYLL, an old English Morality, under a very corrupt title, for the subject of it is the French romance of *Robert le Diable*, an English version of which had been published by Wynkyn de Worde. This dramatic piece was represented at the High Cross in Chester in 1529.

96. ROBERT EARL OF HUNTINGTON'S DOWNFALL, *afterwards called* Robin Hood *of merry Sherwode; with his Love to the chaste* Matilda, *the Lord* Fitzwater's *Daughter, afterwards his Maid* Marian. An historical Play, by Thomas Heywood, 4to. 1601.

97. ROBERT EARL OF HUNTINGTON'S DEATH, *otherwise called* Robin Hood, *of merry* Sherwode, *with the lamentable Tragedy of chaste* Matilda, *his fair Maid* Marian, *poisoned at Dunmow by the King*. An historical Play, by T. Heywood, 4to. 1601. This play and the preceding one are both printed in the old black letter, and are neither of them divided into acts. The first part is introduced by J. Skelton, poet laureat to Henry VIII. and the other by Fryar Tuck. The story on which they both are founded, may be seen in Stow, Speed, Baker, and the other historians of the reign of Richard I.

98. ROBIN CONSCIENCE. An Interlude. Anonymous. 4to. 1624. This piece is entirely allegorical, being a dramatic dialogue of *Robin Conscience*, against his Father *Covetise*, his Mother *Newguise*, and his Sister *Proud Beauty*. I suspect this piece to be much older, a. in the books of the Stationers' Company Aug. 3, 1579, is entered the second booke of *Robyn Conscience*, with songs, in four parts.

99. ROBIN HOOD'S PASTORAL MAY GAMES, 1624.

100. ROBIN HOOD. Opera. Acted at Lee's and Harper's Booth, Bartholomew Fair, 8vo. 1730.

101. ROBIN HOOD AND HIS CREW OF SOLDIERS. An Interlude, 1627. This piece and the last but one are in all the lists, yet I do not find any of the writers who pretend to have seen them. Langbaine and Jacob have mentioned them without date; and it is only in *The British Theatre* that I meet with those above, which from that authority alone therefore I have affixed to them.

After the many proofs which have appeared of Chetwood's want of fidelity, a date cannot be taken merely on his credit. In the books of the Stationers' Company, " A pastoral pleasant comedie of " Robin Hood and Little John," was entered by Edward White, May 18, 1594.

102. ROBINHOOD. A Musical Entertainment, 8vo. 1751. This piece was performed at the Theatre Royal in Drury-Lane, but without any great success, it having little more than musical merit to recommend it, which was not then quite so much the idol of public adoration as it seems at present to be.

X 4   103. Ro-

163. ROBINSON CRUSOE. Pantomime. Acted at Drury-Lane 1781. This is said to be contrived by Mr. Sheridan, whose powers, if it really be his performance, do not seem adapted to the production of such kinds of entertainments. The scenery, by Loutherbourg, has a very pleasing effect, but confidered in every other light it is a truly infipid exhibition.

104. RODOGUNE, or, *The Rival Brothers*. Trag. by S. Afpinwall, 8vo. 1765. This is a tranflation from the French of Corneille. From the preface we learn, that it had been refused by the managers.

105. ROGER AND JOAN, or, *The Country Wedding*. A comic Mafque. Anonymous. 4to. 1739. This very little piece is faid in the title-page to have been acted at the Theatre Royal in Covent-Garden; but by the length of it, which does not exceed about eight pages in quarto printed very loosely, it appears fcarcely fufficient for the entertainment of a whole evening, and therefore I imagine it muft rather have been a fort of interlude between the acts made use of to introduce a ballet, or else have filled up the fpace of time after the play, while the performers were drefling and otherwife preparing for the reprefentation of the farce. The fcene lies in a Country Village, and the mufic was compofed by Mr. Lampe.

106. ROLLO DUKE OF NORMANDY. Trag. by John Fletcher. Acted by his Majefties fervants, 4to. 1640. This was efteemed an excellent tragedy, and, though now laid afide, ufed to be received with great applaufe. The fcene lies in Normandy. The plot is taken from Herodian, lib. iv. and part of the language from Seneca's *Thebais*.

107. THE ROMAN ACTOR. Tr. by Phil. Maffinger. Acted at Black-Friers, 4to. 1629. This play was confidered by its author, and by other dramatic poets, his contemporaries, to have been the moft perfect birth of his *Minerva*, as appears from his own Epiftle dedicatory, and by no lefs than fix feveral copies of verfes prefixed to it. It could not, therefore, fail of meeting with fuccefs in the reprefentation. It was revived with fome alterations, and printed in 8vo. 1722. and even before that time, Mr. Betterton occafioned it to be got up in the theatre, and gained great applaufe and reputation in the part of the *Roman Actor*, which he himfelf performed. The plot of it may be found in the hiftorians of the reign of Domitian, and the fcene lies at Rome.

108. THE ROMAN BRIDE's REVENGE. Trag. by Charles Gildon. Acted at the Theatre Royal, 4to. 1697. This was a very hafty production, having been written in a month, and met with that fuccefs, that fuch precipitancy in works which undoubtedly require the utmoft care in compofition, revifal, and correction, juftly deferves. Yet it is far from being deftitute of merit, the firft and fecond acts, written probably while the author's genius and imagination were in their full glow, being very well executed. Nor is the cataftrophe at all to be found fault with. The moral intended in it, is to fet forth, in the punifhment of one of the principal characters, that no confideration whatfoever fhould induce us to neglect or delay the fervice of our country. The fcene lies in Rome, and part of the plot is taken from *Camera* of Galata.

109. THE ROMAN EMPRESS. Trag. by William Joyner. Acted

at the Theatre Royal, 4to. 1671. This play met with great approbation and success, notwithstanding its first appearance laboured under some inconveniencies. The language of it is poetical, spirited, and masculine, and free from what he calls the jingling antitheses of *Love* and *Honour*; *Terror* and *Compassion* being the alternate sensations he aims at exciting in his auditors. It is not very apparent for what reason the author should alter the names of the characters from those which they bear in history. Yet he tells us, that by the advice of friends he has done so, and that this *Emperor* was one of the greatest that ever Rome boasted. Langbaine conjectures, that under the character of Valentius, the author has intended to draw that of Constantine the Great, and that Crispus and his mother-in-law Fauſtina, lie concealed under those of Florus and Fulvia. The ſcene of this drama, or action, is about the banks of the Tiber; where Hoſtilius and his party are ſuppoſed to be in Rome, or on the Roman ſide of the river; and Valentius with his party encamped on the other ſide, in the nature of beſiegers.

110. THE ROMAN FATHER. Trag. by W. Whitehead. Acted at Drury-Lane, 8vo. 1750. This play is founded on that celebrated incident of the earlieſt period of the Roman hiſtory, the combat between the Horatii and the Curiatii. The ſame ſtory had been long ago made the ſubject of a dramatic piece, by the great French tragic writer, P. Corneille, whoſe Horace is eſteemed amongſt his *Chef d'Oeuvres*. From that tragedy, therefore, Mr. Whitehead confeſſes that he has borrowed the idea of two or three of his moſt intereſting ſcenes. And I muſt confeſs I cannot help wiſhing he had even more cloſely followed the plan of that very capital writer in the conduct of the piece, ſince by confining himſelf entirely to Rome, and the family of the Horatii, he has deprived himſelf of the opportunity of throwing-in that variety of incident and contraſt of character which Corneille's play is poſſeſſed of, in conſequence of his having introduced the young Curiatius, whoſe rugged, hardy valour, though truly heroical, ſets off, in the moſt advantageous manner, the equality and reſolution mingled with a ſuperior tenderneſs and humanity, which ſhines out in the character of the young Horatius. The addition of a ſiſter of Curiatius married to Horatius, in Corneille's tragedy, by ſtrengthening the tie between the families, is alſo a great aggravation of the diſtreſs. I would not, however, here be underſtood to mean any reflection on Mr. Whitehead's tragedy, which has certainly great merit, and obtained the juſt approbation of repeated and judicious audiences. For ſurely to fall ſomewhat ſhort of a Corneille, can be no diſgrace to any writer beneath a Shakſpeare. Nay, in ſome reſpects, the piece before us has the advantage of the French play, the declamatory parts in the laſt act being, in the latter, too long and diffuſe for giving pleaſure in a theatrical repreſentation, however pleaſing they may appear in the cloſet. There are alſo, in general, more poetical beauties in the language of Mr. Whitehead's, than in that of Corneille's tragedy; and, indeed, taking it on the whole, it may be ranked amongſt the beſt of the dramatic pieces of this ſomewhat unprolific age.

111. THE ROMAN GENERALS, or, *The Diſtreſſed Ladies*. Trag. by John

John Dover, 4to. 1667. The plot of this play, as far as it relates to history, may be traced in Plutarch's Lives of Pompey and Cæsar. The author has, however, laid it down as his maxim, neither rigidly to adhere to historical fact, nor wildly to deviate from it. The scene lies in Gallia, Rome, and other parts of Italy. From the general tenor of the prologue and epilogue, it is not unreasonable to collect that the piece was never acted, nor intended to be so, they seeming rather addressed to the reader than the auditor.

112. THE ROMAN MAID. Tr. by Capt. Robert Hurst, 8vo. 1725. This play was acted at the Theatre Royal in Lincoln's-Inn Fields, with very little success.

113. THE ROMAN REVENGE. Trag. by A. Hill, 8vo. 1753. This play was acted at the Theatre at Bath with some success, but is not equal to the generality of its author's works. The plot of it is the death of Julius Cæsar; and he has heightened the distress by a circumstance, which, however, I know not that he has any authority for in history, viz. the making Brutus find himself, after the death of the dictator, to be his natural son. How far such an addition to, or deviation from, recorded facts, is warrantable, or comes within the limits of the *Licentia Poetica*, I have neither room nor inclination to enter into a discussion of in this place.

114. THE ROMAN SACRIFICE. Trag. by William Shirley. Acted at Drury-Lane 1776. Not printed. This piece was performed only four nights, and was very coldly received.

115. THE ROMAN VICTIM. Trag. by William Shirley. This play is promised in the collection of the author's dramatic works.

It appears to have been refused both by Mr. Garrick and Mr. Harris.

116. THE ROMAN VIRGIN, or, *Unjust Judge*. Trag. by Thomas Betterton. Acted at the Duke's Theatre, 4to. 1679. This is only an alteration of Webster's *Appius and Virginia*.

117. THE ROMANCE OF AN HOUR. Com. of two acts, by Hugh Kelly, performed at Covent-Garden, 8vo. 1774. This little comedy is built on one of Marmontel's Tales, and was acted with success.

118. ROME EXCIS'D. A Tragi-comi Ballad Opera, 8vo. 1733. This little piece is entirely political, and was never intended for the stage, being only a satire on the measures then taking by the ministry with regard to the revenue.

119. ROME PRESERV'D. Trag. translated from Voltaire, 8vo. 1760.

120. ROME'S FOLLIES, or, *The Amorous Fryars*. C. by N. N. 4to. 1681. The scene lies in the City of Rome; and the piece is said, in the title-page, to have been acted at a person of a quality's house, but I imagine it was only intended to throw a glance of censure and ridicule on the professors of the Romish religion, which were at that time pretty numerous, and still more increasing in these kingdoms.

121. ROMEO AND JULIET. Trag. by W. Shakspeare. Of this play there are several early editions; one in 4to. a sketch, acted by Lord Hunsdon's servants, 4to. 1597. 4to. 1599. The complete one as acted at the Globe, 4to. 1609. 4to. N. D. 4to. 1637. The fable of this now favourite play is built on a real tragedy that happened about the beginning of the fourteenth

fourteenth century. The story with all its circumstances is given us by Bandello, in one of his Novels, vol. II. Nov. 9. and also by Girolamo de la Corte, in his History of Verona. The scene, in the beginning of the fifth act, is at Mantua; through all the rest of the piece, in and near Verona. As I have mentioned before that this is at present a very favourite play, it will be necessary to take notice what various alterations it has gone through from time to time, and in what form it at present appears, which is considerably different from that in which it was originally written. The tragedy in itself has very striking beauties, yet on the whole is far from being this great author's master-piece. An amazing redundance of fancy shines through the whole diction of the love scenes; yet the overflowings of that fancy in some places rather runs into puerility, and the frequent intervention of rhymes which appears in the original play, and which seems a kind of wantonness in the author, certainly abates of that verisimilitude to natural conversation which ought ever to be maintained in dramatic dialogue, especially where the scene and action fall under the circumstance of domestic life. The characters are some of them very highly painted, particularly those of the two lovers, which perhaps possess more of the romantic, giddy, and irresistible passion of love, when it makes its first attack on very young hearts, than all the labours of an hundred poets since, was all the essence of their love scenes to be collected into one, could possibly convey an idea of. Mercutio too is a character so boldly touched, and so truly spirited, that it has been a surmise of some of the critics, that Shakspeare put him to death in the third act, from a consciousness that it would even exceed the extent of his own powers to support the character through the two last acts, equal to the sample he had given of it in the three former ones. The catastrophe is affecting, and even as it stands in the original is sufficiently dramatic.

"This play, says Dr. Johnson, "is one of the most pleasing of "our author's performances. The "scenes are busy and various, "the incidents numerous and im- "portant, the catastrophe irre- "sistibly affecting, and the pro- "cess of the action carried on "with such probability, at least "with such congruity to popular "opinion, as tragedy requires.

"Here is one of the few at- "tempts of Shakspeare to exhi- "bit the conversation of gentle- "men, to represent the airy "sprightliness of juvenile ele- "gance. Mr. Dryden mentions "a tradition, which might easily "reach his time, of a declaration "made by Shakspeare, that *he was* "*obliged to kill Mercutio in the third* "*act, lest he should have been killed* "*by him.* Yet he thinks him *no* "*such formidable person, but that he* "*might have lived through the play,* "*and died in his bed,* without "danger to a poet. Dryden well "knew, had he been in quest of "truth, that, in a pointed sen- "tence, more regard is common- "ly had to the words than the "thought, and that it is very "seldom to be rigorously under- "stood. Mercutio's wit, gaiety, "and courage, will always pro- "cure him friends that wish him "a longer life; but his death is "not precipitated, he has lived "out the time allotted him in the "construction of the play; nor "do I doubt the ability of Shak-

"speare to have continued his exiſtence, though ſome of his ſallies are perhaps out of the reach of Dryden, whoſe genius was not very fertile of merriment, nor ductile to humour, but acute, argumentative, comprehenſive, and ſublime.

"The Nurſe is one of the characters in which the author delighted: he has, with great ſubtilty of diſtinction, drawn her at once loquacious and ſecret, obſequious and inſolent, truſty and diſhoneſt.

"His comic ſcenes are happily wrought, but his pathetic ſtrains are always polluted with ſome unexpected depravations. His perſons, however diſtreſſed, *have a conceit left them in their miſery, a miſerable conceit.*"

Now for the ſeveral alterations of the foregoing piece, by ſeveral hands.

122. ROMEO AND JULIET. By Ja. Howard, Eſq; who, as Downes, in his *Roſcius Anglicanus*, p. 22. tells us, altered this tragedy into a tragi-comedy, preſerving both Romeo and Juliet alive; ſo that, when the play was revived in Sir William Davenant's company, it was played alternately, viz. tragical one day, and tragi-comical another, for ſeveral days together. This alteration hath never been printed.

123. ROMEO AND JULIET. A Tragedy, reviſed and altered from Shakſpeare, by Mr. Theophilus Cibber; firſt revived (in September, 1744) at the Theatre in the Hay-Market; afterwards acted at Drury-Lane, 8vo. no date [1748.] Subjoined to this is a ſerio-comic apology for part of the life of the author. Very conſiderable alterations and additions were made in this edition; but theſe agree ſo ill with the remainder written by Shakſpeare, that it is impoſſible to read them with any degree of ſatisfaction.

124. ROMEO AND JULIET. A Tragedy. Acted at Drury-Lane, 12mo. 1751. The third of theſe alterations, which is now univerſally and repeatedly performed in all the Britiſh Theatres, and is the work of Mr. Garrick, whoſe perfect acquaintance with the properties of effect, and unqueſtionable judgment as to what will pleaſe an audience, have ſhewn themſelves very conſpicuouſly in this piece. For, without doing much more than reſtoring Shakſpeare to himſelf, and the ſtory to the Novel from which it was originally borrowed, he has rendered the whole more uniform, and worked up the cataſtrophe to a greater degree of diſtreſs than it held in the original; as Juliet's awaking before Romeo's death, and the tranſports of the latter, on ſeeing her revive, over-coming even the very remembrance of the very late act of deſperation he had committed, give ſcope for that ſudden tranſition from rapture to deſpair, which make the recollection, that he *muſt* die, infinitely more affecting, and the diſtreſs of Juliet, as well as his own, much deeper than it is poſſible to be in Shakſpeare's play, where ſhe does not awake till after the poiſon has taken its full effect in the death of Romeo. There is one alteration, however, in this piece, which, I muſt confeſs, does not appear to me altogether ſo neceſſary, viz. the introducing Romeo from the beginning as in love with Juliet, whereas Shakſpeare ſeems to have intended, by making him at firſt enamoured with another (Roſalind), to point out his misfortunes in the conſequence of one paſſion, as a piece of poetical juſtice for his

his inconstancy and falshood in regard to a prior attachment, as Juliet's in some measure are for her breach of filial obedience, and her rashness in the indulgence of a passion, so opposite to the natural interests and connections of her family.

Besides these, two other managers, viz. Mr. Sheridan of the Dublin, and Mr. Lee of the Edinburgh theatre, have each, for the use of their respective companies, made some supposed amendments in this play; but, as neither of them have appeared in print, I can give no further account of them: nor of a third alteration by Mr. Marsh, which he has likewise had the prudence to conceal from the public.

I cannot, however, quite drop this subject without taking notice of one more alteration, though not so professed a one of it, made by a more celebrated pen than any of those I have hitherto mentioned, viz. Mr. Otway, whose Tragedy of CAIUS MARIUS is founded wholly on it, and who has culled all its choicest beauties to engraft them on the stock of a Roman story, with which they have not, nor can have, the least plausible connexion. Yet so little does this play seem to have been known till of very late years, that I have frequently, with surprize, observed quotations of some of its finest passages, particularly the inimitable description of the apothecary's shop, made use of by authors, who have attributed them to Otway, without seeming to have the least knowledge from whence he took them. Yet to do that gentleman himself justice, it must be acknowledged, that in his Prologue he has confessed his having borrowed half his plot from some play of Shakspeare's, although he does not mention this particularly by name.

125. ROMEO AND JULIET. Com. written originally in Spanish, by that celebrated dramatic poet Lopez de Vega, 8vo. 1770.

126. ROMULUS. Trag. by H. Johnson, from the French of Monsieur De La Motte, 8vo. 1721.

127. ROMULUS AND HERSILIA, or, *The Sabine War.* Trag. Anon. Acted at the Duke's Theatre, 4to. 1683. This is a very good play; the plot taken from Livy, Lib. 1. and Ovid's *Metamorphoses*, Lib. 14. The scene lies in Rome, and the Epilogue is written by Mrs. Behn.

128. ROMULUS AND HERSILIA. Tr. by Dr. Ralph Schomberg. Never printed. It was offered to Mr. Garrick, and we doubt not very properly refused by him.

129. ROSALINDA. A Musical Drama, by J. Lockman; set to music by John Christopher Smith, and performed at Hickford's Great Room in Brewers-street, 4to. 1740. Prefixed to this is, "An Enquiry "into the Rise and Progress of "Operas and Oratorios, with "some Reflections on Lyric Poe- "try and Music."

130. ROSAMOND. Opera, by Joseph Addison, 4to. 1707. The plot of this little piece is taken from the English History in the reign of Henry II. and it is observed that it exceeds, in the beauty of the diction, any English performance of the kind. It was, however, very ill set to music, by which means the success it met with fell far short of what its merit might justly have laid a claim to. In the year 1767 it was entirely new set by Dr. Arnold, and performed at Covent-Garden, 8vo. The scene is laid in Woodstock Park. Dr. Johnson observes, that the opera of *Rosamond*,

though

though it is seldom mentioned, is one of the first of Addison's compositions. The subject is well chosen, the fiction is pleasing, and the praise of Marlborough, for which the scene gives opportunity, is, what perhaps every human excellence must be, the product of good-luck improved by genius. The thoughts are sometimes great, and sometimes tender; the versification is easy and gay. There is doubtless some advantage in the shortness of the lines, which there is little temptation to load with expletive epithets. The dialogue seems commonly better than the songs. The two comic characters of Sir Trusty and Grideline, though of no great value, are yet such as the poet intended. Sir Trusty's account of the death of Rosamond is, I think, too grossly absurd. The whole drama is airy and elegant; engaging in its process, and pleasing in its conclusion.

131. ROSANIA, or, *Love's Victory*. Com. by James Shirley. This is mentioned in his poems, but is, I apprehend, no other than *The Doubtful Heir* under a different title.

132. THE ROSE. Com. Op. in two acts, performed at Drury-Lane, 8vo. 1773. The music by Dr. Arne, who is supposed to have been the author of the words also. The title-page, however, ascribes them to a gentleman commoner of Oxford. It was represented only one night.

133. ROSE AND COLIN. Com. Opera, by Charles Dibdin. Acted at Covent-Garden, 8vo. 1778. This is a short piece of one act, translated from the French piece, called, *Rose and Colas*.

134. ROTHERIC O'CONNOR, KING OF CONNAUGHT, or, *The Distress'd Princess*. Trag. by Cha. Shadwell, 12mo. 1720. This tragedy was acted in Dublin, the title points out where the scene is laid, and the plot is borrowed from the Irish Historians. It is far from being a bad play, though, I think not equal to some of his comedies.

135. THE ROVER, or, *The Banish'd Cavaliers*. Com. in two parts, by Mrs. Aphra Behn. Acted at the Duke's Theatre, 4to. 1677 and 1681. These two comedies are both of them very entertaining, and contain much business, bustle, and intrigue, supported with an infinite deal of sprightliness. The basis of them both, however, may be found on a perusal of Killigrew's DON THOMASO, or, *The Wanderer*. The scene of the first part is laid in Naples during the time of Carnival, which is the high season for gallantry; and that of the second at Madrid.

136. THE ROVER, or, *Happiness at Last*. A dramatic Pastoral, designed for the theatre, but never acted, by Samuel Boyce, 4to. 1752.

137. THE ROVER RECLAIM'D, Com. Anonym. 1691. This play I do not find mentioned any where but in *The British Theatre*.

138. THE ROVING HUSBAND RECLAIM'D. A Comedy, *written by a Club of Ladies, in Vindication of virtuous Plays*, 4to. 1704. This play was never acted, nor do I find it in any of the Catalogues; yet Coxeter has it with the above full title, in his MS. Notes.

139. THE ROUND-HEADS, or, *The Good Old Cause*. Com. by Mrs. Behn. Acted at the Duke's Theatre, 4to. 1682. Great part both of the plot and language of this play is borrowed from Tateham's Comedy, called, *The Rump*. Yet, to do Mrs. Behn justice, she has very much improved on her original,

original, having drawn the *Roundheads*, whose characters it was the principal design of both to expose, in much higher colours than her predecessor was able to do. The scene, London.

140. THE ROUT. Farce of two acts. Acted at Drury-Lane, 8vo. 1758. This very insignificant little piece made its first appearance for the benefit of the *Marine Society*, and was said to be written by a *Person of Quality*, and *presented* to that charity, without the least view to private emolument. In some little time afterwards, however, this boasted person of distinction turned out to be no other than the *illustrious* Dr. Hill (of whom see some further mention under ORPHEUS), whose *disinterested* motives to *public benevolence* terminated at last in a demand on the managers for a *private* benefit to himself, by a second representation of the piece. This claim was in some measure complied with, the piece being performed a second time, though it was hissed and hooted throughout every scene. The acknowledged powers of its author,

Spargere qui fomnos cantuque manuque soliebat,

had no success in quieting the audience;

— *nec quid cum juvere in vulnera cantus Somniferi, aut Marsi, quaesitae in montibus herbae.*

Smart, in his *Hilliad*, has characterized the Doctor in the following line, which is equally bitter, witty, and philosophical; and may be applied to his farce as properly as to himself, the former, during its short existence on the stage, being undoubtedly

" Th' insolvent tenant of incumber'd
" space."

He who has read only the present work of Hill will not think the satire of his opponent was too severe, any more than that of Mr. Garrick, who, on the representation of the *Rout*, produced the following epigram:

" For physic and farces, his equal there
" scarce is;
" His farces are physic, his physic a
" farce is."

141. THE ROYAL CAPTIVE. Trag. by John Maxwell, being blind, 8vo. 1745. Printed at York for the benefit of the author.

142. THE ROYAL CAPTIVES. Trag. Acted at the Hay-Market, 8vo. 1729. This play is taken from Euripides, and met with no success in the representation. In the preface the author complains that his piece was performed very imperfectly, some scenes being left out, and others so intolerably mangled, that it was impossible for any body to make any thing of it.

143. THE ROYAL CHACE, or, *Merlin's Cave*. Dram. Entertainment, introduced into the Grotesque Pantomine of Jupiter and Europa. Acted at Covent-Garden, 8vo. 1736. The words by Mr. Phillips.

144. THE ROYAL CHOICE. A Play, by Sir Robert Stapleton. Entered on the books of the Stationers' Company Nov. 29, 1653; but apparently not printed.

145. THE ROYAL COMBAT. Com. by John Ford. Entered on the books of the Stationers' Company June 29, 1660; but probably not printed, it being amongst those destroyed by Mr. Warburton's servant.

146. THE ROYAL CONVERT. Trag. by N. Rowe, 4to. 1707. This play, though not so often acted as some others of this author's pieces, is far from falling short of any one of them in point of merit. The scene of it is laid

in the kingdom of Kent, and the fable fuppofed to be in the time of Hengift, and about twenty years after the firſt invafion of Britain by the Saxons. The characters of Rodogune and Ethelinda are very finely contrafted, as are alfo thofe of Hengiſt and Aribert; the incidents are interefting; the language occafionally fpirited and tender, yet every where poetical; and the cataſtrophe affecting and truly dramatic. Nor do I know any reafon why it fhould not be as great a favourite as either *Jane Shore* or *The Fair Penitent*, unlefs that its being founded on a religious plan renders it lefs agreeable to the general taſte of an audience, than thofe ſtories where love is in fome meafure the bafis of the diſtrefs. It was acted at the Queen's Theatre in the Hay-Market, and with but fmall fuccefs, if we may judge from the motto to it, *Laudatur & alget.*

Dr. Johnfon obeferves, that the fable of this play is drawn from an obfcure and barbarousage, to which fictions are moſt eafily and properly adapted; for when objects are imperfectly feen, they eafily take forms from imagination. The fcene lies among our anceſtors in our own country, and therefore very eafily catches attention. Rodogune is a perfonage truly tragical, of high fpirit, and violent paffions, great with tempeftuous dignity, and wicked with a foul that would have been heroic if it had been virtuous. Rowe does not always remember what his characters require. In *Tamerlane*, there is fome ridiculous mention of the God of Love; and Rodogune, a favage Saxon, talks of Venus, and the eagle that bears the thunder of Jupiter. This play difcovers its own date, by a prediction of the Union, in imitation of Cranmer's prophetic promifes to *Henry the Eighth.* The anticipated bleffings of Union are not very naturally introduced, nor very happily expreffed.

Mr. Gibbon (Hiſtory of the Roman Empire, vol. III. p. 627.) fays, that Procopius may have fuggefted to Mr. Rowe the character and fituation of Rodogune in this tragedy.

147. THE ROYAL CUCKOLD, or, *Great Baſtard.* Tragi-Com. 4to. 1693. This is nothing more than a tranflation from the German, by Mr. Paul Vergerius, and was never acted. It is taken from a book, called *The Secret Hiſtory of Lewis XIV. of France.*

148. THE ROYAL FLIGHT, or, *The Conqueſt of Ireland.* A Farce, 4to. 1690. The title-page of this piece plainly fhews the fubject, and fcene of it, it being evidently defigned to ridicule the conduct of the unfortunate King James II. in his abdication; and the author has drawn moſt of his characters without any difguife or modefty.

149. THE ROYAL GARLAND. An occafional Interlude, in honour of his Danifh Majefty, pertormed at Coyent-Garden, 8vo. 1768.

150. THE ROYALIST. Com. by Thomas Durfey. Acted at the Duke's Theatre, 4to. 1682. This play met with good fuccefs, but like moſt of our author's pieces is collected from novels; Camilla's tricks of impofing on her hufband Sir Oliver Old-Cut, for the love of Sir Charles Kinglove, is borrowed from Boccace's *Decam.* Dec. 7. Nov. 9, and the fong of *Hey Boys up go we,* in the fourth act, ftolen from an eclogue, printed in 4to. 1644. called *The Shepherd's Oracle.*

151. THE ROYAL KING AND THE

THE LOYAL SUBJECT. Tragi-Com. by Thomas Heywood, 4to. 1637. This play was acted with great applause. The plot very much resembles, and is probably borrowed from, Fletcher's LOYAL SUBJECT. The scene, London.

152. THE ROYAL MARRIAGE. A Ballad Opera, of three acts. Anonymous. 8vo. 1736. This piece was never performed, but written in compliment to the marriage between his late Royal Highness Frederick Prince of Wales, and Princess Augusta, of Saxegotha, the late princess-dowager of Wales.

153. THE ROYAL MARTYR, or, *King Charles the First*, by Alexander Fyfe, 4to. 1709. This play was never acted, but the subject speaks itself.

154. *The True Description of a* ROYAL MASQUE, presented at Hampton-Court on the eighth of January, 1604. This piece was personated by the Queen, and eleven of her ladies of honour. Anomymous, 4to. 1604.

155. THE ROYAL MASTER. Tragi-Com. by Ja. Shirley, 4to. 1638. This play was acted at the Theatre in Dublin, and before the Lord Lieutenant at the Castle; and by the several copies of complimentary verses prefixed to it, being no less than ten in number, it is probable that it met with applause. The scene, Naples.

156. THE ROYAL MERCHANT, or, *The Beggar's Bush*. Com. 4to. 1706. by H. N. (I imagine this to be Henry Norris the comedian). This play is only an alteration from Beaumont and Fletcher's BEGGAR'S BUSH, and in this altered form has been frequently performed. The scene is laid in Flanders.

157. THE ROYAL MERCHANT. Opera, by Thomas Hull, founded on Beaumont and Fletcher. Acted at Covent-Garden, 8vo. 1768.

158. THE ROYAL MISCHIEF. Trag. by Mrs. De la Riviere Manley. Acted by his Majesties servants, 4to. 1696. The plot, as the author herself informs us in her preface, is taken from a story in Sir John Chardin's Travels; but she has improved the catastrophe, by punishing the criminal characters for their illicit amours, whereas in the original tale they are suffered to escape. The allegories in it are just, the metaphors beautiful, and the Aristotelian rules of the drama strictly adhered to. The scene, the Castle of Phasia, in Libardian.

159. THE ROYAL SHEPHERD. Opera, by Richard Rolt. Acted at Drury-Lane, 8vo. 1764. Taken from Metastasio. The story, that of Alexander the Great delivering Sidon from the Tyrant Strato. It met with no success.

160. ROYAL SHEPHERDESS. Tragi-Com. by Thomas Shadwell. Acted at the Duke of York's Theatre, 4to. 1669. This play is not Shadwell's own, being, as he himself acknowledges in his Epistle to the reader, taken from a comedy written by M. Fountain, called *The Rewards of Virtue*. It met, however, with considerable applause. The scene lies in Arcadia.

161. THE ROYAL SHEPHERDS. Pastoral, of three acts, by Josias Cunningham, 8vo. 1765.

162. THE ROYAL SLAVE. Tragi-Com. by William Cartwright, 4to. 1639. 4to. 1640. and 8vo. 1651. The first representation of this play was by the students of Christ-Church in Oxford, before King Charles I. and his Queen, on the 30th of August, 1636. And it is very remarkable, that Dr. Busby (afterwards the very celebrated

celebrated master of Westminster-school), who acted a principal part in it, signalized himself so greatly, as did also many of his fellow-students, and the play gave on the whole such general satisfaction to their Majesties and the Court, and that not only for the noblenefs of style in the piece itself, and the ready address and graceful carriage of the performers, but also for the pomp of the scenery, the richness of the habits, and the excellency of the songs, which were set by that admirable composer, Mr. Henry Lawes, that it was universally acknowledged to exceed every thing of that nature that had been seen before. The Queen, in particular, was so extremely delighted with it, that her curiosity was excited to see her own servants, whose profession it was, represent the same piece, in order to be able, from comparison, to form a just idea of the real merit of the performance she had already been witness to. For which purpose she sent for the scenes and habits to Hampton-Court, and commanded her own regular actors to represent the fame, when, by general confent of every one present, the judgement was given in favour of the literary performers, though nothing was wanting on the side of the author, to inform the actors as well as the scholars, in what belonged to the action and delivery of each part; nor can it be imagined that there was any deficiency in point of execution in the former, since so much of their reputation must have been dependent on their shewing a superiority on that occasion. The prologues and epilogues, written for both these representations, are printed with the play.

163. THE ROYAL SUPPLI-ANTS. Trag. by Dr. Delap. Acted at Drury-Lane, 8vo. 1781. This nine-nights' play is taken from the Heraclidæ of Euripides.

164. THE ROYAL VOYAGE, or, *The Irish Expedition*. Tragi-Com. Acted in the years 1689 and 1690, 4to. 1690. The scene of this piece is laid in various places in Ireland; nor can any one be at a loss to know the subject of it, who has the least acquaintance with the affairs of these kingdoms during that period. It was never acted.

165. RUDENS. Com. translated from Plautus, by Lawrence Echard, 1694. This play, together with two others from the same author, are published in a pocket volume, and dedicated to Sir Charles Sedley. Mr. Echard has also added critical remarks to each piece, and a parallel drawn between the writings of Plautus and Terence, the latter of which, as I have observed in another place, he has given the world a compleat translation of.

166. RULE A WIFE AND HAVE A WIFE. Com. by John Fletcher. Acted by his Majesty's servants, 4to. 1640. This is a very pleasing play, and is frequently acted at this time. The plot of Leon's feigned simplicity, in order to gain Margaretta for a wife, and his immediate return to the exertion of a spirited behaviour for the controul of her, create an agreeable surprize, and are truly dramatical. The characters of Estifania and the Copper Captain are also well drawn and lively supported. In a word, this play, though not perfectly regular, may undoubtedly stand in a rank of merit superior to much the greatest part of those which are daily presented on our stage, and that with repeated tokens

kens of approbation. The last act of this piece, and indeed many other parts of it, received great improvements from the hand of Mr. Garrick, by whom it was adapted to the stage, and whose excellent performance of the part of Leon will be long remembered with pleasure.

167. THE RUMP, or, *The Mirrour of the late Times*. Com. by John Tatham. Acted at Dorset-Court, 4to. 1660. This piece was written soon after the Restoration; and the author, being a steady royalist, has endeavoured to paint the Puritans in the strongest and most contemptible colours. This play was revived with alterations by Mrs. Behn, for which, See ROUNDHEADS.

168. "The famous Tragedie
" of the Life and Death of MRS.
" RUMP. Shewing how she was
" brought to bed of a monster,
" with her terrible pangs, bitter
" teeming, hard labour, and la-
" mentable travell, from Ports-
" mouth to Westminster, and the
" great misery she hath endured
" by her ugly, deformed, ill-sha-
" pen, base-begotten brat, or imp
" of reformation, and the great
" care and wonderful pains taken
" by Mr. London Midwife, Mrs.
" Haslerigg, Nurse Gossip Vaine,
" Gossip Scot, and her man Lite-
" sum, Gossip Walton, Gossip
" Martin, Gossip Nevil, Gossip
" Lenthal, secluded Gossip's Ap-
" prentices. Together with the
" exceeding great fright she took
" at a free parliament: and the
" fatal end of that grand tyrant
" O. C. the father of all mur-
" thers, rebellions, treasons, and
" treacheries, committed since the
" year 1648. As it was pre-
" sented on a burning stage, at
" Westminster, the 29th of May
" 1660. 4to. 1660." This long title is prefixed to a trifling piece of eight pages, which is entirely political, and of no value.

169. THE RUNAWAY. Com. by Mrs. Cowley. Acted at Drury-Lane, 8vo. 1776. This piece is supposed to have received some touches from the pen of Mr. Garrick, to which gentleman the authoress acknowledges her obligations in a Dedication. It was performed with a considerable degree of success.

S.

S A

1. THE SACRIFICE. Trag. by Sir Francis Fane, 4to. 1680. This play was never acted, the author having long before devoted himself to a country life, and wanting patience to attend the leisure of the stage. It met, however, with the highest approbation from his contemporary writers; three of whom, viz. Mr. Tate, Mr. Robins, and Mrs. Behn, have paid it the tribute of complimentary verses, which are published with it. The plot is founded on the story of Bajazet and Tamerlane, (and probably might afford

ford the hint to Mr. Rowe, of his admirable Tragedy of *Tamerlane)* for which see the Life of *Tamerlane*, by M. D'Assigny; the same by P. Perondini, Knolles's *Turkish History* of the Life of Bajazet the first, and several other writers. The scene in a revolted Fort in China.

2. THE SACRIFICE, or, *Cupid's Vagaries*. Masque, by Benjamin Victor. Never acted, 8vo. 1776.

3. THE SACRIFICE OF IPHIGENIA. Entertainment of Music, performed at the New Wells, near the London Spaw, Clerkenwell, 12mo. 1750. To this piece are added the songs of a Pantomime, called, *Harlequin Mountebank*, or, *The Squire Electrified*. The music by Dr then Mr. Arne.

4. THE SAD ONE. Trag. by Sir John Suckling, 8vo. 1646. This play was never acted, having been left by the author unfinished. In short, it is rather a sketch or skeleton of a play, than an entire piece; for though it consists of five acts, and seems to have somewhat of a catastrophe, yet none of those acts are of more than half the usual length; nor is the subject of any one scene so much extended on, as it is apparent it was the author's intention to have done. The scene lies in Sicily.

5. THE SAD SHEPHERD, or, *A Tale of Robin Hood*. A Pastoral, by Ben Jonson, Fol. 1640. This piece is printed among this writer's works, but was never acted, as it was left imperfect by him at his death, only two acts and part of a third being finished. The scene is in Sherwood, consisting of a landscape, of a forest, hills, valleys, cottages, a castle, a river, pastures, herds, flocks:—all full of country simplicity.—Robin Hood's bower, his well;—the Witch's *Dimble*, the Swineherd's Oak, and the Hermit's *Cell*.

6. THE SAILORS FAREWELL, or, *The Guinea outfit*. Com. of three acts, by Thomas Boulton, 12mo. 1768. Printed at Liverpool.

7. THE SAILORS OPERA, or, *A Trip to Jamaica*, 12mo. 1745.

8. SAINT ALBONS. Trag. by James Shirley, was entered on the books of the Stationers' Company, Feb. 14, 1639, by William Cooke; but, I believe, not printed.

9. SAINT CICILY, or, *The Converted Twins*. A Christian Trag. by E. M. 4to. 1676. For the story, consult Eusebius, Baronius, Epiphanius, and other writers of Ecclesiastical History, and the various collections of the Saints Lives, published by authors of the Romish church. Scene, Rome. It was published by M. Medbourne.

10. SAINT GEORGE FOR ENGLAND, a play, by W. Smithe, appears to have been among those destroyed by Mr. Warburton's servant.

11. SAINT HELENA, or, *The Life of Love*. Musical Entertainment, by Captain Edward Thompson. Acted at Richmond, and once at Drury-Lane, 1776. Not printed.

12. SAINT JAMES's PARK. C. Anonym. 8vo. 1733. This is a most paltry piece, and was never acted.

13. SAINT PATRICK FOR IRELAND. Historical Play, by James Shirley, 4to. 1640. This play is mentioned as Shirley's by all the writers, and they all speak of it as a first part, which it is also called in the title-page, and the promise of a second part is given in the Prologue. Yet none of them pretend

tend to know whether such second part was ever executed or not, excepting Gildon, who positively asserts that such second part was designed by the author for the press, but never published. For the plot of the play, see Bede's Life of St. Patrick, and others of the Romish Legends. The play is now in print, and common to be met with in Ireland, it having been republished there, about thirty years ago, by Mr. Chetwood.

14. SAINT PATRICK's DAY, or, *The Scheming Lieutenant.* Farce, by Richard Brinsley Sheridan, Esq. Acted at Covent-Garden, May 2, 1775. Not printed. This piece was originally represented at the benefit of Mr. Clinch, who seems to have been favoured with it in consequence of his performance of the Irishman in Mr. Sheridan's play of *The Rivals.*

15. SALISBURY PLAIN. Com. was entered on the books of the Stationers' Company, Nov. 29, 1653, but, I believe, not printed.

16. SALMACIDA SPOLIA. A Masque. Anonym. 4to. 1639. This Masque, though printed without any author's name to it, ought to be arranged among the works of Sir William Davenant, since whatever was either spoken or sung in it was written by that gentleman. It was presented by the King and Queen's Majesties at Whitehall on Tuesday the 21st of January 1639. The scenes and machines, with their descriptions and ornaments, were invented by Inigo Jones, and the music composed by Mr. Lewis Richard.

17. THE SALOPIAN SQUIRE, or, *The Joyous Miller.* A Dramatic Tale, by E. Dower, 8vo. 1739. The author of this piece has annexed to it the reasons for its not making its appearance on the stage, which, with the true virulence of a disappointed poet, he attributes to party, bigotry, and malevolence in the manager who refused it. In vindication however of the gentleman so accused, it will be needful only to peruse the piece itself, to find much more substantial reasons for that rejection than those which its author has assigned.

18. SAMPSON AGONISTES. A dramatic poem, by John Milton, 8vo. 1670. This piece is written in imitation of the Greek tragic poets, more particularly Æschylus. The measure is not regular, being composed of every kind indiscriminately blended together. The speaking scenes are relieved and explained by *Choruses,* and all the regular constraint of division into acts and scenes is totally avoided, the poem having never been intended by the author for the stage, who strongly laboured to render it admirable for the closet. So noble, so just, so elegant, so poetical is the diction of it, that the great Mr. Dryden, whose imagination might be supposed to be equal to that of any man, has transferred many thoughts of this piece into his tragedy of *Aureng-zebe.* The foundation of the story is in holy writ, see Judges, ch. xiii. and the scene is laid at or near the gates of Gaza. I remember to have seen in the possession of a gentleman in Dublin (one Mr. Dixon) an alteration of this poem, said by himself to be his own, so as to render it fit for the stage; and the same gentleman also shewed me a bill for the intended performance (which was, through some dispute among the proprietors of the theatre, entirely laid aside) in which, from the number of characters, and the apparent strength to sup-

port them, it appeared to have been cast to the greatest advantage possible, every performer of importance, whether actor, singer, or dancer, having somewhat allotted to them towards the illustration of it. This representation, if I mistake not, was intended for the year 1741-2.

19. SANCHO AT COURT, or, *The Mock Governor*. An Opera Comedy, by James Ayres, 8vo. 1742. The title of this piece sufficiently points out the plan of it. It was intended to be acted at Drury-Lane, and in the preface great complaints are made against the manager for not bringing it on the stage.

20. SAPHO AND PHAO. Com. by John Lyly, 4to. 1584. This old play was first presented before Queen Elizabeth on a Shrove-Tuesday, and afterwards at the Black-Friers Theatre. The plot is taken from one of Ovid's Epistles. In this first edition, and another in 1591, the author's name is omitted, and the piece was by some means or other attributed to Mr. Richard Edwards. This mistake, however, is rectified by the edition of 1632, in which this and five more plays by the same author were all published together in one volume in twelves. The prologue and epilogues to them all are written in prose.

21. SATIROMASTIX, or, *The Untrussing of the humourous Poet*. Acted publickly by the Lord Chamberlain's servants, and privately by the children of Paul's, 4to. 1602. by Thomas Dekker. This is no more than a retaliation on Ben Jonson, who, in his *Poetaster*, had severely and with a good deal of ill-nature lashed our author under the character of Crispinus, which he has in this play returned by introducing Ben under the title of *Horace*, jun.

22. THE SAVAGE, or, *The Force of Nature*, 8vo. 1736. This piece, which was never acted, is inserted by the author of *The British Theatre* among the writings of Mr. James Miller; yet I can by no means help thinking it a mistake, as I have not the least remembrance of such a piece being ever mentioned to me, though long intimate in the family, as being his. By the title it is apparently a translation, or somewhat like it, of *The Arlequin Sauvage* of Mr. De L'Isle; and as Mr. Miller the year before had made use of every valuable incident of that piece in a comedy he had brought on the stage, but which failed of success, called *Art and Nature*, it is not very probable that he should so immediately afterwards proceed on the same plan again, or put himself to the trouble of a translation for the press alone, of a piece which he had but just before paraphrased and extended upon for the stage. It is therefore much more probable that it was the work of some other person, who imagined that on the strength of Mr. Miller's play it might not be disagreeable to the public to see Mr. De L'Isle's farce in its original form. I imagine this piece was never printed, though it is advertised with other plays, printed for J. Watts, at the beginning of Havard's *King Charles the First*.

23. SAUL. Trag. by Aaron Hill. Of this intended tragedy the author finished no more than one act, which is to be found in the last volume of his works published in two volumes, 8vo.

24. KING SAUL. Trag. written by a deceased person of honour, and now made public at the request

quest of several men of quality, who have highly approved of it, 4to. 1703. This play is dedicated by the publisher Henry Playford to the Countess of Burlington, who is therein said to be related to the noble person who was supposed to be the author of it. I know not on what foundation, but this play has been ascribed to Dr. Trapp.

25. SAUL AND JONATHAN. Trag. by Edward Crane, of Manchester, 8vo. 1761. Printed at Manchester, in a volume of Poetical Miscellanies, by the same author.

26. SAWNEY THE SCOT, or, *The Taming of the Shrew*. Com. by John Lacy. Acted at Drury-Lane, 4to. 1698. 4to. 1708. This is only an alteration, without much amendment, of Shakspeare's comedy of the last-mentioned title. It met, however, with very good success.

27. SCANDERBEG. Trag. by William Havard, 8vo. 1733. This play is founded on the same plan with Lillo's *Christian Hero*, being built on the life of the famous George Castriot, king of Epirus, who, on account of his illustrious actions, which in great measure resembled those of Alexander the Great, had the title of Scanderbeg (or Lord Alexander) universally allowed to him. It was acted at the Theatre in Goodman's Fields, but with no very good success.

28. SCANDERBEG, or, *Love and Liberty*. by Thomas Whincop, 8vo. 1747. This tragedy has the same foundation for its plot with the last-mentioned one, but has kept much closer to the history. It was never acted, but was published by subscription after the author's death, for the benefit of the widow. Annexed to it is a list of the English dramatic authors, with some account of their lives and writings, which, though in general fuller than most of the lists of that kind,

by coming down nearer to the present time, yet is by no means either compleat or correct. In the preface great fault is found with Mr. Havard's play above-mentioned, and some censure thrown on Mr. Lillo, and an insinuation given of his not having acted with perfect candour to the author; but with what justice I shall not pretend to determine.

29. SCARAMOUCH, *a Philosopher*, HARLEQUIN, *a School-Boy, Bravo, Merchant, and Magician*. Com. by Edward Ravenscroft. Acted at the Theatre Royal. 4to. 1677. The author boasts of having written this piece after the Italian manner, and by that means brought a new species of drama on the English stage; but complains in his prologue of having been forestalled by the representation of Otway's *Cheats of Scapin*, at the Duke's house. Yet it is certain that this comedy is made up of the compounded plots of three plays of Moliere, viz. *The Marriage Forcé*; *The Bourgeois Gentilhomme*; and *The Fourberies de Scapin*. Nay, Langbaine goes so far as to challenge the author to prove any part of a scene in it that can be called the genuine offspring of his own brain, styling him rather the midwife than parent of the piece.

30. THE SCHEMERS, or, *The City Match*. Com. Acted at Drury-Lane, 8vo. 1755. This is Jasper Maine's *City Match* altered, and was both acted and printed for the benefit of the Lock-Hospital. The alterer is said to have been William Bromfield, Esq.

31. THE SCHEMING VALET, or, *Brother and Sister*. Interlude, extracted from Moliere, printed in *The Theatrical Museum*, 8vo. 1776.

32. THE SCHOLAR. Com. by Richard Lovelace. Acted at Gloucester-

cester-Hall and Salisbury-Court. Not printed.

33. THE SCHOOL BOY. or, *The Comical Rival.* A Com. Acted at Drury-Lane, 4to. 1707. This comedy is little more than the plot of Major Rakish and his Son, and the Widow Manlove in *Woman's Wit, or The Lady in Fashion,* a comedy, written by the same author, taken verbatim, and thrown by itself into the form of a farce, under which appearance it had better success than the entire comedy, and is now frequently performed; whereas the other has been long thrown entirely aside. The characters of Young Rakish and the Major are themselves in great measure to be considered as copies, as any one may be convinced who will carefully examine Carlisle's *Fortune Hunters,* the character of Daredevil in Otway's *Soldiers Fortune,* and those of Sir Thomas Revel and his Son in Mountford's *Greenwich Park.*

34. "THE SCHOOL BOY'S "MASQUE, by Thomas Spateman. Designed for the Diversion of Youth and their Excitement to Learning, 8vo. 1747."

35. THE SCHOOL FOR ACTION. Com. by Sir Richard Steel, left unfinished by him at his death.

36. THE SCHOOL FOR ELOQUENCE. Interlude by Mrs. Cowley. Acted at Drury-Lane, April 4, 1780, for Mr. Brereton's benefit. Not printed. This piece was intended to ridicule the number of disputing societies, which at this time were opened and frequented.

37. THE SCHOOL FOR FATHERS. Com. Opera, by Isaac Bickerstaffe. Acted at Drury-Lane, 8vo. 1770. This is only *Lionel and Clarissa,* with some slight alterations.

38. THE SCHOOL FOR GUARDIANS. Com. by Arthur Murphy, Esq. Acted at Covent-Garden, 8vo. 1767. This comedy is taken from three plays of Moliere's, viz. *L'Ecole des Femmes, L'Etourdie,* and *L'Ecole des Maris.* It lingered on the stage for six nights, and then was laid aside.

39. A SCHOOL FOR HUSBANDS. Com. by J. Ozell. This is only a translation of Moliere's *Ecole des Maris.*

40. THE SCHOOL FOR LOVERS. Com. by W. Whitehead. Acted at Drury-Lane, 8vo. 1762. This is the last dramatic work but one of our present laureat, and his first attempt in the walks of comedy. In an advertisement prefixed to it, he acknowledges it to have received its first foundation in a dramatic piece written, but not intended for the stage, by M. de Fontenelle, to whose memory he dedicates this piece, subscribing himself a *Lover of Simplicity.* What species of *Drama,* however, it ought to be classed in, is somewhat difficult to determine, since, though it is styled a comedy, the risible faculties have much less opportunity of exertion than the tender feelings of the heart, and the catastrophe, though happy in the main, and suitable to poetical justice, is not completely so, since two amiable characters are left, the one entirely unprovided for, and the other in a situation far from agreeable, viz. that of only being witness to a degree of happiness in the possession of others, which, with respect to herself, she must imagine out of reach, or at least deferred for a considerable period of time. Those who are acquainted with the play will readily conceive that the characters I mean are Bellmour and Araminta; and as to Modely, though he has, through the course of the piece, appeared to have foibles, yet, as they have not arisen from

from any badness of heart, and that the open sincerity of his repentance is too apparent to every auditor, not to render him deserving of a restoration to esteem, the author might perhaps have waived some little of his punishment, and restored his Araminta also to his arms. What the author, however, seems to have principally aimed at, viz. delicacy, sentiment, and the consequence of instruction in the conduct of a generous and well-placed passion, he has undoubtedly most eminently succeeded in. His Celia and Sir John Dorilant, and more especially the latter, are characters most perfectly amiable and worthy of imitation; and to remove at once the great cavil of the critics, who seemed with respect to this piece to be at a loss where to fix a censure, if a dramatic piece has those essential good qualities of affording at once a sensibility to the heart, a lesson to the understanding, and an agreeable amusement to the senses, of what importance is it to look back to what title the author has thought proper to give it?

41. THE SCHOOL FOR RAKES. Com. by Mrs. Elizabeth Griffiths. Acted at Drury-Lane, 8vo. 1769. This play was performed with considerable success. The hint of it was taken from *Eugenie*, by Monf. Beaumarchais.

42. THE SCHOOL FOR SCANDAL. Com. by Richard Brinsley Sheridan, Esq. Acted at Drury-Lane 1776. Any attempt to be particular in the praise of this comedy, would be at once difficult and unnecessary. No piece ever equalled it in success on the stage, and very few are superior to it in point of intrinsic merit. The policy of our earliest theatres being at present revived, *The School for Scandal* is still unprinted, and therefore escapes that minuteness of criticism of which in our idea it has no reason to be afraid.

43. THE SCHOOL FOR SCANDAL. Com. 8vo. 1778. A paltry catchpenny, intended to be imposed on the public as the genuine production of Mr. Sheridan. This despicable piece is political.

44. THE SCHOOL FOR SCANDAL SCANDALIZED. Interlude. Acted at Mr. Lewis's benefit at Covent-Garden, March 1780. Not printed.

45. SCHOOL FOR WOMEN. C. by J. Ozell. This is a translation of Moliere's *Ecole des Femmes*. As is also

46. THE SCHOOL FOR WOMEN CRITICIZ'D, of a little piece called the *Critique de l'Ecole des Femmes*, written likewise by Moliere, and englished by the same gentleman. Neither of these pieces was ever intended for the English stage in their present form, being only translations calculated for the acquiring an acquaintance with that celebrated French poet in the closet.

47. THE SCHOOL FOR WIVES. Com. translated from the French by Robert Lloyd, and printed in *The St. James's Magazine*, vol. I. 1763. This was published merely to shew how much Mr. Murphy had borrowed in composing *The Way to keep him*.

48. THE SCHOOL FOR WIVES. Com. by Hugh Kelly. Acted at Drury-Lane, 8vo. 1774. The hard treatment Mr. Kelly's comedy of *A Word to the Wise* met with from the public, induced him to produce the present in the name of Mr. Addington. He asserts, that it is unborrowed from any other writer. The success of it was fully equal to its merit.

49. THE SCHOOL OF COMPLIMENT.

MENT. Com. by James Shirley. Acted at the private house, Drury-Lane, 4to. 1631. 4to. 1637. and in 4to. 1667. under the title of *Love Tricks*, or, *The School of Compliments*, as acted at the Duke of York's Theatre in Little Lincoln's-Inn Fields. The author in a prologue declares this to be the *First Fruits of his Muse*, and *that be meant not to swear himself a Factor to the Scene*. Yet the success the first attempt met with probably induced him to change this intention, and devote himself a very industrious one, as the multitude of plays he afterwards wrote sufficiently evince him to have been.

50. SCHOOL PLAY. An Interlude. Anonymous. 8vo. 1664. This little piece, which consists of only five scenes, was prepared for, and performed in, a private grammar school in Middlesex in the year 1663, and I suppose was written by the master of the said School. In it is presented the anomaly of the chiefest part of grammar, and it is accommodated to that book which the author says is of the most use and best authority in England, viz. the *Grammatica Regia*.

51. SCIPIO AFRICANUS. Trag. by Charles Beckingham, 12mo. 1718. This play was acted at the Theatre in Lincoln's-Inn Fields with considerable success, and deservedly. For though the author was not above nineteen years of age when he wrote it, yet he has been happy in his diction, proper in his expressions, and just in his sentiments. His plot is founded on historical facts, and those such as are well suited to form the subject of a dramatic piece. His action is uniform and entire, his episodes judicious, his characters well drawn, and his unities perfectly preserved. So that, on the whole, it may certainly be pronounced an excellent tragedy, conformable to the rules of the drama and the precepts of modern criticism.

52. THE SCRIBLER. Com. 12mo. 1751. Printed at Dublin, but it does not appear to have been acted.

53. THE SCORNFUL LADY. Com. by Beaumont and Fletcher. Acted at Black-Friers, 4to. 1616. This play was esteemed an exceeding good one, and even within very late years has been performed with great applause. Yet Mr. Dryden, in his *Dramatic Essay*, p. 35. finds fault with it for want of art in the conclusion, with reference to Morecraft the usurer, whose conversion, as he observes, seems a little forced. The scene lies in London.

54. THE SCOTS FIGARIES, or, *A Knot of Knaves*. Com. by John Tateham, 4to. 1652. 12mo. 1735. This play is great part of it written in the Scotch dialect, and the author, who was a strong Cavalier, and had the highest detestation for the Scots, has drawn the characters of them and of the *Puritans* in this piece in very contemptible as well as hateful colours.

55. THE SCOTTISH POLITIC PRESBYTER SLAIN BY AN ENGLISH INDEPENDENT, or, *The Independent's Victory over the Presbyterian Party*, &c. Tragi-Com. Anonymous. 4to. 1647. This is one among the numerous sarcastical pieces which the disturbances and heartburnings both in church and state of that unhappy period gave birth to.

56. THE SCOWERERS. Com. by Thomas Shadwell. Acted by their Majesties servants, 4to. 1691. This play contains a great deal of low humour; yet, although Langbaine entirely acquits our author

of

of plagiarism with respect to it, the character of Eugenia seems to be pretty closely copied from Harriot, in Sir George Etherege's *Man of Mode*.

57. THE SCULLER. A play, by John Taylor the water-poet, is mentioned as being in the Bodleian library. See *Hyde's Catalogue*.

58. THE SEA VOYAGE. Com. Beaumont and Fletcher, Fol. 1647. The design of this play is borrowed from Shakspeare's *Tempest*, and the scene lies, as it does in that play, first at Sea, and afterwards on a Desert Island. It was revived with considerable alterations for the worse by Mr. Durfey in 1686.

59. THE SEARCH AFTER HAPPINESS. Pastoral Drama, by Miss Hannah More, 8vo. 1773. This pastoral was composed by the authoress at the age of eighteen years, and recited by a party of young ladies, for whose use it was originally written.

60. SEBASTIAN. Trag. by G. P. Toosey, 8vo. 1772.

61. THE SECOND MAIDEN'S TRAGEDY. This play is now in MS. in the library of Lord Shelburne, and is one of those which escaped the general havock made by Mr. Warburton's servant. It was entered on the books of the Stationers' Company Sept. 9, 1653, but had been licenced so long before as October 31, 1611. The name of the author in the title-page seems, from the traces of the letters, originally to have been Thomas Goff, but this is carefully obliterated, and George Chapman substituted in its stead, which has again been blotted out to make room for William Shakspeare. The latter name, however, is written in a modern character, and with ink of a different colour from the rest. I do not, however, believe this piece to have been the composition either of Goff or Chapman. It is in many parts distinguished by an elegance and tenderness superior to theirs, and is no where disgraced by such ridiculous extravagances as characterize their known productions. From particular marks on the copy, it appears to have been acted. As a specimen of this curious production, the reader will hardly be displeased with the following extract:

" Enter the Tyrant agen at a
" farder dore, which opened brings
" hym to the tombe where the
" lady lies buried. The toombe
" here discovered richly sett
" forthe.

" *Tyrant.* Softlie, softlie;
" Lets give this place the peace that it re-
" quires;
" The vaults e'en chide our steps with
" murmuring sounds,
" As making bould so late:—It must be
" donne,
" The monument wooes me; I must runne
" and kisse it;
" Now trust me if the teares do not e'en
" stand
" Upon the marble: What flow springs
" have I?
" 'Twas weeping to itself before I came.
" How pity strikes e'en through insensible
" things,
" And makes them shame our dullness!
" Thow howse of seilence and the calmes
" of rest
" After tempestuous life, I clayme of thee
" A mistres, one of the most beauteous
" sleepers
" That ever lay so colde, not yet due to
" thee,
" By naturall death, but cruellie forc'd
" hether
" Many a yeare before the world could
" spare her.
" We misse her mongst the glories of our
" courte,
" When they be numbred up. All thy
" full strength,
" Thow grey-eyde monument, shall not
" keep her from us.
" Strike, villaines, thoe the eccho raile
" us all
" Into ridiculous deafnes; pierce the
" jawes
" Of this could ponderous creature.—
" O,

SE

" O, the moone rifes: What reflection
" Is throwre around this sanctified build-
" inge!
" E'en in a twincklinge how the monu-
" ments glitter,
" As if death's pallaces were all maffie
" fylver,
" And fcorn'd the name of marble!"

This play confifts of two diftinct plots; one borrowed from the ftory of *The Curious Impertinent* in Don Quixote; the other, which exhibits the conduct of the tyrant, refpecting the dead body of his miftrefs, from Camoens's *Lufiad*, which the reader will find admirably tranflated by Mr. Mickle.

62. SECOND THOUGHTS ARE BEST. Com. by Mrs. Cowley. See *The World as it goes.*

63. SECOND THOUGHT IS BEST. Com. Opera, by John Hough, Efq. Acted at Drury-Lane. March 30, 1778, at Mifs Younge's benefit, 8vo.

64. THE SECRET EXPEDITION. Farce, of two acts, 8vo. 1757. A political performance occafioned by the failure of an expedition to the coaft of France.

65. SECRET LOVE, or, *The Maiden Queen.* Tragi-Com. by J. Dryden. Acted at the Theatre Royal, 4to. 1668. 4to. 1691. The plot of the ferious part of this play is founded on a novel, called the Hiftory of Cleobuline Queen of Corinth, Part 7. Book 7. under whofe character that of the celebrated Chriftina of Sweden has been confidently affirmed to be reprefented. The characters of Celadon, Florimel, Olinda, and Sabina, are borrowed from the Hiftory of Pififtrata and Corintha in the Grand Cyrus, Part 9. Book 3. and that of the French Marquis from Ibrahim, Part 2. Book 1. The fcene laid in Sicily.

66. THE SECRET PLOT. Trag. of three acts. Written by Rupert Green, Dec. 30, 1776, aged eight

SE

years and eleven months, 12mo, 1777. The printing of this piece is one of thofe foolifh inftances of parental vanity which nothing can juftify or excufe. As the author may probably live long enough to feel the ridicule which this conduct of his parents is likely to draw upon him, we cannot but feel fome concern on his account. As Uncle Toby obferved, when he was told of an infant who had produced a work on the day he was born, " they fhould have wiped " it up, and faid nothing of the " matter."

67. SEJANUS. Trag. by Francis Gentleman, 8vo. 1752. This tragedy is an alteration of Ben Jonfon's play, of which anon. It never made its appearance on either of the London theatres, but, if I do not miftake, I have heard it was acted at Bath with fome degree of applaufe.

68. SEJANUS HIS FALL. Trag. by Ben Jonfon, 4to. 1605. This play was firft acted in 1603, and is ufhered into the world by no lefs than nine copies of commendatory verfes. It has indeed a great fhare of merit. The plot is founded on hiftory, the ftory being to be feen in the Annals of Tacitus, and Suetonius's Life of Tiberius. The author has difplayed great learning, and made an advantageous ufe of his acquaintance with the ancients; yet fearful, as it fhould feem by the preface, of being taxed by the critics with a plagiarifm which he thought himfelf by no means entitled to be afhamed of, he has pointed out all his quotations and authorities.

69. THE SELF RIVAL. Com. by Mrs. Mary Davys. This piece was never acted, but was intended for the Theatre Royal in Drury-Lane. It is printed with another play and the reft of this lady's works,

works, which were published in two volumes, 8vo. 1725. The scene, London.

70. "The First Part of the Tragicall Raigne of SELIMUS, sometime Emperour of the Turkes, and grand-father to him that now raigneth. Wherein is shewne how he most unnaturally raised warres against his owne father Bajazet, and prevailing therein, in the end caused him to be poisoned; also with the murthering of his two brethren Corcutus and Acomat." Acted by the Queen's players, 4to. 1594. The plot of this play is taken from the Turkish histories of the reign of the Emperor Selimus I. It is sometimes ascribed to Thomas Goffe, who, from his then age, could not possibly be the author of it.

71. SELIMA AND AZOR. Dram. Romance. Acted at Drury-Lane 1776. The songs only printed in 8vo. A pompous nothing, pilfered from the French, and said to be the work of Sir George Collier. By the assistance of Loutherburgh's pencil and Mrs. Baddeley's voice, it escaped the contempt to which on all other accounts it was intitled.

72. SELINDRA. Tragi-Com. by Sir William Killegrew, 8vo. 1664. Fol. 1666, Scene, Byzantium.

73. SEMELE. An Opera, by W. Congreve. This short piece was performed and printed in 4to. 1707.

74. SEMIRAMIS. Trag. translated from Voltaire, 8vo. 1760.

75. SEMIRAMIS. Trag. translated from Voltaire, and printed in Dr. Franklin's edition of that author.

76. SEMIRAMIS. Trag. by George Edward Ayscough. Acted at Drury-Lane, 8vo. 1776. The present tragedy, as written by Voltaire, has a considerable degree of dramatic merit, which is all evaporated through the wretchedness of this translation from a translation, and by injudicious changes in the conduct of the fable. The ghost of Ninus, on his first appearance at Paris, was by no means treated with such civility as might have been expected to be shewn by a polite nation to so great a stranger on their stage. The phantom indeed, contrary to the rule his predecessors had consented to observe, bolted out at noonday, and in the midst of all the assembled Satraps of the realm. Captain Ayscough, however, obliged him to entertain his widow and his son with only a private exhibition. In this scene, the figure and post of the Assyrian monarch exactly resembled those of an old Chelsea pensioner employed to watch a church-yard, and bursting from a sentry-box to catch the persons who came to steal bodies for the surgeons. The Captain's play, in short, like himself and other parasites of the late Lord Lyttelton, was every way contemptible; though it is plain that he thought differently, as he appeared, during the first night of its representation, in various parts of the house, thrusting out his head to engage the attention and receive the homage of the spectators. The theatre on this occasion was filled with his brother officers, who were all so sick of their duty under him, that they never returned to it a second time. Our author therefore gained only a few pounds by all his three benefits, being oblig'd to employ the profits of one to make up deficiencies in the other two, when there was not money enough in the house to defray its nightly expences. This Fool of fashion has

done

done yet more extensive mischief; having made the story of Ninus and Semiramis so disgusting, that, should it be undertaken by a more skilful hand, it would fail, for some years at least, in its power to attract an audience.

77. SEPARATE MAINTENANCE. Com. by George Colman, Esq. Acted at the Hay-Market 1779. The characters of genteel life are not sufficiently distinct from each other to afford much entertainment to an English audience. For this reason, we think this performance not the most pleasing of Mr. Colman's dramatic works. The part of Leveret, supposed to represent a coxcomb still living, is, however, well drawn and supported. The scene of the swathing, taken from *The Spectator*, is disgusting in a public exhibition.

78. OF THE SEPULTURE AND RESURRECTION. Two Comedies, by Bishop Bale. These two pieces stand on the list this right reverend father has given us of his own writings, and which is all the information we have concerning them. Yet I cannot here avoid dropping one observation, which is, that in the titles of these and some other of the very early writings of this kind, we frequently find the name of comedy given to pieces, whose subjects are apparently of so very grave and serious a nature, as by no means to admit of the least supposition of humour or pleasantry being thrown into them; I cannot help therefore conjecturing that the word *Comedy* had not at that time the limited sense it has at present, but must in all probability have been the usual term to express what we now mean by a play in general; and this seems the more probable, since to this day it conveys the very same sense in certain instances in another language, where the visiting the theatre, be the piece comic or tragic, is frequently expressed by the phrase *Aller à la Comedie*.

79. THE SEQUEL OF HENRY THE FOURTH, *with the Humours of Sir John Falstaffe and Justice Shallow*, altered from Shakspeare, by Mr. Betterton. Acted at Drury-Lane, 8vo. no date. [1719.]

80. A SEQUEL TO THE OPERA OF FLORA. Acted at Lincoln's-Inn Fields, 8vo. 1732. By the author of Flora, says the title-page, Chetwood ascribes to Mr. John Leigh, *Hob's Wedding* 1721, which is nearly the same performance as the present, but without the songs.

81. THE SERAGLIO. A comic Opera, by Captain Edward Thompson. Acted at Covent-Garden, 8vo. 1776. This writer, by sometimes flattering, and sometimes abusing managers, contrived to get two or three of his pieces on the stage. The present one, like the rest, was commended only by its author in the news-papers. The subject is such as must naturally have engaged the attention of one who has boastfully called himself *The Poet of the Stews*.

82. SERTORIUS. Tr. by John Bancroft. Acted at the Theatre Royal, 4to. 1679. The plot of this tragedy is founded on Plutarch's Life of Sertorius, Velleius Paterculus, Florus, and other historians. The scene lies in Lusitania, and the epilogue is written by Ravenscroft. The elder Corneille has a play on the same subject, but Mr. Bancroft does not seem to have borrowed any thing from him.

83. SESOSTRIS, or, *Royalty in Disguise*. Trag. by John Sturmy, 8vo. 1728. This play was acted with some success at the Theatre Royal in Lincoln's-Inn Fields, and

though

though it is not in itself a piece of any great merit in respect to language or poetical execution, yet it seems to have furnished hints to some of our later tragic writers, who, having had greater abilities, have made a more masterly use of the very same incidents that compose the plot of this tragedy. In short, Merope and Barbarossa seem both greatly indebted to this piece. The scene is laid in Egypt, where Omar having deposed and murdered the former King Pharnaces, and usurped the throne from his Widow Nitocris, is still unsatisfied till he can close the scene of blood by the death of her Son Sesostris, who, through the care of Phares, an old servant of the king's, had been preserved from the general slaughter of the royal race, and bred up at a distance from the court. Sesostris returning to Egypt, in order to assert his rights, meets with Omar's son, who, having attacked him, falls a victim to his valour, and the conqueror making himself master of a ring, letter, and other credentials belonging to the son of Omar, proceeds on his expedition, and by the advice of Phares passes on Omar for his own son (whom he had not seen from infancy) and the slayer of Sesostris. This imposition, however, being at length discovered, the tyrant's rage dooms him an immediate sacrifice at the temple of Isis; but as the fatal act is just on the verge of being executed, Sesostris, full of a supernatural ardor, seizes on the knife of sacrifice, and, plunging it in the tyrant's heart, at once frees the nation from oppression, and restores himself to the throne, his right by birth.

How near these incidents to the plays I have mentioned! Sesostris' introduction to Omar as the murderer of himself, and the love which Phares's daughter has for him, bear the strongest resemblance to Selim's disguise and Irene's passion, in Barbarossa, at the same time, that the confirmation to Nitocris of her son's death, by means of the sword and jewels, and Sesostris's heroic action at the altar, are scarcely at all different from the distress of Merope, and the death of Poliphontes by the hand of Eumenes. I know not whether this play, or M. Voltaire's *Merope*, was first written; but I am apt to believe the latter, and if so, this is only built on the foundation of the French tragedy, and it is to M. de Voltaire that the abovementioned plays are indebted for their origins. (Voltaire's *Merope* was not finished until the year 1736; but as there were plays on this subject by Gilbert 1643, by Chapelle 1683, by La Grange 1691, and the Marquiss Maffei, whose play Voltaire professed to translate, it is not very probable that he availed himself of Sesostris.)

84. SETHONA. Trag. by Alexander Dow. Acted at Drury-Lane, 8vo. 1774. This play may properly be styled a faggot of utter improbabilities, connected by a band of the strongest Northern fustian. Overawed by Scottish influence, Mr. Garrick prevailed on himself to receive it; but though his theatre was *apparently* full several times during its nine nights' run, it brought so little cash into his treasury, that he would not have lamented its earlier condemnation. It expired on his premises, but hardly left enough behind it to defray the expences of its funeral. Sethona, and its predecessor Zingis, exhibit striking instances of the national partiality with which Scotsmen labour for the promotion of each other. Mr.

Mr. Dow has been represented by persons who knew him well during his first residence in the East-Indies, as a man utterly unqualified for the production of any work of learning or fancy, either in prose or metre. At his return to England however, he stood forward as the historian of Indostan, and then as the author of Zingis and the drama before us. These phænomena perhaps are to be solved by our recollection of his strict intimacy with two of his own countrymen, the one a translator, the other a dramatic poet. Though these gentlemen were candidates for literary fame, yet between them they contrived to transfer as much of it as would set up a needy brother in trade, and afford a degree of distinction and consequence sufficient to befriend his future prospects of advancement.

85. THE SEVEN CHAMPIONS OF CHRISTENDOME. By John Kirke. Acted at the Cockpit, and at the Bull in St. John's-street, 4to. 1638. The plot of this piece is taken from a well-known book in prose which bears the same title, and from Heylin's History of St. George. It is written in a mixed style, for which the author himself apologizes in his epistle dedicatory, by observing that the nature of the work being history, it consists of many parts, not walking in one direct path of comedy or tragedy, but having a larger field to trace, which should yield more pleasure to the reader; novelty and variety being the only objects these our times are taken with. The tragedy may be too dull and solid; the comedy too sharp and bitter; but a well-mixed portion of either, doubtless, would make the sweetest harmony.

86. THE SEVEN CHIEFS A-GAINST THEBES. Trag. translated from Æschylus, by R. Potter, 4to. 1777.

87. THE SEVEN DEADLY SINS. A play, by Richard Tarlton. This play was never printed. See vol. I. p. 442.

88. SEVENTEEN HUNDRED AND TWENTY, or, *The Historic, Satiric, Tragi, Comic, Humours of Exchange-Alley*. Com. by Francis Hawling. Acted at Drury-Lane 1723. Not printed.

89. THE SEVERAL AFFAIRS. Com. by Thomas Meriton. This piece was never acted, nor ever appeared in print, but as the author himself informs us in the dedication to another play of his, called *The Wandring Lover*, was only reserved as a Pocket companion for the amusement of his private friends. The stupidity of the title, however, affords a most contemptible idea of the piece, and leaves us some reason to congratulate ourselves on the not having been in the number of Mr. Meriton's friends.

90. THE SEVERAL WITS. C. by the Duchess of Newcastle, Fol. 1662.

91. SHAKESPEARE'S JUBILEE. Masque, by George Savile Carey, 8vo. 1769.

92. THE SHAM BEGGAR. Com. in two acts. Acted at Dublin, 8vo. 1756.

93. THE SHAM FIGHT, or, *Political Humbug*. A State Farce, in two acts. Acted by some persons of distinction in the M—d—n and elsewhere, 8vo. 1756.

94. THE SHAM LAWYER, or, *The Lucky Extravagant*. Com. by Dr. James Drake. As it WAS DAMNABLY ACTED at Drury-Lane, says the title-page, 4to. 1697. This play is mostly borrowed from two comedies of Beaumont and Fletcher, viz. *The Spanish Curate*, and *Wit without Money*. The first
title

title of this play having a reference to the plot of the former; and the second to that of the latter of these comedies. The scene laid in London.

95. THE SHAM PRINCE, or, News from Passau. Com. by Charles Shadwell, 12mo. 1720. This play was written in five days, and acted in Dublin; the design of it being to expose a public cheat, who had at that time passed himself on the Irish nation as a person of the first importance, and by that means imposed on many to their great loss and injury. The scene is laid in Dublin, and the time of action five hours.

96. THE SHARPER. Com. by Michael Clancy. This play was acted at Smock-Alley, Dublin, and printed at the end of the author's life, 8vo. 1750. The plot of it is founded on some of the exploits of the infamously famous colonel Chartres.

97. THE SHARPERS. A Ballad Opera, by Matthew Gardiner, 8vo. 1740. This piece is by an Irish author, and therefore might possibly be both published and performed in Dublin; but I do not find it taken notice of in any of the English Lists, nor indeed any where but by the author of *The British Theatre*.

98. THE SHE GALLANTS. C. by Lord Lansdowne. Acted at Lincoln's-Inn Fields, 4to. 1696. This Comedy was written when the author was extremely young, yet contains an infinite deal of wit, fine satire, and great knowledge of mankind. It was acted with considerable applause, notwithstanding that envy of its merit raised a party against it, who misrepresented it, as designing, in some of the characters, to reflect on particular persons, and more especially on the government: but when it comes to be considered that it was written above a dozen years before it was performed, and at a time when neither the same government subsisted, nor the persons supposed to be aimed at had been any way noted; and that moreover it was not composed with any design to be made public, but only as a private amusement, any impartial judge must surely acquit his lordship of the charge laid against him. Part of the episode of *The four Sisters* seems borrowed from the French Marquis in the Romance of *Ibrahim*. See *Once a Lover always a Lover*.

99. THE SHE GALLANT, or, Square Toes outwitted. Com. of two acts, performed at Smock-Alley, Dublin, 8vo. 1767.

100. THE SHEEP SHEARING, or, Florizel and Perdita. Pastoral Comedy. This is taken from Shakspeare's *Winter's Tale*, and was first acted at Mr. Barry's benefit about 1754. It has been printed often in Dublin, particularly, 12mo. 1767.

101. THE SHEEP SHEARING. Dramatic Pastoral in three acts, taken from Shakspeare, by Geo. Colman. Acted at the Hay-Market, 1777, 8vo. This is borrowed from *The Winter's Tale*, and met with so cold a reception, that it appeared only one night.

102. THE SHEPHERDESS OF THE ALPS. Com. Opera, by Charles Dibdin. Acted at Covent-Garden, 8vo. 1780. Like the rest of this writer's pieces, it was taken from the French, and was dismissed from public view after three nights' representation.

103. THE SHEPHERD'S ARTIFICE. Dramatic Pastoral, by C. Dibdin. Acted at Covent-Garden, 8vo. 1765. A very trifling insipid performance.

104. THE SHEPHERD'S COURT-SHIP.

SHIP. Mufical Paftoral of four Interludes, by William Shirley. Not acted, nor yet printed, but is promifed in an edition of the author's dramatic works.

105. THE SHEPHERD'S HOLIDAY. Paft. Tragi-Com. by Jofeph Rutter. Acted before their Majefties at Whitehall, 8vo. 1635. This play has only the initials J. R. in the title-page; but Kirkman, whofe authority in general is a very good one, has afcribed it to this gentleman, and all the other writers have followed his example. The piece is written in blank verfe, and Langbaine ftyles it the nobler fort of paftoral. It is alfo recommended by two copies of verfes, the one from Ben Jonfon, who calls the author *his dear Son* (in the Mufes) *and his right learned Friend*, and the other from Thomas May. The fcene lies in Arcadia, and at the end of the piece is a paftoral elegy on the death of the Lady Venetia Digby, written in the character of her hufband Sir Kenelm Digby, Knt. to whom this play is dedicated.

106. THE SHEPHERD's LOTTERY. A Mufical Entertainment, by Mr. Mendez. Acted at Drury-Lane, 8vo. 1751. This little piece is in the fame ftyle of writing with the *Chaplet*, another piece of the fame author, but I do not think it quite equal to it. There are, however, feveral pretty fongs in it, and the mufical compofition is very pleafing. It met with good fuccefs at firft, but has not been often repeated fince the feafon it made its appearance in.

107. THE SHEPHERD's PARADICE. A Paftoral, by Walter Montague, 8vo. 1629. This piece was acted privately before king Charles I. by the Queen and her Ladies of Honour, whofe names are fet down in the Dramatis Perfonæ. It is, however, very defervedly ridiculed by Sir John Suckling in his *Seffion of the Poets*, as being perfectly unintelligible.

108. SHE STOOPS TO CONQUER, or, *The Miftakes of a Night*. Com. by Dr. Goldfmith. Acted at Covent-Garden, 8vo. 1773. The prefent dramatic piece is, by fome criticks, confidered as a farce, but ftill it muft be ranked among the farces of a man of genius. One of the moft ludicrous circumftances it contains (that of the robbery) is borrowed from *Albumazar*. It met with great fuccefs, and reftored the public tafte to the good opinion of our author.

109. SHE VENTURES, AND HE WINS. Com. Acted at Lincoln's-Inn Fields, 4to. 1696. This play was written by a young lady who figns herfelf Ariadne. The fcene lies in London, and the plot is taken from a Novel written by Mr. Oldys, called, *The Fair Extravagant*, or, *The Humorous Bride*. Mr. Motteux wrote the Epilogue.

110. SHE WOU'D IF SHE COU'D. Com. by Sir George Etheridge. Acted at the Duke of York's Theatre, 4to. 1671. This play has been for fome time laid afide, yet it is undoubtedly a very good one, and at the time it was written was efteemed as one of the firft rank. Nay, Shadwell, in the preface to his *Humourifts*, declares it to be the beft dramatic piece produced from the reftoration of the ftage to that time. Yet Dennis, in his epiftle dedicatory to *The Comical Gallant*, fays, that though it *was efteemed by the men of fenfe for the truenefs of fome of its characters, and the purity, freenefs, and eafy grace of its dialogue*, yet on its firft appearance it was *barbaroufly treated* by the audience.

111. SHE

111. SHE WOU'D AND SHE WOU'D NOT, or, *The Kind Impostor.* Com. by C. Cibber. Acted at Drury-Lane, 4to. 1703. This is a very busy, sprightly, and entertaining comedy, but the plot of it is borrowed either from Leonard's *Counterfeits*, or else from the Novel of the *Trapanner trapanned*, on which that comedy itself was built. The scene lies at Madrid.

112. THE SHIPWRECK. Com. translated from Plautus, by Bonnel Thornton, printed in his edition, 8vo. 1767.

113. THE SHIPWRECK. Dramatic Piece, by William Hyland, Farmer in Suffex, 8vo. 1746.

114. A SHOEMAKER'S A GENTLEMAN. Com. by William Rowley. Acted at the Red Bull, 4to. 1638. The plot of this play is founded on a Novel in 4to. called *Crispin and Crispianus*, or, *The History of the Gentle Craft*. It consists of a good deal of low humour, and it appears from Langbaine to have been a great favourite among the strolling companies in the country, and that some of the most comical scenes in it used commonly to be selected out, and performed by way of droll at Bartholomew and Southwark Fairs.

115. THE SHOEMAKER'S HOLIDAY, or, *The Gentle Craft, with the humorous Life of Simon Fyre, Shoemaker, and Lord Mayor of London.* Com. Acted before the Queen, by Thomas Earl of Nottingham, Lord High Admiral his servants, on New-Year's Day at night, 4to. 1600. 4to 1610. 4to. 1631. 4to. 1657. This play has been attributed to Dr. Parson Holiday. It is dedicated to *all Good Fellows, Professors of the Gentle Craft, of what degree soever;* and in the dedication the argument of the piece is laid down. It is printed in the black letter, and not divided into acts.

116. SHUFFLING, CUTTING, AND DEALING in a Game of Pickquet, being acted from the year 1653 to 1658. By O. P. and others with great applause. By Henry Neville, 4to. 1650.

117. SICELIDES. A Piscatory Drama or Pastoral, by Phineas Fletcher, 4to. 1631. This piece was acted in King's College, Cambridge, and is printed without any author's name. It was intended originally to be performed before King James the First on the 13th of March, 1614; but his majesty leaving the university sooner, it was not then represented. The serious parts of it are mostly written in rhyme, with choruses between the acts. Perianus's telling Armillus the story of Glaucus Scylla and Circe, in the first act, is taken from Ovid's *Metamorphoses*, Lib. 12. And Atychus's fighting with and killing the Ork that was to have devoured Olynda, is an imitation of the story of Perseus and Andromeda in Ovid's *Metamorphoses*, Book 4. or the deliverance of Angelica from the monster by Ruggiero, in the *Orlando Furioso*, Cant. 10. The scene lies in Sicily, the time two hours.

118. THE SICILIAN, or *Love makes a Painter*, by J. Ozell. This is a translation for the closet only of Moliere's *Sicilien, ou l'Amour Peintre*, not intended for the stage; but Mr. Crown, in his *Country Wit*, and Sir Richard Steele, in his *Tender Husband*, have both borrowed incidents, and indeed whole scenes, from this play. It consists of twenty scenes, not divided into acts; and the general scene is in Sicily.

119. THE SICILIAN USURPER. Trag. by N. Tate, 4to. 1691.

1691. This is nothing more than an alteration of Shakspeare's Richard II. It appears to have been acted only once or twice, when it was forbidden by authority; on which account the author has added to it a prefatory epistle in vindication of himself, with respect to the said prohibition. The scene is laid in England. It was published originally in 4to. 1681, under the title of *King Richard the Second*.

120. SICILY AND NAPLES, or, *The Fatal Union*. Trag. by S. H. A. B. 4to. 1640. This play is recommended by seven copies of verses prefixed to it. The scene, Naples.

121. THE SIEGE. Tragi-Com. by Sir William Davenant, Fol. 1679. Scene, Pisa.

122. THE SIEGE, or *Love's Convert*. Tragi-Com. by William Cartwright, 8vo. 1651. This play is dedicated in verse to King Charles I. The scene lies at Byzantium; and the story of Misander and Leucatia is founded on that of Pausanias and Cleonice in Plutarch's life of Cymon, as is the injunction which the rich widow Pyle lays upon her lovers, in the Decameron of Boccace, Dec. 9. Nov. 1.

123. THE SIEGE OF ALEPPO. Trag. by William Hawkins, 8vo. 1758. Printed in the second volume of Miscellanies, published by the author in that year. The fable, and the whole construction of the play, except the reality of the siege, are purely fictitious.

124. THE SIEGE OF AQUILEIA. Trag. by J. Home, 8vo. 1760. This play was performed with success at the Theatre Royal in Drury-Lane. It is the third dramatic piece produced by this Caledonian bard. It is greatly preferable to the *Agis*, but much inferior to the *Douglas* of the same author. From the title one would reasonably expect to find in it the several circumstances of the siege whose title it bears, when the city of Aquileia was held out by the legions of Gordianus against the gigantic tyrant Maximin: and such, from the first setting out of it, we are permitted to expect; but every incident in this play deviates from the historical facts which we have on record in regard to that siege; yet as they all agree with those of one much nearer to our own times, and nearer connected with the history of the author's own country, viz. the siege of Berwick, defended by Seton against the arms of our Edward III. it is not surely an improbable conjecture to suppose that Mr. Home received his first hint from that story; but as by pursuing it under the real characters, he must have painted one of our English monarchs (and him indeed one classed amongst the heroes of the British Annals) in the light in which in more than this one instance he appeared to be, viz. a tyrant, and an exerter of brutal power, without any consideration of the feelings of humanity; he chose, rather than pay so ill a compliment to an English audience, to preserve the circumstances only, changing the scenes of action to one that had some little kind of analogy with it. The unities are well preserved, and some of the sentimental parts of the language are fine. But on the whole, the incidents are too few, the distress too much the same from beginning to end, and the catastrophe too early pointed out to the audience. Besides which, it may be added, that the character of Æmilius bears too strong a resemblance

to that of the Old Horatius in Whitehead's *Roman Father*, though it would be paying the last-named character a bad compliment to set this in point of execution in any degree of competition with it.

125. THE SIEGE OF BABYLON. Tragi-Com. by Samuel Pordage. Acted at the Duke's Theatre, 4to. 1678. This play is founded on the Romance of Cassandra. The siege lies in Babylon, and the fields adjacent.

126. THE SIEGE OF CALAIS. Trag. by Charles Denis, translated from the French of M. De Belloy, with Historical Notes, 8vo. 1765. Not acted.

127. THE SIEGE OF CONSTANTINOPLE. Trag. 4to. 1675. Acted at the Duke's Theatre. This play, though published anonymous, is said by Downes, in the *Roscius Anglicanus*, to be written by Nevil Paine. The plot may be found by perusing Heylin's *Cosmography*, Knolles's *Turkish History*, &c. The scene, Constantinople.

128. THE SIEGE OF DAMASCUS. Trag. by John Hughes, Acted at Drury-Lane, 8vo. 1720. This play was, and still continues to be, acted with general approbation. It is generally allowed, that the characters in this tragedy are finely varied and distinguished; that the sentiments are just and well adapted to the characters; that it abounds with beautiful descriptions, apt allusions to the manners and opinions of the times where the scene is laid, and with noble morals; that the diction is pure, unaffected, and sublime, without any meteors of style or ambitious ornaments; and that the plot is conducted in a simple and clear manner. When it was offered to the managers of Drury-Lane house in the year 1718, they refused to act it, unless the author made an alteration in the character of Phocyas, who, in the original, had been prevailed upon to profess himself a Mahometan, pretending he could not be a hero if he changed his religion, and that the audience would not bear the sight of him after it, in how lively a manner soever his remorse and repentance might be described. The author (being then in a very languishing condition) finding, if he did not comply, his relations would probably lose the benefit of the play, consented, though with reluctance, to new model the character of Phocyas. The scenes, however, as they were originally written, are printed in the third volume of *Letters by several eminent Persons deceased*, 8vo. 1773. On the first night's performance of the play, Feb. 17, 1719-20, the author died.

129. THE SIEGE OF DERRY. Tragi-Com. Anonymous, 1692. This is an exceeding bad play, and was never acted; but as it was written very near the period of the transaction which it describes, no bad idea may be formed from it of the distresses which the garrison and inhabitants of that city underwent during that famous siege. See further under PIETY AND VALOUR.

130. THE SIEGE OF GIBRALTER. Musical Farce, by F. Pilon. Acted at Covent-Garden, 8vo. 1780. The author of this piece had been more successful in some former temp... than in the present, ... trifling and conce...

131. THE S... SALEM, BY FITE Trag. by Mary ... Prefixed to this p... troduction, is, " " Mystery and M... " craft."

132. THE SIEGE OF JERUSALEM. Trag. 8vo. 1774. Of this piece, which is said to be the production of Lady Strathmore, a few copies only were printed. It has not been published.

133. THE SIEGE OF MEMPHIS, or, *The Ambitious Queen*. Trag. by Thomas Durfey. Acted at the Theatre Royal, 4to. 1676. This play is written in heroic verse, and as Mr. Durfey's genius apparently lay much more to comic humour than tragic power, it is not much to be wondered that he should, in his attempts of the latter kind, run into somewhat of fustian and bombast. However, the judgement of an audience, which on the whole is generally right, pointed out to him his mistake in the indifferent success this piece met with. The plot is in some measure borrowed from history, and the scene is Memphis besieged.

134. THE SIEGE AND SURRENDER OF MONS. Tragi-Com. Anonymous. 4to. 1691. The plot of it is founded on the siege of Mons by the French, in the year 1641. And the author's intention, as he himself expresses it in the the title-page, was to expose the villany of the priests, and the intrigues of the French. The scene lies in Mons, and the French camp before it.

135. THE SIEGE OF RHODES. A Play in two parts, by Sir William Davenant, 4to. 1656. and 4to. 1663. Both these plays met with great approbation. They were written during the time of the civil wars, when the stage lay under a prohibition, and indeed all the *Belles Lettres* were at a stand, and consequently made not their appearance till after the Restoration, at Lincoln's-Inn Fields, when Sir William himself obtained the management of the theatre. The plot, as far as it has a connection with history, is to be found in the several historians who have given an account of this remarkable siege in the reign of Solyman the Second, who took this city in the year 1522. The scene, Rhodes, and camp near it.

136. THE SIEGE OF SINOPE. Trag. by Mrs. Brooke. Acted at Covent-Garden, 8vo. 1781. Taken from Metastasio, and not worthy the reputation which the authoress had deservedly acquired by her former productions.

137. THE SIEGE OF TAMOR. Trag. by Gorges Edmond Howard, 12mo. 1773. Printed at Dublin. This tragedy is founded upon a transaction in the Irish Annals of the 9th century. It does not appear to have been acted.

138. THE SIEGE OF TROY. A Dramatic Performance. Acted in Mrs. Mynns's Booth, Bartholomew-Fair, by Elk. Settle, 8vo. 1707.

139. THE SIEGE OF TROY, A small Drama subjoined to a sixpenny history of the destruction of that city.

140. THE SIEGE OF URBIN. Tragi-Com. by Sir William Killigrew, Fol. 1666. Scene, Pisa.

141. THE SIEGE OF THE CASTLE OF ÆSCULAPIUS. Heroic Comedy. Acted at the Theatre in Warwick-Lane, 8vo. 1768. This relates to the differences between the Fellows of the College of Physicians and the Licentiates.

142. THE SILVER AGE. A History, by Thomas Heywood, 4to. 1613. This is the second of a series of historical dramas which this author has pursued, and which contain on the whole the greatest part of the Heathen mythology. This part contains the Loves of Jupiter and Alcmena, the Birth of Hercules, and the Rape of Proserpine,

pine, concluding with the Arraignment of the Moon. In the pursuance of a plan of this kind it was impossible to avoid making use of the facts which history pointed out to the author, and those assistances which the ancient writers seemed to hold forth to his acceptance; nor can he by any means be chargeable with plagiarism for so doing. In the intrigue of Jupiter and Alcmena therefore he has borrowed some passages from the *Amphitruo* of Plautus; the Rape of *Proserpine* is greatly enriched by taking in the account which Ovid has given of that transaction in his *Metamorphoses*; and other parts of the piece are much advantaged by quotations from the legends of the poets.

143. OF SIMON THE LEPER. One Comedy, by Bishop Bale. Named only in his catalogue of his own works.

144. SIR ANTONY LOVE, or, *The Rambling Lady*. Com. by Thomas Southerne. Acted at the Theatre Royal, 4to. 1691. 4to. 1698. This play met with very great applause. The author, in his Dedication, makes his acknowledgments to Mrs. Mountfort, for her excellent performance of Sir Antony the principal character. The scene, Montpelier.

145. SIR BARNABY WHIGG, or, *No Wit like a Woman's*. Com. by Thomas Durfey. Acted at the Theatre Royal, 4to. 1681. The principal plot of this play is founded on a novel of Monf. St. Evremond, called *The Double Cuckold*; and part of the humour of Capt. Porpuss is borrowed from Marmion's comedy of *The Fine Companion*. Scene, London.

146. SIR CLYOMON, *Knight of the Golden Shield, Son to the King of Denmark; and Clamydes the White Knight, Son to the King of Suavia (both valiant Knights), their History*. Acted by her Majesties players. Anonymous. 4to. 1599. This is a very indifferent play, written in verse, and in the language more obsolete than the date seems to warrant, and is very disagreeable in the reading.

147. SIR COURTLY NICE, or, *It cannot be*. Com. by J. Crowne, 4to. 1685. This play was written at the command of King Charles II. The plot and part of the play is taken from a Spanish comedy, called *No pued-esser*, or *It cannot be*, and from a comedy, called *Tarugo's Wiles*. The song of *Stop-Thief* is a translation, or rather paraphrase of Mascarille's *Au Voleur* in Moliere's *Precieuses ridicules*. The character of Crack is admirably kept up; but the chief merit of the play is in the very fine contrast supported between the two characters of Hothead and Testimony, characters which even now give pleasure; but at those times, when fanaticism was arisen to a very absurd height, must certainly have done great credit to the author's power of execution.

148. *The History of* SIR FRANCIS DRAKE. Exprest by instrumental and vocal Music, and by art of perspective in Scenes, &c. The first part. Represented daily at the Cockpit, in Drury-Lane, at three in the afternoon punctually, 4to. 1659.

149. SIR GIDDY WHIM, or, *The Lucky Amour*. Com. Anonymous, 4to. 1703. This piece was never acted.

150. SIR GYLES GOOSECAPPE, Knight. Com. Anonym. 4to. 1606. 4to. 1636. This play was presented by the children of the Chapel.

151. SIR HARRY GAYLOVE, or, *Comedy in Embrio*. By the author of Clarinda Cathcart and Alicia Montague, 8vo. 1772. This

This play was printed in Scotland, but not acted. In the preface, the author complains of the managers of the three London theatres, for refusing her the advantages of representing her performance.

152. SIR HARRY WILDAIR, being the sequel of *The Trip to the Jubilee*, by George Farquhar. Acted at Drury-Lane, 4to. 1701. This comedy is a continuation of *The Constant Couple*, and hath several of the same characters. Yet, although the success and real merit of the first part so much insured success to this as to afford it a run of nine nights to crouded audiences, yet it was by no means equal in merit to that first part, nor is it now ever performed, although *The Constant Couple* still remains one of the most favoured pieces on the list of acting plays. From a peculiar happiness in hitting the character of Jubilee Dicky in these plays, the celebrated Mr. Henry Norris, the comedian, gained so much reputation, as occasioned his own christian name to be sunk in that of his character, and his being ever after distinguished by the name of Dicky Norris; under which name, at the head of a play-bill, a benefit for that gentleman was advertised.

153. SIR HERCULES BUFFOON, or, *The Poetical Squire*. Com. by J. Lacy. Acted at the Duke's Theatre, 4to. 1684. This play was not published, nor brought on the stage, till about three years after the author's decease. The prologue was written by Mr. Durfey, and contains a great compliment to the author, in his capacity of an actor. Jos. Haynes, the comedian, wrote the *Epilogue*, and spoke both that and the prologue.

154. SIR JOHN COCKLE AT COURT. Farce, by Robert Dodsley, 8vo. 1737. This little piece is a sequel to *The King and the Miller of Mansfield*, in which the Miller, newly a knight, comes up to London, with his family, to pay his compliments to the King. It is not, however, equal in merit to the first part, for though the King's disguising himself in order to put Sir John's integrity to the test, and the latter resisting every temptation, not only of bribery, but of flattery also, is ingenious, and gives an opportunity for many admirable strokes both of sentiment and satire, yet there is a simplicity, and fitness for the drama, in the story of the first part, that it is scarcely possible to come up to, in the circumstances which arise from the incidents of the latter.

155. "The first Part of the " true and honourable History of " the Life of SIR JOHN OLD-" CASTLE, the good Lord Cob-" ham." Acted by the Earl of Nottingham the Lord High Admiral's servants, 4to. 1600. This is one of the seven plays discarded from Shakspeare's works by most of the editors, yet it was undoubtedly published in his lifetime with his name. Mr. Malone says, the hand of Shakspeare is not to be traced in any part of this play; and Dr. Farmer supposes it to be the production of Thomas Heywood, whose manner it resembles.

156. SIR JOHN OLDCASTLE. A Play, Part II. Mr. Malone supposes this second part to have once existed. If however it did, it is now lost.

157. SIR JOHN OLDCASTLE. Trag. by Thomas Brereton. This play is noticed in several catalogues, but none of them give the date of it. As it has not fallen into my hands, I am unable to supply any account of it.

158. SIR

158. SIR MARTIN MAR-ALL, or, *The feign'd Innocence*. Com. by J. Dryden. Acted at the Duke's Theatre, 4to. 1668. 4to. 1691. The plot and great part of the language of Sir Martin and his Man Warner, are borrowed from Quinault's *Amant indiscret*, and the *Etourdi of Moliere*. Warner's playing on the lute instead of his master, and being surprized by his folly, is taken from M. du Parc's *Francion*, Book 7. and Old Moody and Sir John, being hoisted up in their altitudes, owes its origin to a like incident in Marmion's *Antiquary*. Downes says, the Duke of Newcastle gave this play to Dryden, who adapted it to the stage; and it is remarkable, that it is entered on the books of the Stationers' Company as the production of that nobleman.

159. SIR MARTIN MAR-ALL. Com. by J. Ozell. This is only a literal translation of Moliere's *Etourdi*, to which I suppose Mr. Ozell gave the above title, from the hint of Dryden's comedy.

160. SIR MARTYN SKINK, *the Life and Death of, with the Warres of the Low Countries*. A Play, by Richard Broome and Thomas Heywood. Entered on the books of the Stationers' Company April 8, 1654; but, I believe, not printed.

161. SIR PATIENT FANCY. Com. by Mrs. Behn. Acted at the Duke's Theatre, 4to. 1678. The hint of Sir Patient Fancy is borrowed from Moliere's *Malade imaginaire*; and those of Sir Credulous Easy and his Groom Curry, from the M. Pourceaugnac of the same author. Those last characters have also been made use of by Brome in his *Damoiselle*. Mr. Miller also, in his comedy of THE MOTHER-IN-LAW, or, *The Doctor the Disease*, has availed himself of both these plots, and blended them together much after the same manner that Mrs. Behn has done in this. The scene lies in two different houses in London.

162. SIR ROGER DT COVERLY, or, *The Merry Christmas*. A dramatic Entertainment of two acts, by Mr. Dorman, 1740. 8vo. This piece was never acted.

163. SIR ROGER DE COVERLY. Com. by James Miller. Not acted or printed. In a preface to this author's Miscellanies, he says that this play was written at the desire of Mrs. Oldfield, who was to have performed the Widow; the part of Will Honeycomb was also intended for Wilks, and Sir Roger for Mr. Cibber. The deaths, however, of the two former, and the retirement of the latter from the stage, prevented its representation; and probably the copy is now lost.

164. SIR ROGER DE COVERLY. Com. by Dr. Dodd. Not acted or printed. This piece is said to have been in the managers' hands, at the very time when its unfortunate author was taken into custody.

165. SIR SALOMON, or, *The Cautious Coxcomb*. Com. Acted at the Duke of York's Theatre, 4to. 1671. 4to. 1691. This play is very little more than a translation from the *Ecole des Femmes* of Moliere, and is attributed to John Caryll, who, in the prologue to it, owns it to be a translation. It met with some enemies at first, but, notwithstanding, made its part good in the representation; scene lies in Lo[...]

166. SIR T[...] Play under this [...] tant in *The* [...] MS. 7308.) but n[...] lished.

167. SIR THOMAS OVERBURY. Trag. by Richard Savage, 8vo. 1724. This play was acted at the Theatre Royal in Drury-Lane, and the author performed the principal part in it himself, but without success, both his voice and aspect being very much against him, neither of them being at all agreeable.

168. SIR THOMAS OVERBURY. Trag. Acted at Covent-Garden, 8vo. 1777. See Vol. I. p. 392.

169. SIR WALTER RALEIGH. Trag. by George Sewell, 8vo. 1719. This play, the title of which points out its plot, was acted at Lincoln's-Fields Theatre with very great success. It is extremely well written; the lines, with which the fourth act of it concludes have been justly celebrated for novelty of thought and elegance of expression.

170. SIR WILLIAM WALLACE. Trag. by Mr. Jackson. Acted at Edinburgh 1780. but not printed.

171. THE SISTERS. Com. by Mrs. Charlotte Lenox, 8vo. 1769. This comedy was taken from the authoress's own novel, intituled *Henrietta*. Though it was treated severely, and performed but one night at Covent-Garden, it is written with a considerable degree of good sense and elegance. Dr. Goldsmith's Epilogue to it is, perhaps, the best that has appeared in the course of the last thirty years.

172. THE SISTERS. Com. by James Shirley. Acted at the private house, Black-Friers, 8vo. 1652. Scene, Parma.

173. THE SISTERS. C. translated from the French, and printed in the second volume of Foote's *Comic Theatre*.

174. SIX DAYS ADVENTURE. or, *The New Utopia*. Com. by Edward Howard. Acted at the Duke of York's Theatre, 4to° 1671. This play miscarried in the representation; and the witty Lord Rochester wrote a sharp invective against it, notwithstanding which, when it appeared in print, it was ushered into the world with four recommendatory copies of verses, by Mrs. Behn, Ravenscroft, and others. The scene, Utopia.

175. THE SLEEP-WALKER. Com. translated from the French of *Pont de Vile*, by Lady Craven, 12mo. 1778. Printed at Strawberry-Hill, but not published.

176. THE SLIGHTED MAID. Com. by Sir Robert Stapylton. Acted at Lincoln's-Inn Fields, 4to. 1663. The scene of this play is laid in Naples. And the epitaph made by Decio, upon Iberio and Pyramons, is borrowed from Martial's celebrated epigram of Arria and Pætus, lib. i. ep. 14.

177. THE SLIP. Farce, by Christopher Bullock, 12mo. 1715. This piece was acted with applause at Lincoln's-Inn Fields; it is entirely taken from Middleton's *Mad World my Masters*.

178. THE SMUGGLERS. A Farce, of three acts, by Thomas Odell, 8vo. 1729. Acted with some success at the Little Theatre in the Hay-Market.

179. THE SNAKE IN THE GRASS. A Dramatic Entertainment of a new species, being neither Tragedy, Comedy, Pantomime, Farce, Ballad, or Opera, by Aaron Hill, 8vo. 1760. This was never acted, but is printed with the author's other works. The intention of it is, in a satirical and emblematical manner, to point out the false taste prevailing in the present age, hinting that opera has assumed the seat of tragedy, and pantomime that of comedy, in the regions of British genius; and that genuine wit, humour,

mour, and poetry, have no chance for being attended to by audiences, who, to make use of Hamlet's phrase, are "*capable of nothing but inexplicable dumb show and noise.*"

180. THE SNUFF-BOX, or, *A Trip to Bath*. Com. in two acts, by William Heard. Acted at the Hay-Market, 8vo. 1775.

181. THE SOCIABLE COMPANIONS, or, *The Female Wits*. Com. by the Duchess of Newcastle, Fol. 1662?

182. SOCRATES. A Dramatic Poem, by Amyas Bushe, Esq. A. M. and F. R. S. 4to. 1758.

183. SOCRATES. Trag. translated from the French of Voltaire, 12mo. 1760. This was printed originally in France as a translation from a MS. left by James Thomson, author of *The Seasons*.

184. SOCRATES. Dramatic Performance, translated from Voltaire, and printed in Dr. Franklin's edition of that author.

185. SOCRATES TRIUMPHANT, or, *The Danger of being wise in a Commonwealth of Fools*. Trag. Anonymous, 8vo. 1716. This piece was never acted, but was written by an officer of the army, and printed at the end of a collection of "Military and other Poems upon several Occasions, and to several Persons." The scene, Athens.

186. THE SODERED CITIZEN, or, *The Crafty Merchant*. Com. by Shakerly Marmyon, Entered on the books of the Stationers' Company June 29, 1660; and was amongst the plays destroyed by Mr. Warburton's servant.

187. SODOM. A Play, by Mr. Fishbourne. At what time this infamous piece was published I know not; but the bookseller, with a view of making it sell, by passing it on the public as Lord Rochester's, put the letters E. R. in the title-page; but, licentious as that nobleman was in his morals, he was ashamed of being supposed the author of so very obscene and shocking a piece of work as this; and therefore he wrote a copy of verses to disclaim it. Nor has it indeed any of his lordship's wit, to make atonement for its most abominable obscenity.

188. THE SOLDIER. Trag. by Richard Lovelace. Not printed.

189. SOLDIER's FORTUNE. C. by Thomas Otway. Acted at the Duke's Theatre, 4to. 1681. The plot of this play is by no means new, the several incidents in it being almost all of them borrowed. For instance, Lady Dunce's making her husband an agent for the conveyance of the ring and letter to her gallant Capt. Beaugard, is evidently taken from Moliere's *Ecole des Maris*, and had besides been made use of in some English plays before, particularly in *The Fawne*, and in Flora's *Vagaries*. The original story from which Moliere himself probably borrowed the hint, may be seen in Boccace, Dec. 3. Nov. 3. Sir Davy's bolting out of his closet, and surprising his Lady and Beaugard kissing, and her behaviour on that occasion, is borrowed from the story of Millamant, or *The Rampant Lady*, in Scarron's *Comical Romance*. The character of Bloody Bones is much like that of Bravo in *The Antiquary*, and Courtine's conduct under Silvia's balcony has a great resemblance to Monsieur Thomas' carriage to his mistress in Fletcher's comedy of that name.

There is a sequel to this play which is called THE ATHEIST, or the second part of *The Soldier's Fortune*, 4to. 1684. The plot of which, so far as relates to the amours of Beaugard and Portia, is founded on Scarron's novel of

The

The Invisible Mistress. Both these plays have wit and a great deal of busy and intricate intrigue, but are so very loose in respect to sentiment and moral, that they are now entirely laid aside.

190. THE SOLDIER'S LAST STAKE. Com. by Giles Jacob. This piece, I believe, never made its appearance to the world; yet I could not avoid taking notice of it, as the author himself in his *Political Register*, 8vo. 1719. p. 318. mentions his having such a play by him ready for the stage.

191. THE SOLICITOUS CITIZEN, or, *The Devil to do about Dr. S—c—l.* A Com. 8vo. no date.

192. SOLIMAN AND PERSEDA, *The Tragedie of* (Anonym. 4to. no date), *wherein is laide open Love's Constancy, Fortune's Inconstancy, and Death's Triumphs.* This old piece is not divided into acts; and Langbaine supposes it was never acted. Mr. Hawkins, in the Origin of the English Drama, vol. II. p. 197. conjectures it to be one of the productions of Thomas Kyd, author of *The Spanish Tragedy*; and this may be probably true, as it is entered on the books of the Stationers' Company Nov. 20, 1592, being the same year as that play.

193. KING SOLOMON'S WISDOM. Interlude, 4to. no date. Printed with other pieces attributed to Robert Cox, comedian.

194. SOLON, or, *Philosophy no Defence against Love.* Trag.-Com. by Martin Bladen, 4to. 1705. This piece was never acted, and even printed unknown to the author. The scene lies in Athens; and in the third act is a masque of *Orpheus and Euridice.*

195. THE SOMEWHAT. A Dram. Piece, by Edward Barnard. Printed in a volume, intituled, *Virtue the Source of Pleasure*, 8vo. 1757.

196. THE SON-IN-LAW. Farce, by J. Keefe. Acted at the Hay-Market 1779. The songs only printed. This piece was extremely successful in its representation, and does no small credit to the talents of its author.

197. THE SONG OF SOLOMON. Drama, by J. Bland, 8vo. 1750.

198. THE SOPHISTER. Com. Anonymous. 4to. 1639. This play was acted at one of the universities, and has a prologue spoken by Mercury, as the God of Eloquence, and addressed to the Academical Auditory. At the end of a book, this play is said to be written by Dr. Z. (probably Dr. Zouch.)

199. SOPHOMPANEAS, or, *Joseph.* Trag. by Francis Goldsmith, 8vo. no date. This is only a translation from Hugo Grotius, with critical remarks and annotations.

200. SOPHONISBA, or, *Hannibal's Overthrow.* Trag. by Nath. Lee. Acted at Drury-Lane, 4to. 1676. 4to. 1697. This tragedy is written in rhyme, yet it met with great applause, especially from the female and the more tender part of the audience. The loves of Sophonisba and Masinissa are delicately and affectingly managed; but the author has greatly deviated from the idea history gives us of the characters of Scipio and Hannibal, in the manner he has here represented them, yet perhaps he might in some measure be drawn into this error by following too closely the example set him by Lord Orrery in his romance of *Parthenissa*, wherein he has made Hannibal as much of a whining lover towards his Izadora, as Lee has done with regard to Rosalinda. The histories of Scipio and Hannibal are to be found by perusing Plutarch and Cornelius Nepos; and the story of Masinissa and Sophonisba

nisba is very nearly related by Petrarcha, in his *Trionfo D'Amore*, C. 2. The scene of the play, Zama.

201. SOPHONISBA. Trag. by James Thomson, 8vo. 1730. This play was acted at Drury-Lane Theatre with very great applause, and is founded on the same story with the foregoing piece. Yet it was not without its enemies, a very severe criticism being published against it; and, to say truth, though the author has in good measure avoided the rants and wild extravagances which break forth continually in Lee's Tragedy, yet at the same time he falls greatly short of him in poetical beauties and luxuriance of imagination. And on the whole it will not perhaps be doing Mr. Thomson any injustice, to say, that had he never published his Seasons and some other Poems, but confined his pen to dramatic writing only, he would not have stood in that rank of poetical fame which he now holds in the annals of Parnassus. Dr. Johnson observes, that every rehearsal of this tragedy was dignified with a splendid audience, collected to anticipate the delight that was preparing for the public. It was observed, however, that nobody was much affected, and that the company rose as from a moral lecture; that it had upon the stage no unusual degree of success. Slight accidents will operate upon the taste of pleasure. There was a feeble line in the play:

O, Sophonisba, Sophonisba, O!

This gave occasion to a waggish parody,

O, Jemmy Thomson, Jemmy Thomson, O!

which for a while was echoed through the town.

Dr. Johnson likewise observes he had been told by Savage, that of the Prologue to *Sophonisba* the first part was written by Pope, who could not be persuaded to finish it; and that the concluding lines were added by Mallet.

202. THE SOPHY. Trag. by Sir John Denham. Acted at Black-Friers, Fol. 1642. This tragedy is built on the same story in Herbert's Travels, on which Baron has constructed his tragedy of *Mirza*. It is, however, very differently handled by the two authors. And Baron objects on this account, that Denham has deviated from the truth of history in making Abbas die in his tragedy, whereas he really survived several years after the murder of his son. This, however, is no more than a *Licentia poetica*, which has ever been considered warrantable, and which on the present occasion is made use of only for the sake of dramatic justice.

203. SOPHY MIRZA. Tr. This play is on the same subject as Sir John Denham's. It was begun by Mr. Hughes, who wrote two acts of it, and finished by his brother-in-law Mr. William Duncombe, in the hands of whose son it now remains in manuscript.

204. THE SOT. Burletta; acted at the Hay-Market, 8vo. 1775. See SQUIRE BADGER.

205. SOUTH-SEA, or, *The Biters bit*. A Farce, by William Rufus Chetwood, 8vo. 1720. This piece was not intended for the stage, but only designed as a satire on the South-Sea project, and the inconceivable bubbles of that æra of folly and credulity.

206. THE SOUTH-BRITON. C. of five acts; performed at Smock-Alley Theatre, Dublin, 8vo. 1774. The title-page of this piece speaks of it as the performance of a lady. It was acted at Covent-Garden one night for the benefit of Mrs. Bulkeley.

207. SOUTH-

207. SOUTHWARK FAIR, or, *The Sheep-shearing*. An Opera, by Charles Coffey, 8vo. 1729. This piece consists only of three scenes, and is said to have been acted by Mr. Reynolds's company from the Hay-Market; but at what place it was presented, or with what success, I know not, although I am apt to conjecture that it might have been performed as a kind of droll at one of the booths in the Borough-Fair.

208. THE SPANISH BARBER, or, *The Fruitless Precaution*. C. by G. Colman. Acted at the Hay-Market 1777. This is a very pleasing though farcical performance, and was taken from the *Barbier de Seville* of Monf. Beaumarchais.

209. THE SPANISH BAWD, *represented in* Celestina, *or the Tragicke Comedy of* Calisto *and* Melibea; *wherein is contained, besides the Pleasantnesse and Sweetenesse of the Stile, many philosophical Sentences, and profitable Instructions necessary for the younger Sort: Shewing the Deceits and Subtilties housed in the Bosoms of false Servants and Cunny-catching Bawds.* Fol. 1631. This play is the longest that was ever published, consisting of twenty-one acts. It was written originally in Spanish, by El Bachiler Fernanda de Roxas de la Puebla de Montalvan, whose name is discoverable by the beginning of every line in an acrostic or copy of verses prefixed to the work. The translator also, James Mabbe, pretends to be a Spaniard, and has taken on himself the disguised name of Don Diego Puedeser. The scene lies in Spain.

210. THE SPANISH CURATE. Com. by Beaumont and Fletcher, Fol. 1647. This is a good comedy, and although it is not new on the list of acting plays, it was at many different times after the death of its author revived, and always with success. The plot of Don Henrique, Ascanio, Violante, and Jacintha, is borrowed from Gerardo's *History of Don John*, p. 202. and that of Leandro, Bartolus, Amaramha, and Lopez, from the *Spanish Curate* of the same author, p. 214.

211. THE SPANISH DUKE OF LERMA. A Play, by Henry Shirley. Entered on the books of the Stationers' Company, Sept. 9, 1653, but not printed.

212. THE SPANISH FRYAR, or, *The Double Discovery*. Trag.-Com. by John Dryden. Acted at the Duke's Theatre, 4to. 1681. 4to. 1686. 4to. 1690. Langbaine charges the author of this play with casting a reflection on the whole body of the clergy in his character of Dominick the Fryar, and seems to imagine it a piece of revenge practised for some opposition he met with in his attempt to take orders. However that might be with respect to Mr. Dryden in particular, I cannot pretend to say, but this one point appears evident to me, viz. that the satire thrown out in it is only general against those amongst the clergy who disgrace their cloth by wicked and unbecoming actions; and is by no means pointed at, or can any way affect, the sacred function in itself. That there have been such characters as Father Dominick among the priests of all religions, and more especially those of the Romish church, to whom the practice of confession affords more frequent opportunities and uninterrupted scope for such kind of conduct, no man in his senses will, I believe, attempt to deny; and if so, how or where can they be more properly exposed than on the stage? but can that be said to cast any reflection on the much greater number of valuable, well-meaning

meaning and truly religious among the divine professors?—No surely. Yet the *qui capit ille facit* is a maxim so perfectly founded in truth, that I am ever apt to suspect some consciousness in themselves of the truth of particular satire in those persons who appear over angry at hints thrown out in general only. This play considered in itself has perhaps as much merit as any that this author has given to the world. The characters of Torrismond and Leonora in the tragic part are tender and poetical, yet there are some ideas and descriptions thrown out by the latter towards the beginning of the third act, which are rather too warm and luxuriant to bear repetition on a public stage, and are therefore now omitted in the acting. But the whole comedy is natural, lively, entertaining, and highly finished both with respect to plot, character, and language. The scene lies in Arragon, and the plot of the comic parts is founded on a Novel, called *The Pilgrim*, written by M. St. Bremond.

213. THE SPANISH GYPSIE. Com. by Thomas Middleton and William Rowley. Acted at Drury-Lane and Salisbury-Court, 4to. 1653. 4to. 1661. The plot of this play with respect to the story of Roderigo and Clara, if not borrowed from, has at least a very near resemblance to a Novel of Cervantes, called *The Force of Blood*. The scene lies at Alicant.

214. THE SPANISH LADY. Musical Entertainment, by Tho. Hill. Acted at Covent-Garden, 8vo. 1769. This piece was originally written on receiving the news of a signal conquest gained in the Spanish West-Indies by the English forces in 1762. It was afterwards acted in 1765, once for the author's benefit.

215. THE SPANISH PURCHAS. A play in the list of those destroyed by Mr. Warburton's servant.

216. THE SPANISH ROGUE. Com. by Thomas Duffet, 4to. 1674. This play is written after the manner of most of the French comedies, in rhyme, but is the only instance I know of that kind among the English ones. It is the best of all this author's dramatic works, yet met with very indifferent success. The scene in Spain. It is dedicated to Madam Ellen Guyn.

217. THE SPANISH SOULDIER. Trag. by Thomas Dekker, entered on the books of the Stationers' Company, May 16, 1631, by John Jackman; but, I believe, never printed. See THE NOBLE SPANISH SOULDIER.

218. SPANISH TRAGEDY. See JERONYMO.

219. THE SPANISH TRAGEDY, or, *Hieronimo is mad again, Containing the lamentable end of Don Horatio and Belimperia. With the pitiful Death of Hieronimo*, by Thomas Kyd, 4to. 1603. 4to. 1615. 4to. 1618. 4to. 1623. 4to. 1633. This play was the object of ridicule to almost every writer of the times. Philips and Winstanley ascribe it, but erroneously, to Thomas Smith. Heywood, however, declares it to be the production of Kyd. It had been acted several years before its appearance in print, and we are told in Dekkar's *Satiromastrix*, that Ben Jonson originally performed the part of Hieronimo.

220. THE SPANISH VICEROY, or, *The Honour of Woman*. Com. by Philip Massinger. Entered on the books of the Stationers' Company, Sept. 9, 1653, and was amongst those destroyed by Mr. Warburton's servant.

221. THE SPANISH WIVES. Farce,

Farce, of three acts, by Mrs. Mary Pix, 4to. 1696. The scene of this little piece is laid at Barcelona, and the plot of it borrowed from the same Novel of the *Pilgrim*, on which that of the *Spanish Fryar* is also built. It was acted at Dorset-Gardens.

222. THE SPARAGUS GARDEN. Com. by Richard Brome. Acted in the year 1635, by the then Company of Revels at Salisbury-Court, 4to. 1640.

223. THE SPARTAN DAME. Trag. by Thomas Southerne. Acted at Drury-Lane, 8vo. 1719. This play was written the year before the Restoration, but, on what account I know not, prohibited the stage till the above year, when it made its appearance with universal and indeed merited applause. The subject of it is taken from Plutarch's Life of Agis, in which the character of Chelonis, with respect to the virtuous duties both of a wife and daughter, are a sufficient authority for the picture Mr. Southerne has drawn of an excellent woman in the heroine of his tragedy. It is not now however on the acting list.

224. THE SPARTAN LADIES. Com. by Lodowick Carlell. For some mention of this play see Humphry Moseley's Catalogue at the end of Middleton's Comedy of *More Dissemblers besides Women*, which is the only place in which I find it named. It was entered on the books of the Stationers' Company, Sept. 4. 1646.

225. SPEECHES AT PRINCE HENRY'S BARRIERS. By Ben Jonson, Fol. 1640. These speeches are not much dramatic, being only some compliments paid to Prince Henry, the eldest son of King James I; but as they are printed with the rest of Jonson's works, I could not help thinking them deserving of a mention here.

226. THE SPENDTHRIFT. C. Anonym. 1680. This I find mentioned only in *The British Theatre*.

227. THE SPENDTHRIFT. C. by Matthew Draper. Acted at the Hay-Market, 8vo. 1731. The hint of this play is taken from Shakspeare's *London Prodigal*.

228. THE SPENDTHRIFT. C. translated from the French, and printed in Foote's *Comic Theatre*, vol. I.

229. THE SPENDTHRIFT, or, *A Christmas Gambol.* Farce, by Dr. Kenrick. Acted at Covent-Garden 1778. Not printed. This was taken from Charles Johnson's *Country Lasses*, and was acted only two nights.

230. THE SPIGHTFUL SISTER. Com. by Abr. Bailey, 4to. 1667. The author of this play is allowed by both Langbaine and Jacob to be free from plagiarism, what he has written being all his own, and his characters, particularly those of Lord Occus and Winifred, to be truly original. Jacob however concludes, and with reason, from its being printed without either prologue, epilogue, or dedication, that it never made an appearance on the stage.

231. THE SPIRIT OF CONTRADICTION. Farce, of two acts, by a Gentleman of Cambridge, 8vo. 1760. This farce made its appearance at the Theatre Royal in Covent-Garden, but with very little success. Nor indeed did it deserve a better fate than it met with, there being neither plot, character, wit, humour, nor language through the whole, excepting some little of the virago spirit kept up in the character of Mrs. Partlett, who, from the making it a settled principle to contradict to the utmost the inclinations of every other

other person, is tricked into the compelling her daughter to a match with the m.. the loves, but whom her mother is made to believe she has the utmost dislike to. Mr. Rich is said to have had some hand in this Farce.

232. THE SPIRITUAL MINOR. Com. 8vo. 1763. A low and stupid imitation of Foote's *Minor*.

233. THE SPLEEN, or *Islington Spaw*. A Comic Piece, of two acts, by George Colman, performed at Drury-Lane, 8vo. 1756. A performance which will not lessen the established fame of its ingenious author, though it did not meet with equal success with other of his performances.

234. THE SPOUTER, or, *The Triple Revenge*. Comic Farce, in two acts, 8vo. 1756. A whimsical production of Mr. Murphy, with the connivance of Mr. Garrick. The chief personages in this piece were designed as representations of living authors and managers. Garrick himself, Rich, Foote, and young Cibber, are all the objects of its merriment, which is unmixed with the least offensive severity, as will be supposed from the circumstance of their leaders having been privy to the publication.

235. THE SPOUTER, or, *The Double Revenge*. Comic Farce, in three acts, by Henry Dell, 8vo. 1756.

236. THE SPRING. Pastoral, by James Harris, Esq. Acted at Drury-Lane, 4to. 1763.

237. SPRING'S GLORY, vindicating Love by Temperance, against the Tenet, "fine Cerere & Baccho "friget Venus." Moralized in a Maske, by Thomas Nabbes, 4to. 1638. The title of this piece so amply explains the subject it is written on, that I need say nothing more in regard to it. At the end

of it are printed Poems, Epigrams, Elegies, and Epithalamiums of the same author.

238. THE SQUIRE OF ALSATIA. Com. by Thomas Shadwell. Acted by their Majesties servants, 4to. 1688. This play is founded on the *Adelphi* of Terence, the characters of the two elder Belfonds being exactly those of the Micio and Demea, and the two younger. Belfonds the Eschinus and Ctesipho of that celebrated Comedy. Mr. Shadwell has however certainly, if not improved on those characters in their intrinsic merit, at least so far modernized and moulded them to the present taste, as to render them much more palatable to an audience in general, than they appear to be in their ancient habits. This play met with good success, and is still at times performed to universal satisfaction. The scene lies in Alsatia, the cant name for White Fryars; and the author has introduced so much of the cant or gamblers' language, as to have rendered it necessary to prefix a glossary for the leading the reader through a labyrinth of uncommon and unintelligible jargon.

239. SQUIRE BADGER. Burletta, in two parts. Acted at the Hay-Market, 8vo. 1772. The music of this piece was composed by Dr. Arne, who probably also wrote the words. It is taken from Fielding's *Don Quixote in England*, and was afterwards brought out under the title of *The Sot*.

240. THE SQUIRE BURLESQUED, or, *The Sharpers outwitted*. Com. by Bartholomew Bourgeois, 8vo. 1765.

241. SQUIRE OLD-SAP, or, *The Night Adventures*. Com. by Thomas Durfey. Acted at the Duke's Theatre, 4to. 1679. This play is greatly obliged to several

Novels

Novels and other Dramas for the composition of its plot, which is very intricate and busy. For instance, the character of Squire Old-Sap, and the incident of Pimpo's tying him to the tree in the first act, is borrowed from *The Comical History of Francion*. Tricklove's cheating Old-Sap with the bell, and Pimpo's standing in Henry's place, is related in Boccace's Novels, Dec. 7. Nov. 8. and in Fontaine's Tale of *La Gageure des trois Commeres*: and Tricklove's contrivance with Welford for having Old-Sap beaten in her cloaths in the same act, and which is also an incident in Fletcher's *Woman pleas'd*, Ravenscroft's *London Cuckolds*, and some other Comedies, is evidently taken from Boccace, Dec. 7. Nov. 7.

242. THE STAGE BEAU TOSS'D IN A BLANKET, or, *The Hypocrite a la Mode*. Com. Anonym. 4to. 1704. This piece, though without a name, was written by the humorous Tom Brown. It consists of three acts only, and is a satire on Jeremy Collier, who wrote a severe book against the stage and dramatic writers, called, *A short View of the Immorality and Prophaneness of the English Stage*. Mr. Brown has dedicated his piece to Christopher Rich, Esq; patentee of the Theatre Royal, and father of the late patentee of Covent-Garden Theatre.

243. THE STAGE COACH. Farce, by George Farquhar, 4to. 1710. In this little piece he was assisted by Mr. Motteux; yet after all it is nothing more than a plagiarism, the whole plot of it, and some entire scenes, particularly one between Captain Basil and Nicodemus Somebody, being borrowed from a little French piece, called *Les Caresses d'Orleans*. The scene is laid in an inn on the road, and the time about three hours, viz. from the coming in of the coach to its stage, till about midnight.

244. THE STATE FARCE, or, *They are all come home*, 8vo. 1757.

245. THE STAGE MUTINEERS, or, *A Playhouse to be Let*. A Tragi-Comi-Farcical Ballad Opera. Acted at Covent-Garden. Anonym. [1733] 8vo. This piece is only a burlesque on a contest between the manager of one of the theatres and his performers, at the head of the male-content part of whom Mr. Theophilus Cibber at that time stood in a very conspicuous light, and is in this piece characterized by the name of Ancient Pistol, all the speeches put into his mouth being thrown into the bombastic or mock tragedy style which Shakspeare has given to that character in his two parts of Henry IV. and the *Merry Wives of Windsor*. As in all disputes of this kind both sides are generally to blame, I shall not here attempt to enter on the merits of the cause, but content myself with observing that the Farce under our present consideration seems to be written in favour of the performers. The scene lies in the playhouse at the time of rehearsal.

246. THE STAPLE OF NEWS. Com. by Ben Jonson, Fol. 1631. This play, though not printed till the above date, was first acted in the year 1625. He has introduced in this Comedy four Gossips, by way of interlocutors, who remain on the stage during the whole representation, and make comments and criticisms on all the several incidents of the piece. It, however, is not the only instance of this kind of conduct, he having done the very same thing in two other plays, viz. *Every Man out of his Humour*, and the

the *Magnetic Lady*; and Fletcher in his *Knight of the burning Pestle* has followed the very same example. Scene, London. It is entered on the books of the Stationers' Company, April 14, 1616.

247. THE STATE JUGGLER, or, *Sir Politic Ribband*. A new Excise Opera. Anonym. 8vo. 1733. This is one of those pieces in which Sir Robert Walpole, then prime minister, was abused, in regard to the jobs which the public imagined were going forwards with respect to the excise and other branches of the public revenues.

248. THE STATE OF INNOCENCE, or, *The Fall of Man*. An Opera, 4to. 1676. 4to. 1677. 4to. 1691. This piece was never performed, the subject being too solemn, and the characters of a nature that would render it almost blasphemy for any person to attempt the representation of them. It is written in heroic verse or rhyme, and the plot is founded on Milton's *Paradise Lost*, from which he has even borrowed many beauties in regard to his language and sentiments. Some of the nicer and more delicate critics have found fault with this Opera, charging the author with anachronism and absurdity in introducing Lucifer conversing about the world, its form, matter, and vicissitudes, at a time previous to its creation, or at least to the possibility of his knowing any thing concerning it. And indeed Mr. Dryden seems himself to have been aware of its lying open to such kind of objections, by his having prefixed to it an apology for *Heroic Poetry*, and for the *Licentia Poetica*, of which he had indeed made a most ample use in this piece. On the whole, however, it has undoubtedly very great beauties, and is very highly commended by Nat. Lee, in a copy of verses published with it; nor is it at all detracting from its merit to own, that we are by no means blind to some few faults that it may have. As Dr Johnson truly observes, is is termed by Dryden an opera: it is rather a tragedy in heroic rhyme, but of which the personages are such as cannot decently be represented on the stage. Some such production was for seen by Marvel, who writes thus to Milton:

"Or if a work so infinite be spann'd,
"Jealous I was lest some less skilful
"hand,
"Such as disquiet always what is well,
"And by ill-imitating would excel,
"Might hence presume the whole crea-
"tion's day
"To change in scenes, and show it in a
"play."

It is one of Dryden's hasty productions; for the heat of his imagination raised it in a month.

249. THE STATE OF PHYSIC. Com. Anonym. 8vo. 1742. This piece was never acted, nor do I know who was the author, yet I conjecture it must have been some person of the faculty, since, if I may be allowed a paltry quibble, it is apparent, that even in the very title-page, to make use of the vulgar phrase, *He talks like an apothecary*.

250. THE STATESMAN FOILED. A Musical Com. of two acts, by Robert Dossie; performed at the Hay-Market, 8vo. 1768. The music by Mr. Rush.

251. THE STATUTE. Pastoral Masque, privately performed with applause, 8vo. 1777.

252. *King* STEPHEN, *the History of*. A Play, by William Shakspeare. Entered on the books of the Stationers' Company June 29, 1660, but not printed. It cannot but be a subject of regret, that this performance is lost to the world. Should it exist in any library, it is hoped

hoped that the proprietor will gratify the general curiosity by the publication of it.

253. *Saint* STEPHEN's GREEN, or, *The Generous Lovers*. Com. by William Philips, Esq. 8vo. 1720. This piece was never acted, nor have I ever seen it. It is mentioned in none of the catalogues but *The British Theatre*; from which, and the title, I should be apt to conclude the author an Irishman, the scene of action of his piece being laid in a place which is, with respect to Dublin, nearly the same as the Mall in St. James's Park is with regard to London; that is to say, the theatre for the playing off all the various turns of vanity, affectation, and gallantry, and the scene of thousands of assignations and intrigues.

254. THE STEP-MOTHER. Tragi-Com. by Sir Robert Stapylton, 4to. 1664. Acted at Lincoln's-Inn Fields, by the Duke of York's servants. Though Sir Robert did not put his name to this play, yet the prologue, which expressly declares it to be written by the author of *The Slighted Maid*, authorizes my giving the credit of it to this gentleman. The scene lies at Verulam, or St. Alban's; and the instrumental, vocal, and recitative music, were composed by Mr. Locke. Two masques are inserted in the body of the play, viz. one in the third act, called *Apollo's Masque*, the scene of which is a grove, wherein is a laurel tree and three poplar trees; the other is called *Diana's Masque*, in which a hawthorn tree is made the grand scene of action.

255. THE STOCK-JOBBERS, or, *The Humours of Exchange-Alley*. Com. of three acts. Anonym. 8vo. 1720. This is one more of the pieces written on the follies of the year 1720, but which, like the rest of them, was never acted.

256. THE STOLEN HEIRESS, or, *The Salamanca Doctor out-plotted*. Com. by Susanna Centlivre. Acted at Lincoln's-Inn Fields. No date, 4to. [1703.] Scene, Palermo.

257. STONEHENGE. Pastoral, by John Speed. Acted before Dr. Richard Baylie, the president and fellows of the College of St. John's, Oxford, in their common refectory, at what time, says Wood, the said Doctor was returned from Salisbury, after he had been installed Dean thereof, anno 1635. Not printed.

258. THE STRANGE DISCOVERY. Tragi-Com. 4to. 1640. This play has the letter J. G. Gent. prefixed to it as the initials of the author's name, and in some copies of this only edition the name J. Gough at length. The plot, and great part of the language, is taken from the tenth book of *Theagenes* and *Chariclea*, or Heliodorus's *Ethiopic History*, which is looked on to be one of the most ancient, and is unquestionably one of the finest romances extant. It is to be had in English, the first five books being translated by a person of quality, the remaining five by Mr. Tate, 8vo. 1686. The scene in the beginning and end of this play lies in Ethiopia, in the other parts of it in England and Greece.

259. THE STRATFORD JUBILEE. Com. of two acts, by Francis Gentleman, as it hath been lately exhibited at Stratford upon Avon with great applause. To which is prefixed, Scrub's *Trip to the Jubilee*, 8vo. 1769.

260. THE STROLLERS. Farce. Acted at Drury-Lane. This is only an extract of some particular scenes from a comedy written by John

John Durant Breval, called *The Play's the Plot*, published in 1718. It has sometimes been acted with the addition of another little piece, called *The Mock Countess*.

261. THE STROLLER'S PACKET BROKE OPEN. 12mo. 1742. This is nothing more than a small collection of drolls, calculated for Bartholomew-Fair, and other fairs and country villages, being certain select scenes borrowed from different comedies, and put together so as to form short pieces, easily represented by four or five persons only, in the very same manner as those published by Kirkman and Cox, and mentioned in the foregoing part of this work, under the title of *Sport upon Sport*. The pieces contained in this collection are only seven. Their titles and the dramas they are borrowed from as follows:

1. *The Bilker bilk'd*, or *The Banquet of Wiles*. — from — *The Match in Newgate* of C. Bullock.

2. *The Braggadocio*, or *His Worship the Cully*. — from — Congreve's *Old Batchelor*.

3. *The Feign'd Shipwreck*, or *The Imaginary Heir*. — from — *The Elder Brother* of Beaumont and Fletcher.

4. *The Guardians over-reach'd in their own Humour*, or *The Lover metamorphos'd*. — from — Mrs. Centlivre's *Bold Stroke for a Wife*.

5. *The Litigious Suitor defeated*, or *A New Way to get a Wife*. — from — Bullock's *Woman's a Riddle*.

6. *The Sexes mismatch'd*, or *A New Way to get a Husband*. — from — Southerne's *Oroonoko*, and the *Monsieur Thomas* of Beaumont and Fletcher.

7. *The Witchcraft of Love*, or *Stratagem upon Stratagem*. — from — Mrs. Centlivre's *Man's bewitch'd*, or *The Devil to do about her*.

262. THE STUDENTS. Com. altered from Shakspeare's *Love's Labour Lost*, and adapted to the stage, 8vo. 1762.

263. THE STURDY BEGGARS. A New Ballad Opera. Dedicated to the Lord Mayor, Aldermen, &c. of London, 8vo. 1733. This piece was written on occasion of the Excise-Bill.

264. THE SUBJECTS' JOY FOR THE KING'S RESTORATION. A sacred Masque, by Dr. Anthony Sadler, 4to. 1661. gratefully made public for his sacred Majesty. The plot of this piece is founded on the 1st Kings, ch. xi. 12. and 2 Chronicles, ch. xiii. And the scene, for the *Land*, in *Canaan*, for the *Place*, in *Bethel*, and for the *Person*, in *Jeroboam*.

265. THE SUCCESSFUL PIRATE. A Play, by Charles Johnson. Acted at Drury-Lane, 4to. 1713. This play is taken from an old one written by Lodowick Carlell, called *Arviragus and Philicia*. The scene, the City of Saint Lawrence in the Island of Madagascar.

266. THE SUCCESSFUL STRANGERS. Trag-Com. by William Mountfort. Acted at Drury-Lane, 4to. 1696. This play is much superior to *The Injur'd Lovers* of the same author; yet he is by no means clear from the charge of plagiarism with regard to his plot, however original his language and conduct of the piece may be; the design of the catastrophe being evidently borrowed from Scarron's Novel, called *The Rival Brothers*.

267. THE SUICIDE. A Com. in four acts, by George Colman. Acted at the Hay-Market, 1773. Not printed. The author of this piece may be considered as one of the best judges of the writing of any dramatist now living. Although none of the characters can be taken of as new, yet the business of the

drama is conducted with so much judgement, that we cannot but esteem this very pleasing comedy as little inferior to the best of Mr. Colman's productions. The quarrelling scene between the poet and the player, is taken from *Joseph Andrews*, and the duel from *The Coxcomb* of Beaumont and Fletcher.

268. THE SULLEN LOVERS, or, *Impertinents*. Com. by Thomas Shadwell. Acted at the Duke of York's Theatre, 4to. 1668. The author owns in his preface that he had received a hint from the report of Moliere's *Les Facheux*, on which he had founded the plot of this comedy; but at the same time declares, that he had pursued that hint in the formation of great part of his own play before the French one ever came into his hands. Be this, however, as it may, he has certainly made very good use of whatever assistances he borrowed, having rendered his own piece extremely regular and entertaining. The place of the scene in London, the time supposed in the month of March in the year 1667-8.

269. THE SULTAN, or, *Love and Fame*. Trag. by Francis Gentleman. Acted at the Hay-Market, 8vo. 1770. This play was written about the year 1755, and has been frequently acted at Bath, York, and Scarborough. The plot is founded in Turkish history.

270. THE SULTANA. Farce. Acted at Drury-Lane 1775. A frivolous raree-show performance, which but for the splendor of its scenery, and the sprightliness of a female performer, would have met with early condemnation. It is founded on a tale of Marmontel; was at first said to be composed by some flimzy man of quality; but was afterwards known to be the work of Cickerstaff.

271. THE SULTANESS. Trag. by Charles Johnson, 8vo. 1717. This is little more than a translation of *The Bajazet* of Racine; a piece which of itself is esteemed the very worst of that author's writings; and as Mr. Johnson's talent seemed to consist much more in comedy than tragedy, it is not much to be wondered at if this play, thus served up at second-hand by so indifferent a cook, should rather form an insipid and distasteful dish; yet it was performed at Drury-Lane Theatre with no very bad success. The concluding lines to the prologue probably occasioned the author, many years after, to be introduced into *The Dunciad*:

"At least, 'tis hop'd, he'll meet a kinder
"fate,
"Who strives some standard author to
"translate,
"Than they, who give you, without
"once repenting,
"Long-labour'd nonsense of their own
"inventing.
"Such wags have been, who boldly durst
"adventure
"To club a farce by tripartite indenture:
"But, let them share their dividend of
"praise,
"And their own fool's cap wear instead
"of bays."

272. SUMMER AMUSEMENT, or, *An Adventure at Margate*. Com. Opera, by Messieurs Andrews and Miles. Acted at the Hay-Market 1779. The subject of this piece is of high importance, and the manner in which it is treated will undoubtedly countenance the joint labours of the brace of authors, whose names it has been our office to record.

273. THE SUMMER'S TALE. Musical Com. of three acts, by Richard Cumberland, Esq. Acted at Covent-Garden, 8vo. 1765. This comedy met with but a cold reception, though it was performed nine nights.

274. SUMMER'S LAST WILL AND

AND TESTAMENT. Com. by Thomas Nash, 4to. 1600.

275. THE SUN's DARLING. A Masque, by John Ford and Thomas Dekker. Acted at Whitehall, and afterwards at the Cockpit in Drury-Lane, 4to. 1656. 4to. 1657. The plan of this masque alludes to the four seasons of the year. The explanation of the design is to be seen prefixed to the Dramatis Personæ. It was not published till after the death of the authors.

276. THE SUPERANNUATED GALLANT. Farce, by Joseph Reed, 12mo. about 1746. This piece is by the same author as the *Register Office* and *Madrigal* and *Trulietta*, mentioned before. It was never acted.

277. THE SUPPLICANTS. Tr. translated from Æschylus, by R. Potter, 4to 1777.

278. THE SUPPOSES. Com. by George Gascoigne, 4to. 1566. This is one of the earliest dramatic pieces which can properly be called plays in the English language, and was acted at Gray's-Inn. It is a translation from an Italian comedy, by the celebrated Ariosto. The prologue to it is written in prose, which, though not customary at this time, has been followed by some other of our dramatic writers, particularly Cockayne, in the prologue to *Trappolin suppos'd a Prince*; and Tate, in his epilogue to *Duke and no Duke*. Shakspeare has also given us an example of an epilogue in prose, which is even to this day constantly spoken to the play, and seems now to be considered as part of it, viz. the long speech of Rosalind, at the conclusion of his comedy of *As you like it*.

279. SUPPOSED INCONSTANCY. A Play; entered on the books of the Stationers' Company Nov. 29, 1653, but not printed.

280. THE SURPRISAL. Com by Sir Robert Howard, Fol. 1665. The scene, Sienna.

281. SUSANNA. By Thomas Garter, 4to. 1578. The running title of this play is, *The Commody of the moste vertuous and godlye Susanna*. The Dramatis Personæ is printed in the title-page, wherein it is also said that eight persons may easily play it. It is written in metre, printed in the old black letter, and not divided into acts, three great tokens of its being a very ancient piece. The playe of *Susanna* was entered, by Thomas Colwell, in the books of the Stationers' Company 1568 to 1569.

282. SUSANNA, or, *Innocence Preserv'd*. Musical Drama, by Elizabeth Tollet, 12mo. 1755. Printed in a Collection of Poems published that year.

283. SUSANNA'S TEARS. Both Langbaine and Jacob mention a piece of this name; but as they neither of them pretend to have seen it, I am apt to believe that it may be the last-mentioned play but one, either with an altered title in some later edition, or coming to their knowledge only by report, and with a wrong name.

284. SUSPICIOUS HUSBAND. Com. by Dr. Benjamin Hoadly, 8vo. 1747. This comedy was first presented at Covent-Garden house, and appears to have one standard proof of merit, which is, that although, on the first night it was performed, it seemed threatened with considerable opposition; yet, from the time the curtain rose, it gradually overcame all prejudice against it, met with universal applause, and continues to this day one of the most favourite pieces with the public, being as frequently presented to crowded theatres as any one modern comedy on the list. To speak impartially

of it, however, its merit is rather pleasing than striking, and the busy activity of the plot takes off our attention to the want of design, character, and language, which even its best friends must confess to be discoverable on a more rigid scrutiny. Yet the audience is kept constantly alive; and as the principal intent of comedy is to entertain, and afford the care-tired mind a few hours of dissipation, a piece consisting of a number of lively busy scenes, intermingled with easy sprightly conversation and characters, which, if not glaring, are at least not unnatural, will frequently answer that purpose more effectually than a comedy of more complete and laboured regularity, and therefore surely lays a very just claim to our approbation and thanks. Yet this play is not entirely devoid of merit with respect to character, since that of Ranger, though not new, is absolutely well drawn, and may, I think, be placed as the most perfect portrait of the lively, honest, and undesigning rake of the present age; nor can Mr. Garrick's inimitable performance of that character, which indeed was in great measure the support of the piece during its first run, be ever forgotten, while one person survives who has seen him in it. Clarinda is an amiable, lively, and honest coquet; and Strictland, though evidently copied from Ben Jonson's Kitely in *Every Man in his Humour*, and indeed greatly inferior to that character, has nevertheless some scenes in which the agitations of a weak mind, affected with that most tormenting of all passions, *Jealousy*, are far from being badly expressed; nor can I bring a more convincing argument to prove this assertion, than the universal reputation the performing of that character brought to an actor of no very capital share of merit in other parts, viz. Mr. Bridgewater, who, during the run of this comedy, obtained so much of the public approbation by his performance of Mr. Strictland, as even in an advertisement of his benefit to assign that approbation as a reason for his making choice of this play rather than any other. The scene lies in London, and the time about thirty-six hours.

285. THE SUSPICIOUS HUSBAND CRITICIZED, or, *The Plague of Envy*. Farce, by Charles Macklin, 1747. This piece was acted at the Theatre Royal in Drury-Lane, and is, as it styles itself, a criticism on the foregoing play. It hath never appeared in print.

286. THE SWAGGERING DAMSEL. Com. by Robert Chamberlaine, 4to. 1640. It is uncertain whether this play was ever acted; but it is ushered into the world by five recommendatory copies of verses, one of which is written by Mr. Rawlins, and is in requital for one prefixed by our author to that gentleman's tragedy of *The Rebellion*. This custom of authors complimenting each other, was formerly greatly in vogue; and we see Dryden, Lee, Jonson, Fletcher, &c. alternately paying this tribute to each other's merits. It seems, however, to be now laid aside, the writers of the present age appearing more zealously to make it their endeavour to point out to the public how very small a share of genius is possessed by every author but himself; and so successfully do they pursue this candid plan, that generally at the conclusion of every contest of this kind, the world becomes perfectly convinced of the justice of their assertions, and is ready to believe that

that every individual among them has spoken the truth in his turn.

287. SWETNAM THE WOMAN-HATER ARRAIGN'D BY WOMEN. Com. Acted at the Red Bull by the late Queen's servants. Anonymous. 4to. 1620. This play is chiefly intended to lash a very scandalous pamphlet against the female sex, written by one Joseph Swetnam, intituled, *The Arraignment of lewd, idle, froward, and inconstant Women*. The plot, however, is built on an old Spanish book, called *Historia da Aurelia, y Isabella Hija del Rey de Escotia*, &c. The scene, in Sicily.

288. THE SWINDLERS. Farce. Acted at Drury-Lane, April 25, 1774, for the benefit of Mr. Baddeley, but not printed.

289. THE SWITZER. A play, by Arthur Wilson. Entered on the books of the Stationers' Company Sept. 4, 1646, but not printed.

290. SWORDS INTO ANCHORS. Com. by Mr. Blanch, 4to. 1725. This play was never acted, nor indeed could any thing but the dotage of an author towards the offspring of his brain, produced by a hasty delivery when its parent was seventy-five years of age, excuse the folly of having suffered it to appear in print. The plot is nothing more than the introducing an officer of rank and fortune, who having fallen in love with the daughter of a merchant, in order to oblige the old gentleman and his daughter, throws up his commission, and on quitting the army disposes of his money to the purposes of commerce. There is nothing dramatic in the whole piece; but if we may judge of the author's disposition from his writing, he appears to have been very fond of the convivial pleasures, having introduced eating and drinking into almost every scene.

291. THE SYLPH. Com. Piece, in one act, translated from Fagan, 8vo. 1771.

292. SYLLA. A Dramatic Entertainment, by Mr. Derrick, 8vo. 1753. This is only a translation, not designed for the stage, of a kind of Opera written originally in French by the King of Prussia.

293. SYLLA's GHOST. A Dramatic Satyrical Piece. Anonym. 1689. This piece I have never seen, nor can form any idea of its design. I find it mentioned only in *The British Theatre*.

294. SYLVIA, or, *The Country Burial*. A Ballad Opera, by Geo. Lillo, 8vo. 1731. This was one of the pieces which the general vogue of these ballad Operas occasioned by the success of *The Beggar's Opera* being brought forth into the world. It was performed at Lincoln's-Inn Fields Theatre, but with no very great success.

295. THE SYRACUSAN. Trag. by Dr. Dodd. This piece was never either acted or printed. It was written while the author was an under-graduate at Cambridge, and was sold in 1750 to Mr. Watts the printer. On the author's taking orders in 1751, he withdrew the copy from the hands of the managers, and returned the money the printer had advanced. It was founded on a fictitious story, and was intended to be performed with choruses. Probably it may still remain in manuscript.

296. THE SYRENS. Masque, in two acts, by Captain Edward Thompson, performed at Covent-Garden, 8vo. 1776. This piece, after being thrice performed, was dismissed with the contempt it so well deserved.

T.

T.

T A

1. **A** TALE OF A TUB. Com. by Ben Jonſon, Fol. 1640. The ſcene, Finſbury Hundred. This is not one of our author's beſt pieces, being chiefly confined to low humour.

2. TAMBERLAIN THE GREAT or, *The Scythian Shepherd*. Trag in two parts, by Chriſt. Marloe, 4to. 1590—1593. The full titles of theſe two plays are as follows, viz. Of the firſt part. *Tamberlaine the Great, who from a Scythian Shepherd, by his rare and wonderful Conqueſts, became a moſt puiſſant and mighty Monarque, And (for his Tyranny and Terrour in War) was termed the Scourge of God, divided into two Tragical-Diſcourſes*, 4to. 1590. Of the ſecond part. *Of the Bloodie Conqueſts of mighty Tamberlaine, with his impaſſionate Fury for the Death of his Lady and Love, the fair Zenocrate; his Fourme of Exhortation to his three ſons, and the Maner of his own Death*, 1593. The ſcene of both theſe pieces lies in Perſia, and they are both printed in the old black letter. The plot is taken from the Life of Tamerlane, as related by Knolles and other Hiſtorians of the Turkiſh affairs.

3. TAMBERLANE THE GREAT. Trag. by Charles Saunders. Acted at the Theatre Royal, 4to. 1681. This was eſteemed a very good play, and was highly commended by Banks and other his contemporary writers. The author himſelf confeſſes his deſign to be taken from a Novel, called

T A

Tamerlane and Aſteria. Epilogue by Dryden.

4. TAMERLANE. Trag. by N. Rowe. Acted at Lincoln's-Inn Fields, 4to. 1702. This play was written in compliment to King William III. whoſe character the author intended to diſplay under that of Tamerlane. It was received with great applauſe at its firſt appearance, and ſtill continues to be an admired play. In purſuance of Mr. Rowe's intended compliment, it has been a conſtant cuſtom at all the theatres both in London and Dublin, to repreſent it on the 4th of November, which was that monarch's birth-day. In Dublin more eſpecially it is made one of what is called the *Government Nights* at the theatre, when the Lord Lieutenant, or in his abſence the Lords Juſtices, pay the ladies the compliment of rendering the boxes entirely free to ſuch of them as chuſe to come to the houſe. Nor has it been unuſual in ſome theatres to perform this play on the ſucceeding night alſo, which is the anniverſary of his firſt landing on the Engliſh coaſt.

Dr. Johnſon obſerves, that the virtues of Tamerlane ſeem to have been arbitrarily aſſigned him by his poet, for we know not that hiſtory gives him any other qualities than thoſe which make a conqueror. The faſhion however of the time was, to accumulate upon Lewis all that can raiſe horror and deteſtation; and whatever

ever good was witheld from him, that it might not be thrown away, was bestowed upon K ng William. This was the tragedy which Rowe valued most, and that which probably, by the help of political auxiliaries, excited most applause; but occasional poetry must often content itself with occasional praise. Tamerlane has for a long time been acted only once a year, on the night when King William landed. Our quarrel with Lewis has been long over, and it now gratifies neither zeal nor malice to see him painted with aggravated features, like a Saracen upon a sign.

Dr. Warton, in his Essay on the Genius and Writings of Pope, p. 271. remarks, that there is a want of unity in *The Fable of Tamerlane*, and that such a furious character as that of Bajazet is easily drawn and easily acted.

5. THE TAMING OF THE SHREW. A pleasant conceited Historie. As it hath beene sundry times acted by the right honourable the Earle of Pembrooke his servants, 4to. 1607. This play is a different one from Shakspeare's, and supposed to be prior to it. The merit of it in any other light than being what our great bard availed himself of, is but slender. It has lately been reprinted by Mr. Nichols.

6. THE TAMING OF THE SHREW. Com. by William Shakspeare. Acted at the Black-Friers and the Globe, Fol. 1623. This is very far from being a regular play, yet has many very great beauties in it. The plot of the drunken Tinker's being taken up by the Lord, and made to imagine himself a man of quality, is borrowed from Goulart's *Histoires admirables*. The scene, in the latter end of the third and the beginning of the 4th acts, is at Petrucio's house in the country; for the rest of the play, at Padua. This Comedy has been the groundwork of some other pieces, particularly *Sawney the Scot*, *The Cobler of Preston*, and *Catharine and Petruchio*; among which the last is much the most regular and perfect Drama that has ever been formed from it. See further under its own title.

Dr. Johnson says, "Of this " play the two plots are so well " united, that they can hardly be " called two without injury to " the art with which they are in- " terwoven. The attention is en- " tertained with all the variety of " a double plot, yet is not dis- " tracted by unconnected inci- " dents.

" The part between Katherine " and Petruchio is eminently " spritely and diverting. At the " marriage of Bianca, the arrival " of the real father perhaps pro- " duces more perplexity than " pleasure. The whole play is " very popular and diverting."

7. TANCRED. Trag. by Sir Henry Wotton, composed when the author was a young man at Queen's College, but never printed.

8. TANCRED AND GISMUND. Trag. This play was the work of five gentlemen of the Inner Temple, and was performed there before Queen Elizabeth in the year 1568. It was afterwards revived and polished by Robert Wilmot, the author of the 5th act, and printed in 4to. 1592. It is founded on Boccace's Novels, Dec. 4. Nov. 1. which story is very finely related by Dryden in his Fables, under the title of *Sigismunda and Guiscardo*. Mrs. Centlivre has also taken the very same story for the basis of her tragedy, called *The Cruel Gift*.

9. TAN-

9. TANCRED AND SIGISMUNDA. Trag. by James Thomson. Acted at Drury-Lane, 8vo. 1744. The plot of this play is taken from the Novel of *Gil Blas*. It is one of the best of this author's dramatic pieces, and met with very good success. The characters are well supported, yet they are not sufficiently new and striking. The loves of Tancred and Sigismunda are tender, pathetic and affecting; yet there is too little variety of incident or surprize, to preserve the attention of an audience sufficiently to it; and the language is in many places poetical and flowery, yet in the general too declamatory and sentimental. On the whole, therefore, the piece, though far from wanting some share of merit, appears heavy and dragging in the representation, and seems therefore better adapted to the closet than the theatre.

10. TARTUFFE, or, *The French Puritan*. Com. by Math. Medbourne. Acted at the Theatre Royal, 4to. 1670. This play is an improved translation of Moliere's *Tartuffe*, and according to the author's own account met with very great applause, and indeed it is no great wonder that any piece which was written against the French Hugonots, who bore a strong resemblance to the English Puritans, should give pleasure at a period when every motive was made use of to render that class of people detestable throughout the kingdom. It must, however, be confessed, that the original *Tartuffe* is a master-piece in the dramatic way, and to it we stand indebted for a comedy as excellent in our own language, viz. *The Nonjuror* of Colley Cibber.

11. TARTUFFE, or, *The Hypocrite*. Com. by J. Ozell. This is only a literal translation from Moliere.

12. TARUGO'S WILES, or, *The Coffee-house*. Com. by Sir Thomas St. Serfe. Acted at the Duke of York's Theatre, 4to. 1668. Great part of the plot of this play is founded on a Spanish Comedy, called *Ne Pued esser*, or, *It cannot be*; from which, or from the piece before us, Mr. Crown has borrowed his Sir Courtly Nice, at least as far as relates to Lord Bellguard and Crack, which are extremely resembling Don Patricio and Tarugo; in this, Sir Thomas has in his third act introduced a coffee-house scene, which is admirably finished. In a word, this piece, if not intitled to the *first*, may, without presumption, lay claim to a place in the *second* rank of our dramatic writings; and the ingenious Earl of Dorset, when Lord Buckhurst, paid a strong testimonial to its merit in a copy of verses to the author on its publication. The scene is laid in Madrid.

13. TASTE. Com. of two acts, by Samuel Foote. Acted at Drury-Lane, 8vo. 1752. This piece and its profits were given by its author to Mr. Worsdale the painter, who acted the part of Lady Pentweasle in it with great applause. The general intention of it is to point out the numerous impositions that persons of fortune and fashion daily suffer in the pursuit of what is called *Taste*, or a love of *Virtù*, from the tricks and confederacies of painters, auctioneers, *Medal Dealers*, &c. and to shew the absurdity of placing an inestimable value on, and giving immense prizes for, a parcel of maimed busts, erazed pictures, and inexplicable coins, only because they have the mere name and appearance of antiquity, while the more

more perfect and really valuable performances of the most capital artists of our own age and country, if known to be such, are totally despised and neglected, and the artists themselves suffered to pass through life unnoticed and discouraged; these points Mr. Foote has in this Farce set forth in a very just, and at the same time a very humorous light; but whether the generality of the audience did not relish, or perhaps did not understand this confined satire, or that, understanding it, they were so wedded to the infatuation of being imposed on, that they were unwilling to subscribe to the justice of it, I will not pretend to determine; but it met with some opposition for a night or two, and during the whole run of it, which was not a long one, found at best but a cold and distasteful reception.

14. THE TAXES. Dramatic Entertainment, by Dr. Bacon, 8vo. 1757.

15. THE TAYLORS. Trag. for warm weather. Acted at the Hay-Market, 8vo. 1778. This piece was first acted July 2, 1767, at a time when there had been great disturbances between the master Taylors and their journeymen about wages. The author of it hath kept himself concealed; but the manner in which it came to the manager is said to have been as follows: A short time before its appearance, Mr. Foote received the manuscript from Mr. Dodsley's shop, offering it for his acceptance, with a request at the same time, that if it was not approved, it might be returned in the manner it came to him. Mr. Foote, on perusing it, was much pleased with the performance, ordered it immediately into rehearsal, and took the principal character himself. It was acted with some applause, and having since been abridged by Mr. Colman, with some additional touches from his pen, generally makes a part of the summer entertainments at the Hay-Market.

16. TCHOO CHI COU ELL, or, *The Little Orphan of the Family of Tchoo*. Trag. 8vo. 1737. This is nothing more than a literal translation from the Chinese language of the tragedy in the first volume of Du Halde's *History of China*, by R. Brookes.

17. TEAGUE'S RAMBLE TO LONDON. Interlude. Acted at the Hay-Market 1770. Not printed.

18. THE TEARS AND TRIUMPHS OF PARNASSUS. Ode, by Robert Lloyd; performed at Drury-Lane, 4to. 1760.

19. TEXNOΓAMIA, or, *The Marriage of the Arts*. Com. by Barton Holiday, 4to. 1618. 4to. 1630. This piece was acted by the students of Christ-Church, Oxford, before the university at Shrove-Tide. It is entirely figurative, all the liberal arts being personated in it; and the author has displayed great learning in the contexture of his play, having introduced many things from the ancients, particularly two odes from *Anacreon*, which he has inserted, one in his second, and the other in his third act. The challenge of Logicus to Poeta is an elegant and ingenious imitation of that from Damætas to Clinias in Sir Philip Sidney's celebrated *Arcadia*. The scene, *Insula fortunata*.

20. TELEMACHUS. Masque, by George Graham, 4to. 1763.

21. THE TELLTALE. Com. advertised at the end of *Wit and Drollery*, 12mo. 1661, as then in the press. It, however, did not appear

pear in print; but is probably the same piece as now remains in MS. in the possession of Mr. Malone.

22. TEMPE RESTOR'D. A Masque. 4to. 1631. This piece was presented before K. Charles I. at Whitehall on Shrove-Tuesday, 1631, by the Queen and fourteen of her ladies. It is founded on the story of Circe as related in the 14th Book of Ovid's *Metamorphosis*. The words were written by Mr. Aurelian Townshend; but the subject and allegory of the masque, with the descriptions and apparatus of the scenes, were invented by Inigo Jones.

23. THE TEMPEST. A Com. by William Shakspeare, Fol. 1623. This is a very admirable play, and is one instance, among many, of our author's creative faculty, who sometimes seems wantonly, as if tired with rummaging in nature's storehouse for his characters, to prefer the forming of such as she never dreamt of, in order to shew his own power of making them act and speak just as she would have done had she thought proper to have given them existence. One of these characters is Caliban in this play, than which nothing surely can be more *outré*, and at the same time nothing more perfectly natural. His Ariel is another of these instances, and is the most amazing contrast to the heavy earth-born clod I have been mentioning; all his descriptions, and indeed every word he speaks, appearing to partake of the properties of that light and invisible element which he is the inhabitant of. Nor is his Miranda less deserving of notice, her simplicity and natural sensations under the circumstances he has placed her in, being such as no one since, though many writers have attempted an imitation of the character, has ever been able to arrive at. The scene is at first on board a vessel in a storm at sea; through all the rest of the play, in a desert island.

Dr. Johnson says, "It is observed of *The Tempest*, that its "plan is regular; this the author "of *The Revisal* thinks, what I "think too, an accidental effect "of the story, not intended or re-"garded by our author. But "whatever might be Shakspeare's "intention in forming or adopt-"ing the plot, he has made it in-"strumental to the production of "many characters, diversified with "boundless invention, and pre-"served with profound skill in na-"ture, extensive knowledge of "opinions, and accurate observa-"tion of life. In a single drama "are here exhibited princes, cour-"tiers, and sailors, all speaking in "their real characters. There is "the agency of airy spirits, and of "an earthly goblin. The opera-"tions of magic, the tumults of a "storm, the adventures of a desert "island, the native effusion of "untaught affection, the punish-"ment of guilt, and the final "happiness of the pair for whom "our passions and reason are "equally interested."

24. THE TEMPEST, or, *The Inchanted Island*. Com. by J. Dryden. Acted at Dorset-Gardens, 4to. 1670. 4to. 1690. The whole ground-work of this play is built on the fore-mentioned one of Shakspeare, the greatest part of the language and some entire scenes being copied *verbatim* from it. Mr. Dryden has, however, made a considerable alteration in the plot and conduct of the play, and introduced three entire new characters, viz. a sister to Miranda, who, like her,

has

has never seen a man; a youth, who has never beheld a woman; and a female monster, sister and companion to Caliban; besides which, he has somewhat enlarged on the characters of the sailors, greatly extended the musical parts, and terminated the whole with a kind of masque. In short, he has, on the whole, rendered it more shewy, more intricate, and fitter to keep up the general attention of the audience; and yet, to the immortal evidence of Shakspeare's superior abilities over every other genius, we cannot but observe that the work of this very great poet Mr. Dryden, interwoven as it is with the very texture of Shakspeare's play, and fine as it must be considered taken singly, appears here but as patch-work, as a fruit entirely unequal to the noble stock on which it is engraffed. Mr. Dryden, in his preface, observes, that Fletcher in his *Sea Voyage*, and Sir John Suckling in his *Goblins*, have borrowed very considerably from Shakspeare's *Tempest*. Sir William Davenant had some share with Dryden in this alteration.

25. THE TEMPEST. Opera, 8vo. 1756. by David Garrick, esq. This is only the principal scenes of Shakspeare's *Tempest*, thrown into the form of an opera, by the addition of many new songs. It was performed at the Theatre Royal in Drury-Lane with success.

26. THE TEMPLE BEAU. Com. by Henry Fielding. Acted at Goodman's Fields, 8vo. 1729. Mr. Murphy observes, that this play contains a great deal of spirit and real humour—not but it must be acknowledged, that the picture of a Temple Rake, since exhibited by the late Dr. Hoadly in *The Suspicious Husband*, has more of what the Italians call *Fortunato* than can be allowed to the careless and hasty pencil of Mr. Fielding.

27. THE TEMPLE OF DULLNESS, with the Humours of Signor Capochio and Signora Dorinna. A Comic Opera. Acted at Drury-Lane, 4to. 1745.

28. THE TEMPLE OF HYMEN. A Masque, with the landing of the Queen, by John Wignell, performed at Shuter's Booth-Fair in Bartholomew-Fair 1761. Printed in this writer's Poems, 8vo. 1762.

29. THE TEMPLE OF LOVE. A Masque. Presented by the Queen's Majesty and her ladies at Whitehall on Shrove-Tuesday 1634. By Inigo Jones and William Davenant, 4to. 1634. The names of the several performers are at the end of this masque.

30. TEMPLE OF LOVE. Pastoral Opera, englished from the Italian. All sung to the same music, by Signior J. Saggione; performed at the Hay-Market, 4to. 1706. By Peter Motteux. Prologue spoken by Mr. Booth. This piece is taken from the Italian. The scene lies in Arcadia, and the time of action the same with that of the representation.

31. THE TEMPLE OF PEACE. Masque of one act, performed at Dublin, 8vo. 1749.

32. OF THE TEMPTATION OF CHRIST. A dramatic piece, by Bishop Bale, mentioned only in his own list.

33. THE TENDER HUSBAND, or, *The Accomplished Fools*. Com. by Sir Richard Steele. Acted at Drury-Lane, 4to. 1705. Some part of this play, particularly the incident of Clerimont's disguising himself and painting his mistress's picture, is borrowed from Moliere's *Sicilien ou L'Amour Peintre*.
The

The prologue is written by Mr. Addison, to whom the play is dedicated.

34. TERAMINTA. An English Opera, by Mr. H. Carey, 8vo. 1732. This piece was performed at the Theatre in Lincoln's-Inn Fields. The music by Mr. J. C. Smith.

35. TETHYS' FESTIVAL, or, *The Queen's Wake*, celebrated at Whitehall the 5th day of June, 1610; devised by Samuel Daniel, 4to. 1610. This piece was written and performed on occasion of creating King James's eldest son Henry Prince of Wales.

36. THE THEATRES. Farce. Anonymous, 8vo. 1733. This is in the list of *The British Theatre*, but without any farther particulars. It was never acted, and I suppose was only a party-affair, relating to the theatrical contests of that time.

37. THE THEATRICAL CANDIDATES. Prel. by David Garrick, Esq. Acted at Drury-Lane, 8vo. 1775.

38. THE THEATRICAL MANAGER. Dram. Satire, 8vo. 1751. Abuse on Mr. Garrick.

39. THEBAIS. Trag. by Tho. Newton, 4to. 1581. This is a translation from one of the tragedies published as Seneca's, although, from some inconsistencies between the catastrophe of this and that of *Oedipus*, it is scarcely reasonable to imagine them both the work of the same author.

40. THELYPTHORA, or, *More Wives than One*. Farce, by F. Pilon. Acted at Covent-Garden, 1781. The popularity of Mr. Madan's book, with the same title as this piece, and the novelty of its doctrine, seemed to point them out as good subjects for comic ridicule. The author on this occasion was not so lucky as he had formerly been. His piece was represented once, and attempted a second time, but without success.

41. THEMISTOCLES, *the Lover of his Country*. A Trag. 1729. 8vo. by Dr. Samuel Madden. Acted with some success at the Theatre in Lincoln's-Inn Fields.

42. THEODORIC KING OF DENMARK. Trag. by a young Gentlewoman, 8vo. 1752. Who this young gentlewoman was I know not, but suppose her to have been a native of Ireland, as the piece was published in Dublin. The plot of this play is built on a novel, intituled *Ildegerte*. The scene, Denmark.

43. THEODOSIUS, or, *The Force of Love*. Trag. by Nath Lee. Acted at the Duke's Theatre, 4to. 1680. 4to. 1692. This play met with great and deserved success, and is to this day a very favourite tragedy with most of the sensible part of the audience. The passions are very finely touched in it, and the language in many parts extremely beautiful. Every thing that relates to the loves of Varanes, Athenais, and Theodosius, is uniform, noble, and affecting; yet even all these beauties cannot bribe me from remarking how very unequal to these is the episode of the loves of Marcian and Pulcheria, which is in itself so trifling, and so unconnected and unnecessary to the main plot of the play, that, with a very little alteration, those two characters, and every thing that relates to them, might be entirely omitted, and the piece rendered the better for the want of them. Marcian's behaviour to Theodosius is not only inconsistent with probability, but such as renders the latter too contemptible for the sufferance of an audience

after

after it, to admit him again on the stage; and Pulcheria's banishing the general only to have an opportunity of recalling him to surprize him by making him her husband, has something in it so truly ludicrous and puerile, that one should imagine it rather the treatment of a skittish boarding-school miss to some pretty master just come home to a holiday breaking-up, than that of a princess, to whom the empire of the world was to devolve, towards a hardy soldier, whose arms that world had trembled at the sound of. It were therefore to be wished, that this slight hint might induce some person equal to the task, to undertake an alteration of it, by curtailing these superfluous excrescences, and filling up the hiatus they would leave, with some incidents that might have more uniformity and connection with the general design of the play. The ground-work of it is built on the romance of Pharamond, in which the History of Varanes is to be seen, Part 3. Book 3. of Martian in Part 7. Book 1. and of Theodosius in Part 7. Book 3. The scene lies at Constantinople. It is also assisted in the representation by several entertainments of singing in the solemnity of church music, composed by the celebrated Hen. Purcell, being the first he ever composed for the stage. There is a play on the same story by Massinger. See EMPEROR OF THE EAST.

44. THERSYTES, *his Humours and Conceits.* An Interlude. Anonymous. 1598.

45. THE THIRTIETH OF OCTOBER. A Play. Entered on the books of the Stationers' Company in the year 1560; but not printed.

46. THOMAS AND SALLY. A Musical Entertainment, 8vo. 1761. This little piece was performed at Covent-Garden Theatre with great success. It was written by Mr. Isaac Bickerstaff. The plot is very simple, being no more than a country squire's attempting the virtue of a young girl in the neighbourhood, who, after resisting all the persuasions of an old woman who pleads in the squire's favour, is at last rescued from intended violence by the timely approach of a youth, for whom she had long maintained a pure and unaltered passion. The songs are pleasing, and the music well adapted to the present taste.

47. THOMASO, or, *The Wanderer.* Com. in two parts, by Thomas Killigrew. Fol. 1664. The author of this play has borrowed several of his decorations from others, particularly a song on jealousy from Mr. Carew, and another song from Fletcher's play of the Captain. He has, besides, taken not only the design of his character of Lopus, but even many of the very words, from that of Jonson's *Volpone.* But as he seems very ready candidly to confess his thefts, and that what he has thus borrowed he applies to very good purpose, he may surely be excused. Both these pieces were written at Madrid, which city he has made the scene of action in them.

48. THOMYRIS QUEEN OF SCYTHIA. An Opera, by P. Motteux, 4to. 1707. This was performed at the Theatre Royal in Drury-Lane, and was one of the attempts made at that time for the introduction of English operas after the manner of the Italian. The scene lies in the part of Scythia inhabited by the Massagetes.

49. THORNEY ABBEY, or, *The London Maid.* Trag. by T. W. 12mo. 1662. Who the author of this piece was I know not, but it

is printed with the *Marriage Broker* and *Grim the Collier of Croydon*, under the title of *Gratiæ Theatrales*, or, *A choice Ternary of English Plays, composed upon especial Occasions by several ingenious Persons.* The scene of the piece we are now speaking of, is laid in London.

50. THE THRACIAN WONDER. A comical History, by John Webster and William Rowley, 4to. 1661. This play was acted with great applause. It is one of those published by Kirkman after the author's death.

51. THE THREE CONJURERS. A political Interlude, stolen from Shakspeare, 4to. 1763. A squib thrown at Lord Bute.

52. THREE HOURS AFTER MARRIAGE. Com. of three acts, by Messrs. Gay, Pope, and Arbuthnot. Acted at Drury-Lane, 8vo. 1717. This little piece, the joint produce of this triumvirate of first-rate wits, was very deservedly damned. The consequence of which was the giving Mr. Pope so great a disgust to the stage, that he never attempted any thing in the dramatic way afterwards; and, indeed, he seems, through the course of his satirical writings, to have shewn a more peculiar degree of spleen against those authors who happened to meet with success in this walk, in which he had so conspicuously failed. Yet it is far from improbable, that had he thought it worth his while singly to have taken the pains of writing a dramatic piece, he might have succeeded equally, if not fu-superior to any of his contemporaries. Though this piece was printed under the name of Gay, his hand is not very discernible in any part of it. We may however observe, that the character of Sir Tremendous, being apparently designed for Dennis, was in all probability introduced by Pope. Fossile, who was meant as the representative of Dr. Woodward, might likewise have been the production of Arbuthnot, who through the knowledge incident to his profession was enabled to furnish a sufficient train of physical terms and observations. Phœbe Clinket also should seem to have been intended as a ridicule on one of the females whose petulant attacks had irritated the little bard of Twickenham. Cibber informs us, that his own quarrel with him was occasioned by a joke thrown into the Rehearsal, at the expence of this unsuccessful performance.

53. A right excellent and famous Comedy, called, THE THREE LADIES OF LONDON. Wherein is notablie declared and set forth how by meanes of Lucar, Love and Conscience is so corrupted, that the one is married to Dissimulation, the other fraught with all abhomination. A perfect patterne for all estates to looke into, and a worke right worthie to be marked. Written by R. W. as it hath been publiquely plaied.

At London. Printed by Robert Warde, dwelling neere Holburne Conduit, at the signe of the Talbot, 1584.

The characters in this piece are, Fame. Love. Conscience. Dissimulation, having on a farmer's long coate, and a cap, and his poll and beard painted motley. Simplicitie, like a Miller all mealy, with a wand in his hande. Fraud, with a sword and buckler, like a Ruffin. Symonie. Lady Lucar. Mercadore, like an Italian merchant. Artifex, an Artificer. A Lawyer. Sinceritie. Hospitalitie. Sir Nicholas Nemo. Peter Pleasen.an, like a priest. Gerountes, tres, a Jewe. Coggin, Dissimulation's man. Tom Beggar. Wily Will. Judge of Turkie. Serviceable Diligence, a Constable. Clarke of the Size, &c.—*Paule Bucke.*

Of this morality there is another copy printed in 1592.

55. *The pleasant and stately Morall of the* THREE LORDES AND THREE LADIES OF LONDON, *with the great joy and pompe solempnized at their Mariages. Commically interlaced with much honest Mirth for pleasure and recreation, among many morall observations and other important matters of due regard.* By R. W. 4to. bl. l. 1590.

The actors names.

Policie. ⎫
Pompe. ⎬ the three Lords of London.
Pleasure. ⎭

Wit. ⎫
Wealth. ⎬ their pages.
Wil. ⎭

Nemo, a grave old man.

Love. ⎫
Lucre. ⎬ three Ladies of London.
Conscience. ⎭

Honest Industrie. ⎫
Pure Zeale. ⎬ three Sages.
Sinceritie. ⎭

Desire. ⎫
Delight. ⎬ three Lords of Lincolne.
Devotion. ⎭

Sorrowe, a jayler.
Simplicity, a poore Freeman of London.
Paineful Penurie, his wife.
Diligence, a poste or an officer.

Fealtie. ⎫
Shealtie. ⎬ two heraldes at armes.

Fraud. ⎫
Usurie. ⎬
Dissimulation. ⎬ Foure Gallantes.
Simony. ⎭

Falshood. ⎫
Double dealing. ⎬ two that belong to Fraud and Dissimulation.

54. THE THREE LAWS OF NATURE, MOSES, AND CHRIST, *corrupted by the Sodomites, Pharasies, and Papists.* Com. 4to. 1558. 4to. 1562. See Ames, p. 317. Former catalogues style it, *The Laws of Nature.*

56. THE THREE OLD WOMEN WEATHERWISE. An Interlude, by George Savile Carey. Acted at the Hay-Market, 8vo. 1770.

57. THREE WEEKS AFTER MARRIAGE. Com. of two acts, by Arthur Murphy, performed at Covent-Garden, 8vo. 1776. This piece affords a very striking proof of the capriciousness of public taste, and the injustice of some public determinations. It is no other than the *What we must all come to,* of the same author, with only a new title. On its first appearance it was condemned almost without a hearing, and lay dormant for several years, until Mr. Lewis ventured to produce it again at his benefit, when it met with universal applause, and still continues to be favourably received.

58. THIERRY AND THEODORET. Trag. by Beaumont and Fletcher. Acted at the Black-Friers, 4to. 1621. 4to. 1648. 4to. 1649.

1649. The plot of this play may be seen by consulting De Serres, Mezeray, and other of the French writers on the reign of Clotaire II. and the scene lies in France. In the folio edition of these authors' works in 1679, the editor, either defignedly, or from fome careleſsneſs of the compoſitor, has omitted a great part of the laſt act, which contains the King's behaviour during the operation of the poiſon adminiſtered to him by his mother, and which is as affecting as any part of the play.

59. THYESTES. Trag. by Jaſper Heywood, 8vo. 1560. This is only a tranſlation from the *Thyeſtes* of Seneca. It was not intended for the ſtage; yet the author has taken fome liberty with his original, having added a whole ſcene at the end of the fifth act, in which Thyeſtes bewails his own miſery, and imprecates the vengeance of heaven on Atreus. The ſcene, Argos. This is a very old, and, I believe, the firſt Engliſh tranſlation of this play, and is printed in the black letter.

60. THYESTES. Trag. by James Wright, 12mo 1674. This is another tranſlation of the ſame play, writ (ſays the tranſlator) many years ſince, though corrected, and rendered into ſomewhat a more faſhionable garb than its firſt dreſs, at the intervals of a more profitable ſtudy the laſt long vacation, before 'twas publiſhed.

61. THYESTES. Tr. by John Crown. Acted at the Theatre Royal, 4to. 1681. This is the only piece on this ſtory that has made its appearance on the Engliſh ſtage, where it met with good ſucceſs. The foundation of it is laid in Seneca's Tragedy, and he has in ſome meaſure imitated that author in the ſuperſtructure. There are, however, two plays on the ſame ſubject, the one in French, the other in Spaniſh; but how far our author has been obliged to either of them I know not, neither of them having fallen in my way. The ſcene lies at Atreus's court in Argos.

62. THYRSIS. Paſtoral, by John Oldmixon, 4to. See *The Novelty*, by Mocteaux.

63. TIDE TARRIETH FOR NO MAN. *A moſt pleaſaunte and merry Comedie, ryght Pithy and fulle of Delighte*, by George Wapul, 4to. 161.. This piece I never ſaw. But as it is entered by Hugh Jackſon, Oct. 26, 1576, on the books of the Stationers' Company, I imagine it to be older.

64. TIME VINDICATED TO HIMSELF AND HIS HONOURS. A Maſque, by Ben Jonſon, preſented at court on Twelfth-Night, 1623.

65. TIMANTHES. Trag. by John Hoole. Acted at Covent-Garden, 8vo. 1770. This ſecond tragedy by the worthy and ingenious Mr. Hoole, like his firſt, is the child of Metaſtaſio, and indeed has all the features of its parent. There is, however, too ſtrong "a ſpice of your opera" in it, to render it a very acceptable entertainment to an Engliſh audience; and yet it was played with ſome degree of ſucceſs at Covent-Garden.

66. THE TIMES. Com. by Mrs. Elizabeth Griffiths. Acted at Drury-Lane, 8vo. 1779. This piece, like moſt other of the ſame author's, is taken from the French. It poſſeſſes as much merit, but was not acted with equal ſucceſs to ſome of her former pieces.

67. TIMOLEON. Trag. by Benj. Martyn, 8vo. 1730. This play was acted at Drury-Lane Theatre with ſome ſucceſs. The plot of it is taken from hiſtory, the language

guage is not unpoetical, and there are some strokes of liberty in it that do credit to its author.

68. TIMOLEON, or, *The Revolution*. Tragi-Com. Anonymous. 1697. The comic parts of this play are intended as a satire on mercenary courtiers, who prefer money to merit. The story of the tragic part is from Cornelius Nepos, Plutarch's Life of Timoleon, &c. The scene in Syracuse.

69. TIMON. Com. Not printed. This piece, which still remains in manuscript, from the hand-writing is supposed to be of the age of Shakspeare. See Mr. Malone's Attempt, &c. p. 338.

70. TIMON IN LOVE, or, *The Innocent Theft*. Com. by J. Kelly, 8vo. 1733. This play was acted at Drury-Lane with indifferent success. It is a translation, with but little alteration, of *The Timon Misantrope* of M. De L'Isle; a piece which, in itself, has very great merit; but how much it might lose of its effect in a translation, I cannot form any judgement of.

71. TIMON OF ATHENS. Tr. by William Shakspeare. Fol. 1623. There are some passages in this play equal to any thing this author ever wrote, particularly Timon's grace, and his several curses; nor was there ever perhaps an higher finished character than that of Apemantus. Yet it is not without some faults in point of regularity. The story may be found in Lucian's *Dialogues*, Plutarch's Life of M. Anthony, &c. The scene lies in Athens and the woods adjacent. Dr. Johnson observes, this play " is a domestic " tragedy, and therefore strongly " fastens on the attention of the " reader. In the plan there is " not much art, but the incidents " are natural, and the characters " various and exact. The cata- " strophe affords a very powerful " warning against that ostenta- " tious liberality which scatters " bounty, but confers no benefits, " and buys flattery, but not friend- " ship."

72. THE HISTORY OF TIMON OF ATHENS, *the Manhater*, made into a play, as the alterer modestly phrases it, by Thomas Shadwell. Acted at the Duke's Theatre, 4to. 1678. This tragedy is borrowed from the foregoing one, but is not near so good a play, almost every thing that is valuable in it being what the author has taken verbatim from Shakspeare.

73. TIMON OF ATHENS. Altered from Shakspeare and Shadwell, by James Love. Acted at Richmond, 8vo. 1768.

74. TIMON OF ATHENS. Tr. Altered from Shakspeare, by R. Cumberland. Acted at Drury-Lane, 8vo. 1771. but with little success.

75. 'TIS BETTER THAN IT WAS. Com. by George Digby, earl of Bristol. This play is mentioned by Downes, p. 26. as being *made out of Spanish*, and acted at the Duke's Theatre between 1662 and 1665. Not printed.

76. 'TIS GOOD SLEEPING IN A WHOLE SKIN. Com. by W. Wager. This was amongst those destroyed by Mr. Warburton's servant.

77. 'TIS PITY SHE'S A WHORE. Trag. by John Ford. Acted at the Phœnix, Drury-Lane, 4to. 1633. I cannot help considering this play as the masterpiece of this great author's works. There are some particulars in it both with respect to conduct, character, spirit, and poetry, that would have done honour to the pen of the immortal Shakspeare himself. Langbaine has, however, pointed

pointed out a fault, which I must, though unwillingly, subscribe to, and which relates to a very essential point, viz. the morals of the play; which is, his having painted the incestuous love between Giovanni and his sister Annabella, in much too beautiful colours; and, indeed, the author himself seems by his title to have been aware of this objection, and conscious that he has rendered the last-mentioned character, notwithstanding all her faults, so very lovely, that every auditor would naturally cry out to himself, *'Tis Pity she's a Whore.* In consequence of this incestuous passion also, on which the whole plot of the play turns, the catastrophe of it is too shocking for an audience to bear, notwithstanding every recollection of its being no more than fiction.

78. 'TIS WELL IF IT TAKES. Com. by William Taverner, 8vo. 1719. This play was acted with success at the theatre in Lincoln's-Inn Fields, yet, like most of its author's pieces, quickly sunk into oblivion, and has not been revived since.

79. 'TIS WELL ITS NO WORSE. Com. by Isaac Bickerstaffe. Acted at Drury Lane, 8vo. 1770. The original of this play is *El Escondido y la Tapada* of Calderon. It was not unsuccessfully performed.

80. TITHONUS AND AURORA. Entertainment of Music, set by J. Dunn, and performed at Sadler's Wells, 12mo. 1746.

81. TITERUS AND GALATEA. Com. entered by Gab. Cawood on the books of the Stationers' Company, April 1, 1585, but, I believe, not printed.

82. TITTLE TATTLE, or, *Style a la Mode.* Farce, 8vo. 1749.

This is no other than Extracts from Swift's *Polite Conversation*.

83. TITUS. Opera, translated from Metastasio, by John Hoole, 8vo. 1768.

84. TITUS ANDRONICUS. Trag. by William Shakspeare. Acted by the servants of the Earls of Pembroke, Derby, and Essex, 4to. 1594. 4to. 1611. This play has by some been denied to be Shakspeare's; and Ravenscroft, in the epistle to his alteration of it, too positively asserted that it was not originally Shakspeare's, but brought by a private author to be acted, and that he only gave some master-touches to one or two of the principal parts or characters. However, as Theobald admitted it into his edition of this author's works, I cannot think myself entitled to deny it a place. It is true, there is somewhat more extravagant in the plot, and more horrid in the catastrophe, than in most of Shakspeare's Tragedies; but as we know that he sometimes gave an unlimited scope to his imagination, and as there are some things in the characters of Aaron, Tamora, and Titus, which are scarce to be equalled, I think we can hardly deny our homage to those stamps of sterling merit which appear upon it, nor our acquiescence to the opinion of a critic so well acquainted with the manner of our author as Mr. Theobald unquestionably was. Later criticks of abilities, much superior to Mr. Theobald's, have, however, given very different opinions on this subject. See Dr. Johnson's, Dr. Farmer's, Mr. Steevens's, and Mr. Malone's sentiments on the same subject at the end of this play, in the last edition of Shakspeare. The scene lies in Rome, and the plot borrowed, but

very

very slightly, from the Roman history of the latter empire.

85. TITUS ANDRONICUS, or, *The Rape of Lavinia*. Trag. by Edward Ravenscroft. Acted at the Theatre Royal, 4to. 1687. Mr. Steevens, in his notes on Titus Andronicus, has given specimens of the changes made by Ravenscroft; among others, the following speech by the Moor after the Empress had stabbed her child:

"She has out-done me, ev'n in mine
"own art,
"Out-done me in murder—kill'd her
"own child.
"Give it me—I'll eat it."

"It rarely happens that a dra-
"matic piece is altered with the
"same spirit that it was written;
"but Titus Andronicus has un-
"doubtedly fallen into the hands
"of one whose feelings were con-
"genial with those of the original
"author."

86. TITUS AND BERENICE. Trag. by Thomas Otway, 4to. 1677. This is a translation, with some few alterations, from a tragedy of the same name by M. Racine. The plot is taken from Suetonius's *Life of Titus*, Josephus's *Wars of the Jews*, &c. The scene, Rome. Though the original consists of the usual number of acts, this play is divided into no more than three, and is written in rhyme.

87. TITUS VESPASIAN. Trag. by John Cleland, 8vo. 1760. This piece is an enlarged translation from the *Clemenza di Tito* of Metastasio. It was offered to the manager of Drury-Lane Theatre, who refused it. Yet it is by no means destitute of merit.

88. THE TOBACCONIST. Com. of two acts, by Francis Gentleman, altered from Ben Jonson's *Alchymist*. Acted at the Hay-Market and Edinburgh, 8vo. 1771.

89. TOMBO CHIQUI, or, *The American Savage*. A dramatic Entertainment, in three acts, by John Cleland, 8vo. 1758. This is no more than a translation of the *Arlequin Sauvage* of De L'Isle.

90. TOM ESSENCE, or, *The Modish Wife*. Com. Acted at the Duke's Theatre, 4to. 1677. One Mr. Rawlins is said to be the author of this play, which is founded on two French comedies, viz. the *Cocu imaginaire* of of Moliere, and the *D. Cæsar d'Alvaros* of Thomas Corneille, the part of Loveall's intrigue with Luce being borrowed from the latter, and the whole affair of Tom Essence and his wife from the former, or from Sir W. Davenant's fifth act of the *Playhouse to be Lett*, which is a translation from it.

91. TOM JONES. Com. Opera, by Joseph Reed. Acted at Covent-Garden, 8vo. 1769. This is taken from Fielding's novel, with the same title, and was received with considerable applause.

92. TOM THUMB. Burletta, by Kane O'hara. Acted at Covent-Garden, 1780. An alteration of Fielding's *Tom Thumb*, with the addition of songs. It met with great success.

93. TOME TYLERE AND HIS WYFE. *A passing merrie Interlude*. Anonymous, 1598. This play has been attributed, but, I believe, without foundation, to William Waver. The plot of it resembles M. Poisson's *Le Sot vengé*, and the intent of it is to represent and humble a shrew. It was reprinted in the black letter in 4to. 1661. and in the title-page of that edition it is said to have been written and acted an hundred and thirty years before.

94. TONY LUMPKIN IN TOWN, or, *The Dilettanti*. Farce, by J. Keefe. Acted at the Hay-Market 1778, printed 8vo. 1780. A very humorous

humorous production, which received the applause it deserved.

95. THE TOOTH-DRAWER. C. advertised at the end of *Wit and Drollery*, 1661, as then in the press; but, I believe, never printed.

96. TOTTENHAM COURT. C. by Thomas Nabbes, 4to. 1638. 12mo. 1718. Scene, Tottenham Court and the fields about it. Acted 1633, in Salisbury Court.

97. THE TOUCHSTONE. A Pantomime. Acted at Covent-Garden 1779.

98. THE TOURNAMENT. Interlude, 8vo. 1777. This is one of the pieces published under the name of Thomas Rowley, a Priest, of the fifteenth century. It is now generally acknowledged to be the production of T. Chatterton.

99. THE TOWN FOP, or, *Sir Timothy Tawdrey*. Com. by Mrs. Aphra Behn. Acted at the Duke's Theatre, 4to. 1677. Great part of this play, not only with respect to plot but language also, is borrowed from George Wilkins's Comedy, called, *The Miseries of Enforced Marriage*. Scene, Covent-Garden.

100. THE TOWN SHIFTS, or, *Suburb Justice*. Com. by Edward Revet. Acted at the Duke's Theatre, 4to. 1671. Langbaine speaks highly in favour of this play as an instructive and moral piece; and particularly commends the author for the signature of one of his characters, viz. Lovewell, who, though reduced to poverty, not only maintains himself the principles of innate honesty and integrity, but even takes great pains in the persuading his two friends and comrades, Friendly and Faithful, to the practice of the same. The whole piece, according to the preface, was begun and finished in a fortnight.

101. THE TOWN UNMASKED Com. This play is mentioned in no catalogue, nor has it ever been seen in print. It is, however, enumerated in a list of publications at the beginning of *The Ladies Visiting Day*, 170.

102. THE TOY. A Play. Is mentioned by Mr. Malone amongst the unprinted dramas, whose titles have fallen under his notice.

103. THE TOYSHOP. Farce, by Robert Dodsley, 8vo. 1735. The hint of this elegant and sensible little piece seems built on Randolph's *Muses Looking-Glass*. The author of it, however, has so perfectly modernized it, and adapted the satire to the peculiar manner and follies of the times he writes to, that he has made it perfectly his own, and rendered it one of the justest; and at the same time the best-natured rebukes that fashionable absurdity perhaps ever met with. The merit of this piece recommended its author to the notice of Mr. Pope, who, by stirring up this little spark of genius, then almost lost in obscurity, was the means of giving to the world, not only a man whose own abilities were sufficient to entitle him to its warmest regards, but also a zealous promoter in the course of his business of the cause of literary worth, wherever to be found, as the several collections he has himself made for the preservation of the minutiæ, if we may so call them, of capital merit, and his numerous publications of more essential works, bear ample evidence of. *The Toyshop* was acted at Covent-Garden Theatre with very great success.

104. TRACHINEÆ. Tr. translated from Sophocles, by George Adams, 8vo. 1729.

105. TRACHINEÆ. Tr. translated

lated from Sophocles, by Dr. Thomas Franklin, 4to. 1759.

106. THE TRAGEDY OF TRAGEDIES, or, *The Life and Death of Tom Thumb the Great*, 8vo. 1731. with annotations by *Scriblerus secundus*. This piece first made its appearance in the Little Theatre in the Hay-Market, in the year 1730, in one act only; but in the above-mentioned year the success it had met with before, induced the author to enlarge it to the extent of three acts, and bring it on the stage again, first in the Hay-Market, and afterwards in Drury-Lane Theatre. It is perhaps one of the best burlesques that ever appeared in this or any other language, and may properly be considered as a sequel to the Duke of Buckingham's *Rehearsal*, as it has taken in the absurdities of almost all the writers of tragedy from the period where that piece stops. The scene between Glumdalca and Huncamunca, is a most admirable parody on the celebrated meeting between Octavia and Cleopatra in Dryden's *All for Love*. His love-scenes, his rage, his marriage, his battle, and his bloody catastrophe, are such strong imitations of the tragic rules pursued by the writers of that time, that the satire conveyed in them cannot escape the observation of any one ever so little conversant with the writers of about half a century past. His *similes* are beautiful, yet truly ludicrous, and point out strongly the absurdity of a too frequent use of that image in speech. In a word, this piece possesses in the highest degree the principal merit of true burlesque, viz. that while it points out the faults of every other writer, it leaves no room for the discovery of any in itself. To those who can relish the satire conveyed in it, it is truly delightful, and to those who do not even understand every turn of its humour, it will ever appear at the least agreeable.

107. TRAGOPODAGRA, or, *The Gout*. Trag. translated from Lucian, by Dr. Thomas Franklin, 4to. 1781.

108. TRAPPOLIN SUPPOSED A PRINCE. Tragi-Com. by Sir Aston Cockain, 12mo. 1658. The author of this piece borrowed his design from an Italian Tragi-Com. called *Trappolino creduto Principe*, which he saw twice acted during his residence at Venice; the original plot of which, as far as it relates to Trappolin in his judicial character, &c. is borrowed from a story in the *Contes D'Ouville*. It is, however, a most absurd piece of work, every rule of character, probability, and even possibility, being absolutely broken through, and very little wit or humour to compensate for such irregularity. Yet, as its absurdities are of a kind adapted to excite the laughter of the vulgar, it has been revived at divers times with little alteration and by different titles, and is even now a standard farce at both theatres, though in a very curtailed and and mangled manner, under the title of *Duke and no Duke*.

109. THE TRAVELS OF THE THREE ENGLISH BROTHERS, Sir *Thomas, Sir Anthony, and Sir Robert Shirley*. An Historical Play, by John Daye, 4to. 1607. Our author was assisted in this play by W. Rowley and George Wilkins. The real history of these three famous Brethren, on which the plot of this piece is founded, may be seen in Fuller's account of the Worthies of Sussex, and in many of the English chronicles. The entry of this play, in the books of the Stationers' Company, mentions that it was played at the Curtain Theatre.

110. THE TRAYTOR. Trag. by

by Ja. Shirley, 4to. 1635. Scene, London. This play was originally written by one Rivers, a Jesuit, but is greatly altered by its present author, and highly recommended in a copy of verses, by W. Atkins, of Gray's-Inn. It was also published in 4to. 1692. with alterations, amendments, and additions, as acted at the Theatre Royal; and again in 8vo. 1718. as acted at Lincoln's-Inn Fields.

111. THE TRAYTOR. Trag. Acted at Lincoln's-Inn Fields. Revived with alterations, 8vo. 1718. This is Shirley or Rivers's play, altered, as Coxeter says, by Christopher Bullock.

112. THE TRAYTOR TO HIMSELF, or, *Man's Heart his greatest Enemy*. A moral Interlude, by William Johns, 4to. 1678. This piece is written in rhyme, and is intended to represent the careless, hardened, returning, despairing, and renewed heart; with intermasques of interpretations at the close of each several act. It was performed by the boys of the public school of Evesham at a breaking-up, and published so as to render it useful on the occasion. It contains many moral and instructive sentences, well adapted to the capacities of youths, but has nothing in it remarkable, excepting its being written without any women's parts, after the manner of Plautus's *Captivi*; and for this the author (who was master of the school) assigns as a reason that he did not think female characters fit to put on boys. The prologue is in parts, spoken by four boys.

113. THE TREACHERIES OF THE PAPYSTS. A dramatic piece, by Bishop Bale. See his own catalogue copied in *The British Theatre*.

114. THE TREACHEROUS BROTHERS, Trag. by George Powell. Acted at the Theatre Royal, 4to. 1696. The foundation of this tragedy is taken from a romance, called *The Wall Flower*, written by Dr. Baily, as will appear by comparing the sleeping potion given to Iltocles and Semantha in this play with that administered to Honoria, Amarissa, and Hortensia in the novel. The scene lies in Cyprus. The author being an actor, two of his brother comedians have on this occasion shewn their regard to him; the one, Mr. John Hodgson, in a commendatory copy of Latin verses prefixed to the play, and the other Mr. W. Mountfort, by furnishing it with a prologue and epilogue.

115. THE TREACHEROUS HUSBAND. Trag. by Samuel Davey, 8vo. 1737. The author of this tragedy being a native of Ireland, and our acquaintance with the transactions of the Irish Theatre being very imperfect, I know not whether it was ever acted. It has not, however, made its appearance even in print in these kingdoms.

116. THE TREASURE. Com. translated from Plautus, by Bonael Thornton. 8vo. 1767.

117. TRICK FOR TRICK, or, *The Debauch'd Hypocrite*. Com. by Thomas Durfey. Acted at the Theatre Royal, 4to. 1678. This is very little more than a revival of Beaumont and Fletcher's *Monf. Thomas*, though Mr. Durfey has scarcely had candour enough to acknowledge the theft.

118. A TRICK TO CATCH THE OLD ONE. Com. by Thomas Middleton. Acted both at Paul's and Black-Friers, 4to. 1608. 4to. 1616. This is an excellent old play, and appears to have been greatly in vogue at the time it was written.

119. TRICK UPON TRICK, or, *Squire Brainless*. Com. by Aaron Hill.

Hill. As this gentleman's turn of writing does not seem at all adapted to comedy, there being a peculiar pointed sententiousness in his style, which even in tragedy, though powerful, has somewhat of stiffness and obscurity about it, it is not much to be wondered, that this attempt in the easy unrestrained walk of comedy, great as his merit and success in the opposite cast might be, met not with so favourable a reception as the generality of his pieces, before and since, have done. In short, it made its appearance at the Theatre Royal in Drury-Lane, but was damned the very first night.

120. TRICK UPON TRICK. A Com. of two acts, by R. Fabian, 1735. 8vo. This piece made its appearance at Drury-Lane. On the first night an accident happened, which would of itself have prevented its being performed again. Mr. Macklin and Mr. Hallam, who performed the parts of servants, quarrelling behind the scenes about a wig, Mr. Macklin had the misfortune to run a stick into Hallam's eye, which occasioned his death. Mr. Macklin was tried for this fact, and found guilty of manslaughter.

121. TRICK UPON TRICK, or, *The Vintner outwitted*, 8vo. 1742. This little piece, which was printed at York, and published by Mr. Joseph Yarrow, is word for word the same with the droll borrowed from *The Match in Newgate*, and which I have before-mentioned under the title of *The Biter bit'd*, or, *A Banquet of Wiles*. See *Stroller's Packet broke open*. Both were published about the same time; but I imagine Mr. Yarrow's to have been somewhat before the other. I remember to have seen the piece itself acted at York, by the title of *The Vintner in the Suds*.

122. THE TRIPLE MARRIAGE. Com. translated from the French of *Destouches*; and printed in Foote's *Comic Theatre*, vol. I.

123. A TRIP TO CALAIS. C. by Samuel Foote, 8vo. 1778. This comedy was intended for representation, in 1776, at the Hay-Market, but containing a character designed for a lady of quality, she had interest enough to prevent its obtaining a licence. It was afterwards altered, and acted under the title of *The Capuchin*.

124. THE TRIP TO PORTSMOUTH. A Sketch of one act, with songs, by George Alexander Stevens, performed at the Hay-Market, 8vo. 1773.

125. A TRIP TO SCARBOROUGH. Com. by Richard Brinsley Sheridan, Esq. Acted at Drury-Lane 1776. An alteration of Vanbrugh's *Relapse*; but such a one as will add little to the reputation of the gentleman whose name it bears. Indeed, he has been heard in conversation to confess, that he had spoiled Vanbrugh's Play.

126. A TRIP TO SCOTLAND. Farce, by William Whitehead, Esq. Acted at Drury-Lane, 8vo. 1770. One of the best farces of the present times.

127. THE TRIUMPHANT WIDOW, or, *The Medley of Humours*. Com. by William Duke of Newcastle. Acted at the Duke's Theatre, 4to. 1677. This is esteemed an excellent play, though now never acted; and Mr. Shadwell had so high an opinion of it, that he has transcribed great part of it into his *Bury Fair*.

128. THE TRIUMPH OF BEAUTY. A Masque, by Ja. Shirley, 8vo. 1646. This piece is printed together with some Poems of the author's, and esteemed of less consequence than the generality of his dramatic works. It was written

ten purposely for the private recreation of some young gentlemen, who themselves personated it. Part of it seems borrowed from Lucian's *Dialogues*, and part from Shakspeare's *Midsummer Night's Dream*. The subject of it is the very well known story of *The Judgement of Paris*.

129. TRIUMPHS OF THE GOUT, a mock tragedy, translated from the Greek of Lucian, by Gilbert West, Esq. 4to. 1749. Printed with his translation of *Pindar*. Lucian had composed an entire drama upon this subject; but as only the beginning of this piece remains, Mr. West has translated it, and with little alteration, has made it a part of the same Greek author's other drama, whose subject is the *Triumph of the Gout* over physic.

130. THE TRIUMPHS OF HYMEN. Masque, by J. Wignell, 8vo. 1762. Printed with his Poems.

131. THE TRIUMPHS OF LOVE AND HONOUR. A Play, by Tho. Cooke, 8vo. 1731. Acted at the Theatre Royal in Drury-Lane, but without success. To the end are added, "Considerations on the Stage and on the Advantages which arise to a Nation from the Encouragement of Arts."

132. THE TRIUMPH OF PEACE. A Masque, by Ja. Shirley, 4to. 1633. This masque was presented before the King and Queen at the Banqueting-House at Whitehall, by the Gentlemen of the Four Inns of Court, on the 3d of Feb. 1633. The machinery and decorations were under the conduct of Inigo Jones, and the music composed by W. Lawes and Simon Ives, the two greatest masters of that time. The masquers went in a solemn cavalcade from Ely-House to Whitehall; and the author himself tells us, that for the variety of the shews, and the richness of the habits, this masque was the most magnificent of any that had been brought to court in his time. The names of every one of the masquers, with the house or inn of court to which they belonged, and an epigram addressed to each, may be seen in a little book, written by Francis Lenton, called, *The Inns of Court Anagrammatist*, or, *The Masquers masqued in Anagrammas*, 4to. 1634. See Warton's *History of Poetry*, vol. II. 400.

133. THE TRIUMPH OF PEACE. A Masque, by Robert Dodsley, 4to. 1749. This was written on occasion of the signing the treaty of peace at Aix la Chapelle. It was set to music by Dr. Arne, and performed at Drury-Lane.

134. THE TRIUMPHS OF THE PRINCE D'AMOUR. A Masque, by Sir W. Davenant, 4to. 1635. This masque was written in three days, at the request of the members of the Inner Temple, by whom it was presented for the entertainment of the Prince Elector at his highness's palace in the Middle Temple, on the 24th of February, 1635. The music of the songs and symphonies was set by Messrs. Henry and William Lawes. The Masquers names are annexed at the end of the piece.

135. THE TRIUMPHS OF VIRTUE. Tragi-Com. Anonymous. 4to. Acted at the Theatre Royal, 1697. The scene of this play is laid at Naples, and the comic parts of it seem partly borrowed from Fletcher's *Wit without Money*.

136. TROADES. Trag. 12mo. 1660. This piece is published with Poems upon several occasions, and has the letters S. P. which all the writers explain to be Samuel Pordage. It is a translation from Seneca,

Seneca, with a comment annexed. The scene, Troy.

137. TROADES, or, *The Royal Captives*. Trag. by Sir Edward Sherbourne, 8vo. 1649. 8vo. 1701. This is a critical translation, with remarks, of the same piece with the foregoing.

138. TROADES. Trag. translated from Euripides, 8vo. 1780. Printed with three other plays by the same author.

139. TROAS. Trag. by Jasper Heywood, 4to. 1581. This is a translation from Seneca, in which, however, the translator has taken considerable liberties with his author. For instance, he has added threescore lines of his own to the chorus of the first act; a whole scene in the beginning of the second, in which he introduces the Ghost of Achilles rising from hell to require the sacrifice of Polyxena; and three stanzas to the chorus of the said act. Besides which, he has substituted a chorus of his own, in the room of that to the third act, which, consisting wholly of the names of foreign countries, he imagined would appear, as it really is, extremely tedious.

140. TROAS. Tr. translated from Seneca, by J. T. 4to. 1656. None of these translations were ever intended for the stage. In a copy of this play, which came out of the library of a man of rank, the name of the translator (J. Talbot) was added in MS.

141. TROILUS AND CRESSIDA. Trag. by W. Shakspeare, 4to. 1609. This is, perhaps, the most irregular of all Shakspeare's plays, being not even divided into acts; yet it contains an infinite number of beauties. The characters of the several Greeks and Trojans are finely drawn and nicely distinguished; and the heroism of the greatest part of them finely contrasted by the brutishness of Thersites, and the contemptible levity of Pandarus. Cressida's love in the first part of the play, and her inconstancy in the sequel, bespeak the author perfectly acquainted with the female heart: Troilus's conviction of her falshood is admirably conducted; and his behaviour on the occasion, such as a lover of the complexion he at first appears would naturally fall into. The scene lies in Troy and the Grecian camp, alternately.

Dr. Johnson says, "This play "is more correctly written than "most of Shakspeare's compositions, but it is not one of those "in which either the extent of "his views or elevation of his "fancy is fully displayed. As "the story abounded with materials, he has exerted little invention; but he has diversified "his characters with great variety, and preserved them with "great exactness. His vicious "characters sometimes disgust, but "cannot corrupt, for both Cressida and Pandarus are detested "and contemned. The comic "characters seem to have been "the favourites of the writer; "they are of the superficial kind, "and exhibit more of manners "than nature; but they are copiously filled and powerfully "impressed. Shakspeare has in "his story followed for the greater "part the old book of Caxton, "which was then very popular; "but the character of Thersites, "of which it makes no mention, "is a proof that this play was "written after Chapman had "published his version of Homer."

142. TROILUS AND CRESSIDA, or, *Truth found too late*. Trag. by J. Dryden. Acted at the Duke's Theatre, 4to. 1679. This is only

an alteration from Shakſpeare's above-mentioned play, in which Mr. Dryden has reduced the piece into a more regular form, lopped off the redundancies, and added ſome ſcenes entirely his own. But how far he has improved the play in general, I ſhall leave to the critics, not taking on myſelf in this place to determine.

143. THE TROOPER'S OPERA. Anonymous. 1736. Whether this piece has the length of a complete opera, or only that of a ballad farce, I know not, but imagine it was never acted, as I find it no where mentioned but in *The Britiſh Theatre*.

144. THE TRUE BORN SCOTCHMAN. Com. by Charles Macklin. Acted in Ireland about 1774. Thoſe who have ſeen or read this play ſpeak of it in terms of the higheſt approbation. The principal character was repreſented by the author, and the whole piece met with great applauſe. Mr. Macklin had been endeavouring to obtain a licence for this performance in England, but hitherto without effect.

145. THE TRUE WIDOW. C. by Thomas Shadwell. Acted at the Duke's Theatre, 4to. 1679. The plot of this piece is entirely invention, not having been borrowed from any one; and Langbaine gives it a very high commendation, ſaying, that it has as much true comedy, and the characters and humours in it as well drawn, as any dramatic piece of that age. It did not, however, meet with ſucceſs in the repreſentation. The ſcene, London.

146. The Hiſtory of the TRYALL OF CHEVALRY. *With the Life and Death of Cavaliero Dicke Bowyer. As it hath bin lately acted by the Right Honourable the Earl of Darby* his ſervants. Winſtanley and Philips have aſcribed this piece to William Wayer; but Langbaine imagines it not to be written by that author.

147. *A new and mery Enterlude, called,* THE TRYALL OF TREASURE, *newly ſet foorth, and never before this tyme imprinted.* The names of the plaiers. Firſt. Sturdines, Contention, Viſitation, Time. The ſecond. Luſt, Sapience, Conſolation. The thirde. The Preface, Juſt, Pleaſure, Gredy gutte. The fourth. Elation, Truſt, a woman, and Treaſure, a woman. The fifth. Inclination, the Vice. Imprinted at London in Paule's Churchyarde, at the ſigne of the Lucrece by Thomas Purfoote. 1567.

148. THE TRYAL OF THE TIME-KILLERS. Com. of five acts, by Dr. Bacon, 8vo. 1757.

149. TRYPHON. Tr. by Roger Earl of Orrery. Fol. 1672. The hiſtory of this uſurper is taken from the firſt book of *Maccabees, Joſephus,* Book 23, &c. It was performed at the Duke of York's Theatre with great ſucceſs.

150. TUMBLE DOWN DICK, or, *Phaeton in the Suds.* Farce, by Henry Fielding, 8vo. 1737. This piece was acted at the Little Theatre in the Hay-Market, and was written in ridicule of an unſucceſsful pantomime, performed at Drury-Lane houſe, called, *The Fall of Phaeton.*

151. TUNBRIDGE WELLS, or, *A Day's Courtſhip.* C. Acted at the Duke's Theatre, 4to. 1678. This play has been attributed to Mr. Rawlins, although in the title-page it is ſaid to be written by a perſon of quality. It ſeems intended as a kind of imitation of Shadwell's *Epſom Wells,* but falls greatly

greatly short of the merit and humour of that comedy.

152. TUNBRIDGE WALKS, or, *The Yeoman of Kent*. Com. by Thomas Baker. Acted at the Theatre Royal, 4to. 1703. This is an entertaining and well-conducted play, and contains a great deal of true character and pointed satire. But one circumstance which I have heard relating to it is somewhat extraordinary, viz. that the character of Maiden, which is perhaps the original of almost all the Fribbles, Beau Mizens, &c. that have been drawn since, and in which effeminacy is carried to an height beyond what any one could conceive to exist in any man in real life, was absolutely, and without exaggeration, a portrait of the author's own former character, whose understanding having at length pointed out to him the folly he had so long been guilty of, he reformed it altogether in his subsequent behaviour, and wrote this character, in order to set it forth in the most ridiculous light, and warn others from that rock of contempt, which he had himself for some time been wrecked upon. The scene lies at Tunbridge, and the time twelve hours.

153. TURNCOAT. A Parody on the Tragedy of *Athelstan*, 8vo. 1756.

154. THE TURKISH COURT, or, *The London 'Prentice*. A Burlesque Satirical Piece, by Mrs. Latitia Pilkington, 1748. This was performed only at the Little Theatre in Capel-street, Dublin, but was never printed.

155. THE TUSCAN TREATY, or, *Tarquin's Overthrow*. Trag. 8vo. 1733. This play was acted at Covent-Garden. It was written by a gentleman then deceased, and revised and altered by William Bond, esq. The story of it is founded on the Roman history, soon after the expulsion of the Tarquins. Prologue by A. Hill.

156. THE TUTOR. Farce; acted at Drury-Lane, 1765. This piece was brought out under the patronage of Mr. Colman. The author is unknown, but it was acted only two nights.

157. A TUTOR FOR THE BEAUS, or, *Love in a Labyrinth*. A Comedy, by J. Hewitt. Acted at Lincoln's-Inn Fields, 8vo. 1737. The plot of it, as the author himself confesses, is taken partly from M. de Boissy's *François a Londres*, and partly from a Spanish comedy. It is, however, on the whole, a very indifferent performance.

158. TWELFTH-NIGHT, or, *What you will*. Com. by William Shakspeare. Fol. 1623. This comedy with respect to its general plot, is, I believe, taken from Belleforest's Novels, Tom. 4. Hist. 7. but the mistakes arising from Viola's change of habit, and true resemblance to her brother Sebastian, seem to owe their origin to the *Menæchmi* of Plautus, which not only Shakspeare, but several others of our dramatic writers, have since borrowed from. There is somewhat singularly ridiculous and pleasant in the character of the fantastical Steward Malvolio; and the trick played him by Sir Toby Belch, and Maria, contains great humour, and somewhat of originality in the contrivance, which cannot fail of affording continual entertainment to an audience. This play has at different times even lately been revived, particularly on Twelfth-Night, to which period, however, it has no kind of reference in any thing but its name. The scene lies in a city on the coast of Illyria.

Dr.

Dr. Johnson says, "This play is in the graver part elegant and easy, and in some of the lighter scenes exquisitely humorous. Ague-cheek is drawn with great propriety, but his character is, in a great measure, that of natural fatuity, and is therefore not the proper prey of a satirist. The soliloquy of Malvolio is truly comic; he is betrayed to ridicule merely by his pride. The marriage of Olivia, and the succeeding perplexity, though well enough contrived to divert on the stage, wants credibility, and fails to produce the proper instruction required in the drama, as it exhibits no just picture of life."

159. THE TWIN BROTHERS. Com. translated from Plautus, by Richard Warner, 8vo. 1773. vol. III.

160. TWIN RIVALS. Com. by George Farquhar. Acted at Drury-Lane, 4to. 1703. This play met with very great success, and is said by the critics to be the most regular and compleat of all this author's dramatic works. Yet I must confess I cannot readily acquiesce with that judgement; for although it may, perhaps, be allowed that his younger Wou'dbe, Mrs. Midnight, and Teague, are more highly drawn characters, than any in his other comedies, it will probably appear on a strict scrutiny, that they are so only, because they are more out of real life, more *outré*, or if you please, more unnatural. There are as many improbabilities in the conduct of the plot, (the greatest fault that can be laid to Farquhar's charge in general) as in almost any comedy he has wrote, and many more than are to be found in one much livelier play of his writing, viz. THE RECRUITING OFFICER. I am not, however, for taking from the merit of this, which must be allowed to have many very great beauties in it; but I think my opinion of its not being the best piece he has wrote, seems to stand confirmed by one of the strongest proofs possible to be brought, which is the pecuniary profits of managers, who have never found it so well worth while to direct the frequent repetition of this play, as they have, and daily do, of the STRATAGEM, RECRUITING OFFICER, CONSTANT COUPLE, &c.

161. THE TWINS. Tragi-Com. by William Rider. Acted at the private house, Salisbury-Court, 4to. 1655. Langbaine suspects this play to be much older than the annexed date implies it to be: yet neither the plot nor language of it are by any means contemptible. The scene, Italy.

162. TWO ANGRY WOMEN OF ABINGTON. Com. by Henry Porter, 4to. 1599. This play is not divided into acts. The full title runs thus: *A pleasant History, called, The two angrie Women of* ABINGTON; *with the humorous Mirth of* DICK COOMES *and* NICHOLAS PROVERBS, *two Serving Men.* Acted by Lord Nottingham, Lord High Admiral's servants. Scene lies in London.

163. THE TWO ENGLISH GENTLEMEN, or, *The Sham Funeral*. Com. by James Stewart, 8vo. 1774. This despicable piece was acted one night at the Hay-Market, by a set of performers every way worthy of the author.

164. THE TWO GENTLEMEN OF VERONA. Com. by William Shakspeare. Fol. 1623. This is a very fine play, the plot simple and natural; the characters perfectly marked, and the language poetical and affecting. The falsehood

hood of Protheus to his friend Valentine and Miſtreſs Julia, his remorſe and ſelf-reproaches on that head, and his converſion to truth, to love, and friendſhip afterwards, are admirably conducted. The characters of Valentine and Protheus are truly genteel, and rendered amiable throughout all the tranſactions of the piece, even in deſpight of the temporary falſhood of the latter; and the humour of their two ſervants, Launce and Speed, are very beautifully ſet as ſhades to the ſenſibility and brilliancy of their more ſentimental behaviour. This has been looked on by ſome authors to have been the firſt piece that Shakſpeare wrote; if ſo, what an amazing ſoar of imagination did his genius take at its firſt flight! The ſcene ſometimes in Verona, ſometimes in Milan.

Dr. Johnſon ſays, " In this play " there is a ſtrange mixture of " knowledge and ignorance, of " care and negligence. The ver- " ſification is often excellent, the " alluſions are learned and juſt ; " but the author conveys his he- " roes by ſea from one inland " town to another in the ſame " country ; he places the emperor " at Milan, and ſends his young " men to attend him, but never " mentions him more ; he makes " Protheus, after an interview " with Silvia, ſay he has only ſeen " her picture ; and, if we may " credit the old copies, he has, " by miſtaking places, left his " ſcenery inextricable. The rea- " ſon of all this confuſion ſeems " to be, that he took his ſtory " from a novel, which he ſome- " times followed, and ſometimes " forſook, ſometimes remembered, " and ſometimes forgot.

" That this play is rightly at- " tributed to Shakſpeare, I have Vol. II.

" little doubt. If it be taken from " him, to whom ſhall it be given ? " This queſtion may be aſked of " all the diſputed plays, except " *Titus Andronicus*; and it will " be found more credible, that " Shakſpeare might ſometimes " ſink below his higheſt flights, " than that any other ſhould riſe " up to his loweſt."

165. THE TWO GENTLEMEN OF VERONA. Com. by Shakſpeare; with alterations and additions by Benjamin Victor. Acted at Drury-Lane, 8vo. 1763. *Non tali auxilio*. A more able and judicious nand than Mr. Victor's would prove inſufficient to raiſe this play into dramatic conſequence. Many parts of it that appear beautiful in the cloſet, on the ſtage produce no effect.

166. THE TWO HARLEQUINS. A Farce of three acts, 8vo. 1718. This piece was written by M. le Noble, and acted by the king's Italian comedians at Paris, and afterwards performed at the theatre in Lincoln's-Inn Fields by ſome French ſtrollers. In this edition of it, the French, and a bad Engliſh tranſlation by one Mr. Brown (being merely literal), are printed in oppoſite pages to each other, as in the Italian Opera acted at the King's Theatre in the Hay-Market. The ſcene, Paris.

167. *The Hſtory of the* Two MAIDS OF MOORE CLACKE, *with the Life and ſimple manner of John in the Hoſpital*. Played by the children of the King's Majeſtie, Revels. Written by Robert Armin, 4to. 1609.

168. THE TWO MERRY MILK-MAIDS, or *The beſt Words wear the Garland*. Com. by J. C. Acted by the company of the Revels, 4to. 1620. 4to. 1661. Part of the plot of this play, viz. the promiſe of enjoyment given by

Deriganus

Dorigena to Dorillus, of his enjoying her, when he should bring her in January a garland, containing all sorts of flowers, and its consequence, is founded on Boccace's Novels, Dec. 10. Nov. 5. which is also the foundation of Fletcher's *Four Plays in one*, and other comedies. The scene laid in Saxony.

169. THE TWO NOBLE KINSMEN. Tragi-Com. by J. Fletcher and William Shakspeare. Acted at the Black-Friers, 4to. 1634. The story of this play is taken from Chaucer's *Palamon and Arcite*, or, *The Knight's Tale*. The editor of Beaumont and Fletcher's works, in 1778, has taken some pains to prove that Shakspeare had no hand in this work. The scene near Athens.

170. THE TWO MISERS. Musical Farce, by Kane Ohara. Acted at Covent-Garden, 8vo. 1775. This was taken from *Les Deux Avares* of Falbaire.

171. TWO PLOTS DISCOVERED, A THIRD PAYS FOR ALL. Com. Intended (by the author, I suppose) to be acted at Covent-Garden: by G. P. 12mo. 1742. It is scarcely possible to conceive any thing more contemptible than this piece; it would therefore be an absolute loss of time both to myself and the reader to take any farther notice of it.

172. THE TWO QUEENS OF BRENTFORD, or, *Bayes no Poetaster*. Musical Farce, or Comical Opera, being the sequel of *The Rehearsal*, by Thomas Durfey, 8vo. 1721. Printed with other pieces by the author, who says *it was once very near being acted as being rehearsed upon the stage, but afterwards laid by, some accidents happening in the play-house*.

173. THE TWO SYNNES OF KING DAVYD. Interlude. Not printed, but entered by Thomas Hackett on the books of the Stationers' Company in the year 1561.

174. TWO LAMENTABLE TRAGEDIES IN ONE. by Robert Yarrington, 4to. 1601. This piece is written on the story of two horrid murthers perpetrated not long before; the one of Mr. Beech, a chandler, in Thames-street, and his boy, committed by Thomas Mern; the other, of a young child, murthered in a wood by two ruffians, by the consent of his uncle.

175. TWO WISE MEN, AND ALL THE REST FOOLS. A comical Moral, censuring the follies of that age, by George Chapman, 4to. 1619. The Prologue and Epilogue to this play are written in prose; which practice, as I have elsewhere observed, several poets have gone into: but there is one particular, in which this piece differs from all other plays in our own or any other language, which is, its extending to seven acts, in opposition to the positive direction of Horace, with respect to their number, who absolutely limits it to five. It is on tradition, however, only, that this piece is ranked amongst Chapman's writings, it being published without any author's name, or even so much as a mention of the place where it was printed.

176. THE TWYNNES TRAGEDYS. by   Niccols. This play is entered on the books of the Stationers' Company, Feb. 15, 1611, by Edward Blunt, but, I believe, never printed.

177. TYRANNY TRIUMPHANT! AND LIBERTY LOST; THE MUSES RUN MAD; APOLLO STRUCK DUMB; AND ALL COVENT-GARDEN CONFOUNDED. A Farce, by Fitzcrambo, esq; secretary to the Minor Poets, 8vo. 1743.

1743. This relates to the disputes between the managers and the players.

178. TYRANNICAL GOVERNMENT ANATOMIZ'D, or, *A Discourse concerning evil Counsellors: being the Life and Death of John the Baptist, and presented to the King's most excellent Majesty, by the author.* Anonym. 4to. 1641. This piece, by the title, date, and subject, may be suspected to convey some concealed meaning, not improbably being intended to give a secret hint to King Charles I. then in the bursting out of his troubles, of the danger he incurred from the counsels of some about him; and, indeed, the story of John Baptist, who lost his head by the instigation of Herodias, seems figuratively to glance at the Queen's influence, and the execution of the Earl of Stafford. The piece, which is only a translation from Buchanan, was printed by order of the House of Commons. It is divided into five short acts, which are called parts, and was republished by Francis Peck, in 1740, on very slender grounds as the production of Milton. The scene in Judæa.

179. TYRANNIC LOVE, or, *The Royal Martyr.* Trag. by John Dryden. Acted at the Theatre Royal, 4to. 1672. 4to. 1686. This play is written in rhyme, yet has many things in it extremely pleasing. The plot of it is founded on history, and the scene laid in Maximin's camp, under the walls of Aquileia.

"This tragedy (as Dr. Johnson observes) is conspicuous for many passages of strength and elegance, and many of empty noise and ridiculous turbulence. The rants of Maximin have been always the sport of criticism; and were at length, if Dryden's own confession may be trusted, the shame of the writer."

180. THE TYRANT KING OF CRETE. Trag. by Sir Charles Sedley. I know not whether this play was ever acted, but am rather inclined to believe it was not, neither that nor the GRUMBLER having made their appearance in print, till they were published together, with the most of Sir Charles's works, in 2 vols. 8vo. 1719.

181. THE TYRANT. Trag. by Philip Massinger. Entered on the books of the Stationers' Company, June 29, 1660; and was in the number destroyed by Mr. Warburton's servant.

V.

V A

1. **VALENTIA**, or, *The Fatal Birth-Day.* Trag. by P. Stewart, 8vo. 1772.

2. VALENTINE AND ORSON. A famous History, played by her Majesties players. Was entered, by William White, on the books of the Stationers' Company, March 31, 1600; but, I believe, not printed. An enterlude with the same title,

and perhaps the same piece, was entered, May 23, 1595, by Thomas Goffon and Raffe Hancock.

3. VALENTINE's DAY. Musical Drama, by William Heard. Acted at Drury-Lane, 8vo. 1776. This was acted only one night at Mr. Reddish's benefit.

4. VALENTINIAN. Trag. by Beaumont and Fletcher, Fol. 1647. This play is founded on history, and was acted at first with considerable applause.

5. VALENTINIAN. A Tragedy. Acted at the Theatre Royal, 4to. 1685. These alterations were made by the Earl of Rochester, of whom there is an account in the preface by a friend. Whoever reads the speech with which the first scene of the second act of this piece concludes, will find no difficulty in conceiving that *Sodom* (an infamous drama already mentioned) might be the work of Rochester; though, his lordship disclaiming any share in it, it has been since attributed to another hand.

6. THE VALIANT SCOT, A Play, by J. W. gent. 4to. 1637. For the plot of this piece, see the Scotch History of Sir William Wallace.

7. THE VALIANT WELCHMAN, or, *The Chronicle History of the Life and valiant Deeds of Caradoc the Great, King of Cambria, now called Wales*. Tragi-Com. by R. A. gent. 4to. 1615. 4to. 1663. The plot of this piece is taken from Tacitus's *Annals*, Book 12. Milton's *History of England*, &c.

8. VANELIA, or, *The Amours of the Great*. Opera, 8vo. 1732. Court scandal.

9. VANQUISH'D LOVE, or, *The Jealous Queen*, by Mess. Dan. Bellany, sen. and jun. Whether this piece is tragedy or comedy, it is not very easy to determine by the title; though it seems to carry with it most of the air of the former. It was never acted, but is published with the other dramatic and poetical works of this united father and son, in 2 vols. 8vo. 1746.

10. VANELLA. Trag. 8vo. 1736. This piece was never intended for the stage; but has a reference to the story of Miss Vane, an unfortunate young lady, who was said to have had an amorous connection with a certain very great personage, whose marriage at the time of writing this piece, as it was the public concern, so likewise was it the public topic of conversation; and gave too bold a scope for the tongues and pens of the censorious and malevolent to make free with every circumstance that had any the most distant reference to the important event:

"For *Vane* con'd tell what ills from
" Beauty spring,
" And Sedley curs'd the form that
" pleas'd a King."
Johnson's *Vanity of Human Wishes*.

11. THE VARIETY. Com. by William Duke of Newcastle, 12mo. 1649. This play was acted with very great applause at Black-Friers, and is printed with *The Country Captain*.

12. VENICE PRESERVED, or, *A Plot discovered*. Trag. by Thomas Otway. Acted at the Duke's Theatre, 4to. 1682. This tragedy, which is still a very favourite one with the public, is borrowed, with respect to the plan of it at least, from a little book that relates the circumstances of the Spanish conspiracy at Venice, i. e. the Abbé de St. Real's *Histoire de la conjuration de Marquis de Bedemar*. The speech of Renault to the Conspirators, is translated word for word from this author, whom

whom Voltaire is willing to rank with Salluſt, declaring at the ſame time this his work is far ſuperior to that of Otway, as well as to *Manlius*, a French tragedy on the ſame ſubject, diſguiſed under Roman names, &c. It has been remarked, however, that though on the whole the incidents of Otway's piece are intereſting, and the cataſtrophe affecting, there is not one truly valuable character in the whole drama, except that of Belvidera. The ſcene lies in Venice. This tragedy, ſays Dr. Johnſon, ſtill continues to be one of the favourites of the public, notwithſtanding the want of morality in the original deſign, and the deſpicable ſcenes of vile comedy with which Otway has diverſified his tragic action. By comparing this with the *Orphan*, it will appear that his images were by time become ſtronger, and his language more energetic. The publick ſeems to judge rightly of the faults and excellencies of this play, that it is the work of a man not attentive to decency, nor zealous for virtue, but of one who conceived forcibly, and drew originally, by conſulting nature in his own breaſt.

13. VENUS AND ADONIS, or, *The Maid's Philoſophy*, 8vo. 1659. and 4to. no date. This is one among ſix pieces ſuppoſed to be written by Robert Cox the comedian, and printed in the ſecond part of *Sport upon Sport*.

14 VENUS AND ADONIS. Maſque, by Samuel Holland, 12mo. 1660. Printed in a book, called, " Romancio-Maſtix, or, " A Romance on Romances."

15. VENUS AND ADONIS, or, *The Triumphs of Love*. A Mock Opera, by Martin Powell. Acted at Punch's Theatre, in Covent-Garden, 8vo. 1713.

16. VENUS AND ADONIS. A Maſque, by C. Cibber, 8vo. 1715. This piece was preſented at the Theatre Royal in Drury-Lane with no very great ſucceſs. The muſic by Dr. Pepuſch. The ſcene in the Idalian woods.

17. A VERY GOOD WIFE. C. by George Powell. Acted at the Theatre Royal. 4to. 1693. Coxeter ſays, that whole pages of this play are borrowed from Richard Brome. The prologue is written by Congreve, and the ſcene lies in the Park.

18. A VERY WOMAN, or, *The Prince of Tarent*. Tragi-Com. by Phil. Maſſinger, 8vo. 1655. The author in his prologue confeſſes this play to be founded on a ſubject which had long before appeared upon the ſtage, but does not tell us what piece it was borrowed from; yet on a compariſon of this Tragi-Com. with Sir Aſton Cockain's *Obſtinate Lady*, their plots will be found ſo nearly reſembling, that it muſt appear probable they both derived their hints from the ſame original. The ſcene, Sicily.

19. THE VESTAL VIRGIN, or, *The Roman Ladies*. Trag. by Sir Robert Howard. Fol. 1665. The ſcene of this play lies in Rome; and the author has written two fifth acts to it, the one of which ends tragically, and the other ſucceſsfully, probably in imitation of Sir John Suckling's *Aglaura*; and I do not think it in the leaſt unlikely, that theſe different acts might at different times be performed in the play, ſo alternately to ſuit the various taſtes of the audience, as we find that to have been expreſsly the practice with regard to *Romeo and Juliet*, as altered by Mr James Howard, which ſee under our account of that play.

20. THE VESTAL VIRGIN. Trag. by Henry Brooke, eſq. 8vo. 1778. Not acted; but printed

in his works, in four volumes, 8vo.

21. VICE RECLAIM'D, or, *The Paſſionate Miſtreſs*. C. by Richard Wilkinſon. Acted at the Theatre Royal, 4to. 1703. Though this play made its appearance at a very diſadvantageous ſeaſon of the year, it met with very good ſucceſs. It is not, however, now acted. The ſcene lies in London. The time twelve hours.

22. THE VICTIM. Trag. by Charles Johnſon. Acted at Drury-Lane, 12mo. 1714. Mr. Boyer, in the ſecond edition of his *Achilles*, charges our author with plagiariſm from that tragedy, but I confeſs I cannot ſee much juſtice in his accuſation, both plays being equally borrowed from the *Iphigenie* of Racine. The epilogue by Mr. Cibber.

23. VICTORIOUS LOVE. Trag. by William Walker. Acted at Drury-Lane, 4to. 1698. This play is a kind of imitation of Southerne's *Oroonoko*. The author wrote it in three weeks' time at nineteen years of age, and acted a part in it himſelf. The ſcene is the Banza or palace of Tombult. The time, the ſame with that of the repreſentation.

24. THE VILLAGERS. Farce, of two acts, taken from *The Village Opera*. Acted at Drury-Lane, for Mrs. Pritchard's benefit, about the year 1759. Not printed.

25. THE VILLAGE CONJURER. Interlude, tranſlated from J. J. Rouſſeau, 12mo. 1767. printed in the tranſlation of Rouſſeau's works. This piece was originally acted at Fontainbleau the 18th and 24th of October, and by the Academy of Muſic the 1ſt of March, 1753.

26. THE VILLAGE OPERA, by Charles Johnſon. Acted at Drury-Lane, 8vo. 1729. This is one of the many imitations of *The Beg-gar's Opera*. It is far from being devoid of merit, yet met with very indifferent ſucceſs. It was from this piece, that Mr. Bickerſtaff's much applauded Opera of *Love in a Village* was taken.

27. THE VILLAGE WEDDING, or, *The Faithful Country Maid*. Paſtoral Entertainment of Muſic, by James Love. Acted at Richmond, 8vo. 1767.

28. THE VILLAIN. Trag. by Thomas Porter, 4to. 1663. This play was acted at the Duke of York's Theatre for ten nights ſucceſſively to crouded audiences, which at that period was meeting with very great ſucceſs. It is in itſelf a very good piece, yet owed great part of its good fortune, to the excellent performance of Mr. Sandford, in the part of Maligni, the villain, and of Meſſieurs Betterton and Price, in thoſe of Monſ. Briſac and Coligni the ſcrivener's ſon. The ſcene, Tours. The epilogue by Sir W. Davenant.

29. THE VINTNER TRICK'D. Farce, by H. Ward, 8vo. This is nothing more than the ſingle plot of the Vintner and Sharper, extracted from *The Match in Newgate*, and made into a farce. This plot is itſelf borrowed from Mulligrub and Cockledemoy in Marſton's *Dutch Courtezan*.

30. VIRGINIA. Trag. by Mr. Criſp, 8vo. 1754. This tragedy is built on the celebrated ſtory of Virginius's killing his daughter, to preſerve her from the luſt of Appius the decemvir. The ſcene lies in Rome, and the time is nearly that of the repreſentation. It was acted at the Theatre Royal in Drury-Lane with ſome ſucceſs and indeed not undeſervedly. Yet it is by no means to be ranked as a firſt-rate tragedy. Nor has it been without ſome degree of ſurprize that I have frequently obſerved

served, that, although this story is, perhaps, in itself, and with no other circumstances than those which the historians have plainly related in regard to it, most truly dramatic, and formed as it were to be the subject of a tragedy, the best of any we meet with throughout the Greek or Roman history, yet no one of the many writers who have hitherto fixed on it with that view, have so far succeeded in the execution of the design, as to furnish us with a capital or standard play on the subject. Perhaps, indeed, this failure may in some measure have arisen from their having all deviated from, or added circumstances to, a story, which was in itself too simple, and yet, at the same time, too complete to be advantaged by any alteration. How much is it to be lamented, that the immortal Shakspeare, who had in so many instances made history his own; or that the pathetic Rowe, whose merit in scenes of domestic distress, and the conduct of historical incidents, and who has even hinted at this very story in his *Fair Penitent*; had not undertaken the task, and given us, by that means, as frequent occasion of sympathising with the distress of a *Virginia*, as we have at present of weeping for a *Juliet* or a *Desdemona*, a *Jane Shore* or a *Califta*.

31. VIRGINIA. Trag. by Mrs. Frances Brooke, 8vo. 1756. This play, considering it as written by a lady, is far from being devoid of merit. It was not, however, brought on the stage.

32. THE VIRGIN MARTYR. Trag. by Phil. Massinger and Thomas Dekker. Acted by the servants of the Revels, 4to. 1622. 4to. 1651. 4to. 1661. The scene lies in Cæsarea, and the plot is from the Martyrologies of the tenth Persecution in the time of Dioclesian and Maximin, particularly Eusebius's *Hist.* lib. viii. cap. 17. Rosweidus, Valesius, &c.

33. THE VIRGIN PROPHETESS, or, *The Fate of Troy*. An Opera, by Elk. Settle, 4to. 1701. This piece was performed at the Theatre Royal. The plot is on the story of Cassandra, and the scene in Troy and the Grecian camp before it. It is dedicated to Sir Charles Duncomb, knt.

34. THE VIRGIN QUEEN. T. by Richard Barford, 8vo. 1729. Acted at the Theatre Royal in Lincoln's-Inn Fields. Scene, a room in the royal palace of Susa.

35. THE VIRGIN WIDOW. C. by Francis Quarles, 4to. 1649. This piece, which is the only dramatic attempt of our author, is rather an interlude than a regular play, and was not brought on the stage at any of the theatres; from the information, however, of the Stationer, we learn, " that it had " been sometimes at Chelsea pri" vately acted (by a company of " young gentlemen) with good " approvement."

36. VIRTUE BETRAY'D, or, *Anna Bullen*. Tr. by John Banks. Acted at the Duke's Theatre, 4to. 1682. This play met with great success at its first representation, more particularly becoming a favourite with the fair sex. In short, it has that kind of merit which the most of this author's pieces possess, viz. a happiness in the choice of its story, and a pathetical manner of conducting the plot, which seldom fails of engaging the hearts, and drawing tears from the eyes of the audience, even in despight of the greatest deficiency both of poetry and nature in the language.

37. THE VIRTUOSO. Com. by Thomas Shadwell. Acted at

the Duke's Theatre, 4to. 1676. This play contains an infinite deal of true humour, and a great variety of characters, highly drawn, and perfectly original, particularly those of Sir Nicholas Gimcrack and Sir Formal Trifle, which had been hitherto untouched upon, though of a kind that were very frequent at that period, when the studies of Natural History and Experimental Philosophy, being then but in their infancy in these kingdoms, hurried the professors of them, who were frequently men of shallow abilities, and capable of minuteness only, into a thousand absurdities, which, in this more enlightened age, where every one assumes the liberty which Nature has bestowed on him, of enquiring and thinking for himself, those useful investigations of the proceedings of Nature have become entirely cleared from. It met with great approbation, more especially from the university of Oxford; and Langbaine, in his account of this play, gives its author this commendation, "that none since Jonson's time had ever drawn so many different characters of humours, and with such success." Scene, London.

38. THE VIRTUOUS OCTAVIA. Tragi-Com. by Sam. Brandon, 12mo. 1598. The plot of this play is taken from Suetonius's Life of Augustus and Plutarch's Life of Marc Antony. It is written in alternate verse, with a chorus at the end of each act; and, at the end of the whole, are printed two epistles between Octavia and her husband M. Antony, written in imitation of Ovid's manner, but in long Alexandrine verse. This play was never acted, yet it seems to have been held in some estimation from two commendatory copies of verses which are prefixed to it; and so high an opinion does its author appear to have had of its merit, that, besides his *Prosopopeia al Libro*, at the beginning of the book, he has concluded the whole with this presumptuous Italian sentence, *L'Acqua non temo de l'eterno Oblio*; an instance among many of the vanity of authors, who flatter themselves into an imaginary immortality, which frequently terminates even before the close of their mortal existence, much less extends beyonds it; as is the case with this writer, who, now, in a century and half, has found that oblivion, which he thus sets at defiance for eternity, so entirely overwhelming his works, that, excepting in the records of a few writers, who have taken on themselves the perpetuating those particulars, his very name lives not within remembrance. The scene in Rome.

39. THE VIRTUOUS WIFE, or, *Good Luck at last*. Com. by Tho. Durfey, 4to. 1680. This is as entertaining a comedy as any which this author has written; yet is he not entirely free from plagiarism in it, having borrowed several hints from Marston's *Fawn*, and the character of Beaufort from that of Palamede in Dryden's *Marriage à la Mode*. The scene lies at Chelsea.

40. THE VISION OF DELIGHT. Masque, by Ben Jonson. Fol. 1641. Presented at court in Christmas, 1617.

41. THE VISION OF THE TWELVE GODDESSES. Masque, by Samuel Daniel, 4to. 1623. Presented by the queen and her ladies at Hampton-Court on the 8th of January. This piece was at first unwarrantably published without the author's leave, from a spurious and incorrect copy, which had

had been by some means or other procured by an indiscreet and presumptuous printer; which obliged the author, in order to wipe off the prejudice which both the masque and the invention had suffered from that edition, to republish it from his own copy. The design of the piece is to represent, under the shapes, and in the persons of the twelve Goddesses, the figure of those blessings which the nation enjoyed in peace under the reign of King James I. Power being represented by Juno, wisdom and defence by Pallas, and so of the rest. This and the many other compliments paid to that weak and pedantic monarch by the poets and other writers of that time, are a proof how constant an attendant flattery is on greatness, and how little judgement is to be formed of the real characters of princes from the praises so lavishly bestowed on them by their contemporaries; adulations being as duly paid to the worst as to the best, and a Nero and a Caligula being as highly exalted by the flatterers of their own times, as a Titus or an Antonine.

42. ULYSSES. Trag. by Nich. Rowe, 4to. 1706. The scene of this play is laid in Ithaca, and the plot borrowed from the *Odyssey*. It was acted at the Queen's Theatre in the Hay-Market with success; but is not the best of this author's pieces. It is sometimes presented at the theatres in Dublin, but has not lately been acted in London. This tragedy, says Dr. Johnson, with the common fate of mythological stories, is now generally neglected. We have been too early acquainted with the poetical heroes to expect any pleasure from their revival; to shew them as they have already been shewn, is to disgust by repetition; to give them new qualities or new adventures, is to offend by violating received notions.

43. ULYSSES. Opera, performed at Lincoln's-Inn Fields, 4to. 1733. The words by Mr. Humphreys. The music, by John Christopher Smith, jun.

44. THE UNEASY MAN. C. translated from St. Foix, 8vo. 1771.

45. THE UNFORTUNATE LOVERS. Trag. by Sir William Davenant. Acted at the Black-Friers, 4to. 1643. Scene, Verona.

46. THE UNFORTUNATE DUTCHESS OF MALFY, or, *The Unfortunate Brothers*. Tr. Anon. 4to. 1708. This play was acted at the Queen's Theatre in the Hay-Market, and is dedicated by the publisher, one Hugh Newman, to the Duke of Beaufort. But it seems to be no other than Webster's *Dutchess of Malfy* revived, with the addition of a second title.

47. THE UNFORTUNATE MOTHER. Trag. by Tho. Nabbes, 4to. 1640. This play was never acted, but set down according to the intention of the author; yet it has three several commendatory copies of verses prefixed to it, and a proem in verse by the author, justifying it to be written according to the rules of art. The scene lies at the court of Ferrara. Langbaine, by some mistake or other, has called it *The Unfortunate Lover*.

48. THE UNFORTUNATE SHEPHERD. A Pastoral, by John Tutchin, 8vo. 1685. Printed with his poems.

49. THE UNFORTUNATE USURPER. Trag. Anonym. 4to. 1663. The scene lies at Constantinople, and the plot of it is historical, being founded on the story of *Andronicus Comnenius*. It is not, however,

however, so good a play as Wilson's on the same subject (which see in its place), yet has some merit in a parallel drawn in Act 5. Scene 8. between those times and the period of the rebellion and civil wars of Charles the 1st's reign.

50. THE UNGRATEFUL FAVOURITE. Trag. Anonym. 4to. 1664. This play is said to be written by a person of honour; but I do not find it was ever acted. The scene is laid in Naples, and the plot may be traced in Guicciardini, and other of the Italian Historians.

51. THE UNHAPPY FATHER. Trag. by Mary Leapor, 8vo. 1751. Printed in the second volume of her poems, published after her death.

52. THE UNHAPPY FAIR IRENE, *The Tragedy of*, by Gilbert Swinhoe, 4to. 1658. The plot of this play is founded on the Turkish History, in the reign of Mahomet I. yet is probably borrowed from one of Bandello's Novels, where the story is told at large, as it is also by William Painter, in his *Palace of Pleasure*, Nov. 40. The play is but an indifferent one, yet may in some measure stand excused, as three several copies of verses, which are prefixed to it in compliment to the author, all take notice of his being very young. The scene, Hadrianople.

53. THE UNHAPPY FAVOURITE, or *The Earl of Essex*. Tr. by John Banks. Acted at the Theatre Royal, 4to. 1685. This tragedy is possessed of the same kind of merit with the *Virtue betray'd* of the same author (which see above); and it met with the same success, having constantly a very strong influence on the tenderer passions of the audience. The Prologue was written by Dryden. The scene lies in London. How far other English authors have succeeded in the prosecution of the same design, may be seen under *Earl of Essex*. Yet thus much must be confessed in honour to Mr. Banks, that both Jones and Brooke have been greatly obliged to his play, both of them having not only very nearly followed him in his plot and conduct, but having even adopted his very thoughts, and in many places copied whole periods from him. Two French writers, viz. Monf. Calprenade and T. Corneille, and one Italian author, have written dramatic pieces on the same story, which is perhaps as well adapted to the theatre as any incident in the English History.

54. THE UNHAPPY KINDNESS, or, *A Fruitless Revenge*. Tr. by Thomas Scott. Acted at Drury-Lane, 4to. 1697. This is only an alteration of Fletcher's *Wife for a Month*; in which, however, the character of the wife, in provoking the husband to ease her of her maidenhead, is considerably heightened and improved. The scene lies in Naples.

55. THE UNHAPPY PENITENT. Trag. by Mrs. Cath. Trotter, afterwards Cockburne. Acted at Drury-Lane, 4to. 1701. The scene, France.

56. THE UNINHABITED ISLAND. Drama, translated from Metastasio, by Anna Williams. Printed in a Collection of Miscellanies by her, 4to. 1766.

57. THE UNIVERSAL GALLANT, or, *The Different Husbands*. Com. by Henry Fielding, esq. Acted at Drury-Lane, 8vo. 1734. By an advertisement prefixed to this play, we find that it met with very severe treatment from the audience.

58. THE UNIVERSAL PASSION. Com. by James Miller. Acted

Acted at Drury-Lane, 8vo. 1737. This play met with good succefs, being brought on the ftage before the author had incurred that indignation from the town which fome of his later pieces fo feelingly experienced the weight of. The approbation it met with, however, was no more than a juft tribute to the immortal Shakfpeare, from whom all its chief merit is derived, it being no more than an alteration of that author's *Much ado about Nothing*, which having been itfelf revived and frequently performed within thefe few years, this comedy has confequently been quite fet afide. Whincop has, by miftake, called it an alteration of *All's Well that ends Well*.

59. THE UNNATURAL BROTHER. Trag. by Dr. Edward Filmer. Acted at Lincoln's-Inn Fields, 4to. 1697. This play is on the whole heavy, cold, and enervate, yet is not without fome paffages that do great honour to the underftanding and fenfibility of its author. The plot is from the celebrated Romance of Caffandra; and the fcene lies at a caftle about a league diftant from Lyons in France.

60. THE UNNATURAL COMBAT. Trag. by Phil. Maffinger. Acted at the Globe, 4to. 1639. This tragedy is a very admirable one, and may almoft be efteemed the very beft of this great author's pieces. The accufations of the father againft his own fon, through an apparent zeal for the public fervice, are artfully and glorioufly handled, and, at the fame time, the refentments of the fon againft that father for fome horrid crime, which the author has delicately avoided any perfect explanation of, yet left it within the reach of conjecture, are raifed to a height of heroifm, which makes us almoft forget the criminal appearance of a fon's pointing his fword againft a parent's bofom. The confequences of the combat are affecting and finely fupported. The language, through the whole, is nervous and poetical, and the characters ftriking and ftrongly marked; yet, if the piece can be faid to have a fault, it is fome kind of incompleatnefs in the winding up of the cataftrophe. This, however, is greatly recompenfed by the beauties I have before-mentioned; and I cannot help thinking that, with very little alteration, it might be rendered a valuable acquifition to the prefent ftage. It has neither Prologue nor Epilogue, " having been com- " pofed" (to ufe the author's own words) " at a time when fuch *By-* " *Ornaments* were not advanced " above the fabrick of the whole " work." From which paffage we may, by inference, difcover nearly at what period thefe *By-Ornaments*, as he calls them, came into that general ufe in which they have defcended down to our our times. The fcene lies at Marfeilles.

61. THE UNNATURAL MOTHER. Trag. Anon. 4to. 1698. This play was written by a young lady, and acted at Lincoln's-Inn Fields. The fcene is laid in Levo, a province in the kingdom of Sion; and fome part of the plot is borrowed from Settle's *Princefs of Perfia*, particularly Babhameah's being put on a couch with a black flave, and there found afleep, which is the very fame with the incident of Cleomira and Virantes in that play. Gildon finds great fault with this tragedy, and exclaims loudly againft the public tafte for the fuccefs it met with, and againft the author, for having drawn, in the character of Calla-

peia the *Unnatural Mother*, such a picture of vice as never was paralleled in Nature, or if it was, ought rather to have been exposed on a public gallows than exhibited on a private stage. The author of *The British Theatre*, Whincop, and Jacob, have all, by mistake, called this play the *Unfortunate Mother*, though the last-mentioned author has it in his index by the proper title. In his work, therefore, it was probably no more than an error of the press, overlooked and uncorrected by the author; an error, however, which the other two writers literally copied without giving themselves the trouble to make farther enquiry about it. A hint by the bye how little dependence is to be had on their authorities.

62. THE UNNATURAL TRAGEDY, by Margaret Dutchess of Newcastle. Fol. 1662. There is nothing very particular in this play, farther than some censures which her grace has taken occasion to cast on Camden's *Britannia* in her second act. The Prologue and Epilogue are written by the duke her husband.

63. VOLPONE, or, *The Fox*. Com. by Ben Jonson. Acted by the King's servants, 4to. 1605. This comedy is joined by the critics with the *Alchymist* and *Silent Woman*, as the Chef d'Oeuvres of this celebrated poet; and, indeed, it is scarcely possible to conceive a piece more highly finished, both in point of language and character, than this comedy. The plot is perfectly original, and the circumstance of Volpone's taking advantage of the viciousness and depravity of the human mind in others, yet being himself made a dupe to the subtilty of his creature Mosca, is admirably conceived, and as inimitably executed.

Yet, with all these perfections, this piece does and ever will share the same fate with the other dramatic works of its author, viz. that whatever delight and rapture they may give to the true critic in his closet, from the correctness exerted and the erudition displayed in them; yet, there still runs through them all an unemassioned coldness in the language, a laboured stiffness in the conduct, and a deficiency of incident and interest in the catastrophe, that robs the auditor in the representation of those pleasing, those unaccountable sensations he constantly receives from the flashes of nature, passion, and imagination, with which he is frequently struck, not only in the writings of the unequalled Shakspeare, but even in those of authors, whose fame, either for genius or accuracy, is by no means to be ranked with that of the bard under our present consideration. To write to the judgement, is one thing, to the feelings of the heart, another; and it will consequently be found, that the comedies of Cibber, Vanbrugh, and Congreve, will, on the *Dicies repetita*, afford an increase of pleasure to the very same audiences, who would pass over even a second representation of any one of Jonson's most celebrated pieces with coldness and indifference.

64. THE VOLUNTEERS, or, *The Stock-Jobbers*. Com. by Thomas Shadwell. Acted by their Majesties servants, 4to. 1693. This comedy was not acted till after the author's death, and is dedicated by his widow to Queen Mary. The hint of Sir Timothy Catril in it seems to have been borrowed from Fletcher's *Little French Lawyer*. The prologue by Mr. Durfey.

65. THE VOLUNTEERS, or, *Taylors to Arms*. Com. of one act, by

by G. Downing. Acted at Covent-Garden, 8vo. 1780. This performance, though called a Comedy, is in fact no more than a trifling prelude introduced at the benefit of Mr. Quick.

66. THE VOW-BREAKER, or, *The Fair Maid of Clifton in Nottinghamshire*. Trag. by William Sampson, 4to. 1636. This play met with very good success. The plot of it seems to be founded on fact; a ballad was composed on the same subject.

67. THE UPHOLSTERER, or, *What News?* Farce, of two acts, by A. Murphy, 8vo. 1758. This piece was first acted at Mr. Mossop's benefit at Drury-Lane, and met with very good success, and indeed deservedly, as it, with very great humour, exposes the absurdity of that insatiable appetite for news, so prevalent among mankind in general, and that folly, which seems in some measure peculiar to our own nation, of giving way to an absurd anxiety for the concerns of the public, and the transactions of the various potentates of the world, even to the neglect and ruin of domestic affairs and family interest; and that, in persons totally ignorant, not only of the proceedings of a ministry, but even of any of those springs by which the wheels of government ought to be actuated. The characters employed to point out the ridiculousness of this passion, are an old Upholsterer, who, at the very time when a statute of bankruptcy is issued against him, shews no concern for himself or his family, but condoles himself with the consideration that his name will be read in the news-papers, together with those of the several princes of Europe, yet is breaking his rest night and day with anxiety for our German allies, and laying schemes for the payment of the national debt;—a bedlamite barber, who leaves his shop, and a customer in it half shaved, to communicate to his neighbour the ominous gravity of a great man's butler, whom he had shaved that morning;—and an hireling political scribbler, who, though retained on both sides, betrays his ignorance of the meaning of the very terms of that jargon he so lavishly pours forth to confound the understandings, and corrupt the principles, of readers as ignorant as himself. These characters, it is true, are somewhat *outré*, and touched up in the most glaring colours; yet, as the scenes in which they are introduced have great effect, being truly comic and entertaining, this can scarcely be considered as a fault, since follies of this nature call such a dimness before the eyes of their possessors, as is not to be cleared away, nor themselves brought to see them at all, but by the assistance of magnifying glasses. In short, till we can make fools laugh at their own folly, there can be no hopes of their being cured of it; and though their hides may happen to be so tough that a feather cannot tickle them, yet a curry-comb may chance to make them feel the same sensation, and produce the effect desired.

68. THE USURPER. Trag. by Edward Howard. Acted at the Theatre Royal, 4to. 1668. The scene of this play lies in Sicily; and the plot is founded on the story of Damocles the Syracusan, under whose character, it is supposed, the author intended to point that of Oliver Cromwell.

69. THE USURPER DETECTED, or, *Right will prevail*. A comic, tragical Farce, of two acts, 8vo. 1718. The scene, Urbino. The characters,

characters, the Chevallier St. George, Lord Marr, the Duke of Ormond, &c. The author of *The British Theatre* has mentioned a play with both these titles, which he calls a Tragi-Comedy, and gives it the date of 1660. I suspect no play of that date is in being, as it is not mentioned by Langbaine.

70. THE USURPERS, or, *The Coffee-House Politicians*, A Farce. Anonymous. 1749.

W.

W A

1. THE WALKING STATUE, or, *The Devil in the Wine Cellar*. Farce, by A. Hill, 4to. no date. This little farce is printed at the end of, and was, I believe, annexed in the representation to *Elfrid*, or *The Fair Inconstant*, of the same author. The plot of it is totally farcical, and the incidents beyond the limits of probability, nay, even of possibility; yet there is somewhat laughable in the incident of passing a living man on the father as a statue or automaton, and the consequence of it, though somewhat too low for a dramatic piece of any kind of regularity, may, nevertheless, be endured, by considering this as a kind of speaking pantomime, which may surely be as readily admitted of, and allowed as instructive, at least, as those where the particular gentleman has no other method of expressing his sensations and sentiments, than the very ingenious one of gestures and grimaces.

2. THE WALKS OF ISLINGTON AND HOGSDON, *with the Humours of Wood-street Compter*. Com. by Thomas Jordan, 4to. 1657. The title of this play seems to promise nothing more than the very lowest kind of humour, yet its success was surprisingly great, having taken a run of nineteen days together, with extraordinary applause. At the end of it is a licence for its being acted, signed Henry Herbert. Dated August 2, 1641.

3. THE WANDERING LOVER. Tragi-Com. by Thomas Meriton, 4to. 1658. This play is said to have been acted at sundry places *privately*, by the *Author* and his *Friends*, with great applause; probably because no other persons would have either *acted* or *applauded* it; for we may surely acquiesce with Langbaine's opinion of the author, viz. "That he is the "meanest dramatic writer England "ever produced; and, if he is to "be allowed a poet, *of all men that "are, were, or ever shall be, the very "dullest.*"

4. THE WANDERING LOVERS, or, *The Painter*. Com. by Philip Massinger. Entered on the books of the Stationers' Company, Sept. 9, 1653; but not printed.

5. THE WANTON COUNTESS, or, *Ten Thousand Pounds for a Pregnancy*. A Ballad Opera, 8vo. 1733. This piece was never intended for the stage, but written for the propagation of some tale of private scandal in the court annals of that time;

time; but what that was, is neither my business to enquire, nor my inclination to perpetuate.

6. THE WANTON JESUIT, or, *Innocence seduced*. Ballad Opera. Acted at the Hay-Market, 8vo. 1731. This opera was occasioned by the affair of Father Gerard and Miss Cadiere.

7. A WARNING FOR FAIR WOMEN. Tr. Anonym. 4to. 1599. This is a very old play, which was considerably in vogue in Queen Elizabeth's time. It is full of dumb shews, which was the fashion of those earlier periods, and is not divided into acts. The plot of it is founded on a real fact, which, I suppose, was then familiar in the memories of many, containing, as it tells us in the title-page, *The most tragical and lamentable Murder of Mr. George Sanders, of London, Merchant, nigh Shooter's Hill; consented unto by his own Wife, and acted by M. Brown, Mrs. Drury, and Trusty Roger, Agents therein; with their several Ends.* Acted by the Lord Chamberlain's servants. It is printed in the old black letter. The prologue and epilogue spoken by *Tragedy*.

8. THE WARRES OF CYRUS, KING OF PERSIA, AGAINST ANTIOCHUS, KING OF ASYRIA, *with the tragical Ende of Panthæa*. Trag. Anonymous. 4to. 1594. This play was acted by the children of her Majesty's Chapel.

9. THE WARY WIDOW, or, *Sir Noisy Parrot*. Com. by Henry Higden. Acted at Drury-Lane, 4to. 1693. This is very far from being the worst of our English comedies, and is ushered into the world by several complimentary copies of verses, and a prologue written by Sir Charles Sedley. Yet it was damned the first night, owing to a very extraordinary circumstance, which was, that the author had introduced so much drinking of punch into his play, that the performers got drunk during the acting it, and were unable to go through with their parts; on which account, and the treatment the audience gave them by hisses and catcalls in consequence of it, the house was obliged to be dismissed at the end of the third act.

10. THE WATERMAN, or, *The First of August*. Ballad Opera, by Charles Dibdin. Acted at the Hay-Market, 8vo. 1774.

11. WAT TYLER AND JACK STRAW, or, *The Mob Reformers*. Dramatic Entertainment, performed at Pinkethman and Giffard's Booth in Bartholomew Fair, 8vo. 1730.

12. THE WAY OF THE WORLD, Com. by W. Congreve. Acted at Lincoln's-Inn Fields, 4to. 1700. This is the last play this author wrote, and perhaps the best; the language is pure, the wit genuine, the characters natural, and the painting highly finished; yet, such is the strange capriciousness of public taste, that, notwithstanding the great and deserved reputation this author had acquired by his three former comedies, this before us met with but indifferent success; while his *Mourning Bride*, a piece of not the twentieth part of its merit, was in the full meridian of applause. It is not very improbable that this testimonial of want of judgement in the audience, might be the motive for the author's quitting the stage so early; for, though he was at that time in the prime of life, not above twenty-seven years of age, and lived about twenty-nine years afterwards, he never obliged the public with any other dramatic piece. Time, however, has since opened the eyes of the town to its perfections; and it

is now as frequently performed as any of his other plays.

13. THE WAY TO KEEP HIM. Com. in three acts, by A. Murphy, 8vo. 1760. This piece made its first appearance in this form at Drury-Lane Theatre, as a subsequent entertainment to *The Desert Island* of the same author. The intention of it is to point out to the married part of the female sex, how much unhappiness they frequently create to themselves, by neglecting, *after* marriage, to make use of the same arts, the same assiduity to please, the same elegance in the decoration of their persons, and the same complacency and blandishments in their temper and behaviour, to *preserve* the *Affections* of the *Husband*, as they had *before* it put in practice to *awaken* the *Passions* of the *Lover*. This doctrine is here enforced by the example of a gentleman of amiable qualities, and a natural liveliness of turn; yet, according to his own declarations, strongly inclinable to domestic happiness, driven, by this mistaken conduct in his wife, from his home, and a valuable woman the mistress of that home, into gallantries with other women, and a total indifference to his wife. The design has great merit, and the execution of it is pleasingly conducted. The principal characters are well drawn; some of the incidents sufficiently surprizing and interesting, and the denouement attended with circumstances which render it truly comic. And, although the language may not abound with the studied wit of Congreve or Wycherley, yet it is a natural and easy dialogue, and properly adapted to that domestic life which it is intended to represent.

14. THE WAY TO KEEP HIM. A Com. by A. Murphy, esq. Acted at Drury-Lane, 8vo. 1761. This is the foregoing piece enlarged into a regular comedy of five acts, by the addition of two principal characters, viz. Sir Bashful Constant and his Lady. The former of which is a gentleman, who, though passionately fond of his wife, yet, from a fear of being laughed at by the gay world for uxoriousness, is perpetually assuming the tyrant, and treating her, at least before company, with great unkindness. The manner in which the author has interwoven this character with the rest of the plot, is productive of scenes which certainly add greatly to the *Vis comica* of the piece; but how far it is, on the whole, improved by that addition, is a point of controversy among the critics, which I shall not here take upon myself to determine. Some of them have charged the author with having drawn a character entirely out of nature, at the same time that he has been taxed by others with intending it for a person really existing. From both these accusations, however, he will surely stand acquitted, when I have made one remark, which is, that however Mr. Murphy may have touched up and heightened it, either from his own imagination, or from real life, the ground-work of the character itself, and of several of the incidents, is to be found in M. de la Chauffee's character of D'Urval, in his comedy, called *Le Prejugé alamode*.

15. THE WEAKEST GOETH TO THE WALL. Anonymous. Acted by the Earl of Oxford, Lord great Chamberlain of England's servants, 4to. 1600, 4to. 1618. The scene of this piece lies in Burgundy.

16. THE WEATHERCOCK. Musical Entertainment, by Th. Forest.

Forc'd. Acted at Covent-Garden, 8vo. 1775. This was performed about three or four times, and then laid aside. It is a very poor production.

17. THE WEDDING. Com. by Ja. Shirley. Acted at the Phœnix, Drury-Lane, 4to. 1629. 4to. 1633. 4to. 1660. This is a very good play; the scene lies in London.

18. THE WEDDING. See *Country Wedding*, which is the same performance acted at a different Theatre. This being represented at Lincoln's-Inn Fields; that at Drury-Lane.

19. THE WEDDING DAY. C. by Henry Fielding. Acted at Drury-Lane, 8vo. 1742. This was the last dramatic piece of this author; and, as if he had exhausted the whole of his comic humour in his former works, it is by much the dullest of them all. Its success was equal to its merit, being acted only six nights. The author says, in the Preface to his Miscellanies, that he did not receive 50 *l.* from the house for it. Prefixed to it, however, is a prologue of some humour, in doggrel verse, which was spoken by Mr. Macklin.

20. THE WEDDING NIGHT. Farce, by —— Cobb. Acted at the Hay-Market, 1780. Not printed.

21. THE WEDDING RING. Com. Opera, in two acts, by Charles Dibdin, performed at Drury-Lane, 8vo. 1773. The hint of this piece, which met with some success, was taken from *Il Filosofo di Campagna*.

22. THE WELCH, or, *Grub-street Opera*. This piece I have before spoken of, under the title of *The Grub-street Opera*, the first name being only prefixed to the other in the title-page. It was written by Henry Fielding, but is one of the most indifferent of his works.

23. WESTWARD HOE. Com. by Thomas Decker and John Webster, 4to. 1607. Many times acted with good success by the children of Paul's.

24. THE WEST-INDIAN. C. by Richard Cumberland, esq. Acted at Drury-Lane, 8vo. 1771. This comedy may be considered as one of the best which the present times have produced. The frequency of its representation renders it sufficiently known. It was performed with very great and deserved success.

25. WESTON'S RETURN FROM THE UNIVERSITIES OF PARNASSUS. Interlude, performed at the Hay-Market for that actor's benefit, 1775. Not printed.

26. WEXFORD WELLS. Com. by Matthew Concanen, 8vo. 1721. This play was never represented in London; but, the author being an Irishman, it probably made its appearance on the Dublin Theatre. It is written in imitation of Tunbridge and Epsom Wells, but is not equal in merit to either of them.

27. THE WHAT D'YE CALL IT. A Tragi-Comi-Pastoral Farce, by John Gay. Acted at Drury-Lane, 8vo. 1715. This ingenious and entertaining little piece, which is to this day frequently performed, is an inoffensive and good-natured burlesque on the absurdities in some of the tragedies then the most in favour, particularly *Venice preserv'd*, the principal characters in which are ridiculed with much humour and some justice, in the parts of Filbert, Peascod, and Kitty Carrot. There is great originality in the manner of it, great poetry in the language, and true satire in the conduct of it, on which accounts, though it may be "Caviare to the Multitude," it will ever be "sure to please the better Few."

28. WHAT

28. WHAT YOU WILL. Com. by John Marston, 4to. 1607. 12mo. 1633. Langbaine mentions this comedy as one of the best of the author's writing. Some part of the plot, however, viz. that of Francisco's assuming the person and humour of Albano, is borrowed from Plautus's *Amphitrio*, and has been also since made use of in other plays.

29. WHAT WE MUST ALL COME TO. A Comedy, in two acts, performed at the Theatre Royal in Covent-Garden, 8vo. 1764. This was introduced as a tail-piece to *No one's Enemy but his own*, and acted at the same time; but shared in the condemnation, although it was generally thought to have had merit enough to entitle it to a better fate: but this comes of keeping bad company! The vice of gaming is admirably ridiculed in it; and the character of Druget, the over-grown rich citizen, (who, with an hundred thousand pounds in his pocket, retires to his country-house, close by the side of a dusty road, within four or five miles of London) is very well drawn.

30. WHEN YOU SEE ME, YOU KNOW ME, or, *The famous Chronicle Historie of King Henry VIII. with the Birth and virtuous Life of Edward Prince of Wales*, by Sam. Rowley, 4to. 1632. The plot of this play is taken from Lord Herbert's Life of Henry VIII. and other English Historians. The scene lies in England.

31. WHIG AND TORY. Com. by Benjamin Griffin, 8vo. 1720. Acted at the Theatre in Lincoln's-Inn Fields, with no very extraordinary success.

32. THE WHIM, or, *The Miser's Retreat*. A Farce, altered from the French of *La Maison Rustique*. Acted at Goodman's Fields, 8vo. 1734.

33. THE WHIMSICAL LOVERS, or, *The Double Infidelity*. Com. translated from the French, and printed in Foote's *Comic Theatre*.

34. THE WHITE DEVIL, or, *The Tragedy of Paulo Giordano Ursini, Duke of Brachiano; with the Life and Death of Vittoria Corombona, the famous Venetian Courtezan*. Trag. by John Webster. Acted by the Queen's servants, 4to. 1612. 4to. 1631. The scene, Italy.

35. *The History of* RICHARD WHITTINGTON, *of his lowe byrthe, his great fortune, as yt was plaied by the Prynce's servants*. This play is entered on the books of the Stationers' Company, by Thomas Payrer, Feb. 8, 1604, but was, I believe, not printed.

36. THE WHORE OF BABYLON. A History, by Tho. Deeker, 4to. 1607. I know not whether this play was ever acted, but the general tenor of it is to illustrate the virtues of Queen Elizabeth, and, under feigned names, to expose the machinations of the Roman Catholics of that time, more especially the Jesuits, and set forth the dangers which that great Queen escaped from their evil designs against her person. The Queen is represented under the character of Titania, a title which seems to have been fixed on her by the poets of that time: Spenser having first set the example; and Shakspeare and Decker following it, the one in his *Midsummer Night's Dream*, and the other in the piece before us. Rome is stiled Babylon, Campiano the Jesuit, Campeius, Dr. Parry, Paridel, &c.

37. THE WHORE OF BABYLON. Com. said to be written by King Edward VI. but not printed.

38. WHO'S

38. WHO'S THE DUPE? Farce, by Mrs. Cowley. Acted at Drury-Lane, 8vo. 1779. This piece was acted with confiderable applaufe.

39. THE WIDOW. Com. by Ben Jonfon, 4to. 1652. Though I have named Jonfon as the author of this play, it was the refult of the joint labours of him, Fletcher, and Middleton, but was not publifhed till after all their deaths, when Alexander Gough, a great admirer of dramatic writings, procured this, and fome other MSS. of the like kind, for Mofeley the bookfeller, who caufed them to be printed and publifhed.

40. A WIDOW AND NO WIDOW. Com. by Mr. Jodrell. Acted at the Hay-Market, 1779. Printed, 8vo. 1780. The late Mr. Foote was unrivalled in the art of introducing known characters, and applying temporary allufions in his dramas. Mr. Jodrell has taken the fame road; and the prefent fpecimen of his art affords us fome expectations of future entertainment.

41. THE WIDOW BEWITCH'D. Com. by John Mottley, 8vo. 1730. This play was acted at the Theatre in Goodman's-Fields, and met with very good fuccefs.

42. THE WIDOW OF DELPHI. Mufical Com. by Richard Cumberland, efq. Acted at Covent-Garden, 1780. The fongs only printed. This piece, though great expectations were formed from it, met with little fuccefs. The author, who feems to have been determined to avoid the imputation of too much fentiment, has thereby run into the oppofite extreme. This performance is alfo cenfurable, on account of fome loofe expreffions contained in it.

43. THE WIDOW RANTER, or, *The Hiftory of Bacon in Virginia.* Tragi-Com. by Mrs. Behn. Acted by their Majefties fervants, 4to. 1690. This piece was not publifhed till after the author's deceafe, who died in 1689. The tragedy part of it, particularly the cataftrophe of Bacon, is borrowed from the well-known ftory of Caffius, who, on the fuppofition of his friend Brutus's being defeated, caufed himfelf to be put to death by the hand of his freedman Dandorus. The fcene is laid in Bacon's camp in Virginia. The comic part entirely invention. The Prologue is written by Dryden.

44. THE WIDOW OF WALLINGFORD. Com. of two acts, 8vo. No date [1775]. This piece, in the title-page, is faid to have been performed in the neighbourhood of Wallingford by a fet of gentlemen and ladies.

45. THE WIDOW'S PRIZE. C. Entered on the books of the Stationers' Company, the 9th day of September, 1653; and was amongft thofe deftroyed by Mr. Warburton's fervant.

46. THE WIDOW'S TEARS. Com. by George Chapman. Acted at Black and White-Friers, 4to. 1612. Some parts of this play are very fine, and the incidents affecting and interefting. Yet the cataftrophe, with refpect to Cynthia and her hufband, is rather flubbered over and inconclufive; the plot of Lyfander and Cynthia, is taken from the ftory of the Ephefian Matron, related in *Petronius Arbiter.*

47. THE WIDOW'S WISH, or, *An Equipage of Lovers.* A Farce, by Henry Ward. Acted at York, 8vo. 1746.

48. THE WIDOWED WIFE: C. by Dr. Kenrick. Acted at Drury-Lane, 8vo. 1768. A piece which reached nine nights with little applaufe,

plause, and has not since been heard of. It is of the Novel species of drama, tedious and uninteresting. To Mr. Garrick's alterations much of its success may be ascribed; though the author, with a degree of gratitude peculiar to himself, charges some of its faults, and consequently its lukewarm reception, to the very person to whom he had been so materially indebted.

49. A WIFE AND NO WIFE. Farce, by Charles Coffey, 8vo. 1732. This piece was never acted.

50. A WIFE FOR A MONTH. Tragi-Com. by Beaumont and Fletcher. Fol. 1647. This play is a very good one. The plot of it, as far as relates to the story of Alphonso, his character, and the treatment he meets with from his brother Frederic, is borrowed from the History of Sancho VIII. King of Leon, which may be seen in *Mariana*, and *Lewis de Mayerne Turquet*. The scene lies in Naples.

51. A WIFE IN THE RIGHT. Com. by Mrs. Elizabeth Griffiths, 8vo. 1772. This play was performed one night only at Covent-Garden. The author, in her preface, complains of the injury her play received by the negligence and intemperance of Mr. Shuter, who, being called to an account by the audience on that evening, became so confused, that he not only forgot his part, but lost all idea of the character he was to represent.

52. THE WIFE OF BATH. C. by John Gay, 4to. 1713. This piece was acted at the Theatre Royal in Drury-Lane, but met with very indifferent success. It was the author's first dramatic attempt, yet its failure did not discourage him from pursuing that way of writing in which he was afterwards so fortunate.

53. THE WIFE OF BATH. A Com. by John Gay. Acted at Lincoln's-Inn Fields, 8vo. 1730. This is the same piece, revised and altered by the author. On this its second appearance it met with the very same, or rather worse, treatment from the audience, than it had done before, notwithstanding the merit of *The Beggar's Opera* had raised Mr. Gay's reputation at that time to the most exalted height. The scene is laid at an Inn on the road between London and Canterbury, and the time twelve hours, being from nine o'clock at night to nine the next morning.

54. THE WIFE's RELIEF, or, *The Husband's Cure*. Com. by Charles Johnson. Acted at Drury-Lane, 4to. 1712. This is a very entertaining play, and used to be frequently represented. The scene lies in Covent-Garden; and the plot, characters, and most part of the language, are borrowed from Shirley's *Gamester*.

55. A WIFE TO BE LET. Com. by Mrs. Elizabeth Haywood, 8vo. 1724. This comedy was acted at Drury-Lane Theatre in the summer, with but middling success; which might, however, in some measure, be owing to the season, and the small merit of the performers. The author herself performed a principal part in it, but met with little approbation.

56. A WIFE WELL MANAGED. Farce, by H. Carey. No date. Whether ever acted I know not.

57. A WIFE WELL MANAGED. Farce, by Mrs. Centlivre. This was acted at Drury-Lane, and printed, 12mo. 1715.

58. THE WILD GALLANT. C. Acted at the Theatre Royal, 4to. 1669. This was Mr. Dryden's

first

first attempt in dramatic writing. He began with no happy auguries; for his performance was so much difapproved, that he was compelled to recall it, and change it from its imperfect state to the form in which it now appears, and which is yet fufficiently defective to vindicate the criticks. The fcene lies in London; and the plot, as the author confefies, is borrowed. It was firft acted in 1663.

59. THE WILD GOOSE CHACE. Com. by Beaumont and Fletcher. Fol. 1679. This is one of the beft of the writings of thefe united poets. It was very frequently performed, with univerfal approbation; and about a dozen years ago was revived by Mrs. Clive, for her benefit. From it Farquhar has borrowed almoft the whole of the four firft acts of his INCONSTANT. The fcene lies in Paris.

60. A WILL OR NO WILL, or, *A New Cafe for the Lawyers*. Farce, by Charles Macklin. This piece has been frequently acted at the author's benefits, but has not yet made its appearance in print.

61. WILLIAM AND LUCY. Opera. An attempt to fuit the ftyle of the Scotch mufic, by Mr. Paton, 8vo. 1780. Printed at Edinburgh. Taken from the ballad of *Auld Robin Gray*.

62. WILLIAM AND NANNY. Ballad Farce, in two acts, by R. Goodenough, efq. Acted at Covent-Garden, 8vo. 1779.

63. WILTSHIRE TOM. An Entertainment at Court, printed in 4to. N. D. This is one of thofe pieces afcribed to Robert Cox, comedian.

64. " A Pleafant Comedie, called, WILY BEGUILDE. The chief actors be thefe: A Poore Scholler, a rich Foole, and a Knave at a Shifte." 4to. 1606. 4to. 1623. 4to. 1635. 4to. 1638. Not divided into acts.

65. WINE, BEER, ALE, AND TOBACCO, CONTENDING FOR SUPERIORITY. An Interlude, or more properly a Dialogue. Anon. 4to. 1658.

66. WIN HER AND TAKE HER, or, *Fools will be meddling*. Com. Anonym. Acted at the Theatre Royal, 4to, 1691. This play is dedicated to Lord Danby, by Underhill, the player; and Coxeter, in his MS. Notes, attributes it to Mr. John Smith, the author of *Cytherea*; in which latter affertion he was miftaken, there being two different authors of the fame name. See Wood's *Fafti*, vol. II. p. 228. The Epilogue was written by Mr. Durfey, and the plot of the piece feems partly borrowed from Shadwell's *Virtuofo*; at leaft the character of Wafpifh, throughout all his humours and misfortunes, bears a ftrong refemblance to Snarl, in that comedy.

67. THE WINTER'S TALE. Tragi-Com. by William Shakfpeare. Fol. 1623. This is one of the moft irregular of this author's pieces, the unities of time and place being fo greatly infringed, that the former extends from before the birth of Perdita till the period of her marriage, and the choice of the latter, for the fcenes of the play, is fixed at fome times in Sicily, and at others in Bithynia. From thefe confiderations I fuppofe it is, that fome of the critics have been induced to fufpect its being Shakfpeare's. There are, however, fo many amazing beauties glittering through the different parts of it, as amply make amends for thefe trivial deformities, and ftamp on it the moft indelible marks of its authenticity. Nay, fo redundant are thofe beauties, that they have afforded

afforded scope for the forming of two regular dramatic pieces from this single one; Mr. Garrick having reduced the principal part of the plot, viz. that of Leontes's jealousy, and the divorce and justification of Hermione, into a tragic piece of three acts, which he brought on the stage, reserving to it its original title, (though afterwards published under that of *Florizel and Perdita*) in the year 1756, and which met with very good success; and some other author having, from the comic parts of it, formed a very complete and entertaining Farce, called, THE SHEEPSHEARING, or, *Florizel and Perdita*. The plot of the whole, is borrowed from Rob. Green's Novel of *Dorastus and Faunia*.

68. THE WINTER'S TALE. A Play, altered from Shakspeare, by Charles Marsh, 8vo. 1756. Not acted.

69. THE WISDOM OF DR. DODIPOLE. Com. Acted by the children of Paul's, 4to. 1600. That part of the plot of this piece, in which Earl Cassimeere's generosity induces him to marry the deformed Cornelia, and share his estate with her father Flores, when under affliction by being arrested by the duke's commands, is borrowed from the story of *Zenothemis* and *Menecrates*, told us by Lucian.

70. THE WISE WOMAN OF HOGSDON. Com. by Thomas Haywood, 4to. 1638. This play met with good success, and is commended in a copy of verses to the author. Scene, Hogsdon.

71. THE WISHES, or, *Harlequin's Mouth opened*. Com. by Mr. Bentley, 1761. This play has not yet made its appearance in print, but was brought on the stage at Drury-Lane Theatre by the company under the management of Mess. Foote and Murphy. It is written in imitation of the Italian comedy; Harlequin, Pantaloon, Pierrot, Mezzetin, Columbine, &c. being introduced into it as speaking characters. It contains, in many parts of it, very just satire and solid sense; and gives evident testimony of the author's learning, knowledge, understanding, and critical judgement; yet the deficiency of incident which appears in it, as well as of that lively kind of wit which is one of the essentials of perfect comedy, added to the extravagance and oddity of a set of characters which the English audience had been accustomed to see only in the light of mute mimics, and consequently could not easily connect the idea of sense or understanding to, seem, in great measure, to justify that coldness, with which the piece was received by the town. In a word, though far from being destitute of merit, it is certainly better adapted to the closet than the stage, and is one proof, among many, that dramatic writings require a peculiar species of genius which neither learning nor criticism can create, and an idea of public taste which only a peculiar attention to, and observation of that taste, can ever bestow. It was reported that a man of quality [Lord Melcomb], nay, it was even hinted that a still *greater Personage*, had some hand in the composition of this comedy. Be that as it will, however, it is certain that the former interested himself very greatly in the bringing it in a proper manner on the stage, and that the royal favour extended itself to the author in a very handsome present, in consequence of which he resigned the profits of his third night (which, however, did not prove very considerable) to the

advantage

advantage of the performers. The prologue and epilogue were written by Mr. Cumberland.

72. THE WISHES OF A FREE PEOPLE. A dramatic Poem, 8vo. 1761. This piece, though published anonymous, is said to be the work of Dr. Hiffernan, a gentleman whom I have had occasion to mention once before in this work, under the NEW HIPPOCRATES. It is intended as a compliment to the Princess Charlotte of Mecklemburgh, now our most gracious Queen, on her landing and marriage. The design is certainly laudable; but I am sorry to say, that the execution of it is so very undramatic, and contains so little either of poetry or imagination, that it stands itself as a sufficient answer to the charge the author has, in a postscript to it, thrown on the managers of both the Theatres, for refusing to bring it on the stage. Prefixed to it is a dedication to the Queen in French, for which the author has quoted, as a precedent, M. de Voltaire's English dedication of his *Henriade* to Queen Caroline.

73. THE WITCH OF EDMONTON. Tragi-Com. by William Rowley, 4to. 1658. This piece is said, in the title-page, to be founded on a known true story. It met with singular applause, being often acted at the Cockpit in Drury-Lane, and once at Court. The scene lies in the town of Edmonton. Although the above-named author had the chief hand in this play, yet he received considerable assistance in it from Ford and Decker, both whose names are equally mentioned with his in the title-page.

74. THE WITCHES. Pantomime. Acted at Drury-Lane, 1765.

75. WIT AT A PINCH, or, *The Lucky Prodigal.* Com. Acted at Lincoln's-Inn Fields, 12mo. 1715.

76. WIT AT SEVERAL WEAPONS, Com. by Beaumont and Fletcher. Fol. 1647. This play was esteemed an entertaining one, and from it has Sir William Davenant borrowed the characters of the Elder Pallatine, and Sir Morglay Thwack, in his comedy, called *The Wits.*

77. WIT FOR MONEY, or, *Poet Stutter.* Anonymous. 4to. 1691. This is rather a dialogue than a dramatic performance. It contains reflections on some plays then lately acted, and particularly on *Love for Money,* or, *The Boarding-School,* by Tom Durfey, who is intended by *Poet Stutter.*

78. WIT IN A CONSTABLE. Com. by Henry Glapthorne. Acted at the Cockpit in Drury-Lane, 4to. 1640. The scene, London.

79. THE WIT OF A WOMAN. Com. Anonym. 4to. 1604. This is styled by the author a pleasant merry comedy; but Langbaine gives it us as his opinion, that it by no means deserves that character.

80. THE WIT OF A WOMAN. Com. 4to. 1705. At the end of the play of *The Cares of Love,* T. Walker, gent. is mentioned as the author of this comedy. It was performed at the Theatre in Little Lincoln's Inn Fields.

81. WIT WITHOUT MONEY. Com. by Beaumont and Fletcher. Acted at Drury-Lane, 4to. 1639. 4'o. 1661. This comedy is a very entertaining one, and is among the number of the few pieces written by these authors, which are even now represented on the London stages. The scene of it lies in London. The character of Valentine, who renounces all patrimony, and resolves to live by his wit, is whimsical, yet spirited and pleasing.

fing, as is also that of the Widow, who is won by the bluntness and open sincerity of his behaviour. There is likewise true humour in several of the inferior characters.

82. WIT WITHOUT MONEY. Com. (with alterations and amendments by some persons of quality). Acted at the Hay-Market, 4to. no date.

83. WITT IN A MADNESS. A Play. Entered on the books of the Stationers' Company, by Mr. Constable, March 19, 1639; together with *The Sparagus Garden*, and *The Antipodes*, by Richard Brome, and probably by the same author.

84. WIT'S LAST STAKE. Farce, by Thomas King. Acted at Drury-Lane, 8vo. 1769. Taken from *Le Legataire Universel* of Monf. Regnard, and first acted at Mr. Cautherly's benefit.

85. WIT'S LED BY THE NOSE, or, *A Poet's Revenge*. Tragi-Com. Acted at the Theatre Royal, 4to. 1678. See LOVE'S VICTORY.

86. THE WITS. Com. by Sir W. Davenant. Acted at Black-Friers, 4to. 1636. This was esteemed a good play, and met with good success. The scene is laid in London, but some part of the plot, as I have hinted before, was borrowed from Beaumont and Fletcher's *Wit at several Weapons*. It is highly commended in a copy of verses written by Mr. Thomas Carew.

87. THE WITS, or, *Sport upon Sport*. 8vo. 1673. This is only a collection of various drolls and farces, frequently presented by strollers at fairs. They consist chiefly of scenes (all of them comic) borrowed from the celebrated plays of Shakspeare, Fletcher, Marston, Shirley, &c. and presented by themselves under new titles. The edition here mentioned is the best, but not the first; and in one of the former editions there is a table prefixed, which shews from what play each droll is borrowed. The editor of this collection was one Francis Kirkman, a bookseller, and a very great admirer of dramatic writings. The names of the various pieces, with their respective origins, I shall here set down, as taken from the above-mentioned tables, viz.

1. *The Bouncing Knight*—from—Shakspeare's *Henry* IV. Part I.
2. *The Bubble*—from—Cooke's *Green's Tuquoque.*
3. *Joe Cammen*—from—Beaumont and Fletcher's *Philaster.*
4. *The Empirick*—from—Ben Jonson's *Alchymist.*
5. *An Equal Match*—from—Beaumont and Fletcher's *Rule a Wife and have a Wife.*
6. *The False Heir*—from—Fletcher's *Scornful Lady.*
7. *Forc'd Valour*—from—*The Humorous Lieutenant*, of Beaumont and Fletcher.
8. *The French Dancing-Master*—from—the Duke of Newcastle's *Variety.*
9. *The Grave-makers*—from—Shakspeare's *Hamlet.*
10. *Jenkins's Love Course*—from—*The School of Complements*, by James Shirley.
11. *Invisible Smirk*—from—*The Two merry Milkmaids.*
12. *The Lame Commonwealth*—from—Beaumont and Fletcher's *Beggar's Bush.*
13. *The Landlady*—from—*The Chances*, of the same authors.
14. *The Mock Testator*—from—*The Spanish Curate*, of the same.
15. *A Prince in Conceit*—from—*Shirley's Opportunity.*
16. *Simpleton, Simpkin, Hobbinol, and Swabber*—from—Cox's *Diana and Actæon*, &c.
17. *The Stallion*—from—*The Curious*

Custom of the Country, by Beaumont and Fletcher.

18. *The Surprize* — from — *Father's own Son*, a play which we cannot find any where mentioned but in this list.

19. *The Testy Lover* — from — Beaumont and Fletcher's *Maid's Tragedy*. And,

20. *Three Merry Boys* — from — *The Bloody Brother*, of the same.

There is also a second part of *Sport upon Sport*, published in 1672, which contains eleven pieces, supposed to be written by Robert Cox, the comedian; the titles of which are printed in the first volume of this work, p. 103.

88. WITS CABAL. Com. in two parts, by the Duchess of Newcastle. Fol. 1662.

89. A WITTY COMBAT, or, *The Female Victor*. Tragi-Com. by T. P. 4to. 1663. This play was acted by persons of quality, in the Whitsun Week, with great applause. The plot of it is founded on the story of Mary Carleton, the German princess, whose life is formed into a novel, and printed in 8vo. 1673.

90. THE WITTY FAIR ONE. Com. by James Shirley. Acted at the private house, Drury-Lane, 4to. 1633.

91. THE WIVES EXCUSE, or, *Cuckolds make themselves*. Com. by Thomas Southerne. Acted at Drury-Lane, 4to. 1692. There is a great deal of gay, lively conversation in this play, much true wit, and less licentiousness intermingled with that wit than is to be found in the greatest part of this author's comic writings. The scene lies in London.

92. THE WIVES REVENGE. Com. Opera, by Charles Dibdin. Acted at Covent-Garden, 8vo. 1778.

93. THE WOER. Com. by George Puttenham; mentioned in his *Art of Poetry*, but not printed.

94. WOMAN CAPTAIN. Com. by Thomas Shadwell. Acted at the Duke's Theatre, 4to. 1680. This play met with very good success in the representation, and, indeed, although it may fall short of the merit of his *Virtuoso*, *Squire of Alsatia*, and some few others of his dramatic pieces, yet it has considerable worth, in the variety of its characters, and the multiplicity of its incidents. The scene in London.

95. THE WOMAN HATER. C. by John Fletcher, 4to. 1607. 4to. 1649. In the composition of this piece, Mr. Fletcher had no assistances. It is a very good comedy, and met with success. After the Restoration it was revived by Sir William Davenant, with the addition of a new prologue, instead of the original one, which had been in prose. The scene lies in Milain.

96. THE WOMAN IN THE MOON. Com. by John Lyly, 4to. 1597.

97. A WOMAN KILL'D WITH KINDNESS. Trag. by Thomas Heywood. Acted by the Queen's servants, 4to. 1617. I cannot help looking on this play as one of the best of this author's writing. For although there is, perhaps, too much perplexity in it, arising from the great variety of incidents which are blended together, yet there are some scenes and numberless speeches in it which would have done no dishonour to the pen of Shakspeare himself. Mrs. Francford's seduction by Wendoll, might perhaps, with more propriety, have been extended on, and have given scope for more argument on the side of her lover, and a more gradual yielding on hers, as her conquest at present appears somewhat

what too easy for a woman who ever before appears so amiable. But nothing can be finer than her consciousness of guilt, her remorse, and self-accusations after it; and the manner of her death, in consequence of her husband's lenity and affection, is beautifully conceived, and finely executed, and leaves us still prejudiced in favour of a character, which, in the former parts of the play, every one must have been attached to by the most rational partiality. In a word, was this part of the plot to be modernized by some able band, it might undoubtedly furnish materials for a very fine tragedy. As to the other plot of the quarrel between Sir Charles Mountford and Sir Francis Acton, it might well be dispensed with, as having too little connexion with the more important design of the piece, and, indeed, the pleadings of Sir Charles with his sister, to give up her person to Acton for the discharge of his debt, and ransom of his liberty, and her reflections on the proposal, seem borrowed in some degree from the scenes between Claudio and Isabella in Shakspeare's *Measure for Measure*.

98. THE WOMAN MADE A JUSTICE. Com. by Thomas Betterton. This comedy was brought on the stage by its author, but never printed, on which account it is out of my power to give any particular detail of its plan or merits; but as all the other pieces which this gentleman produced were no more than translations or alterations of the works of others, I cannot help conjecturing this to have been of the same kind, and that it most probably might owe its origin to some or other of the older dramatic poets.

99. THE WOMAN TURN'D BULLY. Com. Anonymous. 1675. Acted at the Duke of York's Theatre.

100. WOMAN'S A RIDDLE. C. by Christ. Bullock. Acted at Lincoln's-Inn Fields Theatre, 4to. 1717. It was, however, the occasion of some disputes between Mr. Christopher Bullock, the nominal author, and who brought it on the stage, and Mr. Savage, who laid an equal claim to the property of the piece. The real fact was as follows; the play itself was not the work of either of these gentlemen, but a translation from a Spanish comedy, called, *La Dama Duenda*, or, *Woman's the Devil*. This translation had been executed by Mrs. Price, lady of baron Price, one of the judges of the court of Exchequer, who, being a perfect mistress of that language had performed it by way of *Passe Tems* to herself. This lady, either through forgetfulness or inadvertency, had bestowed three several copies of her translation on three different persons, in which number both the above mentioned gentlemen were included. But Mr. Bullock getting the start, partly perhaps by industry, and partly through his influence in a theatre in which he was at that time a performer, made some considerable alterations in the MS. and brought it out in the form in which it then appeared, and in which it to this day makes its appearance with success on the stage.

101. A WOMAN IS A WEATHER-COCK. C. by Nath. Field. Acted before the King at Whitehall, and divers times privately at the White-Friers, by the children of her Majesties Revels, 4to. 1612. This play is dedicated to any Woman that has not been a weather-cock; and is highly commended, in a complimentary copy of verses to the author, by George Chapman.

102. THE

102. THE WOMAN'S LAW. A Play. Entered on the books of the Stationers' Company, Nov. 29, 1653; but not printed.

103. WOMAN'S MASTERPIECE. A play under this title was entered on the books of the Stationers' Company, Nov. 29, 1653; but not printed.

104. THE WOMAN'S MISTAKEN. Com. by Drew and Davenport. Entered on the books of the Stationers' Company, Sept. 9, 1653; but, I believe, not printed.

105. THE WOMAN'S PLOT. Com. was acted at Court 1621; and was one of the dramatic pieces destroyed by Mr. Warburton's servant. In that gentleman's catalogue of lost plays, this is ascribed to Philip Massinger.

106. THE WOMAN'S PRIZE, or, *The Tamer tam'd*. Com. by John Fletcher, Fol. 1647. This piece is a kind of sequel to Shakspeare's *Taming of the Shrew*, in which Catherine being supposed dead, and Petruchio again married to a young woman of a mild and gentle disposition, she, in combination with two or three more of her female companions, forms a plot to break the violent and tyrannical temper of her husband, and bring him to the same degree of submission to her will, as he had before done with his former wife in her compliance to his: and this design is at length, through a variety of incidents, brought perfectly to bear. The play, in itself, is more regular and compact than *The Taming of the Shrew*, yet has not, on the whole, so many beauties as are to be met with in that comedy. The scene lies in London; and the whole is the work of Mr. Fletcher, unassisted by, and, I believe, written after the death of his partner Mr. Beaumont.

107. A WOMAN'S REVENGE, or, *A Match in Newgate*. Com. in three acts, by Christopher Bullock. Acted at Lincoln's-Inn Fields, 12mo. 1715. This is only an alteration from an alteration made by Mr. Betterton, of Marston's *Dutch Courtezan*, which I have mentioned under the title of *The Revenge*.

108. THE WOMAN OF TASTE, or, *The Yorkshire Lady*. Ballad Opera, 12mo. 1739. Printed in a collection, called, "The Curiosity, "or Gentleman and Ladies Library."

109. THE WOMAN'S TOO HARD FOR HIM. Com. Acted at Court 1621; but, I believe, not printed.

110. WOMAN'S WIT, or, *The Lady in Fashion*. Com. by Colley Cibber. Acted at the Theatre Royal, 4to. 1697. This is very far from being the best of this author's comic pieces, nor is he entirely clear from the charge of borrowing in it; the characters of Major Rakish and his Son, and their courtship of the Widow Manlove, being pretty evidently copied from Sir Thomas Revel and his Son, in Mountford's *Greenwich Park*, and from Carlisle's comedy of *The Fortunehunters*. This part of the plot Mr. Cibber has detached from the rest of the play, and formed it into a farce by itself, under the title of *The School-Boy*, which see in its place. The author himself had the candour to acknowledge this piece defective, and that it came out too hastily after his first play. See Apol. 217. The scene, St. James's, and the time of action five hours.

111. WOMEN BEWARE WOMEN. Trag. by Thomas Middleton, 8vo. 1657. The plot of this play is founded on a romance called *Hippolito and Isabella*; and the scene laid in Florence. How high a rank of estimation this piece

piece stood in with the publick at its first coming out, may be gathered from the words of Mr. Richards, a contemporary poet, who closes a copy of verses in praise of it with these words, "Ne'er Tragedy came off with more Applause."

112. WOMEN PLEAS'D. Tragi-Com. by Beaumont and Fletcher. Fol. 1647. The plan of the comedy parts of this play, between Bartello, Lopez, Isabella, and Claudio, is compiled from three or four different Novels of Boccace; and that of the serious parts, relating to Silvio and Belvidera, more especially as to the incidents of the last act, may be traced in Chaucer's *Wife of Bath's Tale*. According to the best of my judgement, this play may very justly be ranked with several of the pieces of these authors which are better known, and even frequently represented; nor can I help thinking that, without any further alteration than a judicious curtailing of some particular passages, or what is understood in the theatrical language, by *properly cutting* this play, it might be rendered, on a revival, a very agreeable entertainment even to the nice-stomached audiences of the present age. This play was revived about thirty or forty years since at Drury-Lane, but with no success.

113. THE WOMEN'S CONQUEST. Tragi-Com. by Edward Howard. Acted at the Duke of York's Theatre, 4to. 1671. This piece, from the character given of it by Langbaine and Jacob, appears to have been the best of this gentleman's dramatic works. The scene in Scythia.

114. THE WONDER, A WOMAN KEEPS A SECRET. Com. by Mrs. Centlivre. Acted at Drury-Lane, 4to. 1714. This comedy had very good success at first, is still frequently acted, and is indeed one of the best of Mrs. Centlivre's plays. The plot is intricate and ingenious, yet clear and distinct both in its conduct and catastrophe; the language is in general more correct than she usually renders it; and the characters, particularly those of the jealous Don Felix and Colonel Briton's Highland Servant Gibby, are justly drawn, and very well finished. I know not, however, whether the whole merit of this contrivance is to be attributed to Mrs. Centlivre, as there are some circumstances in the concealment of Isabella, Violante's fidelity to her trust, and the perplexities which arise therefrom, that seem to bear a resemblance to one part of the plot of a play of Lord Digby's, called, *Elvira*, or, *The Worst not always true*. The scene lies at Lisbon. Mr. Garrick has thrown a new lustre on this comedy, by reviving it with some judicious alterations, and by his inimitable performance of Don Felix.

115. THE WONDER, AN HONEST YORKSHIREMAN. Ballad Opera, by Henry Carey. Acted at the Theatres, 8vo. 1736. The author apologises for his piece being published so late, from his apprehensions of piratical booksellers.

116. THE WONDERS OF DERBYSHIRE. A Pantomime. Acted at Drury-Lane, 1779.

117. THE WONDER OF A KINGDOM. Tragi-Com. by Tho. Decker, 4to. 1636. Langbaine gives this play a good character.

118. WONDER OF WOMEN, or, *Sophonisba*, her Tragedy, by John Marston. Acted at Black-Fryers, 4to. 1606. 12mo. 1633. The plot of this play is taken from Livy, Polybius,

Polybius, and other Historians, and the scene laid in Libya; but that the author had not rigidly adhered to historical facts, may be gathered from his own words in his epistle to the reader, in which he tells us, that he "has not laboured in it to tye himself to relate every thing as an Historian, but to enlarge every thing as a Poet."

119. WONDERS IN THE SUN, or, *The Kingdom of Birds*. A Comic Opera, by Thomas Durfey, 4to. 1706. This whimsical piece was performed at the Queen's Theatre in the Hay-Market. It is dedicated to the celebrated society of the *Kit Cat Club*, and illustrated with a great variety of songs in all kinds (set to music) by several of the most eminent wits of the age, who lent the author their assistance.

120. A WORD TO THE WISE, Com. by Hugh Kelly. Acted at Drury-Lane, 8vo. 1770. This play being produced at a time when political disputes ran very high, and the author of it being suspected to have written on the unpopular side, a party was formed to prevent its representation. It with difficulty was dragged through the first night; but the second proved fatal to it. The author, however, was consoled for his disappointment by a very large subscription to the publication.

121. WORDS MADE VISIBLE, or, *Grammar and Rhetoric accommodated to the Lives and Manners of Men*, in two parts, by Samuel Shaw, 8vo. 1679. This piece has scarcely a right to be enumerated among the productions of the drama; for, although we are told in the title-page that it was represented in a country school for the entertainment and edification of the spectators, yet the author himself terms it no more than a mere *Colloquium Scholasticum puerile*; written, I suppose, by the master, for the improvement of his pupils in the knowledge of grammar and the practice of oratory; an example not unworthy of imitation by some of the present instructors of youth.

122. THE WORLD AS IT GOES, or, *A Party to Montpelier*. Com. by Mrs. Cowley. Acted at Covent-Garden, 1781. The success of this Lady's former performance, instead of producing caution, seems to have inspired a degree of confidence which has been almost fatal to her reputation. The present hasty, indecent, and worthless composition received its sentence from a very candid and impartial audience, who appeared to condemn with reluctance what it was impossible to applaud. Yet, such is the fondness of authors for their own productions, that, not satisfied with the first trial, this play a little altered, and not with much advantage to it, was brought out once more, under the title of *Second Thoughts are best*, and received its final condemnation from an audience equally candid with the former.

123. THE WORLD IN THE MOON. A Dramatic Comic Opera, by Elk. Settle. Acted at Dorset Gardens, 4to. 1697. The author, in his Dedication to Christ. Rich, esq; the Patentee, says, that the model of the scenes of his play, was something of an original.

124. "*Courtly Masque*; the Device called, THE WORLD TOSS'D AT TENNIS. As it hath beene divers times presented to the contentment of many noble and worthy spectators: by the Prince's servants; invented and set down by Thomas Middleton and William Rowley, gent." 4to.

4to. N. D. [1620]. It is entered on the books of the Stationers' Company, July 4, in that year.

125. THE WORLD'S IDOL, or, *Plutus the God of Wealth*. Com. from the Greek of Aristophanes, by H. H. B. 1650, 8vo.

126. WORSE AND WORSE. C. by George Digby, Earl of Bristol. Acted at the Duke's Theatre between 1662 and 1665. This play is only mentioned by Downes, who says *it was made out of the* Spanish. It seems not to have been printed.

127. THE WOUNDS OF CIVIL WAR, *lively set forth in the true Tragedies of Marius and Sylla*, by Thomas Lodge. Acted by the Lord Admiral's servants, 4to. 1594. The plot of this piece is taken from Plutarch, Sallust, &c.

128. THE WRANGLING LOVERS, or, *The Invisible Mistress*. Com. by Edward Ravenscroft. Acted at the Duke's Theatre, 4to. 1677. The scene of this comedy is laid at Toledo, and the original of its plot may be traced in a Spanish Romance, called *Deceptio Visus*, or, *seeing and believing are two Things*. But, as Corneille has taken the same Romance for the ground-work of his *Engagemens du Hazard*, and Moliere for that of his *Depit amoureux*, it is probable that Mr. Ravenscroft might rather set these great dramatic writers before him in forming the model of this piece, than the author of the Novel. The writer of *Woman's a Riddle* seems also in her turn to have borrowed some hints from Mr. Ravenscroft.

129. THE WRANGLING LOVERS, or, *Like Master, like Man*. Farce, by William Lyon, comedian, 8vo. 1745. Printed at Edinburgh. This is taken from Vanbrugh's *Mistake*.

130. WYAT'S HISTORY, 4to. 1607. The whole title of this piece is as follows. *The famous History of Sir* Thomas Wyat, *with the Coronation of Queen* Mary, *and the coming in of King* Philip, plaied by the Queen Majesties servants. Written by Thomas Dickers [Dekker] and John Webster.

131. WYTLES. A Play never printed; but entered on the books of the Stationers' Company in the year 1560.

X.

1. XERXES. Trag. by Colley Cibber, 4to. 1699. This tragedy made its first appearance at Lincoln's-Inn Fields House, but with no success, making a stand of only one night, as may be gathered from an inventory of theatrical goods to be sold, humorously related by *The Tatler*, in which, among other things, are, "*The Imperial Robes of Xerxes, never wore but once*." The scene lies in Persia, and the plot is borrowed from the Persian History, but so little did this author's genius lie towards tragedy, that I can

can by no means pretend to vindicate it from the dislike shewn to it by the audience.

2. XIMENA, or, *The Heroic Daughter*. Trag. by C. Cibber. Acted at Drury-Lane, 8vo. 1719. This play was the production of the same author with the foregoing; but did not meet with much better fortune. For which reason I suppose it was, that it made not its appearance in print till about two years after it had been acted on the stage. The author has prefixed a Dedication to Sir Rich. Steele, in which he pays that gentleman a very exalted compliment at the expence of a much superior writer, viz. Mr. Addison, whom he figures under the allegory of a *Wren*, whom the former had mounted aloft on his *Eagle Back*. But, whether he afterwards became reconciled to Mr. Addison, or, that the general allowance given to his merit, rendered Mr. Cibber ashamed of this extravagant invective, he thought proper, in the quarto edition of a select number of his plays, to omit this Dedication. The tragedy itself, as to the plot and great part of the language, is borrowed from the *Cid* of M. Corneille.

Y.

YO

1. THE YORKSHIRE GENTLEWOMAN, AND HER SON. Trag. by George Chapman. Entered on the books of the Stationers' Company, June 29, 1660; but probably now lost.

2. A YORKSHIRE TRAGEDY. Not so new as lamentable and true, by William Shakspeare. Acted at the Globe, 4to. 1608. 4to. 1619. This is one of the seven pieces denied by some of the commentators to have been Shakspeare's. Mr. Steevens, however, after a very careful examination of it, has given his opinion in favour of its authenticity. It appears to have been grounded on an event which happened in the year 1604, and made with three other pieces the entertainment of an afternoon. On it Mr. Mitchell formed the groundwork of his *Fatal Extravagance*.

3. THE YOUNG ADMIRAL. Tragi-Com. by James Shirley. Acted at the private house, Drury-Lane, 4to. 1637. Scene, Naples.

4. THE YOUNG HYPOCRITE. Com. translated from the French by Samuel Foote, and printed in *The Comic Theatre*, vol. I. This, we are assured, was the only piece in this collection which was really translated by Mr. Foote.

5. THE YOUNG KING, or, *The Mistake*. Tragi-Com. by Mrs. Behn. Acted at the Duke's Theatre. 4to. 1683. 4to. 1698. The plot of this play, which is very far from being a bad one, is borrowed from the history of Alcamenes and Menalippa in M. Calprenade's celebrated romance of *Cleopatra*, p. 8. and the character of the Young King bears some resemblance to Hippolito in Dryden's *Tempest*.

Tempest. The scene is laid in the Court of Daca between the two armies just before the town, and the authoress has dedicated the play, under the fictitious name of Philaster, to some gentleman who appears to have been her very particular friend, not improbably a lover.

6. THE YOUNGER BROTHER. Com. Entered on the books of the Stationers' Company, Nov. 29, 1653; but, I believe, not printed.

7. The YOUNGER BROTHER, or, *The Amorous Jilt*. Com. by Mrs. Behn. Acted at the Theatre Royal, 4to. 1696. This play, though written ten years before her death, was not published till after that event. It seems to have been a favourite of its author, and is indeed not devoid of merit, the two first acts particularly abounding with very lively and pleasing wit. It did not, however, meet with success, probably owing to some heavy scenes in blank verse between Mirtilla and Prince Frederic. The plot is founded on some facts within her own knowledge, in the story of a brother of Colonel Henry Martin and a particular Lady, and which may be also found related, after the manner of the Atalantis, in a Novel called *Hattige*, or, *The Amours of the King of Tameran*. Prefixed to this play is a life of its author.

8. THE YOUNGER BROTHER, or, *The Sham Marquis*. Com. Anon. 8vo. 1719. This piece was acted at Lincoln's-Inn Fields Theatre, but without success.

9. YOUR FIVE GALLANTS. Com. by Thomas Middleton. Acted at Black-Friers, 4to. N. D. This play, though published without a date, appears, by the entries of the Stationers' Company, to have been printed in the year 1607.

10. YOUTH's COMEDY, or, *The Soul's Tryals and Triumph*. A dramatic Poem, with divers meditations intermixed upon several subjects. Set forth to help and encourage those that are seeking a heavenly country. By the author of *Youth's Tragedy*, 8vo. 1680.

11. YOUTH's GLORY AND DEATH's BANQUET. Trag. in two parts, by the dutchess of Newcastle. Fol. 1662. All the songs and verses in the second, and two scenes, together with the speeches in favour of Mademoiselle Sans-pareille in the first of these two pieces, were written by the duke.

12. YOUTH's TRAGEDY. A Poem, drawn up by way of Dialogue between Youth, the Devil, Wisdom, Time, Death, the Soul, and the Nuncius. By T. S. 4to. 1671.

Z.

Z A

1. ZARA. Trag. by A. Hill. 8vo. 1735. This piece is a very good one, although founded on the principles of religious party, which are generally apt to throw an air of enthusiasm and bigotry into those dramatic works which are built upon them. It is borrowed originally from the *Zaire* of M. de Voltaire, an author who, while

while he resided in England, imbibed so much of the spirit of British liberty, that his writings seem almost always calculated for the meridian of London. Mr. Hill, however, has made this, as well as his other translations, so much his own, that it is hard to determine which of the two may most properly be called the author of this play. At its first representation, a young gentleman, a relation of the author's, attempted the character of Osman, but without success, though great pains had been taken with him in it by Mr. Hill himself; who was perhaps, though not an actor, one of the best judges of theatrical abilities, and the requisites for an actor, of any man these kingdoms ever produced. It was besides remarkable for another extraordinary event, viz. the appearance of Mrs. Cibber, whose wonderful abilities in theatrical life have since rendered themselves so conspicuous; the part of Zara being her first attempt in tragedy.

2. ZARA. Trag. translated from Voltaire; and printed in Dr. Franklin's edition of that author.

3. ZELIDA. Trag. 8vo. 1772. Printed at Oxford.

4. ZELMANE, or, *The Corinthian Queen*. Trag. 4to. 1705. This play was acted at the Theatre in Lincoln's-Inn Fields; it was left unfinished by Mr. M——t (probably Mr. Mountfort); but it does not appear by whom it was compleated. Scene, Corinth.

5. ZENOBIA. Trag. by Arth. Murphy, esq. Acted at Drury-Lane, 8vo. 1768. This play is dedicated to Mrs. Dancer, now Mrs. Crawford; and was acted with great and deserved success.

6. LA ZINGARA, or, *The Gipsy*. Burletta, performed at Marybone-Gardens, Aug. 21, 1773. 4to.

7. ZINGIS. Trag. by Alex. Dow. Acted at Drury-Lane, 8vo, 1769. The story taken from *Tarich Mogulistan*, or, *The History of the Mogul Tartars*, written in the Persian Language.

Tumour without magnificence, and circumlocution untinctured with poetry, are the true characteristicks of the play now under consideration. Our ears are cudgelled with the uncouth names that perpetually occur in it; but as to the fortunes of the personages who bear them, we remain in a state of perfect indifference. It is of little moment to us (said the first of English criticks, in ridicule of the noisy lines the piece abounds with)

"How 'gainst the Nirons the bold
"Naimans stood,
"And red Tartares foam'd with Om-
"rahs' blood."

Some unlucky blunder, however, of a Naiman, or a Niron, (no matter which) on the first night of representation, convulsed the audience with laughter to a degree that was nearly fatal to any second appearance of these Asiatic warriors. The play indeed met with inconsiderable success afterwards. Though it was allowed the usual run, the spectators were continually asking each other what it was about; and no satisfactory answer being ever afforded to the repeated question, they at last deserted it as a species of tragedy which, with their best efforts, they could not understand.

Some wag also molested the first appearance of this drama with sportive verses address'd to Mr. Dow in one of the news-papers. He immediately waited on the printer, to intercede for better treatment; and carried a friend or two with him on the occasion. But the

the complaints of thefe gentlemen were fo much louder than thofe of the oftenfible bard, that honeft Mr. Type could eafily diftinguifh the real parents from the pretended father of the piece.

8. ZOBEIDE. Trag. by Jofeph Cradock. Acted at Covent-Garden, 8vo. 1771. The play before us is an imitation of *Les Scythes*, a dramatic piece, which Voltaire did not originally intend for the ftage, being convinced that the manners of it were too fimple, and the plot infufficiently ftored with incidents, to engage the attention of an audience. It is indeed a beautiful outline, but we defpair of feeing it properly filled up. There is always hazard in adopting the unfinifhed plan of any great mafter in his art. A fubject which the fertile genius of Voltaire could not diverfify and enlarge, muft in its own nature be fcanty and barren. Had he been able to complete his defign in a manner correfponding with his private ideas of excellence, he would not have left this tragedy in a ftate of avowed imperfection. Mr. Cradock has done fufficient juftice to his original, and, as we are informed, received the thanks of Voltaire on the occafion.

9. ZORAIDA. Trag. by W. Hodfon. Acted at Drury-Lane, 8vo. 1780. This tragedy has no farther foundation in hiftory than that Selim I. one of the Ottoman emperors, befieged and fubdued Cairo, and by that event reduced Egypt under his dominion. The reft, as the author afferts, is invention. The fuccefs of this piece was but fmall, it being only eight times reprefented. Annexed to it are fome obfervations on Tragedy in general.

LATIN

LATIN PLAYS,

Written by ENGLISH AUTHORS.

A B

ABSALON. Trag. by John Watson, afterwards bishop of Winchester. N. P.

ALBA. A Pastoral Comedy, acted in Christ-Church Hall, Oxford, before King James I. in 1605. In this dramatic piece, five men, almost naked, appearing on the stage as part of the representation, gave great offence to the queen and maids of honor: while the king, whose delicacy was not easily shocked at other times, concurred with the ladies, and availing himself of this lucky circumstance, peevishly expressed his wishes to depart before the piece was half finished, for he had already sat four hours in the morning and afternoon, with infinite satisfaction, to hear syllogisms in jurisprudence and theology.

ARCHIPROPHETA, *five Johannes Baptista*, a Latin Tragedy, written in 1547, by Nicholas Grimald, one of the first students of Christ-Church, Oxford, which probably was acted in the refectory there. It is dedicated to the dean, Dr. Richard Cox, and was printed at Cologne, 1548, 8vo. This play coincided with his plan of a rhetorical lecture, which he had set up in the college.

B

BELLUM GRAMMATICALE. C. Acted before Queen Elizabeth, Sunday the 24th of September, 1592. The writer, who mentions this representation, says it was but meanly performed, though most graciously and with great patience heard by her majesty. See Peck's *Desiderata Curiosa*, annexed to his *Life of Oliver Cromwell*, p. 21.

C

CANCER. Comœdia, 8vo. 1648. This is printed with *Loiola*, *Stoicus Vapulans*, and *Paria*.

CATO. Trag. translated into Latin without the love scenes, 8vo. 1764.

CLEOPHILUS. Comœdia, 4to. 1650.

CORNELIANUM DOLIUM. Comœdia lepidissima optimorum judiciis approbata. 8vo. 1638. This play I have not seen. It is entered on the books of the Stationers' Company, March 30, 1638.

D

DIDO. A Latin Tragedy, acted before Queen Elizabeth in the magnificent chapel of King's College, Cambridge, when she honoured that university with a visit in 1564. Mr. Warton, in his *History of English Poetry*, vol. II. p. 383, describes it as a performance in English, but he is mistaken. It appears from a Latin account of her majesty's reception, &c. at Cambridge, written by Nicholas Robinson, afterwards bishop of Bangor, that *Dido* was composed by one of the fellows of King's College. See MSS. Baker, 7037, p. 203. The author of this *opus venustum et elegans*, for so it is styled, we may suppose to have been John Ritwise, who was elected fellow of King's in 1507; and acccording to A. Wood, "made the tragedy of "*Dido* out of Virgil, and acted "the same with the scholars of his "school [St. Paul's, of which he "was appointed master in 1522] "before Cardinal Wolsey, with "great applause." What will serve to countenance this supposition, is, that the members of the college already mentioned, have been ever famous for their classical attachments, and the elegance of their latinity.

DIDO. A Tragedy presented in Christ-Church Hall, by some of the scholars of that society and of St. John's College, before Albertus de Alasco, a Polish Prince Palatine, in 1583. Whether this play was composed in English or Latin, is uncertain. It cannot be the *Dido* of Nash and Marloe, because that piece affords no room for the scenery described as follows by Holingshead, Chron. III. 1355, "wherein the queene's banket "(with Eneas narration of the "destruction of Troie) was livelie "described in a marchpaine pat- "terne; there was also a goodlie "fight of hunters with full crie "of a kennel of hounds, Mercurie "and Iris descending and ascend- "ing from and to an high place, "the tempest wherein it hailed "small confects, rained rosewater, "and snew an artificiall kind of "snow, all strange, marvellous, "and abundant." It was hardly the same play that was acted before Queen Elizabeth at Cambridge in 1564, as Oxford could have furnished poets enough without being indebted to a rival university on such a public occasion.

E

ÆMILIA. Com. by Mr. Cecill, of St. John's College, Cambridge; acted before King James I. March 7, 1614, at Trinity College Hall. Not printed.

F

FRAUS HONESTA. Comœdia Cantabrigiæ olim acta. Authore Magistro Stubbe, Collegii Trinitatis Socio. 8vo. 1632. It was entered on the books of the Stationers' Company Sept. 28, 1631.

H

HERMOTHUS. Com. by Geo. Wilde; several times acted, but not printed.

HEZEKIAH, a Tragedy (whether in English or Latin, is unknown), was performed in King's College Chapel, Cambridge, before Queen Elizabeth, in the year 1564, together with two other dramatic pieces. This magnificent Gothic building was lighted by the royal guards, during the time of exhibition, each of them bearing a staff-torch in his hand. See Peck's *Desid. Cur.* p. 36. Num. xv.

I

JEPTHA, a Tragedy. This is taken from the eleventh chapter of the book of *Judges*, and was written both in Latin and Greek, and dedicated to King Henry VIII. about the year 1546, by a very grave and learned divine, John Christopherson, one of the first fellows of Trinity College in Cambridge, afterwards master, dean of Norwich, and bishop of Chichester. It was probably composed as a Christmas play for the same society.

IGNORAMUS. Comœdia coram Regia Majestate Jacobi, Regis Angliæ, &c. 8vo. 1630. This play

play was written by George Ruggles, of Clare Hall, Cambridge; and was acted before King James I. Thursday, the 8th of March, 1614, in Trinity College Hall. The names of the original actors are preserved in the Supplement to Mr. Granger's *Biographical History of England*, p. 146. See Dodsley's *Collection of Old Plays*, edit. 1780. vol. VII. p. 126.

L

LABYRINTHUS. A Latin Comedy; was entered on the books of the Stationers' Company July 17, 1635.

LOILA. Com. 8vo. 1648. This play may be ascribed to Dr. Lacket, and by the prologues appears to have been acted first Feb. 28, 1622, and afterwards before King James I. March 12, 1622. It was a university play; but whether it was performed at Oxford or Cambridge, is not certain.

M

MARCUS GEMINUS. A Latin Comedy; acted in Christ-Church Hall, Oxford, before Queen Elizabeth in 1556. See Peshall's *History of Oxford*, p. 226.

"MELANTHE. Fabula pasto-
"ralis acta, cum Jacobus Magnæ
"Brit. Franc. & Hiberniæ Rex
"Cantabrigiam suum nuper in-
"viserat, ibidemque musarum at-
"que animi gratia dies quinque
"commoraretur. Egerunt Alumni
"Coll. San. et individuæ Trini-
"tatis Cantabrigiæ, 4to. 1615."
This play written by Mr. Brookes, of Trinity College, was acted before King James I. Friday, the 10th of March, 1614. A person who was present says it was excellently written, and as well acted, which gave great contentment as well to the king as to the rest.

MELEAGER. A Tragedy in Latin, by William Gager; acted at Christ-Church, before Lord Leicester, Sir Philip Sidney, and other distinguished persons, in 1581, 4to. 1592.

N

NAUFRAGIUM JOCULARE. Comœdia: Publice coram Academicis acta, in Collegio S. S. et individuæ Trinitatis, 4to. Nonas Feb. An. Dom. 1638. Authore Abrahamo Cowley, 12mo. 1638. Dr. Johnson observes, that this comedy is written without attention to the ancient models; for it is not loose verse, but mere prose. It was printed, with a dedication in verse to Dr. Comber, master of the college; but having neither the facility of a popular, nor the accuracy of a learned work, it seems to be now universally neglected.

"NERO. Tragœdia Nova,
"Matthæo Gwinne, Med. Doct.
"Collegii Divi Joannis Præcur-
"soris, apud Oxonienses Socio.
"Collecta e Tacito, Suetonio,
"Dione, Seneca, 4to. 1603."

P

PANMACHIUS. This Latin Comedy was acted at Christ's College, in Cambridge, in 1544, and was laid before the privy council by Bishop Gardiner, chancellor of the university, as a dangerous libel, containing many offensive reflections on the papistic ceremonies yet unabolished.

This mode of attack (as Mr. Warton observes) was seldom returned by the opposite party. The catholic worship, founded on sensible representations, afforded a much better hold for ridicule, than the religion of some of the sects of the reformers, which was of a more simple and spiritual nature. But this is said of the infancy of the stage. In the next century, fanaticism was brought on the English theatre with great success, when polished manners had introduced humour into comedy, and character had taken place of spectacle. There are, however, two English Interludes, one in the reign of Henry VIII, called *Every Man*; the other of that of Edward VI, called *Lusty Juventus*, written by R. Weever: the former defends, and the latter attacks the church of Rome.

De PAPATU. Tragedy, by Nicholas Udall, master of Eton about the year 1540; written probably to be acted by his scholars.

PARIA; acted coram sereniss. Rege Carolo. Authore Tho. Vincent, Trin. Colleg. Socio, 8vo. 1648.

PEDANTIUS. Comedy in Latin; was entered on the books of the Stationers' Company Feb. 9, 1630.

PROGNE. A Latin Tragedy; acted in the magnificent hall at Christ-Church, Oxford, before Queen Elizabeth, in the year 1566. See Peshall's *History of Oxford*, p. 229.

R

REGICIDIUM. Tragi-Com. à R. Braithwaite, 8vo. 1665.

RICHARDUS TERTIUS. A Latin Tragedy, by Henry Lacy, Fellow of Trinity College, Cambridge, 1586. This is among the Harleian MSS. in *The British Museum*, N° 6926, and contains many curious stage-directions like the following:

"After the like noyse made
"agayne, lett souldiours runne
"from the fielde over the stage on
"after an another, flinginge of
"their harneys, and at length
"some come haltinge as wounded."

Another copy of the same piece, entitled *Richardus Tertius, Tragedia, in tres actiones divisa*, is to be found likewise in the Harleian Collection, N° 2412.

RIVALES. A Comedy in Latin, by William Gager, presented in Christ Church Hall, Oxford, by some of the scholars of that society, and of St. John's College, before Albertus de Alasco, a Polish Prince Palatine, in 1583. See Peck's *Desiderata Curiosa*, annexed to his *Life of Oliver Cromwell*, p. 21.

ROXANA. Tragœdia, a plagiarii unguibus vindicata, aucta & agnita ab Authore Gulielmo Alabastro, 12mo. 1632. See vol. I. p. 5.

S

SENILE ODIUM. Comœdia Cantabridgiæ publicè Academicis recitata in Collegio Reginali ab ejusdem Collegii juventute. Autore P. Hausted, 12mo. 1633.

SIMO. Comœdia, 4to. 1652.

SPURIUS. Com. by Peter Heylin, 1616. N. P.

STOICUS VAPULANS. Olim Cantabrigiæ, actus in Collegio S. Johannis Evangelistæ. Ab ejusdem Collegii juventute, 8vo. 1648.

T

THEOMACHIA. Com. by Peter Heylin, 1618. N. P.

V

"VERTUMNUS, sive Annus
"Recurrens Oxonii: 29 Augusti,
"Anno 1605, coram Jacobo
"Rege, Henrico Principe, Pro-
"ceribus, a Joanniensibus in
"Scena recitatur, ab uno scriptus,
"Phrasi Comica prope Tragicis
"senariis, 4to. 1607." This was written by Dr. Matthew Gwinne, and was acted with great applause.

VERTUMNUS.

VERTUMNUS. This dramatic piece was exhibited in Christ-Church Hall, Oxford, before King James I. in 1605; but although *learnedly penned* in Latin, and by a Doctor of Divinity, could not keep the king awake, who was wearied in consequence of having executed the office of moderator all that day at the disputations in St. Mary's Church. This seems to have been a different performance from the former.

ULYSSES REDUX. A Tragedy in Latin, by William Wager; when or on what occasion it was written and performed, is uncertain. It must have been acted, however, between 1574 and 1590.

ORATORIOS.

A C

THESE performances were not originally defigned to have been enumerated in the prefent Catalogue; but, being of a dramatic caft, it was apprehended that the exclufion of them might be deemed a defect in the work. The prefent Editor has therefore endeavoured to obtain as complete a lift of them as he was able. This fpecies of the drama was introduced into England by Mr. Handel, and carried on during his life with great fuccefs. It was borrowed from the *concert fpirituel* of our volatile neighbours on the continent, but conducted in a manner more agreeable to the native gravity and folidity of this nation. It has been fuggefted, that action and gefticulation accommodated to fituation and fentiments, joined with dreffes conformable to the characters reprefented, would render the reprefentations more expreffive and perfect, and confequently the entertainment much more rational and improving. How far fuch an innovation might with propriety be admitted, we can only conjecture. The fafhion about Oratorios feems much on the decline, and it may require the genius of another Handel to reftore them to their former credit and reputation.

A

ACIS AND GALATEA. See p. 2. This was originally fet to mufic by Mr. Handel, for the duke of Chandos, about the year 1731.

ALEXANDER BALUS. Orat. by Dr. Morell, fet to mufic by Handel; acted at Covent-Garden 1748.

ALEXANDER'S FEAST. Orat. fet to mufic by Handel; acted at Covent-Garden 1736. This excellent Ode had formerly been altered for mufic by Mr. Hughes.

ALFRED THE GREAT. Orat. fet to mufic by Dr. Arne, and acted at Drury-Lane about 1761, 4to. This is taken from Mallet's Play of *Alfred*.

ALLEGRO ED IL PENSEROSO. Orat. taken from Milton; fet by Mr. Handel, acted 1739.

ATHALIAH. Orat. fet by Mr. Handel; and performed at Oxford at the time of the Public Act in July 1733. The words by Mr. Humphreys, 4to. 1733.

B

BELSHAZZAR. Orat. fet by Mr. Handel, 4to. 1745.

C

THE CURE OF SAUL. A Sacred Ode, by Dr. Brown, 4to. 1764. This piece was originally compofed by the author himfelf, by felecting different parts of Mr. Handel's Works, and adapting them to his own performance. In this ftate it was firft acted at Drury-Lane with fmall fuccefs. It was afterwards new fet (1767) by Dr. Arnold, and performed at the Hay-Market.

D

D

DAVID'S LAMENTATION. Orat. by John Lockman; performed at Covent-Garden, 4to. 1740.

DEBORAH. Orat. by Mr. Humphreys; set by Mr. Handel, 1732.

E

ESTHER. Orat. by Mr. Humphreys; set by Mr. Handel, performed at the Hay-Market, 4to. 1732. It had been originally composed for the duke of Chandos, and performed at Cannons.

F

THE FORCE OF TRUTH. Orat. by Dr. John Hoadly; set by Dr. Greene, 8vo. 1764.

H

HANNAH. Orat. by Christop. Smart; set by Mr. Worgan; and performed at the Hay-Market, 4to. 1764.

I

JEPHTHA. Orat. by Dr. John Hoadly; set by Dr. Greene, 8vo. 1737.

JEPHTHA. Orat. by Dr. Morell; set by Mr. Handel, performed at Covent-Garden, 4to. 1751. During the composition of this Oratorio, Mr. Handel became blind.

JOSEPH AND HIS BRETHREN. Orat. by Mr. James Miller; set by Mr. Handel, and performed at Covent-Garden, 4to. 1744.

JOSHUA. Orat. set by Mr. Handel, performed at Covent-Garden, 4to. 1748.

ISRAEL IN BABYLON. Orat. set by Mr. Handel, performed at Covent-Garden, 4to.

ISRAEL IN ÆGYPT. Orat. set by Mr. Handel, performed at Lincoln's-Inn Fields, 4to. 1740.

JUDAS MACCABEUS. Orat. by Dr. Morell; set by Mr. Handel, performed at Covent-Garden, 4to. 1746. This Oratorio was written at the request of Mr. Handel, and by the recommendation of Prince Frederick. The plan of it was designed as a compliment to the duke of Cumberland, upon his returning victorious from Scotland. The success of it was very great, there being above 400 l. in the house on the 30th night of its representation. That incomparable Air, "*Wise men flattering may deceive us;*" and the Chorus, "*Sion now her head shall raise*," were the last Mr. Handel ever composed. They were designed for *Belshazzar*; but that not being performed, they were introduced in the present Oratorio.

JUDITH. Orat. by William Huggins, esq; set by William de Fesch, 8vo. 1733. This piece was performed with scenes and other decorations, but met with no success. Prefixed to it is a plate by the author's friend, Mr. Hogarth.

JUDITH. Orat. by Isaac Bickerstaffe; set by Dr. Arne, and performed at the Lock Hospital Chapel, Feb. 29, 1764, 4to. This piece was likewise again revived, and performed at the Church of Stratford upon Avon, Sept. 6, 1769, upon occasion of the Jubilee in honour of the memory of Shakspeare.

M

MANASSES. Oratorio.

MESSIAH. Orat. set by Mr. Handel. The words selected by Mr. Jennens. This excellent Oratorio was originally performed about the year 1741; but by some unaccountable caprice in the public taste, met with a very cold reception. The composer thereupon went over to Dublin, where it was honoured with universal applause; and, on his return to England, it found all the approbation it

N A

It was entitled to, and has ever since been the favourite of the admirers of this species of composition.

N

NABAL. Orat. by Dr. Morell; set by Mr. Smith to the music of some old genuine performances of Mr. Handel. It was performed at Covent Garden, 4to. 1764.

NEW OCCASIONAL ORATORIO. Set by Mr. Handel, and performed at Covent-Garden, 4to. 1746. This was brought forward on occasion of the victory gained at Culloden by the duke of Cumberland.

O

OMNIPOTENCE. Oratorio, 4to.

P

PARADISE LOST. Orat. by Benjamin Stillingfleet; set by Mr. Smith, and performed at Covent-Garden, 4to. 1760. The words of this piece were altered and adapted to the stage from Milton.

THE PRODIGAL SON. Orat. by Thomas Hull; set by Dr. Arnold, and performed at Covent-Garden, 4to.

R

REBECCA. Orat. set by Mr. Smith, and performed at Covent-Garden, 4to. 1761.

RUTH. Orat. by Henry Brooke, esq; printed in his Works, 8vo. 1778.

S

SAMPSON. Orat. by Newburgh Hamilton; set by Mr. Handel, and performed at Covent-Garden, 4to. 1742.

SAUL. Orat. set by Mr. Handel, and performed at the Hay-Market, 4to. 1738.

SEMELE. Orat. set by Mr. Handel, and performed at Covent-Garden, 4to. 1743. This is Con-

TH

greve's piece of the same name, something altered.

SOLOMON. Orat. set by Mr. Handel, and performed at Covent-Garden, 4to. 1748.

SOLOMON. Serenata, by Edward Moore; set by Dr. Boyce, 4to.

SUSANNAH. Orat. set by Mr. Handel, and performed at Covent-Garden, 4to. 1743.

T

THEODORA. Orat. by Dr. Morell; set by Mr. Handel, and performed at Covent-Garden, 4to. 1749. I am informed, that Mr. Handel valued this Oratorio more than any other performance of the same kind. Being once asked, whether he did not consider the grand chorus in *The Messiah* as his masterpiece; "no, says he, I "think the chorus at the end of "the second part in *Theodora* far "beyond it," "*He saw the lovely Youth, &c.*" The following anecdote is given from undoubted authority. The second representation of this piece was very thinly attended, though the Princess Amelia was present. A gentleman, who was on intimate terms of friendship with Mr. Handel, imagining it to be a losing night, was willing to avoid speaking to him that evening; but he observing him at some distance, went up to him and said, "Will you "be here next Friday night?" I will play it *to you*. He was answered, that a person of note from the city had undertaken to engage for all the boxes, if it was represented again. "He is a fool, "replied Handel, the Jews will not "come to it (as to *Judas Maccabeus*), because it is a Christian "story; and the ladies will not "come, because it is a virtuous "one."

THE

THE TRIUMPH OF TIME AND TRUTH. Orat. by Dr. Morell; set by Mr. Handel, and performed at Covent-Garden, 4to. 1757. The words of this piece were entirely adapted to the mufic of *Il Trionfo del Tempo*, compofed at Rome about 1707.

THE TRIUMPH OF TRUTH. Orat. by George Jefferys, efq; printed in his Works, 4to. 1754.

Z

ZIMRI. An Oratorio, performed at Covent-Garden, and fet by Mr. Stanley, 4to. 1760. This piece, though anonymous, was written by Dr. Hawkefworth. Yet, like moft of the pieces compofed for the fake of mufic, found has been too much confidered in it to give fcope for very ftrong teftimonials of that genius which the author has fhewn in many of his other writings. Nor can I indeed greatly approve of the choice of the fubject. For although it is borrowed from the facred writings, and that hiftorical fact is fufficient to authorize the cataftrophe, yet the circumftances of a father, (*Zuran*) and he a prince, a chief of a powerful people, urging his daughter to proftitution, the daughter glorying in that proftitution, not from affection to her lover, but for the deftruction of a nation at variance with her own, together with the conclufion of the whole infamous bargain in the transfixion of them both in the very act of tranfport, feems to me to have fomewhat too grofs to fuit a drama intended to ferve the purpofes of religion, and deftined to be reprefented in a time of mortification, penance and abftinence from every human, or at leaft corporeal defire.

APPENDIX

[428]

APPENDIX

TO

THE SECOND VOLUME.

A B

ABRADATES AND PANTHEA. Trag. Acted by the scholars of St. Paul's school in 1770. Not printed.

THE AGREEABLE SURPRIZE. Farce, by J. Keefe. Acted at the Hay-Market, 1781. Not printed. This was the second little piece produced by the same author in one season. It is much inferior to his former performances, and highly exceptionable for the indecency of some parts of it. The character of Lingo, however, was represented by Mr. Edwin with so much real humour, that the audience forgot the absurdity both of the fable itself, and the conduct of it.

AGRIPPINA. Trag. in rhime, by John Lord Hervey. Not printed. This performance still remains unpublished in the possession of the Bristol family. See Walpole's Anecdotes, vol. II. p. 149.

ALCESTIS. Trag. translated from Euripides, by R. Potter, 4to. 1781.

ALEXAS, or, *The Chaste Gallant*, by Philip Massinger. By this title Massinger's *Bashful Lover* seems sometimes to have been called.

ALL UP AT STOCKWELL, or, *The Ghost no Conjurer*. Interlude. Acted at Drury-Lane, at a benefit, 1772. Not printed.

THE AMBIGUOUS LOVER. F.

B E

by Miss Sheridan. Acted at Crow-Street, 1781. Not printed.

ANTIGONE. Trag. translated from Sophocles, by George Adams, 8vo. 1729.

ANTIGONE. Trag. translated from Sophocles, by T. Franklin, 4to. 1759.

ARTHUR. Trag. See *The Misfortunes of Arthur*.

B

THE BACCHÆ. Trag. translated from Euripides, by R. Potter, 4to 1781.

BARNABY BRITTLE. Farce. Acted at Covent-Garden, 1781. This worthless piece is taken from the George Dandin, of Moliere; and was acted for Mr. Quick's benefit.

THE BARON KINKVERVANKOTSDORSPRAKENGATCHDERN. Musical Com. by Miles Peter Andrews. Acted at the Hay-Market, 8vo. 1781. This piece was taken from a Novel, written by Lady Craven. It was performed only once, though twice afterwards it was attempted to be forced on the publick.

BEAUTY AND GOOD PROPERTIES OF WOMEN. See *The Craft of Rhetorick*.

THE BELLES STRATAGEM. C. Acted by his Majesty's servants, 8vo. 1781. This despicable performance

formance is only mentioned to prevent the reader from being imposed upon by it. Whoever purchases it as Mrs. Cowley's play of the same name, will find they have been grossly defrauded of their money.

THE BOLD BEAUCHAMPS. An ancient play; probably not now extant, but mentioned in *The Knight of the Burning Pestle*, 1613. See also Dodsley's *Collection of Old Plays*, edit. 1780, vol. X. p. 172.

THE BRITISH STAGE, or, *The Exploits of Harlequin*. Farce, 8vo. 1724. The title-page of this piece declares it to have been performed by a company of wonderful comedians at both theatres with universal applause, and that it was designed as an after-entertainment for the audiences of *Harlequin Doctor Faustus* and *The Necromancer*.

C

CARDENIO. See *The History of Cardenio*. This play was acted at Court in the year 1613.

CASTARA, or, *Cruelty without Lust*. A Play, entered on the books of the Stationers' Company Nov. 29, 1653; but probably never printed.

CHIT CHAT. Interlude. Acted at Covent-Garden, 1781, for a benefit; but not printed.

CHRISTIANETTA. A Play, by Richard Brome; entered on the books of the Stationers' Company August 4, 1640; but probably not printed.

THE CITY SHUFFLER. A Play probably never printed. It was amongst those destroyed by Mr. Warburton's servant.

THE CONCEITED DUKE. A Play, that formerly belonged to the Cockpit Theatre. It is, however, probably no other than *The Noble Gentleman* of Beaumont and Fletcher.

THE CONCEITS. A Play; entered on the books of the Stationers' Company, by R. Marriot, Nov. 29, 1653; but probably not printed.

THE CONVERTED COURTEZAN. The first Part of Dekker's *Honest Whore* was originally printed under this title, but in what year is uncertain, the only copy I have seen wanting the title-page. I suspect, however, that it was printed in 1605.

CORNELIA. See *Pompey the Great*.

THE COUNTRYMAN. A Play; entered on the books of the Stationers' Company, Sept. 9, 1653; but probably not printed.

THE COXCOMBS. A Farce, by Francis Gentleman. Acted at the Hay-Market, 1771. Not printed. This was an alteration of part of Ben Jonson's *Epicoene*, and was performed only one night at a benefit.

THE CRADLE OF SECURITIE. An Interlude, mentioned in the manuscript Tragedy of Sir Thomas More, (MSS. Harl. 7368.); but probably never printed.

CUPID AND PSYCHE. A Play, by Thomas Heywood. Never printed. See his *Dialogues and Dramas*, p. 238. edit. 1637.

THE CYPRIAN CONQUEROR, or, *Faithless Relict*. A Play, now in *The British Museum*, MSS. Sloane, 3709. xxii R.

D

DAMNATION, or, *Hissing hot*. Interlude, by Charles Stuart. Acted at the Hay-Market, 1781; for the benefit of Mr. Bannister, August 29, 1781.

DARYUS. Interlude. See *King Daryus*.

THE DEAD ALIVE. A Farce, by John Keefe. Acted at the Hay-Market, 1781. Not printed. The abilities

abilities of this writer are admirably calculated for the species of entertainment which he has hitherto attempted. The flight sketches of character which he has produced are strongly marked; the incidents, though extravagant, within the limits of possibility, and the humour, though not of the most delicate sort, yet still restrained by the rules of decency. The present performance was excellently acted, but not so generally approved as *The Son-in-Law*.

DEMETRIUS AND MARSINA, or, *The Imperial Imposter and unhappy Heroine*. Trag. formerly in the possession of John Warburton, esq; and sold by auction among his books and MSS. about the year 1759. This play has not been printed.

THE DESTRUCTION OF JERUSALEM; by Thomas Legge. This piece, which was written in the time of Queen Elizabeth, is mentioned in Kirkman's Catalogue, 1661. Probably it was in MS. and he had then thoughts of putting it to the press; but, I believe, it was never printed.

DISSIPATION. Com. by Miles Peter Andrews. Acted at Drury-Lane, 8vo. 1781. This play is borrowed from Garrick's *Bon Ton*, and several other pieces. The reception it met with did great credit to the good nature of the audiences before which it was represented.

E

ECHO AND NARCISSUS. Dramatic Pastoral, of three acts, by Richard Graves, 8vo. 1780. This piece was printed in the second volume of *Euphrosine*, or, *Amusements on the Road of Life*. It was never acted, nor even set to music.

THE ELECTION. Entertainment, of two acts, by Richard Cumberland. Not printed; but privately performed at Mr. Hanbury's, Kelmarsh, Northamptonshire, in 1774.

ENGLAND'S JOY. A Play, acted at the Swan, but probably never printed. See Dodsley's *Collection of Old Plays*, vol. X. p. 172. vol. XII. p. 425. edit. 1780.

A *Worke in Ryme contayning an* ENTERLUDE OF MYNDES, *witnessing the Man's Fall from God and Christ*. Set forth by H. N. (Henry Nicholas), and by him newly perused and amended. Translated out of base Almayne into English. No date, but printed in 1574.

The honorable ENTERTAINMENT, given to the Queene's Majestie, in progresse at Elvetham, in Hampshire, by the right honorable the Earl of Hertford, 4to. 1591.

THE EXCISEMAN. Farce, by ——— Knap. Acted at Covent-Garden, 1780. Not printed. A very contemptible performance, which met with its just fate on the first night's exhibition.

F

THE FABII. An antient Drama, performed before the year 1580. See Stephen Gosson's *School of Abuse*, 1579.

THE FAIRY QUEEN. A Play, in the list of those destroyed by Mr. Warburton's servant. It was probably not printed.

THE FAIRY TALE. A dramatic Performance, by George Colman. Acted at Drury-Lane, 8vo. 1764. On the ill success of the *Midsummer's Night Dream*, altered by this gentleman, the above Drama was taken from it, and performed with great applause.

THE FATHER'S OWN SON. A Play, formerly in the possession of the

F L

the company performing at the Cockpit Theatre. See Malone's *Supplement to Shakspeare*, vol. I. p. 392.

FLORIMENE. Paſtoral, preſented by the Queen's commandment before the King at Whitehall, 4to. 1635.

THE FLYING VOICE. A Play, by Ralph Wood. One of thoſe deſtroyed by Mr. Warburton's ſervant.

THE FORTITUDE OF JUDITH. Trag. by Ralph Radcliff. Not printed.

FRIENDSHIP OF TITUS AND GISIPPUS. Com. by the ſame author. Not printed.

G

THE GENERAL. A Play, mentioned by James Shirley, in his Poems; but probably never printed.

The true Hiſtorie of GEORGE GRANDERBURYE, as played by the Right Hon. the Earl of Oxenforde's ſervants. Not printed. (See Mr. Malone's *Supplement to Shakspeare*, vol. I. p. 78.)

THE GREAT MAN. Trag. Anonymous. One of thoſe deſtroyed by Mr. Warburton's ſervant.

GUISE. A Play with this title is mentioned in Kirkman's Catalogue, 1661. It was probably written by Henry Shirley. See vol. I. p. 418.

H

THE HERACLIDÆ. Tragedy, tranſlated from Euripides, by R. Potter, 4to. 1781.

HERCULES. Trag. tranſlated from Euripides, by R. Potter, 4to. 1781.

HENRY IV. An Old Play, in which was introduced the depoſing of King Richard II. This piece

L O

was prior to Shakſpeare's *King Henry* IV. It was performed at Lord Eſſex's Houſe the night before his inſurrection, and was even then conſidered as an ancient Drama. See *The Supplements to Shakspeare*, vol. I. p. 381.

HIPPOLYTUS. Trag. tranſlated from Euripides, by R. Potter, 4to. 1781.

HIT THE NAILE O' THE HEAD. An Interlude, not noticed in any Catalogue ancient or modern, but mentioned in the Tragedy of *Sir Thomas More*, MSS. Harl. Nº 7368.

I

INTERLUDE CONCERNING THE LAWS OF NATURE. See *The Three Laws of Nature*, poſt.

INTERLUDE OF NATURE. See *Nature*, poſt.

INTERLUDE OF THE FOUR ELEMENTS. See *A new Interlude and a merry, &c.* p. 250.

ION. Trag. tranſlated from Euripides, by R. Potter, 4to. 1781.

JOSEPH. A piece with this title is mentioned in all the Catalogues. It is Goldſmith's *Sophompaneas*.

K

KENSINGTON GARDENS, or, *The Walking Jockey*. Interlude, by ―― Cobb. Acted at the Hay-Market, 1781. N. P. This was acted for Mr. Wilſon's benefit.

L

LANNIVE'S FESTIVALS. Of this piece I can give no account. It is in none of the Catalogues; but I am aſſured that it exiſts.

LOVE IN DISGUISE. Opera, by Henry Lucas. Acted at Dublin about the year 1776; but I am uncertain whether printed or not.

LOVE

LOVE WILL FIND OUT THE WAY. Comic Opera, by Thomas Hull. Acted at Covent-Garden, 1777. The Songs only printed. This piece was with difficulty dragged through nine nights. It is no more than Mr. Murphy's *School for Guardians* with the addition of Songs.

M

THE MAN OF THE WORLD. A Comedy, by Charles Macklin. Acted at Covent-Garden, 1781. Not printed. This play, which in respect to originality, force of mind, and well-adapted satire, may dispute the palm with any dramatic piece that has appeared within the compass of half a century, was received with the loudest acclamations in Ireland about ten years ago, under the title of *The True-born Scotchman*. In London, however, an official leave for its exhibition was repeatedly denied; and our audiences are indebted for the pleasure they have since derived from it, to the death of Mr. Capell, the late sub-licenser of the Theatres Royal. This scrupulous petty place-man had long preferred what he conceived to be the bias of a court, to the innocent gratification of the public. His sagacity on a former occasion also, should not be forgotten. He once prohibited the rehearsal of an Opera, because he thought the situation of *Pharnaces* too nearly resembled that of the *Young Pretender*; nor, till a minister of state interposed his authority, would our guardian eunuch of the stage indulge the lovers of music with this favourite entertainment.—Peace to his ashes! He has consigned the care of his own works to the publisher as well as ostensible author of Mr. Geo. H—ge's Letter to himself. Provident dulness could have dug no deeper grave for its literary remains.

But to resume our subject. We hope the reception lately afforded to Mr. Macklin's Comedy, as well as to his own performance of the principal part in it, has gratified his warmest expectations. Before the conclusion of his Epilogue had reminded us how much our fathers were delighted by the efforts of his youth, we felt an weak propension to reward the labours of his age. *The Man of the World* indeed, began its career during the last weeks of an expiring season; yet are we confident that the length and vigour of its course are reserved for the present winter. The actors, in general, were fortunate in the characters they attempted; but if words proportioned to the exertions of Miss Younge were at command, *she* should receive more distinct applause:

"Her worth demands it all,
"Pure and unmix'd on her the sacred
"drops should fall."

Her modes of pleasing, diversified with endless variety, seem to have reached their highest point; and, on this occasion, were invigorated by ardent zeal for the success of our meritorious veteran. Her professional excellence therefore must be satisfied with only partial acknowledgement, as justice compels us to divide our praise between the lustre of her talents and the goodness of her heart.—Mr. Macklin, we are sure, will pardon us for blending our tribute to this lady's merit with his own commendation; and, like the venerable Tiresias reclining on a daughter, will gratefully confess how far he owes the stability of his piece to the support of a female hand.

A MASQUE,

A MASQUE, by R. Govell. One of those destroyed by Mr. Warburton's servant.

MEDEA. Trag. translated from Euripides, by R. Potter, 4to. 1781.

THE MELANCHOLY KNIGHT, by Samuel Rowland. Entered on the Stationers' Books, Dec. 2, 1615. Probably grounded on *The History of Don Quixote*; a translation of which work appeared in 1612.

THE MENTALIST. Dram. Satire, by Francis Gentleman. Acted at Manchester. Not printed.

N

NATHAN THE WISE. Philosophical Drama, translated from the German of G. E. Lessing, late Librarian to the duke of Brunswick, by R. E. Raspe, 8vo. 1781. The translator of this Drama says, that it was not written for the stage, but was intended as an antidote against that rancour of religious bigotry, with which the Jews are still treated in many parts of Germany. He likewise very humanely adds, "it is to be hoped that Nathan will be suffered to counteract the poison which barbarous ages have left in the minds of fanatics, and Shakspeare and political factions may, some time or other, stir up again and put into fermentation."

NATURE. A goodly interlude of Nature, compyled by Mayster Henry Medwall, chapleyn to the right reverent Father in God, Johan Merton, somtyme cardynall and archbyshop of Canterbury. Fo. No date.

The names of the Players.

Nature.	Wreth.	Lyberalyte.
Man.	Envy.	Chastyte.
Reson.	Slouth.	Good Occupacyon.
Sensualyte.	Glotony.	Shamefastnes.
Innocencye.	Humylyte.	Mundus.
Worldly Affeccyon.	Charyte.	Pacyence.
Bodyly Lust.	Abstynence.	Pryde.

NINEVEH'S REPENTANCE. This piece is no where mentioned, except in the Catalogue annexed to *The Careless Shepherdess*, Com. 1656.

NOTHING IMPOSSIBLE TO LOVE. Tragi-Com. by Robert Le Greene. This was one of the plays destroyed by Mr. Warburton's servant.

O

OTHO AND RUTHA. Dramatic Tale, by a Lady, 8vo. 1781.

P

THE PHOENICIAN VIRGINS. Trag. translated from Euripides, by R. Potter, 4to. 1781.

Vol. II.

PRELUDIO, by George Colman. Acted at the Hay-Market 1781. This trifle was produced merely to usher to the publick the disgusting representation of *The Beggar's Opera*, with the characters reversed.

THE PRISONER'S OPERA, with other entertainments, performed at Sadler's Wells, 8vo. 1730.

THE PROUD WYVES PATER NOSTER. A Play, entered on the Stationers' Books in 1559.

R

KING RICHARD THE SECOND. Trag. altered from Shakspeare, by Francis Gentleman. Acted at Bath about the year 1754. Not printed.

F f THE

THE RIDICULOUS GUARDIAN. Comic Burletta, acted at the Hay-Market, 4to. 1761.

RIPE FRUIT, or, *The Marriage Act*. Interlude, by Charles Stuart. Acted at the Hay-Market, 1781, for the benefit of Mr. Wilson.

S

THE SCHOOLE MODERATOR. Of this Play I can give no account; but it is in Mr. Garrick's Collection.

SEE ME, AND SEE ME NOT. This is the running title of *Hans Beer Pot*.

SEVENTEEN HUNDRED AND EIGHTY-ONE. Farce, acted at Covent-Garden, at a benefit, 1781. Not printed.

The Life and Death of Master Shore, and Jane Shore his Wife, as it was lately acted by the Earle of Derbie his servants. Entered on the Stationers' Books, Aug. 28, 1599. This Play is mentioned in *The Knight of the Burning Pestle*, and appears to be the second part of Heywood's *Edward the Fourth*.

THE SILVER TANKARD. Musical Farce, by Lady Craven. Acted at the Hay-Market, 1781. Not printed. With great difficulty, and some management, this piece was heard throughout on the first night. The natural tenderness with which an English audience will always treat the work of a lady, could alone have preserved such an insipid trifle from immediate condemnation.

THE SUPPLICANTS. Tragedy, translated from Euripides, by R. Potter, 4to. 1781.

T

THE THEATRE OF EDUCATION, translated from the French of *The Countess of Gengis*, 4 vols. 8vo. 1781. This Collection consists of a number of small dramatic pieces, calculated for the instruction of Youth. They are, says the editor, "only moral treatises brought into action; and it is hoped that young people may find lessons in them, both entertaining and instructive. Besides, in playing these pieces, in learning them by heart, several advantages may be found; such as, engraving excellent principles upon their minds, exercising their memories, forming their pronunciation, and giving them a graceful pleasing manner." It is but justice to add, that on this occasion the editor has said no more than what the merit of the collection will amply justify. The following is a list of these petite dramas:

Vol. I.

1. *Hagar in the Desert*. A Serious Dialogue.
2. *The Beauty and the Monster*. Com. in two acts.
3. *The Phials*. Com. in one act.
4. *The Happy Island*. Com. in two acts.
5. *The Spoiled Child*. Com. in two acts.
6. *The Effects of Curiosity*. Com. in two acts.
7. *The Dangers of the World*. Com. in three acts.

Vol. II.

1. *The Blind Woman of Spa*. Com. in one act.
2. *The Dove*. Com. in one act.
3. *Cecilia, or, The Sacrifice of Friendship*. Com. in one act.
4. *The Generous Enemies*. Com. in two acts.
5. *The Good Mother*. Com. in three acts.
6. *The Busy Body*. Com. in two acts.

Vol. III.

1. *The Children's Ball, or, The Duel*. Com. in two acts.

2. *The*

T U

2. *The Traveller.* Com. in two acts.
3. *Tatleth.* Com. in two acts.
4. *The False-Friends.* Com. in two acts.
5. *The Judge.* Com. in three acts.

Vol. IV.
1. *The Queen of the Rose of Salency.* Com. in two acts.
2. *The Milliner.* Com. in one act.
3. *The Linen-Draper.* Com. in two acts.
4. *The Bookseller.* Com. in one act.
5. *The Truly wise Man.* Com. in two acts.
6. *The Portrait, or, The Generous Rival.* Com. in three acts.

THE TOY. This Play is mentioned by James Shirley in his Poems, 8vo, 1646. It was never printed.

THE TURKISH MAHOMET, AND HIREN THE FAIRE GREEK. A Play, by George Peele. Never published. See Mr. Malone's *Supplement* to the last edition of Shakspeare, vol. I. p. 191.

V

THE VESTAL. Tragedy, by Henry Glapthorne. One of those destroyed by Mr. Warburton's servant.

W

WHO'D HAVE THOUGHT IT? Farce, by —— Cobb. Acted at Covent-Garden, 1781. Not printed. This piece was performed at the benefit of Mr. Wilson, and once afterwards at the Hay Market.

A WOMAN WILL HAVE HER WILL. A Comedy, entered on the Stationers' Books, by W. White, Aug. 3, 1601.

THE WORLD. A Play, that formerly belonged to the Cockpit Theatre. See *Supplement to Shakspeare*, last edit. vol. I. p. 392.

Z

ZAPHIRA. Trag. by Francis Gentleman. Acted at Bath about 1754. Not printed. This piece was on the same story as *Barbarossa*, which it preceded in the presentation.

ADDITIONS

[436]

ADDITIONS AND CORRECTIONS

TO

THE SECOND VOLUME.

A B

PAGE 1. col. 2. ABRAHAM's SACRIFICE.] Oldys took his account of this piece from Chetwood, who probably forged the title and date that he has affixed to it in *The British Theatre*.

P. 5. col. 1. AGLAURA. This Play was first printed in fol. 1639.

P. 8. col. 1. ALEXIS'S PARADISE.] For 1722 read 1732.

P. 16. col. 1. ANDRIA.] For 1737 read 1627.

P. 18. col. 1. ANTONIO AND MELLIDA. This Play is to precede ANTONIO'S REVENGE.

B

P. 33. N° 72. THE BLOODY BANQUET.] In addition to what has been already said concerning this play, we may add, that it was probably written by Robert Davenport, being enumerated with some other of his pieces in a list of Plays that formerly belonged to the Cockpit Theatre. The letters T. D. were perhaps printed by mistake in the title-page instead of R. D. See Mr. Malone's *Supplement to Shakspeare*, vol. I. p. 393.

C

P. 40. N° 3. CÆSAR AND POMPEY, &c.] There was another edition, apparently an earlier one, without a date. There

C O

was also a very ancient Play on this subject, intituled, *The History of Cæsar and Pompey*, exhibited before 1580. See Gosson's *School of Abuse*.

N° 55. N° 109. CINNA's CONSPIRACY.] In a Pamphlet, by Daniel Defoe, written about 1713, this play is ascribed to Colley Cibber, who spoke the Prologue.

P. 60. N° 158. THE COMBATE OF CAPPS.] The date which Chetwood affixed to this piece (1582) was certainly a forgery. Kirkman mentions it as a Masque, but it can scarcely be called a dramatic piece, being only the skeleton or argument of a very absurd play with a few songs intermixed, and would therefore not be entitled to a place in this work, were it not necessary to take notice of the errors of former Catalogues. The full title is as follows: PRINCEPS RHETORICUS, or, Πιλομαχια. Ye COMBAT OF CAPS. Drawn forth into arguments, general and special. In usum Scholæ Masonensis, et in gratiam totius auditorii Mercurialis. Veni, vide London. Printed for H. R. at the three pigeons in Saint Paul's Church-yard, 1648.

P. 62. N° 170. THE COMMON'S CONDITION.] A Pleasant Comedie called COMMON CONDITIONS.

TIONS. This play (of which the copy before me wants both the first and concluding leaves) is to all appearance as ancient as *Gammer Gurton*, or any other comic piece in the English language. The original entry of it on the books of the Stationers' Company, is perhaps earlier than any part of their records now remaining; and yet is it referred to on a subsequent occasion, as follows: "July 26, 1576. John Hunter enters —A new and pleasant comedie or plaie, after the manner of *Common Condycyons*." The scene lies in Arabia. The characters of the drama are—

Unthrift. ⎫
Shifte.   ⎬ Thieves in the disguise of Tinkers.
Drifte.   ⎭

Sedmond.—a Knight.
Clarifia.—his Sister.
Common Conditions.—a clown or buffoon.
Galiarbus.—a Phrygian; father to Sedmond and Clarisia.
Lamphedon. ——a Phrygian knight.
Nomides.—the same.
Sabia.—a young Lady in love with him, and sometimes passing under the name of Metrea.
Mountagos.—father to Sabia. He seems designed for a Frenchman.
Cardolus.—Governor of the Isle of Marofus,
Lomia.—a Naturall.
Leolthenes.—a Knight, her master.
Pirates, Mariners, Maller, Boatswain, Ship-boy, &c.

Between the acts of this piece there are no intervals; nor is there much connection between the different couples of lovers, except such as is brought about by the good and ill offices of *Common Conditions*, who assists the interests of some, and perplexes that of others. The present drama, however, exhibits perhaps the earliest examples of naval dialogue on the stage, as well as of the English language distorted by foreign pronunciation.

P. 67. N° 204. THE CONTENTION BETWEENE LIBERALITIE AND PRODIGALITIE.] This piece, by a passage about the conclusion of it, appears to have been written in the 43d year of Queen Elizabeth's reign, consequently about the time of its publication. The original compiler of the present work was deceived by Chetwood, whom he has followed in asserting that *Liberalitie and Prodigalitie*, a masque of much moralitie, was printed in 1550. There is no such masque. The drama abovementioned is a comedy, nor has any edition but that of 1602 been hitherto discovered.

P. 70. N° 232. THE COSTLY WHORE.] This Play was attributed by Philips to Rob. Mead only, because in Kirkman's Catalogue it followed Mead's *Combat of Love and Friendship*. See article BREWER. Appendix to vol. I.

P. 72. N° 248. THE COUNTRY GIRL.] In the title-page of this piece are only the letters T. B. which were probably inserted by the Bookseller, who knew the author by the familiar appellation of Tony Brewer.

P. 76. N° 281. CROMWELL LORD THOMAS.] This play was first printed in 1602, and is said in the title-page to be written by W. S.

P. 77. N° 292. THE CRUEL DEBTOR.] The date affixed to this piece (1669) was one of Chetwond's forgeries, as appears clearly from the entry on the Stationers' Books in 1566. From the

C U   H E

the title, he thought himself war-
ranted to call it a *Tragedy*, the
falshood of which deicription
likewife is detected by the entry
already mentioned. Kirkman appears never to have feen this very
rare piece.

P. 78. N° 305. CUPID's
WHIRLIGIG.] It is highly probable that the letters E. S. in the
title-page of this play were intended for Edward Sharpham,
whofe Comedy of *The Fleire* was
entered on the Stationers' Books
about the fame time (1606).

D

P. 82. N° 15. THE DEATH
OF DIDO.] I much queftion whether this piece was printed in
1621. If it had appeared at that
time, it would probably have
been mentioned, by either Kirkman, Langbaine, or Gildon, none
of whom have taken notice of it.
Jacob was the firft who gave the
title of it, and for the date we
have no authority, or, which is
the fame thing, only that of
Chetwood.

P. 90. N° 88. DON QUIX-
OTE.] Philips and Winftanley
afcribe this play to Robert Baron,
without any foundation whatfoever, merely becaufe it happened
in Kirkman's Catalogue to follow
Baron's play, called *Deorum Dona*.
For the fame reafon they have
attributed to him *The Deftruction of
Jerufalem*, a play written before
he was born. They have likewife made him the author of *The
Marriage of Wit and Science*, printed in 1570, becaufe that piece
followed his *Mirza* in the fame
Catalogue.

F

P. 112. N° 8. FAIR AND
FAIR WEATHER.] Dele the article, there being no fuch play.

P. 113. N° 18. THE FAIR PE-
NITENT.] It appears from an
advertifement prefixed to *The
Boudwian*, printed in 1710, that
Mr. Rowe had revifed all Maffinger's plays, and was preparing
an edition of them for the prefs
the very year he died. Perhaps,
therefore, if his own dramas were
accurately examined, he might be
found to have more obligations to
that ancient Poet.

P. 125. N° 127. THE PLEIRE.]
There is an Edition of this play
in 1610.

P. 126. N° 139. A FOOL AND
HER MAIDENHEAD SOON PART-
ED.] This play was probably
written by Robert Davenport, being enumerated with the reft of
his pieces in the Catalogue of
dramatic pieces belonging to the
Cockpit Theatre.

P. 127. N° 158. FORTUNE TO
KNOW, &c.] I fufpect this is the
fame play that has been diftin-
guifhed in the Catalogues by the
title of COMMON's CONDITIONS.
See an account of that piece ante.

P. 134. N° 183. FULGIUS
AND LUCRELLE.] The date
1670 affixed by Chetwood to this
piece is undoubtedly a forgery.
It is mentioned by Kirkman in
his Catalogue 1661, and is probably very ancient. It was, we
may prefume, one of the ten dramatic pieces that he fays he had,
never feen, for he has not annexed any mark to it to afcertain
whether it is a tragedy, a comedy,
or a mafque.

H

P. 144. N° 7. HANS BEER,
POT.] There can be no doubt
concerning the author of this
piece. D. Belchier's name is fubfcribed to the Dedication.

P. 147. N° 40. THE HEC-
TORS.] This piece was attributed

to Edmund Prestwich by Phillips and Winstanley only, because, in Kirkman's Catalogue, it followed the play of *Hippolitus*, written by that author. The date, 1650, is one of Chetwood's forgeries. There is no other play with this title but that printed in 1656, which is anonymous.

P. 155. N° 101. HIREN.] Since the former part of this work was printed off, my conjecture concerning the piece has been confirmed. It is, I find, not a Play, but a Poem, consisting of 114 stanzas. The dedication to the heroicke Heros, Henry Earle of Oxenford, Viscount Bulbeck, &c. begins thus:

  Sir, if my unpolisht pen that dedicates now
  The bashful utterance of a maiden Muse, &c.

The author, William Barksted, is styled in the title-page one of the servants of his Majesty's Revels.

I

P. 165. N° 30. AN ILL BEGINNING, &c.] This play was performed at Court in the year 1613.

Ibid. N° 59. THE IMPERIAL LOVERS.] For IMPERIAL, read IMPERTINENT.

P. 172. N° 104. JOSEPH'S AFFLICTIONS.] This is one of those dramas that Kirkman (the first, I believe, who mentions it) appears not to have seen. It is perhaps a misprint for *Job's Afflictions*; a play written by Ralph Ratcliffe, and probably never printed. See Wood's *Athenæ*, I. 89. There was, however, an ancient Poem, intituled, "The tragedious Troubles of the most chaste and innocent Joseph, son to the most innocent Patriarch Jacob," written by William Forrest, which might have been mistaken for a play. See Wood's *Athenæ*, I. 125.

Ibid. N° 105. THE JOVIAL CREW.] It is quite uncertain when this Interlude was printed. The date affixed to it in the former part of this work (1598) is taken from Chetwood, on whom no reliance whatever can be placed. Langbaine had never seen it. Gildon says it was printed in 1651, and that it exhibits a character of the roaring ranters of that time; but that was the age of Saints, not of ranters. However, this writer mentions the piece so particularly, that it is probable he had seen it.

L

P. 187. N° 44. THE LEVELLERS LEVELL'D.] Wood ascribes this piece to Marchamont Nedham.

P. 189. N° 54. LIKE WILL TO LIKE, &c.] The following is the complete title to this piece:

5. *An Enterlude, intituled,* LIKE WIL TO LIKE, *quod the Devil to the Colier, very godly and ful of plesant mirth. Wherein is declared not onely the punishment followeth those that will rather followe licentious living then to esteem and followe good councel; and what great benefits and commodities they receive that apply them unto vertuous living, and good exercises. Made by* Ulpian Fulwel. Five may easily play this enterlude.

The names of the Players.
The Prologue.
Tom Tospot. }
Hankin Hangman. } for one.
Tom Collier. }
Chance.
Vertuous life. }
God's Promises. } for one.
Cutbert Cutpurse. }
Lucifer.
Ralfe Roister. }
Good Fame. } for one.
Severitie. }

Philip

M A

Philip Fleming.
Pierce Pickpurs. } for another.
Honour.

Nichol Newfangle, the Vice. Imprinted at London, at the long shop adjoyning unto S. Mildred's Churche in the Pultrie, by John Allde. Anno Domini, 1568.

P. 190. N° 56. LINGUA.] See article BREWER. Appendix to vol. I.

P. 202. N° 155. THE LOVE-SICK MAID.] This Comedy was performed at Court, by John Heminge's company, in 1629.

P. 208. N° 202. LUMINALIA.] For 1627 read 1637.

M

P. 217. N° 46. MANHOOD AND WISDOME.] For this date and description we have only Chetwood's authority, who is never to be trusted. The present was, without doubt, one of his many forgeries. The piece was so rare above a hundred years ago, that it appears never to have been seen by Kirkman.

P. 221. N° 83. THE MARRIAGE OF WITTE AND SCIENCE.] The following is the full title of this piece: "A newe and pleasaunt Enterlude, intitled, The MARIAGE of WITTE AND SCIENCE. Imprinted at London, in Fleteſtret, neare unto Sainct Dunstan's Churche, by Thomas Marſhe, (1570.) The Players names. Nature, Witte Will, Studie, Diligence, Instruction, Science, Reason, Experience, Recreation, Shame, Idelnes, Ignoraunce, Tediousnes, with three other women fingers." The date affixed to this piece, in the former part of the present work, (1606.) was taken from Chetwood, and is undoubtedly one of his numerous forgeries.

N

P. 230. N° 151. THE MERRY DEVIL OF EDMONTON.] This Comedy in the original entry on the Stationers' Books in 1608, by Joseph Hunt and Thomas Archer, is said to have been written by T. B. which letters were perhaps placed for *Tony* or Anthony Brewer. The same letters are prefixed to that Author's *Country Girl*. These initials shew, that this piece belongs neither to Shakspeare nor Drayton. H. Moseley indeed entered it on the Stationers' Books Sept. 9, 1653; as the production of the former; and from this circumstance, we may perceive how little credit is due to the other entries of that bookseller about the same time. See *King* STEPHEN, *the History of* —THE HISTORY OF CARDENIO, DUKE HUMPHRY, and IPHIS AND IANTHE, all registered by him as the compositions of our great dramatic Poet. This book (says Anthony Wood, speaking of a novel attributed to Sir Philip Sydney) *coming out so late*, it is to be enquired whether Sir Philip Sydney's name is not set to it for sale-sake, being *a usual thing in these days to set a great name to a book or books, by sharking booksellers or sniveling writers, to get bread.* Athen. Oxon. I. 228.

P. 233. N° 164. MICHAELMAS Term.] The original compiler of this work was mistaken in saying that the play we are now speaking of, is not divided into acts.

P. 247. N° 249. MUSTAPHA.] For 1606 read 1609.

N

P. 254. N° 37. THE NICE WANTON.] It is undoubtedly of much older date than 1634; having been entered on the Stationers' Books in 1559. The date (1634),

O

(1634), as well as the description of the piece, (a pleasaunt comedie) was one of Chetwood's forgeries; neither Kirkman nor Langbaine had seen any such drama, nor is it in Mr. Garrick's Collection.

P. 262. N° 31. THE OLD WIFE'S TALE.] Dele this article, and substitute the following.

THE OLD WIVES TALE, a pleasant conceited Comedie, plaied by the Queenes Majesties players. Written by G. P. [i. e. George Peele.]

Printed at London by John Danter, and are to be sold by Ralph Hancocke and John Hardie, 1595.

Perhaps the reader will join with me in supposing that Milton had read this very scarce dramatic piece, which, among other incidents, exhibits two Brothers wandering in quest of their Sister, whom an enchanter had confined. This enchanter had learned his art from his mother *Meroë*, as Comus had been instructed by his parent *Circe*. The Brothers call out on the Lady's name, and *Echo* replies to them. The Enchanter has given her a potion, which induces oblivion of herself. The Brothers afterwards meet with an Old Man, who is likewise versed in magic, and by listening to his vaticinations, &c. they recover their Sister; but not till the Enchanter's wreath had been torn from his head, his sword wrested from his hand, a glass broken, and a light extinguished.

Principiis quasin debemus grandia parvis!

The names of some of the characters, as Sacripant, Corebus, &c. are adopted from the *Orlando Furioso*.

VOL. II.

P

P. 270. N° 2. PAGEANTS] The first Pageants we meet with in London were exhibited when Henry the Third's Queen, Eleanor, rode through the city to her coronation 1236, and for Edward the First's victory over the Scots, 1298. Another, when the Black Prince made his entry with his royal prisoner 1357. A third, when his son Richard the Second passed along Cheapside 1392, after the citizens had made their submission, and by the Queen's intercession recovered their charter. A fourth, when Henry the Fifth made his entry 1415, after the battle of Agincourt. A Fifth, when Henry the Eighth received the Emperor Charles V. 1522. A sixth, when he and Ann Boleyn passed through the city to her coronation 1532.

"The passage of our most sovereyne lady Queen Elizabeth through the city of London to Westminster the daye before her coronation, 4to. 1558."

The last printed pageant of 1708 has three plates.

The latest attempt at any thing like pageants was in 1761, when his present Majesty honoured the city with a visit; but there were no songs or speeches, only exhibitions of two or three companies.

P. 271. N° 5. PALAMON AND ARCYTE.] The original compiler of this work was misled by Chetwood's account of this piece, which he has followed. It was, I believe, never printed.

P. 275. N° 35. PATIENTE GRIZZELE.] The date which has been affixed to this piece (1603), is taken from Chetwood's *British Theatre*, on which we have seen already no reliance is to be placed. The piece was, in all probability, printed in 1600, in which year it was entered on the books of the Stationers' Company. The play with the same title, written by Ralph Radcliffe, I suspect had also appeared in print, being noticed in Kirkman's Catalogue, under the name of *Old Patient Grizzle.*

R
P. 311. N° 98. ROBIN CONSCIENCE.] The date allotted to it by Chetwood (1624) is one of his forgeries, as may be collected from the entry at Stationers-Hall, and from the silence of Gildon, who appears to have seen this piece, and has affixed no date to it.
Ibid. N° 99. ROBIN HOOD'S PASTORAL.] This date is another of Chetwood's forgeries. The piece is in Mr. Garrick's Collection, and is intitled " *The Play of Robin Hoode; verye proper to be played in Maye Games.*" Imprinted at London, by William Copland; no date, but probably before 1570. It consists of five leaves only.
P. 324. N° 151. ROMEO AND JULIET.] There is a slight mistake in this article. The edition of 1599 is not a sketch, but the complete play, as exhibited in all the subsequent copies.
P. 331. N° 70. THE SCULLER.] Dele this article, there being no such play.

S
P. 333. N° 57. SELIMUS.] There was another edition of this tragedy in 1638, with the initials T. G. added to it by the printer, to impose the piece on the publick as the production of Thomas Goff, who had written two other plays founded on *The Turkish His-*

tory. Hence it was attributed to him by Langbaine and other biographers.
P. 348. N° 192. SOLIMAN AND PERSEDA.] This Tragedy was printed in 1599. The date is at the end of it.

T
P. 369. N° 44. THERSYTES.] What the real date of this piece may be, is uncertain; that which has been ascribed to it being taken from Chetwood, in whom no confidence ought to be placed. The quaint addition of *His Humours and Conceits* is probably the offspring of this bookseller's fertile brain.
P. 372. N° 63. TIDE TARRIETH FOR NO MAN.] It appears from Oldys's MSS. that this Comedy was printed in 1576. The date ascribed to it in the former part of this work (1611) was one of Chetwood's falsifications.

W.
P. 402. N° 30. WHEN YOU SEE ME, &c.] This piece could not be taken from Lord Herbert's *History of King Henry* VIII. as the original compiler of the present work supposed the first edition of Rowley's play having been printed in 1605.
P. 411. N° 105. THE WOMAN'S PLOT.] It appears from an entry on the Stationers' Books, by H. Moseley, Sept. 9, 1653, that this is the second title to Massinger's *Very Woman,* which is printed among his Works. In this single instance, therefore, the public has suffered no loss by the carelessness of Mr. Warburton.

www.ingramcontent.com/pod-product-compliance
Lightning Source LLC
Chambersburg PA
CBHW032130010526
44111CB00034B/573